INCOME INEQUALITY

INCOME INEQUALITY

*Economic Disparities and the Middle Class
in Affluent Countries*

Edited by Janet C. Gornick and Markus Jäntti

STANFORD UNIVERSITY PRESS
STANFORD, CALIFORNIA

Stanford University Press
Stanford, California

Fonds National de la
Recherche Luxembourg

Financial support for the publication of this book was provided by the Fonds National de la Recherche Luxembourg.

Printed in the United States of America on acid-free, archival-quality paper

Library of Congress Cataloging-in-Publication Data

Income inequality : economic disparities and the middle class in affluent countries / edited by Janet C. Gornick and Markus Jäntti.

    pages cm
  Includes bibliographical references and index.
  ISBN 978-0-8047-7824-4 (cloth : alk. paper)
  1. Income distribution. 2. Middle class. I. Gornick, Janet C., editor of compilation. II. Jäntii, Markus, 1966– editor of compilation.
  HC79.I5I486 2013
  339.2'2091722—dc23

                                    2013010763

Typeset by Newgen in 10/14 Sabon

For Joachim R. Frick (1962–2011)—scholar, data provider, teacher, advisor, international collaborator, husband, father, and friend.

CONTENTS

Anthony B. Atkinson

I am delighted that one of my first tasks as president of LIS is to contribute the foreword to this book edited by Janet Gornick, director of LIS, and Markus Jäntti, research director. I have been associated with LIS since the early days of its 30-year history, and I have followed with great interest its development and expanding horizons. And, as a researcher, I have benefited much from using LIS data.

The history is important. It is thanks to the farsightedness of LIS's founders, Gaston Schaber, Lee Rainwater (its first research director), and Tim Smeeding (its first director), that researchers today have access to the comparable cross-country data provided by LIS via its two databases— the *Luxembourg Income Study (LIS)* and the *Luxembourg Wealth Study (LWS)*—that have been employed to such advantage in this book. The assembly of microdatasets and, above all, the ex post harmonization of the data according to a common template involve a major investment of time. Such social science infrastructure cannot be created overnight.

We should therefore be looking ahead to future needs and be planning the infrastructural investments that we need to make today. Such planning is particularly important at the present time because of the major threat to one of LIS's core ingredients: the household survey. Despite the advances in technology and methodology, household surveys are labor-intensive and expensive, and around the world national statistical offices are subject to budget cuts. The survey instrument itself faces its own problems in the form of declining response rates and inability to expand the range of questioning to meet the increased need for data linked across different domains. These concerns have led to increased interest in the use of administrative records and to the exploration of data linkage methods. However, it is important that such developments continue to provide individual researchers with the kind of access currently available via LIS.

LIS has been expanding its geographical coverage, and this is most welcome. Thus, while the chapters in this book largely concentrate on high-income countries, future LIS-based research will be able to encompass important middle-income countries. Each such development, however, leads one to ask for more. How else could the scope of LIS be widened? One priority immediately suggests itself. The economic crisis has highlighted the need for both up-to-date data and annual data. The events in which we are interested, such as the financial crisis that began in 2007, do not occur neatly vis-à-vis the intervals between waves of LIS data. Although LIS has shortened the interval from five to three years, more frequent data and more up-to-date data are needed, and this will require additional resources. Expansion means investment.

Substantively, the chapters in this book clearly demonstrate the importance of looking at the distribution as a whole. We cannot focus on just one part of the distribution in isolation. Some economists say that they are concerned about poverty but not about inequality. However, as Richard Tawney famously noted in 1913, "What thoughtful rich people call the problem of poverty, thoughtful poor people call with equal justice a problem of riches." In between is situated the "middle class," and this book reflects increased interest in distributional changes affecting those around the median. For those who see the growth of a middle class as a sign of development and as a guarantee of democracy, there are concerns about the possible "hollowing out of the middle" in high-income countries. It is perhaps reassuring to remind ourselves that such concerns are not new. In *The Grasmere Journal*, Dorothy Wordsworth in May 1800 records that a neighbor "talked much about the alteration of the times and observed that in a short time there would be only two ranks of people, the very rich and the very poor." The difference today is that the observations that we make about "the alteration of the times"—like those in this book—can be more firmly based in empirical evidence.

REFERENCES

Tawney, Richard. 1913. "Poverty as an Industrial Problem," Inaugural Lecture, *Memoranda on the Problems of Poverty*. London: William Morris Press.
Wordsworth, Dorothy. 2002. *The Grasmere and Alfoxden Journals*. Oxford: Oxford University Press.

ACKNOWLEDGMENTS

We are grateful to the LIS staff in Luxembourg—Thierry Kruten, Caroline de Tombeur, Teresa Munzi, Paul Alkemade, Piotr Paradowski, and the rest of the data team—for the inestimable work they do to make the *LIS* and *LWS* microdata comparable across countries and over time.

We thank the LIS staff at the City University of New York—Natascia Boeri, Zack Hollenbeck, Sarah Kostecki, Amalia Leguizamón, Laurie Maldonado, and Berglind Hólm Ragnarsdóttir—for their tireless and creative work in preparing this book.

We appreciate the excellent guidance we received from David Grusky, Kate Wahl, and two anonymous reviewers at Stanford University Press.

We acknowledge the many institutions and individuals who supported LIS's 2010 *Conference on Inequality and the Status of the Middle Class*, including the Luxembourg National Research Fund, the Luxembourg Ministry for Higher Education and Research, the University of Luxembourg, the Alphonse Weicker Foundation, the local discussants, and Paul Krugman of Princeton.

We thank Lee Rainwater, Tim Smeeding, and the late Gaston Schaber, who, 30 years ago this year, decided to build a database of harmonized microdata and grant access to the data to social science researchers around the world.

And last but not least, we are deeply grateful to LIS's many data providers and funders, who are based in more than 40 countries and supranational institutions. Their contributions enable all of us at LIS to carry out our work.

Janet Gornick, LIS Director
Markus Jäntti, LIS Research Director

Janet C. Gornick is a professor of political science and sociology at the Graduate Center of the City University of New York and director of LIS.

Markus Jäntti is a professor of economics at the Swedish Institute for Social Research, Stockholm University, and research director of LIS.

Arthur S. Alderson is a professor of sociology at Indiana University–Bloomington.

Serge Allegrezza is director general of the Luxembourg National Institute for Statistics and Economic Studies (STATEC).

Anthony B. Atkinson is a fellow of Nuffield College, Oxford, and a centennial professor at the London School of Economics in the UK.

Bruce Bradbury is a senior research fellow at the Social Policy Research Centre of the University of New South Wales in Sydney, Australia.

Andrea Brandolini is an economist in the Department for Structural Economic Analysis of the Bank of Italy.

Louis Chauvel is a professor of sociology at the University of Luxembourg.

Helen Connolly is an economist and a former data expert and research associate at LIS.

Kevin Doran is a PhD candidate in the Department of Sociology at Indiana University–Bloomington.

Amaresh Dubey is a professor in the Centre for the Study of Regional Development at Jawaharlal Nehru University and a principal investigator on the India Human Development Survey.

Margarita Estévez-Abe is an associate professor of political science at Maxwell School of Citizenship and Public Affairs, Syracuse University, and chair of Public Policy at Collegio Carlo Alberto in Turin, Italy.

Arden Finn is a researcher at the Southern Africa Labour and Development Research Unit.

Nancy Folbre is a professor of economics at the University of Massachusetts, Amherst.

Joachim R. Frick was deputy director of the Socio-Economic Panel (SOEP) and head of the SOEP Research Data Center (SOEP-RDC) at the DIW Berlin Germany, and acting professor at the Technische Universitaet Berlin.

Markus M. Grabka is senior researcher in the Department of the Socio-Economic Panel (SOEP) at the DIW Berlin Germany and the Technische Universitaet Berlin.

Susan Harkness is a reader in social policy at the University of Bath in the UK.

Tanja Hethey-Maier is a researcher at the Institute for Employment Research (IAB) in Nuremberg, Germany.

David K. Jesuit is a professor of political science and director of the School for Public Service and Global Citizenship at Central Michigan University.

Tamás Keller is a researcher of TÁRKI Social Research Institute in Budapest in Hungary.

Lane Kenworthy is a professor of sociology and political science at the University of Arizona.

Arnaldur Sölvi Kristjánsson is an economist and a researcher at the Social Research Centre at the University of Iceland.

Murray Leibbrandt holds the NRF research chair in poverty and inequality research and is director of the Southern Africa Labour and Development Research Unit in the School of Economics at the University of Cape Town.

Vincent A. Mahler is a professor of political science at Loyola University Chicago.

Colin McKenzie is a professor of economics in the Faculty of Economics, Keio University in Tokyo, Japan.

Teresa Munzi is data team coordinator and research associate at LIS.

Stefán Ólafsson is a professor of sociology and director of the Social Research Centre at the University of Iceland.

Piotr R. Paradowski is data expert and research associate at LIS.

Eva Sierminska is research fellow at CEPS/INSTEAD in Luxembourg and IZA Bonn, and research affiliate at DIW Berlin.

Timothy M. Smeeding is Arts and Sciences Distinguished Professor of Public Affairs and Economics, and director of the Institute for Research on Poverty at the University of Wisconsin–Madison.

István György Tóth is director of TÁRKI Social Research Institute, and Privatdozent, Department of Sociology, Budapest Corvinus University in Hungary.

Philippe Van Kerm is a research economist at CEPS/INSTEAD in Luxembourg.

Reeve Vanneman is a professor of sociology at University of Maryland and a principal investigator on the India Human Development Survey.

Ingrid Woolard is an associate professor in the School of Economics at the University of Cape Town and research associate of the Southern Africa Labour and Development Research Unit at the same institution.

INCOME INEQUALITY

Introduction

Janet C. Gornick and Markus Jäntti

Few social and economic conditions are more compelling or more vexing than inequality. For many, concerns about inequality are largely instrumental. Their unease is focused not on inequality per se but on the possibility that inequality may have troublesome social, economic, and political consequences. For others, the presence of high or increasing levels of inequality raises concerns about equity and justice. These concerns, in turn, prompt questions about whether (or to what extent) public and private institutions function equitably with regard to opportunities, outcomes, or both.

Inequality has long attracted the attention of comparative scholars, especially those interested in studying variation across relatively similar countries. Cross-country comparisons provide a fruitful approach for inequality scholarship, largely because inequality itself varies sharply across countries, even among countries at similar levels of economic development. In addition, many of the institutions widely understood to influence inequality also vary cross-nationally, as do several of the problematic consequences that have been linked to inequality. For these reasons, cross-national comparisons offer a natural framework for inequality research.

This book presents inequality research carried out by 17 established researchers (or research teams), each of which address a different facet of inequality. The collection has several unique features. First, all of the chapters are focused specifically on income inequality. Second, nearly all of the included studies use cross-national research designs; the comparative chapters are complemented by four case studies selected to build upon the explicitly comparative chapters. Third, most of the chapters integrate into their inequality analyses an assessment of the status of the middle class, in most cases defined in relation to the income distribution. As we argue below, many inequality scholars have long focused on poverty, and recently several have assessed the top of the income distribution; empirical studies that integrate questions about inequality with analyses focused on the middle of the income distribution have been remarkably few and far between.

Fourth and finally, all of the chapters use microdata that are available—or will be available—through LIS (formerly known as the Luxembourg Income Study), a longstanding archive that provides researchers with cross-nationally harmonized income and wealth microdata, mostly from high-income countries. As we describe in more detail below, the use of a common data source provides the methodological backbone of this book, as it maximizes the use of common concepts as well as definitional and measurement practices. It also imposes a degree of both geographic and temporal consistency. The 12 cross-national studies (Chapters 1–12) use data drawn from a common group of 28 countries included in the income and/or wealth databases made available through LIS, and they all focus on the time period from about 1980 to about 2004.

While the common use of the LIS data has numerous conceptual and methodological advantages, it also has at least two disadvantages. One is that this collection is limited almost entirely to assessments of high-income countries (as we discuss in detail later in this Introduction). The other is that the time period covered in the harmonized LIS data ends before the start of the global financial crisis that has, not surprisingly, raised a host of new questions about economic well-being across the affected countries. (The reality of data archives such as LIS that harmonize data ex post from a large number of countries is that a lag time of five to seven years is standard.) In this sense, these chapters might be considered as a baseline study that could catalyze a follow-up in a few years.

In the next section, we introduce the focal concept that underlies this book: income inequality. We next offer a brief overview of prior research, discuss measurement and methodological issues, and present empirical snapshots based on the harmonized LIS data. We then introduce the five substantive parts of the book, providing highlights from each chapter. In the Conclusion, we offer a synthesis of findings from across the 17 studies and offer comments about future research directions.

INCOME INEQUALITY

Inequality Matters

In her book on changing U.S. income inequality, Rebecca Blank (2011) identified several claims, primarily instrumental, that should motivate widespread concern about inequality, especially about rising inequality. First, she argued, rising inequality may indicate declining income, and thus decreasing well-being, among individuals and households at the bottom of the income distribution. Rising inequality, more specifically, might signal rising poverty rates. Poverty, in turn, has demonstrably negative consequences for individuals, families, and communities. (For a comprehensive review of the multi-faceted effects of poverty, see the Urban Institute's "Consequences of Poverty" series.[1])

Second, Blank argues, inequality may depress economic mobility, which is generally interpreted as a measure of openness and opportunity in an economy. A substantial and growing literature, much of it cross-national, suggests that high levels of inequality may thwart mobility (see, e.g., Björklund and Jäntti 2009). Focusing on the United States, Blank observes that constraints on mobility, in turn, worsen other types of disparities as well: "Since a disproportionate share of low-income families are headed by people of color . . . , children from these families may face particularly reduced economic opportunities in a time of rising inequality, intensifying racial differences as well" (2011, 5).

Third, inequality might harm economic growth, although Blank acknowledges that both the direction and size of this effect are in dispute. Indeed, the claim that high levels of inequality may depress economic growth has been the subject of an extensive debate in recent years, but there is no clear consensus about how this effect operates (see, e.g., Aghion, Caroli, and García-Peñalosa 1999; Forbes 2000; Voitchovsky 2009). Recent scholarship suggests there is no single answer to this question. Voitchovsky (2005), using data from LIS, found that inequality in the upper end of the distribution increases growth, whereas inequality in the lower end is detrimental to growth. This is consistent with the view that the impact of inequality on growth depends on where in the distribution the inequality resides. As Bowles and Gintis (1998, 13) aptly observed, the prevailing view is probably best summed by concluding that "under favorable circumstances egalitarian outcomes are not incompatible with the rapid growth of productivity and other valued macroeconomic outcomes"; subsequent research has not overturned their observation.

And, in fact, economic growth and trends in income inequality are closely related. Economic growth measures change in aggregate income, while inequality trends capture how that growth accrues differentially to households in different parts of the income distribution. As any change in aggregate income must, by definition, benefit households somewhere in the distribution, economic growth is expected to shift the income distribution. On the assumption that more income growth is beneficial, one reason to be concerned with changing patterns of inequality is that they may indicate differential rates of income growth across the income distribution. If all households' incomes increase at the same pace, then, by definition, inequality is unchanged. If, on the other hand, incomes grow more rapidly among the affluent, inequality increases. If incomes grow more rapidly among the poor, inequality declines. Assessing inequality trends can illuminate how economic growth is distributed across the income spectrum.

The fourth concern that Blank raised is that inequality may have harmful effects on political processes. A core value in many modern societies is that of democracy. What exactly constitutes democracy is subject to intense debate, but a common interpretation is that all persons should enjoy equal political representation. It is, therefore, worrisome that inequality seems to adversely affect political participation and the nature of political decision making. Whether or not the poor vote may be seen as an exercise of choice. But for those who hold fundamental democratic values, it is of concern that when public opinion varies along the income distribution, policy makers (in the United States, at least) respond much more strongly to views held by the affluent than by the poor (see, e.g., Gilens 2005). Bartels (2009) found that U.S. senators appear to be more responsive to the views of the affluent than to those of the middle class; the views held by the bottom third of the income distribution have no apparent effect on senators' voting patterns. Also focused on the U.S. case, Stiglitz (2012, 117) argues that one of the main costs of inequality is that "our democracy is being put at peril." The United States' high level of inequality, Stiglitz concludes, is causing voter disillusionment, widespread distrust, perceptions of unfairness, and ultimately disenfranchisement.

Other instrumental arguments have received much attention in the literature on the adverse consequences of inequality on non-income outcomes.

In their popular book *The Spirit Level*, Wilkinson and Pickett (2009) argue that large income disparities—within a country—have harmful effects on a multitude of outcomes, including physical and mental health, infant mortality and life expectancy, crime and incarceration, and educational performance. Research is ongoing on the association between income inequality and these diverse non-income outcomes. Thus far, there is little consensus regarding the existence of these effects and/or the nature of any underlying causal mechanisms. However, given the high-stakes nature of these claims, they certainly merit our attention.

Yet another reason that scholars should be interested in inequality is that many people are themselves concerned about inequality, so it should be of concern to those who study public opinion and its consequences. McCall and Kenworthy (2009) presented evidence suggesting that (despite popular perceptions to the contrary) Americans do, in fact, care about inequality of outcomes. According to McCall and Kenworthy, Americans in substantial numbers believe that government should address increased inequality, although not necessarily through traditional processes of redistribution. Likewise, cross-national research on attitudes toward inequality also turns up evidence that the widely held belief that Americans are less concerned with inequality of outcomes than are citizens in other countries may not be true. Osberg and Smeeding (2006), for example, reported that across 27 countries (including most *LIS* countries), a clear majority agreed with the statement that "income differences are too large." While a relatively small fraction of U.S. respondents indicated that they strongly agreed with that statement, that fraction was even lower in Germany and Norway. Osberg and Smeeding concluded that citizens in all of the included countries share a general concern for inequality of outcome, specifically with regard to income.

Furthermore, concern about income inequality has risen sharply in several high-income countries since late 2011, when social protests focused on domestic economic issues sprung up in many countries. In the United States, these protests began in September 2011, when a group of activists gathered in lower Manhattan and launched the "Occupy Wall Street" movement, which quickly spread to other U.S. cities and states. Between September and November of 2011, references to income inequality in the American national media increased by a factor of five (Byers 2011). Since then, media coverage about inequality and the declining status of the middle class has been extensive in the United States and in other countries (see, e.g., Giles 2011).

And, of course, there are ample intrinsic reasons to care about inequality. That said, there is, in fact, no clear line between the instrumental and the intrinsic, as they inform each other. Nevertheless, many regard inequality as inherently undesirable, such that, all else equal, more equality is preferred to less. A well-known exposition of this perspective on equality is that outlined in Arthur Okun's (1975) classic book *Equality and Efficiency: The Big Tradeoff*. To Okun, both equality and efficiency (the latter measured with respect to income levels) are desirable, but the pursuit of greater efficiency comes at the cost of more inequality, so a compromise must be sought between the two. Not surprisingly, this assessment—how much leaking from the famous leaky bucket is too much?—can only be settled on normative grounds. Traditionally, those on the political left tend to place relatively more weight on the value of equality, while those on the political right favor efficiency (and unfettered market outcomes more generally).

Indeed, not everyone agrees that income inequality should be a matter for concern. Feldstein (1998) provided one vantage point on why inequality need not prompt worry. He argues that increases in inequality, measured by (for example) the Gini coefficient, should not necessarily be interpreted as problematic. For Feldstein, many who are concerned with inequality are "spiteful egalitarians"—that is, they regard someone with unchanged real income as being worse off if others experience increased income. According to Feldstein's view, the only real distributional concern should be poverty, to the extent that poverty signals absolute deprivation.

Debates about relative deprivation are by no means new. The question as to whether an individual can reasonably feel relatively deprived has been examined in depth by many scholars, perhaps most prominently by Amartya Sen (see, e.g., Sen 1983). Sen often cites a famous passage from *The Wealth of Nations* (Smith 1776/1976) that states that the ability to "appear in public without shame" required access to quite different goods in, say, the Roman empire than in the Scotland and England of the late eighteenth century, and indeed that even Scotland and England were different in this respect. What counts as making ends meet or having a reasonable standard of living can vary significantly both across time and space (on this point, see Frank 2007). This line of thought raises challenges to the notion that only real income levels, or absolute deprivation, matter. Concerns about relative deprivation require that we pay close attention to inequality.

Many schools of political philosophy give inequality of resources a prominent role, although exactly what kind of inequality is thought to be problematic varies. For example, the so-called Rawlsian position, following John Rawls's (1971) *Theory of Justice*, focuses on the standard of living of the least well-off (see Roemer 1996). Importantly, however, the utilitarian position is that, all else equal, more equality is preferred to less. But all else may not be equal. In the event that more inequality is associated with greater mean income, the less equal distribution is chosen only if the adverse distributional consequences do not outweigh the increase in mean income. That is, the utilitarian ethical position is very close to the view put forward by Okun.

Measurement of Income and Its Distribution

The chapters in this book mostly rely on a few key income concepts. The chapters on employment and gender (Chapters 7–9 in Part IV) rely heavily on labor market earnings, with Chapter 8 augmented by the imputed value of unpaid work. The chief measure of income in the rest of the book is household disposable income, adjusted for household size. (In the LIS literature, income adjusted for household size is generally referred to as "equivalized.") Although the chapters on wealth also draw heavily on the concept of net worth (which is defined in detail in Chapter 10), when these authors assess disparities, they generally rely on the income distribution. Only Chapter 5 examines the effects of redistribution per se on inequality; these researchers compare inequality in pre-tax, pre-transfer income with that of post-tax, post-transfer income.

Disposable Income Defined. Using the definition that is standard in the LIS literature, disposable income includes all cash and near-cash earnings, capital income, other private income, public transfers, less direct taxes. This follows closely the international standard for the measurement of disposable income, with the exception of imputed rents, the most important being imputed rents from owner-occupied housing (Expert Group on Household Income Statistics [The Canberra Group] 2001). (See Chapter 12 by Bradbury for more on this.) Other sources of income that may be important are omitted, including non-cash public transfers (in essence, the value of public services), non-cash private income (such as the value of in-kind employer-provided benefits), and unrealized capital gains.

As Atkinson (1997a, 2003) has pointed out, while the income definition used in this book is a common one, other quite reasonable definitions are possible because money income is obviously only a partial measure of economic well-being. On the other hand, Atkinson (2003) also observed that the distribution of disposable income can be relied on as a gauge on inequality based on the revealed preference of governments, which frequently rely on disposable income when producing public inequality statistics.

The case can be made for studying consumption rather than income. The chief difference between household consumption and household income consists of savings and the consumption value of durables. While it is possible that both cross-country variation and within-country changes in the inequality of consumption are different from those for income, no broadly comparable database of household consumption exists. However, in Chapter 12, Bradbury uses *Luxembourg Wealth Study (LWS)* data to examine how inclusion of housing expenditure changes our assessment of the living standards of the elderly. Furthermore, in Chapter 16, Vanneman and Dubey compare inequality results based on consumption versus income, as do Leibbrandt, Finn, and Woolard in Chapter 17.

The Equal-Sharing Assumption. Most income distribution statistics assume, for lack of better information, that all household members share the same standard of living (Jenkins and O'Leary 1998). Most of the chapters make that assumption, as do we in the empirical work presented later in this Introduction. However, Chapters 7 to 9 do address how inequality is affected by differences in spouses' labor market earnings.

Inequality in an Annual Cross Section Compared with Multi-Year Income. We also rely on annual rather than the more long-run measures of income that many economists would argue are more relevant for gauging well-being (see Burkhauser and Couch 2009). Because incomes tend to fluctuate from year to year, the distribution of annual income tends to overstate inequality in permanent income, which is arguably a more reliable or stable measure of individual well-being. Moreover, inequality of annual income may increase over time because transitory shocks are increasing across time rather than because inequality of permanent income is rising. Likewise, differences across countries may be driven by differences in transitory shocks rather than in permanent income.

When it comes to cross-country variation, however, the limited evidence that is available on this score suggests that country inequality rankings—that is, cross-country variation in levels of inequality—are largely unaffected by extending the measurement period of income from one to multiple years (Burkhauser and Poupore 1997; Aaberge et al. 2002). It is possible that changes in inequality are driven, to different degrees, by transitory or permanent variation. While there are some cross-nationally comparable data that allow the examination of longitudinal income inequality, they do not allow for as broad a range of countries to be examined as are examined in this book. Using longitudinal data for Germany, the United Kingdom, and the United States, however, Daly and Valletta (2008) found that changes in transitory earnings did not account for the trend in earnings inequality in these three countries in the 1990s. The variance of annual (age-adjusted, logged) earnings followed roughly the same pattern as do their estimates of permanent earnings inequality, at least among prime-aged male household heads.

The Definition of the Middle Class. Many of the chapters in this book concentrate on the middle class. But what exactly is meant by the "middle class"? There is no consensus on the definition of the middle class, even within disciplinary traditions. Sociologists typically invoke definitions that extend beyond income measures, often incorporating educational attainment and/or occupational characteristics, with the overarching aim of capturing power relations. Economists more often identify the middle class with respect to the income distribution (especially in high-income countries) or vis-à-vis the consumption distribution (typically in lower-income countries). The authors in this book have taken this more economic approach, defining the middle class, specifically, relative to each country's income distribution.[2] As a result, what we (and many of the authors) refer to as the "middle class" might more accurately be described as those households that fall in the "middle"—that is, in the middle of the income distribution. Nevertheless, throughout this book, the terms *middle* and *middle class* are used interchangeably.

The reliance on income-based definitions has two advantages in the context of this book. First, the common data source—the *LIS* and *LWS*

Databases (discussed in the next section)—are most suited to this approach because the income data are extremely detailed, as well as highly standardized, across countries. Constructing cross-nationally comparable measures of education and occupation is much more difficult in the *LIS/LWS* data and, in fact, in all cross-country databases. Second, using this clearly quantifiable income-based framework enables a high level of comparability across the chapters.

Furthermore, within this income-based framework, the authors generally approach defining the middle class in one (or both) of two ways, both of which are common in the relatively limited comparative literature on the middle class (for a review, see Pressman 2007). One approach identifies a portion of the distribution, generally by defining specific decile groups as the middle class.[3] Several chapters use this strategy, in most cases defining the middle class as those households with income between the 20th and 80th percentiles—in other words, "the middle 60." A second approach establishes an interval defined by percentages of median household income. Several chapters use that method, most often defining the middle class as those households with income between 75 and 125 percent of the national median[4]—although some drew different intervals. For example, Frick and Grabka (Chapter 13) chose 70 to 150 percent (further disaggregating into lower-middle, middle-middle, and upper-middle), and Chauvel (Chapter 4), using a similar framework, selected 75 to 250 percent and also disaggregated the middle class into subgroups. Ólafsson and Kristjánsson (Chapter 15) selected 75 to 150 percent when studying Iceland, while Vanneman and Dubey (Chapter 16) used 50 to 200 percent in their study of India (where the distribution is especially skewed).

These two approaches, of course, enable different questions to be answered. Both approaches allow researchers to compare *characteristics* of the middle class (e.g., absolute income levels, intra-household earnings ratios, wealth holdings, political behavior) across countries, time periods, and/or income definitions. The latter approach also enables analysts to compare the *size* of the middle class, likewise across countries, time periods, and/or income definitions. Both sets of questions are raised in this book.

The Global Distribution of Income. What is the appropriate geographical unit for studying inequality? All of the chapters focus on distributions within countries (or, in the case of the chapter on India, within sub-national units). In recent years, there has been a vigorous debate about what has been happening to the world distribution of income—that is, the distribution among all persons in the world (see, e.g., Bourguignon and Morrisson 2002; Milanovic 2007). While that debate has yielded valuable insights, in our view, studies on levels and/or trends in economic well-being within countries—such as we present in this book—are warranted for several reasons. In particular, while economies have become increasingly integrated and interdependent, most economic and social policy making still operates at the national (or sub-national) level. Moreover, even if one were to focus on the world income distribution, the central building block for understanding that consists of the distribution within individual countries.

While the analysis of the distribution of income among all persons in the world has considerable merit—every person's well-being should, after all, matter equally—the examination of income distributions within individual countries is clearly meaningful as well. One reason is that data sources are, almost without exception, national (at least originally), so data definitions and concepts are much more uniform within countries. But importantly, there are relatively few possibilities for, say, UK policymakers to affect the distribution of income in, say, India, although they have a reasonable likelihood of influencing the UK distribution of income. In other words, because policy making is mostly nationally based, it surely makes sense to examine the distribution of economic well-being nationally as well.

Dowrick and Akmal (2005) assessed both inter-country inequality (the inequality of mean income across countries) and global inequality, highlighting problems associated with comparing real incomes across countries. Critiquing both those who use standard estimates of purchasing power parity (PPP)–adjusted exchange rates and current exchange rates, their estimates do suggest a moderate increase in global inequality between 1980 and 1993.

KEY ELEMENTS OF THE BOOK: A SHARED FRAMEWORK AND THE USE OF COMMON DATA

We commissioned the 17 studies that are presented in this book. When we did, we imposed four core requirements. First, a central component of each study had to be income, earnings, and/or wealth inequality—across households, within households, or both. We urged the authors focused on income inequality to emphasize comprehensive measures of income, especially post-tax and post-transfer (disposable) income (see Chapters 1 to 4). We engaged two sets of authors to assess interactions between income inequality and political outcomes (see Chapters 5 and 6). We invited the authors of three of the commissioned chapters to extend their analyses to gender disparities in employment outcomes and specifically to assess the interplay between gender disparities and income inequality more generally (see Chapters 7 to 9). We asked four researchers (or research teams) to focus their inequality analyses on wealth (see Chapters 10 to 13). Finally, we invited four chapters focused on country cases (Chapters 14 to 17), which we introduce below.

Second, the empirical component of each study had to be cross-national in design. Exceptions to this requirement were made for one of the wealth studies (see Chapter 13, which used single-country data to assess a question that has clear implications for cross-national wealth comparisons) and the four single-country studies that close this book. (We return to these below.)

Third, we asked several of the researchers to include within their inequality analyses some assessment of the middle class. While we did not impose a single definition of the middle class, we encouraged authors to define this group with respect to the income distribution.

Finally, we required that the researchers draw heavily on microdata that are available—or will be available—through LIS, a data archive that provides cross-nationally harmonized income and wealth microdata. We invited the contributors to supplement their use of the LIS data with other datasets as well, including either macro-level data or other microdata, provided that they drew mainly on LIS data to analyze inequality levels and trends and/or to define and assess the status of the middle class.

We imposed the use of this common data source to maximize (across the chapters) conceptual commonality, empirical comparability, and geographic and temporal consistency. Relying on LIS data allowed all of these authors to assess inequality with respect to a shared set of income, employment, and wealth concepts. The use of the harmonized LIS data ensured a high degree of comparability in the contents of key variables, across countries and time periods. Furthermore, the common use of LIS data also enhanced consistency across the chapters in the selection of both countries included and time periods studied.

LIS (the institution) is home to two microdatabases: the *Luxembourg Income Study Database* (also known as *LIS*) and the *Luxembourg Wealth*

Study Database (known as *LWS*).[5] (Detailed information is available from http://www.lisdatacenter.org.) These two databases contain microdata from several high- and middle-income countries. The LIS staff gathers datasets and harmonizes them, ex post, into a common template; that means they construct a common set of variables and a standard set of rules that determine the placement and treatment of variables from the original datasets. The LIS staff also makes available an extensive catalogue of documentation that provides information on the scope of the datasets included in the databases, characteristics of the original surveys, the rules of variable construction, variable availability (across datasets), and features of the institutions that correspond to the tax and transfer variables.

The *LIS Database* contains harmonized microdata from a large number of mostly high-income countries. The *LIS* datasets contain variables on market income, public transfers and taxes, household- and person-level characteristics, labor market outcomes, and, in some datasets, expenditures. The *LIS Database* currently includes harmonized microdata from 39 countries: 23 European countries; the United States, Canada, and Australia; Israel and Russia; South Korea and Taiwan; 6 Latin American countries (Brazil, Colombia, Guatemala, Mexico, Peru, and Uruguay); and China, India, and South Africa. These data currently span nine time points: (approximately) 1970–1975, 1980, 1985, 1990, 1995, 2000, 2004, 2007, and 2010. (As this book goes to press, some additional *LIS* microdatasets corresponding to 2007 and 2010 have become available.) Over-time data are not available for all of the countries included in *LIS*, because newly participating countries typically provide data from only the most recent time point. When data are available over time, they are available in the form of repeated cross sections.

The *LWS Database*, a new companion to the *LIS Database*, contains harmonized microdata from several high-income countries. The *LWS* datasets include variables on assets and debt, market and government income, household characteristics, labor market outcomes, and, in some datasets, expenditures and behavioral indicators. The *LWS Database* currently includes harmonized microdata from 12 countries: 9 European countries (Austria, Cyprus, Finland, Germany, Italy, Luxembourg, Norway, Sweden, and the United Kingdom), plus Japan, Canada, and the United States. These *LWS* datasets correspond (variously) to years between 1994 and 2006. As with the *LIS Database*, over-time data are not available for all of the participating countries, and, when available, the data take the form of re-peated cross sections. (See the Appendix to this Introduction, Table A1, for a complete list of countries currently included in the *LIS* and *LWS Databases*, with the standardized two-letter abbreviations that are used throughout this book.)

LIS—Expanding Horizons

LIS has traditionally concentrated its data work on high-income countries. According to the World Bank's country classification system (based on per capita income), of the 39 countries currently in the *LIS Database*, 28 are high-income and 11 are middle-income countries. Those 11 countries in-clude 6 from Latin America, as well as China, India, Romania, Russia, and South Africa. The *LWS* datasets are entirely from high-income countries. A current priority at LIS is adding a substantial number of microdatasets from middle-income countries—first to *LIS* and eventually to *LWS* as well. At press time, that effort is well underway.

The chapters address inequality almost entirely in high-income coun-tries. The 12 comparative chapters (Chapters 1 to 12) utilize datasets from high-income countries, with only two exceptions: one chapter includes Mexico and one includes Russia. This is simply because this group of commissioned authors started their work before a recent spate of middle-income datasets (from Latin America, and India and South Africa, thus far) was added to the LIS data archive.

Finally, among the 17 commissioned chapters are 4 (see Part VI) that assess inequality in selected countries for which microdata had not yet been added to the *LIS Database* when the chapters were commissioned. These countries include Japan (Chapter 14), Iceland (Chapter 15), India (Chap-ter 16), and South Africa (Chapter 17). We selected these four countries for specific reasons. We asked researchers using datasets from Japan and Iceland, both high-income countries, to prepare studies based on them, as they represent two substantively unique and interesting cases with respect to income distribution. In both of these chapters, the authors (using single-country datasets) include some results from after the global financial crisis. We also invited chapters focused on two of the incoming middle-income countries: India and South Africa. These two are included because, like Japan and Iceland, there is widespread interest in their income distribu-tions, especially because rapid change is underway. When this book goes to press, India and South Africa will also be included in the *LIS Database*, and income datasets from Japan and Iceland are in the pipeline and will be added soon.

INCOME INEQUALITY IN CROSS-NATIONAL PERSPECTIVE: A LOOK AT LEVELS AND TRENDS

The Literature

There is a vast and growing literature that documents cross-country variation in income inequality, as well as trends, much of it using the *LIS* microdata. The contributions of *LIS*-based analyses were summarized by Förster and Vleminckx (2004). Research based on *LIS* data has the advantage of using data that have been harmonized in multiple ways—for example, all *LIS* data have been annualized, and standardized income aggregates have been constructed and made available. Other decisions are left to researchers, but the data allow them to implement common practices across the countries included in their analyses, such as the method for adjusting for household size (i.e., the choice of equivalence scale) or, say, how to treat negative or zero incomes.

In their groundbreaking report prepared for the OECD, Atkinson, Rainwater, and Smeeding (1995) used the *LIS* data from the middle 1980s to establish the first widely accepted cross-country rankings of inequality across high-income countries. Using Gini coefficients to measure inequality, they found that the Nordic countries had the least inequality, followed by continental European countries, Canada, Australia, and the southern European countries, with the United States having the highest (Atkinson et al. 1995).

Many researchers have used the *LIS* data to examine and explain inequality levels and changes. Most recently, Immervoll and Richardson (2011) assess whether, and to what extent, government redistributive policies slowed or accelerated the trend toward greater income inequality over the last two to three decades. Wang and Caminada (2011) analyzed income inequality and the redistributive effect of social transfers; using a simulation approach, they decomposed income inequality into income tax and transfer sources. Grimm and colleagues (2009) examined how indices of human development vary across the income distribution. Cowell and Fiorio (2009) developed decomposition techniques to assess changes in inequality in the United States and Finland. Scholtz (2008) analyzed whether inequality change between 1985 and 2005 took place near the bottom or top of the distribution. Orgiazzi, Breen, and García-Peñalosa (2008) examined which income sources accounted for cross-country variation in levels and trends in inequality. Mohl and Pamp (2008) assessed links between inequality and redistributive spending, while Checchi and García-Peñalosa (2008) studied links between labor market institutions and income inequality.

While inequality increased in many (but not all) OECD countries in the late 1990s and early 2000s, the broad pattern of cross-country variation identified by Atkinson and colleagues (1995) and again by Förster and Vleminckx (2004) remains in place (OECD 2008). The focus of much of the research on cross-national variation in inequality has been on examining and accounting for *changes* in income inequality (see, e.g., Atkinson 2003; OECD 2008, 2011a; McCall and Percheski 2010). Accounts of the factors underlying changes in income inequality have focused mainly on developments that shift the distribution of labor market income, demographic factors (especially those that affect the sorting of persons with different earnings capacity into different family types), and changes to taxes and transfers.[6]

Many inequality scholars (mostly using data from sources other than *LIS*) have focused their analyses on specific regions. Gasparini and Lustig (2011) reported that income inequality actually declined in most Latin American countries in the 2000s, after having risen earlier. Surveying inequality changes in central and eastern Europe, Heyns (2005) observed that while most of these former state socialist countries experienced increases in overall inequality, the timing, size, and nature of those increases varied substantially.

Arguably, most assessments of inequality trends in high-income countries have focused on the effect of changes in labor markets—importantly, technological shifts, increased international trade, and changes in institutions affecting wage setting. The three explanations need not be mutually exclusive, and, indeed, Atkinson (1997b, 1999, 2003) has made the case that none of them alone can account for the observed trends in earnings inequality. For example, while increased international trade—globalization— is often thought to account for changes in earnings distributions, Atkinson argued that the observed patterns cannot easily be accounted for within a standard economic model of international trade—that is, the Hecksher-Olin model.

McCall and Percheski (2010) reviewed evidence of how changes in family structure and in married women's labor supply (mostly in the U.S. context) have affected income inequality. While the evidence is not clear-cut, it does appear that decreases in married-couple families have tended to increase inequality, while changes in women's employment behaviors and earnings have tended to decrease inequality. Whether or not marital homogamy (i.e., within-couple similarities) increases or decreases income inequality remains open to debate, and, to the best of our knowledge, little is known about how the pure effect of homogamy varies cross-nationally.

Incomes at the very top of the distribution have been increasing in many countries, something observed first in the United States (Piketty and Saez 2003), and later in many other countries as well (Atkinson and Piketty 2007, 2010). As suggested by McCall and Percheski (2010), explanations for the evolution of incomes at the very top should focus on different factors than those that account for overall inequality. In particular, changes in compensation practices for top private-sector officials and the market for top-end jobs are a common focus in this literature.

Furthermore, labor market income can be, and most likely is, affected by changes in capital markets. Atkinson (1997a) reported that the interest rate can affect the skill premium, which affects both the wage differential among persons with different educational qualifications and how the supply of skills reacts to changes in demand. In particular, the premium to higher education increases when real interest rates increase. Compensation of top private-sector officials may depend on returns in the financial sector as well as, for example, differential tax treatment of different types of compensation.

Mahler (2004) found that the evidence that suggests large inequality effects from globalization tends to be weak, a finding that is supported by Roine, Vlachos, and Waldenström (2009). Gustafsson and Johansson (1999), on the other hand, do find some support for the view that imports of manufactured goods are associated with greater inequality.

Public policy can both counteract and reinforce changes in inequality that stem from the market. For example, progressive income taxes can dampen the effects of increased earnings inequality. Rules that lead capital incomes to be taxed at lower rates than labor earnings again provide incentives to convert executive compensation into capital income (rather than labor income) and will thus lead to greater inequality.

A Contemporary Portrait of Income Inequality Based on LIS Data

We build on existing literature on levels and trends in income inequality, using the *LIS* microdata and drawing on the most recent "wave" of *LIS* data—that is, the data centered on 2004. In Figure I.1, we plot the Gini coefficient for each country against median disposable income, expressed

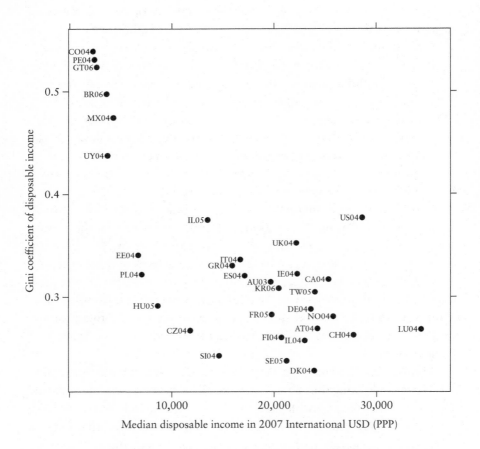

Figure I.1.   Inequality and real income levels—the Gini coefficient and median disposable income in selected countries (approximately 2004)

SOURCE: Authors' calculations from the *LIS Database*.

NOTE: Disposable incomes, adjusted for household size using the square root of household size, have been inflated to within-country 2007 prices using national consumer price indices for all items (IXOB) from OECD (2011b) and have been converted to international dollars using the PPPs for Actual Individual Consumption (A01) in 2007 from OECD (2011c). See Appendix Table A1 to this Introduction for country abbreviations.

in PPP-adjusted income (in 2007 prices). When assessing these inequality estimates, it is useful to keep in mind that they are based on sample data, so they are associated with sampling error. Atkinson (2003) cited evidence to suggest that, with samples of about 30,000, a difference in the Gini coefficient of about 0.01 indicates a statistically significant difference. He further applies the rule of thumb that a difference of about 0.03 is substantively meaningful. Because some of the *LIS* datasets have fewer than 30,000 observations, a conservative reading calls for applying the 0.03 standard.

The broad pattern of cross-country variation in inequality of disposable income has changed little since the publication of Atkinson, Rainwater, and Smeeding (1995), as can be seen in Figure I.1 (see also OECD 2008). Compared to Atkinson and colleagues, we have added data for six Latin American countries—Brazil, Colombia, Guatemala, Peru, Mexico, and Uruguay—that were unavailable in the earlier studies. We have also added several former state socialist countries: the Czech Republic, Estonia, Hungary, Poland, and Slovenia. Taken together, this extended group of countries spans a wide range of real household disposable income, from a low in Colombia of USD2,186 to a high of USD35,001 in Luxembourg (measured after adjusting for purchasing power using OECD PPPs for Actual Individual Consumption).

The country ranking in Figure I.1 indicates that the Latin American countries have inequality levels that are substantially higher than the rest, with Colombia reporting the highest level (0.539), followed by Peru (0.531) and Guatemala (0.528). Mexico, the only Latin American country that is a member of the OECD, tops the OECD inequality rankings with a Gini coefficient of 0.475. The U.S. Gini coefficient is 0.377, which makes it the second most unequal among the OECD countries, followed by Israel (0.375) and the United Kingdom (0.352). The ranking continues with Estonia, Italy, Greece, Poland, Spain, Ireland, Canada, Australia, Korea, and Taiwan, all with Gini coefficients above 0.30. The next group of countries includes Hungary, Germany, France, Norway, Luxembourg, Austria, the Czech Republic, Switzerland, Finland, and the Netherlands, all in close succession. Slovenia (0.243), Sweden (0.238), and Denmark (0.229) have the lowest levels of inequality.

We note that in very few cases do the differences between two adjacent countries exceed the 0.01 rule of thumb for statistical significance, and even more rarely is the economically significant difference of 0.03 exceeded. However, the broad patterns we observe are consistent with evidence from other sources—based, albeit in part, on the same sources (OECD 2008; Ward et al. 2009).

Measured across all these countries, inequality and median income are strongly negatively associated (rank correlation –0.60), and even after omitting the Latin American countries, the correlation is negative (rank correlation –0.26). Of course, we make no claim that this correlation is causal. Whatever relationships underlie this correlation, they are complex and affected by multiple factors.

To shed further light on the distribution of real income across the *LIS* countries, in Figure I.2, we plot the real disposable household income at the 10th, 50th (median income), and 90th percentiles of the distribution in each country, now ordered by the living standard of the 10th percentile. One of the ways in which inequality matters is that for a given level of real median income, greater inequality in a country may indicate that those at the bottom of the distribution have less purchasing power than those in another country with less inequality. For example, while the United States ranks second in median (and 90th percentile) income, it ranks as 14th with respect to the purchasing power of those at the 10th percentile (on this, see e.g., Rainwater and Smeeding, 2003). The U.S. official poverty line in 2007 (converted here from the line for a family of four, using our equivalence scale) is USD10,325, indicating that the 10th percentile incomes are just above the U.S. poverty line in 15 of our study countries—the 13 countries with 10th percentile incomes greater than those in the United States, as well as the United States and France—and are lower in the rest of the countries.

The United States and Luxembourg at USD64,087 and USD62,182, respectively, do have substantially higher real income at the 90th percentile than do the rest of the countries included here. Canada, Switzerland, Taiwan, and the United Kingdom fall next with incomes just below USD50,000. Taken across all countries, however, real income levels at different points in the distribution are quite highly correlated. Even the rank correlation between the 10th and 90th percentiles, which is lower than that of either of these with the median, is 0.88.

In Figure I.3, we summarize trends in income inequality as measured by the Gini coefficient of disposable income for 27 *LIS* countries included in the 2004 wave of the *LIS* data—and for which we have observations at multiple time points. Bearing in mind that inequality often changes episodically rather than in even trends (Atkinson 1997a), the most common pattern in evidence in Figure I.3 is of increasing inequality. There are, however,

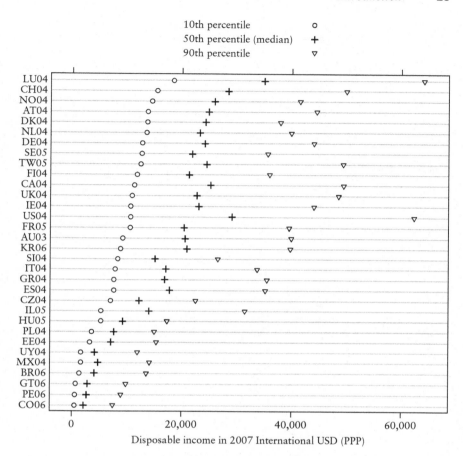

10th percentile   o
50th percentile (median)   +
90th percentile   ▽

Disposable income in 2007 International USD (PPP)

Figure I.2.   Real income in selected parts of the distribution of disposable income—selected countries (approximately 2004)

SOURCE: Authors' calculations from the *LIS Database*.

NOTE: Disposable incomes, adjusted for household size using the square root of household size, have been inflated to within-country 2007 prices using national consumer price indices for all items (IXOB) from OECD (2011b) and have been converted to international dollars using the purchasing power parities for Actual Individual Consumption (A01) in 2007 from OECD (2011c).

many exceptions to this. For example, inequality decreases quite substantially in the 2000s in Switzerland; decreases somewhat in Spain, Greece, Mexico, Sweden, and Slovenia; is nearly flat in Australia; and is even flatter in France, Italy, Ireland, Hungary, and the Netherlands. Among those countries where inequality has risen substantially, especially the United States and the United Kingdom, the change occurred mostly before the 2000s.

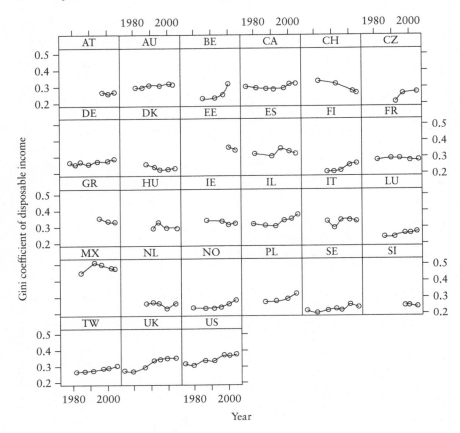

Figure I.3. Inequality trends in comparative perspective—Gini coefficients of disposable income in selected countries in all *LIS* waves

SOURCE: Authors' calculations from the *LIS Database*.

Here, we do not assess the reasons that shape the diverging trends across countries. Instead, we refer the reader to recent work by the OECD (2011a) for a detailed analysis of the trends and the factors underlying them.

SUBSTANTIVE AREAS OF RESEARCH IN THIS BOOK

Income: Trends in Household Income Inequality

Part I focuses on trends in income inequality. The background to Chapter 1, discussed in greater detail above, is that inequality has increased in many

LIS countries, but the shape of that increase varies substantially (Alderson, Beckfield, and Nielsen 2005). In Chapter 1, Arthur Alderson and Kevin Doran examine the shape of changes in the income distribution across *LIS* countries. Their point of departure is that the same change in aggregate inequality, as measured by, for example, the Gini coefficient, can come about in multiple ways, depending on what drivers are affecting the distribution of income. For instance, changes at the top of the distribution, driven by shifts in the compensation of top employees, generate different effects on the shape of the distribution than, for example, changes in the labor market participation of those at the bottom of the distribution. Alderson and Doran use relative distribution methods to explore the changing shape of within-country income distributions over time.

Specifically, they index all *LIS* datasets within a country to a base-year median and examine how subsequent distributions compare with the base-year distribution. In most cases, increased inequality takes place by households moving both toward the top and toward the bottom of the distribution, so the middle tends to hollow out. That hollowing out is usually distributed unevenly; in some countries, such as the United Kingdom and the United States, households have moved more toward the top than toward the bottom ("upgrading"), whereas in other countries, such as Sweden and Germany, there is relatively more movement toward the bottom ("downgrading").

The Middle Class: The Middle Class in the Income Distribution

Part II focuses on inequality and the position of the middle class. The authors in this section extend their inequality analyses in a common direction: they all take a deliberate and sustained look at the middle class. The vast literature on income inequality has long been tied to scholarship on low-income households (see, e.g., Ferreira and Ravallion 2009; Nolan and Marx 2009), and, in fact, the concept of relative poverty—which establishes poverty thresholds relative to the income distribution—is inextricably linked to inequality. Many studies that use the *LIS* data specifically intertwine analyses of inequality and poverty (see, e.g., Smeeding, O'Higgins, and Rainwater 1990; Rainwater and Smeeding 2003; Förster and Vleminckx 2004). Likewise, a spate of recent scholarship on inequality has focused attention on top incomes (see, e.g., Atkinson and Piketty 2007; Leigh 2009). In contrast, while several single-country and cross-national studies of inequality have reported variations on the linked phenomena of polarization and "the hollowing out of the middle," relatively little inequality scholarship has focused its attention on the economic status of the middle class per se—as the authors in this part do systematically.

Although inequality scholarship has given relatively short shrift to the status of the middle class, there is in fact a large literature that concerns the importance of having a strong and stable middle class, and that literature addresses countries at all income levels. Estache and Leipziger (2009), in the introduction to their book *Stuck in the Middle*, observed that the "essential role of the middle class has been recognized by politicians in many regions. It is a recurring theme in the United States [and] in Europe, but it is also an essential concern in many developing regions" (9). In their article "Why You Should Care about the Threatened Middle Class," Littrell and colleagues (2010) emphasized two claims that are widespread in this literature: a strong middle class is a prerequisite for a well-functioning democracy, and a secure middle class is vital for economic growth. Birdsall (2010) argued that the links between the middle-class strength and both democracy and growth operate in both directions; she describes both links as "virtuous circles." Focusing on developing countries, Ravallion (2010) observed that there are intrinsic and instrumental reasons to be concerned with the status of the middle class. He identified the core instrumental arguments for expanding the size of the middle class: fostering entrepreneurship, shifting the composition of consumer demand, and building political support for policy and institutional reforms that are conducive to growth and, in turn, effective in poverty amelioration.

A recent body of scholarship tackles the question of the effects of inequality per se on the well-being of the middle class. Perhaps the most colorful presentation is by Robert Frank in his widely cited 2007 book *Falling Behind: How Rising Inequality Harms the Middle Class*. Frank argues that rising inequality has inflated the ranks of the wealthy, and their high-end consumption patterns have influenced consumption among the middle class. As a result, although middle-income families earn only modestly more than they did in past decades, they have been induced to buy more expensive homes (as well as cars and appliances). Paying for these items squeezes out other types of consumption and drives these middle-class families into debt. Frank sums up his argument: "Increased spending at the top of the income distribution has imposed not only psychological costs on families in the middle, but also more tangible costs. In particular, it has raised the cost of achieving goals that most middle-class families regard as basic" (43).

The central question addressed in Chapter 2 is how the position of the middle class depends on the way it is defined. Chapter 3 examines whether increased income inequality has led to stunted income growth for the middle class. An associated line of inquiry concerns how the life chances of different birth cohorts have changed over time, especially with respect to their chances of attaining a middle-class income position. This question is addressed in Chapter 4.

In Chapter 2, Anthony Atkinson and Andrea Brandolini examine how assessments of characteristics of the middle depend on which definition of the middle class is used. Taking issue with conventionally adopted approaches, they argue for relying on income cutoffs, not proportions of the population (such as the middle 60 percent). Income cutoffs are commonly taken as defining the middle class as individuals with incomes between 75 and 125 percent of median income, but they suggest that the upper threshold needs to be set considerably higher—for example, at 200 percent of the median. This can lead to a different picture of the changes over time. They go on to argue that the middle class should be defined not only in terms of income but also by taking into account occupation and, ideally, wealth holdings as well. The middle-income class includes a substantial fraction of those identified by labor market position to be "working class" and "top class," in addition to those in traditionally middle-class positions. Also, many in the middle-income class turn out to be financially vulnerable in the sense of having low net worth. They conclude that a purely income-based analysis of the middle class may be insufficient and argue for integrating analyses of income, labor market position, and property holding. In this respect, they argue, there needs to be closer integration between the literatures in economics and sociology.

In Chapter 3, Lane Kenworthy assesses whether increased income inequality is associated with slower growth in the real income level of the middle class. Starting from the observation that this is the case in the United States, Kenworthy uses *LIS* data to examine if this also holds in other affluent countries. Examining middle-class real income at the 25th, 50th (median), and 75th percentiles of adjusted disposable household income, he finds that middle-class income growth is only modestly related to changes in levels of inequality. Kenworthy concludes that inequality is not a key driver of changes in absolute income among the middle class.

In Chapter 4, Louis Chauvel examines how those in the middle of the income distribution fare across different birth cohorts. Chauvel distinguishes between the lower-middle class (75 to 125 percent of median income) and the upper-middle class (125 to 250 percent of median income). Chauvel studies four countries, using *LIS* data from the mid-1980s to the mid-2000s, to assess whether changes in the economic fortunes and prospects for middle-class membership of different cohorts vary "episodically" and/or differ by the standard typologies of welfare state regimes. His study countries include Norway (representing the social democratic regime), France (corporatist), Italy (familialistic), and the United States (liberal). Chauvel concludes that France exhibits the greatest instability in age-income profiles, and Norway reports the most stability. In France, the post-war cohort (born during the years 1945 to 1950) is at a considerable advantage, while the cohort born from 1965 to 1970 is at a substantial disadvantage, when these cohorts are followed over time. In a regression analysis of middle-class membership, Chauvel again finds that in France the 1945–1950 cohort stands out as having better fortunes than others, with more pronounced differences across cohorts than in the other countries. Interestingly, while the cohort differences in the odds of being in either the lower-middle or upper-middle class are largest in France, the odds of reaching upper-middle-class membership decline for cohorts born in the 1960s and later in all four countries.

Politics: Inequality, Political Behavior, and Public Opinion

Part III focuses on politics and distribution. As we noted in at the beginning of this Introduction, inequality may affect civic engagement and the political process more generally (Gilens 2005; Blank 2011). There is an extensive theoretical and empirical literature on the interconnections among voting, inequality, and redistribution. (For reviews, see Borck 2007 and Savoia, Easaw, and McKay 2010; see also, for example, Alesina and Rodrik 1994; Benabou 2000; and Perotti 1996.) In earlier research on income inequality, much emphasis was placed on how politics affects inequality—that is, the political determinants of inequality. Mahler (2004), Brady and Leicht (2008), and Bradley and colleagues (2003) examined inequality and redistribution; these researchers concluded that the political composition of national governments affects inequality. More left-leaning governments are associated with less inequality, and right-leaning governments with more. Roine and colleagues (2009), in turn, found that government transfers and progressive taxation substantially redistribute income from the top of the distribution downward.

Most of this cross-national research has been conducted using the country-year as the observation unit. As we pointed out above, similar changes in aggregate inequality can come about in multiple ways, so a more disaggregated approach is advantageous. Moreover, most cross-national research to date has been focused on the effect of politics on inequality and redistribution—the central topic of Chapter 5. We know much less about the reverse process—that is, how inequality affects the formation of political preferences across countries. That is the subject of Chapter 6.

In Chapter 5, Vincent Mahler, David Jesuit, and Piotr Paradowski use *LIS* data from 1980 and later to examine links between government redistribution of income and political participation. They study the way in which redistribution affects income shares and how this has changed over time. They especially emphasize the role of government taxes and transfers in determining who ends up in the middle three income quintile groups (their measure of the middle class). Their results suggest that, over time, redistribution has generally decreased, although, even in the mid-2000s, redistribution still plays a substantial role in evening out the distribution of market income. They use data drawn from surveys of political participation and electoral turnout, ordered by income quintile group, as well as country-period level variables, such as the partisan composition of national government and the strength of labor unions, to assess the determinants of redistribution in different parts of the income distribution. While Mahler and colleagues' results suggest that political participation affects redistribution, the relationship between the two varies across the income distribution and by mode of participation, even within the middle-income classes.

In Chapter 6, István Tóth and Tamás Keller assess how redistributive preferences relate to personal attitudes and perceptions, as well as to the overall inequality in the societies in which people live. The conceptual framework is given by the median voter theorem, which suggests that greater inequality may lead to greater redistribution. Tóth and Keller point out, however, that voters differ along many dimensions other than their actual incomes, all having consequences for actual preferences for redistribution.

In addition, they argue that not only individual attributes but also contextual effects play a role in preference formation. They measure preferences for redistribution and subjective well-being and attitudes, using data from the Eurobarometer survey and income inequality estimated from *LIS* data around 2004. Reliance on Eurobarometer data for preferences and attitudes limits the analysis to only European Union member countries and, because the welfare state attitudes were only surveyed in 2009, to a single time point.

Their findings suggest that a significant part of the large observed cross-country variance of redistributive preference relates to the level of actual (and perceived) inequality in various societies. Those who live in highly unequal countries hold favorable attitudes toward redistribution. The difference in redistributive preference between high- and low-income respondents is largest in countries not with the lowest or highest levels of overall income inequality but those with medium inequality. They also find that the middle class will be more favorable to redistribution if society is perceived to consist of relatively more poor than rich persons. Other findings are largely in line with earlier literature: those with fewer resources and those who expect living standards to decline will be in favor of more redistribution, while those who believe poverty is poor individuals' own fault are less favorably disposed. Their theory-relevant conclusion is that for a better understanding of the preconditions and consequences of the median voter theorem, in addition to the actual income distribution, the self-evaluation of the income skew in general and the median voter in particular should also be analyzed.

Employment: Women's Work, Inequality, and the Economic Status of Families

Part IV addresses the role of women's work in the economic status of families. Two facts are well documented in the comparative literatures on women's employment and family economic security. First, across the industrialized countries, women's attachment to the labor market has increased over the last four decades; most substantially, women's employment rates have risen (especially among married mothers), and gender earnings gaps have narrowed. At the same time, despite making substantial gains, in all high- and middle-income countries, women's employment outcomes still lag men's, especially among the subset of adults who are parents. Compared to their male counterparts, women (especially those with children) are less likely to be employed, they work fewer average hours per week, they are less likely to be employed in remunerative occupations, and on average they earn less, both hourly and annually (see Gornick 2004 for a review; also see Pettit and Hook 2010). While many researchers have assessed gender gaps in employment outcomes overall, others have focused on employment and/or earnings differentials between women and men within couples (see, e.g., Winkler 1998; Smith 2010). Second, rising employment among women implies that women's earnings are an increasingly influential component in household income. Cancian and Reed (2009) report that in the United States, for example, the employment rate of married women with preschool-age children rose from 41 to 68 percent between 1970 and 1990, but then leveled off, showing little change between 1990 and 2006. During that same interval, 1969 to 2006, the poverty rate among families increased modestly. Had female employment not increased during those years, the increase in poverty would have been more than double what it was.[7] Mishel, Bernstein, and Shierholz (2009) further illuminate the U.S. case with a focus on married-couple families with children. They assessed changing income among these families between 1979 and 2006 and found that real family income grew in each quintile group: by 7.4 percent in the bottom fifth, by 24.3 percent in the middle fifth, and by 66.2 percent in the top fifth. Mishel and colleagues report that, in these families, wives' increased contributions to family income were hugely influential. For example, in the middle fifth, that nearly 25 percent increase would have been about only 5 percent in the absence of increasing wives' contribution to household income.

These two literatures together—one on patterns of gender employment gaps across countries and over time and the other on the effect of wives' earnings on household income—combine to motivate a specific question regarding economic outcomes among families headed by couples: what is the impact on income inequality across households of women's changing and/or varying level of engagement in paid work? In short, is women's paid work equalizing or dis-equalizing with regard to inter-household income inequality? This question is addressed in detail in Chapters 7 and 8.

In addition, a growing literature has established that work-family reconciliation policies (such as child care, leave programs, and working time regulation) play a substantial role in shaping women's employment outcomes and, by extension, gender differentials between women and men overall and within couples (for a review of this literature, see Hegewisch and Gornick 2011). A number of scholars have assessed the effects of other institutions, such as public employment, employment protection legislation, and taxation (see, e.g., Gustafsson 1992; Gornick and Jacobs 1998; Jaumotte 2003; OECD 2005, 2006; Rubery 2010). The effect of institutions on wives' contributions to household earnings is central to Chapter 9.

In Chapter 7, Susan Harkness begins by reviewing the growing cross-national literature on the question of the effect of women's employment on inter-household inequality. Although it is often argued, especially in popular discourse, that women's rising employment, combined with homogamy, has increased inter-household income differentials, in fact, several studies (both single-country and cross-national) find otherwise. That is largely because, in most countries, women's increased contributions to household earnings have raised household income at the bottom of the income distribution much more than at the top. In her own empirical work, Harkness assesses the impact of women's earnings on household income inequality, using *LIS* microdata on 17 countries at approximately 2004. She employs both standard decomposition methods and three counterfactuals: no women work for pay; all women work for pay; and employment is unchanged, but there is no gender pay gap. Harkness concludes that, overall, women's employment has an equalizing effect on the income distribution in all countries. If, for example, all women worked for pay (imputing regression-adjusted female wages for the currently non-employed women), total earnings inequality would fall in all countries by an amount ranging from 24 percent in Germany and Luxembourg to over 60 percent in Greece and Italy. She also finds that closing the earnings gap (by imputing regression-adjusted men's earnings to all women) would also have an equalizing effect but one that is smaller than the effect of increased employment rates.

Harkness disaggregates some of her findings by class, taking a close look at middle-earning couples. One key finding is that, in terms of couples' employment patterns, this middle-earning group—defined as the middle three income quintile groups with respect to couples' earnings—resembles the top fifth more than it does the bottom fifth. Across the 17 study countries, in households in the bottom fifth, the minority of households (generally between 20 and 40 percent) include two earners, which is, of course, what places them so low in the distribution. In contrast, in 14 of the 17 countries (all except for three southern European countries), the majority of middle-income couples include two earners, as is the case in all countries for couples in the top fifth of the earnings distribution.

In Chapter 8, Nancy Folbre, Janet Gornick, Helen Connolly, and Teresa Munzi extend Harkness's empirical analysis, using an approach that is unusual in this literature. They start by observing that most studies of the impact of higher, or increasing, levels of women's employment on earnings inequality ignore the amount of time that women, and men, devote to unpaid work. To remedy that, Folbre and colleagues use cross-national time-use microdata to construct estimates of time spent in unpaid child care and domestic work; using aggregate data, they estimate the market value of these unpaid work hours. Then, by matching on subgroup characteristics, they impute the value of unpaid work into the *LIS* microdata; that enables them to assess women's contribution to couples' total market earnings (from paid work), as well as their contribution to couples' "extended" earnings, where extended earnings is the sum of the value of paid and unpaid work. Folbre and colleagues decompose household market earnings and arrive at results similar to Harkness's. They then turn to extended earnings and conclude that incorporating the imputed value of unpaid work has a further equalizing effect on the inter-household income distribution in all countries, albeit to varying degrees across countries.

In Chapter 9, Margarita Estévez-Abe and Tanja Hethey-Maier assess what is essentially the prior question: What institutional factors shape women's employment outcomes and, by extension, women's relative contribution to couples' earnings? Their key findings are that the strictness of labor market regulation (i.e., employment protections) has a significant negative effect on wives' relative contribution to household income, while generous paid leaves increase wives' contributions. Surprisingly, they found no significant effects of the size of the public sector or the generosity of public child care provisions (both expected to boost wives' relative earnings), or of the magnitude of tax penalties on second earnings (expected to depress wives' contributions), although, with all three institutional factors, the coefficients were generally in the expected direction. Estévez-Abe and Hethey-Maier also focus portions of their analysis on middle-class couples, which they define as households with disposable income between 75 and 125 percent of national median household income. Like Harkness, they find that couples report different earnings patterns at different parts of the income distribution and, furthermore, that institutional factors appear to influence the ways couples' earnings patterns vary by class.

Wealth: The Distribution of Assets and Debt

For over two decades, the *LIS Database* has allowed comparative researchers to study income distributions, using harmonized data, across a large number of high-income (and increasingly middle-income) countries. At the same time, there were few options for assessing the distribution of wealth cross-nationally, and most studies that were carried out had to rely on unharmonized data (see, e.g., Guiso, Haliassos, and Jappelli 2001; Jäntti and Sierminska 2008).

The purpose of the *LWS Database*—established in 2007—is to facilitate such cross-national comparisons; for an overview of the data, see Sierminska, Brandolini, and Smeeding (2006). The national wealth datasets that the *LWS Database* contains are, unfortunately, too diverse to allow for a single comprehensive definition of net worth to be created. Nevertheless, a small but growing comparative literature has developed, based on the *LWS* data.

Sierminska, Brandolini, and Smeeding (2006) present estimates of wealth levels across countries; their results indicate that the ordering of countries by wealth inequality is somewhat surprising with respect to what we know about income inequality. For example, they report that Sweden, one of the most equal countries with respect to the income distribution, has the greatest level of wealth inequality. While this is accounted for by a large fraction of households with substantial housing debt, this result raises pressing questions about the links between income and wealth. Moreover, median levels of net worth are exceptionally high in Italy, followed by the United States, which suggests that country rankings by real income levels may be markedly different from those based on wealth. These questions are addressed in detail in Chapters 10 and 11.

Much work remains to be done on developing the concept of net worth to arrive at internationally comparable benchmarks. Two major components of wealth across countries are housing and pension wealth. Housing is included in the *LWS* measures of net worth, although most pensions are not.

Principal residence constitutes between one-half to three-quarters of overall household net worth in most of the *LWS* countries (Sierminska et al.

2006). However, comparisons of income inequality rarely take into account the value of owner-occupied housing. How important this is for cross-country comparisons of economic well-being varies with the prevalence of owner-occupied housing. Variation in home-ownership patterns may also affect comparisons of economic well-being across groups *within* countries, especially the elderly compared to the working-age population. This issue is examined in Chapter 12.

The omission of much pension wealth from net worth comparisons is also problematic. An important source of institutional variation across countries is the income maintenance system for the elderly. It is customary to talk of "pillars" of the pension system. The "first pillar" is defined as the basic (flat-rate and sometimes means-tested) legislated pension. The "second pillar" includes legislated pensions that are conditioned on labor market and earnings histories. The "third pillar" consists of assorted voluntary private and occupational systems. The extent to which future pension rights are defined as part of an individual's or a household's wealth varies across countries. In general, however, net worth excludes the value of "first pillar" and "second pillar" pension wealth, which is especially problematic given that these increasingly provide the bulk of the incomes of the retired; in addition, net worth only infrequently includes "third pillar" pension wealth. And, in fact, the inclusion of pension wealth, where available, in estimates of net worth is not uncontroversial. Pension wealth is like other assets in that it can provide an income stream, but in general pension wealth cannot be sold, and in many cases (this varies from country to country) pension holders have limited, if any, rights to bequeath their pension wealth to family members when they die. Pension wealth is quantitatively important, however, and examining how the distribution of wealth changes when it is added to net worth is a crucial topic in wealth research. This is addressed in Chapter 13.

In Chapter 10, Eva Sierminska, Timothy Smeeding, and Serge Allegrezza examine the net worth of households in Italy, Luxembourg, Sweden, the United Kingdom, and the United States. Specifically, they examine all households as well as single-parent and two-parent families separately. Their analysis focuses on levels of net worth, portfolio composition, and the wealth package of households with an emphasis on home-ownership rates and home values. They find large differences across countries in wealth levels, driven to a great extent by differences in home values. Rates of home ownership vary less; holdings of financial assets account for a relatively small share of cross-country variation in wealth levels. In analyzing the affordability of home ownership across the income distribution, they find that home-value-to-income ratios are highest where home values are highest: in Luxembourg, Italy, and Germany. They conclude that this is also true among the middle class, suggesting that, in these countries, housing is the least affordable for middle-class households.

In Chapter 11, Markus Jäntti, Eva Sierminska, and Philippe Van Kerm use *LWS* data for Germany, Italy, Luxembourg, Sweden, and the United States to explore the joint distribution of income and wealth. Many authors argue that wealth matters because the capacity to finance consumption out of wealth can be important when incomes are low. Examination of the joint distribution of disposable income and net worth can suggest ways in which these two resources capture similar levels of well-being. It turns out that income and wealth are highly, but not perfectly, correlated. Net worth is much more unequally distributed than disposable income, but households at similar income levels have quite varying levels of net worth. Descriptive bivariate regressions of disposable income and net worth against age, education, and family structure variables capture a reasonable fraction of the overall variance of both income and wealth. The coefficient estimates are qualitatively similar, but the differences among groups vary across countries. Even after that part of the similarity in net worth and disposable income that is accounted for by systematic differences across groups defined by age, education, and family structure has been accounted for, net worth and disposable income remain highly positively associated.

In Chapter 12, Bruce Bradbury assesses the role that housing plays in supporting consumption by the elderly. Bradbury notes that home ownership, the rate of which varies substantially across countries, supports consumption by providing a flow of housing services that would otherwise require expenditures on rent. The failure to include such imputed rents from owner-occupied housing may distort the impression of the economic well-being of the elderly, both relative to younger cohorts within countries and relative to the elderly in other countries. Moreover, economic inequality among the elderly may be different if housing consumption is taken into account. Bradbury uses *LWS* data for Canada, Finland, Germany, Italy, Sweden, the United Kingdom, and the United States, along with national data for wealth and income in Australia, to explore to what extent inclusion of housing consumption alters conclusions about the economic well-being of the elderly.

Bradbury concludes that taking housing into account can lead to quite different conclusions about retirement living standards from those found when examining income alone. Taking housing into account means that the "replacement rate" (i.e., the income or consumption level of the elderly relative to the non-aged) is substantially increased in the United States and Australia but unchanged in Sweden. Defining the middle class in terms of the three middle-income quintile groups, Bradbury finds that, among the elderly population, incorporating housing consumption reduces the gaps between the middle, top, and bottom in most countries, and substantially so in Australia. Both Australia and the United States have a particularly high rate of home ownership among the older population. The distributional impact of home ownership on retirement living standards, however, is very different in the two countries. Housing wealth is strongly correlated with income in the United States but weakly correlated in Australia, implying a reinforcing of income-based inequality in the former but not the latter country. Taken together, Bradbury's results suggest that home ownership and housing wealth are of central importance in understanding both the average standard of living of the elderly and the inequality in those living standards.

In Chapter 13, Joachim Frick and Markus Grabka examine how the distribution of net worth in Germany changes when pension wealth is included. Their assessment focuses on a single dataset included in the *LWS Database*: Germany in 2007. This is because the inclusion of pension wealth requires the authors to access microdata on pension entitlements from administrative records that had to be statistically matched onto the data that underlie the German *LWS* dataset, the German Socio-Economic Panel (SOEP). While the exact consequences for the distribution of net worth of adding pension entitlements depends on several assumptions—key being the assumed rate of return to pension assets—it is clear that average net worth is considerably higher, and much more evenly distributed, once it has been augmented by pension wealth.

At the same time, Frick and Grabka find that there are large differences across occupational groups, depending on the generosity of pension arrangements. Adding pension entitlements is especially important for the middle class (defined as falling within the band of 70 to 150 percent of the median). Among the lower middle class (defined as 70 to 90 percent of the median) net worth triples, while it doubles for the upper middle class (defined as 130 to 150 percent of the median). It is also likely that the extent to which net worth changes when pension wealth is incorporated depends on individual labor market histories and on institutional arrangements that regulate how pension entitlements are divided following marital dissolution; as a result, the effect of accounting for pension wealth is likely to be different between men and women. The authors end by strongly recommending that pension entitlements be included in comparisons of net worth across countries.

Country Case Studies: Inequality in Japan, Iceland, India, and South Africa

As noted earlier, we invited four country case study chapters—two from high-income countries (Japan and Iceland) and two from middle-income countries (India and South Africa)—all new or incoming participants in the *LIS* and/or *LWS Databases*. We include chapters on Japan and Iceland because they each provide a unique look at a high-income country that is rarely included in cross-national inequality comparisons. Furthermore, both chapters (using data prior to being harmonized by *LIS*) offer at least a glimpse at post-crisis outcomes. We invited chapters focused on India and South Africa because they are two of the largest middle-income countries and are also among the most interesting due to their rapidly shifting income distributions.

In Chapter 14, Colin McKenzie uses data from two Japanese household panel surveys—the Keio Household Panel Survey (KHPS) for the period 2004–2009 and the Japan Household Panel Survey (JHPS) for 2009—to examine income and consumption inequality levels and trends, income mobility, and the concentration of assets in Japan.

Using annual household income to compute Gini coefficients, McKenzie finds that there is little change in income inequality in Japan during the period 2004–2009. In contrast, short-term income mobility in the middle to late 2000s declined relative to 2000–2001 for all income quintile groups except the top group. Finally, comparing the asset holdings of Japanese households with those in other countries included in the *LWS Database* suggests that Japan falls somewhere in the middle of this cross-national range. The principal residence forms the largest component of Japanese households' wealth portfolio in all quintile groups. McKenzie also finds that debt appears to be concentrated in the 35- to 55-year-old age group. The proportion of Japanese households reporting positive net worth is approximately the same as in Finland and the United Kingdom.

In Chapter 15, Stefán Ólafsson and Arnaldur Kristjánsson use data from the tax authorities in Iceland to examine how inequality evolved between the early 1990s and 2009—that is, before, during, and after the remarkable economic bubble in Iceland that deflated in 2008. They find that, starting from largely Nordic levels of inequality, income inequality in Iceland soared as the bubble built up—with the Gini coefficient increasing from 0.28 in 1992 to 0.44 in 2007 and then decreasing to 0.34 in 2009.

They define the middle class in two different ways—as the three middle-income quintile groups and as those with income in the range of 75 to 150 percent of the median—and find that the bubble did not lead to substantial income growth for the middle class by either definition. For much of the period 1994–2007, the very top income earners in Iceland benefited from far greater income growth than the rest. While the subsequent bust (2007–2009) led to a decline in real income of about a quarter for the top decile group, all earners experienced income declines. The authors also find that the increase in inequality occurred mainly through an increase in financial earnings but was reinforced by a change in the tax regime in 1997, which shifted the burden of taxation toward the middle- and lower-income groups.

In Chapter 16, Reeve Vanneman and Amaresh Dubey assess inequality in India—one of the countries that is central to *LIS*'s expansion into middle-income countries. The authors draw on data from the 2005 India Human Development Survey, the first nationally representative survey that gathered detailed income data in India. After accounting for inter-regional price differences in India, the authors estimate that a lower-bound estimate of the Gini coefficient for income inequality is 0.48—a level that is well above that found in most high-income countries. It is also well above earlier estimates of Indian inequality that relied on expenditure data.

Taking up what they refer to as "horizontal inequality," Vanneman and Dubey assess variation across the Indian states (of which there are 22 after they combined a few smaller states). They find that there is sharp variation across states in both income levels and income inequality—in fact, as much variation as is seen across the high-income countries contained in the *LIS Database*. Households in the highest-income Indian states have three times the median income as those in the low-income states, and Gini coefficients vary, across states, by 17 points. In addition, across states, inequality in the upper part of the income distribution (i.e., between middle-income and affluent households) is almost uncorrelated with inequality in the lower part of the income distribution (i.e., between middle-income and poor households).

Vanneman and Dubey define middle-income households in India as those households whose (size-adjusted) income is above 50 percent and below 200 percent of the all-India median. This interval, they report, contains about 60 percent of Indian households, with about one-fifth falling below and one-fifth falling above. Their analysis highlights the complexity of defining the middle class in a case such as India. They note that although this is a conventional relative definition of the middle class, when they assess real income levels, "this middle-income group is not what would be considered middle class in any global sense." They conclude that a more recognizable "middle class" might actually be those households they have identified as affluent—that is, households with incomes above twice the Indian median.

In Chapter 17, Murray Leibbrandt, Arden Finn, and Ingrid Woolard use survey data from two points in time—1993 and 2008—to assess changing inequality in South Africa. Their analysis is based on income and expenditure data from the 1993 Project for Statistics on Living Standards and Development and the 2008 base wave of the National Income Dynamics Study.

They find that inequality has increased since the end of Apartheid in 1994, due to an increased share of income going to the top decile group. They also report that social grants have become a more important source of income in the lower decile groups. However, income source decompositions reveal that the labor market was and remains the key driver of aggregate inequality. Their results also indicate that inequality within each racial group has risen over time, while between-race inequality has declined. Furthermore, they note that income and expenditure data indicate consistent stories, but the expenditure data suggest larger changes in inequality over time.

Leibbrandt and colleagues observe that operationalizing a concept of the "middle class" in the South African context is a challenging task—largely due to the heavily skewed nature of the income distribution (toward the richest decile group). The consequence of this is that there is little difference between the income accruing to households in the lower, compared

List of countries in the LIS and LWS Databases *with country abbreviations and wave/year correspondence in the* LIS Database

A: COUNTRIES, TWO-LETTER ABBREVIATIONS IN THE *LIS* AND *LWS DATABASES*

Country	Abbreviation	In the LIS/LWS Database
Australia	AU	*LIS*
Austria	AT	*LIS, LWS*
Belgium	BE	*LIS*
Brazil	BR	*LIS*
Canada	CA	*LIS, LWS*
China	CN	*LIS*
Colombia	CO	*LIS*
Cyprus	CY	*LWS*
Czech Republic	CZ	*LIS*
Denmark	DK	*LIS*
Estonia	EE	*LIS*
Finland	FI	*LIS, LWS*
France	FR	*LIS*
Germany	DE	*LIS, LWS*
Greece	GR	*LIS*
Guatemala	GT	*LIS*
Hungary	HU	*LIS*
India	IN	*LIS*
Ireland	IE	*LIS*
Israel	IL	*LIS*
Italy	IT	*LIS, LWS*
Japan	JP	*LWS*
Luxembourg	LU	*LIS, LWS*
Mexico	MX	*LIS*
Netherlands	NL	*LIS*
Norway	NO	*LIS, LWS*
Peru	PE	*LIS*
Poland	PL	*LIS*
Romania	RO	*LIS*
Russia	RU	*LIS*
Slovak Republic	SK	*LIS*
Slovenia	SI	*LIS*
South Africa	ZA	*LIS*
South Korea	KR	*LIS*
Spain	ES	*LIS*
Sweden	SE	*LIS, LWS*
Switzerland	CH	*LIS*
Taiwan	TW	*LIS*
United Kingdom	UK	*LIS, LWS*
United States	US	*LIS, LWS*
Uruguay	UY	*LIS*

(*continued*)

APPENDIX TABLE A1
(Continued)
B: WAVE/YEAR CORRESPONDENCE IN THE
LIS DATABASE

Wave	Year (circa)
Historical	1967–1975
I	1980
II	1985
III	1990
IV	1995
V	2000
VI	2004
VII	2007
VIII	2010

SOURCE: http://www.lisdatacenter.org/our-data/
lis-database/documentation/list-of-datasets/ (*LIS*)
and http://www.lisdatacenter.org/our-data/lws-data
base/documentation/lws-datasets-list/ (*LWS*).

to the middle, decile groups. (This finding echoes the results for India, reported in Chapter 16). Nevertheless, using household income (per capita), they define the middle class as "the middle 60." Using this definition, they assess change over time in the factors allocating individuals into or out of the middle class. They find that rising within-race inequality makes race a weaker predictor of being in the middle class in 2008, compared with 1993. In 2008, all racial groups—except whites—have some members with increased probabilities of exiting the middle class by moving upward and other members with increased probabilities of exiting the middle class by moving downward. In contrast, having tertiary education is shown to un-ambiguously push people out of the middle class and upward.

In closing, these 17 empirical chapters—taken together—demonstrate the advantages of adopting a multi-dimensional approach to the study of inequality—that is, an approach that integrates measures of income, employment, and wealth. This book further extends conventional analyses of inequality by casting a light on the middle of the income distribution—a segment that often receives short shrift in the inequality literature—and by addressing fundamental questions about the interplay between inequality and political outcomes. This multi-dimensional and multi-faceted approach allows us to construct a complex portrait of inequality across high-income countries, as it was on the eve of the global financial crisis that marked the end of the first decade of the twenty-first century.

NOTES

1. This series is available online at http://www.urban.org/poverty/consequencesofpoverty.cfm.

2. Chapter 2, by Atkinson and Brandolini, is a partial exception. In one portion of their empirical analysis, they incorporate information on occupation and wealth.

3. Estache and Leipziger (2009) take this approach as well, but emphasize there is no clear agreement on which deciles to include: "Although there is a wide range of definitions of the middle class, from economic to sociological, we focus here on the most traditional economic definition that defines the middle class in terms of the income decile that the population belongs to. . . . This is itself a subject of debate, since there is no consensus on the specific deciles that define the middle class" (9). Pressman (2007) observes, however, that the middle 60 is the most commonly used definition in this literature.

4. The 75 to 125 percent definition is generally attributed to Lester Thurow, who argued for this definition in 1986 (Wogart 2010).

5. For clarity, when we refer to the institution LIS, it is not italicized. *LIS* and *LWS Databases* are italicized.

6. Burkauser, Feng, and Jenkins (2009) point to a potential problem in studies of inequality trends, at least using U.S. data, which is that top-coding procedures have changed and that may affect both the magnitude and timing of the U.S. trend in inequality.

7. Rising rates of single parenthood operated in the opposite direction—that is, pushing the poverty rate above what it would have been in the absence of changes in family structure. Also see McCall and Percheski (2010) on this point.

For additional results, please see the online appendices by following the link in the listing for Income Inequality *on the Stanford University Press website: http://www.sup.org.*

REFERENCES

Aaberge, Rolf, Anders Björklund, Markus Jäntti, Mårten Palme, Peder J. Pedersen, Nina Smith, and Tom Wennemo. 2002. "Income Inequality and Income Mobility in the Scandinavian Countries Compared to the United States." *Review of Income and Wealth* 48(4): 443–69.

Aghion, Philippe, Eve Caroli, and Cecilia García-Peñalosa. 1999. "Inequality and Growth: The Perspective of the New Growth Theories." *Journal of Economic Literature* 37(4): 1615–60.

Alderson, Arthur, Jason Beckfield, and François Nielsen. 2005. "Exactly How Has Income Inequality Changed? Patterns of Distributional Change in Core Societies." *International Journal of Comparative Sociology* 46(5): 405–23.

Alesina, Alberto, and Dani Rodrik. 1994. "Distributive Politics and Economic Growth." *Quarterly Journal of Economics* 109(2): 465–90.

Atkinson, Anthony B. 1997a. "Bringing Income Distribution in from the Cold." *Economic Journal* 107(441): 297–321.

———. 1997b. *Three Lectures on Poverty in Europe.* Forthcoming. Malden, MA: Blackwell.

———. 1999. *"Is Rising Inequality Inevitable? A Critique of the Transatlantic Consensus."* WIDER annual lectures 3. http://www.wider.unu.edu/publications/annual-lectures/.

———. 2003. "Income Inequality in OECD Countries: Data and Explanations." *CESifo Economic Studies* 49(4): 479–513.

Atkinson, Anthony B., and Thomas Piketty, eds. 2007. *Top Incomes over the 20th Century.* Oxford: Oxford University Press.

———. 2010. *Top Incomes: A Global Perspective.* Oxford: Oxford University Press.

Atkinson, Anthony B., Lee Rainwater, and Timothy M. Smeeding. 1995. *"Income Distribution in the OECD Countries: The Evidence from the Luxembourg Income Study." Social Policy Studies* 18. Paris: OECD.

Bartels, Larry M. 2009. "Economic Inequality and Political Representation." In *The Unsustainable American State*, edited by Lawrence R. Jacobs. Oxford: Oxford University Press.

Benabou, Roland. 2000. "Unequal Societies: Income Distribution and the Social Contract." *American Economic Review* 90(1): 96–129.

Birdsall, Nancy. 2010. *The (Indispensable) Middle Class in Developing Countries, Or the Rich and the Rest, Not the Poor and the Rest.* Washington, DC: Center for Global Development.

Björklund, Anders, and Markus Jäntti. 2009. "Intergenerational Income Mobility and the Role of Family Background." In *Oxford Handbook of Economic Inequality*, edited by Wiemer Salverda, Brian Nolan, and Timothy M. Smeeding. Oxford: Oxford University Press.

Blank, Rebecca M. 2011. *Changing Inequality.* Berkeley: University of California Press.

Borck, Rainald. 2007. "Voting, Inequality and Redistribution." *Journal of Economic Surveys* 21(1): 90–109.

Bourguignon, François, and Christian Morrisson. 2002. "Inequality among World Citizens: 1820–1992." *American Economic Review* 92(4): 727–44.

Bowles, Samuel, and Herbert Gintis. 1998. *"Recasting Egalitarianism: New Rules for Communities, States and Markets."* In *The Real Utopia Series*, edited by Erik Olin Wright. London: Verso.

Bradley, David, Evelyne Huber, Stephanie Moller, Francois Nielsen, and John Stephens. 2003. "Distribution and Redistribution in Postindustrial Democracies." *World Politics* 55(2): 193–228.

Brady, David, and Kevin Leicht. 2008. "Party to Inequality: Right Party Power and Income Inequality in Affluent Western Democracies." *Research in Social Stratification and Mobility* 26(1): 77–106.

Burkhauser, Richard V., Shuaizhang Feng, and Stephen P. Jenkins. 2009. "Using the P90/P10 Ratio to Measure US Inequality Trends with Current Population Survey Data: A View from Inside the Census Bureau Vaults." *Review of Income and Wealth* 55(1): 166–85.

Burkhauser, Richard, and Kenneth Couch. 2009. "Intragenerational Inequality and Intertemporal Mobility." In *Oxford Handbook of Economic Inequality*, edited by Wiemer Salverda, Brian Nolan, and Timothy M. Smeeding. Oxford: Oxford University Press.

Burkhauser, Richard, and John G. Poupore. 1997. "A Cross-National Comparison of Permanent Inequality in the United States and Germany." *Review of Economics and Statistics* 79(1): 10–17.

Byers, Dylan. 2011. "Occupy Wall Street Is Winning." *Politico.* http://www.politico.com/blogs/bensmith/1111/Occupy_Wall_Street_is_winning.html.

Cancian, Maria, and Deborah Reed. 2009. "Changes in Family Structure, Childbearing, and Employment: Implications for the Level and Trend in Poverty." In *Changing Poverty*, edited by Maria Cancian and Sheldon Danziger. New York: Russell Sage Foundation.

Checchi, Daniele, and Cecilia García-Peñalosa. 2008. "Labour Market Institutions and Income Inequality." *LIS* working paper 470. Luxembourg: LIS.

Cowell, Frank A., and Carlo V. Fiorio. 2009. "Inequality Decompositions. A Reconciliation." Working paper 117. Palma de Mallorca, Spain: Society for the Study of Economic Inequality.

Daly, Mary C., and Robert G. Valletta. 2008. "Cross-National Trends in Earnings Inequality and Instability." *Economics Letters* 99(3): 215–19.

Dowrick, Steven, and Muhammad Akmal. 2005. "Contradictory Trends in Global Income Inequality." *Review of Income and Wealth* 51(2): 201–29.

Estache, Antonio, and Danny Leipziger, eds. 2009. *Stuck in the Middle: Is Fiscal Policy Failing the Middle Class?* Washington, DC: Brookings Institution Press.

Expert Group on Household Income Statistics [The Canberra Group]. 2001. *Final Report and Recommendations.* Ottawa: Statistics Canada.

Feldstein, Martin. 1998. "Income Inequality and Poverty." Working paper 6770. Cambridge, MA: National Bureau of Economic Research.

Ferreira, Francisco H. G., and Martin Ravallion. 2009. "Poverty and Inequality: The Global Causes." In *Oxford Handbook of Economic Inequality*, edited by Wiemer Salverda, Brian Nolan, and Timothy M. Smeeding. Oxford: Oxford University Press.

Forbes, Kristin J. 2000. "A Reassessment of the Relationship between Inequality and Growth." *American Economic Review* 90(4): 869–87.

Förster, Michael F., and Koen Vleminckx. 2004. "International Comparisons of Income Inequality and Poverty: Findings from the Luxembourg Income Study." *Socio-Economic Review* 2(2): 191–212.

Frank, Robert. 2007. *Falling Behind: How Rising Inequality Harms the Middle Class.* New York: Russell Sage Foundation.

Gasparini, Leonardo, and Nora Lustig. 2011. "The Rise and Fall of Income Inequality in Latin America." In *Oxford Handbook of Latin American Economics*, edited by Jose A. Ocampo and Jaime Ros. Oxford: Oxford University Press.

Gilens, Martin. 2005. "Inequality and Democratic Responsiveness." *Public Opinion Quarterly* 69(5): 778–96.

Giles, Chris. 2011. "Spectre of Stagnating Incomes Stalks Globe." *Financial Times*. June 27, 2011.

Gornick, Janet C. 2004. "Women's Economic Outcomes, Gender Inequality, and Public Policy: Lessons from the Luxembourg Income Study." *Socio-Economic Review* 2(2): 213–38.

Gornick, Janet C., and Jerry A. Jacobs. 1998. "Gender, the Welfare State, and Public Employment: A Comparative Study of Seven Industrialized Countries." *American Sociological Review* 63(5): 688–710.

Grimm, Michael, Kenneth Harttgen, Stephan Klasen, Mark Misselhorn, Teresa Munzi, and Timothy Smeeding. 2009. "Inequality in Human Development: An Empirical Assessment of Thirty-Two Countries." *LIS* working paper 519. Luxembourg: LIS.

Guiso, Luigi, Michael Haliassos, and Tulio Jappelli, eds. 2001. *Household Portfolios*. Boston: MIT Press.

Gustafsson, Björn, and Mats Johansson. 1999. "In Search of Smoking Guns: What Makes Income Inequality Vary over Time in Different Countries?" *American Sociological Review* 64(4): 585–605.

Gustafsson, Siv S. 1992. "Separate Taxation and Married Women's Labor Supply, A Comparison between West Germany and Sweden." *Journal of Population Economics* 5(1): 61–85.

Hegewisch, Ariane, and Janet C. Gornick. 2011. "The Impact of Work-Family Policies on Women's Employment: A Review of Research from OECD Countries." *Community, Work and Family* 14(2): 119–38.

Heyns, Barbara. 2005. "Emerging Inequalities in Central and Eastern Europe." *Annual Review of Sociology* 31: 163–97.

Immervoll, Herwig, and Linda Richardson. 2011. "Redistribution Policy and Inequality Reduction in OECD Countries: What Has Changed in Two Decades?" Social, Employment and Migration Working papers 122. Paris: OECD.

Jäntti, Markus, and Eva Sierminska. 2008. "Survey Estimates of Wealth Holdings in OECD Countries: Evidence on the Level and Distribution across Selected Countries." In *Personal Wealth from a Global Perspective, edited by* James B. Davies. Oxford: Oxford University Press.

Jaumotte, Florence. 2003. "Female Labour Force Participation: Past Trends and Main Determinants in OECD Countries." Working paper 376. Paris: OECD.

Jenkins, Stephen P., and Nigel C. O'Leary. 1998. "The Incomes of U.K. Women: Limited Progress towards Equality with Men?" In *The Distribution of Wel-*

fare and Household Production, edited by Stephen P. Jenkins, Arie Kapteyn, and Bernard Van Praag. Cambridge: Cambridge University Press.

Leigh, Andrew. 2009. "Top Incomes." In *Oxford Handbook of Economic Inequality*, edited by Wiemer Salverda, Brian Nolan, and Timothy M. Smeeding. Oxford: Oxford University Press.

Littrell, Jill, Fred Brooks, Jan Ivery, and Mary L. Ohmer. 2010. "Why You Should Care about the Threatened Middle Class." *Journal of Sociology and Social Welfare* 37(2): 87–113.

Luxembourg Income Study (LIS) Database, http://www.lisdatacenter.org (multiple countries; microdata last accessed in July 2011). Luxembourg: LIS.

Luxembourg Wealth Study (LWS) Database, http://www.lisdatacenter.org (multiple countries; microdata last accessed in July 2011). Luxembourg: LIS.

Mahler, Vincent A. 2004. "Economic Globalization, Domestic Politics, and Income Inequality in the Developed Countries: A Cross-National Study." *Comparative Political Studies* 37(9): 1025–53.

McCall, Leslie, and Lane Kenworthy. 2009. "American's Social Policy Preferences in the Era of Rising Inequality." *Perspectives on Politics* 7(3): 459–84.

McCall, Leslie, and Christine Percheski. 2010. "Income Inequality: New Trends and Research Directions." *Annual Review of Sociology* 36(1): 329–47.

Milanovic, Branko. 2007. *Worlds Apart: Measuring International and Global Inequality*. Princeton, NJ: Princeton University Press.

Mishel, Lawrence, Jared Bernstein, and Heidi Shierholz. 2009. *The State of Working America 2008/2009*. Washington, DC: Economic Policy Institute.

Mohl, Philipp, and Oliver Pamp. 2008. "Income Inequality and Redistributional Spending: An Empirical Investigation of Competing Theories." *LIS* working paper 491. Luxembourg: LIS.

Nolan, Brian, and Ive Marx. 2009. "Economic Inequality, Poverty, and Social Exclusion." In *Oxford Handbook of Economic Inequality*, edited by Wiemer Salverda, Brian Nolan, and Timothy M. Smeeding. Oxford: Oxford University Press.

Okun, Arthur M. 1975. *Equality and Efficiency: The Big Tradeoff*. Washington, DC: Brookings Institution.

Organisation for Economic Co-operation and Development (OECD). 2005. *Employment Outlook*. Paris: OECD.

———. 2006. *Employment Outlook*. Paris: OECD.

———. 2008. *Growing Unequal? Income Distribution and Poverty in OECD Countries*. Paris: OECD.

———. 2011a. *Divided We Stand: Why Inequality Keeps Rising*. Paris: OECD.

———. 2011b. Prices and Price Indices—Consumer prices. Statistical database. http://stats.oecd.org/Index.aspx?DataSet Code=MEI_PRICES.

———. 2011c. Purchasing Power Parities (PPP) Statistics: 2008 PPP Benchmark results. Statistical database. http://stats.oecd.org/Index.aspx?DataSetCode=PPP2008.

Orgiazzi, Elsa, Richard Breen, and Cecilia García-Peñalosa. 2008. "Factor Components of Inequality: Cross-Country Differences and Time Changes." *LIS* working paper 503. Luxembourg: LIS.

Osberg, Lars, and Timothy Smeeding. 2006. "'Fair' Inequality? Attitudes toward Pay Differentials: The United States in Comparative Perspective." *American Sociological Review* 71(3): 450–73.

Perotti, Roberto. 1996. "Growth, Income Distribution, and Democracy: What the Data Say." *Journal of Economic Growth* 1(2): 149–87.

Pettit, Becky, and Jennifer L. Hook. 2010. *Gendered Tradeoffs: Family, Social Policy, and Economic Inequality in Twenty-One Countries.* New York: Russell Sage Foundation.

Piketty, Thomas, and Emmanuel Saez. 2003. "Income Inequality in the United States, 1913–1998." *Quarterly Journal of Economics* 118(1): 1–39.

Pressman, Steven. 2007. "The Decline of the Middle Class: An International Perspective." *Journal of Economic Issues* 41(1): 181–200.

Rainwater, Lee, and Timothy M. Smeeding. 2003. *Poor Kids in a Rich Country.* New York: Russell Sage Foundation.

Ravallion, Martin. 2010. "The Developing World's Bulging (but Vulnerable) Middle Class." *World Development* 38(4): 445–54.

Rawls, John. 1971. *A Theory of Justice.* Oxford: Oxford University Press.

Roemer, John E. 1996. *Theories of Distributive Justice.* New York: Harvard University Press.

Roine, Jesper, Jonas Vlachos, and Daniel Waldenström. 2009. "The Long-Run Determinants of Inequality: What Can We Learn from Top Income Data?" *Journal of Public Economics* 93(7–8): 974–88.

Rubery, Jill. 2010. "Labour Market Flexibility and Women's Employment." Unpublished paper, prepared for the World Bank.

Savoia, Antonio, Joshy Easaw, and Andrew McKay. 2010. "Inequality, Democracy, and Institutions: A Critical Review of Recent Research." *World Development* 38(2): 142–54.

Scholtz, Hanno. 2008. "Does Inequality Rise from Above or from Below? Understanding Income Skewness Trends in 16 OECD Countries, 1985–2005." *LIS* working paper 504. Luxembourg: LIS.

Sen, Amartya. 1983. "Poor, Relatively Speaking." *Oxford Economic Papers* 35(2): 153–69.

Sierminska, Eva, Andrea Brandolini, and Timothy M. Smeeding. 2006. "Comparing Wealth Distribution across Rich Countries: First Results from the Luxembourg Wealth Study." *LWS* working paper 1. Luxembourg: LIS.

Smeeding, Timothy, Michael O'Higgins, and Lee Rainwater. 1990. *Poverty, Inequality and the Distribution of Income in a Comparative Context: The Luxembourg Income Study (LIS).* London/Washington, DC: Harvester Wheatsheaf/Urban Institute Press.

Smith, Adam. 1776 (1976). *The Wealth of Nations*, edited by Edwin Cannan. Chicago: University of Chicago Press.

Smith, Kristin. 2010. "Wives as Breadwinners: Wives' Share of Family Earnings Hits Historic High during the Second Year of the Great Recession." Fact sheet 20. Durham: Carsey Institute, University of New Hampshire.

Stiglitz, Joseph E. 2012. *The Price of Inequality: How Today's Divided Society Endangers Our Future*. New York: Norton.

Voitchovsky, Sarah. 2005. "Does the Profile of Income Inequality Matter for Economic Growth? Distinguishing between the Effects of Inequality in Different Parts of the Income Distribution." *Journal of Economic Growth* 10(3): 273–96.

———. 2009. "Inequality and Economic Growth." In *Oxford Handbook of Economic Inequality*, edited by Wiemer Salverda, Brian Nolan, and Timothy M. Smeeding. Oxford: Oxford University Press.

Wang, Chen, and Koen Caminada. 2011. "Disentangling Income Inequality and the Redistributive Effect of Social Transfers and Taxes in 36 LIS Countries." Working paper 2. Department of Economics Research Memorandum.

Ward, Terry, Orsolya Lelkes, Holly Sutherland, and István György Tóth, eds. 2009. *European Inequalities: Social Inclusion and Income Distribution in the European Union*. Budapest: Tarki Social Research Institute.

Wilkinson, Roger, and Kate Pickett. 2009. *The Spirit Level—Why Greater Equality Makes Societies Stronger*. New York: Bloomsbury Press.

Winkler, Anne E. 1998. "Earnings of Husbands and Wives in Dual-Earner Families." *Monthly Labor Review* 121(4): 42–48.

Wogart, Jan Peter. 2010. "Global Booms and Busts: How Is Brazil's Middle Class Faring?" *Centro de Economia Politica* 30(3): 381–400.

Part I

INCOME: TRENDS IN HOUSEHOLD INCOME INEQUALITY

CHAPTER ONE

How Has Income Inequality Grown?

The Reshaping of the Income Distribution in *LIS* Countries

Arthur S. Alderson and Kevin Doran

Research on trends in inequality has cumulated to the point that many scholars conclude that income inequality has been growing in the typical society in recent decades (e.g., Cornia and Addison 2003). While this "U-turn" on inequality has received a great deal of social scientific attention in and of itself, it has also spawned growing concern over the status of the middle class. The idea that the middle class might be shrinking or declining began to receive popular attention in the United States in the early 1980s. That is, in the face of rising income inequality, concern about a particular pattern of change in the distribution of income—polarization, or the shift of individuals, households, and families from the middle of the distribution to both the upper and lower tails—began to grow. Noting the transition from an industrial to a service-based economy, Kuttner (1983), for instance, argued that the decline of well-paying manufacturing jobs and lack of unionization in the growing service sector were driving many formerly "middle-class" families into the bottom tail of the income distribution and were polarizing the workforce. In a similar vein, Thurow (1984) reported that between 1967 and 1982, the percentage of U.S. families with incomes between 75 and 125 percent of the median declined from 28.2 percent to 23.7 percent and that the percentage of families falling above and below those bounds grew by roughly equal proportions. Beyond the empirics, concern with income polarization has also been heavily informed by the classic vision of the middle class as a bulwark of political democracy and against social, political, and economic instability (Lipset 1963; see Thurow 1984 and Pressman 2007).

As highlighted by Pressman (2007), academic interest in the fate of the middle class grew across the 1980s and into the 1990s, before declining during the economic expansion of the latter 1990s. In the context of the economic downturn in 2008, the issue once again moved to the center of scholarly and public debate. How should one approach the question of the "hollowing of the middle"?[1] It is clear that conclusions are sensitive to definitions and measurement (McMahon and Tschetter 1986; Horrigan and Haugen 1988). For instance, McMahon and Tschetter (1986), replicating conflicting studies by Lawrence (1984) and Rosenthal (1985) in the United States, demonstrate that, when defined in terms of occupation, no hollowing of the middle is seen from 1973 to 1985, but when it is defined in terms of personal earnings, there is ample evidence of polarization.

More recently, a rough consensus appears to be emerging in studies of income around a "literal" definition that focuses on the fate of the population falling within 75 and 125 percent of the median income (Pressman 2007; Ravallion 2010). However, as a number of commentators have noted (e.g., Wolfson 1994; Jenkins 1995; Foster and Wolfson 2010; Atkinson and Brandolini [see Chapter 2]), this definition often seems to raise as many questions as it answers. Critics have expressed concern regarding the rationale behind the cut points, the nature of the social groups encompassed (and not encompassed) by this income range, the implications of the definition for our understanding of groups above and below 75 to 125 percent of the median, and, ultimately, the sensitivity of the conclusions drawn in such research to the bounds applied.

While debate over conceptualization and operationalization continues, a sketch of recent work on the hollowing of the middle is instructive for the research we conduct in this chapter. While the scholarly debate initially focused nearly entirely on the case of the United States—with some finding empirical support for the hollowing of the middle (e.g., Lawrence 1984; McMahon and Tschetter 1986; Horrigan and Haugen 1988; Davis and Huston 1992) and others finding just the opposite (e.g., Rosenthal 1985; Levy 1987; Kosters and Ross 1988)—some scholars have turned, more recently, to examine the question in a broader, cross-national framework. For example, using data from the *Luxembourg Income Study (LIS) Database* and employing the 75 to 125 percent criterion, Pressman (2007) examines shifts in the size of the middle-income population in 11 countries, employing available data from between 1980 and 2000. Pressman notes that several countries experienced notable reductions in the proportion of their populations falling in the middle of the income distribution (e.g., Sweden, −7.1 percent; United Kingdom and Taiwan, −4.5 percent; Spain, −3.2 percent; and United States, −2.4 percent) and that, where this occurred, it proceeded via a process of polarization, with households shifting into both the upper and lower tails of the income distribution. Pooling data for all 11 countries and weighting by population size, he finds, overall, that downgrading—movement from the middle to the lower tail—exceeded upgrading—movement from the middle to the upper tail—by about a factor of 2 to 1.[2]

ACCOUNTS OF CONTEMPORARY TRENDS
IN WITHIN-NATION INEQUALITY

In accounting for the hollowing of the middle, scholars draw on a range of explanations for trends in income inequality. In other cross-national research and research on trends in inequality in U.S. states and counties, we have worked to integrate three literatures that have emerged around this debate. Our aim is to combine attention to factors affecting the distribution of wages and earnings—which have tended to be the concern of economists—with a focus on a range of institutional, demographic, and compositional factors that both shape the aggregation of wages and earnings into the distribution of household and family income and affect inequality in ways that may be "independent" of the distribution of earnings. Given that we have reviewed these literatures in detail elsewhere (e.g., Moller, Alderson, and Nielsen 2009), we touch here on only the broadest outlines of each.

The first literature is centered in economics and takes as its object the simple fact of rising inequality. A central hypothesis is that wage inequality has risen in many countries because of skill-biased technological change. Technological advancements have increased the demand for highly educated and skilled workers; this demand has outpaced supply and created scarcity rents for the highly skilled (Levy and Murname 1992; Autor, Katz, and Krueger 1998).

The second literature, which is typically oriented toward cross-national comparison, takes as its object the persistent differences in levels of inequality across countries and regions and the heterogeneous inequality experience of different countries and regions. Here one finds a diversity of arguments regarding the role of labor market institutions (e.g., centralized wage-setting, unionization), the process of globalization (e.g., international trade, investment, and migration), and the wave of domestic and international liberalization (e.g., Alderson and Nielsen 2002; Moller et al. 2003; Kenworthy and Pontusson 2005; Brady 2009). This research has increased to such an extent that some scholars have begun to outline a "unified theory" that would explain recent trends in wage inequality, real wages, and unemployment across developed countries. This theory attributes recent inequality trends to the interplay of exogenous shocks—affecting labor supply and demand and the stability of earnings—with the marked differences in the institutional contexts of different countries and regions (Blank 1998; Blau and Kahn 2002; DiPrete et al. 2006). In this perspective, for instance, the effects of skill-biased technological change on inequality might vary substantially depending on the institutional context.

The third literature takes as its object household and family income inequality. While sharing many of the same concerns of the second (e.g., labor market institutions, globalization, etc.), this literature distinctly focuses, for instance, on how socio-demographic factors—the age distribution of the population, the composition of households, assortative mating, racial and ethnic cleavages—generate inequality among households and families that is independent of the distribution of wages and earnings (e.g., Cancian and Reed 2001; McCall 2001; Moller, Alderson, and Nielsen 2009; Blau, Ferber, and Winkler 2010). In the case of the United States, for example, while household and family income inequality rose measurably across the 1970s, the upswing in earnings inequality did not take off until the 1980s. And during the 1980s and early 1990s (when earnings inequality was rising), change in earnings inequality explains only about one-third of the change in family/household income inequality (Burtless 1999).

While research on the issues raised in these literatures has grown at a remarkable pace over the last two decades, we must consider that these explanations often imply very different patterns of distributional change while predicting the same outcome in terms of the behavior of standard summary measures of inequality (e.g., a rise in the Gini coefficient or in the Theil index). Morris, Bernhardt, and Handcock (1994, 206) noted this problem at the very outset of the revival of social scientific interest in income inequality, suggesting that "empirical investigation . . . has been handicapped by methods that are insensitive to [patterns of distributional change]." What is at issue? Consider, for instance, now-standard accounts of the effects of globalization on income inequality in the Global North. They often suggest that globalization is producing an increasingly polarized job distribution, a growing upper tier with high wages and security, a growing bottom tier in low-wage and insecure service positions, and a "shrinking" middle (e.g., Wood 1994). Other accounts, however, imply a rather different pattern of distributional change. The skill-biased technological change explanation we mentioned previously suggests that inequality is rising as a result of upgrading—that is, growth in the upper tail of the distribution that has simply left less skilled workers behind. Similarly, scholars who emphasize the effects of the growth of autocatalytic, "winner-take-all" markets describe a process in which various technological and institutional changes have combined to produce an expanding number of markets in which rewards are concentrated in the hands of a small number of "winners" (Frank and Cook 1995).[3] While implying very different patterns of distributional change—and while these patterns have distinct implications for both policy and distributive justice—these accounts of rising inequality effectively point to the same increase in summary inequality measures as prima facie evidence in support of their premises. As such—and in a world in which high-quality, comparable data on income are scarce—we believe it is useful to occasionally look "behind" the usual summary measures and closely examine the actual pattern of distributional change, attending to change at all points on the distribution and fully exploiting the available information. In short, it is important to examine how income inequality has grown.

In earlier research, we used the available high-quality data from the *LIS Database* to examine the experiences of 16 high-income countries across the period from the late 1960s to the late 1990s (Alderson, Beckfield, and Nielsen 2005). We next expanded our investigation to include seven transitional and middle-income countries (Alderson and Doran 2010). Most recently, we updated our earlier analyses, taking advantage of the latest wave of data from LIS centered around 2004, and began to look at households in interesting social locations (e.g., female-headed households). In investigating the inequality experience of these countries, we seek to understand how inequality grew and to what extent the observed patterns of distributional change are heterogeneous or homogeneous. In this chapter, we address the question "Has the middle hollowed out?"

RELATIVE DISTRIBUTION METHODS AND DATA

To address these questions, we use relative distribution methods. Developed by Handcock and Morris (1999), methods based on the relative distribution powerfully assist in the description of distributional change and enable counterfactual comparison of compositionally adjusted distributions.[4] The basic idea underlying the relative distribution is to take the values of one distribution (the comparison distribution) and express them as positions in another (the reference distribution). Consider two distributions of household income, one measured at $t - 1$ and one at t. Treat the $t - 1$ distribution as the reference distribution and t as the comparison distribution. When there are no differences between the comparison and reference distributions, the relative distribution of the grade-transformed data will be uniform or "flat"—that is, the proportion of households falling within a given quantile's cut points of the reference distribution $t - 1$ at t is the same as at $t - 1$. When there are differences between comparison and reference distributions, the relative distribution will "rise" or "fall"—that is, the proportion of households falling within a given quantile's cut points of the reference distribution $t - 1$ at t will be larger or smaller than at $t - 1$. In this fashion, one can distinguish among growth, stability, and decline at all points on the distribution.[5]

Another advantageous feature of these methods is that one can use the relative data to develop summary measures to characterize any pattern of change that one might be interested in exploring. Handcock and Morris (1999) developed a measure of polarization that captures the degree to which there is divergence from, or convergence toward, the center of the distribution and is thus ideally suited to addressing the question of the "hollowing of the middle." For quantile data Q, the median relative polarization index (MRP) takes the following form (Morris, Bernhardt, and Handcock 1994, 217):

$$\text{MRP}_t(Q) = \frac{4}{Q-2} \left| \frac{i-1/2}{Q} - \frac{1}{2} \right| \times \left(g_t(i) - \frac{Q}{Q-2} \right),$$

where $g_t(i)$ is the relative distribution—the proportion of year t's households whose median-adjusted incomes fall between each pair of quantile cut points, divided by the proportion in the reference year $i = 1, 2, \ldots, Q$, and the adjustment by 1/2 establishes the mid-point for each quantile. The index varies between −1 and 1. It takes the value of 0 when there has been no change in the distribution of household income relative to the reference year. Positive values signify relative polarization (i.e., growth in the tails of the distribution), and negative values signify relative convergence toward the center of the distribution (i.e., less polarization).

The median relative polarization index can be decomposed into the contributions to distributional change made by the segments of the distribution above and below the median (Handcock and Morris 1999), enabling one to distinguish "upgrading" from "downgrading." For quantile data, the lower relative polarization index (LRP) and the upper relative polarization index (URP) are calculated as follows:

$$\frac{\text{LRP}_t}{\text{URP}_t(Q)} = \frac{8}{Q-2} \left| \frac{i-1/2}{Q} - \frac{1}{2} \right| \times \left(g_t(i) - \frac{Q}{Q-2} \right).$$

They have the same theoretical range as the MRP and decompose the overall polarization index (Morris, Bernhardt, and Handcock 1994, 209): $\text{MRP}_t = \text{LRP}_t/2 + \text{URP}_t/2$.

We apply these techniques to data drawn from the *LIS Database* (2010). For each country/year used in the analysis, we generate quantile boundaries for the distribution of household income (equivalent net disposable household income), adjusting for household size using a standard equivalence scale (i.e., the square root of the number of persons in the household).

RESULTS

To introduce the results and illustrate our use of these methods, consider the case of the Czech Republic. Based on the Gini coefficient and other summary measures, we know that the *LIS* data indicate that income inequality rose in the Czech Republic throughout the 1990s, but what exactly happened to the "middle" during the first few years of the transition from communism? In the upper panel of Figure 1.1, we present two probability density functions (PDFs) of the Czech distribution of household income, measured in nominal terms. The solid line, which is labeled the reference year, is the distribution of household income in 1992. The PDF with the dotted line, which we treat as the comparison year, is the distribution in 1996. Examining these two distributions, we see that the reference or 1992

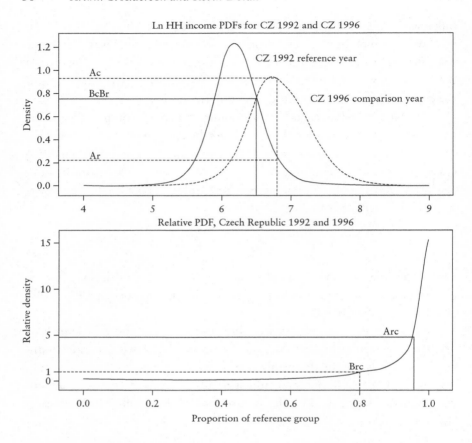

Figure 1.1.   Distribution of household income in the Czech Republic, 1992 and 1996 (top) and relative PDF (bottom)

SOURCE: Authors' calculations from the *LIS Database*.

distribution has a slight right skew, while the comparison distribution has a larger median and variance.

As touched on earlier, the central idea informing relative distribution methods is to take the values of one distribution and express them as positions in another. To illustrate, consider the two vertical lines in the upper panel of Figure 1.1. The dotted line is drawn at the median of the 1996 distribution (approximately 6.8 ln kroner). The solid vertical line is drawn at the point where the 1992 and 1996 distributions intersect (approximately 6.5 ln kroner). On the dotted line, notice the density of the comparison or 1996 distribution, A_C, at this point (approximately 0.87) and the density of the reference or 1992 distribution, A_R, at this same income (approximately 0.20). On the solid line, notice as well the density of the comparison and reference distributions, B_C and B_R, at this income (both approximately 0.74).

With this information, and across the response scale, one can form the relative PDF, which is simply the density ratio at each quantile. At the median of the 1996 distribution, the relative density is $0.87/0.20 = 4.4$. This is illustrated in the bottom panel of Figure 1.1. The relative density at point A_{RC} means there were about 4.4 times more households at this point on the reference distribution in 1996, a point corresponding to the 95th percentile of the 1992 distribution. At the point where the two distributions intersect in the upper panel, the relative density is $0.74/0.74 = 1$. The relative density at point B_{RC} means there were exactly as many households at this point of the reference distribution in 1996 as in 1992, a point corresponding to about the 81st percentile of the 1992 distribution. When the relative density is less than 1, there are fewer comparison observations at this point of the reference distribution (<81st percentile in this case). When the relative density is greater than 1, there are more comparison observations at that point on the reference distribution (>81st percentile in this case).

Returning again to the top panel of Figure 1.1, it is clear that there are two key differences between the 1992 and 1996 distributions of household income, differences that pertain to the first two moments of the distribution. First, there is a change in location: the distribution shifts to the right over time. Second, there is a change in shape: the comparison distribution has greater variance than the reference distribution.

When location or shape shifts operate in isolation, the relative PDF provides a readily interpretable picture of distributional change. In the case of a pure (positive) location shift, the relative distribution is always a simple monotonic increase, while in the case of a pure shape shift, change in shape can be read directly off the relative PDF. Of course, in practical applications, the pattern of distributional change is more complicated. In the case of the Czech Republic between 1992 and 1996, there are both location and shape shifts. In such cases, the relative PDF is less informative, and it is useful to isolate that portion of distributional change that occurs owing to changes in location—a shift in median income—and that portion that occurs owing to change in shape.

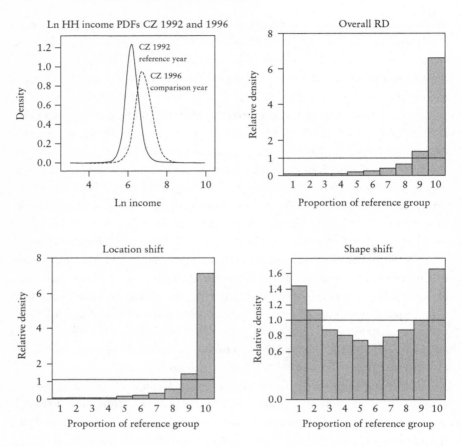

Figure 1.2. Decomposition of overall RD (relative PDF) into location and shape shifts: Czech Republic, 1992–1996

SOURCE: Authors' calculations from the *LIS Database*.

In Figure 1.2, we illustrate the results of decomposing the overall relative density (top right panel) in this fashion.[6] Canceling out differences in shape between the two distributions yields the location shift (lower left panel). Canceling out differences in location between 1992 and 1996 enables one to identify the shape shift (lower right panel). Consistent with what one can glean from the relative PDF (overall RD), there was a sizable shift in location: an increase in median household income between 1992 and 1996. However, the shape shift reveals a pattern of polarization that is not visible in the overall RD. Viewed together, these results indicate that in the course of the upswing in income, some households fell behind, while others shifted toward the top, joining the ranks of those whose income put them in the top decile group in 1992.

Canceling out changes in location and fitting the 1996 data to the 1992 quantile cut points, one can quite readily address the question of the "hollowing" of the middle. As one can note from the lower right panel, the distribution of household income grew more polarized, with about 40 percent more households joining the ranks of those whose median-adjusted income put them in the first decile group in 1992. In the fifth and sixth decile groups, in contrast, there were, respectively, roughly 25 percent and 30 percent fewer households at those locations on the reference or 1992 distribution. In sum, then, between 1992 and 1996, the Gini coefficient of household income inequality in the Czech Republic grew by about 5 Gini points. How did inequality grow? The shape shift reveals the pattern of distributional change that occurred "behind" the increase in the Gini coefficient.[7]

Figures 1.3a and 1.3b examine the shape shift over the longest period available between 1980 and 2004 for three other transitional societies and Taiwan (a) and four high-income countries (Figure 1.3b).[8] To illustrate with the case of the Slovak Republic, look at the first column of Figure 1.3a. The panel in the first row reports the shape change, comparing the 1996 distribution of household income to the reference year distribution of 1992. When the relative density has a value of 1, it means there has been no change at that point on the distribution over the period under consideration. Thus, the ninth decile group contained relatively as many median-adjusted households in 1996 as it did in 1992. Values less than 1 indicate relative decline. Thus, the values for the second through eighth decile groups mean there were fewer households at those points on the 1992 distribution. By 1996, the distribution of households had shifted from these locations to the first and tenth decile groups—the decile groups with RD values greater than 1.

To summarize these changes, we present in the lower panels of Figures 1.3a and 1.3b the change in the Gini coefficient (Gini) and in two versions of the Atkinson index (A) in each country, along with Handcock and Morris's (1999) polarization indices. Between 1992 and 1996, household income inequality in the Slovak Republic grew by 0.052, or by about 5 Gini points. This appears in the first bar on the left in the lower panel of the first column of Figure 1.3a. The Atkinson indices, at $\varepsilon = 0.5$ and 1, appear,

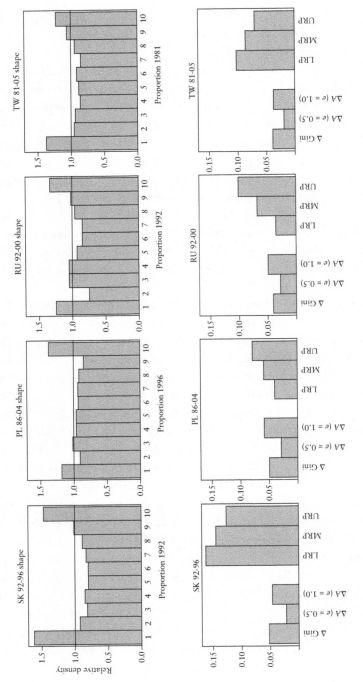

Figure 1.3a. Shape shifts (top) and summary inequality and polarization measures (bottom): Slovak Republic, Poland, Russia, and Taiwan

SOURCE: Authors' calculations from the *LIS Database*.

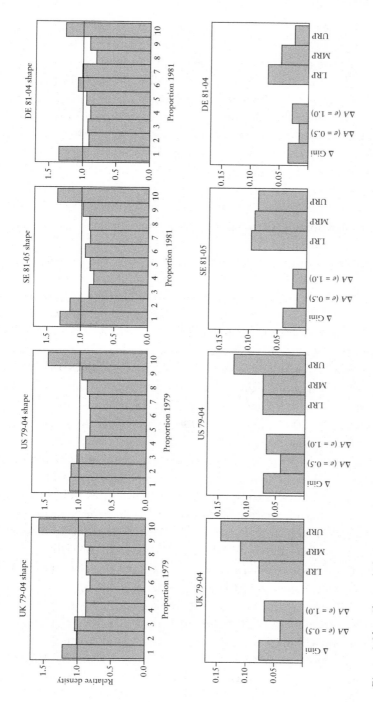

Figure 1.3b. Shape shifts (top) and summary inequality and polarization measures (bottom): United Kingdom, United States, Sweden, and Germany

SOURCE: Authors' calculations from the *LIS Database*.

respectively, in the second and third bars. The mean relative polarization index (MRP) in the fifth bar from the left is positive (0.145). The positive value indicates relative polarization, confirming the visual impression from the panel above (i.e., by 1996, more households fell in the tails of the 1992 distribution, and fewer fell in the middle). Decomposing the MRP into the contributions to distributional change made by the segments of the distribution above and below the median, it appears that "downgrading" dominated "upgrading" in the upswing in inequality in the Slovak Republic: the value of the LRP is greater than the URP: 0.163 and 0.127, respectively. Consistent again with the visual impression from the preceding shape shift, this means that, by 1996, more households had moved toward the lower tail of the 1992 distribution than had moved toward the upper tail in the course of relative polarization.

Results for three other transitional countries and Taiwan are also presented in Figure 1.3a. Countries are presented in order of the size of the change in their Gini coefficients, ranging from the Slovak Republic (ΔGini = 0.052) to Taiwan (ΔGini = 0.038). Note the variation in the inequality experience of the transitional countries. At one extreme, in the short period between 1992 and 1996, the successors to the former Czechoslovakia experienced comparatively intense polarization, surpassing that experienced by the United Kingdom and the United States over the period from 1979 to 2004 (see Figure 1.2 for the Czech Republic). At the other extreme—and over the longer 1986–2004 and 1992–2000 periods—the distributional consequences of transition appear less stark in the cases of Poland and Russia. Here, the increase in inequality has been more modest and polarization is less pronounced. Interestingly, this conclusion is not simply a function of the different time spans under consideration. Over the 1992–1995 period, the MRP in Poland was not appreciably larger (0.064) than the value for the 1986–2004 period (0.059). In Russia, the MRP was indeed larger for the 1992–1995 period (0.092) than for the 1992–2000 period (0.068), but these "early transition" values for Russia and Poland alike are lower than those for the Czech and Slovak Republics (0.152 and 0.145, respectively).

In Figure 1.3b, we present results for four high-income countries, using available data from 1980 to 2004 for the United Kingdom, the United States, Sweden, and Germany.[9] Again, we present countries in order of the size of the change in their Gini coefficients, ranging from the United Kingdom (ΔGini = 0.075) to Germany (ΔGini = 0.034). In the United Kingdom and the United States, where the increase in inequality has been most pronounced, upgrading has taken precedence over downgrading; that is, the shift from the middle to the upper tail has dominated the shift from the middle to the bottom in the course of rising inequality. As with the transitional countries and Taiwan, the experiences of these high-income countries have not been homogeneous. In Sweden, where inequality grew by 4 Gini points between 1980 and 2004, growth in the lower tail was more pronounced than growth in the upper tail. In Germany, the pattern is also distinct: there was relatively little change around the sixth and seventh decile groups by 2004 relative to 1981, fewer households at the second through fifth, eighth, and ninth decile groups and growth in the first and tenth decile groups. Also, while by the Gini coefficient Germany experienced an increase in inequality that was less than half as large as that of the United Kingdom or the United States, the shift of households to the first decile group of the distribution at around 1980 was actually more pronounced in Germany than in the United Kingdom or the United States.

Viewed in toto, the results suggest that rather than solely being a story of "upgrading"—of the movement of a fraction of households into the upper reaches of the distribution owing to skill-biased technological change, the growth of winner-take-all markets, or, in the case of the transitional economies, the relaxation of institutional pressures that had previously compressed the top of the income distribution—the story of rising inequality has been one of polarization. Where the upswing in inequality has been most pronounced—in the United Kingdom, the United States, and the Czech and Slovak Republics—polarization has likewise been most pronounced. Households in all four countries have shifted away from the middle of the distribution toward the tails. In the United Kingdom, the United States, and the Czech Republic, upgrading has dominated downgrading in the course of polarization (i.e., more households shifted up than down), while in the Slovak Republic the opposite occurred (i.e., downgrading was measurably more pronounced than upgrading). Where the upswing in inequality has been more modest—in Poland, Sweden, Russia, Taiwan, and Germany—the pattern of distributional change is also one of polarization. In Poland and Russia, upgrading took precedence over downgrading, while in Sweden, Taiwan, and Germany, downgrading was more prominent.

Looking "behind" standard summary measures, then, we find that the experience of *LIS* countries with rising inequality is not entirely homogeneous (see also Brandolini and Smeeding 2009). While largely a story of polarization, the precise pattern of distributional change varies from country to country. In some countries, more households have "fallen behind" than have "moved ahead," while in others we observe just the opposite. While it is beyond the scope of this chapter to attempt to offer an explanation for these patterns, we have begun to look at some of the "usual suspects" using the same methods. The results to date are interesting. They suggest that there is also a good bit of heterogeneity within and between demographic groups that are often treated as effectively interchangeable in comparative work.

Consider the role of changes in household structure in rising income inequality. In the United States, a number of scholars have noted that the increase in inequality coincided with an increase in the proportion of households headed by single women (e.g., Levy and Michel 1991). In fact, Burtless (1999) estimates that 21 percent of the increase in overall family income inequality between 1979 and 1996 reflected changes in household structure (cf. McLanahan and Percheski 2008). Moller and colleagues (2009) found that over the 1970–2000 period at the U.S. county level, changes in the proportions of households headed by women were strongly associated with changes in family income inequality. But how has the distribution of income among female-headed households changed over time? Where exactly do female-headed households fall in the distribution of other households containing children, and how does this vary cross-nationally?

The upper panel of Figure 1.4 shows the shape shift for female-headed households (FHH) in the United Kingdom and the United States between 1980 and 2004. We define FHH as households containing only women and minor children (i.e., <18 years of age). As one can note, in the United Kingdom, FHHs have converged toward the center of the 1979 distribution. By 2004, there were more median-adjusted FHHs in the fourth through the seventh decile groups and fewer in the first through third, ninth, and tenth decile groups. In the United States, in contrast, we observe a pattern of divergence or polarization. Relative to 1979, some FHHs moved up, but more fell behind, joining the ranks of those FHHs that were in the bottom two decile groups in 1979. In the last few decades, it appears that the experience of the population of lone mothers in the United States systematically differs from that of lone mothers in the United Kingdom.

We can also take FHHs and examine how they differ in shape from other sorts of households. In the lower panel of Figure 1.4, we compare

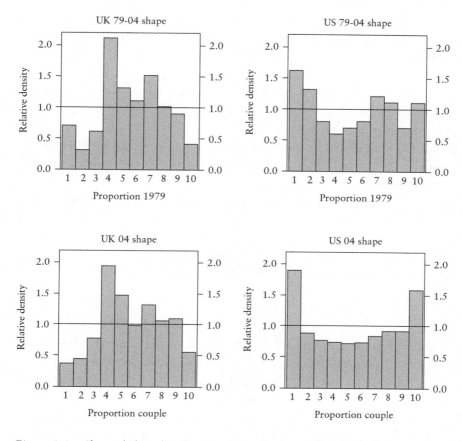

Figure 1.4.   Shape shift in distribution of income among female-headed households, *LIS* data 1980–2004 (top), and female-headed households in the distribution of households containing couples and children, *LIS* data 1980–2004 (bottom)

SOURCE: Authors' calculations from the *LIS Database*.

female-headed households to households containing only couples and their minor children around 2004, canceling out differences in location and fitting the FHH distribution to the quantile cut points of the reference distribution. As one can note, not only is the distribution of income among FHHs converging over time in the United Kingdom (upper panel), but around 2004 it is more homogeneous than the distribution of households containing couples and minor children. There are fewer FHHs at the very top of the distribution of income among households containing couples and minor children and fewer FHHs at the bottom of that distribution as well. In the United States, in contrast, the distribution of income among female-headed households has been polarizing or diverging over time (top row), and around 2004 it is also more polarized than the distribution of households containing couples and minor children: there are more FHHs at both the bottom and the top.

These differences between the United States and the United Kingdom would seem to have a number of implications, but the most obvious is that female-headed households appear to be qualitatively different in each country. In the United Kingdom, FHHs look increasingly similar to one another over time and presently exhibit a distribution that is more homogeneous than that exhibited by other households with children. In the United States, FHHs look increasingly dissimilar over time and exhibit a distribution that is more polarized relative to other households with children.

CONCLUSION

These results have a number of implications for our understanding of inequality in these countries. Considering, again, pure upgrading accounts of the upswing in inequality, our analyses using the *LIS* data indicate that there is more to the story of rising household inequality in these countries than that of the movement of a fraction of households into the upper reaches of the distribution. Rather, we find that the distribution of income is evolving in such a way that households are moving toward the top and the bottom of the distribution relative to the past. Has the middle hollowed out? Our analysis suggests that it has. It is also important to note the fact that when one decomposes observed polarization or "hollowing" into the contributions of the upper and lower tails, the experiences of the countries examined in this chapter are heterogeneous, with upgrading taking precedence over downgrading in the United States, the United Kingdom, the Czech Republic, Poland, and Russia, and downgrading dominating upgrading in the Slovak Republic, Taiwan, Sweden, and Germany. What we find, then, is not entirely inconsistent with the upgrading explanations. Rather, it suggests that factors producing upgrading may simply be "some among many" driving contemporary inequality trends. For instance, when considering the transitional economies, a range of distinctive institutional changes have obviously played a heavy role in reshaping the distribution of income (e.g., Kattuman and Redmond 2001; Večerník 2001; Kislitsyna 2003).

Looking forward, these results also highlight the utility of focusing on change at all points on the distribution as opposed to focusing on summary inequality measures alone (Nielsen 2007). For example, given that it is often difficult to measure in a compelling fashion, arguments about skill-biased technological change are not infrequently arguments about the residual: regress a summary measure of inequality on the "usual suspects" and what remains is deemed "technological change." With the techniques we apply in this chapter, one could more rigorously pursue model-based or residual approaches to assessing the impact of technological change or, indeed, use the relative data to directly relate measures of technology to change at particular points on the distribution. By focusing on the comparison between income distributions rather than on their individual shapes, the analyst is forced to be precise about exactly how different factors should affect inequality. For example, in U.S. research, changes in household structure have regularly been observed to be a major culprit in the upswing in family and household income inequality. Given that female-headed households have lower-than-average incomes, the growth of such households is typically argued to affect the distribution of income by inflating the proportion of poor households (e.g., Nielsen and Alderson 1997). However, when one examines the evolution of the distribution of income among female-headed households over time and places such households in the distribution of other households containing children (Figure 1.4), it is clear that while one part of the often-observed compositional effect of the growth of female-headed households on inequality results from differences in average income between female-headed and other households, another part results from growing inequality within this subset of households and from its polarization relative to other types of households.

A wide variety of explanations have been offered to account for the rise in inequality that is seen in many countries in recent decades. Rather than attempt to adjudicate among these accounts, we examined the data that inform the debate. We have aimed to demonstrate how an examination of the pattern of distributional change occurring "behind" the summary measures can aid in thinking about the phenomenon itself and accounts thereof. A key substantive conclusion emerging from our research using the *LIS* data is that the pattern of distributional change in countries experiencing rising inequality is, in the broadest terms, similar from one country to the next. This similarity is intriguing. It suggests an underlying commonality in the contemporary inequality experience of an otherwise heterogeneous group of countries—ranging from Russia to the United States and from Taiwan to Sweden. In our view, this suggests that common global/transnational processes may be at work: a common set of exogenous factors that have reshaped the distribution of income in otherwise very different countries in a similar fashion.

NOTES

The authors thank Ben Jann for access to the pre-release version of reldist, a Stata program for relative distribution methods.

1. Because this issue is discussed in detail elsewhere in this volume (see Chapter 2), we only briefly touch on it here.

2. While employing different data and metrics, other research on Germany, Canada, and the United Kingdom has yielded results that are consistent with Pressman's (2007) overall conclusion regarding polarization (Jenkins 1995; Grabka and Frick 2008; Foster and Wolfson 2010).

3. In the case of the United States, Piketty and Saez (2003) document the explosive growth of the income share of the top 1 percent across the 1980s and 1990s. It nearly doubled, rising from 8 percent in 1980 to about 15 percent by 1998.

4. These techniques are similar in spirit to those developed in economics by Juhn, Murphy, and Pierce (1993); Lemieux (2002); Machado and Mata (2005); and DiNardo, Fortin, and Lemieux (1996).

5. While introduced here—and illustrated below—in a non-technical fashion, see Handcock and Morris (1999; especially pp. 21–27) for a formal definition of the relative distribution.

6. From this point on, we present the relative data in histogram form to ease presentation and discussion.

7. We treat the relative distribution and the related polarization indices as simple *descriptive statistics* and, as such, definitive in exactly the same sense that the sample mean *is* the sample mean. Unlike the sample mean, however, the sampling distribution of a ratio (e.g., the density ratio at each quantile) or of a function of q ratios (e.g., the polarization indices) is not well understood. These sampling distributions are known to be non-normal, which makes the traditional frequentist approach to statistical inference problematic. An empirical approach to defining the sampling distribution of such statistics, based on re-sampling methods (e.g., the bootstrap), presents an alternative means for moving from description of sample data to inferences about population parameters. These techniques could, of

course, be paired with the relative distribution statistics we report. In this chapter, however, we limit our focus to a simple description of the *LIS* data.

8. One could use any set of comparison and reference years in the *LIS* series for these countries. For the purposes of presentation, we examine the longest span available in each country. For the countries appearing in Figure 1.3b, this decision is consequential, since a substantial proportion of the change in income inequality between 1980 and 2004 in fact occurred between 1980 and 1985 (i.e., 44 percent of the change in the Gini coefficient in the United Kingdom between 1980 and 2004 occurred between 1980 and 1985, with 49 percent in the United States, 52 percent in Sweden, and 47 percent in Germany). The implications of the choice of comparison and reference years for the countries examined in Figure 1.3a are discussed below.

9. *LIS* data centered around 1980 for "Germany" are for West Germany, and *LIS* data centered around 2004 are for reunified Germany.

REFERENCES

Alderson, Arthur S., Jason Beckfield, and François Nielsen. 2005. "Exactly How Has Income Inequality Changed? Patterns of Distributional Change in Core Societies." *International Journal of Comparative Sociology* 46(5–6): 405–23.

Alderson, Arthur S., and Kevin Doran. 2010. "Global Inequality, Within-Nation Inequality, and the Changing Distribution of Income in Seven Transitional and Middle-Income Societies." In *Inequality Beyond Globalization: Economic Changes, Social Transformations and the Dynamics of Inequality*, edited by Christian Suter. Zurich: Lit Verlag.

Alderson, Arthur S., and François Nielsen. 2002. "Globalization and the Great U-Turn: Income Inequality Trends in 16 OECD Countries." *American Journal of Sociology* 107(5): 1244–99.

Atkinson, Anthony B., and Andrea Brandolini. 2013. "On the Identification of the Middle Class." Chapter 2 in this book.

Autor, David H., Lawrence F. Katz, and Alan B. Krueger. 1998. "Computing Inequality: Have Computers Changed the Labor Market?" *Quarterly Journal of Economics* 113(4): 1169–1213.

Blank, Rebecca M. 1998. "Contingent Work in a Changing Labor Market." In *Generating Jobs: How to Increase Demand for Less-Skilled Workers*, edited by Richard B. Freeman and Peter Gottschalk. New York: Russell Sage Foundation.

Blau, Francine D., Marianne A. Ferber, and Anne E. Winkler. 2010. *The Economics of Women, Men, and Work*, 6th ed. Upper Saddle River, NJ: Prentice-Hall.

Blau, Francine D., and Lawrence M. Kahn. 2002. *At Home and Abroad: U.S. Labor Market Performance in International Perspective*. New York: Russell Sage Foundation.

Brady, David. 2009. *Rich Democracies, Poor People: How Politics Explain Poverty*. Oxford: Oxford University Press.

Brandolini, Andrea, and Timothy M. Smeeding. 2009. "Income Inequality in Richer and OECD Countries." In *Oxford Handbook of Economic Inequality*, edited by Wiemer Salverda, Brian Nolan, and Timothy M. Smeeding. Oxford: Oxford University Press.

Burtless, Gary. 1999. "Effect of Growing Wage Disparities and Family Composition Shifts on the Distribution of U.S. Income." *European Economic Review* 43(4–6): 853–65.

Cancian, Maria, and Deborah Reed. 2001. "Changes in Family Structure: Implications for Poverty and Related Policy." In *Understanding Poverty*, edited by Sheldon H. Danziger and Robert H. Haveman. New York: Russell Sage Foundation.

Cornia, Giovanni Andrea, and Tony Addison. 2003. "Income Distribution Changes and their Impact in the Post–World War II Period." Discussion paper 28. Helsinki: World Institute for Development Economics Research (UNU-WIDER).

Davis, Joe C., and John H. Huston. 1992. "The Shrinking Middle-Income Class: A Multivariate Analysis." *Eastern Economic Journal* 18(3): 227–85.

DiNardo, John E., Nicole Fortin, and Thomas Lemieux. 1996. "Labour Market Institutions and the Distribution of Wages, 1973–1992: A Semiparametric Approach." *Econometrica* 64(5): 1001–46.

DiPrete, Thomas A., Dominique Goux, Eric Maurin, and Amélie Quesnel-Vallée. 2006. "Work and Pay in Flexible and Regulated Labor Markets: A Generalized Perspective on Institutional Evolution and Inequality Trends in Europe and the U.S." *Research in Social Stratification and Mobility* 24(3): 311–32.

Foster, James E., and Michael C. Wolfson. 2010. "Polarization and the Decline of the Middle Class: Canada and the U.S." *Journal of Economic Inequality* 8(2): 247–73.

Frank, Robert H., and Phillip J. Cook. 1995. *The Winner-Take-All Society*. New York: Free Press.

Grabka, Markus M., and Joachim R. Frick. 2008. "The Shrinking German Middle Class-Signs of Long-Term Polarization in Disposable Income?" *DIW Berlin Weekly Report* 4: 21–27.

Handcock, Mark S., and Martina Morris. 1999. *Relative Distribution Methods in the Social Sciences*. New York: Springer-Verlag.

Horrigan, Michael W., and Steven E. Haugen. 1988. "The Declining Middle-Class Thesis: A Sensitivity Analysis." *Monthly Labor Review* 111(5): 3–13.

Jenkins, Stephen P. 1995. "Did the Middle Class Shrink During the 1980s? UK Evidence from Kernel Density Estimates." *Economics Letters* 49(4): 407–13.

Juhn, Chinhui, Kevin M. Murphy, and Brooks Pierce. 1993. "Wage Inequality and the Rise in Returns to Skill." *Journal of Political Economy* 101(3): 410–42.

Kattuman, Paul, and Gerry Redmond. 2001. "Income Inequality in Early Transition: The Case of Hungary 1987–1996." *Journal of Comparative Economics* 29(1): 40–65.

Kenworthy, Lane, and Jonas Pontusson. 2005. "Rising Inequality and the Politics of Redistribution in Affluent Countries." *Perspectives on Politics* 3(3): 449–71.

Kislitsyna, Olga. 2003. "Income Inequality in Russia during Transition: How Can It Be Explained?" Working paper 08. Kyiv, Ukraine: Economics Education and Research Consortium (EERC).

Kosters, Marvin H., and Murray N. Ross. 1988. "A Shrinking Middle Class?" *Public Interest* 90 (Winter): 3–27.

Kuttner, Bob. 1983. "The Declining Middle." *Atlantic Monthly* 252 (July): 60–72.

Lawrence, Robert Z. 1984. "Sectoral Shifts and the Size of the Middle Class." *Brookings Review* 3 (Fall): 3–11.

Lemieux, Thomas. 2002. "Decomposing Changes in Wage Distributions: A Unified Approach." *Canadian Journal of Economics* 35(4): 646–88.

Levy, Frank. 1987. "The Middle Class: Is It Really Vanishing?" *Brookings Review* 5 (Summer): 17–21.

Levy, Frank, and Richard C. Michel. 1991. *The Economic Future of American Families: Income and Wealth Trends.* Washington, DC: Urban Institute Press.

Levy, Frank, and Richard J. Murname. 1992. "U.S. Earnings Levels and Earnings Inequality: A Review of Recent Trends and Proposed Explanations." *Journal of Economic Literature* 30(3): 1333–81.

Lipset, Seymour Martin. 1963. *Political Man: The Social Bases of Politics.* Garden City, NY: Anchor Books.

Luxembourg Income Study (LIS) Database, http://www.lisdatacenter.org (multiple countries; microdata last accessed in May 2010). Luxembourg: LIS.

Machado, José A. F., and José Mata. 2005. "Counterfactual Decomposition of Changes in Wage Distributions Using Quantile Regression." *Journal of Applied Econometrics* 20(4): 445–65.

McCall, Leslie. 2001. "Sources of Racial Wage Inequality in Metropolitan Labor Markets: Racial, Ethnic, and Gender Differences." *American Sociological Review* 66(4): 520–42.

McLanahan, Sara, and Christine Percheski. 2008. "Family Structure and the Reproduction of Inequalities." *Annual Review of Sociology* 34: 257–76.

McMahon, Patrick J., and John H. Tschetter. 1986. "The Declining Middle Class: A Further Analysis." *Monthly Labor Review* 109(9): 22–27.

Moller, Stephanie, Arthur S. Alderson, and François Nielsen. 2009. "Changing Patterns of Income Inequality in U.S. Counties, 1970–2000." *American Journal of Sociology* 114(4): 1037–1101.

Moller, Stephanie, David Bradley, Evelyne Huber, François Nielsen, and John Stephens. 2003. "Determinants of Poverty in Advanced Capitalist Democracies." *American Sociological Review* 68(1): 22–51.

Morris, Martina, Annette D. Bernhardt, and Mark S. Handcock. 1994. "Economic Inequality: New Methods for New Trends." *American Sociological Review* 59(2): 205–19.

Nielsen, François. 2007. "Economic Inequality, Pareto, and Sociology: The Route Not Taken." *American Behavioral Scientist* 50(5): 619–38.

Nielsen, François, and Arthur S. Alderson. 1997. "The Kuznets Curve and the Great U-Turn: Patterns of Income Inequality in United States Counties, 1970–90." *American Sociological Review* 62: 12–33.

Piketty, Thomas, and Emmanuel Saez. 2003. "Income Inequality in the United States, 1913–1998." *Quarterly Journal of Economics* 118(1): 1–39.

Pressman, Steven. 2007. "The Decline of the Middle Class: An International Perspective." *Journal of Economic Issues* 41 (March): 181–200.

Ravallion, Martin (2010). "The Developing World's Bulging (but Vulnerable) Middle Class." *World Development* 38(4): 445–54.

Rosenthal, Neal H. 1985. "The Shrinking Middle Class: Myth or Reality?" *Monthly Labor Review* 108(3): 3–10.

Thurow, Lester C. 1984. "The Disappearance of the Middle Class." *New York Times*, February 5, 1984, p. F3.

Večerník, Jiří. 2001. "From Needs to the Market: The Changing Inequality of Household Income in the Czech Transition." *European Societies* 3(2): 191–212.

Wolfson, Michael C. 1994. "When Inequalities Diverge." *American Economic Review* 84(2): 353–58.

Wood, Adrian. 1994. *North-South Trade, Employment, and Inequality*. Oxford: Oxford University Press.

Part II

THE MIDDLE CLASS: THE MIDDLE CLASS IN THE INCOME DISTRIBUTION

CHAPTER TWO

On the Identification of the Middle Class

Anthony B. Atkinson and Andrea Brandolini

The following quote from Robert Solow appears on the cover of Estache and Leipziger's (2009) book *Stuck in the Middle*: "There is no shortage of talk about the middle class—say, the middle 60 percent of income recipients." There is, however, a certain penumbra surrounding the definition of *middle class*. People use the term in many different ways. In his article "Is the British Middle Class an Endangered Species?" in the July 24, 2010, issue of *The Guardian*, Andy Beckett said the following:

> In fact, being middle class has always been a slippery business. Having servants, renting a good property, owning a good property, owning a business, being employed in one of "the professions," how you speak, how you use cutlery—at different times, all these have been regarded as essentials of middle-class life.

It is interesting that income does not feature among these characteristics, suggesting that the layman's perception may well differ from the neat, although narrow, income-based definition favored by economists, as exemplified by Solow's comment above.

In this chapter, our aim is to explore more fully the definition of the middle class. To this end we consider a range of approaches and investigate how far they can be implemented using data from the *Luxembourg Income Study (LIS)* and its twin, the *Luxembourg Wealth Study (LWS)*.[1] We first examine definitions based purely on the dimension of household income, about which much has been written. We then move on to consider the role of property and wealth, which is important in identifying the middle class in popular discourse, as just seen, but which may also be grounded in the economic analysis of household finances. Last, we investigate the importance of the occupational structure. Control over resources and position in the division of labor were at the root of class differences in classical economics, but they receive less attention nowadays, prompting the sociologists' criticism that the over-emphasis on income leads economists to neglect the more fundamental social stratification embodied in labor market relations (e.g., Goldthorpe 2010). Our aim is to elaborate on the meanings and interrelationships of these different concepts, as well as assess the extent to which these classifications overlap. This will eventually lead us, in the final section, to argue for the re-integration of different approaches to the concept of the middle class.

A FIXED-INCOME MIDDLE CLASS

In economics, interest in the middle class appears to stem in part from the perception that past distributional studies focused on the poor at one end and on the rich at the other end, leaving out the middle. Solow's reference to the "middle 60 percent" could be interpreted in this sense, since it is bracketed between the bottom 20 percent (which includes the poor or those at risk of poverty) and the top 20 percent (the well-off). The European Union uses as its main income inequality measure the ratio of the income share of the top 20 percent to that of the bottom 20 percent. Transfers away from the middle 60 percent could, if made proportionately, leave measured income inequality unchanged. They are the "forgotten" middle.

The analysis of the entire income distribution and not just the bottom or the top is indeed revealing. This can be illustrated by combining the income shares of the middle 60 percent of the population, ranked by increasing (equivalized disposable) income, and the shares of the bottom and top 20 percent in 15 countries around 1985 and 2004. The countries used are those for which suitable data are available in the *LIS Database* and that cover a wide spectrum of political, institutional, and economic arrangements,[2] while the two points in time span a period of almost two decades characterized by radical economic and political changes. The variations between these two years provide some information about long-term tendencies, although some caution is needed because the selected years may correspond to different business cycle conditions and need not coincide with the critical junctures that identify the relevant episodes in the evolution of income distribution.[3]

Ranking the 15 countries by increasing size of the income share accruing to the middle 60 percent yields a familiar pattern: in 2004 the Nordic countries have shares of above 55 percent, followed by the corporatist European countries. Canada, Taiwan, Poland, and Italy come next, followed by the United States and the United Kingdom, with shares around 51 percent. Mexico is the country with the smallest middle income share at 44 percent. The difference is sizeable: the UK and U.S. middle class receive a share of total income that is about one-tenth less than that of their Nordic counterparts. There is clearly a strong correspondence between this type of country ranking and that based on the degree of inequality: the correlation coefficient between the income share of the middle 60 percent and the Gini index is negative and well above 0.9 in both years. But it is the *change* in the middle class share that has received the most attention, particularly among those worrying about the disappearing middle. Figure 2.1 shows that the share, defined in this way, has fallen in all countries except Denmark

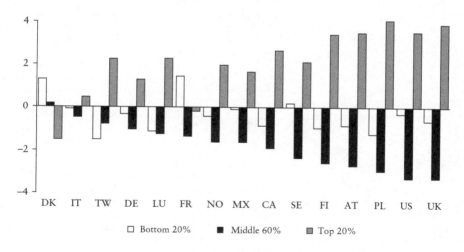

Figure 2.1.   Change in the income share of the bottom, middle, and top income groups in selected *LIS* countries between around 1985 and around 2004 (percentage points)

SOURCE: Authors' calculations from the *LIS Database*.

between the mid-1980s and 2004 and that this loss was consistently to the benefit of the richest one-fifth, except in France.

The evidence of a declining economic status for the middle class is another facet of the trends toward greater inequality prevailing in many countries since the 1980s. This is not, however, the only way in which the middle class can be defined.[4]

FIXING INCOME BOUNDARIES FOR THE MIDDLE CLASS

The approach discussed so far treats the definition of middle class in terms of the cumulative distribution, F, or as Foster and Wolfson (2010) call it, the "people space." Figure 2.2 contains two graphical representations of the income distribution. The cumulative distribution function F, with y on the horizontal axis denoting (equivalized disposable) income expressed as a ratio to the median, is graphed in the right panel. The left panel shows its Lorenz curve, rotated counter-clockwise by 90 degrees so the horizontal axis measures, from right to left, the income share $s(F)$ of the bottom fraction F of the population ranked by increasing income. (Figure 2.2 is drawn using the Danish data for 2004.) The middle class are those between $F_1 = 0.2$ and $F_2 = 0.8$, and their income share is given by the difference $s(F_2) - s(F_1) = s(0.8) - s(0.2)$ in the left part.

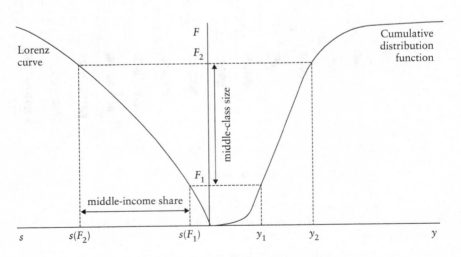

Figure 2.2. Income distribution curves and middle-class identification
SOURCE: Authors' elaboration.

The left-hand part of Figure 2.2 is that on which the income distribution literature tends to concentrate; the right-hand part is more familiar to labor economists, and it tells us *who* belongs to the middle class. Reading the correspondents of F_1 and F_2 on the cumulative distribution function, the middle class are those with income lying between the 20th and 80th percentiles—that is, y_1 and y_2 in the right part. The distance between y_2 and y_1 measures how far apart the two income boundaries of the middle class are. In the more egalitarian countries of northern and central Europe, the richest person in the middle class has an income that is around 1.4 times the median, twice the income of the lowest middle-class person (Figure 2.3). This ratio increases in countries with more unequal distributions, as both

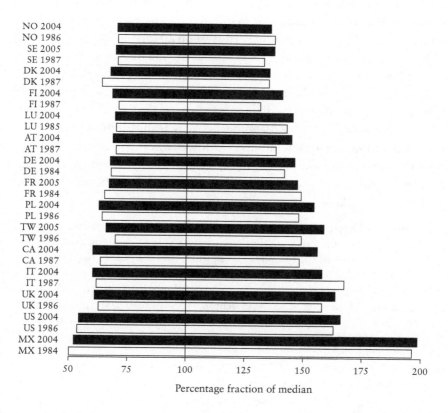

Figure 2.3. Income range of middle 60 percent of population in selected countries around 1985 and 2004 (%)

source: Authors' calculations from the *LIS Database*.

boundaries shift outward: in Mexico the top middle-class income is four times the bottom middle-class income. Changes between the mid-1980s and 2004 are relatively small in comparison to cross-country differences. In the United Kingdom, for instance, the middle 60 percent of the population has an income of between 62 and 158 percent of the median in 1986, but it spans the interval 61 to 164 percent in 2004.

It is not obvious, however, why we should take F as the primitive concept. Indeed, such an identification rules out any discussion of the size of the middle class. The middle class can neither "shrink" nor "expand." Looking at Figure 2.2, we can see that an obvious alternative is to treat y as the primitive concept: the middle class consists of those whose income lies between y_1 and y_2, so the size of the middle class is given by the difference $F_2 - F_1$ (the income share can be read on the horizontal axis of the left part). What are the income limits that define the middle class? The economics literature is said to be "converging" (Ravallion 2010, 446) on the definition of these income limits *relatively*:[5] as 75 percent and 125 percent of the median. These cutoffs typically demarcate a different range than those for the middle 60 percent just observed in Figure 2.3 and, unlike them, are located symmetrically around the median.

This implies that the two approaches may lead to different results. Is there any rationale for these limits? The lower cutoff has a natural linkage with the poverty threshold. Indeed, the Census of Population conducted in Sweden in 1810 contained the following instructions for officials about how to define social classes:

> In order to determine the various statuses of society of households, those who could be called *rich* are those who have a surplus of about 500 rix-dollars in excess of their annual expenditure; the *moderately rich* are those who have less, also those who for their sustenance do not need to incur debts; the *poor* are those who manage not without difficulty: they also include property owners who are in debt in excess of their assets; the *destitute* are those who have to be sustained by gifts and contributions from others. (Soltow 1989, 47)

This may lead us either to accept "the premise that middle-class living standards begin when poverty ends," as Ravallion (2010, 446) states, or to take instead a more conservative approach and fix a level so as "to ensure that the lower endpoint of the middle class represents an income *significantly above the poverty level*," as suggested by Horrigan and

Haugen (1988, 5). In the European Union, the former criterion would bring us to identify the lower bound with the at-risk-of-poverty line, set at 60 percent of the median, whereas the second criterion would rationalize the 75 percent cutoff as defining the "margins" of poverty as plus a quarter of the at-risk-of-poverty line. The middle class can then be said to be those "comfortably" clear of being at-risk-of-poverty.

In contrast, using 125 percent of the median as an upper demarcation has little evident rationale apart from that of symmetry. The middle-class range is in fact relatively short in proportionate terms: 125 is 5/3 times 75. If the lower group had the same proportionate range, then it would extend from 45 percent to 75 percent of the median. Yet, we know that a significant number of people have incomes below 45 percent of the median. At the other extreme, it seems unrealistic to suppose that one-third or more of the population falls in the "upper class," as found by Pressman (2007, 187, Table 2) by applying the 125 percent cutoff to *LIS* data. The rationale just discussed for the bottom cutoff implies that there exists a "lower middle class," comprised of people whose income is in the range of 60 to 75 percent of the median and who are neither poor nor middle class. We could analogously postulate that there is an "upper middle class" between the middle class and the rich by taking the 125 percent cutoff to be a quarter less than the income level that identifies the rich. The implicit "richness line" would equal 167 percent of the median. This would amount to partitioning the population into five rather than three income groups.

By using the 75 and 125 percent cutoffs, we find that the middle class would include at most half of the population in the 15 countries considered here around 2004; it would be as small as one-fourth of the population in Mexico and less than one-third in the United Kingdom and the United States. As a consequence, the upper income group would account for a population share ranging between 27 percent in Denmark, Norway, and Sweden and 39 percent in Mexico. Even splitting this group and setting the richness line at 167 percent of the median as above, the rich would still comprise almost 20 percent of the population in the United Kingdom and the United States, and well above it in Mexico.

If the middle class is to be distinguished from the "rich," a much higher cutoff than 125 percent seems to be required. Grabka and Frick's (2008) results for Germany in 2006 show that one has to go above 150 percent of the median to enter the top 20 percent. Indeed, they choose this income level as the upper limit of the middle class (and 70 percent of the median as the lower limit). Peichl, Schaefer, and Scheicher (2010, 608) further raise the richness line to twice the median, describing it as "arbitrary but common practice," whereas Brzezinski (2010) also considers lines equal to three and four times the median. Danziger, Gottschalk, and Smolensky (1989) define the rich as families with incomes more than nine times the poverty line. Rank and Hirschl (2001) raise this multiplier to ten. With a U.S. poverty line approximately one-third of the median disposable household income (Smeeding 2006), these values imply a cutoff of around 300 percent of median income.

How can these choices of the upper demarcation level be justified?[6] Using a relative measure is common. Over a century ago, Watkins (1907, 3–4) argued that the definition of "rich" is essentially relative: "The rich of former days would not even be 'respectably poor' in New York City today." So y_2 could be taken as rising with the median (or mean). But what percentage of the median should be taken? One criterion considered here is the capacity to employ full-time another person (for personal services, child care, etc.) while allocating a relatively small proportion of the household budget. If the person employed receives a net wage equal to the poverty line, the gross cost would be 60 percent of the median times $1 + \tau$, where τ is additional employment cost. The second parameter is the proportion of total income spent on such personal services, denoted by θ, which, however, has to be small enough to distinguish the well-off from the middle class. The upper threshold is then $(1 + \tau)/\theta$ times 60 percent of the median. So values of τ and θ equal to 25 percent imply a cutoff of three times the median. Lower values for τ (for example, where the outlay is tax deductible) imply a lower cutoff, and lower values of θ imply a higher cutoff. So $\tau = 0$ and $\theta = 0.20$ imply that the cutoff would again be 300 percent of the median, but $\tau = 0.10$ and $\theta = 0.33$ would give a cutoff of 200 percent of the median.

As we raise the upper cutoff to 200 percent of the median, the size of the middle class increases considerably: it reaches 71 percent in Nordic countries and exceeds half of the population even in countries where incomes are distributed more unequally, such as Italy, the United Kingdom, and the United States. The share of the well-off would still be above 10 percent in these three countries; it would fall to 3 to 4 percent only as the upper cutoff is raised to three times the median.

The ranking of the 15 countries is hardly affected by fixing the upper demarcation line alternatively at 125, 167, 200, or 300 percent of the median, and the resulting sizes of the middle class are highly correlated. However, it does not follow that the *changes* in the size of the middle class are the same for all cutoffs. In Italy, for instance, the size of the middle class is unchanged with the 125 percent cutoff, but it increases with the 200 percent cutoff and declines with the 300 percent cutoff. In Norway, it rises with a 125 percent cutoff, but it falls with a 200 or 300 percent cutoff (Figure 2.4, lower panel). Even where the changes are in the same direction, the extent of the variation depends noticeably on the cutoff definition, suggesting different patterns of change of the underlying distribution.

The shrinkage varies in size across countries, but the fact that it is positive in the majority of countries may reinforce the concerns of those

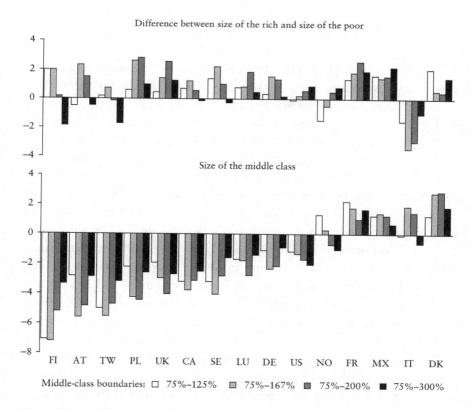

Figure 2.4. Change in population shares for different income cutoffs in selected *LIS* countries between around 1985 and around 2004 (percentage points)

SOURCE: Authors' calculations from the *LIS Database*.

who fear that the middle class is (gradually) disappearing. Is this worry well founded? To some extent, the answer depends on the simultaneous changes in the proportions of the poor and the rich. Regardless of the level of the upper cutoff, in all ten countries where the middle class indisputably shrank, both proportions increased, indicating that the income distribution became more polarized. Yet, the top panel of Figure 2.4 shows that, with few exceptions, the population share of the rich went up more than that of the poor, so the overall net change was toward higher rather than lower income ranges. Italy stands out as the only country where there was a shift from the top to the middle, together with a (more moderate) shift from the middle to the bottom.

THE SHRINKING MIDDLE AND POLARIZATION

In his study of the "shrinking middle class" hypothesis in the United Kingdom during the 1980s, Jenkins (1995, 410) argues that considering the entire income distribution by means of kernel density estimates may reveal information that would be missed by using a specific middle class definition, such as "the shift away from the middle was asymmetric, with the increase in density within the higher income ranges much greater than the increase at the lowest income ranges." This idea is further developed by Burkhauser and colleagues (1999), who use kernel density estimation to compare the income distributions of the United Kingdom and the United States. The comparison of the density functions for 1979 and 1989 enable them to identify two intersections and to show that during the decade, the middle mass shifted toward both the left and right tails but disproportionately more toward the latter in both countries. These intersections are located at 33 and 130 percent of the UK median income, and at 24 and 158 percent of the U.S. median income in 1989. There is no reason to assume that these income levels are those delimiting the middle class: in particular, the lower intersections are well below any standard poverty threshold. However, they tell us that, during those specific episodes, any other pair of cutoffs would yield a lower absolute reduction of the size of the middle class. More interestingly, if both lower and upper cutoffs are set sufficiently higher than these income levels, one may find that the size of the middle class rises rather than declines.

This example illustrates that the arbitrariness of any delimitation of the middle class may lead to contradictory results, as we have seen in the cases of Norway and Italy, where the variation in the share of the middle class changes sign as the upper cutoffs are raised, even in a non-monotonic fashion in Italy. The search for the conditions under which an unambiguous judgment can be reached stimulated Foster and Wolfson's (2010, but originally circulated in 1992) analysis of "polarization," a concept that tries to capture the spreading away from the median that underlies the phenomenon of the vanishing middle class.[7] In addition to exploring partial orderings generated by polarization curves, Foster and Wolfson also proposed an index based on these curves that represents an inverse measure of the size of the middle class.[8] Figure 2.5 reports the change in this index, in the version Wolfson used (1994), between the mid-1980s and the mid-2000s for the 15 countries in our sample, as well as the changes in overall income inequality as measured by the Gini index. The evidence of this figure is in line with that of Figure 2.4: the income distribution became more polarized, and the size of the middle class declined in most countries, but not in Mexico, Norway, Denmark, Italy, and France. The results in Figure 2.4

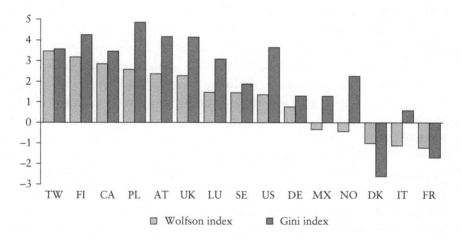

Figure 2.5. Changes in the Wolfson polarization index and the Gini concentration index in selected *LIS* countries between around 1985 and around 2004 (percentage points)

SOURCE: Authors' calculations from the *LIS Database*.

also show that inequality and polarization are interconnected but distinct phenomena, as their variations differed in size and even moved in opposite directions in three countries.

PROPERTY AND THE MIDDLE CLASS

The instructions for the Swedish Census of 1810 were based on the ability to make ends meet, taking as a reference the necessary expenditure. Nothing in those instructions implies that income should be the only variable used in the class definition. Rather, the reference to debts seems to suggest a broader concept of economic resources, incorporating income and wealth and the possibility to access credit. Two centuries later, the official report prepared for the Office of the Vice President of the United States' Middle Class Task Force states, "Middle-class families . . . have certain common aspirations for themselves and their children. They strive for economic stability and therefore desire to own a home and to save for retirement. They want economic opportunities for their children and therefore want to provide them with a college education" (U.S. Department of Commerce, Economics and Statistics Administration 2010, 1). Income alone does not suffice to identify the middle class, defined in this way.

In fact, income is a good proxy of living standards, but it fails to represent the full amount of resources on which individuals rely to cope with the needs of everyday life and to face unexpected events. Individuals may have earnings below the poverty threshold and still reach a decent standard of living thanks to their past savings. A sudden income drop need not result in lower living conditions if they can use accumulated wealth or obtain a bank loan. On the other hand, income can be above the poverty threshold, yet individuals can feel vulnerable because they have no savings with which to face an adverse income shock. Assets and liabilities are fundamental to smoothing out consumption when incomes are volatile, playing an insurance role intertwined with private or public formal insurance mechanisms. More fundamentally, the possession of tangible and intangible assets is a major determinant of personal longer-term prospects. The chances in one's life depend on the set of opportunities open to an individual, which are, in turn, a function of her or his intellectual and material endowments. In the presence of capital market imperfections, individuals with low endowments may be stuck in a poverty trap. Conversely, a minimum endowment may reinforce the sense of responsibility of individuals and their attitude to pursue more efficient behaviors (Bowles and Gintis 1998).

These considerations suggest that middle-class status may be closely linked to the possession of real and financial assets. On one side, the value of wealth holdings may help to define the upper limit of the middle class. As suggested by Atkinson (2008) and Eisenhauer (2008, 2011), the wealthy can be identified as "people who do not need to work"—in other words, individuals whose net worth is large enough to enable them to live off the interest while avoiding paid employment. Atkinson treats as rich those people whose wealth exceeds 30 times the mean income, on the basis of an assumed real after-tax flow of interest of 3.33 percent and taking the average standard of living as a reference. Eisenhauer's wealthy can earn enough on their net worth to be above the poverty threshold: with a poverty line set at 60 percent of the median income and a risk-free net real interest rate of 2 percent, their net worth must exceed 30 (= 0.60/0.02) times the median income. On the other hand, the middle-class condition of being comfortably clear of the risk of poverty hinges on the buffer stocks that would prevent people from falling into poverty should something go wrong. While "income poverty" refers to a static condition where income is insufficient to maintain the minimally acceptable living standard, "asset poverty" captures the exposure to the risk that this standard cannot be secured, for some period of time, if income suddenly falls (Haveman and Wolff 2004; Brandolini, Magri, and Smeeding 2010). The asset-poverty line may then be taken to coincide with a fraction of the standard income-poverty line: one-half means that wealth holdings must be sufficient to maintain the individual at the poverty line for at least six months. The sense of difficulty in coping with negative events associated with asset poverty is at odds with the economic security that is seen as an attribute of the middle class. We may want to exclude all asset-poor individuals from the middle class, even though their incomes are well above the poverty line.

We examine the importance of these issues using the *LWS Database*, which contains household-level data on both income and wealth for ten rich countries.[9] Given data availability, we have selected five countries: Germany (2001), Italy (2004), Norway (2002), Sweden (2002), and the United States (2000). Data for the United States come from the Panel Study of Income Dynamics, a different dataset from the one included in the *LIS Database*, while those for the remaining countries are drawn from the same original sources, although for a slightly earlier year (except for Italy). In spite of these differences, results for the size of the middle class with income cutoffs at 75 and 200 percent of the median are reasonably close to those presented in the previous sections: the larger share of the middle class is observed in the two Nordic countries (around 70 percent), followed by Germany (64 percent), then Italy (58 percent), and finally the United States (54 percent).

Household-level information on wealth is generally reputed to be of lower quality than that on income; moreover, the degree of standardization of definitions and collection procedures is low. Therefore, cross-country comparability is far from perfect, despite the ex post harmonization carried out by *LWS*. In particular, the valuation of real property on a taxable rather than market basis likely leads to an understatement of total wealth in Norway and possibly Sweden, despite the ex post statistical adjustment to market values in the latter country. Wealth is less seriously understated in Germany, where certain items are only recorded for values exceeding a minimum level. Yet, the *LWS* data provide some useful insights on the role of wealth in delimiting the upper limit for the middle class.

Fixing the upper cutoff at 30 times the median income, a couple with two young children would be classified as middle class when their net worth is below 950,000 international dollars at 2004 prices in Italy, 1.2 million in Germany and Sweden, and 1.8 million in Norway and the United States. These values imply that the shares of the well-off go from 3.6 percent in the United States to 6.6 in Germany and 10.6 in Italy: in all three countries they own two-fifths or more of total wealth. (Norway and Sweden are not considered due to the mentioned likely undervaluation of real assets and, therefore, net worth.) The upper income limits of the middle class that correspond to these population proportions are approximately located at twice the median in Italy and Germany and at three and a half times the median in the United States. This evidence provides some support for raising the upper limit of the middle class to at least 200 percent of the median.

At the other extreme, to define asset poverty, we consider both financial assets alone, which include assets that can be easily monetized, and net worth, which includes all marketable assets net of all debts (excluding the value of business equity, which is unavailable in some countries). The former can be seen as an indicator of "emergency fund availability," while the latter is an indicator of "the long-run economic security of families"

(Haveman and Wolff 2004, 151). Consistent with this interpretation, to measure asset poverty, we take a shorter reference period for financial assets (three months) than for net worth (six months), which corresponds to asset poverty thresholds equal to one-fourth and one-half of the income poverty line, respectively. Our estimates show that a considerable proportion of middle-class individuals are asset-poor. When the cutoffs are set at 75 and 200 percent of the median, about half of middle-class Germans and Americans do not have enough financial assets to sustain their standard of living at the poverty line for at least three months, and the size of the middle class shrinks to 32 percent or less. The proportion of asset-poor middle-class Germans and Americans falls to about 30 percent when the focus is on net worth. Financial asset poverty concerns 35 to 40 percent of the Swedish and Norwegian middle-class individuals. Far fewer middle-class Italians are financially vulnerable: 23 percent based on financial assets and 13 percent considering net worth. This reflects the pervasiveness of home ownership and relatively high Italian housing prices but also the segmentation and low generosity of public income-support schemes that induce people to accumulate precautionary savings.[10]

In brief, accounting for wealth helps to qualify purely income-based definitions of the middle class. We have focused on the role of assets either in allowing people to avoid paid employment without jeopardizing their standard of living or in protecting people's standard of living from a sudden drop in their earnings, but other aspects may be relevant, such as the role that wealth plays in sustaining upward mobility. In all five countries examined, the size of the middle class would be significantly cut should we exclude asset-poor individuals to an extent that varies considerably across countries and depends on the wealth measure.

CLASS AND OCCUPATION

The link between income and employment position is undoubtedly close, and both variables can contribute to draw the class distinctions. Yet, their conceptual primacy varies across disciplines. Economists tend to start from income or expenditure. In their study covering 13 developing countries around the world, Banerjee and Duflo (2008) define the middle class as comprising all households with a daily per capita expenditure of between $2 and $10 at purchasing power parities and then proceed to compare their consumption, investment, educational patterns, and occupational status with those of the poor and the well-off. Their conclusion is pertinent to our discussion and worth quoting in full:

> Nothing seems more middle class than the fact of having a steady well-paying job. While there are many petty entrepreneurs among the middle class, most of them do not seem to be capitalists in waiting. They run businesses, but for the most part only because they are still relatively poor and every little bit helps. If they could only find the right salaried job, they might be quite content to shut their business down. If the middle class matters for growth, it is probably not because of its entrepreneurial spirit. (Banerjee and Duflo 2008, 26)

Most sociologists would approach the issue the other way around and focus on the positions in the labor market to fix the demarcation lines across classes. Social differentiation may be specified in terms of occupational prestige and status within a "social-hierarchy approach," or in terms of the employment relations entailed by the position of individuals in the productive process within a "class-structure approach" (Erikson and Goldthorpe 1992, 28–35). Goldthorpe and McKnight (2006) adopt this second approach and show how the employment-based class position impinges on individuals' economic security, economic stability, and economic prospects. This Weberian perspective, which defines classes on the basis of access to and exclusion from certain economic opportunities is, according to Wright (1997, 2009), distinct from the Marxist tradition that "conceives of classes as being structured by mechanisms of domination and exploitation, in which economic positions accord some people power over the lives and activities of others" (Wright 2009, 102). This conceptual distinction aside, Wright (1997) observes that the empirical categories used to estimate the class structure do not dramatically differ between the two perspectives, being largely based on individuals' occupations and employment relations.

Starting with the datasets centered on the year 2004, the *LIS Database* contains much improved coverage of labor market variables. However, original sources were not all designed to provide a careful description of labor market status, not even for the main respondent. Indeed, Mandel and Shalev (2009, 1882–1883) observe that "because the occupational coding schemes utilized in *LIS* datasets are nationally idiosyncratic, carrying out a comprehensive and reliable study of class effects requires utilizing 'income classes'—in the present case, quintiles of hourly earnings." For instance, in May 2011, when the calculations for this chapter were completed, the variable "occupation of the household's head" that would provide the information needed in the class-structure approach presented as many as 496 different categories in the United States and 280 in Germany, but only 31 in France and was missing for Italy and Sweden. The variable "skill level in employment of the household's head" constituted a reasonable substitute for Sweden and Italy, although skill categories differed in number (9 and 14, respectively) and precise definitions. Possibly for this unavoidable patchwork nature, no routine was available to us to compute standard social classifications from the *LIS* data, unlike other comparative projects such as the European Social Survey (see Leiulfsrud, Bison, and Jensberg 2005).

Nonetheless, for the five countries just mentioned, we tried to approximate the simplified version of Goldthorpe's classification to study its overlapping with an income-based class partition. In this classification, the "intermediate class" comprises routine non-manual employees, lower-grade technicians, supervisors of manual workers, and small employers and self-employed workers. This classification is distinct from the "working class" (skilled and unskilled manual workers; low-skilled, routine non-manual workers) on the one hand and the "salariat or service class" (all professionals, administrative and managerial employees, higher-grade technicians, large employers) on the other hand (e.g., Goldthorpe and McKnight 2006, 110, Table 5.1). By combining information on occupation (France, Germany, the United States) or skill level in employment (Italy, Sweden) with information on employment, we apply this classification to all active household heads. Results are therefore not comparable to those presented above, since households of inactive heads are now excluded; moreover, income medians are computed for the restricted group.

According to this classification, the size of the intermediate class ranges from 50 percent in France to 61 percent in Sweden and appears to be far less variable across countries than the size of the income-defined middle class (compare the dotted areas with the narrow bars in Figure 2.6). When the upper-income cutoff is set at 150 percent of the median income, a large part of the intermediate class is located either at the bottom or at the top of the income distribution in Italy and the United States. But when the cutoff is raised to 200 percent, the income-based middle class considerably outweighs the occupation-based middle class in France, Germany, and Sweden. In all countries, the middle class identified on the basis of income includes

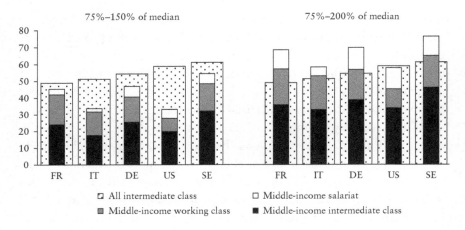

Figure 2.6.   Population shares of occupation-based and income-based middle classes in selected countries around 2004 (%)

SOURCE: Authors' calculations from the *LIS Database.*

a sizeable proportion of the working class, together with some fraction of individuals in the top class. Excluding these two subgroups would reduce the size of the income middle class by between 40 and 50 percent. Bearing in mind the limits in cross-country comparability, the social stratification by occupation and the clustering by income levels do not coincide.

CONCLUSION

The relationship between class and income distribution goes back to the origins of the economic discipline—at least to the famous opening of Ricardo's *Principles of Political Economy and Taxation* (1821) that the principal problem in political economy is to determine the laws that regulate the distribution of "the produce of the earth among . . . the proprietor of the land, the owner of the stock of capital necessary for its cultivation, and the laborers by whose industry it is cultivated." At that time, it may have been reasonable to suppose a close correspondence between social class and position on the income scale. Today, this relationship is blurred by the development of institutions that stand between the productive sector of the economy and the household sector, the state as well as private intermediaries (Atkinson 1983, Ch. 9). The entire social stratification has become more complex: the middle class, the object of this chapter, did not even feature in Ricardo's synthesis.

Nowadays, social class and income distribution largely belong to separate fields of analysis—the former a favorite terrain for sociologists, and the latter a topic largely for economists. Indeed, it is normal among economists to think of classes simply as income groupings. As we have seen, the middle class has been identified by setting limits either in the people space, $F(y)$, or in the income space, y. In the former, the size of the middle class is fixed and attention is focused on the evolution of the income share; in the latter, population size is the main concern. This approach provides an interesting complement to analyses that focus on the bottom or the top of the income distribution.

We have indeed shown that, around 2004, both the size of the middle class (for different income cutoffs) and its income shares are largest in the Nordic countries and corporatist continental European countries; they are smaller in Italy, the United States, the United Kingdom, and especially in Mexico. Moreover, we have observed a downsizing of the middle class between the mid-1980s and the mid-2000s: the middle 60 percent of the population lost income shares to the benefit of the richest top fifth in all countries but Denmark, and the middle class shrank in ten countries, while it expanded in three, as also confirmed by Foster and Wolfson's polarization index.

These results offer a more nuanced view of the recent evolution of economic inequality. On the other hand, when we delve into the composition of middle-income groups, we find that they are internally highly heterogeneous. We have shown this to be the case regarding both wealth holdings and the position in the labor market. Economists often stress the importance of having a large middle class for economic growth, either for its consumption patterns or for its propensity to accumulate human and physical capital, as well as for democracy and the political stability of a society. Yet, it is reasonable to wonder whether a pure income characterization of social classes is analytically satisfactory. Perhaps, it is time to re-integrate analyses of income, wealth, and occupation.

NOTES

We thank Michel Beine, Janet Gornick, Markus Jäntti, and Stephen Jenkins for useful comments on an earlier draft of this chapter. The views expressed here are solely those of the authors; in particular, they do not necessarily reflect those of the Bank of Italy.

1. All estimates are computed from the database as of May 10, 2011, and are reported in the online appendix. Disposable money income is the sum of all cash incomes earned by the household, net of income taxes and social contributions. Net worth includes all real and financial assets except for business equity (unavailable in some countries), net of all liabilities. Income and wealth are divided by the square root of household size and then attributed to each household's member. Zero incomes are dropped, and observations are bottom-coded at 1 percent of the mean equivalent income and top-coded at 10 times the median unadjusted income.

2. Countries and years are Austria (1987, 2004), Canada (1987, 2004), Denmark (1987, 2004), Finland (1987, 2004), France (1984, 2005), Germany (1984, 2004; thus including eastern Länder in 2004 but not in 1984), Italy (1987, 2004), Luxembourg (1985, 2004), Mexico (1984, 2004), Norway (1986, 2004), Poland (1986, 2004), Sweden (1987, 2005), Taiwan (1986, 2005), the United Kingdom (1986, 2004), and the United States (1986, 2004).

3. Moreover, the LIS procedures are such to maximize cross-country comparability for the same wave of data (e.g., Wave VI for data around 2004). This implies that the evidence tends to be less reliable for changes over time than for comparisons across countries, since data cannot be treated as continuous time series (Atkinson 2004). This is especially true for such a long period of time, during which the LIS procedures have been refined but have not always been applied backward. Most surveys have undergone revisions in methods and definitions, and the original datasets in the *LIS Database* may have changed (which is the case in Austria, Canada, and the United Kingdom).

4. Lawrence (1984); Bluestone and Harrison (1988); and Beach, Chaykowski, and Slotsve (1997) define the middle class in terms of labor earnings rather than income. More recently, Autor, Katz, and Kearney (2006); Goos and Manning (2007); and Goos, Manning, and Salomons (2009) examined "job polarization," which is the rise of employment shares in the highest- and lowest-wage occupations at the expense of middle-wage jobs.

5. Absolute income limits are more common in analyses of the middle class in developing countries or at the global level (Milanovic and Yitzhaki 2002; Banerjee and Duflo 2008; Ravallion 2010), but were also used in earlier studies for the United States (Bradbury 1986; Horrigan and Haugen 1988).

6. Medeiros (2006) defines the richness line as that level of income such that the sum of all incomes above it exactly matches the aggregate poverty gap. The problem with this definition is that the affluence score would fall whenever a government reduces poverty. Countries that do well on this account, however, may still have a rich upper class.

7. In a different approach, Esteban and Ray (1994) and later Duclos, Esteban, and Ray (2004, 1747) characterize polarization as "the interplay of two

forces: identification with one's own group and alienation vis-à-vis others"; social classes are endogenously defined but not explicitly identified.

8. Foster and Wolfson's polarization index is equal to $(T - G)\mu/m$, where μ and m are the mean and median incomes, G is the Gini coefficient, and T is the ratio to the mean of the average income distance between those above the median and those below the median. Since the term $(T - G)$ is equal to the Gini coefficient between the upper and lower halves of the distribution minus the weighted inequality within these two subgroups, "more inequality between the upper and lower halves of the distribution will tend to raise both inequality and polarization; a greater level of within-group inequality raises overall inequality, but lowers polarization" (Foster and Wolfson 2010, 266). Wolfson (1994) rewrites the index as $2(1 - 2S_{0.50} - G)\mu/m$, where $S_{0.50}$ denotes the income share of the bottom half of the population.

9. Results are not shown here but are reported in the online appendix.

10. The balance between private wealth and public insurance is closely linked to the "encompassing" nature of welfare state institutions, as discussed by Korpi and Palme (1998).

For additional results, please see the online appendices by following the link in the listing for Income Inequality *on the Stanford University Press website: http:// www.sup.org.*

REFERENCES

Atkinson, Anthony B. 1983. *The Economics of Inequality*, 2nd ed. Oxford: Clarendon Press.

———. 2004. "The Luxembourg Income Study (LIS): Past, Present and Future." *Socio-Economic Review* 2(2): 165–90.

———. 2008. "Concentration among the Rich." In *Personal Wealth from a Global Perspective*, edited by James B. Davies. Oxford: Oxford University Press.

Autor, David H., Lawrence F. Katz, and Melissa S. Kearney. 2006. "The Polarization of the U.S. Labor Market." *American Economic Review Papers and Proceedings* 96(2): 189–94.

Banerjee, Abhijit V., and Esther Duflo. 2008. "What Is Middle Class about the Middle Classes around the World?" *Journal of Economic Perspectives* 22(2): 3–28.

Beach, Charles M., Richard P. Chaykowski, and George A. Slotsve. 1997. "Inequality and Polarization of Male Earnings in the United States, 1968–1990." *North American Journal of Economics and Finance* 8(2): 135–51.

Beckett, Andy. 2010. "Is the British Middle Class an Endangered Species?" *The Guardian*, July 24, 2010, p. 28. http://www.guardian.co.uk/uk/2010/jul/24/middle-class-in-decline-society.

Bluestone, Barry, and Bennett Harrison. 1988. "The Growth of Low-Wage Employment: 1963–86." *American Economic Review Papers and Proceedings* 78(2): 124–28.

Bowles, Samuel, and Herbert Gintis. 1998. "Efficient Redistribution: New Rules for Markets, States and Communities." In *Recasting Egalitarianism: New Rules for Communities, States and Markets*, edited by Erik O. Wright. London: Verso.

Bradbury, Katherine L. 1986. "The Shrinking Middle Class." *New England Economic Review* (September): 41–55.

Brandolini, Andrea, Silvia Magri, and Timothy M. Smeeding. 2010. "Asset-Based Measurement of Poverty." *Journal of Policy Analysis and Management* 29(2): 267–84.

Brzezinski, Michal. 2010. "Income Affluence in Poland." *Social Indicators Research* 99(2): 285–99.

Burkhauser, Richard V., Amy Crews Cutts, Mary C. Daly, and Stephen P. Jenkins. 1999. "Testing the Significance of Income Distribution Changes over the 1980s Business Cycle: A Cross-National Comparison." *Journal of Applied Econometrics* 14(3): 253–72.

Danziger, Sheldon, Peter Gottschalk, and Eugene Smolensky. 1989. "How the Rich Have Fared, 1973–87." *American Economic Review Papers and Proceedings* 79(2): 310–14.

Duclos, Jean-Yves, Joan Esteban, and Debraj Ray. 2004. "Polarization: Concepts, Measurement, Estimation." *Econometrica* 72(6): 1737–72.

Eisenhauer, Joseph G. 2008. "An Economic Definition of the Middle Class." *Forum for Social Economics* 37(2): 103–13.

———. 2011. "The Rich, the Poor, and the Middle Class: Thresholds and Intensity Indices." *Research in Economics* 65(4): 294–304.

Erikson, Robert, and John H. Goldthorpe. 1992. *The Constant Flux: A Study of Class Mobility in Industrial Societies.* Oxford: Clarendon.

Estache, Antonio, and Danny Leipziger, eds. 2009. *Stuck in the Middle: Is Fiscal Policy Failing the Middle Class?* Washington, DC: Brookings Institution Press.

Esteban, Joan-María, and Debraj Ray. 1994. "On the Measurement of Polarization." *Econometrica* 62(4): 819–51.

Foster, James E., and Michael C. Wolfson. 2010. "Polarization and the Decline of the Middle Class: Canada and the U.S." *Journal of Economic Inequality* 8(2): 247–73.

Goldthorpe, John H. 2010. "Analysing Social Inequality: A Critique of Two Recent Contributions from Economics and Epidemiology." *European Sociological Review* 26(6): 731–44.

Goldthorpe, John H., and Abigail McKnight. 2006. "The Economic Basis of Social Class." In *Mobility and Inequality: Frontiers of Research from Sociology and Economics*, edited by Stephen L. Morgan, David B. Grusky, and Gary S. Fields. Stanford, CA: Stanford University Press.

Goos, Maarten, and Alan Manning. 2007. "Lousy and Lovely Jobs: The Rising Polarization of Work in Britain." *Review of Economics and Statistics* 89(1): 118–33.

Goos, Maarten, Alan Manning, and Anna Salomons. 2009. "Job Polarization in Europe." *American Economic Review Papers and Proceedings* 99(2): 58–63.

Grabka, Markus M., and Joachim R. Frick. 2008. "The Shrinking German Middle Class—Signs of Long-Term Polarization in Disposable Income?" *DIW Berlin Weekly Report* 4(4): 21–27.

Haveman, Robert, and Edward N. Wolff. 2004. "The Concept and Measurement of Asset Poverty: Levels, Trends and Composition for the U.S., 1983–2001." *Journal of Economic Inequality* 2(2): 145–69.

Horrigan, Michael W., and Steven E. Haugen. 1988. "The Declining Middle-Class Thesis: A Sensitivity Analysis." *Monthly Labor Review* 111(5): 3–13.

Jenkins, Stephen P. 1995. "Did the Middle Class Shrink during the 1980s? UK Evidence from Kernel Density Estimates." *Economics Letters* 49(4): 407–13.

Korpi, Walter, and Joakim Palme. 1998. "The Paradox of Redistribution and Strategies of Equality: Welfare State Institutions, Inequality, and Poverty in the Western Countries." *American Sociological Review* 63(5): 661–87.

Lawrence, Robert Z. 1984. "Sectoral Shifts and the Size of the Middle Class." *Brookings Review* 3(1): 3–11.

Leiulfsrud, Håkon, Ivano Bison, and Heidi Jensberg. 2005. "Social Class in Europe." *European Social Survey* 2002/3. Trondheim, Norway: NTNU Social Research Ltd.

Luxembourg Income Study (LIS) Database, http://www.lisdatacenter.org (multiple countries; microdata last accessed in July 2011). Luxembourg: LIS.

Luxembourg Wealth Study (LWS) Database, http://www.lisdatacenter.org (multiple countries; microdata last accessed in July 2011). Luxembourg: LIS.

Mandel, Hadas, and Michael Shalev. 2009. "How Welfare States Shape the Gender Pay Gap: A Theoretical and Comparative Analysis." *Social Forces* 87(4): 1873–1911.

Medeiros, Marcelo. 2006. "The Rich and the Poor: The Construction of an Affluence Line from the Poverty Line." *Social Indicators Research* 78(1): 1–18.

Milanovic, Branko, and Shlomo Yitzhaki. 2002. "Decomposing World Income Distribution: Does the World Have a Middle Class?" *Review of Income and Wealth* 48(2): 155–78.

Peichl, Andreas, Thilo Schaefer, and Christoph Scheicher. 2010. "Measuring Richness and Poverty: A Micro Data Application to Europe and Germany." *Review of Income and Wealth* 56(3): 597–619.

Pressman, Steven. 2007. "The Decline of the Middle Class: An International Perspective." *Journal of Economic Issues* 41(1): 181–200.

Rank, Mark R., and Thomas Hirschl. 2001. "Rags or Riches? Estimating the Probabilities of Poverty and Affluence across the Adult American Life Span." *Social Science Quarterly* 82(4): 651–69.

Ravallion, Martin. 2010. "The Developing World's Bulging (but Vulnerable) Middle Class." *World Development* 38(4): 445–54.

Ricardo, David. 1821. *On the Principles of Political Economy and Taxation*, 3rd ed. London: John Murray.

Smeeding, Timothy M. 2006. "Poor People in Rich Nations: The United States in Comparative Perspective." *Journal of Economic Perspectives* 20(1): 69–90.

Soltow, Lee. 1989. "The Rich and the Destitute in Sweden, 1805–1855: A Test of Tocqueville's Inequality Hypotheses." *Economic History Review* 42 (New Series, 1): 43–63.

U.S. Department of Commerce, Economics and Statistics Administration. 2010. *Middle Class in America*. Washington, DC: U.S. Government Printing Office (January).

Watkins, George P. 1907. "The Growth of Large Fortunes." *Publications of the American Economic Association* 8: 1–170.

Wolfson, Michael C. 1994. "When Inequalities Diverge." *American Economic Review Papers and Proceedings* 84(2): 353–858.

Wright, Erik Olin. 1997. *Class Counts: Comparative Studies in Class Analysis*. Cambridge: Cambridge University Press.

———. 2009. "Understanding Class: Towards an Integrated Analytical Approach." *New Left Review* 60 (November–December): 101–16.

CHAPTER THREE

Has Rising Inequality Reduced Middle-Class Income Growth?

Lane Kenworthy

A "top-heavy" rise in income inequality tends to reduce middle-class house-holds' relative incomes, leading them to fall even farther behind those at the top of the income distribution. But what about their absolute incomes? Household income growth is not a zero-sum game because the pie tends to get larger over time. Disproportionately large gains at the top, however, are likely to come at least partly at the expense of those in the middle, resulting in slower growth of income than would have been the case in the absence of rising inequality (Billitteri 2009; Kumhof and Ranciere 2010; Reich 2010; Kenworthy 2011a; Thompson and Leight 2011; Stiglitz 2012).

The U.S. experience fits this hypothesis. Income inequality has increased sharply over the past generation, and income growth for American households in the middle of the distribution has been slow (Mishel, Bernstein, and Shierholz 2009; Kenworthy 2010b). Does this hold if we compare across countries? Has middle-class income growth been slower in countries with larger increases in top-heavy income inequality?

Figure 3.1 shows trends in top-heavy income inequality from the late 1970s to the mid-2000s in six affluent countries. Inequality is measured as the top 1 percent's share of pre-tax income. (Post-tax data on the top 1 percent's share are not available for most countries.) These data are from tax records (Atkinson, Piketty, and Saez 2011; Alvaredo et al. 2012). In the first two countries, the United States and the United Kingdom, top-heavy income inequality soared. In the next two, Canada and Finland, inequality increased moderately. In the last two countries, Germany and the Netherlands, we see little or no rise in inequality.

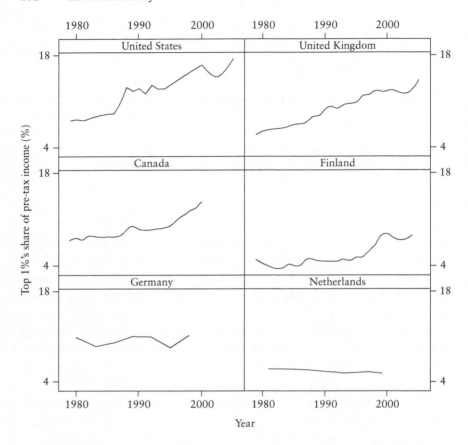

Figure 3.1.   Trends in top-heavy income inequality, six countries, late 1970s to mid-2000s

SOURCE: Author's compilation using data from Alvaredo et al. (2012).
NOTE: Top two countries: large rise in top-heavy income inequality. Middle two countries: moderate rise in inequality. Bottom two countries: no rise in inequality.

Given these trends in inequality, we might expect to find middle-class incomes growing slowest in the United States and the United Kingdom, at an intermediate pace in Canada and Finland, and fastest in Germany and the Netherlands. But this expectation turns out to be wrong. Figure 3.2 shows trends in inflation-adjusted post-tax and post-transfer household income at the 25th, 50th (median), and 75th percentiles of the income dis-

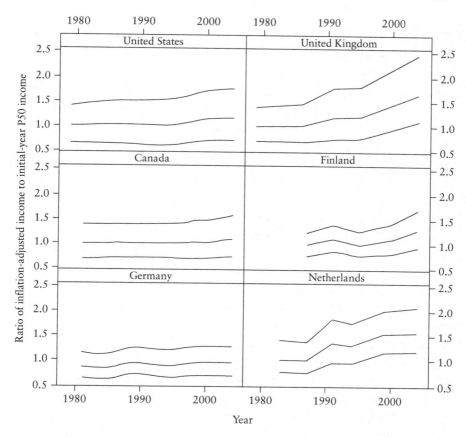

Figure 3.2.   Trends in real incomes of middle-income (25th, 50th, and 75th percentiles) households, six countries, late 1970s to mid-2000s

SOURCE: Author's calculations from the *LIS Database*, Waves I to VI, and the OECD.
NOTE: Lower lines: 25th percentile; middle lines: 50th percentile; top lines: 75th percentile. Post-tax and post-transfer income adjusted for household size.

tribution. In each of the three groups of countries, we observe stagnant middle-class incomes in one country and rapidly growing incomes in the other. Trends in income inequality are of no use in predicting trends in the absolute incomes of middle-class households in these six countries. To understand why, we need a more systematic analysis.

ANALYTICAL STRATEGY

Research on income inequality's consequences has examined countries, regions or states, cities, and individuals. I focus on countries for two reasons. First, countries are the main unit of interest from a policy perspective. Most of the relevant levers for influencing income inequality are at the level of the national government rather than the region or city. Second, the country level is where we now have the best data on income inequality and middle-class incomes. I examine 15 affluent, non-tiny, democratic countries for which data on top-heavy income inequality and middle-class incomes are available: Australia, Canada, Denmark, Finland, France, Germany, Ireland, Italy, the Netherlands, Norway, Spain, Sweden, Switzerland, the United Kingdom, and the United States.

Much existing analysis of the effects of income inequality is comparative but static; it is based on associations across countries or regions at a single point in time (e.g., Wilkinson and Pickett 2009). Cross-sectional correlations can be informative, but they are potentially problematic because countries differ in a variety of ways that we cannot measure very well and that might be the true cause of differences in outcomes such as income growth.

In studying the effects of income inequality in rich countries, there is a better approach. For many countries, we have data for both income inequality and middle-class income growth over a period of nearly three decades. During this period, the degree to which inequality changed varied markedly across these countries. For analytical purposes, this "difference in differences" is useful. If countries with larger increases in inequality experienced more change in the outcome, we can have greater confidence that a causal relationship exists (Allison 1990; Halaby 2004; Angrist and Pischke 2008; Firebaugh 2008; Kenworthy 2011b). Perhaps most important, examining the relationship between changes (first differences, or change scores) in the cause and changes in the outcome takes country "fixed effects"—potentially influential time-invariant factors such as culture—out of play.

Analyzing changes also is more informative for policy analysis. From a policy maker's perspective, knowing that income inequality is bad for middle-class income growth leads to an inference that reducing income inequality (or halting or slowing its rise) would produce a better outcome. But if we have not actually examined what happens when inequality changes, that inference is on less firm footing.

With this type of analysis, the longer the time series, the better. I examine only the period since the 1970s due to data limitations and because many things changed in the rich countries in the 1970s, from productivity slowdown to globalization to massive cultural shifts. These changes were so pronounced that it makes sense to consider the economic and political context since the 1970s as fundamentally different from the period from the 1940s through the 1960s. Rather than maximize the number of data points by including those earlier decades, I take the more cautious approach of confining the analyses to the post-1970s period.

A differences-in-differences analysis presumes that the effect of the cause on the outcome will show up within the measured time period. In some instances we have reason to expect an immediate impact, but that is unlikely to be the case for income inequality. For that reason, the following analysis focuses on change over two and a half decades rather than during a single year or over a five-year period.

THE IMPACT OF RISING TOP INCOME SHARES
ON GROWTH OF MIDDLE-CLASS INCOMES

Figure 3.3 shows changes in median (50th percentile) post-transfer–post-tax household income by changes in the top 1 percent's share of pre-tax income. The actual period covered differs across the countries, so changes in median income and inequality are calculated on an annualized basis. We do not see the expected negative relationship. Moving from the six countries included in Figures 3.1 and 3.2 to a larger set of countries does not alter the conclusion.

In calculating the regression line, Ireland and Norway are omitted because these two countries are statistical outliers. Both had very rapid economic growth during these years, which contributed to a substantial rise in median income. In Norway the source was oil, and in Ireland it was massive foreign investment. Given the exceptional degree of economic growth in these two countries, the pattern across the group of countries as a whole is likely to be more accurately revealed with these two nations excluded.

Why do we not see a negative association in Figure 3.3 between change in top-heavy income inequality and change in middle-class absolute income? One possibility is that the share of income going to those at the top of the distribution actually has no impact on the absolute amount that goes

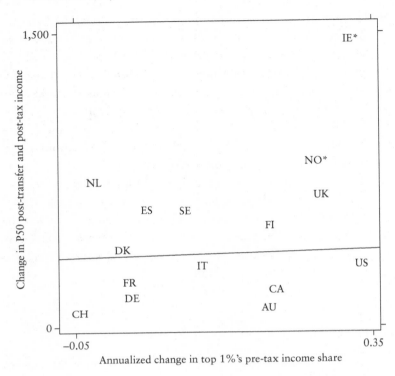

Figure 3.3. Change in median household income by change in top-heavy income inequality, 15 countries, late 1970s to mid-2000s

SOURCE: Author's calculations from the *LIS Database*, Waves I to VI (household income), the OECD (inflation, PPPs), and Alvaredo et al. (2012) (income inequality).

NOTE: Actual years vary somewhat depending on the country, so change is calculated per year. The regression line is calculated with Ireland and Norway excluded. Change in median household income: average change per year in post-tax and post-transfer 50th percentile household income, adjusted for household size and for inflation and converted into U.S. dollars using purchasing power parities. Change in top-heavy income inequality: average change per year in the top 1 percent's income share. For country abbreviations, see Appendix Table A1 in the Introduction to this volume.

to those in the middle. But as noted earlier, that seems unlikely. The other possibility is that there is a negative effect, but it is overshadowed by other factors that influence middle-class incomes.

One such factor could be economic growth. The pace of economic growth has varied across these countries. Even if a rise in top-heavy inequality means that the middle class gets a smaller share of the income gains produced by economic growth, this effect might be swamped by variation across the countries in the pace of economic growth. A good measure of economic growth is change in gross domestic product (GDP) per capita. I use data from the Organisation for Economic Co-operation and Development (OECD) database to calculate per-year change in GDP per capita for each country over the same time period used in Figure 3.3. The first panel in Figure 3.4 shows change in median household income by economic growth. As expected, we see a strong positive association.

Is it a simple mathematical truism that median household income adjusted for change in GDP per capita will rise more slowly in countries in which top-heavy income inequality has grown more rapidly? The answer is no. A rising income share for the richest need not automatically come at the expense of the middle class. It might instead come at the expense of the near rich—say, those in the 90th to 99th percentiles—or at the expense of the poor.

What about the possibility that rising inequality boosts economic growth? If it does, we would not want to control for growth (it is endogenous). Is income inequality good for economic growth? This is a long-standing hypothesis, much debated since the publication of Arthur Okun's (1975) "equality-efficiency tradeoff" book in the mid-1970s. Recent empirical studies have yielded mixed findings (Kenworthy 2004; Voitchovsky 2005; Andrews, Jencks, and Leigh 2011). We thus have no clear answer. Across the 13 countries included in the first chart in Figure 3.4, we see a modestly strong positive association between change in the top 1 percent's share of income and change in GDP per capita (not shown). Whether that indicates a causal relationship is open to debate.

A second potential contributor to changes in median household income is government transfers. In an earlier study (Kenworthy 2010a), I examined the relationship between changes in the top 1 percent's income share and changes in the absolute incomes of households in the bottom 10 percent. It turns out that there is no association across the rich countries. The main determinant of whether and how much absolute incomes in the bottom 10 percent increased over the past generation is net government transfers— cash and near-cash government benefits received minus taxes paid. In some countries net transfers to households in the bottom 10 percent have increased over time, while in others they have tended to remain stagnant. This variation across the countries in changes in net government transfers is not

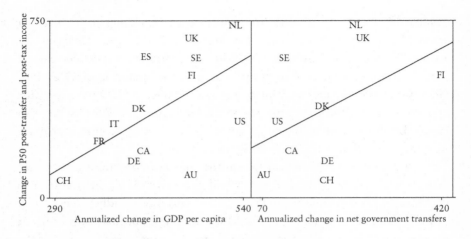

Figure 3.4. Change in median household income by economic growth and by change in net government transfers, 13 countries, late 1970s to mid-2000s

SOURCE: Author's calculations from the *LIS Database*, Waves I to VI (income, government transfers, taxes), and the OECD (economic growth, inflation, PPPs).

NOTE: Actual years vary somewhat depending on the country, so change is calculated per year. Change in median household income: average change per year in post-tax and post-transfer 50th percentile household income, adjusted for household size and for inflation and converted into U.S. dollars using purchasing power parities. Change in GDP per capita: average change per year in per person gross domestic product. Change in net government transfers: average change per year in government transfers received minus taxes paid among households in the lower-middle-income quartile (25th to 50th percentiles). France, Italy, and Spain are missing in the second chart due to lack of net government transfer data.

correlated with changes in top-heavy income inequality. Political choices, rather than constraints or opportunities stemming from the share of income captured by those at the top, have determined the degree to which governments have increased net transfers to the poor.

This could be true in the middle of the income distribution as well. Middle-class households tend to be less reliant than the poor on government transfers, but transfers do account for part of their income. Some in this group receive public pensions and others get unemployment, sickness, or disability benefits. In another recent study (Kenworthy 2011c), I used *LIS* data to examine the sources of the increase in absolute income over time in households between the 25th and 50th percentiles of the income distribution. It turns out that changes in net government transfers have been nearly as important as changes in earnings in accounting for differences across countries in overall income growth for these "lower-middle-income" households.

Indeed, an influential hypothesis predicts that a rise in income inequality in a country will trigger a shift in government policy to increase redistribution, via taxes and transfers, to those in the middle (Meltzer and Richard 1981). This view, often termed the "median-voter theorem," suggests that election outcomes are determined by the median-income voter. When income inequality increases, the median voter will benefit more from redistribution than she or he previously did. Recognizing this, political parties will increase redistribution in order to enhance their electoral fortunes. If this is correct, countries in which the pre-tax income share of the top 1 percent rises will redistribute a growing portion of that group's income to the middle class. This would partially or fully offset the rise in pre-tax income inequality. It could thereby help to account for the lack of association in Figure 3.3 between change in the top 1 percent's pre-tax income share and change in the absolute income of the median household. Then again, earlier studies have found little support for the over-time pattern predicted by the median-voter theorem (Kenworthy and Pontusson 2005; Kenworthy and McCall 2008).

The measure used here is annualized change in average net government transfers received by households between the 25th and 50th percentiles— the lower-middle-quartile group of the income distribution. Again, net government transfers refer to cash and near-cash transfers received minus taxes paid. Unfortunately, this calculation is possible for only ten countries. (For the other countries, earnings and income are reported net of taxes, so it is not possible to cleanly separate out transfers and tax payments.)

The second panel in Figure 3.4 shows a positive association between change in net transfers received by lower-middle-income households and change in median household income. This might help to account for why Finland and the United Kingdom are fairly high on the vertical axis in Figure 3.3 despite relatively sharp increases in their top 1 percent's income share. Net government transfers to lower-middle-income households increased more in these two countries than in most others, helping to offset the declining share of pre-tax income going to those in the middle.

Does controlling for economic growth and change in net government transfers reveal a negative impact of rising top-heavy income inequality on median household income growth? The answer is yes. Figure 3.5 replicates

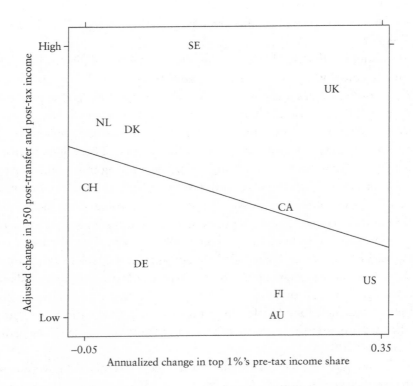

Figure 3.5. Economic growth and net government transfer adjusted change in median household income by change in top-heavy income inequality, ten countries, late 1970s to mid-2000s

SOURCE: Author's calculations from the *LIS Database*, Waves I to VI (income, government transfers, taxes), the OECD (economic growth, inflation, PPPs), and Alvaredo et al. (2012) (income inequality).

NOTE: Actual years vary somewhat depending on the country, so change is calculated per year. Adjusted change in median household income: average change per year in post-tax and post-transfer 50th percentile household income, adjusted for household size and for inflation, converted into U.S. dollars using purchasing power parities, and adjusted for the country's change in GDP per capita and change in net government transfers to households in the lower-middle-income quartile. Change in income inequality: average change per year in the top 1 percent's income share. France, Italy, and Spain are missing due to lack of net government transfer data.

Figure 3.3, but the vertical axis now is change in median household income adjusted for change in GDP per capita and change in net government transfers. (The values on the vertical axis are the residuals from a regression of change in median household income on change in per capita GDP and change in net government transfers.) We now see the expected negative association.

For the ten countries shown in Figure 3.5, a regression of change in median household income on change in the top 1 percent's income share yields a coefficient very close to zero. If we add controls for change in GDP per capita and change in net government transfers, the coefficient for change in the top 1 percent's income share is −530. This suggests that an increase of 1 percentage point in the top 1 percent's share of pre-tax income reduced growth of income for the median household by about USD530. In the most extreme case—the United States—the top 1 percent's pre-tax share increased by 8 percentage points between 1979 and 2004. According to this estimate, that may have reduced median household income growth by a little more than USD4,000. The actual rise in the United States during those years was USD8,000, so the estimated impact of rising income inequality is not trivial.

At the same time, the data suggest that the income-reducing impact of a rise in top-heavy inequality has been overshadowed by the income-boosting impact of economic growth and of increases in net government transfers. That is why we see no (bivariate) association in Figures 3.1, 3.2, and 3.3. And the wide dispersion of the countries around the line in Figure 3.5 tells us that even after adjusting for these other influences, change in top-heavy inequality is not a very good predictor of growth in middle-class incomes.

CONCLUSION

The experience of the world's rich democracies over the past several decades suggests that rising top-heavy income inequality has tended to reduce middle-class income growth. But it also suggests that inequality has not been the key determinant of that growth. Should this lessen our concern about rising inequality?

The sources of worry are threefold. One has to do with fairness, justice, and the influence of luck (Rawls 1971; Jencks et al. 1972). Much of what determines people's earnings and income—intelligence, creativity, physical and social skills, motivation, persistence, confidence, connections, inherited wealth, discrimination—are products of genetics, parents' financial assets and traits, and the quality of one's childhood neighborhood and schools. With few exceptions, these things are not chosen; they are a matter of luck. A non-trivial portion of earnings inequality and income inequality can therefore be said to be undeserved.

Second, an increase in income inequality may cause an increase in inequality of other social, economic, or political outcomes, such as educational attainment, health, and political influence (Neckerman 2004; Bartels 2008; Gilens 2012). The gap in life expectancy or infant mortality between those with high and low incomes may widen. The same is true for college graduation. Perhaps most worrisome, inequality of influence on government policy may rise.

Third, a rise in income inequality may contribute to a worsening of overall or average outcomes (Wilkinson and Pickett 2009). The average level of life expectancy or college completion may decline or rise less rapidly than it otherwise would have. Crime may accelerate. Trust and community may weaken. The middle class may fare worse economically. This brings us back to middle-class income growth. Looking across countries, inequality's effect so far has been overshadowed by the impact of economic growth and of changes in net government transfers. Yet, that will not necessarily hold going forward. Moreover, income is only a partial indicator of living standards. There are other ways in which rising top-heavy income inequality might adversely affect the well-being of middle-class households. Some analysts, most notably Robert Frank (2007), have suggested that inequality hurts the middle class mainly by encouraging excessive spending rather than by reducing income growth.

REFERENCES

Allison, Paul. D. 1990. "Change Scores as Dependent Variables in Regression Analysis." In *Sociological Methodology*, edited by Clifford C. Clogg, 93–114. Oxford: Blackwell.

Alvaredo, Facundo, Anthony B. Atkinson, Thomas Piketty, and Emmanuel Saez. 2012. The World Top Incomes Database. http://g-mond.parisschoolofeconomics.eu/topincomes.

Andrews, Dan, Christopher Jencks, and Andrew Leigh. 2011. "Do Rising Top Incomes Lift All Boats?" *B.E. Journal of Economic Analysis and Policy* 11(1): 6.

Angrist, Joshua D., and Jörn-Steffen Pischke. 2008. *Mostly Harmless Econometrics*. Princeton, NJ: Princeton University Press.

Atkinson, Anthony B., Thomas Piketty, and Emmanuel Saez. 2011. "Top Incomes in the Long Run of History." *Journal of Economic Literature* 49(1): 3–71.

Bartels, Larry M. 2008. *Unequal Democracy*. Princeton, NJ/New York: Princeton University Press/Russell Sage Foundation.

Billitteri, Thomas J. 2009. "Middle-Class Squeeze." *CQ Researcher* 19(9): 201–24.

Firebaugh, Glenn. 2008. *Seven Rules for Social Research*. Princeton, NJ: Princeton University Press.

Frank, Robert H. 2007. *Falling Behind: How Rising Inequality Hurts the Middle Class*. Berkeley: University of California Press.

Gilens, Martin. 2012. *Affluence and Influence*. Princeton, NJ: Princeton University Press.

Halaby, Charles N. 2004. "Panel Models in Sociological Research: Theory into Practice." *Annual Review of Sociology* 30: 507–44.

Jencks, Christopher, Marshall Smith, Henry Acland, Mary Jo Bane, David Cohen, Herbert Gintis, Barbara Heyns, and Stephan Michelson. 1972. *Inequality: A Reassessment of the Effect of Family and Schooling in America*. New York: Basic Books.

Kenworthy, Lane. 2004. *Egalitarian Capitalism*. New York: Russell Sage Foundation.

———. 2010a. "Rising Inequality, Public Policy, and America's Poor." *Challenge* 53(6): 93–109.

———. 2010b. "The Best Inequality Graph, Updated." http://lanekenworthy.net/2010/07/20/the-best-inequality-graph-updated/.

———. 2011a. "Is Winner-Take-All Bad or Good for the Middle Class?" http://lanekenworthy.net/2011/01/11/is-winner-take-all-bad-or-good-for-the-middle-class-evidence-from-baseball/.

———. 2011b. "Step Away from the Pool." Newsletter of the American Political Science Association Organized Section for Qualitative and Multi-Method Research, Fall.

———. 2011c. "When Does Economic Growth Benefit People on Low to Middle Incomes—And Why?" London: Commission on Living Standards, Resolution Foundation, November.

Kenworthy, Lane, and Leslie McCall. 2008. "Inequality, Public Opinion, and Redistribution." *Socio-Economic Review* 6(1): 35–68.

Kenworthy, Lane, and Jonas Pontusson. 2005. "Rising Inequality and the Politics of Redistribution in Affluent Countries." *Perspectives on Politics* 3(3): 449–71.

Kumhof, Michael, and Romain Ranciere. 2010. "Leveraging Inequality." *Finance and Development* 7(4): 28–31.

Luxembourg Income Study (LIS) Database, http://www.lisdatacenter.org (multiple countries; microdata last accessed May 2012). Luxembourg: LIS.

Meltzer, Allan H., and Scott F. Richard. 1981. "A Rational Theory of the Size of Government." *Journal of Political Economy* 89(5): 914–27.

Mishel, Lawrence, Jared Bernstein, and Heidi Shierholz. 2009. *The State of Working America, 2008/2009. An Economic Policy Institute Book*. Ithaca, NY: ILR Press.

Neckerman, Kathryn M., ed. 2004. *Social Inequality*. New York: Russell Sage Foundation.

Okun, Arthur. 1975. *Equality and Efficiency: The Big Tradeoff*. Washington, DC: Brookings Institution.

Organisation for Economic Co-operation and Development (OECD) Database. http://stats.oecd.org (multiple countries; 2012). Paris: OECD.

Rawls, John. 1971. *A Theory of Justice*. Cambridge, MA: Harvard University Press.

Reich, Robert B. 2010. *Aftershock*. New York: Knopf.

Stiglitz, Joseph. 2012. *The Price of Inequality*. New York: Norton.

Thompson, Jeffrey, and Elias Leight. 2011. "Searching for the Supposed Benefits of Higher Inequality: Impacts of Rising Top Shares on the Standard of Living of Low and Middle-Income Families." Working paper 258. Amherst, MA: Political Economy Research Institute, University of Massachusetts–Amherst.

Voitchovsky, Sarah. 2005. "Does the Profile of Income Inequality Matter for Economic Growth?" *Journal of Economic Growth* 10(3): 273–96.

Wilkinson, Richard, and Kate Pickett. 2009. *The Spirit Level: Why Greater Equality Makes Societies Stronger*. New York: Bloomsbury.

CHAPTER FOUR

Welfare Regimes, Cohorts, and the Middle Classes

Louis Chauvel

Middle class is a term that has been used in several different ways in social science. In the British tradition, the middle class generally refers to professionals such as lawyers and upper-level white-collar workers in the financial sector—that is, to various categories that also had been playing a central role in the gentrification of London for the last 30 years (Butler and Robson 2003). In the U.S. tradition, the term usually pertains to associate professionals or managers, and even basic engineers—in other words, various categories of wage earners who live comfortably (Mills 1951). In the standard French or German vision, the middle class could often include even lower technicians and forepersons—a kind of "median" class, rather than a middle one. This ambiguity could result from the fuzzy idea of the "middle": in the continental European tradition, "middle" is "average," whereas in the British and Marxist traditions, "middle" means between the power elite and the "real people." In this chapter, we accept the idea that the middle classes are diverse because we can distinguish with Gustav Schmoller (1897) a lower middle class (close to the median) and an upper middle class (at a level equal to twice the median). Thus, the middle classes are plural, with lower and upper strata, which we must understand for their specificities (Chauvel 2006b).

This chapter offers a comparative analysis of the transformations of the middle classes from the 1980s to the mid-2000s, with a focus on the life chances of birth cohorts. The aim of this contribution is to demonstrate the importance of the year of birth in social dynamics, particularly in terms of opportunities to reach middle-class positions. The main idea here is that in some specific "welfare regimes" (Esping-Andersen 1990), the transformation of the set of social opportunities over the last three decades has had a profound impact on some birth cohorts and not on others. In this respect, in this chapter "social generations" (Mannheim 1928) refer to sets of birth cohorts facing certain social situations and constraints that other social generations did not experience.

Indeed, in most rich countries, the transition from a phase of fast growth—or of "affluent society" (Galbraith 1958)—to slow growth (Krugman 1992) is particularly visible at the median level of post-industrial societies.[1] The transition from a "wage-based society"[2] in the 1960s to a period of increasing inequalities[3] is also of particular interest from a cross-national perspective because national dynamics are diverse. As a consequence, the comparative dynamics of middle-class transformations since the 1980s (Pressman 2007) show a general trend of decline at the median level of the economic scale. However, birth/cohort dynamics have not received sufficient attention, despite their importance in these changes. In the tradition of Age-Period-Cohort analysis (Ryder 1965; Mason et al. 1973; Yang, Fu, and Land 2004), the hypothesis of a long-lasting impact of the period of socialization of young adults on their whole life course and on their long-run life chances could be meaningful. In this respect, cohorts that entered the labor force in a period with a growing, homogeneous middle class will benefit from that context over their entire life span, while the cohorts that experienced a shrinking middle class when they were young adults will suffer in the long run from this adverse context of socialization. In cases of welfare-regime retrenchments, we can expect that younger cohorts are more affected and that older ones avoid adverse consequences. This general idea must, however, be tested in the context of different welfare regimes: different social institutions could generate stronger or weaker cohort effects.

Specifically, in welfare regimes where the first years on the labor market are strategic for future opportunities over the life course (in countries with poor capacities of social "resilience"), the cohorts of young adults who fail at entry into the labor market could become the serial victims of social change. Conversely, in countries where "second chance" policies exist (particularly vocational and continuous education of adults, training, and so-called "flexicurity," including active labor policies of re-inclusion of workers and re-training to maintain skill levels) in particular for adults in difficult or modest socio-economic conditions (as in the Nordic countries), cohort effects could be weaker (Chauvel 2006a, 2010a).

This chapter begins with an analysis of the theoretical linkage between middle-class development, welfare-regime dynamics, and birth-cohort transformation. It then examines the use of an analysis based on the Age-Period-Cohort methodology. Finally, it discusses a comparative analysis of middle-class development by birth cohort, the results of which underscore cross-country differences in the importance of cohort fluctuations.

DEFINITIONS OF MIDDLE CLASSES

The definition of *middle class* varies in the social science literature. While some authors identify the middle class in relation to median income (Pressman 2007), others focus on occupation-based definitions of, for example, an upper middle class of professionals, experts, and upper-level managers. This variation could be explained when we recall the origins of the middle-class debate in social science, with Gustav Schmoller (1897) and his assessment of the Marxist theory of absolute pauperization of the middle class.[4] Schmoller detects the double source of diversity of the middle classes. On the one hand, you have the polarization between a wealth-based old middle class and a wage-based new middle class, with "new" used in the context of the nineteenth century. On the other hand, you have the hierarchic distinction between lower and upper middle classes that identifies the median middle class and the upper middle class, respectively.

I do not focus on the distinction between the "new" versus the "old" middle class, but rather, to distinguish the two hierarchic levels of middle classes ("lower" versus "upper"), I consider first the density of the population around median income and then at the level of twice the median. In this sense, a "lower middle class" is different from an "upper middle class." In a general analysis of the shape of the income distribution, it is possible to relate the density of the "lower" and "upper" middle classes to general inequality. These definitions need discussion because Pressman refers to the individuals who in this study are "upper middle class" as "upper-class" (Pressman 2007, 187). In Chapter 2, Atkinson and Brandolini define the "lower middle class" as persons "whose income is in the range of 60 to 75 percent of the median," even if others would define this latter group as "working class" or even "near poor" (Newman 1999; Newman and Chen 2007). To make sense of our choices, we should analyze the shapes of income distributions.

From a descriptive point of view, inequality can be understood as the stretching of the distribution of income (or other resource) between the extremes; thus, the greater the inequality, the wider the stretching of the middle class between the extremes. But a more accurate observation shows that the middle class is not unique but diverse. This can be illustrated by a theoretical example based on Champernowne/Fisk distributions (Fisk 1961), a family that often provides reasonable models for income distributions. Champernowne showed that the distributions result from quite realistic stochastic models of income dynamics and that they correctly represent the Pareto shape of the upper and lower tails of the distributions, as well as the segments closer to the median. When we simulate these Champernowne/Fisk distributions, the lower middle class is denser when inequality is smaller (measured by the Pareto-Champernowne's alpha), and the upper middle class is larger when inequality is greater, as if the two middle classes were communicating vessels. However, the Champernowne/Fisk distribution is a rough approximation of the empirical distribution of incomes, because inequality could be diverse at the different levels of the curve (Chauvel 1995), and then the transformations of the two middle classes could be less correlated than expected (Figure 4.1). Moreover, at the level of birth cohorts, some cohorts can benefit from economic expansion and have access to the lower and even upper middle classes at the expense of other cohorts that are relatively marginalized. This is why it is crucial to analyze separately the two levels of the middle classes. This distinction could explain why this issue is discussed across different social contexts in countries such as Sweden, Brazil, and China (Li 2009), although the debate does not focus on the same income brackets and social groups.

ECONOMIC TRANSFORMATIONS, STRATIFICATION, AND BIRTH COHORTS

In rich countries, the lower middle class is challenged in many respects, in both social and national contexts (Pressman 2007). The stagnation of wage incomes—especially around the median—and the general trend of increasing disposable income inequality put stress on this social group. The upper middle class—notably of mid-level new entrepreneurs, self-employed professionals—might benefit from the trend of polarization. An important issue here is the problem of birth cohort. In some national contexts (Chauvel

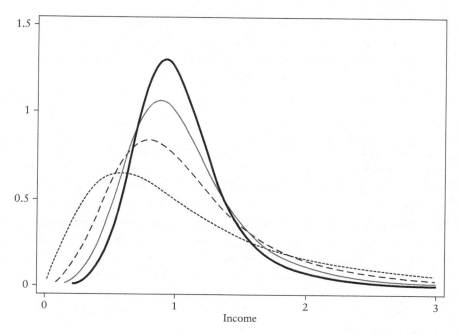

Figure 4.1. Champernowne/Fisk density of income distribution with alpha = 2 (dotted line), 3 (dashed line), 4 (solid line), and 5 (bold solid line)

SOURCE: Author's demonstration.

NOTE: The horizontal axis shows the median-standardized income (1 = median), and the vertical axis shows the density (in percentage points).

2009), we observe a "scarring effect" that characterizes the long-term negative consequences of transitional problems of socialization of some birth cohorts when entering the labor market.[5]

The first hypothesis considered in this chapter is that some periods of time are more open and efficient for the socialization of larger parts of the population into certain subgroups of the middle classes. Lack of opportunities at entry into adulthood can generate long-term scarring effects. These unequal dynamics could generate "social generations" (Mannheim 1928) that benefit from lucky context or, conversely, could generate long-lasting hardship. The more empirically based tradition of Norman Ryder (1965) developed an interest for the analysis of birth cohort as a vehicle of social change, which first impacts the younger generations and then generalizes to the whole society by demographic replacement. If this dynamic is well ascertained in France and in various southern European societies, a more general view is required. Specifically, I assess whether or not cohort is a neutral dimension of the development of the middle classes.

WELFARE REGIMES AND BIRTH COHORT DYNAMICS

A second hypothesis considered in this chapter is that different welfare regimes could have different outcomes in terms of middle-class dynamics, particularly for the opportunities opened to the cohorts of young adults in a context of crisis. The general theory of welfare regimes (Esping-Andersen 1990) proposes a typology of systems of social protection and solidarity underlining differences across clusters of countries. It addresses the diversity of social models of inequality and stratification (Korpi and Palme 1998), solidarity, and systems of protection in many different dimensions of social life: retirement (Myles 1990), health (Bambra 2005), gender inequality (Gornick, Meyers, and Ross 1997), work history (DiPrete 2002), and so on. It is also well known that the life course is deeply influenced by specific welfare regime models (Mayer 2005; Van De Velde 2008). Here I use a later version (Esping-Andersen 1999) that distinguishes among four contrasted regimes, including the familialistic one.[6]

The central idea in this chapter is that status societies, such as those of the conservative and familialistic welfare regimes, as well as the Japanese one (Brinton 2008), provide an institutional context that favors the emergence of deeply contrasted cohorts having diverging social paths and life chances. More resilient societies, where second chances exist (in terms of education or work opportunities), have less cohort-based inequality, notably the social democratic countries and English-speaking liberal countries. In both of these cases, new social or market opportunities over the life course could lessen, at least partially, difficulties in early adulthood. For instance, flexicurity and redistribution of life chances over the life course are social tools in the social democratic countries that can compensate for early difficulties. Somewhat paradoxically, the diversity of market opportunities can produce compensatory effects as well, at least because they have a random component that can reduce early gaps. For this reason, I anticipate stronger cohort fluctuations in France or Italy, which are status-based societies where early adulthood is strategic for the status achievement process, than in Norway or the United States, where resilience is stronger, all else equal. By this latter expression, we mean that the structure of birth cohorts could differ in terms of size, family structure, and level of education, but individuals with the same background will face divergent and fluctuating outcomes because of their specific period of socialization. Both gross and net aspects—that is, both before and after controlling for socio-demographic covariates—could be important, the first one in terms of descriptive differences and the second one for an analysis of relative opportunities or difficulties (relative to individuals of similar social contexts but of different age, period, or cohort).

More precisely, to analyze the probable responses of different welfare regimes to the social transformations of post-industrial societies, I use the standard welfare state typology (Esping-Andersen 1999) and focus on four regimes: the corporatist (or conservative), the liberal, the social democratic, and the familialistic. Examples are provided using France, the United States, Norway, and Italy, respectively. These countries are chosen for their typical behavior in terms of welfare regimes. France is a rigid, status-based society where individuals' trajectories are fixed for life in the process of transition into early adulthood and where young adults face the worst consequences of mass unemployment. The United States is a rich country where the welfare state is obviously undersized. Norway, in turn, is interesting for its capacity (due to its natural resources) to maintain a massive welfare regime even in a period of global crisis. Italy is a case of extreme family solidarity.

Because the *conservative regime* (France) is based on status recognition, its probable response to economic downturn, competition, and economic shortage will be a stronger protection of insiders at the expense of young adults leaving education, of women, and of immigrants, all groups that have fewer opportunities to defend their interests. Youth unemployment is a result of the increasing polarization between protected senior insiders in the labor market and junior outsiders who face an accelerated decline of good jobs; stronger competition among the young generates a decline in wages and retrenchment of social rights. If seniors are victims of early retirement, they enjoy better income protection, and they have opportunities to access comfortable pension schemes and/or acceptable conditions of pre-retirement (generally better than the usual unemployment schemes of younger adults). The cohorts of seniors are more equal because they are the homogeneous cohorts of the "wage-earner society" (Castel 1995) of the "golden period" of the 1960s to the 1980s. This could go with their structuration in a specific "social generation" (Mannheim 1928), having specific objective and subjective traits. We observe a decline in the intra-cohort inequality of French seniors, with better pension schemes available for all, so seniors' relative incomes increase. Conversely, the new cohorts of adults face stronger polarization between winners and losers (Brzinsky-Fay 2007). One aspect I do not discuss here is the declining value of education. A probable collective answer to the difficulties of the young is a massive increase in the post-secondary education of young cohorts (Van De Velde 2008) working in tandem with a lack of improvement in labor market entry. A trend of strong educational inflation—a decline in the nominal value of grades, particularly for the less selective ones—can be observed (Duru-Bellat 2006).

The *liberal regime* (the United States) is characterized by another prob-able answer to the same challenges. The centrality of the market in this regime prompts specific reactions to economic shortages. The main solu-tions are welfare-state retrenchments, need-based redistribution schemes, stronger market competition, and the denunciation of former social rights. Increasing competition between juniors and seniors implies a renegotiation of seniors' better positions, previously obtained in the context of affluence. The consequence is smoother inter-cohort inequality (the new cohorts ben-efit relative to the seniors). However, increasing competition means stronger intra-cohort inequalities, notably within senior age groups, because there are cumulative effects of inequality (DiPrete 2002). In terms of educational value, because there is a stronger link between the individual cost of educa-tion and the expected returns to education (compared to the conservative regime of educational expansion), the market regulation of educational ex-pansion promotes a more stable social and economic value of diploma, with no clear signs of over-education (Chauvel 2010b).

The *social democratic regime* (Norway) is defined by collective goals of long-term stability, progress, and development for all, with a strong sense of collective responsibility. Integrating younger cohorts is considered a pri-ority because failure in the early socialization of young adults is seen as a massive problem for future development of society. High rates of youth un-employment and economic de-valorization of young adults could come with long-term risks of anxiety, self-devaluation of the young, increasing suicide rates, or declines in fertility. To avoid these social risks over the entire life course, the social democratic welfare-state model (notably "second chance" policies) promotes inter-cohort balance (Gooderham and Dale 1995). The consequence is stronger control, relative to the two previous models, of both intra- and inter-cohort inequalities. The increase in the level of education for all could generate a slight process of over-education, defined as an excess level of education in the workforce relative to the prestige of the position and/or the level of wages. Nevertheless, it is shared by all age groups; its specific cohort dimension is not obvious.

The *familialistic regime* (Italy) shares many aspects of the conservative one, but families in this regime are a legitimate institution in the process of the redistribution of resources, both culturally and for the regulatory activities of the state. More precisely, in this regime, some sectors of the economy are heavily protected—mainly the core sectors of the public economy and large companies such as banks, insurance, and so on—and most labor regulations are based on strong seniority rights. In most small and medium-sized companies, regulation is based on family interconnections, where familialism, localism, and long-term fidelity of workers are fundamental institutions that foster stronger social reproduction (Barone and Schizzerotto 2011). In the context of post-affluent societies—and scarce jobs, housing, and other resources—parents of young adults are supposed to offer help and protection, and most families act in conformity with these social pressures. The consequence is a trend of increasing dependence of young adults on their parents until the age of 35 (or even older) in the context of declining wage levels and living standards for the cohorts of new entrants into the labor market.

Consequently, seniors exert political pressure to obtain better pensions to better support their own children. The context of dependency generates stronger constraints for young families, increases the social pressures on women to choose between work and children, and is accompanied by a strong decline in fertility rates, which creates the paradoxical context of "familialism without families" and becomes a major problem in the long-term sustainability of the welfare state. On the other hand, the decline of incomes for young families is offset by the reduction in family size. In this regime, national homogeneity may be weaker compared to other regimes because the inter-provincial imbalances—high unemployment rates in some localities could go with a lack of an adequate workforce in others—are structural traits of a labor market where localism and strong ties are important aspects of social regulations, implying less geographic mobility. Thus, national heterogeneity is greater than in other regimes. Another recent dimension is a strong development of mass tertiary education, which generates a marked trend toward over-education: a large increase in the number of university graduates who cannot find positions in South European countries' labor markets, where small and medium-sized companies seek more specialists and experts than intermediate technical and managing clerks.

AGE-PERIOD-COHORT–DETRENDED COEFFICIENTS METHODOLOGY

I compare the intensity of cohort fluctuations that show the degree to which different birth cohorts faced divergent life chances. The comparative welfare-regime theory of these inter-cohort inequalities would assert that in France and Italy the middle classes increased more intensely for the early baby-boom generations (the young adults of the late 1960s) and that the cohorts born in the 1960s and 1970s are the victims of a backlash in the development of the middle classes. To test the importance of cohorts in the analysis of middle-class dynamics, I consider new aspects of the Age-Period-Cohort (APC) methodology that improved considerably, notably with Yang's recent strategy of analysis (Yang et al. 2004). After an early period of development of APC models (Mason et al. 1973), Yang and her colleagues developed new tools for the identification of APC effects, with the control of individual-level covariates, including the APC-Intrinsic Estimator (APC-IE), which is based on the reduction and identification of age, period, and cohort parameters, with the support of a principal component analysis (PCA) of the APC parameters to tackle the traditional identifying problem. The "intrinsic" character of the parameters in the APC-IE method is still debated (O'Brien 2011). Thus, I developed another tool that is similar in principle and in its capacity to include control variables, such as gender, education, and so on, and based on a generalized linear model with specific constraints that make it possible to disentangle age, period, and cohort fluctuations, called the Age-Period-Cohort–Detrended coefficients model (APCD).

The aim of the APCD is to absorb the linear age, period, and cohort trends (that one cannot disentangle in the general case) and then extract zero-sum and zero-trend coefficients for the three variables to determine specific age, period, and cohort fluctuations. Under these specifications, a cohort effect is defined as null if the coefficients are not statistically significantly different from zero; in that case, no cohort diverges from the linear trend. Conversely, a significant cohort effect refers to fluctuations pertaining to cohorts that diverge from the others. Like the APC-IE model provided in Stata,[7] the APCD accepts various specifications (ordinary least squares, logit, Poisson models, etc.); estimates the sets of age, period, and cohort coefficients after the control of covariates; provides their confidence intervals (here, at the 95 percent level); and offers standard statistical diagnostics. It is likely that some countries, such as France and Italy, will show stronger fluctuations, and others will have flat trends in the cohort coefficients.

DATA AND EMPIRICAL STRATEGY

My definition of the middle class is based on the equivalent disposable income of the household—that is, household income from all private sources, plus public transfers, minus direct taxes and transfers, divided by the square root of household size, rather than on earnings only. This means that the definition of the middle class is based on the level of living and capacity to consume, not on economic rewards based on occupation. Four countries that reflect the different welfare regimes are used. Using the *LIS Database*, I selected countries with datasets from the mid-1980s to the mid-2000s. These datasets provide family structure and educational attainment—household size, gender of the household head, education—that are used as covariates. The samples consist of individuals who are either the head of the household or a partner of the head. Equivalized relative disposable incomes (*erdi*) are standardized around the median of the country/period. The value 1 signifies no divergence to the average, and 1.1 is an increase of approximately 10 percent relative to the median. *Lerdi* is the natural logarithm of equivalized relative disposable income (relative to the country/ period median).

The "lower middle class" consists of those whose erdi is between 0.75 and 1.25 (as in Pressman 2007), and the "upper middle class" includes those whose erdi is between 1.5 and 2.5. This is similar to the definitions used by Pressman (2007) and Atkinson and Brandolini (see Chapter 2). Using this approach reveals the differences in the cohort dynamics of the lower and upper middle classes. To assess cohort dynamics in the four welfare regimes discussed above, we look at France, Italy, Norway,[8] and the United States.

The expected results are that cohorts that get richer on average and that get more unequal are more likely to develop a large upper middle class, while those having a stable economic dynamics and knowing a decline in their intra-cohort inequality compared to the other ones are more likely to have an expanding lower middle class.

The first element of this analysis is descriptive and pertains to the changes in equivalized relative disposable income by age group. These results are similar to those in Chauvel (2009). In the context of contemporary economic transformations, the different welfare regimes analyzed had diverse age distributions with respect to income and different inequalities among age groups. Large differences appear in terms of the structure of the income distribution (Figure 4.2). The curves in Figure 4.2 show changes in the differences between age groups over time: the higher the curve, the better the relative income (0 denotes the average of the year, and +0.1 means 10 percent higher than the average). For instance, the relative income of the 40-year-old French population declined by more than 10 percent.

Italy and France have rather flat between-age-group distribution of resources, while Norway and the United States are characterized by increasing income from age 25 to age 50—the age at which economic resources are highest—followed by a decline. The French and Italian curves fit with the idea of an economic life cycle involving implicit between-age-group redistributions. One could posit, with Lazear (1979), that a more steady linearly increasing shape of career is the result of redistribution from the middle-aged population to the young adults and the seniors, while the Norwegian and U.S. models are closer to a marginal-productivity-based career where midlife is supposed to be more affluent.

If the long-run national structures differ in terms of the age profile of income, we also observe specific dynamics. In general, across all the countries (with the exception of the United States), the seniors who are in their sixties in 2005 are more affluent than those who are in their sixties in 1985, due to the maturing of their retirement systems. Conversely, the birth

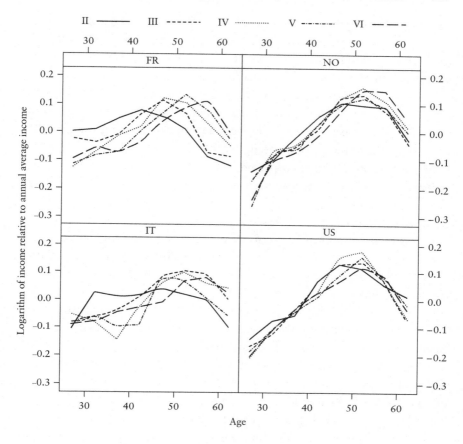

Figure 4.2. Logarithm of equivalized relative disposable income (0 = national median of the period) by age group for Waves II (around 1985: solid lines) to VI (around 2005: long dashed lines)

SOURCE: Author's calculations from the *LIS Database*, Waves II to VI of France, Italy, Norway, and the United States.

NOTE: The horizontal axis shows age, and the vertical axis shows the logarithm of income relative to annual average income. Five periods are represented from 1985 (solid lines) to 2005 (long dashed lines), and the intermediate years are in dotted lines.

cohorts who are in their forties in 2005 are less affluent than the cohorts who are in their forties in 1985. What stands out among the four countries is the visible age transformation in France—a systematic decline in relative terms below age 45 and an increase above—and the more obviously stable configuration seen in the United States, where the 1985 and 2005 outcomes are quite close to each other. The two remaining countries are more moderate with respect to their dynamics: Norway shows almost perfect stability after 1990, and in Italy the steep collapse of the first third of the life course seen between 1985 and 2000 is smaller in 2005.

The most interesting country in terms of cohort dynamics is France, where we observe a wave of affluence at age 40 in 1985, 50 in 1995, and 55 in 2005, which is 14 points higher than the same age group in 1985; conversely, the population at age 40 in 2005 has a relative income 13 points lower than those in the 1985 period. This translates to a 27-point implicit redistribution among age groups, which suggests an extreme transformation of age statuses in France; if juniors were more affluent than seniors in the 1980s, the situation is reversed in 2005.

This relative average situation of age groups has a complementary aspect: the transformation of within-age-group inequality, which is measured with the inter-decile ratio in Figure 4.3. In this graph, the higher the curve, the greater the within-cohort inequality. Here also, inequality varies across time, age groups, and countries. As expected, inequality is generally higher in the United States and lower in Norway. In general, we notice no strong, steady changes in age-specific inequality. At any rate, since the 1980s, inequality in France has declined massively for the seniors and increased slightly for the juniors. The trends in Italy are similar, with a larger increase of inequality for the juniors. This means that the new "fifty-somethings" benefit from more homogeneity, while the younger cohorts face more severe gaps between the top and the bottom. In the United States, the transformation is in the opposite direction, since the new seniors are much more unequal around 2005 than in 1985, and the young are slightly less so. How can we interpret these results? On the one side, the countries in the conservative and familialistic regimes offer stronger and more egalitarian protection to their seniors (Ferrera and Gualmini 2004; Tepe and Vanhuysse 2010), while liberal countries chose the opposite strategy, in which seniors are more dependent on non-public and non-egalitarian protection schemes. In this respect, Norway is more stable.

ESTIMATION RESULTS FROM APCD MODELS

With the help of APCD models, we can examine the importance of cohort fluctuations in terms of relative incomes. I thus investigate whether

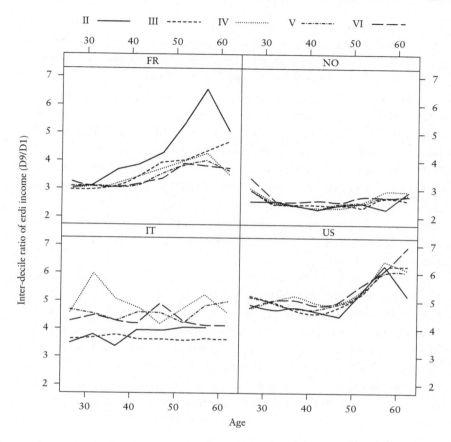

Figure 4.3. Inter-decile ratios of equivalized relative disposable income by age group for Waves II (around 1985: solid lines) to VI (around 2005: long dashed lines)

SOURCE: Author's calculations from the *LIS Database*, Waves II to VI of France, Italy, Norway, and the United States.

NOTE: The horizontal axis shows age, and the vertical axis shows the ratio of the inter-decile ratio D9/D1 of erdi income. Five periods are represented from 1985 (solid lines) to 2005 (long dashed lines), and the intermediate years are in dotted lines.

some cohorts have benefited from exceptional income growth, while others—younger cohorts, in particular—have faced stagnation or backlashes. The models allow us to determine if this is the case even after controlling for education level, household structure (measured by the number of children and partnership status), and the gender of the household head. These controls are important because in many countries different birth cohorts experienced large changes in educational assets and household demographics. The first step is then to estimate between-cohort inequality—that is, the degree to which some cohorts did much better or much worse than others.

The first model in Figure 4.4 accounts for the logarithm of equivalized relative disposable income (erdi) as a continuous variable and graphs its cohort fluctuations after controlling for period and age effects as well as the demographic and educational covariates.[9] The main comparative result is that the cohort differences in economic well-being vary across countries. In France, the cohorts born in the 1940s, including the first cohorts of the baby boom, had higher mean income than later cohorts, resulting in an inverted V–shaped dynamic. After controlling for education and household structure, Figure 4.4 shows an income gap of more than 17 percentage points, with the curve reaching a high of +0.08 and a low of −0.09. Italy has a similar cohort dynamic but with a smoother U-turn, a gap of 14 percentage points between the top and the bottom, and a sharp negative slope concentrated on the cohort born in the 1960s. These cohorts were the first to experience the sharp economic slowdown and expansion of youth unemployment in the 1980s, with deep long-term consequences for those affected. In the United States and Norway, the cohort effects are quite flat. With more detail, significantly negative coefficients pertain to the U.S. cohorts born in the mid-1950s—that is, those who entered adulthood in the long post-Vietnam economic slowdown that appears to be an "age of diminished expectations" (Krugman 1992).

Are there consequences in terms of middle-class dynamics? Figure 4.5 shows the second model that focuses on upper-middle-class positions. The figure estimates an APCD model that accounts for membership in the upper middle class (0/1) using a logit specification. The same cohort coefficients of the APCD-logit model are used that represent the fluctuations of the probabilities of access to the upper middle class after controlling for age and period effects, as well as gender, education, and household structure. Some cohorts have had more opportunities to reach the upper middle class than others. To measure differences in terms of percentage points (relative marginal effects), the coefficient estimates should be divided by a factor of 4.

The cohort coefficients result in rather contrasting transformations. In France, where the cohort variation is largest, the maximum of +0.33 for the cohort born in 1950 falls to −0.22 for the cohort born in 1970, which

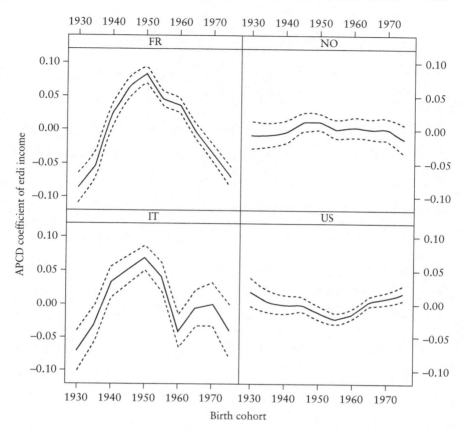

Figure 4.4. Cohort coefficients (bold lines) of the APCD OLS model of the log-equivalized relative disposable income controlled by education, size of household, and gender of the reference person (dotted lines represent the 95 percent confidence intervals)

SOURCE: Author's calculations from the *LIS Database*. Waves II to VI of France, Italy, Norway, and the United States.

NOTE: The horizontal axis shows the birth cohort, and the vertical axis shows the APCD coefficient of the erdi income.

translates to a 13.7 percentage point decrease in the probability of reaching the upper middle class. These differences are both highly statistically significant and substantively important. The curve for the Norway cohorts is similar to the French one but smoother and with a flatter slope. In Italy, the cohort of 1960 had far less access to the upper middle class, but the

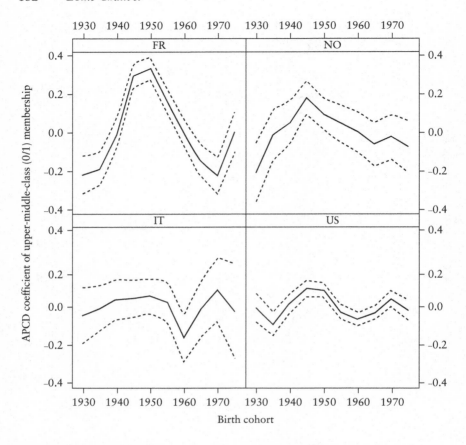

Figure 4.5.   Cohort coefficients (bold lines) of the APCD logit model of upper-middle-class (0/1) membership controlled by education, size of household, and gender of the reference person (dotted lines represent the 95 percent confidence intervals)

SOURCE: Author's calculations from the *LIS Database*, Waves II to VI of France, Italy, Norway, and the United States.

NOTE: The horizontal axis shows the birth cohort, and the vertical axis shows the APCD coefficients of upper-middle-class (0/1) membership.

confidence intervals are wider, making it hard to draw firm conclusions. The U.S. inter-cohort differences are smaller, but the cohorts born around 1960 (the baby-boom generation) show a significant decline in their probability of access to the upper middle class, a result consistent with those of Easterlin (1987). A comparison of these figures regarding upper-middle-class access and the figures pertaining to log income shows that the main determinant of upper-middle-class dynamics is affluence. In this respect, much is given to some birth cohorts, and much is expected of other generations.

The cohort differences in access to the upper middle class are large. Figure 4.6 shows smaller but statistically significant differences that form

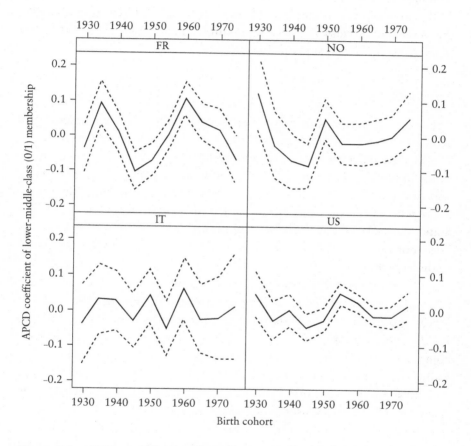

Figure 4.6. Cohort coefficients (bold lines) of the APCD logit model of lower-middle-class (0/1) membership controlled by education, size of household, and gender of the reference person (dotted lines represent the 95 percent confidence intervals)

SOURCE: Author's calculations from the *LIS Database*, Waves II to VI of France, Italy, Norway, and the United States.

NOTE: The horizontal axis shows the birth cohort and the vertical axis shows the APCD coefficient of lower-middle-class (0/1) membership.

a complicated pattern for access to the lower middle class. In the French case, the strong development of upper middle class for the cohorts born in the 1940s was at the expense of the lower middle class. The French cohorts born in the 1960s, whose access to the upper middle class had been barred more frequently, went more often to the lower middle class. We find similar dynamics for the Italian cohorts born in the first half of the 1960s and the 1930s birth cohorts in the United States. However, differences in access to the lower middle class are much more limited and are less significant both in the substantive and statistical sense.

CONCLUSION

The main conclusion is that the responses of middle-class dynamics to the economic slowdown of the post-1970 period vary across welfare regimes. The social democratic welfare regime, exemplified by Norway, seems rather stable in terms of how economic difficulties are distributed across cohorts and that the transformations of both the upper and lower middle classes are not strong. At the opposite end of the inequality spectrum, the United States shows less between-cohort inequality. The parameters for the cohorts born in the 1950s are negative, but their sizes are modest compared to the French ones.

There are more changes in Latin European countries such as France and Italy. The economic slowdown experienced by young Italians in the 1980s (those born in the 1960s) still has consequences for the contemporary middle-aged population. In France, the cohort scars in terms of lower incomes and greater difficulties in reaching upper-middle-class positions are visible over the long run: those born too late, in the 1960s or later, do not equally share the economic position and affluence of earlier cohorts. The French and Italian responses to new challenges are a mix of affluent seniors and deepening difficulties for the younger cohorts (lower relative income, economic dependence, unemployment, plus stronger inequality). This creates a paradoxical situation. The seniors have been living for the last 20 years as if they were in a social democratic country, since they benefit from a more generous system of solidarity, improve their income position, and are more equal (they have more intermediate and upper-middle-class positions). At the same time, the young of the 1980s (today's middle-aged adults) have been durably destabilized, with lower opportunities to climb into the upper classes, higher risks of lower incomes, and stronger inequality, as if they were living in a liberal country. Inside the same country, different cohorts could experience different regimes of welfare, where the generosity for some is based on scarcity for others. Indeed, the problem is thus in terms of welfare regime sustainability, since apparent improvements are at the expense of the newer generations who face the consequences of an increasing public debt that is not devoted to a project of sustainable development over cohorts.

To further investigate how cohort dynamics fare across welfare regimes, more countries should be included. I assessed four countries, but including at least two or three countries from each welfare regime would allow more conclusive findings on the specificities of welfare regimes and not of particular countries. A more exhaustive analysis would also include an assessment of the density at different levels of the income distribution, including the working class and the poor. Also, an APC analysis of the transformation of inequality measures, which is methodologically more complicated, would be useful. One possibility would be to use the Age-Period-Cohort approach to estimate the inter-quantile inequality difference, an unusual statistical approach.

The central point of this conclusion pertains to the long-term sustainability of welfare regimes. To be stable in the long term, a social system must arrange its own reproduction from one generation to the next. In France and Italy, today's seniors benefit from a large welfare state, but the extensive social rights they accumulated were the consequence of their relatively advantaged careers, gained in relative terms at the expense of the young adults of today. The younger cohorts, when they become seniors, are unlikely to have access to rights that are as broad. The large size of the present welfare state will mechanically erode with cohort replacement, since the reproduction of the welfare regime is not ascertained.

In France, where the generational dynamics of the different social strata are parallel, if not similar, the major problem is not so much the generational inequalities as the fact that younger generations heavily support a welfare system that could collapse before they benefit from it. The problem is not stagnation only but a lack of preparation for the long term, at the expense of the most vulnerable groups: the young and recently socialized generations. Here lies the problem of sustainability for the current welfare regime: it appears large, strong, and durable, but its decline is almost certain, and the security it offers to seniors is often at the expense of young cohorts facing radical uncertainty.

In the United States, the case is more complicated. The upper classes enjoy exceptionally good economic positions compared to the rest, while the middle classes see their fortunes stagnate, and the poor are subjected to relative, if not absolute, deprivation. For the moment, this regime is stable and seems durable in the sense that these extreme inequalities continue to develop (Atkinson and Piketty 2010) and reproduce over generations (Ermisch et al. 2012) even in a period of Democratic Party leadership, without deep political backlash. What from a European point of view is unacceptable seems to be largely accepted in the United States, at least for now. By contrast, the social democratic regime suggests that the high levels of social protection, equality, and solidarity could be stable over the generations. That is because newer cohorts benefit from similar conditions and rights as the older cohorts, in a system where seniors and juniors benefit from rather convergent improvement and participate in parallel to the cost of the system. This dynamic is different from those of France and Italy, where the seniors' improvements seem to go along with the juniors' permanent and increasing difficulties. In this respect, in Scandinavian countries, the tradition of negotiations based on long-term visibility and responsibility seems to be an important aspect of their outcomes in terms of shared improvement of human development over generations.

Conversely, the key question is whether younger generations in France or Italy will continue to sustain a system in which their social condition is devalued compared to the older generations, with no clear prospects of improvement. For the moment, these inter-cohort inequalities are accepted because they are generally unknown, their social visibility is low, and their political recognition null, taboo, or perverted. In France and Italy, the trade unions demand a lower retirement age to be able to open more job opportunities to the young; employers' associations support demands for less debt and declining public expenditures to protect "future generations." In neither case is there talk of productive investments, which could diminish the high rates of unemployment among the young. These examples from the conservative and familialistic regimes show that if we want solidarity, there is no other way than to choose a universalistic model (similar to the social democratic one) that equally supports the young, the middle aged, and the elderly in a long-term perspective of socialization.

In terms of consumption, these results provide a better understanding of cross-national variation in living standards over the life course. In France, compared to the United States, the younger generation faces real difficulties, and the current cohort of seniors has benefited from high income and economic homogenization (more equality within the cohort). In France, seniors appear attractive targets for marketing, while the young are often framed in terms of social problems. The Italian situation is similar, but the demographic collapse of the young adult generation (less numerous with fewer children) and their increased dependence on the family reduce the immediate visibility of the social problem. But this problem will persist, raising questions about who will care for the elderly. In contrast, the social democratic system seems to be a stable model of development of a universal solidaristic regime of collective improvement based on a large and homogeneous middle class. The general atmosphere in Scandinavia is more favorable to a socially homogeneous outcome and the development of a "wage-earner middle class" in a knowledge-based society. While recognizing there are limitations to the welfare-regime approach, this analysis suggests that the universalistic welfare regime is sustainable and maintains its own capacity for the long-term development of a large middle class.

NOTES

1. Median family income has regularly increased by 3 percent per year before 1970 and by 0.5 percent since the 1970s. (See Table 696: Money Income of Families—Median Income by Race and Hispanic Origin in Current and Constant (2008) Dollars at http://www.census.gov/compendia/statab/cats/income_expendi tures_poverty_wealth.html.)

2. Based on an ever-stronger intermediate-middle class of wage earners; see, for example, Castel (1995).

3. See, for example, Atkinson and Piketty (2007, 2010) and Piketty (2001a, 2001b).

4. These ideas have been developed by the social democratic revisionism of Bernstein (1899).

5. The expression "scarring effect" has been developed in the context of mass youth unemployment (Ellwood 1982) and more recently by Markus Gangl (2004), who demonstrated the long-lasting scars of social failure at the entry in adulthood. In contrast, "lucky" cohorts benefit from the relative advantage of entry into adulthood during a positive economic context.

6. In the literature on welfare typologies, ideas are more stabilized than words. The comparison of the previous authors shows the diversity of terms used to characterize the welfare regimes. In this respect, the "Nordic" or "Scandinavian" regime is often defined as "social democratic" or even "universalistic." The "liberal" one is often described as "residual" or even "English-speaking family of countries." The "Bismarck," "corporatist," or "continental" type is generally "conservative." Last but not least, the "familialistic" model is "South European" and sometimes "clientelistic," or also "Latin" when it excludes Greece or "Mediterranean" when it excludes Portugal. Thus, references to political theory, geography, linguistic area, or even "civilizations" depend on the authors, and I see no definitive stabilization in this field. I prefer a reference to socio-political theory with "liberal," "social democrat," "conservative," "familialistic" types, but a softer system of appellations could help to understand subtle complexities, since France is close to Germany for its historical Bismarck influence but is also deeply "Latin" and partly "Mediterranean" for some of its secular balance between ("Nordic") rationality and ("southern") clientelism.

7. On the APCD methodology, http://www.louischauvel.org/apcdex.htm gives more information and examples. The APCD is implemented in a Stata ado file that can be downloaded via the command "ssc install apcd" that uses the Stata-constrained general linear model.

8. I selected Norway over the other Nordic countries because the coding of education seems more reliable.

9. The specification of this model is in terms of OLS, and the coefficient must be analyzed as a variation of the log; a coefficient of +0.11 means the erdi increases by 11 percent.

REFERENCES

Atkinson, Anthony, and Thomas Piketty, eds. 2007. *Top Incomes over the Twentieth Century*, Vol. 1. New York: Oxford University Press.
———. 2010. *Top Incomes—A Global Perspective*, Vol. 2. New York: Oxford University Press.
Bambra, Clare. 2005. "Cash Versus Services: 'Worlds of Welfare' and the Decommodification of Cash Benefits and Health Care Services." *Journal of Social Policy* 34(2): 195–213.
Barone, Carlo, and Antonio Schizzerotto. 2011. "Career Mobility, Education, and Intergenerational Reproduction in Five European Societies." *European Societies* 13(3): 331–45.
Bernstein, Eduard. 1899. *Die Voraussetzungen des Sozialismus und die Aufgaben der Sozialdemokratie*. Stuttgart, Germany: Dietz.
Brinton, Mary. 2008. *Lost in Transition: Youth, Education, and Work in Postindustrial Japan*. Tokyo: NTT Press.

Brzinsky-Fay, Christian. 2007. "Lost in Transition? Labour Market Entry Sequences of School Leavers in Europe." *European Sociological Review* 23(4): 409–22.

Butler, Tim, and Garry Robson. 2003. *London Calling: The Middle Classes and the Remaking of Inner London.* Oxford: Berg.

Castel, Robert. 1995. *Les Métamorphoses de la Question Sociale.* Paris: Fayard.

Chauvel, Louis. 1995. *Inégalités Singulières et Plurielles: L'Evolution de la Courbe de Répartition des Revenus. Review 55.* Paris: French Observatory of Economic Conditions.

———. 2006a. "Social Generations, Life Chances and Welfare Regime Sustainability." In *Changing France—The Politics That Markets Make*, edited by Pepper D. Culpepper, Peter A. Hall, and Bruno Palier. Basingstoke, UK: Palgrave Macmillan.

———. 2006b. *Les Classes Moyennes à la Dérive.* Paris: Seuil.

———. 2009. "Comparing Welfare Regime Changes: Living Standards and the Unequal Life Chances of Different Birth Cohorts." In *Consumption and Generational Change—The Rise of Consumer Lifestyles*, edited by Ian Rees Jones, Paul Higgs, and David J. Ekerdt. New Brunswick, NJ: Transaction.

———. 2010a. "The Long-Term Destabilization of Youth, Scarring Effects, and the Future of the Welfare Regime in Post-Trente Glorieuses France." *French Politics, Culture and Society* 28(3): 74–96.

———. 2010b. "Overeducation and Social Generations in France: Welfare Regimes and Intercohort Inequalities in Returns to Education." In *Growing Gaps: Educational Inequality around the World*, edited by Paul Attewell and Katherine S. Newman. Oxford: Oxford University Press.

DiPrete, Thomas A. 2002. "Life Course Risks, Mobility Regimes, and Mobility Consequences: A Comparison of Sweden, Germany, and the U.S." *American Journal of Sociology* 108(2): 267–309.

Duru-Bellat, Marie. 2006. *L'Inflation Scolaire: Les Désillusions de la Méritocratie.* Paris: Seuil.

Easterlin, Richard A. 1987. *Birth and Fortune: The Impact of Number on Personal Welfare.* Chicago: University of Chicago Press.

Ellwood, David T. 1982. "Teenage Unemployment: Permanent Scars or Temporary Blemishes?" In *The Youth Labor Market Problem, Its Nature, Causes, and Consequences*, edited by Richard B. Freeman and David A. Wise. Chicago: University of Chicago Press.

Ermisch, John, Markus Jäntti, Timothy M. Smeeding, and James A. Wilson. 2012. "Advantage in Comparative Perspective." In *From Parents to Children: The Intergenerational Transmission of Advantage*, edited by John Ermisch, Markus Jäntti, and Timothy M. Smeeding. New York: Russell Sage Foundation.

Esping-Andersen, Gøsta. 1990. *The Three Worlds of Welfare Capitalism.* Cambridge: Cambridge University Press.

————. 1999. *Social Foundations of Postindustrial Economies*. Oxford: Oxford University Press.

Ferrera, Maurizio, and Elisabetta Gualmini. 2004. *Rescued by Europe? Social and Labour Market Reforms in Italy from Maastricht to Berlusconi*. Amsterdam: Amsterdam University Press.

Fisk, Peter R. 1961. "The Graduation of Income Distributions." *Econometrica* 29(2): 171–85.

Galbraith, John K. 1958. *The Affluent Society*. New York: Houghton Mifflin.

Gangl, Markus. 2004. "Welfare States and the Scar Effects of Unemployment: A Comparative Analysis of the United States and West Germany." *American Journal of Sociology* 109(6): 1319–64.

Gooderham, Paul N., and Mark Dale. 1995. "The Second-Rate Second Chance? A Comparison of the Fates of Mature Graduates in the Labour Market in Britain and Norway." *International Journal of Lifelong Education* 14(1): 3–21.

Gornick, Janet, Marcia K. Meyers, and Katherine E. Ross. 1997. "Supporting the Employment of Mothers." *Journal of European Social Policy* 7(1): 45–70.

Korpi, Walter, and Joakim Palme. 1998. "The Paradox of Redistribution and Strategies of Equality: Welfare State Institutions. Inequality and Poverty in the Western Countries." *American Sociological Review* 63(5): 661–87.

Krugman, Paul R. 1992. *The Age of Diminished Expectations: U.S. Economic Policy in the 1990s*. Cambridge, MA: MIT Press.

Lazear, Edward P. 1979. "Why Is There Mandatory Retirement?" *Journal of Political Economy* 87(6): 1261–84.

Li, Cheng. 2009. *Formation of Middle Class in Comparative Perspective: Process, Influence and Socioeconomic Consequences*. Beijing: Social Science Academic Press.

Luxembourg Income Study (LIS) Database, http://www.lisdatacenter.org (multiple countries; microdata last accessed in April 2012). Luxembourg: LIS.

Mannheim, Karl. 1928. "Das Problem der Generationen." *Kölner Vierteljahrshefte für Soziologie VII*: 157–85, 309–30.

Mason, Karen O., William M. Mason, Halliman H. Winsborough, and W. Kenneth Poole. 1973. "Some Methodological Issues in Cohort Analysis of Archival Data." *American Sociological Review* 38: 242–58.

Mayer, Karl U. 2005. "Life Courses and Life Chances in a Comparative Perspective." In *Analyzing Inequality: Life Chances and Social Mobility in Comparative Perspective*, edited by Stefan Svallfors. Stanford, CA: Stanford University Press.

Mills, C. Wright. 1951. *White Collar: The American Middle Classes*. London: Oxford University Press.

Myles, John. 1990. "States, Labor Markets and Life Cycles." In *Beyond the Marketplace: Rethinking Economy and Society*, edited by Roger Friedland and A. F. (Sandy) Robertson. New York: Aldine de Gruyter.

Newman, Katherine S. 1999. *Falling from Grace: Downward Mobility in an Age of Affluence*. Berkeley: University of California Press.

Newman, Katherine, and Victor Tan Chen. 2007. *The Missing Class: Portraits of the Near Poor in America*. Boston: Beacon.

O'Brien, Robert. 2011. "Constrained Estimators and Age-Period-Cohort Models." *Sociological Methods and Research* 40(3): 419–52.

Piketty, Thomas. 2001a. "Les Inégalités dans le Long Terme." In *Les Inégalités Economiques*, edited by Tony Atkinson, Michel Glaude, and Lucile Ollier. Paris: Documentation Française.

———. 2001b. *Les Hauts Revenus en France au XXᵉ Siècle: Inégalités et Redistributions, 1901–1998*. Paris: Grasset.

Pressman, Steven. 2007. "The Decline of the Middle Class: An International Perspective." *Journal of Economic Issues* (41)1: 181–200.

———. 2009. "Public Policies and the Middle Class throughout the World in the Mid-2000s." *LIS* working paper 517. Luxembourg: LIS.

Ryder, Norbert B. 1965. "The Cohort as a Concept in the Study of Social Change." *American Sociological Review* 30: 843–61.

Schmoller, Gustav. 1897. *Was verstehen wir Unter dem Mittelstande? Hat Er Im 19. Jahrhundert zu Oder Abgenommen?* Göttingen, Germany: Vandenhoeck und Ruprecht.

Tepe, Markus, and Pieter Vanhuysse. 2010. "Elderly Bias, New Social Risks, and Social Spending: Change and Timing in Eight Programs across Four Worlds of Welfare, 1980–2003." *Journal of European Social Policy* 20(3): 218–34.

Van de Velde, Cécile. 2008. *Devenir Adulte. Sociologie Comparée De La Jeunesse En Europe*. Paris: PUF.

Yang, Yang, Wenjiang J. Fu, and Kenneth C. Land. 2004. "A Methodological Comparison of Age-Period-Cohort Models: The Intrinsic Estimator and Conventional Generalized Linear Models." *Sociological Methodology* 34(1): 75–110.

Part III

POLITICS: INEQUALITY, POLITICAL BEHAVIOR, AND PUBLIC OPINION

CHAPTER FIVE

Political Sources of Government Redistribution in High-Income Countries

Vincent A. Mahler, David K. Jesuit,
and Piotr R. Paradowski

In cross-national empirical work on income inequality and government redistribution, the greatest emphasis has been on the extremes of the income scale. Less work has been done on groups that are neither rich nor poor—the middle class. The lack of attention to this group is unfortunate for several reasons. Most obviously, the middle class, when defined as we do in this chapter as the three middle-income quintile groups, is by far the largest income group, and its fortunes play a correspondingly major role in determining those of society as a whole. In the political sphere, the middle class is a decisive actor in every high-income country, one that has been assiduously courted by both the left and the right—with good reason, since support from at least part of the middle class is an indispensible component of nearly every governing coalition. Beyond this, absolute and relative prosperity of the middle class is widely believed—not least by its own members—to have declined since the early 1980s, after steady improvement in the first part of the post–World War II period.[1] The political causes and implications of this have rarely been explored, at least in cross-national empirical work.

The intention of this chapter is to examine several aspects of middle-class politics and economics in the high-income world over the last 25 years. Specifically, we consider the relationship between, on the one hand, government redistribution toward and away from middle-income groups and, on the other, the degree and nature of political participation by those groups. The analysis employs data from a number of sources, with special reliance on the *Luxembourg Income Study (LIS)*, our source of data on household income, and the Comparative Study of Electoral Systems (CSES) and

145

European Social Survey (ESS), our sources of data on political participation by income group.

The chapter is divided into three parts. The first offers a detailed description of government redistribution as it affects middle-income groups. The second presents the results of a national-level unbalanced pooled cross-sectional/time series analysis of 75 country-years covering the period from 1979 to 2005. This analysis explores the sources of government redistribution as it affects middle-income groups with reference to a number of national-level political and economic variables that have commonly been employed in the literature, including electoral turnout, union density, and the partisan composition of governing cabinets. The third part of the chapter offers a description of cross-national variation in several modes of political participation at the level of income quintile group, including voting, belonging to a labor union, contacting an elected official, and participating in a protest or demonstration. This section includes a multi-level analysis of the 12 countries for which disaggregated data are available for both government redistribution and various modes of political participation.

GOVERNMENT REDISTRIBUTION AND THE MIDDLE CLASS

Our key dependent variable is the extent to which taxes and public social transfers redistribute income toward and away from each of five income quintile groups. Although the sources of cross-national variation in redistribution have been extensively explored for overall inequality and for the poor, less attention has been directed to middle-income groups. In this section, we introduce our measures of government redistribution and describe their effect on income shares in the countries we are examining.

As has been indicated, our basic source of data on household income is the *Luxembourg Income Study (LIS) Database.* In employing *LIS* data to measure government redistribution, the main limiting factor is that in a substantial number of *LIS* datasets income is measured net of taxes, making it impossible to construct a measure that taps the entire redistributive effect of the public sector. Still, more than 70 appropriate ("gross income") datasets remain. In measuring income, we have employed the standard LIS conventions for household size equivalizing, top and bottom coding, income coverage, and so on—that is, those used in computing the widely used *LIS* "Key Figures," which are documented on the LIS website.[2]

The most straightforward, and by far the most common, way of measuring the effect of taxes and social transfers on various income groups is to compute before- and after-government quintile-group shares. This is accomplished by first ranking households according to their pre-tax and pre-transfer income and dividing them into five equal groups, each representing 20 percent of income survey respondents.[3] Next, taxes are deducted and transfers are added to each household's income, and the population is then re-ranked by post-government income and again divided into quintile groups.

In calculating redistribution, we compare the income share of each quintile group before and after transfers have been added and before and after income taxes and social insurance contributions have been deducted.[4] The difference represents the net change in an individual group's income share as a result of transfers and taxes. To cite an example, the share of all income received by the lower middle class, Quintile II (QII), from private sector sources in Canada averaged 10.8 percent across eight *LIS* datasets over the period from 1981 to 2004. When transfers are added and taxes are deducted, this quintile group's share rises to an average of 13.4 percent, for a net gain of 2.6 percentage points. Of course, the net position of an income group with respect to redistribution can be negative as well as positive. For example, QIV in Canada, the upper middle class, received an average of 25.2 percent of all pre-government income, but when transfers were added and taxes were deducted, its share had fallen to 23.5 percent, for a net redistribution value of –1.7 percentage points.

Figures for pre- and post-government quintile group shares, and the difference between them, for each of the 14 countries we examine are presented in Table 5.1. These represent unweighted national means across multiple income datasets, an average of 5.4 per country. Full results for all datasets are available in the online appendix that accompanies this volume.

In describing these figures, we start from the bottom. As can be seen, QI's pre-government income share is very low, in no case more than 3.1 percent for the countries considered—far less than a proportional share of 20 percent. After transfers are added and direct taxes are deducted (for this group it is mainly the former), QI's share in every case increases. However,

TABLE 5.1

Mean pre- and post-government quintile group income shares and redistribution

Country	PRE-GOVERNMENT SHARES					POST-GOVERNMENT SHARES					REDISTRIBUTION BY SHARE				
	QI	QII	QIII	QIV	QV	QI	QII	QIII	QIV	QV	QI	QII	QIII	QIV	QV
Australia	1.3	10.1	17.6	25.8	45.2	7.7	12.9	17.8	23.9	37.7	6.5	2.8	0.1	-1.9	-7.5
Belgium	0.2	8.1	18.5	27.5	45.7	9.9	14.7	18.7	23.4	33.4	9.7	6.6	0.2	-4.2	-12.3
Canada	2.6	10.8	17.6	25.2	43.8	7.8	13.4	18.0	23.5	37.3	5.2	2.6	0.3	-1.7	-6.5
Denmark	1.1	10.6	19.6	26.7	42.1	9.9	15.0	19.1	23.1	32.9	8.8	4.4	-0.5	-3.6	-9.2
Finland	3.1	11.0	18.3	25.5	42.2	10.4	15.1	18.8	22.8	33.0	7.3	4.1	0.5	-2.7	-9.2
France	0.8	8.3	15.3	23.1	52.5	7.4	12.1	15.6	20.3	44.7	6.5	3.7	0.3	-2.8	-7.8
Germany	1.3	10.5	18.1	25.5	44.6	9.3	14.2	17.9	22.7	35.9	8.1	3.7	-0.1	-2.9	-8.7
Ireland	0.5	7.7	16.5	25.7	49.5	7.7	12.3	17.3	23.3	39.4	7.2	4.6	0.7	-2.4	-10.1
Netherlands	1.2	11.2	18.3	25.8	43.5	9.6	14.4	18.0	23.0	35.0	8.4	3.2	-0.3	-2.8	-8.5
Norway	2.4	11.8	18.8	25.3	41.6	9.8	15.0	18.6	22.6	34.0	7.4	3.2	-0.2	-2.7	-7.6
Sweden	1.3	8.9	18.6	26.8	44.4	10.0	15.5	19.0	22.9	32.6	8.8	6.5	0.3	-3.9	-11.8
Switzerland	3.1	12.5	17.9	24.2	42.3	8.6	13.8	17.7	22.5	37.5	5.4	1.3	-0.2	-1.7	-4.9
United Kingdom	0.8	8.2	17.1	26.0	48.0	7.5	12.3	17.0	23.2	40.0	6.8	4.1	0.0	-2.8	-7.9
United States	2.2	9.5	16.3	24.4	47.6	6.1	12.0	17.3	23.7	41.0	3.9	2.5	1.0	-0.7	-6.6
Mean	1.6	9.9	17.7	25.5	45.2	8.7	13.8	17.9	22.9	36.7	7.1	3.8	0.2	-2.6	-8.5
Standard deviation	1.0	1.5	1.1	1.1	3.2	1.3	1.3	0.9	0.9	3.6	1.6	1.5	0.4	0.9	2.0

SOURCE: Authors' calculations from the *LIS Database*. Data for various years between 1979 and 2005.

as displayed in the first column of the third section, the extent to which taxes and transfers improve the poor's income share varies greatly, from a high of 8.8 percent or more (Belgium, Denmark, and Sweden) to a low of about 4 percent (the United States).

What about QII—the lower middle class? As can be seen, net redistribution for this group is also in every case positive. However, the range of percentage improvement again varies widely, with the greatest gains in Belgium and Sweden and the smallest in Switzerland, the United States, Canada, and Australia. QIII is a transitional group with respect to redistribution: net redistribution is positive in 8 and negative or zero in 6 of our 14 countries, although the change in income share is nearly always small. For QIV, net redistribution is in all cases negative, but the degree to which the income share of this group decreases again ranges widely, from less than −1 percent (the United States) to over −4 percent (Belgium). Finally, we consider QV, the highest quintile group. While government redistribution is negative for all countries, the degree to which this is true again varies considerably, from a decline of about 5 percent for Switzerland to one of around 12 percent for Belgium and Sweden.

It is often said, not least by middle-income groups themselves, that the position of the middle class has been eroding over the last two decades in comparison to other groups. Do our figures bear out this widespread perception? One way of considering this, at least in a preliminary way, is to sort the results described above by *LIS* "Wave"; Wave I covers the period around 1980, Wave II around 1985, Wave III around 1990, Wave IV around 1995, Wave V around 2000, and Wave VI around 2004. As can be seen in Figure 5.1, the pre-government income share of QI has indeed eroded sharply over the last 25 years, declining from 2.1 percent of all income around 1980 to 1.2 percent around 2004. Government redistribution toward this quintile group has, however, largely—although not entirely—kept pace with this decline. As for QII and QIII, each has seen its share of pre-government income fall; this is particularly true of QII, a decline that may represent the loss of manufacturing jobs in many high-income countries. For each group, though, government redistribution has largely kept pace, although post-government income shares have declined to some extent. As for QIV, both its pre-government share and the extent of (net negative) government redistribution have changed little over the period. Finally, as can be seen, the big gainers over the last 25 years have been the households in QV, whose

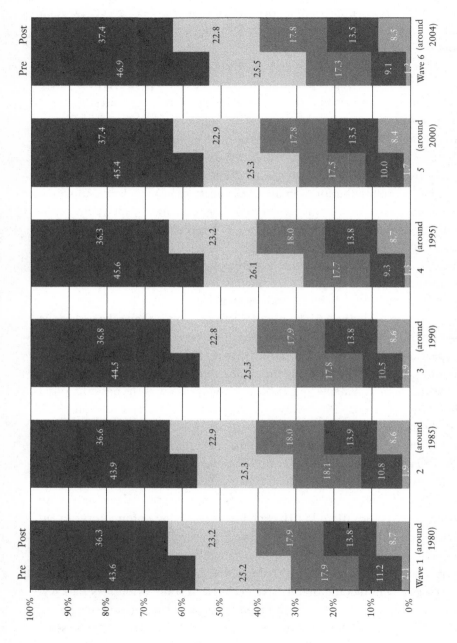

Figure 5.1. Mean pre- and post-government quintile shares by *LIS* wave, 14 countries

SOURCE: Authors' calculations from the *LIS Database*. Data are for various years between 1979 and 2005.

pre-government income share has increased more than 3 percentage points. About two-thirds of this has been "clawed back" by higher taxes or lower transfers, but even after government redistribution, this group's disposable income share has improved substantially, the only quintile group whose income has done so.

To this point we have compared income shares of middle-income groups before and after public social transfers have been added and direct taxes and social insurance contributions deducted. However, such an approach is limited in that, by comparing snapshots of the situation before and after government redistribution, it does not capture the inter-quintile-group dynamics that produced these results. Several measures of income mobility across income groups (rather than, as the term is often used, over time) tap these dynamics, notably the Shorrocks Index (Jenkins and Van Kerm 2006; Morillas 2009). However, none is quite suited to our purposes, since summary measures of this type capture average mobility across all groups. When the focus is on individual income groups, a straightforward way to measure income mobility is to create a quintile transition matrix that reports the percentages of households moving up or down across quintile group boundaries at a given point in time as a result of government redistribution (Burkhauser, Holtz-Eakin, and Rhody 1997).

We made such calculations for the households in our 75 *LIS* income datasets. The results, averaged by country, are reported in Table 5.2. As can be seen, by far the most common outcome is that households remain in the same quintile group after taxes and transfers as before: for a large share of households, on average over 60 percent, government redistribution does not move income recipients very far in either direction. Still, the stability of initial incomes with respect to taxes and transfers does vary across countries. The highest percentage of households that do not move across a quintile group boundary is 78 percent in Australia; also high are the United States (71 percent), Canada (68 percent) and the United Kingdom (64 percent). On the other end of the mobility spectrum are Belgium, Germany, and Sweden, although even in the lowest case—Sweden—nearly 50 percent of all households remain in their pre-government quintile group.

Examining the inter-quintile-group movement that does occur, we begin by focusing on movement up from QI into the broadly defined middle class (QII, QIII, and QIV), a proportion that ranges from more than 11 percent (Belgium and France) to 5 percent (Australia and Finland). Many

TABLE 5.2

Mean quintile group transition matrix for government redistribution

Country	No move	Low to middle	High to middle	Middle to low	Middle to high	In middle: Down	In middle: Up	Net middle
Australia	78.3	5.2	1.4	3.9	1.2	5.2	3.9	1.4
Belgium	50.8	12.6	4.4	7.5	3.9	13.2	7.0	5.6
Canada	68.4	7.3	2.0	5.0	2.0	7.5	7.7	2.2
Denmark	60.3	7.2	3.5	6.7	2.7	12.0	7.1	1.3
Finland	62.6	5.3	3.4	6.6	3.7	10.9	7.4	-1.5
France	51.9	11.3	4.2	8.5	2.9	15.0	4.6	4.1
Germany	51.2	10.0	4.5	8.8	3.7	15.3	5.9	2.0
Ireland	62.3	9.9	2.6	5.8	3.3	7.5	8.4	3.4
Netherlands	56.0	10.8	3.4	6.4	3.6	11.7	7.5	4.2
Norway	61.5	5.8	3.5	5.7	3.6	11.3	8.5	0.1
Sweden	48.3	8.4	4.7	11.9	4.4	13.0	8.9	-3.2
Switzerland	61.2	10.2	2.8	6.8	2.6	10.6	5.0	3.6
United Kingdom	64.0	8.6	2.5	5.9	2.3	8.5	8.1	3.0
United States	70.8	6.8	1.9	4.5	2.1	7.5	6.2	2.1
Mean	60.5	8.5	3.2	6.7	3.0	10.7	6.9	2.0
Standard deviation	8.5	2.3	1.0	2.0	0.9	3.0	1.5	2.4

SOURCE: Authors' calculations from the *LIS Database*. Data for various years between 1979 and 2005.

fewer households move down into the three middle-income groups from the highest quintile than move up into them from the lowest; the percentage share is in all cases less than 5 percent. Somewhat more households move down from the broad middle-income group represented by QII to QIV into the lowest quintile group, a number that ranges from almost 12 percent for Sweden to under 5 percent for the United States and Australia. This is considerably greater than the percentage that moves from the middle three quintile groups into the highest quintile group, which averages 3 percent.

A substantial number of households move within the broad middle-income group represented by QII, QIII, and QIV. Of these, most—an average across all income datasets of 10.7 percent—move down. Somewhat fewer—an average across all *LIS* datasets of just under 7.0 percent—move up. Finally, only a tiny number of households move across three quintile boundaries, from the highest to the lowest quintile group or from the lowest to the highest: in all but one country, the proportion is less than 1 percent (not shown).

Finally, it is possible to offer a summary measure of movement into and out of the broadly defined middle class that reflects the net gain and loss of middle-income groups in comparison to others. In all but two countries, the middle class, broadly defined, experiences a net improvement in its position as a result of taxes and transfers, with positive values ranging from 5.6 percent in Belgium to 0.1 percent in Norway.

To summarize, in this section we attempted to offer an empirical overview of government redistribution as it applies to the middle class, broadly defined. Specifically, we calculated net income redistribution toward and away from individual middle-income groups, as well as the inter-quintile income movements that produced it.

EXPLAINING CROSS-COUNTRY VARIATION IN GOVERNMENT REDISTRIBUTION

Now that we have offered measures of several aspects of government redistribution as it applies to the middle class, it is time to explore the sources of cross-country and over-time variation in redistribution. In the last decade a broad consensus has emerged concerning the main explanatory variables that should be considered. Since these have been described in detail in other works, we offer only a brief discussion at this point.[5]

As we indicated, the central aim of this chapter is to consider whether the extent to which middle-income groups gain or lose from government redistribution is related to the extent to which they express political "voice"— that is, make demands on the political system. The most fundamental way of making such demands in a democracy is by voting; competitive elections are, in fact, one of the essential institutions that distinguish democracies from authoritarian systems. However, there is wide variation across contemporary democracies in average turnout in national elections, ranging from more than 90 percent of the eligible electorate in countries such as Australia to less than 50 percent in Switzerland. It is useful to ask whether this wide variation is related to the equally wide variation in government redistribution. Average turnout at the national level is measured as the share of the eligible population that voted in a national election immediately prior to or in the same year as a given *LIS* dataset. Our measure reflects elections to the lower house of a country's legislature, except in the presidential systems—Finland, France, and the United States—where it represents turnout in presidential elections.[6]

Another perennial theme in the literature looks not to the percentage of the eligible electorate that votes but rather to the ideological orientation of the parties for which they vote. A large body of literature, often called "power resources theory," argues that "it is fruitful to view welfare states as outcomes of, and arenas for, conflicts between class-related socio-economic groups" (Korpi and Palme 2003, 425). Within this tradition, the most common focus has been on the ideological orientation of governing coalitions; indeed, one of the longest-standing preoccupations of political scientists has been the degree to which leftist parties in government drive redistribution or rightist parties forestall it. The alternative possibility is, of course, that the income guarantees of the contemporary welfare state are so ingrained that they are beyond the power of either the left or the right to change, except at the margins. Our measure of partisan orientation, from Armingeon and colleagues (2010), taps the share of left and right parties in governing cabinets in the year of a given *LIS* dataset.

Another much-examined variable said to be associated with government redistribution is membership in labor unions. The expectation is straightforward: organized labor tends to be among the most vigorous supporters of government programs that benefit its members, and it is often argued that the share of the labor force that is organized will be positively related to the size and redistributive nature of social programs. Our measure of union density is from Visser (2009, 15): it taps "net union membership as a proportion [of] wage and salary earners in employment." This measure is closest to the definition we use in the multi-level analysis later in the chapter.

A number of other variables are believed to explain the extent of government redistribution. Perhaps the most straightforward approach is the median voter theorem, first articulated by Meltzer and Richard (1981), which posits that government inequality reduction is positively related to the extent of pre-government inequality (Milanovic 2000, 2010; Scervini 2009). Our measure of pre-government income by quintile group is calculated from *LIS* datasets; as described earlier, it includes market income plus private transfers.

Yet another variable looks to economic globalization. The critique by those skeptical of globalization is clear: in their view, extensive international economic ties trap governments in a "race to the bottom" in the provision of public social benefits, in an effort to retain their country's position in export and capital markets. In measuring economic globalization, we have employed data from the KOF index of globalization (Dreher 2006; Dreher, Gaston, and Martens 2008, updated in 2009). Since trade and foreign direct investment represent very different modes of international integration, we measured them separately, in both cases as a share of GDP. (Separate trade and investment data were supplied to us by Dreher on February 23, 2010.)

Finally, it is necessary to introduce two control variables that together tap the "need" for social benefits in an effort to isolate the extent to which government redistribution is driven by variation in demographic and economic trends across countries. Both control variables come from Armingeon and colleagues (2010). The first is the share of the population that is aged 65 or older, which affects the pension entitlements that are a major component of public benefits in all high-income countries. The second is the unemployment rate, which is linked directly to unemployment compensation and indirectly to a number of other benefits received by households headed by those of working age.

The main results of our analysis are reported in Table 5.3.[7] We begin with QI. Most important for our purposes, we find that both turnout and union density—but not the share of cabinet seats held by leftist parties—are

TABLE 5.3

Pooled cross-sectional time series regression results. Dependent variable: Post-government income quintile shares

Variable	(1) QI	(2) QII	(3) QIII	(4) QIV	(5) QV
Turnout	0.053***	0.018***	−0.010**	−0.026***	−0.048***
	(0.010)	(0.006)	(0.005)	(0.005)	(0.017)
Union density	0.014**	0.026***	0.011***	−0.002	−0.038***
	(0.006)	(0.005)	(0.004)	(0.003)	(0.010)
Left cabinet seats	−0.004	−0.003	−0.001	0.000	0.009
	(0.003)	(0.003)	(0.002)	(0.002)	(0.008)
Trade	0.022***	0.009**	−0.003	−0.009***	−0.019**
	(0.005)	(0.004)	(0.002)	(0.002)	(0.008)
Foreign direct investment	0.008	0.004	0.006	−0.002	−0.032
	0.016	0.010	(0.007)	(0.013)	(0.025)
Percentage population	0.264***	0.209***	−0.040	−0.260***	−0.335***
elderly	(0.054)	(0.049)	(0.029)	(0.032)	(0.113)
Unemployment	−0.015	0.017	0.022	−0.054**	−0.110*
rate	(0.028)	(0.025)	(0.019)	(0.025)	(0.061)
QI share	−0.404***				
(pre-government)	(0.075)				
QII share		−0.579***			
(pre-government)		(0.061)			
QIII share			−0.254**		
(pre-government)			(0.105)		
QIV share				−0.103	
(pre-government)				(0.146)	
QV share					−0.212*
(pre-government)					(0.115)
Constant	−1.925	3.373***	5.560***	6.885**	13.202**
	(1.121)	(1.014)	(1.913)	(2.999)	(4.848)
R^2	0.866	0.899	0.507	0.838	0.699

SOURCE: Authors' statistical analysis using Stata software, as described in text. Data are for various years between 1979 and 2005 from the following sources: turnout (IDEA 2011 and McDonald 2011 [USA]); union density (Visser 2009); left cabinet seats, percentage elderly, and unemployment (Armingeon et al. 2010); trade and foreign direct investment (Dreher 2010). Pre- and post-government income quintile share are authors' calculations from the *LIS Database*.

NOTE: Numbers in parentheses are standard errors; $n = 75$.

*$p < 0.1$; **$p < 0.05$; ***$p < 0.01$.

positively and statistically significantly related to the improvement in this quintile group's income share as a result of taxes and social transfers. Beyond this, the results offer some support for the median voter hypothesis: as the pre-government income share received by households in QI rises, the improvement in that quintile group's income share declines.[8] Finally, we find that the share of the population that is elderly is positively associated with redistribution, as is our trade (but not our foreign direct investment) measure.

What of the QII, the lower middle class? As can be seen, very similar relationships are evident for QII as for QI. In particular, both electoral turnout and union density are positively related to the improvement of this group's income share as a result of government redistribution. As to QIII, there continues to be a significant positive relationship between redistribution and union density—but a negative one for turnout—indicating that the effect of unionization extends fairly high up the income scale. When we reach QIV, however, the relationship between redistribution and unionization disappears, while that for turnout continues to be negative. Finally, both national electoral turnout and union density are significantly negatively related to net redistribution for QV; this is a result primarily of the taxes this group pays to support social transfers benefiting groups lower on the income scale.

These results also highlight a few broader themes. First, and most generally, it seems evident that the middle class is not of one piece. Specifically, QII and QIII have a good deal in common with each other and, at least for some variables, with QI. QIV, on the other hand, even though it extends well into what most people would consider the middle class, tends to have more in common with QV than with the quintile groups below. Although there are exceptions, there does seem to be a demarcation about two-thirds of the way up within our broadly defined middle class, with QII and QIII on one side and QIV on the other.

As to independent variables, it is notable that not a single significant relationship links our variable measuring the partisan composition of governments and net redistribution toward or away from any income quintile group. This may reflect the difficulty governments face in making major cuts—or, for that matter, major enhancements—to longstanding social entitlements, whatever their ideological disposition. There is also some evidence of a positive relationship between international trade (but not foreign direct investment) and government redistribution, which is in the opposite direction from the one globalization critics would lead us to expect. This appears to provide some confirmation of the "domestic compensation" hypothesis, which argues that governments in open economies systematically supply more redistribution than those in less open economies, in an effort to compensate groups that would otherwise suffer most from global competition—thereby maintaining broad public support for a basically liberal system (Ruggie 1982).

As to union density and electoral turnout, the variables that are closest to the concerns of this chapter, it is notable that both are consistently related in the expected direction to net redistribution. With respect to union density, it is of interest that a positive relationship continues through the third quintile group, indicating that, in highly unionized countries, organized labor extends well up the income spectrum. As to turnout, it is positively related to the net share improvement of the bottom two quintile groups and negatively related to that of the top three. This suggests that this mode of political participation, at least measured as a national average, does play a role in explaining cross-national and over-time variation in government redistribution, although other variables clearly matter as well.

A CLOSER LOOK AT POLITICAL PARTICIPATION

The preceding section offered some interesting national-level results in identifying variables that help explain income gains or losses as a result of taxes and social transfers. Although these variables have been much studied, their effect specifically on the middle class has been less frequently considered.

As we showed, the overall level of turnout in national elections is positively related to the net improvement in the income share of QI and QII as a result of taxes and transfers and negatively related to that of QIII, QIV, and QV. What drives this relationship is arguably not so much the level of turnout per se as it is the extent to which low average turnout reflects turnout that is skewed by income. The underlying assumption is that, in the words of Lijphart (1997, 4), "who votes, and who doesn't, has important consequences for who gets elected and for the content of public policies." While this claim is certainly plausible, there are to our knowledge no detailed and fully comparable statistics for turnout by income quintile group for all of the 75 country-years we examine (Pontusson and Rueda 2010).

Until fairly recently, broad cross-national research exploring the relationship between electoral turnout and government redistribution reached something of a dead end at this point. However, in the last decade, the situation has improved as a result of two major research efforts. The first is the Comparative Study of Electoral Systems (CSES), a project in which the most authoritative public opinion surveys administered in many democratic countries at the time of national elections have been harmonized to include a number of questions in common. The second is the European Social

Survey (ESS), a European Union–sponsored poll that asks similar questions about political participation. One major drawback for our purposes is that the CSES and ESS include only recent elections, and their country coverage does not overlap completely with that of *LIS*'s "gross income" datasets. Still, there are 12 countries for which quintile-group-level data are available for both electoral turnout and other modes of political participation (from the CSES or ESS) and gross household income (from *LIS*) for the early and mid-2000s.[9] While this is a much smaller dataset than we have employed so far, it should offer at least some preliminary evidence on the relationship between income and various modes of political participation at a lower level of aggregation than the nation, the usual focus of cross-country work.

It is useful to begin by describing CSES's and ESS's measures of political participation. Of particular value for our purposes is a variable that asks survey respondents to place themselves into one of 5 (CSES) or 12 (ESS) income groups, based on national-level income data. (We have combined ESS income categories into quintile groups to make them consistent with the CSES.) Using these datasets, respondents cannot be placed into income groups as precisely as the *LIS* data allow; for example, income is not equivalized, and, while the ideal is to measure disposable income from all sources, these surveys do not achieve the high level of cross-national comparability that is the hallmark of the *LIS* data. We believe the ESS to be more consistent in this regard and have thus used ESS surveys instead of CSES surveys when both are available for the same election.[10] Finally, note that figures from both sources represent self-reported turnout, which is invariably higher than turnout figures from national electoral rolls, through some combination of selective memory on the part of survey respondents and under-sampling of difficult-to-reach groups.[11]

For our purposes, we are especially interested in political participation by middle-income groups. Our basic intuition is that, to the extent that political variables matter, income groups' net benefit from public sector taxes and transfers will be related to the extent to which they make—or fail to make—demands on politicians in an effort to further their economic interest. In the words of Key (1949, 527)—referring to elections but easily applied to other modes of participation—"the blunt truth is that politicians are under no compulsion to pay much heed to classes and groups of citizens who do not vote."

We begin with the most widespread form of political participation: voting in national elections. This is ultimately the most powerful mode of all, since only by this means are political leaders selected—and rejected. On the other hand, a vote is a blunt instrument; the message it is intended to convey, as well as the one received by elected officials, can vary greatly. Although economic well-being is almost always a major consideration in voting, so too are national security, cultural issues, regional or ethnic identity, and a host of other factors.

Still, it is worth exploring the extent to which voting varies across income groups, with particular reference to the middle classes, shown in Figure 5.2. As can be seen, in several countries self-reported electoral participation is very high: above 90 percent.[12] In these countries there is little room for turnout to vary by income. In others, though, average turnout is much lower. Most prominent among the latter countries are Switzerland, the United States, Finland, and the United Kingdom. As can be seen, there is a substantial income skew to electoral participation in these countries. For example, across all income quintile groups, the difference between average turnout in the lowest and highest groups is about 30 percentage points in the United States, 20 in Germany, 17 in Switzerland, and 13 in Finland. On the other hand, in a number of high-turnout countries, income is only modestly related to turnout, with less than a 10 percentage point difference across the income spectrum.

What of the middle-income groups specifically? As can be seen, the turnout rate of the three middle-income quintile groups is substantially below that of the highest quintile group in the United States—over 20 percentage points for QII. A similar gap is evident in Switzerland, another country with low average turnout. In other countries, there is typically only a modest gap between participation by middle-income groups and those above or below them on the income scale. In general, QIV is a good deal more similar to QV than are QII and QIII, a pattern similar to that found in our national-level analysis.

There are, of course, other ways of participating politically beyond the powerful, but blunt, instrument represented by a vote (Verba, Schlozman, and Brady 2005). Several of these are reflected in CSES and ESS survey questions that ask respondents whether they belong to a labor union, have contacted an elected or public official, or have participated in a demonstration or protest during the last five years. Most interesting for our purposes

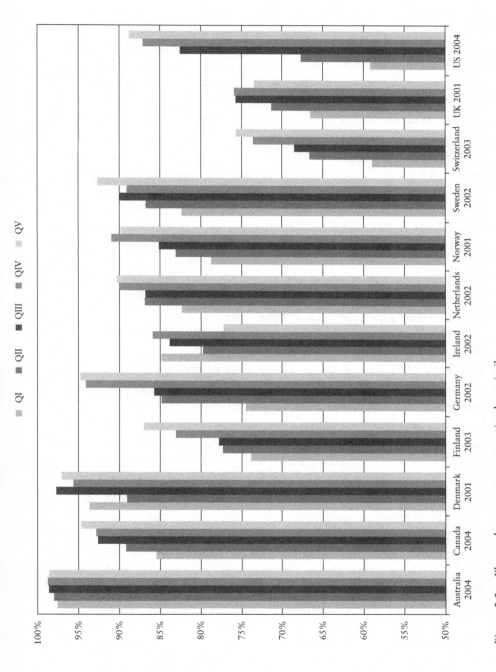

Figure 5.2. Electoral turnout, percent voting by quintile

s o u r c e : Authors' calculations from the ESS and the CSES (Australia, Canada, Ireland, and the United States).

is membership in labor unions, which are generally the largest membership group in affluent countries that have an explicit interest in distributive issues. As is well known, average levels of union membership vary enormously across countries; in CSES and ESS surveys, fewer than 11 percent of Americans report that they belong to a union, while more than 60 percent of Danes and Swedes say they do. However, there is also a great deal of cross-class variation in union membership. In most countries with medium to high levels of union density, membership is relatively low in the bottom quintile group, whose members typically have only a limited attachment to the workforce, then rises in QII, peaks in QIII and QIV, and remains relatively high even in QV.

Yet another measure of political participation is the extent to which respondents report that they have directly contacted an elected or other public official during the last five years. Again, there are fairly large cross-national differences—although it should be noted that fewer than half of all respondents report that they have engaged in this activity in even the highest-contacting countries. The highest values are for liberal regimes, including Australia, Canada, and the United States. In countries with high average participation of this type, there is typically little difference in participation between the middle- and highest-income quintile groups. One exception is the United States, where those in the highest-income group contact elected or other public officials at a much higher rate than those of any other, even the third and fourth quintile groups just below.

What of participation in protests and demonstrations, a form of direct democracy that may indicate frustration with the ordinary institutional channels for political participation? None of our 12 countries registers a high value on this variable (the highest national average is under 15 percent), although Finland, the Netherlands, the United Kingdom, and the United States are near the bottom. Clearly, mass participation of this sort is not a major part of contemporary politics, at least in these 12 countries. As to the middle classes, a rather striking fact is that the rate of participation in protests and demonstrations in most cases rises as one moves up the income scale. Clearly, this is not a strategy employed exclusively, or even mainly, by society's least advantaged members.

To conclude this section on participation, we describe the results of a multi-level analysis that includes household-level demographic variables from *LIS* and quintile-group-level political variables from the CSES and the

ESS in an effort to explain cross-household and cross-country variation in government redistribution in the context of a merged dataset of Wave VI *LIS* datasets from 12 countries. Our dependent variable measures net redistribution within households resulting from direct taxes and payroll contributions, as well as social transfers. Specifically, we subtract household direct taxes paid from total social transfers received and then divide by household gross income. This value is then multiplied by 100 to yield a percentage. Thus, a household that receives all of its income from the state and pays no taxes would have a net redistribution value equal to 100 percent. Conversely, a household that receives no social transfers but pays a quarter of its market income in taxes would have a score equal to –25 percent.

We employ three independent variables at the household level that are hypothesized to play a major role in explaining variation in the net redistributive position of a household. The first two are the number of persons in the household who are 65 or older and 18 or younger—demographic variables that drive entitlements for public pensions, child allowances, and the like, but are largely beyond the ability of policy makers to influence. The third is a dummy variable that equals 0 if there are no earners in the household, which would be expected to drive up unemployment-related transfers, and 1 otherwise. In a perfect world, we would also have individual-level data on political participation. However, since we must rely on CSES and ESS data that are aggregated at the quintile group level, we have assigned the average level of turnout and so on for an income quintile group in a given country to all of the *LIS* households in the corresponding quintile group. Finally, we pooled data for our 12 countries and then examined each quintile group separately, conducting five multi-level analyses for each of four modes of participation—20 in all.[13]

Table 5.4 reports the results of the multi-level models.[14] Beginning with the individual-level (level-one) variables, we can see that households with more elderly persons experience greater net redistribution than those with fewer elderly members, as do households that do not include any earners. These relationships are significant at the $p < 0.01$ level in every equation—not surprising given that these variables measure the retired and unemployed. In addition, households with children are net beneficiaries of redistribution in the bottom quintile group. However, in QIII the direction of the relationship reverses, and it is not in evidence for QII, QIV, or QV. While on the surface this appears somewhat puzzling, it may reflect the fact

TABLE 5.4

Multi-level models, household redistribution for 12 countries. Dependent variable: Net household redistribution

Income group	No earners	Child	Number elderly	Constant	Turnout	Union density	Contact	Protest	Intercept variance (level 2)	Residual variance (level 1)	Proportional reduction in variance (level 2)	Proportional reduction in variance (level 1)	R^2
QI $n = 7,201$	55.549*** (3.189)	3.095*** (1.292)	8.143*** (1.550)	-22.697 (26.378)	0.518** (0.303)				97.237*** (40.148)	981.192*** (53.723)	0.478	0.454	0.456
	55.567*** (3.201)	3.099*** (1.292)	8.133*** (1.548)	10.259 (9.055)		0.335* (0.263)			113.717** (56.346)	981.192*** (16.366)	0.389	0.454	0.447
	55.557*** (3.199)	3.096*** (1.292)	8.142*** (1.544)	10.621* (7.455)			0.435* (0.326)		128.632* (83.564)	981.191*** (53.727)	0.309	0.454	0.440
	55.560*** (3.200)	3.098*** (1.291)	8.140*** (1.545)	17.977*** (9.166)				-0.026 (0.965)	134.008** (80.860)	981.191*** (53.726)	0.280	0.454	0.437
QII $n = 7,201$	56.671*** (3.998)	0.793 (0.927)	11.062*** (2.173)	-5.705 (22.593)	0.139 (0.255)				79.715** (38.430)	784.907*** (44.236)	0.559	0.570	0.569
	56.676*** (4.001)	0.794 (0.927)	11.062*** (2.173)	3.352 (5.581)		0.071 (0.126)			79.520* (38.270)	784.907*** (44.239)	0.560	0.570	0.570
	56.676*** (3.999)	0.794 (0.927)	11.060*** (2.172)	-0.188 (5.796)			0.297 (0.293)		76.225** (37.228)	784.907*** (44.237)	0.578	0.570	0.571
	56.673*** (4.002)	0.792 (0.927)	11.063*** (2.173)	10.320** (6.069)				-0.690* (0.506)	74.628* (33.306)	784.907*** (44.240)	0.587	0.570	0.572
QIII $n = 7,200$	47.632*** (5.897)	-0.227 (0.862)	18.074*** (2.415)	10.726 (24.743)	-0.226 (0.274)				37.405* (18.689)	582.880*** (45.365)	0.459	0.550	0.545
	47.635*** (5.896)	-0.229 (0.863)	18.073*** (2.414)	-6.963** (3.990)		-0.042 (0.085)			40.179* (18.045)	582.880*** (45.362)	0.419	0.550	0.543
	47.635*** (5.899)	-0.229 (0.863)	18.074*** (2.415)	-6.583** (4.243)			-0.095 (0.170)		40.464** (19.554)	582.880*** (45.361)	0.415	0.550	0.543
	47.632*** (5.894)	-0.230 (0.863)	18.077*** (2.415)	-4.540** (2.580)				-0.522*** (0.224)	36.074** (20.109)	582.880*** (45.362)	0.478	0.550	0.546

QIV n = 7,203	44.925*** (6.201)	18.871*** (1.979)	-3.061 (16.371)	-0.151 (0.183)				18.950** (7.260)	387.699*** (45.675)	0.480	0.534	0.532
	44.930*** (6.200)	18.868*** (1.978)	-15.220*** (3.042)		-0.028 (0.086)			19.842*** (7.135)	387.699*** (45.673)	0.455	0.534	0.531
	44.922*** (6.203)	18.872*** (1.978)	-12.811*** (3.580)			-0.146* (0.102)		19.139** (8.949)	387.699*** (45.673)	0.475	0.534	0.531
	44.928*** (6.203)	18.873*** (1.980)	-13.557*** (2.121)				-0.310*** (0.115)	17.746** (8.528)	387.699*** (45.666)	0.513	0.534	0.533
QV n = 7,195	44.081*** (9.029)	14.223*** (1.318)	-5.618 (9.163)	-0.197** (0.103)				3.786** (1.870)	283.831*** (36.879)	0.759	0.450	0.459
	44.073*** (9.038)	14.204*** (1.321)	-21.817*** (1.823)		-0.031 (0.044)			5.921*** (2.120)	283.831*** (36.913)	0.623	0.450	0.455
	44.079*** (9.034)	14.207*** (1.320)	-20.766*** (2.475)			-0.078 (0.063)		5.885** (3.160)	283.831*** (36.902)	0.626	0.450	0.455
	44.085*** (9.036)	14.204*** (1.324)	-21.651*** (1.260)				-0.155* (0.087)	5.862** (3.188)	283.831*** (36.900)	0.627	0.450	0.455

SOURCE: Authors' statistical analysis using Stata software, as described in the text. Data for various years between 2003 and 2005 from the following sources: turnout, union density, contact, and protest are authors' calculations from the ESS and the CSES (Australia, Canada, Ireland, and the United States); no earners, child, number elderly, and household redistribution are authors' calculations from the LIS Database.

NOTE: Robust standard errors are given in parentheses.

*p < 0.1 (one-tailed test); **p < 0.05; ***p < 0.01.

that while every affluent country supports the elderly and unemployed, in some countries child allowances or tax credits do not exist and in others they are means-tested.

What of political participation? We begin by examining electoral turnout. Consistent with our pooled cross-sectional time-series results reported in Table 5.3, the estimate is positive and significant in the first quintile group but negative and significant in the fifth quintile group. Thus, voter mobilization is associated with more redistribution toward the bottom quintile group and away from the top group. A similar but weaker finding concerns union membership: union density is positive and significantly related to redistribution in the lowest quintile group but becomes insignificant above that.

As to the other modes of participation, we find only a single significant relationship in the predicted (positive) direction: a greater frequency of contact by individuals in the bottom quintile group is associated with more net redistribution to households in that group. We also find a significant negative relationship between participation in protests or demonstrations and net redistribution in all but the first quintile group, perhaps suggesting that members of the middle class (but not the poor) who feel that they receive less than their "fair share" of government resources resort to extra-institutional protest. Finally, contacting public officials is negatively associated with income redistribution in the fourth quintile group, which may conceivably be motivated by citizens' backlash over their perceived "unfair" burden.

Overall, the results of the multi-level models lend some—although hardly overwhelming—support to the notion that greater political participation by income groups promotes redistribution toward those groups.[15] True, the vast majority of variation across individuals in their net redistributive position is the product of their own situation—that is, whether they belong to a group, such as the elderly or the unemployed, that receives benefits in every developed country. Moreover, even at the level of countries, a substantial share of the variation in government redistribution is explained by cross-national demographic differences. Still, of the second-level (cross-country) variation in redistribution that does exist, a fair amount is explained by variation in rates of political participation. The degree to which this is true does, however, vary by quintile group and by model. In sum, considering political participation does make a modest but real—and often neglected—contribution to the explanation of income redistribution at the household level.

CONCLUSION

As was indicated at the beginning, this chapter has sought to contribute to the literature on the middle class in several ways. The first and most straightforward has been to provide figures for government redistribution calculated from 75 *Luxembourg Income Study* datasets. In contrast to most measures of redistribution, which either examine the entire income spectrum or concentrate on the poor, our focus has been on the three middle-income quintile groups. In measuring redistribution, we have added cash public sector benefits to, and deducted direct taxes and social insurance contributions from, households' pre-government income, re-ranking households after transfers have been added and taxes deducted. In addition, we have computed a quintile group transition matrix which tracks movement of households across quintile group boundaries as a result of government redistribution.

The second part of the chapter offers a country-level empirical analysis exploring the effect of several variables on the gains and losses from government fiscal policies experienced by the middle-income quintile groups. Among the more notable results are our finding that electoral turnout plays a role in explaining middle-income groups' relative gains or losses as a result of taxes and transfers; our finding that union density is not only positively associated with redistribution but that this relationship is largely a middle-class phenomenon that extends farther up the income scale than is the case with our other variables; our failure to find strong effects in either direction arising from the partisan orientation of the government in power at the time of a *LIS* dataset; and, most broadly, our finding that for many variables, the second and third income quintile groups tend to have more in common with one another than with the fourth quintile group.

Finally, we examine quintile-group averages representing several modes of political participation for the 12 countries for which both *LIS* income datasets and election surveys from the CSES and ESS are available for about the same point in time. In this analysis, we focus not only on much-studied variables like electoral turnout and union membership, but also on such modes of participation as individually contacting an elected or public official and participating in a protest or demonstration. This discussion ends with a multi-level analysis that includes both household-level income variables from *LIS* datasets and quintile-group-level variables measuring various modes of participation from the CSES and ESS. Our expectation that participation would be positively related to redistribution was only partially borne out, certainly to a smaller degree than we had anticipated—perhaps because of the small number of countries included in our analysis and the fact that participation is, of necessity, measured only at the quintile group level.

In sum, this chapter has focused on the relationship between political participation and government redistribution as it affects the middle class, a group that has been neglected in the large empirical literature on this topic—if not in the public debate. Our hope is that the data that we have compiled—much of it to our knowledge unavailable elsewhere—will help to inform a research enterprise that will continue to grow in importance in the coming years.

NOTES

Jesuit and Mahler would like to acknowledge the support of LIS Visiting Scholars grant that permitted them to visit LIS in March 2010.

1. There are a number of commentators observing this trend, most notably Frank (2007), Krugman (2009), Fukuyama (2012), and Stiglitz (2012). Regarding perceptions by members of the middle class about their own economic standing, see Pew Research Center (2008) and Dougherty and Bennhold (*New York Times,* May 1, 2008).

2. See http://www.lisdatacenter.org/data-access/key-figures/inequality -and-poverty/.

3. Pre-government income is defined to include income from market sources as well as private inter-household transfers, such as gifts, inheritances, alimony, and child support. Households reporting zero pre-government income are included, but those reporting zero disposable income are dropped.

4. In an earlier version of this chapter, we computed separate figures for "pensionless" redistribution, as described in Jesuit and Mahler (2010).

5. Examples of recent work on the topic include Bradley et al. (2003), Pontusson (2005), Iversen (2005), Kenworthy (2008), and Kristal (2010).

6. To enhance comparability, we focus on contests where the highest elected office is at stake, as most other research in this area has done (Powell 1986; Jackman 1987; Jackman and Miller 1995). Figures for all countries but the United States are from the International Institute for Democracy and Electoral Assistance

(IDEA) (2011). They measure the share of voters in the registered electorate except in France and the United States, where registration is not automatic; in these countries, they reflect the share of voters in the voting-age population. U.S. figures are from McDonald (2011); they have been adjusted to exclude non-citizens and persons ineligible to vote because of imprisonment, a prior felony conviction, and so on.

7. Because our *LIS* datasets constitute an unbalanced pool (i.e., the years of *LIS* datasets vary slightly, and not all countries are represented by datasets in all years), the analysis employs OLS regression with Huber White "sandwich" robust standard errors clustered by country. Similar studies that employ this method include Bradley et al. (2003), Kenworthy and Pontusson (2005), and Brooks and Manza (2007).

8. The inclusion of pre-government quintile share as an independent variable raises the possibility that this variable will be correlated with the error term, causing inconsistent estimates. We have explored this possibility and found that this correlation is in no case strong and that the exclusion of this variable does not have a major effect on the results. On the other hand, omitting the pre-government variable creates problems of omitted-variable specification error: for all quintiles but QIII, a Ramsey specification error test (ovtest in Stata) indicates that the null hypothesis of no-omitted-variable specification should not be rejected when the pre-government variable is included but should be rejected when it is not.

9. We include all 12 high-income countries from *LIS* Wave VI for which gross income data were available.

10. CSES is used for Australia, Canada, the United States, and Ireland (because ESS lacks income data). ESS is used for the rest.

11. On the other hand, aggregate statistics also have problems, particularly in measuring the denominator of turnout rates. Registration lists or census figures, for example, may be out of date, including some persons who have recently died or moved, making turnout rates appear lower than they actually are. For a detailed discussion of measuring turnout, see Franklin (2004).

12. It should be noted that voting is compulsory in Australia (and also Belgium, for which we do not have quintile-level figures), although penalties for non-compliance are modest.

13. We inflated each *LIS* dataset to the total population, and then we randomly selected a sample equal to 3,000 cases for each country. Households were selected with equal probability and without replacement using SAS software. See the online appendix for details on the multi-level analysis.

14. The null or unconditional models are available in the online appendix. The null model is used to compute the proportional reduction in variance explained by the covariates at each level and overall; these statistics are reported in Table 5.4.

15. The Wald statistic and likelihood-ratio tests for each of the models allow us to reject the joint null hypothesis that all coefficients are equal to zero.

For additional results, please see the online appendices by following the link in the listing for Income Inequality *on the Stanford University Press website: http:// www.sup.org.*

REFERENCES

Armingeon, Klaus, Philipp Leimgruber, Michelle Beyeler, and Sarah Menegale. 2010. Comparative Political Data Set, 1960–2008. Berne, Switzerland: Institute of Political Science, University of Berne. http://www.ipw.unibe.ch/ content/team/klaus_armingeon/comparative_political_data_sets/index_eng .html.

Bradley, David, Evelyne Huber, Stephanie Moller, François Nielsen, and John D. Stephens. 2003. "Distribution and Redistribution in Postindustrial Democracies." *World Politics* 55(2): 193–228.

Brooks, Clem, and Jeff Manza. 2007. *Why Welfare States Persist: The Importance of Public Opinion in Democracies.* Chicago: University of Chicago Press.

Burkhauser, Richard V., Douglas Holtz-Eakin, and Stephen E. Rhody. 1997. "Labor Earnings Mobility and Inequality in the United States and Germany during the Growth Years of the 1980s." *International Economic Review* 38(4): 775–94.

Comparative Study of Electoral Systems (CSES). 2011. www.cses.org.

Dougherty, Carter, and Katrin Bennhold. 2008. "Squeezed in Europe." *New York Times*, May 1.

Dreher, Axel. 2006. "Does Globalization Affect Growth? Evidence from a New Index of Globalization." *Applied Economics* 38(10): 1091–1110.

———. 2010. Personal communication on February 23, 2010.

Dreher, Axel, Noel Gaston, and Pim Martens. 2008. *Measuring Globalization: Gauging Its Consequences.* New York: Springer.

European Social Survey. 2011. www.europeansocialsurvey.org.

Frank, Robert. 2007. *Falling Behind: How Rising Inequality Harms the Middle Class.* Berkeley: University of California Press.

Franklin, Mark N. 2004. *Voter Turnout and the Dynamics of Electoral Competition in Established Democracies.* New York: Cambridge University Press.

Fukuyama, Francis. 2012. "The Future of History: Can Liberal Democracy Survive the Decline of the Middle Class?" *Foreign Affairs* 91(1): 53–61.

International Institute for Democracy and Electoral Assistance (IDEA). 2011. Voter Turnout Database. www.idea.int.

Iversen, Torben. 2005. *Capitalism, Democracy and Welfare.* New York: Cambridge University Press.

Jackman, Robert W. 1987. "Political Institutions and Voter Turnout in the Industrial Democracies." *American Political Science Review* 81(2): 405–23.

Jackman, Robert W., and Ross A. Miller. 1995. "Voter Turnout in the Industrial Democracies during the 1980s." *Comparative Political Studies* 27(4): 467–92.

Jenkins, Stephen P., and Philippe Van Kerm. 2006. "Trends in Income Inequality, Pro-Poor Income Growth and Income Mobility." *Oxford Economic Papers* 58(3): 531–48.

Jesuit, David K., and Vincent A. Mahler. 2010. "Comparing Government Redistribution across Countries: The Problem of Second Order Effects." *Social Science Quarterly* 91(5): 1390–1404.

Kenworthy, Lane. 2008. *Jobs with Equality.* New York: Oxford University Press.

Kenworthy, Lane, and Jonas Pontusson. 2005. "Rising Inequality and the Politics of Redistribution in Affluent Countries." *Perspectives on Politics* 3(3): 449–71.

Key, Valdimer O. 1949. *Southern Politics in State and Nation.* New York: Vintage.

Korpi, Walter, and Joakim Palme. 2003. "New Politics and Class Politics in the Context of Austerity and Globalization: Welfare State Regress in 18 Countries, 1975–95." *American Political Science Review* 97(3): 425–46.

Kristal, Tali. 2010. "Good Times, Bad Times: Postwar Labor's Share of National Income in Capitalist Democracies." *American Sociological Review* 75(5): 729–63.

Krugman, Paul. 2009. *The Conscience of a Liberal.* New York: Norton.

Lijphart, Arend. 1997. "Unequal Participation: Democracy's Unsolved Dilemma." *American Political Science Review* 91(1): 1–14.

Luxembourg Income Study (LIS) Database, http://www.lisdatacenter.org (multiple countries; microdata last accessed in July 2011). Luxembourg: LIS.

McDonald, Michael. 2011. United States Elections Project. http://elections.gmu .edu/ voter_turnout.htm.

Meltzer, Alan H., and Scott F. Richard. 1981. "A Rational Theory of the Size of Government." *Journal of Political Economy* 89(5): 914–27.

Milanovic, Branko. 2000. "The Median Voter Hypothesis, Income Inequality, and Income Redistribution: An Empirical Test with the Required Data." *European Journal of Political Economy* 16(3): 367–410.

———. 2010. "Four Critiques of the Redistribution Hypothesis: An Assessment." *European Journal of Political Economy* 26(1): 147–54.

Morillas, Juan Rafael. 2009. "Redistribution as an Income Mobility Process: The Identification and Measurement of Redistribution." *LIS* working paper 513. Luxembourg: LIS.

Pew Research Center. 2008. *Inside the Middle Class: Bad Times Hit the Good Life.* Washington, DC: Pew Research Center.

Pontusson, Jonas. 2005. *Inequality and Prosperity: Social Europe vs. Liberal America.* Ithaca, NY: Cornell University Press.

Pontusson, Jonas, and David Rueda. 2010. "The Politics of Inequality: Voter Mobilization and Left Parties in Industrial States." *Comparative Political Studies* 43(6): 675–705.

Powell, G. Bingham, Jr. 1986. "American Voter Turnout in Comparative Perspective." *American Political Science Review* 80(1): 17–43.

Ruggie, John Gerard. 1982. "International Regimes, Transactions, and Change: Embedded Liberalism in the Postwar Economic Order." *International Organization* 36(2): 379–415.

Scervini, Francesco. 2009. "The Empirics of the Median Voter: Democracy, Redistribution and the Role of the Middle Class." *LIS* working paper 516. Luxembourg: LIS.

Stiglitz, Joseph E. 2012. *The Price of Inequality: How Today's Divided Society Endangers Our Future.* New York: Norton.

Verba, Sidney, Kay Lehman Schlozman, and Henry Brady. 2005. "Political Equality: What Do We Know about It?" In *Social Inequality*, edited by Kathryn M. Neckerman. New York: Russell Sage Foundation.

Visser, Jelle. 2009. ICTWSS: Database on Institutional Characteristics of Trade Unions, Wage Setting. State Intervention and Social Pacts in 34 Countries between 1960 and 2007 (Version 2, January 2009). http://www.uva-aias.net/208.

CHAPTER SIX

Income Distribution, Inequality Perceptions, and Redistributive Preferences in European Countries

István György Tóth and Tamás Keller

European governments, despite being faced by increasing austerity pressure, also need to implement reform policies in ways that incorporate the electorate's demand for redistribution as an important parameter. The development and execution of reforms may, however, turn out to be especially difficult when electorates *perceive* that inequality is rising, regardless of what actual inequality statistics signal. Hence, the study of the link between the degree of inequality and the demand for redistribution becomes particularly appealing for the social sciences.

Earlier literature offers various theoretical frameworks for understanding the relationship among inequality, popular welfare attitudes, and redistributive policies. The well-known Meltzer-Richard (hereafter: MR) paradigm, which applies the median voter theorem to redistributive policies, predicts that greater levels of inequality lead to greater redistribution because low-income citizens outvote those with above-average incomes (Meltzer and Richard 1981). Not surprisingly, this relationship does not always hold empirically. The chain of causation between inequality and redistribution is complicated, with many intermediate steps, a fact that makes us cautious in interpreting any correlations between the two variables.

With this in mind, we have two primary goals in this chapter. First, we join those who have tried to refine the predictions of the MR theorem via a more detailed understanding of the structure of inequality on the one hand and the structure of redistributive preferences on the other hand. Second, we attempt to refine the understanding of income inequality, with the aim of better identifying the context that may drive respondents' opinions (and, consequently, voters' decisions).

173

RESEARCH QUESTION: WHAT ARE THE DETERMINANTS
OF PREFERENCES FOR REDISTRIBUTION?

Meltzer and Richard (1981) argue that greater inequality leads to greater demand for redistribution. If income inequality—measured as the distance between the median and the average incomes—increased, a self-interested median voter—also assumed to be the median income recipient—would prefer greater redistribution through higher taxes and transfers than a person with an income above the median. Though this predicts more redistribution in countries with greater inequality, the evidence is mixed (for reviews, see Borck 2007; Kenworthy and McCall 2007; Keely and Tan 2008; Alesina and Giuliano 2009; Lupu and Pontusson 2009; McCarty and Pontusson 2009; Senik 2009).

The lack of a strong correlation between pre-tax and pre-transfer inequality and the level of redistribution (however we define it) does not in itself mean that the hypothesis is wrong. To explore the usefulness of the hypothesis about how inequality affects redistribution, we need to think through the long causal chain that links the two variables.

Micro Aspects

Do individuals' income rank predict their redistributive preferences reasonably well? If microdata tests showed a significant negative correlation, we could conclude that higher-income people prefer less redistribution and lower-income people prefer higher levels of redistribution. For this "pure material self-interest" argument, however, factors other than income or wealth might matter as well. For instance, one might expect different attitudes toward redistribution from employees with permanent contracts, the self-employed, or those who primarily and permanently earn income from welfare-state provisions. Additionally, the class positions of respondents may matter to a great extent.

Second, as the correlation linking material position and welfare attitudes is quite weak, another question emerges: what explains the deviations? How can it be that some of the relatively rich (income above the median) may support redistribution, while others with low (below median) incomes may not particularly like the idea of high levels of redistribution? The potential reasons for these differences include perceptual problems (when people underestimate or overestimate their actual positions in the income ranking), conditional preference formation (relative to others, or relative to past experiences or future expectations), and motivations other than pure self-interest (Tóth 2006, 2008). We focus on some of these factors below.

Bénabou and Ok (2001) developed a formal model of the relationship between redistributive claims and rational expectations of the *prospect for upward mobility* (the so-called POUM model). Low-income persons may not be in favor of redistribution if they expect improvements in their positions, while some of the above median persons, if facing the risk of income loss, support redistribution. People motivated by POUM may expect absolute income gains in the future, or they may expect relative gains as compared to others, with both of these expectations resulting in an acceptance of less redistribution. However, testing the model empirically, Ravallion and Lokshin (2000) found that a very high proportion of Russians in 1996 favored redistribution, including some of the rich. Alesina and La Ferrara (2005) stress that deviations from predictions based on the income position of voters might stem from social mobility experiences. We call these subjective variables *"expectation"* in our analysis.[1]

Human conduct, in addition to financial motives, may also be driven by preferences embedded in the general value systems people endorse. General egalitarian attitudes lead to a critique of the reward system of market economies and a preference for redistribution to correct for failures that the market creates or overlooks. In other cases, in certain regimes (such as in transition countries experiencing a move from communism to a capitalistic social order), the moral authority of the free market may form the basis for inequality evaluations (Kelley and Zagorski 2005). Corneo and Grüner (2002) and Fong (2001, 2006), using International Social Survey Programme (ISSP) data, find that public values (social preferences) also play a significant role in shaping preferences for redistribution. Further, the large literature on the legitimation of welfare states assumes that people have aesthetic preferences for certain arrangements in the social fabric— that is, they also derive guidance from ideological value systems when forming their opinion on welfare state expenditures. Svallfors (1997) shows that while the level of support is related to welfare regimes (Esping-Andersen 1990; Ferrara 1996; Bonoli 1997), the typology itself is of little use in explaining group differences in welfare attitudes. Rather, class divisions and gender explain differing attitudes toward the welfare state across various welfare regimes. (On other aspects of class positions, see Svallfors 1997; Kumlin and Svallfors 2008).

In other studies, greater demand for redistribution is also attributed to cultural values and socialization. Alesina and Fuchs-Schündeln (2005) and Suhrcke (2001) both find significant effects for the East-West dummy variable when regressed on inequality or redistribution preferences.[2] Gijsberts (2002) points out that observed differences in inequality aversion between market economies and the previous socialist countries are not due to differences in social structure but rather to socialization and values. Luttmer and Singhal (2008) draw attention to the persistence of general attitudes toward the state in the case of immigrants. We call these arguments *social context/ values explanations*.

In addition to beliefs about the fairness of the economic system (also assumed to contribute to less demand for redistribution; see Fong 2001, 2006; and Alesina and La Ferrara 2005), a related issue is the popular evaluation of conditions of getting ahead in society. Should people, in general, attribute poverty to lack of effort, support for redistribution will diminish. Alternatively, there can be more support for redistribution when there is a general belief that poverty is the result of bad luck rather than lack of individual effort. Piketty (1995) also derived the demand for redistribution from experiences of social mobility and beliefs about whether effort and luck determine individual success. Fong (2001) observes that preferences for redistribution are influenced by social values and beliefs, particularly on how social agents perceive determinants of poverty and affluence in their societies: do they associate poverty with bad luck or lack of effort? Coming from a different perspective, Alesina and Glaeser (2006) and Osberg and Smeeding (2006) both point out that the personal and social reasons attributed to poverty are significant determinants of inequality evaluations and redistribution preferences. We call these *failure attribution arguments*, referring to the fact that poverty might be explained by private failures (bad luck, laziness, etc.) or by failures of the social system (injustices, exclusion tendencies, etc.).[3]

Macro (Contextual) Aspects

Preferences for redistribution may be conditional upon the general societal context (most notably, on the level of actual inequalities). Greater levels of visible inequality might have an independent effect on a person's preference for redistribution, regardless of where the preferences originate from (aesthetic, solidaristic, or referential). While not necessarily exogenous, arguments about what may affect redistributive preferences include, for example, conditional consumption utility (Duesenberry 1949), relative deprivation (Runciman 1966), reference groups (Merton 1968), and "tunnel effects" (Hirschman 1973). Senik (2005) reviews a great deal of empirical evidence and finds that studies on "comparison incomes" in the Netherlands, Germany, the United Kingdom, and the United States show negative signs. That is, the larger the gap between one's own income and that of the reference group, the lower the satisfaction of income and life prospect will be. However, she cites studies in transition countries, including Hungary, Russia, Poland, and the Baltic countries, showing positive signs for reference incomes (Senik 2006).

Translation Mechanisms: Extending Prior Analyses

A largely institutional question also emerges: how are redistributive preferences of the electorate transformed into policy when actual decisions on public expenditure preferences are formed? Outcomes of the democratic policy formation process (via elections) depend, for example, on differential political participation of both the affluent and the poorer segments of a society (Bénabou 2000) that may lead to either more or less redistribution than predicted by the MR model. Larcinese (2007) argues that the turnout plays a major role in defining electoral outcomes and subsequent public spending priorities (see also Mahler 2006; Lupu and Pontusson 2011; Mahler, Jesuit, and Paradowski 2013).

There are also many contextual differences among the various countries or country groupings in Europe that shape attitudes toward redistribution.[4] The European Union includes countries with a long history of democratic governments, along with countries that have experienced major economic, political, and societal changes in the past few decades. Also, various regions of the European Union have different cultural attitudes toward inequality that might be reflected in cross-country differences between, say, continental European countries and those in the Mediterranean group, between those with more liberal welfare regimes of the Anglo-Saxon countries and the social democratic Nordic welfare regimes. The size and incidence of the welfare state depend on many different parameters of the public decision mechanisms (i.e., on the political system as a whole), a feature that warrants caution for the interpretation of our findings in the subsequent sections.

OPERATIONALIZATION, DATA, AND DEFINITIONS

The data we use come from several large cross-national datasets. For attitudes, we use the 2009 Special Eurobarometer survey on poverty and social exclusion (Reference number: 321, wave: EB.72.1; hereafter: EB.72.1), which contains a series of questions on redistributive attitudes, inequality perceptions, evaluations of social policies, and poverty alleviation instruments applied in the member states.[5] For country-level contextual information (level of actual income inequalities and of poverty rates), we use data from the *Luxembourg Income Study Database* (hereafter: *LIS*).

The Empirical Model Used in the Analysis

As introduced above, our aim is to explore determinants of redistributive preferences; thus, we address three questions in this chapter:

> Q1: At the micro level (individual level), what socio-economic characteristics, perceptions, motivational aspects, and other attitudes drive (or are associated with) the formation of redistributive preferences?
>
> Q2: How do various contextual factors (most importantly, aggregate income inequalities) shape redistributive preferences?
>
> Q3: What effect does the structure of inequality have on the attitudes of the middle-income classes?

We want to predict individual-level redistributive preferences using individual attributes and contextual variables (e.g., country-level inequality measures). To answer Q1 (i.e., about the effects of individual attributes on redistributive preferences), we estimate a simple OLS regression. Because we assumed that observations within countries are correlated in some unknown way, we clustered the standard errors by country in our OLS estimations. To be able to answer Q2 and Q3, we used multi-level regressions.

The Dependent Variable: Redistribution

Redistribution can take many forms. Direct transfers from rich to poor constitute only a fraction of the total welfare state intervention. Governments provide various in-kind benefits (e.g., education, health), lifetime consumption smoothing mechanisms (e.g., pensions, child benefits), and insurance against various risks (e.g., sickness, unemployment), and they use many other forms for spending taxpayers' contributions on various common goods and services. When "redistribution" is mentioned (and measured, for example, by the share of public expenditures in GDP), it is in general the combination of these provisions that is implied (in addition to various other non-welfare expenditures such as agricultural subsidies, costs of various protectionist measures, etc.). In this chapter, we use a complex definition to capture a broader notion of redistribution (within the limits of data availability). In what follows, information from five questions about the state, market, and redistribution are combined into a Redistributive Preference Index (RPI):[6]

1. Answers to the general (conventionally used) statement about the desirability ensuring that the wealth of the country is redistributed in a fair way to all citizens (on a 4-point scale from "totally agree" to "totally disagree").

2.–4. Answers to three questions to reveal agreement with normative judgments on the potential desirability of state involvement in providing jobs for citizens, education finance, and social expenditures (close-ended choices between state and market ends of various trade-off questions).

5. Answers to a question about the general attitude toward the role of the state in providing for citizens versus the citizens' responsibility for their own fates.

We take the first principal component of the above five variables as our dependent variable, RPI (noted above).[7]

Explanatory Variables

Theoretical considerations lead us to differentiate between level 1 (individual) and level 2 (country) units of analysis, where individuals are nested into country-level samples, in a multi-level model structure.[8]

Micro (level 1) variables. The available variable structure of the EB.72.1 makes it possible to reflect some (though, unfortunately, not all) aspects of the potential individual-level determinants of redistributive preference.

The *basic socio-demographic variables* (age, education, gender, location, household size) are self-explanatory. We use these as controls to support the analysis of the effects of the other factor groupings.[9]

The *material status index* is created by combining answers to four questions—a general 10-point scale consisting of the self-assessed evaluation of the material situation, the self-assessed difference between own income and the lowest net monthly income needed for a minimum acceptable standard of living, and the ability to "make ends meet." As these are all subjective assessments, one might think this creates problems for interpretation. We have no alternative because the EB.72.1 contains no objective income variables. More importantly, however, we think it is appropriate to include the subjective variables. Those voting at a ballot are unlikely to have accurate information about the "real" income distribution, or their position within it, so they rely on subjective assessments. While their estimates are likely imprecise, that is all the information they have in both the opinion poll and when casting their vote. Therefore, using subjective assessments to measure their material position is no sacrifice in this analysis.[10] There is also a potential problem with the *"expectations"* variable. As no information on subjective mobility is available, the "12-month expectations for the situation to get better, same, or worse" is not sufficient to measure POUM because the question does not ask about relative comparisons. We have no other choice, so we need to keep in mind its insufficiency of subjective assessments when interpreting the results.

The *failure attribution* variable in terms of poverty is based on a question about why there are poor people. Some of the choices provided—they are unlucky, lazy, and lack willpower, or there is much injustice in the society—suggest how the respondents might attribute the cause of poverty. Also, a question on how respondents view poverty—do they believe the statement that poverty is an "inevitable part of progress"?—was included in this variable.

Within the *social context/values* bracket we have the respondents' general subjective evaluations of the circumstances in their country—poverty is "widespread" in their country; "a lot of tension between rich/poor, manager/worker, young/old, and different racial and ethnic groups"—taken as a sign of frustration with aspects of the surrounding social environments. It is important to note that these are not contextual variables per se, but they are individuals' attitudes/evaluations of the social context.

Finally, *inequality sensitivity* is a 0/1-coded variable indicating if someone "completely agrees" that "income differences between people are far too large." We include this variable last in our models because it may not be independent of redistributive preferences, in part because inequality affects personal well-being (Senik 2005, 2009; Clark, Frijters, and Shields 2007) and in part because in the evaluation of income distribution, there is always a relative comparison element that may be directly related to redistributive claims (Senik 2006; Tóth 2006).

Contextual Variables: Inequality Measures

As perceived levels of inequality may differ from the actual level of inequality, it is important to find out what objective inequality measures correlate with perceptional measures. In an earlier paper (Medgyesi, Keller, and Tóth 2009), we found that specific aspects of the income distribution—for example, the relative poverty rate—seem to be more highly correlated with inequality perceptions than overall measures such as the Gini coefficient. We assumed this might be caused by cognitive factors, such as the respondents' ability to perceive inequality in terms of simple social distances, rather than by complicated welfare and inequality indices. We therefore use distance-based rather than variance-based inequality measures to capture objective inequality, although because of its general popularity in the literature, we also include the Gini coefficient. We decided to use the ratios of the 5th and 95th percentiles to the median and to each other (P50/P5, P95/P50, and P95/P5) to measure distances between the middle, the poor, and the rich (all calculated using the *LIS Database*).[11] We expect this approach to be more appropriate for testing the MR predictions as well, as inequalities in MR are also defined in terms of distances (between the average and the median) in the distribution.[12]

To measure how country-level objective inequality influences people's RPI—that is, to what extent some of these inherently contextual variables impact country differences, after controlling for micro-drivers of attitude differences—we substituted the country dummies in our full model (Model VI) with various kinds of distance-based inequality measures (some of them being sensitive to the upper and some sensitive to the lower tails of the income distribution).[13]

Our assumption is that macro-level inequality will have an effect on preferences for redistribution. However, this may easily work in the opposite direction. This kind of reverse causality works in a "historical" perspective: long-term redistributive tendencies (socialization) in a country might lead to a higher level of redistribution, resulting in lower levels of inequality. We return to this issue later in our analysis.

INEQUALITY, INEQUALITY PERCEPTIONS, AND
REDISTRIBUTIVE ATTITUDES ACROSS COUNTRIES

In an earlier paper (Medgyesi et al. 2009) based on the same EB survey, we found that preferences for redistribution, measured as the share of those who are in full agreement for the necessity of redistributing from the rich to the poor, are strongest in some Eastern European countries, including Hungary and Latvia, while some other former transition countries, such as the Czech and Slovak Republics, report redistributive preferences that are among the lowest in Europe. The share of those calling for government intervention exceeds 70 percent in Greece and Hungary, while it is only around 30 percent in the Czech Republic and Denmark (Medgyesi et al. 2009). The country averages of the composite RPI, the dependent variable in the present analysis, also have significant cross-country variance (Figure 6.1). RPI values are highest in Greece, Cyprus, and Hungary,

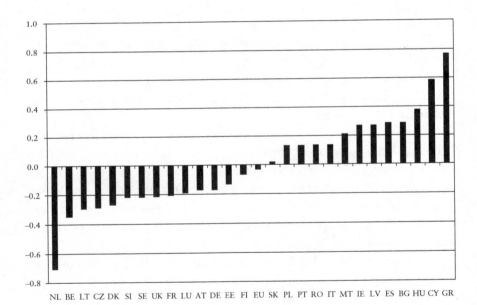

Figure 6.1. Values of the dependent variable (RPI) for EU countries (PCA load scores)

SOURCE: Special Eurobarometer survey on poverty and social exclusion, 2009; EB.72.1; authors' calculations.

followed by Bulgaria, Spain, Latvia, and Ireland. The lowest RPI value is found in the Netherlands,[14] followed by Belgium, the Czech Republic, and Denmark—countries with relatively extensive welfare states—along with Lithuania.

In general, the correlation between RPI and income inequality[15] is sizeable (we present the results on P50/P05 in Figure 6.2). Higher P50/P05 ratios correspond to higher redistributive preference indices, the two extreme

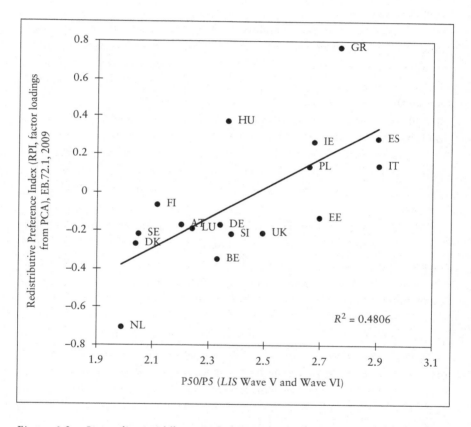

Figure 6.2. Inequality (middle-poor distance) and redistributive preference index (RPI) in European countries (*LIS* Wave V and Wave VI, the most recent available)

SOURCE: *Y* axis: Special Eurobarometer survey on poverty and social exclusion, 2009; reference number: 321; wave: EB.72.1; authors' calculations. X axis: *LIS Database* (Wave VI, around 2004, for countries: AT, DE, DK, ES, FI, GR, HU, IT, LU, PL, SE, UK; and Wave V, around 1999, for countries: BE, EE, IE, NL, SI). Luxembourg: Authors' calculations from the *LIS Database*.

values being Greece (high inequality and high RPI) and the Netherlands (low inequality and low RPI).[16]

In substantive terms, the results show that societies where the income distance between the poorest and the middle is the largest also have the highest demand for redistribution. At the same time, it is interesting that the ratio of rich to middle income (the P95/P50) has only half as large an influence on RPI than has the P50/P5 ratio (Tóth and Keller 2011). Preference for redistribution is thus more influenced by inequality below than above the median.

A correlation between inequality and country-level redistributive preferences does not, of course, necessarily mean that one causes the other; among other possibilities, causality could run in either direction. Persons in high-inequality countries may demand social policy measures, but it may also be that long-term egalitarian attitudes in a country shape the current patterns of the income distribution. If, for example, a country's widespread and long-standing pro-redistribution attitudes provide a supportive climate for politicians offering the electorate extensive social policies, objective income differences will, in the long run, be lower than in countries with less egalitarian attitudes. Determining the direction of causality is challenging, and we can only speculate.

We explored a few possibilities suggested in the literature (see Wooldridge 2009, for example) but found no conclusive results. Our search for an appropriate instrument—a variable correlated with inequality but not with RPI—was unsuccessful,[17] and the experiment with a longitudinal (quasi panel of countries) dataset that would capture change over time was also unsuccessful.[18]

Finding an adequate covariate that captures the reverse impact—from preferences to inequality—could help, so we experimented with two potential candidates for this. The first was a total social protection expenditures variable (SOCEXP, measured in percentages of GDP), which can be understood as a product of past welfare policy in a given country. Should SOCEXP be a good aggregate measure of past redistributive preferences, there would be a positive empirical relationship between SOCEXP and RPI (higher preferences implying higher redistribution). However, this is not the case, as the correlation between SOCEXP, averaged across 1990–2008, and RPI is negative at -0.45 ($p = 0.07$), so we cannot apply this method either.[19] Applying the same logic in another manner, we use a welfare-regime typology (five regimes[20]), assuming that institutionalized welfare regimes are also a product of historic popular preferences expressed through elections. When controlling for welfare regimes, country-level income inequality ceases to be a significant predictor of RPI. However, this estimation is far from perfect, as there may be multicollinearity between welfare regimes and inequality. To conclude: reverse causality is a likely possibility and deserves further attention. Nevertheless, in what follows, we assume that causality, in general, goes from inequality to preferences and not the other way round.

ACCOUNTING FOR MICRO-CORRELATES OF REDISTRIBUTIVE PREFERENCE: ANSWERING Q1

To test the effects of socio-economic factors, we estimate simple pooled OLS regressions (using all available EU member states, with country dummies introduced to control for possible country fixed effects). Unstandardized parameter estimates (B coefficients) for the pooled sample are shown in Table 6.1. The different models reveal how estimates change with the addition of new variables. The first, with country dummies, and the second, with the socio-demographic variables, identify cross-country differences and include several control variables. From Model III to Model VII, additional groups of variables—material self-interest, subjective expectations, failure-attribution attitudes, general social/cultural attitudes, and inequality aversion—are included.[21]

The performance of the basic model (country dummies only) is not very strong, with only 7 percent of the variance in RPI explained. This increases with the introduction of additional sets of variables: in the "full" Model VI, 21 percent of the variance of RPI is accounted for, which, for a model with variables reflecting attitudes, is quite high.

The subsequent introduction of additional variable blocks leads us to a number of findings. The demographic variables reveal significant gender differences in redistributive attitudes: men are much less in favor of redistribution than are women. Age is rarely statistically significant, which is an interesting finding. It should be noted that elements of RPI include jobs provisions, higher education involvement, health care, and social spending, but there is no mention of pensions. Also, while the 61–70 age category contains a different mix of the employed and those out of the labor force,

TABLE 6.1

OLS estimates, dependent variable: Demand for redistribution index (pooled regression for the complete EU)

	Model I Basic model	Model II Demography	Model III Material self-interest	Model IV Expectations	Model V Failure attribution	Model VI Social context/value	Model VII Inequality sensitivity
(Constant)	-0.17***	-0.1*	0.2**	0.12	-0.04	-0.21***	-0.42***
Male		-0.13***	-0.09***	-0.08***	-0.07***	-0.06***	-0.05***
Age: 18–30		0.02	0.04	0.06*	0.06	0.05	0.05
Age: 31–40		0.05	0.04	0.05*	0.06*	0.06**	0.06*
Age: 51–60		0.06	0.06	0.06	0.05	0.05	0.04
Age: 61–70		-0.07	-0.07	-0.07	-0.05	-0.04	-0.05
Age: 71+		-0.06	-0.06	-0.06	-0.04	-0.02	-0.03
Primary education		0.15***	0.09***	0.08***	0.09**	0.09***	0.08***
Tertiary education		-0.22***	-0.17***	-0.16***	-0.16***	-0.13***	-0.12***
Village		-0.05	-0.03	-0.03	-0.02	-0.03	-0.04
Large town		-0.02	-0.01	0	-0.01	-0.02	-0.02
Household size		0	0.01	0.01	0.01	0.01	0.01
Self-employed			-0.19***	-0.18***	-0.18***	-0.17***	-0.16***
Not in work			0.12***	0.12***	0.12***	0.11***	0.1***
Retired			0.02	0.02	0.01	0	-0.01
Student			-0.08*	-0.07*	-0.07**	-0.03	-0.01
Material status			-0.1***	-0.08***	-0.07***	-0.06***	-0.05***
Expectation: gets better				0.04	0.04	0.03	0
Expectation: gets worse				0.24***	0.18***	0.13**	0.12**
Gets better × material status				-0.03*	-0.02	-0.02	-0.02
Gets worse × material status				-0.05*	-0.04	-0.03	-0.03
Poor are lazy.					-0.25***	-0.25***	-0.24***
They are poor because of the injustice in our society.					0.29***	0.27***	0.23***
They are poor because this is an inevitable part of progress.					-0.07**		-0.07**

						17.60% col	20.61% col
Poverty is very widespread.						0.22***	0.17***
Tension between rich and poor						0.14***	0.11***
Tension between old people and young people						0	0.01
Tension between management and workers						0.1***	0.06*
Tension between different racial and ethnic groups						0.03	0.01
Nowadays income differences between people are far too large.							0.38***
Adjusted R^2	6.92%	8.59%	11.11%	11.33%	15.74%	17.60%	20.61%
N	25,988	25,138	24,570	23,631	22,116	22,116	21,899

SOURCE: Special Eurobarometer survey on poverty and social exclusion, 2009; EB.72.1; author's calculations.

NOTE: In each model we controlled for between-country differences because we used country dummies with the reference to Germany. Regression coefficients for country dummies are not included in this table.

Reference categories: female; age 41–50; secondary school; small town; employed; future expectation: the same; poverty attribution: unlucky.

Standard errors are clustered by countries; robust standard error is used.

*$p < 0.1$; **$p < 0.05$; ***$p < 0.01$. All models are significant at the 0.001 level.

depending on retirement age provisions in the country, the youngest age cohort is also quite heterogeneous, depending on the phase of the education expansion process. Considering educational attainment, the more educated are less in favor of redistribution, while the parameter estimates for the less educated are positive and statistically significant for those with only primary education. There are no significant differences between those living in villages and large towns, compared to the omitted category, and those living in cities. Household size cannot be treated as a significant factor in this specification either.

The introduction of material self-interest variables brings about a moderate increase in the variance explained from 9 to 11 percent. The self-employed are less likely to support redistribution than the employed, while those who are not working are more so. Persons with fewer material resources have a significantly larger appetite for redistribution than those in the middle. Those at the higher end show substantially less support for redistribution.

The introduction of subjective expectations brings about a small decline in the effect of the material positions and shows the expected signs. Those who expect a worsening position are more likely to support redistribution. The difference in attitudes between those who evaluate their prospects one year ahead positively from those who do not expect any change is insignificant but in the expected negative direction.

The introduction of the failure attribution variables brings about an additional 4.4 percentage point increase in the variance. Those who believe that the poor are poor because of laziness have much less taste for redistribution, even when compared to those who believe poverty to be caused by bad luck. Those who believe that poverty is a consequence of societal injustice have a much greater redistributive preference.

The variables reflecting the general evaluation of the social context bring another large increase in the explained variance. People evaluating poverty as a problem in the country and/or those who think there are large tensions between the rich and the poor and between the managers and the workers are more pro-redistributive than others. Our estimates did not show perceived ethnic tensions to be statistically significant.[22]

In our last model (Model VII), we added the inequality sensitivity variable. Those who think prevailing income inequality is too large have a very strong taste for redistribution. Since the unconditional correlation between

RPI and inequality sensitivity is quite large (0.26), we do not draw definite conclusions from this result, but it is noteworthy that people with high inequality sensitivity also have a stronger preference for redistribution, with other differences held constant.

REDISTRIBUTIVE PREFERENCE AND MACRO DETERMINANTS: ANSWERING Q2

The Impact of Country-Level Contextual Variables on Redistributive Preferences by Material Status

Knowing that there is cross-country variance of intercepts—the country fixed effects in the previous OLS models—we now examine to what extent country-level inequality accounts for this variance. We investigate whether inequality has an effect on RPI and whether the slope of RPI by material status differs across inequality regimes.

As reported in Table 6.2, inequality measures (see column B) do have an influence on the respondent's RPI. In countries with greater inequality, respondents are more in favor of redistribution. Decomposing the total between-country variance into a part that is transmitted through the different inequality measures and into another that is not reveals (see column G) that between-country differences in RPI can in part be attributed to inequality levels. The proportion of variance explained by between-country differences is reduced by between 13 and 41 percent when controlling for different inequality measures. For example, P50/P5 accounts for around 41 percent of the total between-country RPI differences.

The Relationship between Redistributive Preferences and Material Status in Different Inequality Regimes

To find out how social differentials between high- and low-material-status people in RPI differ across inequality regimes, we estimate the interaction between the country-level inequality and RPI by material status. We classify countries into three inequality groups: Denmark, Finland, the Netherlands, and Sweden, where P95/P5[23] is smaller than 4.77 ("low inequality"); Austria, Belgium, Germany, Hungary, Ireland, Luxembourg, and Slovenia, where P95/P5 is between 4.77 and 6.61 ("middle inequality"); and Estonia, Greece, Italy, Poland, Spain, and the United Kingdom, where P95/P5 is greater than 6.61 ("high inequality").

TABLE 6.2

Multi-level random intercept models using different inequality measures (estimations for 17 countries of the EU)

	A	B	C	D	E	F	G
Model	Inequality measure	Inequality measure's estimated fixed effect	Material status's estimated fixed effect	Estimated random intercept (country level)	Estimated random residual (country level)	Proportion of variance attributed to the random between-country effect (%)	Proportion of between-country random effect transmitted through the inequality measure (%)
Calculation						$D / (D + E)$	$1 - (F / 7.78\%)$
Model VI				0.07***	0.83***	7.78	
Model VI_A	P95/P5	0.17***	−0.06***	0.05**	0.83***	5.68	26.95
Model VI_B	P95/P50	0.69**	−0.05***	0.06**	0.83***	6.74	13.32
Model VI_C	P50/P5	0.72***	−0.05***	0.04**	0.83***	4.60	40.89
Model VI_D	Gini	5.09**	−0.05***	0.06**	0.83***	6.74	13.32

SOURCE: Individual-level variables: Special Eurobarometer survey on poverty and social exclusion, 2009. Reference number: 321; wave: EB.72.1; authors' calculations. Inequality measures: LIS Database (Wave VI, around 2004, for countries: AT, DE, DK, ES, FI, GR, HU, IT, LU, PL, SE, UK; and Wave V, around 1999, for countries: BE, EE, IE, NL, SI). Luxembourg: Authors' calculations from the LIS Database.

NOTE: Restricted maximum likelihood estimation (REML), dependent variable: RPI. For further control variables included in the equations, see Model VI. Regression parameters for all the other control variables are not included in this table.

*$p < 0.1$; **$p < 0.05$; ***$p < 0.01$. All models are significant at the 0.001 level.

We estimate the nonparametric smooth relating RPI to the material status index (using lowess) for the three groups, shown in Figure 6.3.[24] The three curves suggest that slopes differ slightly across these groups. RPI seems to fall more steeply with material status among citizens in the middle inequality group, so the difference between high- and low-income-status respondents' redistributive preferences is larger in this group of countries. In high- and low-inequality countries, the differences by material position are smaller. It is also noteworthy that high-income status respondents in very unequal societies have, on average, nearly the same preference for redistribution as those of low-income status in more equal countries.

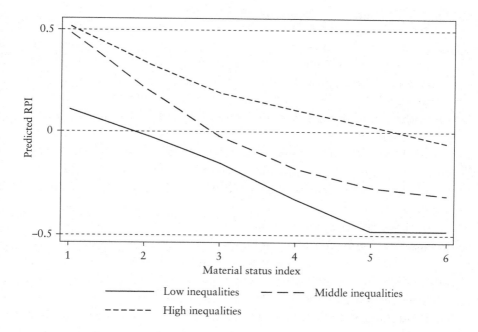

Figure 6.3. Predicted RPI and material status in different inequality regimes—nonparametric lowess smoothing

SOURCE: Inequality measure (95th percentile/5th percentile): *LIS Database* (Wave VI, around 2004, for countries: AT, DE, DK, ES, FI, GR, HU, IT, LU, PL, SE, UK; and Wave V, around 1999, for countries: BE, EE, IE, NL, SI). Luxembourg: Authors' calculations from the *LIS Database*. Material status index: Special Eurobarometer survey on poverty and social exclusion, 2009; reference number: 321; wave: EB.72.1.

NOTE: Authors' own classification based on P95/P5 inequality measure. Low-inequality countries: DK, NL, SE, FI; middle-inequality countries: SI, AT, BE, LU, DE, HU, IE; high-inequality countries: PL, UK, ES, GR, IT, EE.

Using multi-level regression models (Model VI), we estimated the slope of material status in low-, middle-, and high-inequality countries. In low-inequality countries, rich and poor people do not differ from each other ($B = -0.05$; $p > 0.1$), and in countries with a medium level of inequality the differences between rich and poor are larger ($B = -0.1$; $p < 0.01$) than in high-inequality countries ($B = -0.02$; $p < 0.05$).

THE STRUCTURE OF INEQUALITY AND THE VOTES OF THE MIDDLE CLASSES: ANSWERING Q3

The position of the median voter is always relative (to the poor and to the rich). Depending on the actual structure of inequality, the median voter's preferences may resemble those of the higher or those of the lower income groups. Lupu and Pontusson (2011) argue that when income distance between the poor and the middle-income group is small, members of the middle-income group might feel more affinity with the poor (because there is a greater probability for them to become poor). This may motivate them to vote with the poor when redistribution is on the political agenda. When, in turn, the objective position of those in the middle is closer to the affluent, they tend (in coalition with the affluent) to outvote the poor in terms of the redistribution. In other words, for redistributive preference, social affinity with the poor is the inverse of social affinity with the affluent (Lupu and Pontusson 2011).

In this section, we explore the social affinity hypothesis put forward by Lupu and Pontusson by examining how the structure of inequality is related to self-interest—in other words, measured by the impact of material status. We apply the following two-step procedure. First, we estimate the RPI differences between low- and middle-material-status groups on the one hand and middle- and high-material-status groups on the other. All other Model VI variables were included. Material status is recoded into three categories: 1 = low; 2, 3, 4 = middle; and 5, 6 = high. High-status persons are excluded from the analysis when we examine RPI differences between low- and middle-income-status respondents, and those with low status are excluded from the analysis of differences between middle- and high-status persons. We thus ran two separate models for each country. In these models, the coefficient estimates show average differences in RPI relative to the middle class, controlling for all variables included in Model VI. These coefficients are then regressed on the P95/P50 and P50/P5 calculated from the *LIS Database*. We weighted the second-step regressions with the inverse of the standard errors from the first step.

If the data support the social affinity hypothesis, we should observe a positive relationship between the RPI differences between low- and middle-income respondents and the P50/P5 inequality measure because the difference in redistributive appetite is hypothesized to be small in relatively equal societies but large in relatively unequal societies. Following the same logic, the relationship between the high- and middle-income respondent is expected to be negative because, compared to the middle, the redistributive preferences of high-income respondents are smaller in countries where the P95/P50 indicator is relatively high.

Figure 6.4 shows the values of the parameter estimates from Model VI (along with their confidence intervals), against inequality at the bottom (P50/P5) and the top (P95/P50). According to the left diagram, the greater inequality is at the bottom, the smaller the difference is between middle- and low-material-status people. This is not consistent with the Lupu and Pontusson (2011) hypothesis about the affinity of the bottom and the middle. If we examine the left diagram more carefully, we find that in countries where P50/P5 is small, low-income status respondents require more redistribution than those in the middle. However, when inequality at the bottom increases (i.e., relatively larger P50/P5 ratio), the difference in the redistributive preferences between the two groups is eliminated. This finding is parallel to our earlier finding (Medgyesi et al. 2009) and also to the result in the previous section: when inequality rises, especially at the bottom of the distribution, redistributive appetites increase generally (and, therefore, social distances in RPI get smaller). Our findings are robust to both using inequality measures from the EU-SILC database and to grouping the material status variable differently. The coefficient estimate on P50/P5 in the model where we regressed RPI differences between middle- and low-income-status respondents on the two inequality measures (P50/P5 and P95/P50) is −0.24 ($p = 0.02$; $N = 17$). However, we do not obtain the same differences in RPI between middle- and high-status respondents and inequality above the median (P95/P50). (See the panel on the right in Figure 6.4.)

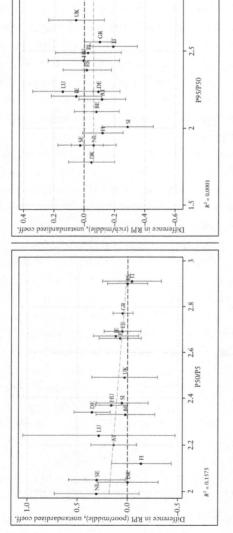

Figure 6.4. Structure of inequality and redistributive preference

SOURCE: Y axis: Special Eurobarometer survey on poverty and social exclusion, 2009; reference number: 321; wave: EB.72.1; authors' calculations.

X axis: *LIS Database* (Wave VI, around 2004, for countries: AT, DE, DK, ES, FI, GR, HU, IT, LU, PL, SE, UK; and Wave V, around 1999, for countries: BE, EE, IE, NL, SI). Luxembourg: Authors' calculations from the *LIS Database*.

NOTE: Parameter estimates (betas) for the middle class versus the low-status groups (left panel) and for the middle class versus the high-status groups (right panel) by the size of inequality at the bottom (left) and at the top (right). The unstandardized regression coefficients are calculated from country-level OLS regressions, using Model VI (see Table 6.1). Material status is recoded into three categories: 1 = low; 2, 3, 4 = middle; 5, 6 = high. High-status persons are excluded from the analysis for the left graph, and low-status people are excluded from the analysis for the right.

CONCLUSION

In this chapter, we analyzed how redistributive preference relates to actual income and to its distribution. To measure the relationship at the macro level, we defined distance-based measures of income inequality (P ratios, based on data from *LIS*) and tested them for their direct and contextual effects on aggregate (country-level) and individual-level redistributive claims. These inequality measures allow reflections of the structure of inequality, as they capture social distances. We argued that for an analysis of people's attitudes across the distribution, we need to use a measure that captures *their* perspectives. This helped, in particular, to identify the relative position of the middle, covering the median voter, whose role may be pivotal.

To measure redistributive preference, we developed a composite index based on an extended definition that captures a broad range of public activities and expenditures, including employment, health, education, and other general redistributive items, apart from the conventionally used redistribution items.

At the macro level, we find there is continued high support for state redistribution in many European countries but that cross-country variation is also high. Preferences for redistribution correspond to several aspects of inequality—most notably, to the extent and depth of relative poverty. Redistributive preferences at the micro level, while mostly derived from rational self-interest—and measured by material position, labor market status, expected mobility—are also driven by attitudes about the role of personal responsibility in one's fate and by beliefs about causes of poverty and the like. This latter factor was found to be one of the strongest individual determinants: the more people believe poverty is caused by personal reasons, like bad luck, laziness, and so forth, the less they support redistribution. By contrast, believing that society operates on unjust or otherwise disliked principles increases the demand for redistribution. This is in line with Piketty (1995), who explained that individual beliefs about the role of effort in social mobility are strongly linked to experiences of upward mobility and thus have an effect on redistributive preferences. Also, our results are similar to those by Corneo and Grüner (2002), who found that, all else equal, those who perceive that hard work is important for getting ahead in life have a lower preference for redistribution.

While the affluent, the middle, and the poor in every country have different attitudes toward inequality, with the "rich" showing less appetite for redistribution, the distance between attitudes also seems to some extent to be determined by the distance between relative positions. In countries with greater overall inequality, redistributive preferences of the rich, the middle, and the poor are higher. However, although the difference between rich and poor is larger in medium-inequality than in high-inequality countries, we cannot draw definitive conclusions on this issue.

The attitudes of the middle-income group are especially important, primarily because of the political consequences of their standing. Redistributive preferences of those in the middle seem to be higher if they live in a society where many people feel poor and only a few feel rich—in other words, inequalities are perceived to be higher in general. Furthermore, when the distance between the poor (P5) and the middle (P50) is larger, the average difference in redistributive preference between the middle and the poor is smaller, along with a general increase in the redistributive appetite. This has implications for both the political process and the theory of redistribution. Simply put, in more unequal societies, especially where inequality is characterized by greater poverty, as opposed to greater distances between the middle and the top, the role of election turnout and of the capability of the political system to translate demand/preferences to actual redistribution becomes more pronounced. As for the theoretical implications, for the MR paradigm to hold, in addition to the objective income situation of the electorate, the self-evaluation of the income skew in general and the median voter in particular should also be taken into account.

NOTES

This paper was prepared in the FP7 project "Growing Inequalities' Impacts" (acronym: Gini; for details, see www.gini-research.org). We are grateful for the comments we received from Giacomo Corneo, Janet Gornick, Dániel Horn, Markus Jäntti, Márton Medgyesi, Jonas Pontusson, and Herman Van De Werfhorst. They bear no responsibility whatsoever for the remaining errors.

1. The extent that POUM will hold is likely dependent on the general risk aversion of various segments of society. The interaction between POUM and risk aversion, for example, accentuates high risk holders' fears of downward mobility, pushing their demand for redistribution higher.

2. Murthi and Tiongson (2008), however, find little evidence for a "socialist legacy" in general.

3. Alesina and Giuliano (2009) point out that respondents may sometimes have conflicting interests and trade-offs within these motives for preferences. We know very little about the dynamics of these, however.

4. Also, subjective, non-economic cleavages and socio-political contexts produce significant cross-country variance in heavily redistribution-favoring regions (regarding Latin America, see Ardanaz 2009).

5. In an earlier paper, we analyzed inequality attitudes in detail in a research note within the frame of the Social Situation Observatory, a regular monitoring exercise of income and living conditions in EU countries (see Medgyesi et al. 2009).

6. The questions were Q14, Qa25_a, Qa25_b, Qa25_c, and Qa25_d from EB 72.1.

7. The variance explained is about one-third of the total variance of the five elementary variables. This improves to around 40 percent when excluding the variable on preferences for social expenditures with price tags applied. However, our concept is to measure an overall index of redistributive preference as it occurs in the "real" world (including taste for vertical redistribution, provision of various in-kind services, public provision for education and labor market measures, etc.). This, however, is a difficult trade-off. Clearly, RPI combines various policy measures with very different potential distributional implications, catching the preferences of very different social groups. However, at this stage, because we want to capture an overall demand for state redistribution, we stick to a broader definition. Should the issue be an attempt for reforms, where politicians start communicating packages with trade-offs between the various expenditure items, a more refined categorization might be warranted. The strongest correlate (with RPI) is the question on the general requirement that the state has a duty to provide for its citizens to a maximum extent ($r = 0.74$).

8. See Snijders and Bosker (1999) and Snijders (2003). Notations here follow those suggested by Snijders (2003).

9. In EB, unlike in many other opinion surveys, the bottom age limit is set at 15. This clearly causes problems for interpretation. However, we excluded those between the ages of 15 and 18. We limited the problem, but this does not fully solve it.

10. The relationship between subjectively defined material status on the one hand and the RPI on the other hand might transmit influences in both ways. The main assumption of the "material self-interest" argument is that people with lower levels of economic resources will demand higher levels of redistribution. But what if a general attitude toward larger state involvement makes people say they are in worse economic conditions than they actually are? In this case, the causality goes the other way round. Besides registering this type of endogeneity problem, we cannot offer really good treatment to this in the context of the current chapter.

11. Lancee and Werfhorst (2010) suggest a measure to calculate the mean distance from the median income (MDMI). However, because it combines

distance and variance and does not simply measure the distance of the median from the extremes, it seems too complex for our purposes. After considering P90/P10, P90/P50, and P50/P10, we preferred measures with a larger variance and a higher covariance with RPI. The measures we used would certainly be more risky when measuring income distribution differences, but for the current purpose (i.e., to serve as right-hand variables), there is no risk.

12. Lupu and Pontusson (2011) also argue that for the formulation process of redistributive preferences, much depends on the distances between the middle class and the upper and lower tails of the distribution. Once the distance between the median and the lower half of income distribution is small, middle-class people feel more affinity to the poor and vote for more redistribution, compared to the rich. On the contrary, if the distance between the middle class and the upper half of the income distribution is small, middle-class people join the rich in voting for less redistribution (contra the poor). We turn back to this later in the analysis.

13. Note that because every inequality measure comes from the *LIS Database*, only 17 of the EU27 countries remain in the analysis. Countries from *LIS* Wave VI are AT, DE, DK, ES, FI, GR, HU, IT LV, PL, SE, UK, and countries from *LIS* Wave V are BE, EE, IE, NL, and SI.

14. This comes partly from the very low level of agreement of the Dutch to the statement "Government should take more responsibility to ensure that everyone is provided for." Taking this variable out of RPI would decrease the level of the Dutch "anti-redistributive" attitudes, but otherwise it would not fundamentally change the country ranking.

15. We refer to data from *LIS* Waves V and VI (whichever is more recent for the various European countries for which we have attitude data).

16. For various other inequality measures, we found that the fit of the regression of P95/P5 on RPI (country averages) is somewhat larger than that of Gini on RPI, a feature probably due to the fact that while the Gini, as a measure, is balanced and symmetrical, the other inequality measure is more sensitive to alterations in the skew and to changes at the two tails of the distribution.

17. Running regressions with a good instrumental variable—which correlates with inequality but not correlated with RPI—on which the chosen inequality measure could be regressed and then using the predicted value to sort out reverse causality directions could be helpful. However, as we did not find such an instrument, we could not employ the appropriate method (two-staged least square estimations).

18. To explore this, we had to use other datasets to substitute RPI with the percentage of those who "totally agreed" with the statement that "government should reduce differences in income levels" coming from the European Social Survey (ESS) round 3 (2006) and round 4 (2008), and we collected time period S80/S20 data from published Eurostat EU-SILC indicators. However, we could collect data for only 16 European countries, and in the case of Hungary there was an unrealistically large change in the S80/S20 indicator, while in Bulgaria there was

a more than 15 percentage point increase in RPI. We considered this too large a data shift (as a kind of measurement error or noise), so we discontinued this experiment.

19. However, we have to emphasize that although the connection between SOCEXP 2008 and RPI is not significant ($r = -0.24$; $p = 0.35$), averaging SOCEXP in a larger time period would result in statistically significant coefficients. (Averaging SOCEXP between 1997 and 2008 would result in a -0.42 correlation coefficient with RPI ($p = 0.1$).) We conclude that reverse causality might be a problem to be addressed later.

20. These variables correspond to the conventional classification originated from Esping-Andersen's seminal work (1990) on the three worlds of welfare capitalism, but we combine a territorial division with the original typology, adding the post-transition countries (CEE and Baltics as well), but also the countries from the Mediterranean tier (see Ferrara 1996; Bonoli 1997; Boeri 2002 for more on these typologies). Anglo-Saxon: UK, IE; East European (ex-communist): EE, HU, PL, SI; Continental: AT, DE, NL, BE, LU; Mediterranean: ES, IT, GR; Scandinavian: DK, FI, SE.

21. We checked for multicollinearity, but VIF is always under the critical value, even in Model VII.

22. Starting from Alesina, Glaeser, and Sacerdote (2001), country-level racial heterogeneity is increasingly offered to explain the cross-country (mostly between Europe and U.S.) differences in size of redistribution and of welfare states, the causal link being attached to the popular belief that racial minorities benefit disproportionately from welfare expenditures (see also Dahlberg, Edmark, and Lundquist 2011; Mau 2007). To proxy the perceived problems caused by ethnic heterogeneity, we aggregated a question: there is a "lot of tension" between "different racial and ethnic groups" (QA 15_4) to arrive at a country-level variable. At this level we found a negative (but not significant) correlation between RPI and ethnic tensions ($r = -0.17$; $p = 0.39$). The direction of the correlation is, however, in line with the predictions: the higher the perceived tension between ethnic groups, the less redistribution that will be desired. When, in addition to the set of other control variables (all as in Model VI) of our multivariate model, we include the country-level aggregated ethnic tension ($B = -1.02$; $p = 0.21$), the sign of the individual-level ethnic tension variable was negative ($B = -0.38$; $p > 0.001$) and their interaction ($B = 1.05$; $p > 0.001$) was significant and positive, indicating that a high level of perceived ethnic tensions will lead to decreased redistributive taste, with higher tensions predicting more widespread consensus on it.

23. We use this indicator for the presentation because of its larger variance. We tested the other three, but the selection does not bias the main messages.

24. "Lowess" (locally weighted nonparametric regression) estimates of coefficients localize subsets in the dataset and gradually develop a function that best explains the variation in the data points. We predict RPI with various inequality measures for breakdowns by the respondents' material status.

REFERENCES

Alesina, Alberto, and Nicola Fuchs-Schündeln. 2005. "Good Bye Lenin (or Not?): The Effect of Communism on People's Preferences." Working paper 11700. Cambridge, MA: National Bureau of Economic Research (NBER).

Alesina, Alberto, and Paula Giuliano. 2009. "Preferences for Redistribution." Working paper 14825. Cambridge, MA: National Bureau of Economic Research (NBER).

Alesina, Alberto, and Edward Glaeser. 2006. *Fighting Poverty in the U.S. and Europe: A World of Difference.* Oxford: Oxford University Press.

Alesina, Alberto, Edward Glaeser, and Bruce Sacerdote. 2001. "Why Doesn't the United States Have a European-Style Welfare State?" *Brookings Papers on Economic Activity* 2. Washington, DC: Brookings Institution.

Alesina, Alberto, and Eliana La Ferrara. 2005. "Preferences for Redistribution in the Land of Opportunities." *Journal of Public Economics* 89(5–6): 897–931.

Ardanaz, Martin. 2009 "Preferences for Redistribution in the Land of Inequalities." Unpublished manuscript. Columbia University, New York.

Bénabou, Ronald. 2000. "Unequal Societies: Income Distribution and the Social Contract." *American Economic Review* 90(1): 96–129.

Bénabou, Ronald, and Efe Ok. 2001. "Social Mobility and the Demand for Redistribution: The Poum Hypothesis." *Quarterly Journal of Economics* 116(2): 447–87.

Boeri, Tito. 2002. "Let Social Policy Models Compete and Europe Will Win." Paper presented to a conference at the John F. Kennedy School of Government, Harvard University. Cambridge, MA (April 11–12, 2002).

Bonoli, Giuliano. 1997. "Classifying Welfare States: A Two-Dimension Approach." *Journal of Social Policy* 26: 351–72.

Borck, Rainald. 2007. "Voting, Inequality and Redistribution." *Journal of Economic Surveys* 21(1): 90–109.

Clark, Andrew E., Paul Frijters, and Michael A. Shields. 2007. "Relative Income, Happiness and Utility: An Explanation for the Easterlin Paradox and Other Puzzles." *Journal of Economic Literature* 46(1): 95–144.

Corneo, Giacomo, and Hans Peter Grüner. 2002. "Individual Preferences for Political Redistribution." *Journal of Public Economics* 83: 83–107.

Dahlberg, Matz, Karin Edmark, and Heléne Lundquist. 2011. "Ethnic Diversity and Preferences for Redistribution." *Department of Economics* working paper 2011:1. Uppsala, Sweden: Uppsala University, Center for Labor Studies.

Duesenberry, James. 1949. *Income, Savings and the Theory of Consumer Behavior (Economic Studies No. 87).* Cambridge, MA: Harvard University Press.

Esping-Andersen, Gosta. 1990. *The Three Worlds of Welfare Capitalism.* Princeton, NJ: Princeton University Press.

European Commission. 2009. Special Eurobarometer Survey on Poverty and Social Exclusion. Reference number: 321, wave: EB.72.1. http://ec.europa.eu/public_opinion/archives/eb_special_339_320_en.htm.

Ferrara, Maurizio. 1996. "The Southern Model of Welfare in Social Europe." *Journal of European Social Policy* 6(1): 17–37.

Fong, Christina M. 2001. "Social Preferences, Self-Interest, and the Demand for Redistribution." *Journal of Public Economics* 82(2): 225–46.

———. 2006. "Prospective Mobility, Fairness, and the Demand for Redistribution." *Department of Social and Decision Sciences* working paper. Pittsburgh: Carnegie Mellon University.

Gijsberts, Merove. 2002. "The Legitimation of Income Inequality in State-Socialist and Market Societies." *Acta Sociologica* 45(4): 269–85.

Hirschman, Albert O. 1973. "Changing Tolerance for Income Inequality in the Course of Economic Development." *Quarterly Journal of Economics* 87(4): 544–66.

Keely, Louise C., and Chih M. Tan. 2008. "Understanding Preferences for Income Redistribution" *Journal of Public Economics* 92(5–6): 944–61.

Kelley, Jonathan, and Krzysztof Zagorski. 2005. "Economic Change and the Legitimation of Inequality: The Transition from Socialism to the Free Market in Central-East Europe." In *Research in Social Stratification and Mobility*, Vol. 22, edited by David B. Bills. Oxford: Elsevier.

Kenworthy, Lane, and Leslie McCall. 2007. "Inequality, Public Opinion, and Redistribution." *LIS* working paper 459. Luxembourg: LIS.

Kumlin, Staffan, and Stefan Svallfors. 2008. "Social Stratification and Political Articulation: Why Attitudinal Class, Differences Vary Across Countries." *LIS* working paper 484. Luxembourg: LIS.

Lancee, Bram, and Herman Werfhorst. 2010. "Inequality and Participation: A Comparison of 24 European Countries." *Gini Discussion Paper* 6. Amsterdam: AIAS.

Larcinese, Valentino. 2007. "Voting over Redistribution and the Size of the Welfare State: The Role of Turnout." *Political Studies* 55(3): 568–85.

Lupu, Noam, and Jonas Pontusson. 2009. "The Structure of Inequality and Demand for Redistribution." Paper presented at the Conference on Inequality and Institutions. Oxford (May 8–9, 2009).

———. 2011. "The Stucture of Inequality and the Politics of Redistribution." *American Political Science Review* 105(2): 316–36.

Luttmer, Erzo, and Monica Singhal. 2008. "Culture, Context, and the Taste for Redistribution." Working paper 14268. Cambridge, MA: National Bureau of Economic Research (NBER).

Luxembourg Income Study (LIS) Database, http://www.lisdatacenter.org (multiple countries; microdata last accessed in July 2011). Luxembourg: LIS.

Mahler, Vincent A. 2006. "Electoral Turnout and Income Redistribution by the State: A Cross-National Analysis of the Developed Democracies." *LIS* working paper 455. Luxembourg: LIS.

Mahler, Vincent A., David K. Jesuit, and Piotr R. Paradowski. 2013. "Political Sources of Government Redistribution in High-Income Countries." Chapter 5 in this book.

Mau, Steffen. 2007. "Ethnic Diversity and Welfare State Solidarity in Europe." Paper prepared for the AGF Midpoint Conference. Berlin (November 29–30, 2007).

McCarty, Nolan, and Jonas Pontusson. 2009. "The Political Economy of Inequality and Redistribution." In *The Oxford Handbook of Economic Inequality*, edited by Wiemer Salverda, Brian Nolan, and Timothy M. Smeeding. Oxford: Oxford University Press.

Medgyesi, Márton, Tamás Keller, and István György Tóth. 2009. "Analysing the Link between Measured and Perceived Income Inequality in European Countries." *The Network on Income Distribution and Living Conditions of the European Observatory on the Social Situation and Demography* research note 8. Brussels: European Commission.

Meltzer, Allan H., and Scott F. Richard. 1981. "A Rational Theory of the Size of Government." *Journal of Political Economy* (89)5: 914–27.

Merton, Robert K. 1968. *Social Theory and Social Structure*. Glencoe, IL: Free Press.

Murthi, Mamta, and Erwin R. Tiongson. 2008. "Attitudes to Equality: The 'Socialist Legacy' Revisited." *The World Bank Policy Research* working paper 4529. Washington, DC: World Bank.

Osberg, Lars, and Timothy M. Smeeding. 2006. "'Fair' Inequality? Attitudes toward Pay Differentials: The United States in Comparative Perspective." *American Sociological Review* 71(3): 450–73.

Piketty, Thomas. 1995. "Social Mobility and Redistributive Politics." *Quarterly Journal of Economics* 110(3): 551–84.

Ravallion, Martin, and Michael Loskhin. 2000. "Who Wants to Redistribute? The Tunnel Effect in 1990s Russia." *Journal of Public Economics* 76: 87–104.

Runciman, Garry W. 1966. *Relative Deprivation and Social Justice*. London: Routledge and Kegan Paul.

Senik, Claudia. 2005. "Income Distribution and Well-Being: What Can We Learn from Subjective Data?" *Journal of Economic Surveys* 19(1): 43–63.

———. 2006. "Ambition and Jealousy: Income Interactions in the 'Old' Europe versus the 'New' Europe and the United States." Discussion paper 2083. Bonn, Germany: Institute for the Study of Labor (IZA).

———. 2009. "Income Distribution and Subjective Happiness: A Survey." *OECD Social, Employment and Migration* working paper 96. Paris: OECD.

Snijders, Tom A. B. 2003. "Multilevel Analysis." In *The SAGE Encyclopedia of Social Science Research Methods*, Vol. 2, edited by Michael Lewis-Beck, Alan E. Bryman, and Tim F. Liao. New York: Sage.

Snijders, Tom A. B., and Roel Bosker. 1999. *Multilevel Analysis: An Introduction to Basic and Advanced Multilevel Modeling*. New York: Sage.

Suhrcke, Marc. 2001. "Preferences for Inequality. East vs. West." *Innocenti* working paper 89. Florence, Italy: UNICEF International Child Development Centre.

Svallfors, Stefan. 1997. "Worlds of Welfare and Attitudes to Redistribution: A Comparison of Eight Western Nations." *European Sociological Review* 13(3): 283–304.

Tóth, István György. 2006. "Measured and Perceived Income Distribution: Tunnel Effect, Reference Group Shifts and Skill Biased Transition in Hungary, 1987–2005." Paper presented at the 29th IARIW General Conference. Joensuu (August 20–26, 2006).

———. 2008. "The Demand for Redistribution: A Test on Hungarian Data" *Sociologický časopis/Czech Sociological Review* 44(6): 491–509.

Tóth, István György, and Tamás Keller. 2011. "Income Distributions, Inequality Perceptions and Redistributive Claims in European Societies." *Gini Discussion Paper* 7. Amsterdam: AIAS. http://www.gini-research.org/system/uploads/244/original/DP_7_-_Toth_Keller.pdf?1301398757

Wooldridge, Jeffrey M. 2009. *Introductory Econometrics: A Modern Approach.* Lexington, KY: South Western Cengage Learning.

Part IV

EMPLOYMENT: WOMEN'S WORK, INEQUALITY, AND THE ECONOMIC STATUS OF FAMILIES

CHAPTER SEVEN

Women's Employment and Household Income Inequality

Susan Harkness

While recent decades have seen rapid growth in female employment across all industrialized countries, significant differences remain. Employment rates, estimated using *LIS* data, range from just 50 percent in Greece, Italy, and Spain to over 80 percent in Denmark and 90 percent in Sweden. At the same time, income inequality has been rising in most countries, but, again, marked differences exist (Esping-Andersen 2007). This chapter looks at how rising female employment has influenced the overall growth in earnings inequality across couples. It looks first at how the economic role of women in couples varies across countries and at how this role differs for those at the bottom, middle, and top of the income distribution. It then goes on to look at how differences in female employment and earnings across countries influence the level of earnings inequality.

Using *Luxembourg Income Study (LIS)* data for 17 industrialized countries, I found a high degree of homogeneity among middle-earning families across countries. I also found that women are increasingly participating in the labor market alongside men in most developed countries (with the exception of southern Europe), although hours and earnings differences between men and women remain substantial everywhere. Among low-income women with partners, there is much greater heterogeneity in employment and earnings. Assessing the influence of female earnings on inequality, I found that female employment is an important factor in reducing earnings inequality across couples in all countries. I believe that boosting employment would further reduce inequality, and this would have a greater effect than eliminating the gender pay gap.

This chapter reviews the literature and describes broad trends in female employment and inequality across countries. Data and methods for determining trends are described. Data from the *Luxembourg Income Study (LIS) Database* are used to assess cross-country differences in couples' employment patterns and income composition, examining in particular differences among middle-income couples. The importance of employment and earnings on overall earnings inequality among couples is assessed, and various counterfactals that show how changes in female employment and earnings may influence the overall distribution of couples' earnings are considered.

LITERATURE REVIEW AND BACKGROUND

Literature Review

There is a large and growing literature on cross-national variation in inter-household income inequality (see, for example, Gottschalk and Smeeding 1997; Atkinson and Brandolini 2001; Rainwater and Smeeding 2003; Smeeding 2004; Brandolini and Smeeding 2008), with recent studies suggesting that rising inequality has been widespread (Esping-Andersen 2007).[1] Key drivers of increasing income inequality have included growing wage inequality, unemployment, and an increasing polarization of households into the "work-rich" and "work-poor" (Gottschalk 1997; Gregg and Wadsworth 2001). Some studies have suggested that as the rise in male wage inequality has tended to mirror the rise in household income inequality, male wages may have been the dominant factor driving rising income inequality. More recently, Gottschalk and Danziger (2005) showed that were it not for other changes—in female earnings inequality and hours of work, in particular—income inequality would have risen even more.

Alongside rising male wage inequality, a second key economic trend has been the growth in female employment across industrialized countries. Yet, the roles of female employment and earnings in shaping household income inequality remain relatively under-explored. Many studies have examined cross-country variation in gender pay inequalities, including several that used *LIS* data. These find that although women do worse than men in the labor market and are more likely to be in poverty in nearly every *LIS* country surveyed, for every time period, outcomes vary enormously across countries (see Gornick 2004 for a review). Yet, substantial differences in employment rates and pay gaps across countries exist, too,[2] and there is evidence of growing inequality among women in terms of both employment and earnings (Blau and Kahn 2007). Several studies have looked at the influence of income components on overall inequality (for example, Shorrocks 1983; Lerman and Yitzhaki 1985; Jenkins 1995; Lam 1997; Jäntti 1997; Cancian and Reed 1998; and more recently, Breen, García-Peñalosa, and Orgiazzi 2008). These suggest that growing earnings inequality has been a major source of rising inter-household income inequality. This is in part a result of rising wage inequality among those in the workforce. However, in some countries, unemployment and inactivity matter more. In the United Kingdom, for example, there is evidence of increasing polarization of work across households, with wives of employed men being more likely to work than wives of the unemployed, and non-employment being particularly high among single-adult and, in particular single-parent households (Gregg and Wadsworth 2001). There is also evidence of an increasing correlation between the employment behaviors and earnings of husbands and wives (for the United States, see Lam 1997 and Cancian and Reed 1998, 1999; Reed and Cancian 2001; for cross-national evidence, see Esping-Andersen 2007), while in the United States, there is evidence that marriage is more common among high-earning men (Burtless 1996). These trends all have implications for the distribution of household income.

The evidence on the actual contribution of women's earnings to income inequality is mixed, with results varying depending on the measure of income used, the sample covered, and the country studied. The earliest studies for the United States found a negative relationship between husbands' earnings and wives' labor supply, with wives' earnings exerting a small equalizing effect on the distribution of household income across couples (Danziger 1980). More recent studies found similarly equalizing effects among married couples using U.S. data for the 1970s and 1980s (see, for example, Cancian, Danziger, and Gottschalk 1992; Cancian and Reed 1998). When the sample is extended to look at all households—those including single adults and married couples—Shorrocks (1983), Lerman and Yitzhaki (1985), and more recently Karoly and Burtless (1995) found an increasing correlation between husbands' and wives' earnings over time. This means female pay has exerted an increasingly dis-equalizing effect on the distribution of household income from 1979 onward. But Cancian and

Reed (1999), again looking at all families (single and married), find that despite a rise in the correlation between husbands' and wives' earnings, wives' earnings explain only a small part of the observed overall rise in family income inequality. They attribute the difference between their results and those of Karoly and Burtless partly to the time period used, but more importantly to the use of the Gini decomposition, a technique that, they argue, does not adequately separate married and single people and does not fully decompose inequality by income source.

Using similar comparisons to Cancian and Reed's 1999 study—which contrasts actual household inequality with that which would exist in the absence of female earnings—several studies find similar equalizing effects for couples in Italy (Del Boca and Pasqua 2003), Norway (Birkelund and Mastekaasa 2011), and the United Kingdom (Harkness, Machin, and Waldfogel 1997). Harkness and colleagues' findings contrast with Jenkins's (1995) results that used earlier data (for the 1970s and 1980s) and, using the Shorrocks decomposition (discussed in greater detail in the following section), found rising wives' employment to have an increasingly dis-equalizing effect on household inequality across all families.[3]

Cross-nationally, Cancian and Schoeni (1998) used *LIS* data from the late 1970s/early 1980s to look at the contribution of female earnings to total earnings inequality across working-age couple-headed households. They found wives' earnings to have a mitigating effect on inequality in all ten countries studied, in spite of wide variations in employment and earnings shares.[4] This equalizing effect occurred even though spouses' earnings were increasingly (positively) correlated—tending to raise levels of inequality—as this effect was offset by the increasing levels of wives' wage inequality and their rising income shares. As a result, the overall effect of spouses' earnings on inequality tended to become more equalizing with time.[5] More recently, Pasqua (2008), using European Community Household Panel (ECHP) data, showed that rising female employment has tended to reduce inequality across couples. She also found, as in other studies, that male wage inequality explains the major part of income inequality in all countries. This is in line with Reed and Cancian's (2001) conclusion that to understand the causes of rising family income inequality over the last three decades, one should concentrate on the causes of rising male wage inequality. Using similar methods, Esping-Andersen (2007) used the difference between the variance of total earnings and the variance of male earnings to estimate the impact of female earnings on overall (couple) family earnings inequality.[6] Using ECHP data for 1993 and 2001, he finds a positive correlation between the earnings and employment of husbands and wives for all countries except Germany (where the labor supply was positively but the earnings were negatively correlated). Comparing the variance of total earnings and husbands' earnings, he concludes that wives' earnings increased inequality among couples in France, Germany, Italy, Spain, and the United Kingdom, but were equalizing for the United States, Sweden, and, in 2001 only, Denmark.[7] These findings contrast with several of those reported in other studies and described above.

These cross-country comparisons all look at couples only. A growing number of studies, using a variety of methods, have looked at how demographic change has affected inequality—both within and across countries. Decomposing across family types, these studies suggest that demographic changes, and indeed the rise in dual-earner households, did little to explain rising household income inequality (for cross-country analyses, see Jäntti 1997 and Pasqua 2008; for analysis in the United Kingdom, see Jenkins 1995; for Australia, see Johnson and Wilkins 2003; in the United States, see Burtless 2009 and Gottschalk and Danziger 2005). Indeed, Jäntti concludes that changes in women's hours of work and earnings were more important in accounting for rising inter-household inequality than were changes in female labor force participation. Gornick and Jäntti's empirical work, and their review of the LIS literature, suggest that labor market and social policy institutions are more important than demography in accounting for cross-national variation in child poverty.[8] Nordic institutions, they argue, are particularly favorable to children's economic well-being because they enable wives' employment.

A cursory look at cross-country data on rates of female employment and levels of income inequality confirm the picture suggested above; across countries, there is a clear inverse relationship between levels of household inequality and rates of female employment. Some clear cross-country groupings also emerge, including Nordic countries with high levels of female employment and low inequality, Anglo-American countries with slightly lower levels of employment and high income inequality, central/northern European countries with similar employment levels to Anglo-American countries but lower income inequality, and southern European countries with low employment rates and high income inequality.

A key question, then, is to what extent does cross-national variation in female employment and earnings drive cross-national variation in inter-household income inequality? The studies reviewed above suggest that women with higher earnings power are most likely to work for pay. *LIS* data show that for better-educated women, employment rates are high in all countries, ranging from 75 percent in Spain to over 90 percent in Austria and Denmark.[9] On the other hand, employment rates among the lower educated vary enormously, from under 40 percent in Italy and Spain to over 70 percent in France and Finland. This unequal distribution of work across women suggests that female employment could exacerbate inequality. However, other factors matter, too, and, the following sections assess the impact of these differences in employment on overall patterns of inequality.

DATA AND METHOD

Data and Definitions

The remainder of this chapter uses microdata for 17 industrialized countries from the *LIS Database*.[10] The latest wave of data (Wave VI; the year of data collection ranges from 2003 to 2005) is available for Australia, Canada, the United Kingdom (UK), the United States (U.S.), Ireland, Austria, France, Germany, Luxembourg, the Netherlands, Greece, Italy, Spain, Denmark, Finland, Norway, and Sweden.

Cross-national comparisons of inequality depend crucially on how income is measured (Atkinson and Brandolini 2001; Smeeding 2004; Brandolini and Smeeding 2008). A key advantage of the *LIS* data is that comparable income measures are constructed across countries, allowing inequality comparisons. This study looks at earnings inequalities across working-age heterosexual couple-headed households. The sample includes all couples where the head of the household and the spouse are both between the ages of 18 and 59, although those families where either partner is attending school full-time are also excluded. Households' earnings are measured as the sum of the head and spouses' net earnings.[11] In order to ensure our data are not unduly influenced by very high earnings households in the top percentile group of earnings are dropped. Data are then weighted using household weights.

I define *middle-income* households as those families headed by a couple whose total earnings fall within the middle 60 percent of the couples' earnings distribution. Thus, when considering middle-income households, my analysis focuses on couples who are typical of the countries' population and are neither among the poorest nor the richest 20 percent of couples.

I was not able to identify family units from the *LIS* datasets. My analysis is instead conducted at the level of the household, with marital status defined by the status of the household head. *LIS* data on work hours were unavailable in the Nordic countries, so I was not able to examine differences in "work intensity" for these countries. If working hours were included in the data, however, I reported that information.

To clarify the presentation of the results, four country groupings are used: Anglo-American, continental European, southern European, and Nordic countries. These correspond broadly to Esping-Andersen's (1990, 1999) welfare state regime types, where each regime is typified by similar sets of social policies and corresponding socio-economic and employment outcomes. For example, in Nordic countries, demand from large public sector employers and extensive service provision is expected to lead to high employment levels, while the lowest employment rates are expected in continental and southern Europe, where female employees have historically been marginalized and mothers encouraged to stay at home. Women in Anglo-American countries are expected to occupy an intermediate position, although in some liberal countries women's labor market performance has been strong in spite of a lack of support for working mothers.[12]

Esping-Andersen's typology has been criticized by those who have increasingly turned their attention to gender and the welfare state (Sainsbury 1999; Daly and Rake 2003). Gornick, Meyers, and Ross (1997) argue that Esping-Andersen's clusters "fail to cohere with policies that affect women's employment." In spite of this limitation, the regime types offer the simplest model by which to classify these countries, and it is used here to present the results. The countries included in the analysis, by regime type, are Anglo-American, including Australia (2003), Canada (2004), Ireland (2004), the United Kingdom (2004), and the United States (2004); continental Europe, including Austria (2000), France (2005), Germany (2004), Luxembourg (2004), and the Netherlands (2004); southern Europe, including Greece (2004), Spain (2004), and Italy (2004); and Nordic, including Norway (2004), Sweden (2005), Finland (2000), and Denmark (2004).

Inequality Measures and Decomposition Methods

The measure of inequality used throughout this chapter is half the squared coefficent of variation, which is denoted throughout as I2. This commonly used inequality index equals the variance normalized by two times the square of the mean; $I2 = \sigma^2/2\mu^2$. A common decomposition method used to attribute inequality to different income components is the Shorrock's decomposition (Shorrocks 1982). However, while the Shorrock's decomposition provides a useful tool with which to analyze the contribution of female earnings to total earnings inequality, one problem with this approach is that as long as the correlation of factor income with total income is positive, the contribution of any income component k to total income inequality must be positive.[13] As Lam (1997) clearly shows, this is typically not the case. This can be seen by expanding out the squared coefficient of variation. Assuming two income components, male and female earnings, the squared coefficient of variation for couples' earnings can be written as:

$$C_t^2 = C_b^2 s_b^2 + C_w^2 s_w^2 + 2\rho_{bw} s_b s_w C_b C_w.$$

Here, C_i^2 is the squared coefficient of variation of factor i, s_i is its share in couples' earnings, and ρ_{ij} is the correlation of income components i and j. The contribution of female earnings to inequality thus depends on (1) the share of female earnings, (2) the squared coefficient of variation, and (3) the correlation of female earnings with male earnings. Lam notes, "A common misconception . . . is that if $C_w > C_b$ and $\rho > 0$, then wives' income will tend to be dis-equalizing." Instead, as he shows, income pooling usually leads to an equalizing effect on the distribution of income. A simple example of this is where it is assumed that male and female earnings are equal ($s_w = s_b = 0.5$) with the same covariance ($C_w = C_b$). In this case:

$$C_t^2 = 0.5 C_b^2 (1 + \rho) \leq C_b^2.$$

In this example, as long as male and female earnings are less than perfectly correlated, female earnings exert an equalizing effect on the overall distribution; only when male and female earnings are perfectly correlated will inequality be as great as that when no women work. Therefore, $C_w > C_b$ is a necessary but not sufficient condition for female earnings to increase overall inequality. An imperfect correlation of women's earnings with other income sources will tend to have an equalizing effect on the overall income distribution, and according to Lam (1997, 1026), "This pooling effect exerts a powerful tendency for combined family income to be more equal than the income of either husbands or wives taken separately."

The decomposition approach taken by Lam and described above is used to analyze the contribution of male and female earnings to inequality. The contribution of female earnings shares, male and female earnings inequality, and the correlation of partners' earnings were all used to assess the implications of each of these for couples' earnings inequality. The second part of the analysis looks at how changes in female employment and earnings could influence overall levels of earnings inequality by taking three stark examples: what would happen to total earnings inequality if (1) no women work for pay (female earnings are zero); (2) all women work for pay (wages being predicted for non-workers from a female wage equation); and (3) there is no gender pay gap (female wages being predicted from the male wage equation, assuming employment is unchanged).[14] These exercises are essentially accounting identities and do not take into account behavioral responses. In particular, they embody the strong assumption that male employment and earnings would not change in response to changes in female earnings. While the counterfactuals represent extreme positions, they are nonetheless useful because they tell us by how much and in what direction earnings inequality would change under such conditions.

FAMILY EMPLOYMENT PATTERNS, HOURS OF WORK, AND EARNINGS AMONG COUPLES

This section describes cross-national variation in couples' employment patterns, hours of work, and earnings, looking specifically at middle-income couples. While in many countries unemployment, for example, influences the overall number of women at work and the number of "workless" households, the position of those in the middle of the income distribution can tell us more about the typical economic status of women in couples and about variation in women's economic status across countries.

Family Employment Patterns

Among middle-income couples, there are significant variations in work patterns across countries, as Figure 7.1 illustrates. While in southern Europe fewer than one-half of all couples have two earners, and there are a large

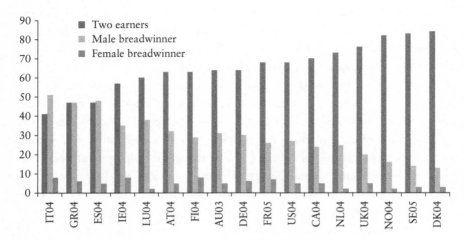

Figure 7.1. Cross-country employment shares among middle-income couples, around 2004

SOURCE: Author's calculations from the *LIS Database*.

number of male breadwinner (MBW) couples (defined as couples where only the man has a paying job), elsewhere the two-earner model is most common. In the Nordic countries (with the exception of Finland), over 80 percent of middle-income couples have two earners. In these countries, the share of MBW families is low at just over 10 percent. Anglo-American countries, with the exception of Ireland, also have a high share of dual-earner families, while in most continental European countries this share is lower. Everywhere the number of families that are middle income and have a sole female earner (descibed here as female breadwinner families) is small.

How are household employment patterns related to their position in the income distribution? Table 7.1 shows household work patterns for those in the bottom quintile group, in the middle of the earnings distribution, and in the top quintile group. Table 7.1 also shows variations in employment patterns among couples across countries for those in the bottom 20 percent of the earnings distribution, the middle 60 percent, and the top 20 percent of earners. Among the poorest households, many families have either no earners or a single earner, while for the richest 20 percent of families, a large majority have two earners (and almost none have a single female earner).

TABLE 7.1

Family employment patterns among the poorest, middle, and top earnings quintile groups (couple families), around 2004

Head and spouse's earnings	ANGLO-AMERICAN					CONTINENTAL EUROPE					SOUTHERN EUROPE			NORDIC COUNTRIES			
	AU03	CA04	IE04	UK04	US04	AT04	FR05	DE04	LU04	NL04	GR04	IT04	ES04	DK04	FI04	NO04	SE05
The bottom 20%																	
Two earners	33	39	14	33	24	38	24	35	22	46	32	24	20	32	25	39	33
Male breadwinner	20	29	41	24	39	21	26	19	35	25	42	41	39	28	29	29	32
Female breadwinner	7	12	1	9	17	15	17	17	14	12	5	5	7	17	11	14	15
No earner	40	21	44	34	20	25	33	29	28	18	21	31	34	24	35	18	19
"The middle class" (middle 60%)																	
Two earners	64	70	57	76	68	63	68	64	60	73	47	41	47	84	63	82	83
Male breadwinner	31	24	35	20	27	32	26	30	38	25	47	51	48	13	29	16	14
Female breadwinner	5	5	8	5	5	5	7	6	2	2	6	8	5	3	8	2	3
The top 20%																	
Two earners	91	92	88	90	80	91	89	82	76	89	87	89	85	99	98	95	99
Male breadwinner	9	8	12	10	20	9	10	18	23	11	13	11	15	1	2	5	1
Female breadwinner	0	0	0	1	1	0	0	0	1	0	0	0	0	0	0	0	0

SOURCE: Author's calculations from the *LIS Database*.

Living in a couple with two earners appears therefore to provide considerable protection against the risk of falling into the lowest income quintile groups, and it is the norm among the most well-off households, even in southern European countries, where the MBW model dominates.

Working Hours

Not only are there significant differences in employment patterns across countries, but hours of work, or work intensity, vary widely, too. Published data show wide variation in the incidence of part-time work across countries. The share of female employees working part-time ranges from 55 percent in the Netherlands, around 40 percent in Australia and the United Kingdom, to just 13 percent in the United States, 16 percent in Spain, and fewer than 10 percent in Sweden.[15] Here, I assess how average working hours vary across countries. Table 7.2 reports working hours for men and women in middle-income couples. Unfortunately, data on working hours are not available in the *LIS Database* for the Nordic countries, and this analysis is confined to the other three country groupings. Among these 13 countries, partners' usual work hours among middle-income families range from an average of 50 in France, 52 in the Netherlands, 54 in Italy, and 56 in Australia to 68 hours in the United States and the United Kingdom. These differences are mainly driven by differences in women's working hours (which range from 14 hours in France and the Netherlands to 26 hours in the United Kingdom and the United States), although variations across countries in men's working hours also matter but to a lesser extent and range from 35 to 42 hours a week. These averages include families where men or women do not work for pay and therefore have zero hours (although our middle-income families, by definition, contain at least one earner).

These averages therefore reflect both differences in participation and hours of work (although, by definition, all middle-income families have positive total earnings). In order to strip out participation effects, I also look at hours of work only among two-earner couples. From these results, it is clear that in Spain and Greece, while female employment rates may be low, women who do work tend to work long hours. Average hours are also relatively long in Anglo-American countries (with the exception of Ireland), Greece, Spain, and France, while in the Netherlands and Germany, women on average work shorter hours. Among couples where both are employed, therefore, work hours are longest in Greece, Spain, and the United States (at 81 hours) and shortest in the Netherlands (65 hours) and Germany (71 hours). The last two columns in Table 7.2 report correlations between partners' work hours for all couples and for those where both partners work (included are couples from across the income distribution rather than just those in the middle of the earnings distribution). Both for the full sample, which includes couples with no earnings, and for families where both partners work, hours of work are positively correlated among couples, with the exception of France and the Netherlands, where those with zero hours are included.

Earnings

Cross-country variation in household employment and hours of work are reflected in the composition of couples' earnings, although the relationship between the two is not always clear-cut. Table 7.3 reports the average female earnings shares in middle-earning couples. The range is considerable: in Luxembourg, the Netherlands, Austria, Spain, and Germany, women's earnings comprise around one-quarter of family earnings, implying that male earnings are on average three times greater (comprising 75 percent of total earnings) than those of their partners. Women contribute most to the family budget in Denmark, Finland, and Ireland, where the female earnings share rises to 40 percent. However, even in these countries, male earnings are on average 50 percent higher (comprising 60 percent of total earnings) than those of their partners.

I also report the share of women in middle-income households who outearn their partners. The results again are somewhat surprising and show that women are most likely to have earnings higher than their partners among the middle class in Anglo-American countries, while women in Nordic and southern European countries also have a high probability of outearning their partners. On the other hand, with the exception of France, the chances of women outearning their partners are lowest in continental European countries.

Studies in the United States have suggested an increasing correlation between the potential earnings of husbands and wives, or greater assortative mating (Burtless 2009). Table 7.3 also reports correlation coefficients for partners' earnings for all couples—those with any positive earnings and those where both partners have positive earnings. The signs of these

TABLE 7.2

Middle-income couples' usual working hours and the correlation of work hours for all couples, around 2004

| | MIDDLE-INCOME COUPLES | | | | | | ALL COUPLES | |
| | Usual working hours (including women with zero hours) | | | Usual working hours (male and female hours > 0) | | | Correlation male and female hours (including zero hours) | Correlation male and female hours (male and female hours > 0) |
	Male	Female	Total	Male	Female	Total		
FR05	36	14	50	39	36	75	−0.059*	0.153**
NL04	38	14	52	39	26	65	−0.023**	0.089**
IT04	38	16	54	41	33	74	0.114**	0.252**
AU03	36	20	56	41	31	72	0.211**	0.065**
CA04	35	22	57	42	34	76	0.254**	0.083**
IE04	39	18	57	43	29	72	0.116**	0.094**
AT04	40	19	59	43	32	75	0.097**	0.191**
DE04	41	19	60	44	27	71	0.068**	0.069**
ES04	42	18	60	45	36	81	0.079**	0.151**
GR04	42	19	61	45	36	81	0.276**	0.143**
LU04	42	20	62	43	32	75	0.139**	0.183**
US04	42	26	68	44	37	81	0.019**	0.038**
UK04	42	26	68	45	32	77	0.203**	0.054**

SOURCE: Author's calculations from the LIS Database.

*$p < 0.1$; **$p < 0.05$.

TABLE 7.3

Women's share of family earnings among middle-income couples and partners' earnings correlations for all couples, around 2004

	MIDDLE-INCOME COUPLES			ALL COUPLES	
	Female earnings share (%)	Percentage of women earning more than their partner	Correlation of partners' earnings (including couples with no earnings)	Correlation of partners' earnings (couples with earnings > 0)	Correlation of partners' earnings (both partners earning > 0)
Anglo American					
AU03	37	27	0.166**	−0.095**	0.133**
CA04	33	25	0.106**	−0.002**	0.158**
IE04	40	34	0.077**	−0.196**	0.111*
UK04	37	26	0.123**	−0.079**	0.140**
US04	32	23	−0.034**	−0.116**	0.030**
Continental Europe					
AT04	28	18	0.061**	−0.103**	0.263**
FR05	35	24	0.175**	0.024	0.301**
DE04	27	19	−0.018*	−0.143**	0.025*
LU04	23	12	0.102**	−0.026	0.323**
NL04	26	13	0.013	−0.125**	0.025*
Southern Europe					
GR04	30	24	0.224**	−0.128**	0.460**
IT04	30	24	0.204**	−0.102**	0.328**
ES04	26	20	0.176**	−0.042**	0.361**
Nordic countries					
DK04	40	25	0.260**	0.102**	0.202**
FI04	40	28	0.227**	0.041**	0.238**
NO04	34	19	0.156**	0.027**	0.142**
SE05	36	20	0.263**	0.150**	0.224**

SOURCE: Author's calculations from the LIS Database.
*p < 0.1; **p < 0.05.

correlations vary across samples; for all couples there tends to be a positive correlation between partners' earnings, although Germany and the United States show small negative correlations. This suggests that in most countries partners' employment statuses are correlated—that is, non-employed men partnering with non-employed women—a correlation that has been discussed extensively elsewhere (see, for example, Juhn and Potter 2007). When only families with positive total earnings are included, however, the relationship is reversed in most countries. The exceptions to this are the Nordic countries and France, where the relationship remains positive. This suggests that, in many countries, women opt out of paid work when their partners earn more. However, the final correlation, which considers only couples where both partners have positive earnings, is positive in all countries. This tells us that male and female earnings tend to move together when both work and suggests assortative mating among working couples.

The picture painted in this section suggests a complex relationship among the three: while participation rates vary across countries, in countries where women work more often, such as in the Netherlands, their hours of work tend to be relatively short and earnings shares relatively low. On the other hand, in countries such as Spain and Greece, where women work less often, those who do work tend to have longer hours and higher earnings shares. For southern European countries, the result is a high degree of inequality among women compared to that in other regions. These differences may have implications for cross-country variations in the role that female earnings play in contributing to overall earnings inequality across couples.

INEQUALITY OF INCOME COMPONENTS AND FAMILY
INEQUALITY

This section looks at how female earnings affect earnings inequality across couples. The decomposition method described above showed that the influence of (male) female earnings on inequality depended on their share of total earnings, the distribution, and the correlation with their partners' earnings. I report these components of the decomposition in Table 7.4, which ranks households by inequality of total earnings and, as would be expected, indicates that Nordic countries have the most equal distribution of total earnings (including families with zero earnings), while southern

TABLE 7.4

Decomposing earnings inequality: Partners' earnings correlations; women's earnings shares; and male, female, and total earnings inequality, around 2004 (all working-age households)

	I2 total earnings	Rank	I2 male earnings	Rank	I2 female earnings	Rank	Female share of earnings (%)	Correlation male and female earnings
Norway	0.122	1	0.179	1	0.265	2	35	0.141
Denmark	0.129	2	0.187	3	0.228	1	41	0.260
Sweden	0.137	3	0.179	1	0.279	3	41	0.264
Finland	0.178	4	0.246	5	0.365	4	43	0.215
Netherlands	0.188	5	0.259	6	0.582	9	26	0.051
Luxembourg	0.194	6	0.235	4	0.819	14	26	0.060
Austria	0.195	7	0.271	7	0.577	8	32	0.064
Germany	0.221	8	0.319	9	0.774	13	23	-0.031
Australia	0.227	9	0.312	8	0.526	7	36	0.167
Canada	0.228	10	0.329	10	0.586	10	33	0.089
United Kingdom	0.244	11	0.373	13	0.509	5	36	0.125
France	0.245	12	0.344	12	0.513	6	37	0.195
United States	0.282	13	0.459	15	0.686	11	21	-0.021
Spain	0.295	14	0.343	11	0.965	15	31	0.158
Ireland	0.301	15	0.440	14	0.730	12	36	0.100
Italy	0.383	16	0.478	16	0.997	16	33	0.196
Greece	0.459	17	0.550	17	1.225	17	33	0.221

SOURCE: Author's calculations from the LIS Database.

European and Anglo-American countries are most unequal. The level of male earnings inequality, as predicted above, is in all cases higher than that of total earnings inequality, while female earnings are more unequally distributed again. Female earnings inequality is greatest in Greece, Spain, and Italy (where there are large numbers of women with no earnings, while among those who do work, hours of work and pay are relatively high) and in Anglo-American countries, in particular the United States, where levels of employment are relatively high but earnings are unequally distributed.

Female earnings inequality is most likely to lead to a rise in couples' earnings inequality when the share of female earnings in total income is high and female earnings are positively correlated with other income. Women's earnings share among all couples ranges from an average of 21 percent in the United States and 23 percent in Germany to 41 percent and above in Denmark, Finland, and Sweden. The correlation of female earnings with male earnings also shows a mixed picture. In the majority of countries, the correlation is positive, with the correlation being greatest and therefore contributing to increasing inequality most in Denmark, Finland, Sweden, and Greece. In the United States and Germany, however, the correlation is negative, although the sizes of the coefficients are small, with wives of lower-earning men more likely to work and therefore exerting a more equalizing affect on overall earnings inequality.

How would changes in female employment and earnings affect overall income inequality? I attempt to answer this question by looking at three counterfactual examples to determine what would happen to inequality if (1) no women work (female earnings are zero), (2) all women work (with wages predicted for non-workers from a female wage equation),[16] and (3) there is no gender pay gap (assuming employment is unchanged).[17] While these examples illustrate what would happen to inequality under extreme scenarios, they are nonetheless informative because they give us an indication of both the sign and magnitude of the potential effect that changes in the pay gap, or increases in female labor supply, could have on earnings inequality.

Results for these scenarios are reported in Table 7.5.[18] Looking at all couples, the first counterfactual shows that if women had no earnings, couples' earnings inequality would increase in all countries by between 20 percent in Greece and 63 percent in the United States. Women's employment therefore currently has an equalizing effect on income inequality in all

TABLE 7.5

Income inequality under three counterfactuals, around 2004

		HALF-SQUARED COEFFICIENT OF VARIATION				
		COUNTERFACTUAL WHERE:				
	Actual	NO WOMEN WORK		ALL WOMEN WORK		NO GENDER PAY GAP	
	I2	I2	Percentage change	I2	Percentage change	I2	Percentage change
Norway	0.122	0.179	47	0.088	−28	0.104	−15
Denmark	0.129	0.187	45	0.083	−36	0.133	3
Sweden	0.137	0.179	31	0.096	−30	0.116	−15
Finland	0.178	0.246	38	0.120	−33	0.191	7
Netherlands	0.188	0.259	38	0.138	−27	0.174	−7
Luxembourg	0.194	0.235	21	0.147	−24	0.168	−13
Austria	0.195	0.271	39	0.123	−37	0.171	−12
Germany	0.221	0.319	44	0.168	−24	0.212	−4
Australia	0.227	0.312	37	0.121	−47	0.206	−9
Canada	0.228	0.329	44	0.160	−30	0.196	−14
United Kingdom	0.244	0.373	53	0.164	−33	0.219	−10
France	0.245	0.344	40	0.159	−35	0.212	−13
United States	0.282	0.459	63	0.219	−22	0.279	−1
Spain	0.295	0.343	16	0.159	−46	0.257	−13
Ireland	0.301	0.440	46	0.166	−45	0.268	−11
Italy	0.383	0.478	25	0.144	−62	0.365	−5
Greece	0.459	0.550	20	0.184	−60	0.440	−4

SOURCE: Author's calculations from the LIS Database.

countries. The second counterfactual considers what would happen to inequality if all women worked. I do this by imputing wages for non-working women from the estimated country-specific female wage equations. Under this scenario, total earnings inequality would fall in all countries by between 22 and 24 percent in Germany, Luxembourg, and the United States to over 60 percent in Greece and Italy. This counterfactual also suggests that female pay exerts a strongly equalizing force on household earnings inequality. Moreover, the effects tend to be larger in those countries where female employment is currently low and their earnings, under the first counterfactual scenario, exerted a relatively small influence on inequality.

The final counterfactual assesses the impact of closing the gender pay gap on overall inequality, assuming no change in employment behaviors. Closing the pay gap is likely to have less effect on overall inequality if there are large gaps in employment between high- and low-educated women, such as those seen in southern European countries, or if there is a high degree of assortative mating, as in some Nordic countries. A wage equation is estimated for all male household heads and is used to predict wages for all working women.[19] Note that changes in predicted female earnings may result either because of an increase in hourly earnings or because of a change in weekly working hours. This third counterfactual suggests that in all countries except Denmark and Finland, total earnings inequality among couples would fall if the pay gap were closed. For Denmark and Finland, reducing the pay gap increases overall earnings inequality by a small amount. In some countries, such as the United Kingdom, where part-time work is concentrated within low-paid jobs and among relatively low-income families, closing the earnings gap has a relatively larger effect on reducing inequality. However, in all cases the effect on inequality is smaller than that of raising employment participation. Note that this counterfactual assumes no change in female employment.

Contrasting the three counterfactuals suggests slightly different influences of female employment and earnings across countries. In the United States, if women did not work, the effect on earnings inequality would be greatest because rates of participation are currently high, and this, combined with the negative correlation of partners' earnings, means that female work currently exerts a strong reducing effect on earnings inequality. While raising employment further would reduce inequality even more, eliminating the pay gap would have only a small influence on inequality. By contrast, in many southern European countries, low levels of employment and the positive correlation between partners' earnings mean that if women did not work, inequality would rise only a little. Boosting female employment in southern European countries could, however, substantially reduce inequality. In the Nordic countries, where there is a relatively high correlation between partners' earnings, boosting female employment would also reduce inequality. Finally, reducing the pay gap would have the biggest influence in countries where the pay gap is large and/or many women work part-time.

CONCLUSION

Aggregate data show a clear inverse relationship between female employment and earnings inequality. This chapter looks further at this relationship, examining the influence of women's earnings and employment on earnings inequality across couples. Data on working patterns have shown that for middle-income couples, the norm across the majority of countries studied here, with the exception of those in southern Europe, is for both partners to work. Having two earners provides considerable protection against the risk of falling into the lowest-income quintile groups and also substantially increases the likelihood of being among the most well-off. However, even where women have high participation rates, hours of work and earnings remain considerably lower than those of their male partners. Across these countries, in middle-income households, male hours of work are on average between 50 and 100 percent higher than those of their female partners. Similarly, the earnings shares of men are on average at least 50 percent higher than those of their partners in Denmark, Finland, and Ireland and up to three times higher in Luxembourg, the Netherlands, Spain, and Germany.

These results indicate that women with higher earnings power are most likely to work in all countries. However, employment rates among the less educated vary enormously, from under 40 percent in Italy and Spain to over 70 percent in Finland. While this unequal distribution of work across women might suggest that female employment could exacerbate inequality, the findings reported here suggest that this is not the case. In all countries, female employment and earnings tend to reduce earnings inequalities across couples, although in countries where participation rates are low, such as the southern European countries studied here, the effects are smaller. The results also suggest that in all countries increasing female employment could have a very substantial inequality-reducing effect, with particularly large effects where employment rates are currently low. The analysis has also shown that closing the pay gap could also help reduce inequality. However, in all countries, the effect would be much smaller than that of raising employment.

Esping-Andersen (2007) concludes, "Even if women's wages improve relative to males', the profile of female labor supply is such that it is more likely to heighten than to abate inequality. The conditions required for an equalizing effect are quite steep: namely, maximum Nordic-type female participation with a fairly symmetric distribution of work intensity across households." The results in this chapter suggest that this is only partially true. First, as my results showed, closing the pay gap would have only a small impact on inter-household income inequality. Second, in all of the 17 countries studied, the effect of female earnings on couples' earnings inequality was equalizing, and this was true regardless of employment levels. Moreover, it is not the case that female earnings always have the most equalizing effects in countries with high employment rates, although it remains the case that increasing female employment rates and reducing the employment gap between high- and low-educated women would reduce couples' earnings inequality.

Perhaps one of the most surprising findings here is just how much lower women's earnings are relative to their partners across all of these countries, including the Nordic ones. In addition, the Nordic countries tend to have relatively high correlations between the earnings of married men and women. These results suggest that the low levels of inequality seen in the Nordic countries are supported by low rates of wage inequality, not by higher levels of gender equality or equality among women. In contrast, the role of women's employment in the United States is largely equalizing and tends to reduce wage inequality. However, in all countries, raising female employment and reducing employment inequality among women would have a substantial impact on reducing couples' earnings inequality and a far larger impact than reducing the gender pay gap.

NOTES

1. Esping-Andersen (2007) finds that Gini coefficients for gross income grew by 6 percent and 7 percent between 1980 and 2000 in Denmark and Italy and in

excess of 20 percent in other countries, including the United Kingdom, the United States, Germany, and Sweden.

2. However, the correlation between these two measures is weak. For example, in Spain and Italy, the gender pay gap is low, but so too are female employment rates. Petrongolo and Olivetti (2008) suggest that the combination of low pay gaps and high employment rates can be explained by the non-random selection of women into employment: wage gaps are small because women who would have low earnings if they worked are not observed in the wage distribution.

3. Although increasing the equality of wives' earnings helped to reduce inequality, this was offset by both an increase in the share of female income in total income and an increase in the correlation of husbands' and wives' earnings.

4. Countries studied were Australia, Canada, the United States, the United Kingdom, Switzerland, France, Germany, Israel, Sweden, and the Netherlands. Female earnings reduced total earnings inequality by 18 and 26 percent, except in Sweden, where the effect was larger.

5. Indeed, Cancian and Schoeni show that the correlation of spouses' earnings would have to double for the effect of wives' earnings to become dis-equalizing.

6. Where total earnings are more equally distributed than male earnings, the effect of female pay is assumed to be equalizing, with the percentage difference in these variances taken to be the impact of female pay on income inequality.

7. Note that Esping-Andersen's 2007 study uses the coefficient of variation in his analysis of cross-country differences in the contribution of female earnings to inequality. These numbers suggest that earnings inequality has been falling in several countries (including Sweden), contrary to other studies, and that inequality is higher in Sweden than elsewhere. The coefficient of variation is used to measure inequality but is highly sensitive to outliers. The results suggest that outliers are substantially influencing the results, particularly for Nordic countries where income data are register data rather than survey data (and therefore record some very high-income values that are not typically included in survey data).

8. For example, Bradbury and Jäntti (1999) find that variations in welfare state institutions matter but not as much as variations in market income. Rainwater and Smeeding (2003) find earnings and transfers are important in explaining cross-country differences in child poverty.

9. The source is the *LIS* "Gender Key Figures" and "Inequality and Poverty Key Figures." These are available at http://www.lisdatacenter.org/data-access/key-figures/.

10. The analysis is confined to high-income countries. Because employment and inequality may have been driven by different factors than those of interest here, eastern European countries are also excluded.

11. Note that net earnings are estimated for Greece, Spain, France, Ireland, the United Kingdom, Austria, Luxembourg, and Italy. This was done by estimating the tax and social contributions paid on earnings by the head and spouse,

from reported information on taxation, and deducting this from the head and spouses' reported gross earnings. Total taxes paid on earnings are estimated by multiplying total taxes paid by the proportion of household income that comes from earnings.

12. This may be in part due to low levels of employment protection boosting women's labor rmarket positions (see Estevez-Abe and Hethey 2008).

13. Shorrocks showed that for all standard inequality indices, the share of total inequality accounted for by factor k is given by:

$$S_k = \frac{\text{cov}(Y^k, Y)}{\sigma^2(Y)} = \rho(Y^k, Y) \cdot \frac{\mu_y^k}{\mu_y} \cdot \frac{CV(Y_k)}{CV(Y)},$$

where $\rho(Y^k, Y)$ is the correlation of income Y_k with total income Y; μ_y^k/μ_y is the income share of component k; and $CV(Y_k)/CV(Y)$ is the relative covariance of factor k compared to that of total income (see Jenkins and Van Kerm 2009 for further details).

14. Wages are estimated for all non-employed women by imputing wages from a wage equation estimated for all working women. This regresses the log of wages on a quadratic in age, a set of education dummy variables, and dummy variables for being partnered and for the presence of children in the household. To estimate wages when there is no pay gap, I estimate the male wage equation, with the log wage being a function of the same characteristics as previously, and this wage equation then being used to predict the wage that working women would receive in the absence of the pay gap. Note that because hours information is incomplete for several of the countries, this wage equation is based on weekly wages and therefore also implies that there is no hours of work gap among those employed.

15. Source: OECD Labour Market Statistics. Data are for 1999.

16. Wages are estimated for all non-employed women by imputing wages from a wage equation estimated for all working women. This regresses the log of wages on a quadratic in age, a set of education dummy variables, and dummy variables for being partnered and for the presence of children in the household

17. Wages are predicted for all working women using the male wage equation.

18. I also conducted a similar exercise using the Gini coefficient using counterfactuals (1) and (2), which produced very similar results.

19. The wage equation is as described for female wages.

REFERENCES

Atkinson, Anthony, and Andrea Brandolini. 2001. "Promises and Pitfalls in the Use of Secondary Data Sets: Income Inequality in OECD Countries as a Case Study." *Journal of Economic Literature* 39(3): 771–99.

Birkelund, Gunn, and Arne Mastekaasa. 2010. "The Equalizing Effect of Wives' Earnings on Inequalities in Earnings among Households: Norway 1974–2004." *European Societies* 13(2): 219–37.

Blau, Francine, and Lawrence Kahn. 2007. "Changes in the Labor Supply Behavior of Married Women: 1980–2000." *Journal of Labor Economics* 25(3): 393–438.

Bradbury, Bruce, and Markus Jäntti. 1999. "Child Poverty across Industrialized Nations." *Innocenti* occasional paper 71. Florence, Italy: UNICEF International Child Development Centre.

Brandolini, Andrea, and Timothy Smeeding. 2008. "Inequality: International Evidence." In *New Palgrave Dictionary of Economics*, edited by Steven Durlauf and Lawrence Blume. New York: Palgrave Macmillan.

Breen, Richard, Cecilia García-Peñalosa, and Elsa Orgiazzi. 2008. "Factor Components of Inequality: Cross-Country Differences and Time Changes." *LIS* working paper 503. Luxembourg: LIS.

Burtless, Gary. 1996. "Trends in the Level and Distribution of U.S. Living Standards: 1973–1993." *Eastern Economic Journal* 22(3): 271–90.

———. 2009. "Demographic Transformations and Economic Inequality." In *The Oxford Handbook of Inequality*, edited by Weimer Salverda, Brian Nolan, and Timothy Smeeding. Oxford: Oxford University Press.

Cancian, Maria, Sheldon Danziger, and Peter Gottschalk. 1992. "Working Wives and Family Income Inequality among Married Couples." In *Uneven Tides: Rising Inequality in America*, edited by Sheldon Danziger and Peter Gottschalk. New York: Russell Sage Foundation.

Cancian, Maria, and Deborah Reed. 1998. "Assessing the Effect of Wives' Earnings on Family Income Inequality." *Review of Economics and Statistics* 80(1): 73–79.

———. 1999. "The Impact of Wives' Earnings on Income Inequality: Issues and Estimates." *Demography* 36(3): 173–84.

Cancian, Maria, and Robert Schoeni. 1998. "Wives' Earnings and the Level and Distribution of Married Couples' Earnings in Developed Countries." *Journal of Income Distribution* 8(1): 45–61.

Daly, Mary, and Katherine Rake. 2003. *Gender and the Welfare State: Care, Work and Welfare in Europe and the USA*. Cambridge: Polity.

Danziger, Sheldon. 1980. "Do Working Wives Increase Family Income Inequality?" *Journal of Human Resources* 15(3): 444–51.

Del Boca, Daniela, and Sylvia Pasqua. 2003. "Employment Patterns of Husbands and Wives and Family Income Distribution in Italy (1977–98)." *Review of Income and Wealth* 49(2): 221–45.

Esping-Andersen, Gøsta, 1990. *The Three Worlds of Welfare Capitalism*. Princeton, NJ: Princeton University Press.

———. 1999. *Social Foundations of Post-Industrial Economics*. Princeton, NJ: Princeton University Press.

———. 2007. "Sociological Explanations of Changing Income Distributions." *American Behavioral Scientist* 50(5): 639–58.

Estevez-Abe, Margarita, and Tanja Hethey. 2008. "How Policies Affect Women's Economic Position within the Family: Labor Market Institutions and Wives' Contribution to Household Income." *LIS* working paper 505. Luxembourg: LIS.

Gornick, Janet. 2004. "Women's Economic Outcomes, Gender Inequality and Public Policy: Findings from the Luxembourg Income Study." *Socio-Economic Review* 2(2): 213–38.

Gornick, Janet, and Markus Jäntti. 2009. "Child Poverty in Upper Income Countries: Lessons from the Luxembourg Income Study." In *From Child Welfare to Child Well-Being: An International Perspective on Knowledge in the Service of Making Policy*, edited by Sheila Kamerman, Shelley Phipps, and Asher Ben-Ariel. New York: Springer.

Gornick, Janet, Marcia Meyers, and Katherin Ross. 1997. "Supporting the Employment of Mothers: Policy Variation across Fourteen Welfare States." *Journal of European Social Policy* 7(1): 45–70.

Gottschalk, Peter. 1997. "Inequality, Income Growth, and Mobility: The Basic Facts." *Journal of Economic Perspectives* 11(2): 21–40.

Gottschalk, Peter, and Sheldon Danziger. 2005. "Inequality of Wage Rates, Earnings and Family Income in the United States, 1975–2002." *Review of Income and Wealth* 51(2): 231–54.

Gottschalk, Peter, and Timothy M. Smeeding. 1997. "Cross-National Comparisons of Earnings and Income Inequality." *Journal of Economic Literature* 35(2): 633–87.

Gregg, Paul, and Jonathan Wadsworth. 2001. "Everything You Ever Wanted to Know about Measuring Worklessness and Polarization at the Household Level but Were Afraid to Ask." *Oxford Bulletin of Economics and Statistics* 63(0): 777–806.

Harkness, Susan, Stephen Machin, and Jane Waldfogel. 1997. "Evaluating the Pin Money Hypothesis." *Journal of Population Economics* 10(2): 137–58.

Jäntti, Markus. 1997. "Inequality in Five Countries in the 1980s: The Role of Demographic Shifts, Markets and Government Policies." *Economica* 64(255): 415–40.

Jenkins, Stephen. 1995. "Accounting for Inequality Trends: Decomposition Analyses for the UK, 1971–86." *Economica* 62(245): 29–63.

Jenkins, Stephen, and Phillipe Van Kerm. 2009. "The Measurement of Economic Inequality." In *The Oxford Handbook of Inequality*, edited by Weimer Salverda, Brian Nolan, and Timothy Smeeding. Oxford: Oxford University Press.

Johnson, David, and Roger Wilkins. 2003. "The Effects of Changes in Family Composition and Employment Patterns on the Distribution of Income in Australia: 1982 to 1997–1998." Working paper 19. Melbourne: Melbourne Institute of Applied Economic and Social Research.

Juhn, Chinhui, and Simon Potter. 2007. "Is There Still an Added-Worker Effect?" Staff report 310. New York: Federal Reserve Bank of New York.

Karoly, Lynn, and Gary Burtless. 1995. "Demographic Change, Rising Earnings Inequality, and the Distribution of Personal Well-Being, 1959–1989." *Demography* 32(3): 379–406.

Lam, David. 1997. "Demographic Variables and Income Inequality." In *Handbook of Population and Family Economics*, edited by Mark Rosenzweig and Oded Stark. Amsterdam: Elsevier.

Lerman, Robert, and Shlomo Yitzhaki. 1985. "Income Inequality Effects by Income Source: A New Approach and Applications to the United States." *Review of Economics and Statistics* 67(1): 151–56.

Luxembourg Income Study (LIS) Database, http://www.lisdatacenter.org (multiple countries; microdata last accessed in March 2011). Luxembourg: LIS.

Pasqua, Sylvia. 2008. "Wives' Work and Income Distribution in European Countries." *European Journal of Comparative Economics* 5(2): 197–226.

Petrongolo, Barbara, and Claudia Olivetti. 2008. "Unequal Pay or Unequal Employment? A Cross-Country Analysis of Gender Gaps." *Journal of Labor Economics* 26(4): 621–54.

Rainwater, Lee, and Timothy Smeeding. 2003. *Poor Kids in a Rich Country: America's Children in a Comparative Perspective*. New York: Russell Sage Foundation.

Reed, Deborah, and Maria Cancian. 2001. "Sources of Inequality: Measuring the Contribution of Income Sources to Rising Family Income Inequality." *Review of Income and Wealth* 47(3): 321–33.

Sainsbury, Diane. 1999. *Gender and Welfare State Regimes*. Oxford: Oxford University Press.

Shorrocks, Anthony. 1982. "Inequality Decomposition by Factor Components." *Econometrica* 50(1): 193–211.

———. 1983. "The Impact of Income Components on the Distribution of Family Incomes." *Quarterly Journal of Economics* 98(2): 311–26.

Smeeding, Timothy. 2004. "Twenty Years of Research in Income Inequality, Poverty and Redistribution in the Developed World: Introduction and Overview." *Socio-Economic Review* 2(2): 149–63.

CHAPTER EIGHT

Women's Employment, Unpaid Work, and Economic Inequality

Nancy Folbre, Janet C. Gornick, Helen Connolly, and Teresa Munzi

How does the level of women's employment affect economic well-being? Most explorations of this question focus on the distribution of market earnings, especially on the consequences of women's increasing engagement in market work, ignoring the possible impact of changes in the value of women's non-market work. Yet, recent calculations of the market value of unpaid work based on data collected from time-use surveys reveal its significant magnitude: between about 20 and 50 percent of conventionally measured gross domestic product (GDP) (Landefeld and McCulla 2000; Giannelli, Mangiavacchi, and Piccoli 2010). Given that household sector income constitutes roughly 70 percent of GDP, clearly, accounting for unpaid work would increase the magnitude of household income even more. Further, many studies show that increases in the time women devote to paid work are associated with declines in overall household time devoted to unpaid work. A full assessment of the impact of women's rising employment on inequality (see Chapter 7) requires attention to the possible countervailing effects of declines in the value of home-produced goods and services.

In this chapter, we move toward such an assessment in eight European countries and the United States. Focusing on heterosexual married/cohabiting couples, we compare estimates of the level and inequality of household market earnings with estimates of "extended earnings"—that is, market earnings plus estimates of the value of non-market work.[1] We estimate the value of non-market work by applying estimates of average time devoted to household work and child care based on data from the Harmonized European Time Use Survey (HETUS) and the American Time Use Survey (ATUS) to married couples whose microdata are included in the *Luxembourg Income Study (LIS) Database.* We provide lower-bound replacement-cost estimates of the market value of this work and examine implications for several different measures of inequality.

Hours of non-market work are more evenly distributed across households than are hours of market work, vary relatively little in terms of market value, and are negatively correlated with hours of market work. Therefore, higher levels of non-market work in a country have an equalizing effect, with important implications for inter-country rankings of equality that vary according to methods of valuation. Our estimates illustrate a range of possible magnitudes of this equalizing effect. They suggest that failure to take the value of unpaid work into account confounds conventional market income-based estimates of the effect of changes in women's employment on economic inequality.

We begin with a discussion of economic well-being that clarifies our definition of extended earnings and our choice of replacement-cost estimates for the value of non-market work. We then review the two different lines of empirical research alluded to above: studies of the impact of increases in women's employment on the level and inequality of household earnings, and studies of the impact of non-market work on a household's extended earnings. In the following section, we consider some important methodological issues, such as the measurement and valuation of non-market work and the possible implications of differing economies of scale for consumption based on market income versus household production. We next discuss our empirical results. In the conclusion, we explain why our estimates are relevant to broader discussions of the impact of changes in women's roles on inequality in economic well-being.

DEFINITION AND MEASUREMENT OF DIFFERENCES IN ECONOMIC WELL-BEING

Defining Extended Earnings

Economic well-being can be defined and measured in many different ways. Economists have traditionally relied on measures of market income (money that comes into a household) or consumption expenditure (money that goes out of a household), but a growing body of research emphasizes what happens within the household itself (Folbre 2009). The value of household production can be seen as a form of implicit income or as a contribution to household consumption. "Work" can be defined as an activity that, in principle, someone else could be paid to perform. By this definition, the overall amount of time devoted to household work in many rich countries approximates the overall amount of time devoted to market work (Burda, Hamermesh, and Weil 2007, Tables 1 and 2). Further, investments in household capital (housing and consumer durables) are substantial. In principle, most economists agree that household production makes significant contributions to household consumption of goods and services and therefore enhances living standards.

Economists disagree, however, on both theoretical and methodological issues concerning the measurement and valuation of household production. Neoclassical models of household production based on Becker (1965) typically begin with the assumption of household utility maximization and apply that logic to valuation. This approach has two important implications for measurement. First, because time devoted to leisure yields direct utility to households, many neoclassical models assign a value to leisure as well as to household production, providing an estimate of what is often termed "full income." Second, because households presumably compare the utility they gain from both leisure and household production to the utility they would gain from their next best alternative, both leisure and household production are often valued according to the opportunity cost of the individuals engaging in them—typically, the estimated wage in market employment. This approach emphasizes the subjective value that households place on their own activities, yielding a measure of utility that is interesting to compare with direct reports of happiness or satisfaction yielded by new survey methodologies (Kahneman et al. 2004).

This subjective emphasis on utility or psychological well-being can be contrasted with the emphasis on material living standards characteristic of classical political economy, rooted in consideration of physiological and social needs (for more discussion, see Folbre 2008). National income accounts—and related measures such as market income and consumption expenditures—are purely descriptive categories that are not based on any assumptions regarding utility maximization. The same is true of survey measures of household earnings or consumption. These measures are based mostly on market prices, and they do not include any consideration of individual utility in the form of consumer surplus. For this reason, an important study published by the National Academy of Sciences (Abraham and Mackie 2004) recommends that valuation of non-market activities for national income accounting purposes should not include the valuation of leisure time and should be based on the logic of replacement cost rather than opportunity cost. That is, if the household did produce its own goods and services, what would it cost to replace these with purchases of comparable goods and services?

As we shall see, a precise answer to this question is difficult to come by, especially because the value of household production is affected not only by inputs of unpaid work but also by household technology and productivity. Furthermore, the challenge of accurately measuring income available for the consumption of goods and services is not limited to the valuation of household production alone. In principle, a measure of extended income should be based on the sum of after-tax earnings, other after-tax income (including government transfers), and the value of in-kind services provided by the government, including health care, child care, and elder care, as well as the value of home production. Indeed, omission of the value of government-provided services directly parallels omission of the value of unpaid work—most obviously in the case of child care and elder care (Esping-Andersen 2009). Any empirical venture into the measurement of extended earnings requires considerable methodological humility. On the other hand, conventional estimates of well-being based on market earnings alone can be seriously misleading.

The Impact of Women's Employment on Household Earnings

Focus on market earnings is a prominent feature of most research on the impact of women's employment on the level and distribution of economic well-being. Measurement of increases in family earnings is straightforward for married/cohabiting couples because it simply involves the addition of married women's earnings to those of their husbands (the implications are less straightforward for families or couples who are less likely to pool their income). In most high-income countries, increases in both women's employment and their earnings have contributed to substantial increases in family earnings since the 1960s, although assessment of this trend is complicated by countervailing trends in household structure, such as increases in the percentage of families maintained by mothers alone.

A focus on the market earnings of married couples clarifies the issue at hand: as married women have entered paid employment, they have reduced the amount of time they devote to non-market work. The historical record is particularly clear for the United States (Bianchi, Robinson, and Milkie 2006). Thus, it seems likely that declines in the value of unpaid work have partially countervailed increases in market earnings—requiring married-couple families to spend more money on substitutes for previously home-produced services, such as convenience foods, restaurant meals, and child care services. Likewise, differences in the value of unpaid work could confound comparisons of earnings between dual-earner married couples and those including a full-time homemaker who devotes more time than her employed counterpart to services such as meal preparation and child care.

In principle, the methodology applied to analyses of the impact of married women's employment on family market earnings can be extended to analyses of its impact on household extended earnings. As a result, a review of this literature yields important insights, particularly for analyses of effects on inequality. First (and most intuitively), this literature sometimes deploys counterfactuals: what would the distribution of family earnings among married couple households look like if (a) women had no earnings or (b) women's earnings were higher (all else equal). Second, this literature often compares the variance of overall earnings with the variance of men's earnings or decomposes a measure of inequality, such as the squared coefficient of variation, into its component parts, making it possible to compare the impact of changes in the level of inequality among women and men, the inequality between women and men, and the correlation between spouses' earnings.

For instance, in their analysis of changes in family income inequality among married couples in the United States, Cancian, Danziger, and Gottschalk (1993) found that increases in women's employment and earnings lowered market earnings inequality overall, with considerable variation among racial/ethnic groups. Their decomposition of the squared coefficient of variation of earnings showed that greater female employment reduced the overall inequality in women's earnings (because fewer women had zero earnings), an effect that outweighed the effect of increased correlation between the earnings of wives and husbands (a result of assortative mating, especially more highly educated women married to more highly educated men).

Similarly, Cancian and Schoeni (1992), examining differences in married-couple incomes across 11 countries (including changes over time in 4 countries) based on *LIS* data, found that wives' earnings reduced overall income inequality, though to varying degrees. They conclude that the correlation between the earnings of married husbands and wives would need to be considerably higher (at least double) to counter the equalizing effect of wives' earnings.

In a more recent *LIS* study, Harkness (see Chapter 7) investigated the relationship between female earnings and household income inequality using microdata for 17 rich countries. Using both of the counterfactuals described above, as well as a decomposition of the squared coefficient of variation, she found that, in all countries, female earnings exert an equalizing force—although of quite different magnitudes across countries.

However, Harkness also acknowledges important variation across studies, based on variation in measures used. Esping-Andersen (2008), for example, compares the variance of total earnings with that of husbands' earnings across several countries, in 1993 and 2001, and concludes that wives' earnings increased inequality among couples in France, Germany, Italy, Spain, and the United Kingdom, but decreased inequality in the United States, Sweden, and, in 2001 only, Denmark. Both the cross-country variation and the sensitivity to different measures of inequality suggest that the effects of increased female employment on extended earnings could be quite different from the effects on market earnings.

The Impact of Valuation of Unpaid Work on Earnings and Earnings Inequality

Estimates of the value of unpaid work show that it increases family earnings fairly uniformly, but more so in countries with lower levels of female employment. Freeman and Schettkat (2002), for example, found that the value of extended earnings relative to market earnings was significantly greater in Germany than in the United States. On the other hand, time devoted to non-market work did not decline proportionately with time devoted to market employment, and it remained relatively high even in high-income economies (Folbre and Yoon 2008).

Efforts to value unpaid work generally find that imputations of its market value have an equalizing effect on the distribution of family "extended earnings," defined as the sum of market earnings and the imputed value of unpaid work (Aslaksen and Koren 1996; Gottschalk and Mayer 2002; Frazis and Stewart 2006; Frick, Grabka, and Groh-Samberg 2009). Somewhat surprisingly, however, low-income households in the United States do not seem to devote significantly more time to household production (including child care) than do high-income households, and unemployed men do not perform significantly more housework than those who are employed (Frazis and Stewart 2006). The equalizing effect of valuing unpaid work results primarily from the addition of a large relatively constant value to most household incomes.

The size of this equalizing effect, however, varies considerably. Some evidence suggests that the distribution of unpaid work across U.S. households has become slightly more unequal over time (Zick, Bryant, and Srisukhumbowornchai 2008). Furthermore, the size of the equalizing effect depends heavily on assumptions used in valuing non-market work time, ranging from valuation methods to considerations of joint production and possibly diminishing productivity (Frick, Grabka, and Groh-Samberg 2009).

Changes in the size of married-couple households may also have implications for economies of scale in household production. While economists know little about the extent of economies of scale in household production, assumptions regarding their impact are built into standard equivalence scales, which assume that many can live more cheaply than one. There are almost certainly greater economies of scale in household production than in market purchases: the marginal cost of adding another person to the home dinner table is much smaller than that of adding him or her to a restaurant tab. In meal preparation, economies of scale in time far exceed economies of scale from consumption alone (Vernon 2005).

Likewise, in countries where child care imposes costs on parents, the marginal cash expenditure cost of putting a young child into paid child care is often greater than the time cost of adding another child to the household. Hence, a shift away from household production toward market production almost certainly reduces overall household economies of scale in consumption. As a result, large families—such as those with more than two children—that rely more heavily on market earnings may actually be worse off in terms of extended earnings than large families with higher levels of household-produced services.

CONSTRUCTING MEASURES OF EXTENDED EARNINGS

In order to focus on unpaid work, which varies most among working-age women in couple-headed households, we focus on married/cohabiting couples, aged 25 to 59 and living in households with no other adults. We generate estimates of the amount of unpaid work per adult, based on data from the HETUS and the ATUS, and we link these to estimates of the earnings of married/cohabiting couples in the *LIS Database*. (A similar methodology is applied in Giannelli et al. 2010, linking the HETUS with the EU household survey, EU-SILC.)[2] We chose the following countries based largely on the temporal proximity of the HETUS/ATUS and *LIS* datasets (typically no more than one year apart): Finland, France, Germany, Italy, Poland, Spain, Sweden, the United Kingdom, and the United States. These nine countries vary considerably in their levels of female employment and non-market work.

The HETUS asked a representative sample of respondents to describe their activities on a randomly chosen day, which could fall during the week or on the weekend. The HETUS database offers consistent harmonized measures of time use; although its interface does not allow direct analysis of the microdata, users are able to construct tables. We use the ATUS microdata to provide comparable estimates of time use for the United States. It is important to note that time designated as "child care" is limited to activities such as feeding, cleaning, bathing, talking to, or transporting a child. Supervisory or "on-call" responsibilities are not included. Also, housework conducted on behalf of a child—such as meal preparation, laundry, or picking up toys, is coded as housework, not as child care.

We estimated mean time devoted to unpaid work activities for individuals based on their employment characteristics, the presence of children, and the age of the youngest, distinguishing between two types of unpaid work: housework and child care. The sum of average unpaid work hours by husbands and wives, with given employment and family size characteristics, provides an estimate of the household's total unpaid work hours. Because we cannot clearly identify other adults living with married/cohabiting couples in the HETUS data, to measure their distinctive pattern of unpaid work, we excluded all couple-headed households in which another adult was a resident. This exclusion leads to an underestimate of the total quantity of unpaid work in countries where extended families are common, such as Poland (where more than 45 percent of men and women living in a household with a child live in a household with more than two adults).

We matched estimates of married/cohabiting individuals' time use from the HETUS/ATUS to married/cohabiting individuals included the *LIS* datasets, based on their individual employment and child-related characteristics. The time-use and income surveys were typically conducted no more than one year apart. It is important to note that estimates of hours devoted to unpaid work are based on averages for different categories of individuals, which substantially reduces overall variation in both hours and imputed earnings. At the same time, most estimates of hours devoted to paid work are also based on self-reported averages or responses to questions regarding "usual" hours of work. We multiplied the number of unpaid work hours per household by the national minimum wage in each country, aiming for a lower-bound estimate of the value of that unpaid work. In several cases, we converted a monthly minimum wage to an hourly wage based on assumptions regarding hours of work. This replacement cost estimate yields imputed values well below the actual cost of hiring a replacement worker because they ignore the value of employer contributions other than wages. We add the estimated value of unpaid work to net earnings (earnings less taxes and social contributions) to estimate extended earnings per household. Finally, we compare measures of the level and distribution of extended earnings for partnered couples, with measures based only on market earnings.

RESULTS

In this results section, we first provide an overview of our estimates of time use based on the HETUS and the ATUS. Second, we provide estimates of the value of unpaid and extended earnings across countries. Third, we examine variation in the distribution of market earnings and extended earnings across countries, demonstrating the equalizing effect of unpaid work.

Time Use

The basic distribution of average work time across the nine countries reveals a familiar pattern (Table 8.1). Men devote more time, on average, to paid work, and women to unpaid work. However, in every country, men devote an average of at least 2 hours a day, or 14 hours per week, to unpaid work. In every country (results not shown in table), the likelihood of performing some unpaid work on the time diary day was far higher than the likelihood of carrying out paid work. In these demographic categories (which exclude single-parent households), men work slightly more total hours per day than

TABLE 8.1

Paid work hours, unpaid work hours, and total work hours, 1999–2004 (married/cohabiting adults, aged 25–59, no other adults in household)

	PAID WORK HOURS		UNPAID WORK HOURS		TOTAL WORK HOURS		UNPAID AS PERCENTAGE OF TOTAL	
	Women	Men	Women	Men	Women	Men	Women	Men
Finland 1999–2000	3.4	5.6	4.7	3.0	8.1	8.5	58.5	34.7
France 1998–1999	3.0	5.6	5.1	2.5	8.1	8.1	62.8	30.4
Germany 2001–2002	2.1	5.0	5.6	3.0	7.7	8.0	72.2	37.2
Italy 2002–2003	2.4	6.3	6.8	2.1	9.2	8.4	73.7	24.9
Poland 2003–2004	2.8	5.7	5.8	3.2	8.6	8.8	67.9	36.1
Spain 2002–2003	2.4	6.0	6.2	2.3	8.7	8.3	71.7	28.0
Sweden 2000–2001	3.3	5.3	4.7	3.2	8.0	8.5	58.4	37.7
United Kingdom 2000–2001	3.0	5.7	5.2	2.9	8.2	8.6	63.3	34.2
United States 2003	3.4	5.8	5.0	2.9	8.4	8.7	59.1	33.5

SOURCE: Authors' calculations using HETUS and ATUS.

do women in every country except France (where there is no difference), Italy, and Spain.

The last column in Table 8.1 presents estimates of unpaid work hours as a percentage of total work hours, by gender. This provides the best summary comparison of variation across countries: Finland, Sweden, and the United States represent the most "marketized" countries for women, with women devoting less than 60 percent of their total work time to unpaid work. At the other end of the spectrum lie Germany, Italy, and Spain, where women devote more than 70 percent of their work time to unpaid work. Variation among men is more limited and follows a less distinct pattern. Men's time devoted to unpaid work is smallest in percentage terms (below 30 percent) in Italy and Spain (perhaps because women do so much more in those countries), but it is over 35 percent in Poland, Germany, and Sweden. Interestingly, in the two Nordic countries, a low percentage (of unpaid to total hours) for women is counterbalanced by a high percentage for men, but in Poland and Germany, both men's and women's participation in unpaid work is relatively high.

In all of these countries, time devoted to housework and child care varies inversely with time devoted to paid work, and it increases with the presence of young children (see the online appendix, Table 8.A1); in addition, the hours of the self-employed more closely resemble those of full-time rather than part-time employees. Another way of describing the trade-off between hours of paid and unpaid work central to our concern in this chapter lies in the correlation, within countries, between paid and unpaid work hours across the employment/family structure categories. While we do not report results for all countries here, our calculations indicate that this correlation is negative and greater than -0.70 for women and men in every country except Sweden (where it is only -0.36 for women). In countries where the level of unpaid work is high in absolute and relative terms, such as Italy, Germany, and Spain, the negative correlation for women exceeds -0.80. In other words, the higher the level of unpaid work, the more it is reduced when paid work increases. In Sweden, women who engage in an additional hour of paid work reduce their unpaid work by only about half an hour—perhaps because they are not doing much to begin with. In Italy, Germany, and Spain, an hour of paid work seems to have a stronger negative effect on unpaid work. This relationship deserves further scrutiny using micro-level data.

Virtually every study reviewed for this chapter shows that non-market work has an equalizing effect on women's total hours of work, as women with no paid work hours work almost as long, overall, as those who combine paid and unpaid work. Furthermore, those who are employed part-time typically put in more hours of unpaid work than those who work for pay full-time, and they log as many or more total work hours as those who are not employed. This pattern helps explain the potentially significant equalizing effect of any positive valuation of women's unpaid work on the level of extended earnings.

Levels of Extended Earnings

Next, we impute our findings on unpaid work hours into the *LIS* micro-data. To do that, we created "synthetic" couples, characterized by their individual paid work hours and the presence and age of their children, and we assigned estimates of unpaid work hours (from the HETUS and the ATUS) to the individuals in the *LIS* datasets.[3] Cross-national variation in couples' average total work hours is not very different from variation in paid work hours, but, by virtually any replacement cost valuation, there is much less inequality in the value of unpaid than paid work hours because virtually everyone engages in at least some unpaid work. As a result, we expect considerable equalization both within and across countries when we shift from market earnings to extended earnings.

Given estimates of unpaid work hours, the next step in constructing an estimate of extended earnings is choosing a set of replacement cost wages for the unpaid work. In an ideal world, we would utilize quality-adjusted measures of wages for both housework and child care. In this world, we make the best of what is available, choosing a lower-bound estimate based on national minimum wages converted to purchasing power parity (PPP)-adjusted 2005 U.S. dollars.[4]

The hourly minimum wage ranges from USD2.43 in Poland and USD4.19 in Spain, on the low end, to USD8.82 in Germany and USD9.07 in France, on the high end. The United States ranks seventh at USD5.98 (Table 8.2). The simple cross-country average is USD6.64.[5] In a previous version of this chapter, we explored the effect of using gender-specific median wages rather than national minimum wages, and we found results comparable to those we report below in terms of overall patterns. However, the cross-country variation here is somewhat different, because the value

TABLE 8.2

Earnings from paid work, estimated earnings from unpaid work, and extended earnings, 1999–2004 (married/cohabiting adults, aged 25–59, no other adults in household; earnings expressed in PPP-adjusted 2005 U.S. dollars)

	National minimum wage	Paid work — Average annual earnings (net of taxes and social contributions), zeros included	Unpaid work — Average replacement cost value of unpaid work (valued at minimum wage)	Extended earnings — Sum of earnings from paid and unpaid work (prior two columns)	Ratio of extended earnings to earnings from paid work
WOMEN					
Finland 2000	$6.93	$12,229	$ 8,701	$20,930	1.71
France 2000	$9.07	$15,160	$13,001	$28,161	1.86
Germany 2000	$8.82	$ 9,678	$14,046	$23,724	2.45
Italy 2004	$6.39	$ 8,946	$11,543	$20,488	2.29
Poland 2004	$2.43	$ 3,656	$ 3,985	$ 7,641	2.09
Spain 2004	$4.19	$ 9,995	$ 6,565	$16,560	1.66
Sweden 2000	$7.73	$12,215	$ 9,844	$22,058	1.81
United Kingdom 1999	$8.20	$12,241	$11,922	$24,166	1.97
United States 2004	$5.98	$19,510	$ 7,435	$26,945	1.38
Average	**$6.64**	**$11,514**	**$ 9,671**	**$21,186**	**1.91**
MEN					
Finland 2000	$6.93	$18,012	$ 4,992	$23,003	1.28
France 2000	$9.07	$23,891	$ 6,223	$30,114	1.26
Germany 2000	$8.82	$27,548	$ 8,715	$36,263	1.32
Italy 2004	$6.39	$21,101	$ 3,472	$24,574	1.16
Poland 2004	$2.43	$ 6,219	$ 2,064	$ 8,284	1.33
Spain 2004	$4.19	$20,436	$ 2,698	$23,134	1.13
Sweden 2000	$7.73	$20,117	$ 7,011	$27,128	1.35
United Kingdom 1999	$8.20	$27,880	$ 6,924	$34,808	1.25
United States 2004	$5.98	$44,835	$ 4,667	$49,502	1.10
Average	**$6.64**	**$23,338**	**$ 5,196**	**$28,534**	**1.24**

SOURCE: National minimum wage from ILO Minimum Wage Data Base (http://www.ilo.org/travaildatabase/servlet/minimumwages). Other columns based on authors' calculations from HETUS, ATUS, and the LIS Database.

NOTE: In Finland, Germany, and Italy, minimum wages are based on collective agreements of unskilled labor in the metal-working sector. Annual earnings are defined as the sum of total annual net income from dependent employment (wages and other payments from employer after deduction of income taxes and social contributions) and annual income from self-employment, converted into 2005 local currency using national CPI indices and into 2005 PPP U.S. dollars using the OECD/EUROSTAT purchasing power parities for final expenditure on GDP conversion rates. Note that wage income was collected net of taxes and contributions only in Italy; in other countries, gross wage income was netted down using taxes and contribution amounts in the same proportion as wage income in taxable income.

of the minimum wage, relative to the median wage, varies across countries. The minimum wage may be more appropriate for some countries than for others, but the same is true of any single wage rate. Use of a minimum wage sets a very low value on women's unpaid work and thus represents a lower-bound estimate of the effect we seek to measure.

We define an individual's extended earnings as the sum of his or her after-tax (net) annual earnings from paid work and the replacement cost estimate of his or her unpaid work (see Table 8.2). Women's mean annual earnings from paid work (including zero values) range from USD3,656 in Poland to USD19,510 in the United States; the unweighted cross-country average is USD11,514. Men's mean annual earnings (including zero values) are substantially higher: the cross-country average is USD23,338. However, the average value of women's unpaid work is considerably higher than men's. On an annual basis, it ranges from a low of USD3,985 in Poland to a high of USD14,046 in Germany.

The best indicator of the relative contribution of market and extended earnings of individuals is the ratio between the two. Across the countries in this study, adding the value of women's unpaid work to their earnings has the effect, on average, of almost doubling the estimate of their contributions, with a ratio of extended earnings to market earnings of 1.91 (see Table 8.2). While the effect on men's contribution is smaller, it remains substantial. Across all countries, the average value of men's extended earnings is between 10 percent and 35 percent higher than the value of their market earnings, with a ratio of extended earnings to market earnings of 1.24.

We next shift to analyses at the household level (Table 8.3).[6] Consideration of unpaid work substantially modifies estimates of women's contribution to household economic well-being, based on market earnings, and the relative ranking of countries with respect to the share of resources contributed by women. As reported in Table 8.3, women generally contribute less than 40 percent of market earnings—on the high side in Finland, France, Sweden, and Poland (37 to 40 percent) and on the low side in Germany, Spain, and Italy (25 to 28 percent), with the United States and the United Kingdom in between (31 percent). Women's contribution to extended earnings, using our minimum wage valuation, is highest in France (55 percent), followed by Italy, Finland, and Poland (47–49 percent), and lowest in the United States (38 percent).

TABLE 8.3
Women's contributions to couples' market earnings and extended earnings,
1999–2004 (married/cohabiting adults, aged 25–59, no other adults
in household; includes observations with zero earnings)

	Women's contribution to couples' market earnings (%)	Women's contribution to couples' extended earnings (%)
FINLAND 2000		
Neither employed	38	56
Man employed, woman not employed	6	40
Man employed, woman employed PT	37	48
Man employed, woman employed FT	45	49
Man not employed, woman employed PT	85	62
Man not employed, woman employed FT	90	63
All couples	40	48
FRANCE 2000		
Neither employed	43	45
Man employed, woman not employed	9	46
Man employed, woman employed PT	32	49
Man employed, woman employed FT	44	64
Man not employed, woman employed PT	92	56
Man not employed, woman employed FT	74	48
All couples	38	55
GERMANY 2000		
Neither employed	0	53
Man employed, woman not employed	0	33
Man employed, woman employed PT	22	36
Man employed, woman employed FT	43	46
Man not employed, woman employed PT	100	55
Man not employed, woman employed FT	100	62
All couples	28	41
ITALY 2004		
Neither employed	0	63
Man employed, woman not employed	0	43
Man employed, woman employed PT	32	46
Man employed, woman employed FT	44	49
Man not employed, woman employed PT	97	69
Man not employed, woman employed FT	93	60
All couples	25	47
POLAND 2004		
Neither employed	19	57
Man employed, woman not employed	1	42
Man employed, woman employed PT	39	45
Man employed, woman employed FT	47	50
Man not employed, woman employed PT	91	57
Man not employed, woman employed FT	98	65
All couples	37	49

(*continued*)

TABLE 8.3 *(Continued)*

	Women's contribution to couples' market earnings (%)	Women's contribution to couples' extended earnings (%)
SPAIN 2004		
Neither employed	23	52
Man employed, woman not employed	7	34
Man employed, woman employed PT	29	38
Man employed, woman employed FT	45	48
Man not employed, woman employed PT	63	55
Man not employed, woman employed FT	70	58
All couples	**29**	**42**
SWEDEN 2000		
Neither employed	29	53
Man employed, woman not employed	5	35
Man employed, woman employed PT	33	43
Man employed, woman employed FT	42	46
Man not employed, woman employed PT	89	60
Man not employed, woman employed FT	93	66
All couples	**38**	**45**
UNITED KINGDOM 1999		
Neither employed	0	55
Man employed, woman not employed	0	32
Man employed, woman employed PT	27	40
Man employed, woman employed FT	43	46
Man not employed, woman employed PT	100	61
Man not employed, woman employed FT	99	68
All couples	**31**	**43**
UNITED STATES 2004		
Neither employed	25	48
Man employed, woman not employed	5	22
Man employed, woman employed PT	24	31
Man employed, woman employed FT	42	44
Man not employed, woman employed PT	65	54
Man not employed, woman employed FT	77	65
All couples	**31**	**38**

SOURCE: Authors' calculations from HETUS, ATUS, and the *LIS Database*.

NOTE: PT = part-time employed women, defined as women working fewer than 30 hours in paid employment. FT = full-time employed women, defined as women working at least 30 hours in paid employment, or any number of hours in self-employment.

The use of extended earnings brings women's relative economic contribution to couples close to 50 percent in most countries, consistent with the idea of "partnership." Note that, among households in which men are not employed, women's relative contribution to extended earnings is greater than 50 percent, nearly everywhere, even if they are not themselves employed.[7] Unpaid work may play an important role in buffering the impact of unemployment or loss of market earnings, although it obviously does not represent a perfect substitute, as it relies heavily on inputs purchased with market earnings—for example, you cannot prepare a meal if you cannot buy food (Folbre 2009).

The Distribution of Extended Earnings

Our results on the inequality of market versus extended earnings are presented in Table 8.4, and three core findings are evident. First, the distribution of extended earnings is far more equal than the distribution of market earnings alone in all of the countries that we examine, across five different measures of inequality: the Gini coefficient, one-half the squared coefficient of variation ($CV^2/2$), and the logarithm of the ratio of average earnings of the 90th percentile relative to the 10th percentile, the 90th percentile relative to the 50th percentile, and the 50th percentile relative to the 10th percentile. The consistent results across these measures suggest that this result is quite robust.

Second, the effect of shifting to our broader earnings indicator varies across countries. The magnitude of the difference between the two indicators can be most easily interpreted using the Gini coefficient. One property of the Gini is that its value, doubled, indicates the average expected income difference between two randomly drawn households, expressed as a percent of average income. That means that, in the United States, shifting from market to extended earnings reduces that average expected difference by about 12.6 percentage points (6.28×2). At the other extreme, in Poland, shifting from market to extended earnings reduces the average expected difference in income by about 38.4 percentage points (19.19×2).

Although the effect of shifting from market to extended earnings varies substantially across these countries, the cross-national rankings with respect to levels of inequality are, in fact, fairly similar regardless of which income measure is used. The United States is the most notable exception. Consider the Gini coefficients vis-à-vis market earnings: the most unequal countries are Poland (ranked 1st), the United Kingdom (2nd), and the United States (3rd), and the most equal are France (7th), Sweden (8th), and Finland (9th). When we shift to extended earnings, the United States becomes the most unequal, still followed by Poland and the United Kingdom, and the most equal three countries remain the same (although France and Sweden

TABLE 8.4

Inequality of market earnings compared to inequality of extended earnings, 1999–2004
(households with married/cohabiting adults, aged 25–59, no other adults in household)

	GINI COEFFICIENT			CV²/2			LN(P90/P10)			LN(P90/P50)			LN(P50/P10)		
	ME	EE	ME − EE	ME	EE	ME − EE	ME	EE	ME − EE	ME	EE	ME − EE	ME	EE	ME − EE
Finland 2000	28.62	19.64	8.98	0.17	0.08	0.09	1.30	0.89	0.41	0.49	0.40	0.10	0.81	0.49	0.32
France 2000	30.14	19.90	10.24	0.17	0.07	0.10	1.40	0.89	0.51	0.65	0.48	0.18	0.75	0.42	0.33
Germany 2000	35.63	21.22	14.41	0.28	0.10	0.18	1.51	0.92	0.59	0.72	0.48	0.24	0.79	0.45	0.34
Italy 2004	37.06	23.32	13.74	0.56	0.23	0.33	1.52	0.90	0.62	0.69	0.46	0.23	0.83	0.44	0.39
Poland 2004	46.41	27.22	19.19	0.49	0.17	0.32	1.71	1.22	0.49	0.85	0.59	0.25	0.86	0.63	0.23
Spain 2004	34.01	25.06	8.94	0.21	0.11	0.09	1.53	1.13	0.40	0.70	0.55	0.15	0.83	0.58	0.25
Sweden 2000	29.08	20.07	9.00	0.18	0.08	0.10	1.27	0.90	0.38	0.54	0.43	0.11	0.73	0.47	0.26
United Kingdom 1999	38.26	25.64	12.62	0.49	0.22	0.27	1.52	1.05	0.46	0.68	0.51	0.17	0.84	0.54	0.29
United States 2004	37.29	31.01	6.28	0.37	0.26	0.11	1.64	1.34	0.30	0.69	0.60	0.09	0.95	0.74	0.21

SOURCE: Authors' calculations from HETUS, ATUS, and the LIS Database.

NOTE: ME = market earnings; EE = extended earnings; ME − EE = difference between market earnings and extended earnings.

switch places). The sizable shift in the U.S. position is due at least in part to the low minimum wage in the United States, which reduces the imputed value of the unpaid work that is carried out in American homes—and, in turn, reduces the equalizing effect of shifting from market to extended earnings. The relatively low share of unpaid work in total work time, in the United States, further reduces (relative to other countries) the effect on the well-being distribution that results from shifting to the more comprehensive earnings measure.

The $CV^2/2$ results are similar. For most countries, the cross-national ranking is largely the same (i.e., within one rank position), regardless of which income indicator is used (market versus extended). Again, the United States is a noted exception: it shifts from the fourth most unequal country (with respect to market earnings) to the most unequal (vis-à-vis extended earnings).

Third, the effect of shifting to extended earnings is different in different parts of the income distribution. The most striking finding is that, in all countries except Poland, the effect of incorporating the value of unpaid work is greater in the bottom half of the income distribution; that is, the difference between inequality of market versus extended earnings is greater for ln(P50/P10) (the ratio of the middle to the near-bottom) than for ln(P90/P50) (the ratio of the near-top to the middle). The impact is greater in the lower half of the distribution, largely because the value of unpaid work varies less than the value of market earnings—that is, it is more constant—so adding it to market earnings disproportionately affects lower-income households. The value of unpaid work varies less, partly because (as noted above) we imputed group averages and partly because there is a minimum amount of domestic work that, essentially, must be done in all households.

Considering the difference in country rankings is again illuminating. Among lower-income households (see the P50/P10 column), market earnings are most unequal in the United States and most equal in Sweden. When we shift to extended earnings, the United States is still the most unequal among these countries, but now three countries have more equal distributions than does Sweden: France, Germany, and Italy. This re-ranking is driven by the fact that in these three continental European countries, unpaid work constitutes a larger share of total work time than it does in Sweden (see Table 8.1), so accounting for unpaid work has a stronger equalizing effect (than it does in Sweden).

The results in the upper-half of the distribution are different. Considering market earnings, the United States is tied (with Italy) for the fourth most unequal, lagging Germany, Poland, and Spain. When we shift to extended earnings, the United States again becomes the most unequal. Again, that could be attributed to two factors: the low minimum wage in the United States reduces the equalizing impact of the shift to extended earnings, and the relatively low share of total work in the United States that is unpaid (especially among women) also reduces the equalizing impact of moving to an extended earnings definition.

One way to unravel the complex effects of changes in women's increased participation in paid work on earnings inequality among couple-headed households is to use an inequality measure that can easily be decomposed into components, such as the level of women's earnings, the relative share of women's earnings, and the correlation between men's and women's earnings (Cancian et al. 1993; see Chapter 7). Expanding this decomposition to simultaneously consider the effects of differences in market earnings and extended earnings for both men and women is beyond the scope of our analysis here, but we provide three separate decompositions of one-half the squared coefficient of variation ($CV^2/2$), examining market earnings decomposed by gender (see Table 8.5, panel A), extended earnings decomposed by gender (panel B), and extended earnings (women and men together) decomposed by market versus non-market work (panel C).

We follow the same method as Harkness in Chapter 7 and present results for four countries—France, Italy, Spain, and the United States—that are based on the same *LIS* datasets. However, our analysis focuses on a different universe of households: our age range is different from hers (households with couples where at least one is between 25 and 59 rather than both between ages 18 and 59). We excluded households with any adults outside of the primary couple, while she excluded those in which a member of the couple was engaged full-time in education. Both studies estimate net wages from gross earnings based on earnings shares, but our definition of net earnings includes self-employment income. As a result of these differences, our estimates for these four countries differ from hers (compare her Table 7.4 with our Table 8.5, panel A).

Nonetheless, our results for the decomposition of market earnings are basically consistent with hers, showing wide variation across countries in the relative equality of men's and women's market earnings, the female

TABLE 8.5
*Decomposition of household inequality, measured by CV²/2, 2000–2004
(households with married/cohabiting adults, aged 25–59, no other adults in household)*

A: MARKET EARNINGS DECOMPOSED BY GENDER

	Total market earnings	Rank	Men's market earnings	Rank	Women's market earnings	Rank	Women's share of market earnings (%)	Correlations between men's and women's market earnings
France 2000	0.17	1	0.23	3	0.30	2	39	0.30
Finland 2000	0.17	2	0.22	1	0.30	3	41	0.35
Sweden 2000	0.18	3	0.27	4	0.27	1	38	0.28
Spain 2004	0.21	4	0.23	2	0.59	4	34	0.26
Germany 2000	0.28	5	0.37	5	0.88	7	28	0.07
United States 2004	0.37	6	0.56	6	0.98	9	31	0.05
Poland 2004	0.49	7	0.71	7	0.91	8	38	0.21
United Kingdom 1999	0.49	8	0.77	8	0.71	5	32	0.17
Italy 2004	0.56	9	0.86	9	0.74	6	30	0.23

B: EXTENDED EARNINGS DECOMPOSED BY GENDER

	Total extended earnings	Rank	Men's extended earnings	Rank	Women's extended earnings	Rank	Women's share of extended earnings (%)	Correlations between men's and women's extended earnings
France 2000	0.07	1	0.14	2	0.08	1	48	0.35
Finland 2000	0.08	2	0.13	1	0.10	3	48	0.40
Sweden 2000	0.08	3	0.15	3	0.09	2	45	0.32
Spain 2004	0.11	5	0.18	4	0.19	8	42	0.29
Germany 2000	0.10	4	0.19	5	0.14	5	40	0.13
United States 2004	0.26	9	0.46	7	0.51	9	36	0.06
Poland 2004	0.17	6	0.39	6	0.18	7	48	0.25
United Kingdom 1999	0.22	7	0.49	8	0.18	6	41	0.19
Italy 2004	0.23	8	0.63	9	0.11	4	46	0.25

share of couples' market earnings, and the correlation between male and female market earnings. Female market earnings are more unequally distributed than those of men in most countries, primarily because they are more likely to take a zero or low value as a result of non-participation or low participation in market work. The United Kingdom and Italy are exceptions here, with lower inequality among female market earnings than male market earnings, as is Sweden, where there is no difference.

TABLE 8.5 (*Continued*)

C: EXTENDED EARNINGS DECOMPOSED BY TYPE OF EARNINGS (MARKET VERSUS UNPAID)

	Total extended earnings	Rank	Market earnings	Rank	Value of unpaid work	Rank	Value of unpaid work as share of total earnings (%)	Correlation between market earnings and value of unpaid work
France 2000	0.07	1	0.29	2	0.11	7	33	−0.36
Finland 2000	0.08	2	0.27	1	0.08	5	31	−0.33
Sweden 2000	0.08	3	0.31	3	0.03	1	34	−0.20
Spain 2004	0.11	5	0.39	4	0.15	8	23	−0.48
Germany 2000	0.10	4	0.62	5	0.07	4	38	−0.53
United States 2004	0.26	9	0.79	6	0.06	2	16	−0.29
Poland 2004	0.17	6	0.84	7	0.11	6	38	−0.35
United Kingdom 1999	0.22	7	0.93	8	0.06	2	31	−0.32
Italy 2004	0.23	8	1.05	9	0.21	9	33	−0.36

SOURCE: Authors' calculations from HETUS, ATUS, and the *LIS Database*.

Consistent with findings reported earlier, the inequality of extended earnings is much lower overall (see Table 8.5, panel B). Not surprisingly, the differences are much greater for women than for men in couples because virtually all women perform a substantial amount of unpaid work. We can infer that much of the equalizing effect of unpaid work derives from these differences because the correlations between male and female extended earnings are slightly higher than for market earnings for all countries That is, highly productive women (defined in terms of extended, rather than market, earnings) are slightly more likely to be coupled with highly productive men than high-market-earning women with high-market-earning men.

Also consistent with earlier findings, the distribution of the sum of partners' extended earnings is far more equal than with respect to market earnings, and the correlations between market and non-market earnings are negative in every instance (see Table 8.5, panel C). That is, on the household level, higher market earnings are associated with lower non-market earnings. The size of these correlations varies substantially across countries. They are highest in Germany (−0.53) and Spain (−0.48), both countries in which women contribute a relatively low share of market earnings (see Table 8.5, panel A) and where women's market earnings are relatively unequal.

CONCLUSION

Our analysis clearly demonstrates the substantial equalizing effect of unpaid work on economic well-being, within nine high-income countries. It also demonstrates the limitations of any analysis of the impact of women's employment and/or earnings on inter-household inequality of economic well-being that fails to take into account unpaid work. Obviously, much depends on the method of valuation used, and our estimates are based on a simple replacement cost analysis using national minimum wages. The shape of inequality in market earnings exerts a strong influence both directly, because market earnings dominate extended earnings, and indirectly, through its impact on the national minimum wage (which, in turn, affects our valuation of unpaid work). Yet, our primary conclusion is supported by a simple analysis of the distribution of total work hours across couples, which vary considerably less than do paid work hours.

These cross-sectional findings have important implications for analyses of the impact of changes in women's participation in paid employment and in their earnings over time. As women reallocate their time from unpaid to paid work, household inequality is likely to increase, both because the hours of paid work are distributed more unequally than hours of unpaid work and because the imputed hourly value of unpaid work (valued at the national minimum wage) varies less than market wages. Our decomposition of the half squared coefficient of variation shows that the extended earnings of men and women are correlated more strongly than are market earnings. However, this effect is not strong enough to countervail the greater inequality associated with the greater relative importance of market earnings.

The impact of declining levels of unpaid work over time on all aspects of household living standards deserves more careful consideration. There is something fundamentally misleading about measuring gains to family earnings provided by increases in women's employment that do not account for the reduction in living standards resulting from declines in time devoted to unpaid work. As our use of "synthetic" households demonstrates, the availability of new time-use data makes it easier to impute the contribution of unpaid work even where such data are not directly linked to household or individual market earnings.

In closing, we reiterate the many limitations of our analysis for an analysis of living standards. Our measures of time devoted to unpaid work per household, calculations of household market earnings, and imputations of the value of unpaid work are all approximate. We set aside issues of equivalence scales, despite our intuition that such scales probably differ for consumption based on income from market earnings compared to unpaid work. We do not consider differences in household capital or technology, which affect the productivity of unpaid work in the home. We do not include any measure of the receipt of government services, such as child care, that provide valuable substitutes for unpaid work and profoundly affect household living standards. Nonetheless, we hope that our results will motivate researchers to develop stronger methods for measuring and valuing unpaid work and will encourage scholars to include unpaid work in their assessments of the distribution of well-being across households.

NOTES

1. Throughout this chapter, we use the terms *market work* and *paid work* interchangeably. Likewise, we use the terms *non-market work* and *unpaid work* interchangeably.

2. For a basic description of the Harmonized European Time Use Survey (HETUS), see https://www.h2.scb.se/tus/tus/doc/Metadata.pdf. For a basic description of the American Time Use Survey (ATUS), see http://www.bls.gov/tus/. For an overview of the *LIS Database*, see https://www.lisdatacenter.org. To carry out the analyses in this paper, we used the HETUS online table maker; the microdata are not distributed. To conduct analyses based on the ATUS and the *LIS* data, we worked directly in the microdata.

3. All of our estimates of time use are based on the HETUS or the ATUS. As noted in the text, to construct estimates of extended earnings, we link estimates of average time devoted to housework and child care for married/cohabiting couples with no other adult present to households, in the *LIS Database*, with similar employment and family structure characteristics. Average weekly paid work hours are included in the *LIS* datasets for all but three of the countries in our study. Among these, estimates of paid work hours differ between the two data sources by less than 10 percent for men and women in most countries, with the salient exception of Germany, where the HETUS results record paid work hours about 20 percent lower than the *LIS* survey for both men and women. Because an underestimate of paid work hours is likely to be associated with an overestimate of unpaid work hours, the value of extended earnings may be biased upward for Germany.

4. We are aware, of course, that cross-national variations in regulations, policies, and labor market structures mean that "in the real world," child care workers' earnings, relative to their country's minimum wage, vary substantially across countries. Our estimations do not take these national features into account.

5. The minimum wage data came from the ILO Minimum Wage Data Base (http://www.ilo.org/travaildatabase/servlet/minimumwages). These national-level indicators were originally expressed in national currency units for 2004 (Italy and Sweden), 2005 (Finland, Germany, and Poland), 2006 (the United Kingdom), and 2007 (France and the United States); we deflated them to 2005 prices (using IMF CPI indices) and then converted them into PPP-adjusted U.S. dollars, using 2005 consumption PPPs from the World Penn Tables. These minimum wages were originally expressed on an hourly basis in all countries except Germany, Italy, Poland, and Spain; in these four cases, we converted monthly figures into an hourly standard by assuming a 40-hour workweek, except in France, where we assumed a 35-hour workweek.

In the countries where there is no national minimum wage fixed by an authority (i.e., Finland, Germany, and Italy), we chose one of the sectoral collective agreements given by the ILO, specifically the one referring to the most unskilled workers in the metalworking industry.

6. None of the estimates of market or extended earnings discussed in this paper have been adjusted for household size, despite considerable variation across partnered households in number of children. A standard equivalence adjustment, often used in the analysis of *LIS* data, divides household income by the square root of the number of household members. This adjustment implies considerable economies of scale in household consumption. For instance, it assumes that the earnings of a household with four people should be divided by 2 (the square root of 4). In other words, this household is assumed to require only twice as much money to live as well as a one-person household. Such assumptions are difficult to test empirically, in part because money and time are substitutes.

Indeed, the relatively generous economies of scale assumed by this standard equivalence scale, which has been widely applied for more than 40 years, may reflect a world in which most married women stayed home and specialized in household production. In general, meal preparation, shopping, and child care enjoy significant economies of scale; the marginal cost of adding another household member is typically far lower than the average cost. As women have entered paid employment, however, households have become more likely to purchase meals away from home and to purchase substitutes for family care. Market purchases of meals and other services do not typically afford a "discount" for larger households and may therefore reduce household economies of scale—a trend consistent with the decrease in household size that typically accompanies economic development and increases in women's employment. We hope to explore this issue in future research.

7. Note that in some countries (i.e., Finland, France, Poland, Spain, Sweden, and the United States), couples coded as "neither employed" can still have market earnings, and thus it is meaningful to calculate women's contributions to those market earnings (as we do in Table 8.3). The reason for this is that in these datasets, the employment status reference period (e.g., "at present") falls outside

the earnings reference period (e.g., "last year"). Thus, among these couples, even though neither is employed during the employment reference period, many had market earnings during the (usually earlier) earnings reference period.

For additional results, please see the online appendices by following the link in the listing for Income Inequality *on the Stanford University Press website: http:// www.sup.org.*

REFERENCES

Abraham, Katherine, and Christopher Mackie. 2004. *Beyond the Market. Designing Nonmarket Accounts for the United States.* Washington, DC: National Academies Press.

American Time Use Survey (ATUS). 2012. http://www.bls.gov/tus/.

Aslaksen, Iulie, and Charlotte Koren. 1996. "Unpaid Household Work and the Distribution of Extended Income: The Norwegian Experience." *Feminist Economics* 2/3 (November): 65–80.

Becker, Gary. 1965. "A Theory of the Allocation of Time." *Economic Journal* 75: 493–517.

Bianchi, Suzanne, John. P. Robinson, and Melissa A. Milkie. 2006. *Changing Rhythms of American Family Life.* New York: Russell Sage.

Burda, Michael, Daniel S. Hamermesh, and Philippe Weil. 2007. "Total Work, Gender and Social Norms." Working paper 13000. Cambridge, MA: National Bureau of Economic Research (NBER).

Cancian, Maria, Sheldon Danziger, and Peter Gottschalk. 1993. "Working Wives and Family Income Inequality among Married Couples." In *Uneven Tides: Rising Inequality in America,* edited by Peter Gottschalk and Sheldon Danziger. New York: Russell Sage Foundation.

Cancian, Maria, and Robert Schoeni. 1992. "Female Earnings and the Level and Distribution of Household Income in Developed Countries." *LIS* working paper 84. Luxembourg: LIS.

Esping-Andersen, Gøsta. 2008. "Sociological Explanations of Changing Income Distributions." *American Behavioral Scientist* 50(5): 639–58.

———. 2009. "Economic Inequality and the Welfare State." In *The Oxford Handbook of Economic Inequality,* edited by Wiemer Salverda, Brian Nolan, and Timothy M. Smeeding. Oxford: Oxford University Press.

Folbre, Nancy. 2008. *Valuing Children: Rethinking the Economics of the Family.* Cambridge, MA: Harvard University Press.

———. 2009. "Inequality and Time Use in the Household." In *The Oxford Handbook of Economic Inequality,* edited by Wiemer Salverda, Brian Nolan, and Timothy M. Smeeding. Oxford: Oxford University Press.

Folbre, Nancy, and Jayoung Yoon. 2008. "Economic Development and Time Devoted to Direct Unpaid Care Activities: An Analysis of the Harmonized European Time Use Survey (HETUS)." Paper prepared for the United Nations Research Institute for Social Development (UNRISD) Flagship Report on Poverty.

Frazis, Harley, and Jay Stewart. 2006. "How Does Household Production Affect Earnings Inequality? Evidence from the American Time Use Survey." Working paper 393. Washington, DC: U.S. Bureau of Labor Statistics.

Freeman, Richard, and Ronald Schettkat. 2002. "Marketization of Production and the U.S.-Europe Employment Gap." Working paper 8797. Cambridge, MA: National Bureau of Economic Research (NBER).

Frick, Joachim, Markus M. Grabka, and Olaf Groh-Samberg. 2009. "The Impact of Home Production on Economic Inequality in Germany." Discussion paper 4023. Bonn, Germany: Institute for the Study of Labor (IZA).

Giannelli, Gianna C., Lucia Mangiavacchi, and Luca Piccoli. 2010. "GDP and the Value of Family Caretaking: How Much Does Europe Care?" Discussion paper 5046. Bonn, Germany: Institute for the Study of Labor (IZA).

Gottschalk, Peter, and Susan Mayer. 2002. "Changes in Home Production and Trends in Economic Inequality." In *The New Economics of Rising Inequalities*, edited by Daniel Cohen, Thomas Piketty, and Gilles Saint-Paul. New York: Oxford University Press.

Harkness, Susan. 2013. "Women's Employment and Household Income Inequality." Chapter 7 in this book.

Harmonized European Time Use Survey (HETUS). 2012. https://www.h2.scb.se/tus/tus/.

Kahneman, Daniel, Alan B. Krueger, David A. Schkade, Norbert Schwarz, and Arthur A. Stone. 2004. "Toward National Well-Being Accounts." *American Economic Review* 94(2): 429–34.

Landefeld, Steven, and Stephanie McCulla. 2000. "Accounting for Nonmarket Household Production within a National Accounts Framework." *Review of Income and Wealth* 46(3): 289–307.

Luxembourg Income Study (LIS) Database, http://www.lisdatacenter.org (multiple countries; microdata last accessed in July 2011). Luxembourg: LIS.

Vernon, Victoria. 2005. "Food Expenditure, Food Preparation Time, and Household Economies of Scale." *IDEAS* working paper. St. Louis, MO: Federal Reserve Bank Research Division.

Zick, Cathleen D., W. Keith Bryant, and Sivithee Srisukhumbowornchai. 2008. "Does Housework Matter Anymore? The Shifting Impact of Housework on Economic Inequality." *Review of Economics of the Household* 6(1): 1–28.

CHAPTER NINE

Women's Work, Family Earnings, and Public Policy

Margarita Estévez-Abe and Tanja Hethey-Maier

WOMEN'S ECONOMIC POSITION WITHIN THE FAMILY

Male breadwinner households are more prevalent in some countries than in others. Even when both spouses—or partners—work, the degree to which women contribute to the family income varies from country to country. This chapter poses two questions: How does a woman's economic status in a married or cohabiting couple vary from country to country? What labor market institutions and social policies affect women's economic status in the family? The analysis is conducted for 16 OECD countries using data from the *Luxembourg Income Study (LIS) Database*, around 2004.

Scholars have noted the role of the welfare state in reducing women's economic dependency on their husbands (Sorensen and McLanahan 1987; Hobson 1990; Bianchi, Casper, and Peltola 1996, 1999; Stier and Mandel 2003). Typically, they conceptualize the wife's dependency in terms of the gap between the husband's and wife's earnings, as a percentage of family earnings. When the gap is small, women are independent; when the gap is large, women are dependent. Bianchi and colleagues (1996, 1999) applied Gøsta Esping-Andersen's three welfare state regimes—social democratic, liberal, and conservative—to explain the mean economic dependency levels of wives in different high-income countries (see Esping-Andersen 1990). In applying Esping-Andersen's taxonomy to explain wives' dependency on their husbands, Bianchi and colleagues expected wives in social democratic welfare states to be the most independent. Publicly provided child care and generous paid maternity and parental leaves actively enhance mothers' labor market attachment and thus women's relative economic position in the family. The tax systems in social democratic countries promote wives' employment because taxes are individual-based and thus do not penalize working wives in the way household-based income tax does. They expect conservative welfare states to do just the opposite. In such states, policies are geared toward discouraging wives from working. In contrast, liberal welfare states—relatively small welfare states in predominantly English-speaking countries—are gender-neutral. Their policies neither promote nor discourage female employment. Thus, Bianchi and colleagues expected wives in conservative welfare states in continental European countries to be the least independent.[1]

Figure 9.1 illustrates cross-national variation in the shares of three different types of heterosexual married and cohabiting couples.[2] The bars on the left show the shares of heterosexual "male-breadwinner households," in which wives' contribution to family earnings is less than 30 percent. (For the sake of simplicity, we refer to female and male partners who are not married but cohabit as "wives" and "husbands.") The bars on the right indicate the shares of what we call "female-breadwinner households," in which husbands' earnings fall below 30 percent of the family earnings. The bars in the middle represent the shares of "egalitarian households," where wives' earnings constitute equal to or more than 30 percent but less than 70 percent of the family earnings. Figure 9.1 sorts countries into three groups that correspond to Esping-Andersen's three welfare regimes. The social democratic regime, which consists of the Nordic countries—Denmark, Finland, Norway, and Sweden—appears to be the most gender egalitarian. The share of male-breadwinner families is comparatively low, and the shares of egalitarian and female-breadwinner households are high. In Denmark and Sweden, roughly 60 percent of all married and cohabiting couples form egalitarian households. In Finland and Norway, close to 50 percent are egalitarian households. On average, liberal countries (English-speaking countries) grouped on the left-hand side of the figure appear to be more egalitarian than the conservative countries (Austria, Belgium, France, Germany, Italy, the Netherlands, and Spain) grouped on the right-hand side. The shares of male-breadwinner households are lower among liberal countries than in conservative ones. The shares of egalitarian households are also higher in liberal countries.

While Esping-Andersen's three welfare regimes roughly correspond to the three clusters of countries in Figure 9.1, some questions remain. There is

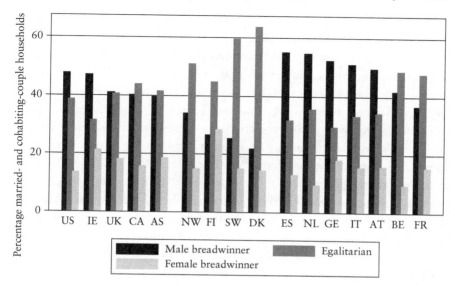

Figure 9.1.   Cross-national variation in types of households, around 2004

SOURCE: Authors' calculations from the *LIS Database*.

NOTE: Male breadwinner refers to couples in which wives' contribution to family earnings is less than 30 percent; female breadwinner refers to couples in which husbands' earnings fall below 30 percent of the family earnings; and egalitarian refers to couples in which wives' earnings constitute between 30 and 70 percent of family earnings.

a significant degree of intra-group variation when we look at the conservative group: Belgium and France stand out for their egalitarianism. Married and cohabiting couples in Belgium and France are much more egalitarian than those in other conservative countries. Furthermore, the percentages of male breadwinner households are much lower in Belgium and France than in other conservative countries; instead, they are roughly the same as in liberal countries. These intra-group variations are large enough to challenge Esping-Andersen's three regimes. As Gornick, Meyers, and Ross (1997) and Morgan (2006) demonstrate in their critique of Esping-Andersen, both Belgium and France provide relatively generous work-family reconciliation policies, although they are not social democratic welfare states. As Gornick's findings indicate, specific welfare-state characteristics matter more than overall welfare-state types in influencing women's—and, in particular, mothers'—employment (Gornick et al. 1997; Gornick 1999). Characteristics such as publicly provided child care and generous paid maternity and parental leaves promote women's employment, regardless of whether or not a country is social democratic.

However, neither Esping-Andersen's original taxonomy nor the concept of work-family reconciliation policies developed by Gornick and colleagues explain why liberal countries should be more gender-neutral than conservative countries. Esping-Andersen's later work addresses this question more directly by using the concept of "de-familialization."[3] Esping-Andersen's original taxonomy was constructed on the basis of two concepts: "de-commodification" and "stratification." Ann Orloff (1993) aptly criticized these concepts for their male-worker-centric perspective. In response, Esping-Andersen tried to demonstrate how his three worlds of welfare regimes could accommodate a feminist perspective. He popularized the term "de-familialization" to capture how the welfare state or the market might take over the family's welfare functions—that is, women's unpaid care services for the family. Liberal welfare states de-familialize women's unpaid care work via the private market. Social democratic welfare states, in turn, de-familialize women's unpaid care work via the welfare state by providing public child care, for instance. This is why, even though public policy support for working mothers is lacking in liberal welfare states, mothers in these countries find child care services in the private market. These services allow them to balance family and work by private means (Esping-Andersen 1999). In contrast, conservative welfare states (in continental European countries) provide little non-family-based welfare provision—either state- or market-based.

Although Esping-Andersen concedes that Belgium and France represent instances of conservative countries that de-familialize child care, he considers his three welfare regimes to represent distinctive labor market regimes with very specific gendered outcomes. The economic dynamics that brings about de-familialization are complex, but Esping-Andersen points to the importance of labor market factors that are independent from the effects of work-family reconciliation policies (Esping-Andersen 1999; see Chapters 6 and 7). We follow Esping-Andersen's lead. In the rest of this chapter, we explore how labor market issues might impact women's economic standing within the marriage.

As the following section discusses in greater detail, social policies are not the only institutional features that affect women's economic position within the marriage. We also need to take into consideration labor market institutions. The labor market structure may affect both the supply and demand of female labor, as well as women's earnings. The combination of these factors together influences wives' economic standing within the marriage.

LABOR MARKET INSTITUTIONS AND WOMEN'S ECONOMIC POSITION IN THE FAMILY

Broadly speaking, two issues stand out when thinking about wives' economic position vis-à-vis their husbands: wives' employment status and their earnings. Given the current context, in which women's tasks performed at home go unpaid, for women to achieve economic parity at home, they must first find paid work.[4] Once they are employed outside their home, it also matters how their wage levels compare to men's wage levels.

Most comparative studies on female employment rates have focused on the role of work-family reconciliation policies. The general finding is that generous public child care and family leave provisions enhance women's labor market attachment (Gornick et al. 1997; Daly 2000; Gornick and Meyers 2003). Gornick and colleagues (1997) show that these policies reduce the child penalty in women's labor force participation rates. As already mentioned, these policies do not, however, explain why women's labor force attachment is relatively strong in liberal countries—that is, countries that do not provide work-family reconciliation policies.[5]

Existing literature on labor market rigidities suggests that restrictions on hiring and firing might have important labor market consequences. Could some of these consequences be gendered? Strict employment protection means high costs of hiring and firing. Employers, anticipating difficulties in adjusting the workforce in possible future downturns, will refrain from hiring too many workers even when times are good. Hence, scholars have pointed out that strict employment protection may reduce overall employment levels (OECD 1994, Part II; Siebert 1997; Elsmeskov, Martin, and Scarpetta 1998; Saint-Paul 2000; Boeri and Van Ours 2008, among others).[6] Additionally, when employment protection is very strong, wages of workers with permanent contracts (i.e., insiders) will increase beyond the levels likely to emerge in competitive labor markets. This occurs because even when labor is abundant, employers have little power to adjust the wage levels of labor market insiders. Relatively speaking, unskilled workers (more abundant) with permanent contracts become more costly vis-à-vis skilled workers (more scarce) than in more competitive markets. Although most of these studies attempt to explain high levels of structural unemployment in continental Europe (i.e., Eurosclerosis), it is possible to identify the gender implications of strict employment protection.

Two main issues that arise are particularly relevant to the economic position of women within the family. First, even if young women were able to get permanent contracts—in the absence of adequately paid maternity leaves with strong employment protection—they may be more likely to quit their jobs once childbirth is near. Once they quit, it might become hard for them to go back to good jobs with permanent contracts. In other words, they risk becoming labor market outsiders—being under-employed and under-paid. Second, strict employment protection might mean that men, who are less likely to interrupt their work lives for family reasons, become the majority in the insider labor market. This is likely to increase the odds of male-breadwinner families. Strict employment protection might make the male-breadwinner household a more viable option by protecting the sole breadwinner's employment and earnings.[7] In short, in the absence of adequate policy intervention to protect and assist the jobs of working mothers, strict employment protection can be expected to increase women's economic dependence on their husbands and male partners.

Aside from the strictness of employment protection, there are other labor market characteristics that might affect gender relations. Wage bargaining institutions might also have direct and indirect effects on how wives might be able to contribute to family earnings. Scholars have found that countries with decentralized wage setting institutions have greater degrees of wage inequality than countries with centralized wage setting institutions. Rosenfeld and Kallenberg (1990) and Blau and Kahn (1992) found that centralized wage-setting systems generally reduce gender wage gaps by compressing the wage structure. It follows that women who live in countries with a more compressed wage structure (i.e., more wage equality) are more likely to achieve economic parity vis-à-vis their male partners than in countries with a dispersed wage structure (i.e., greater wage inequality). However, Esping-Andersen's argument about market-based de-familialization suggests an alternative scenario (Esping-Andersen 1999). We can consider wage equality as capturing ordinary families' ability to purchase market-based personal services. In other words, when wage inequality is small, married women will not be able to "outsource" their unpaid hours devoted to family care and domestic chores because the cost of such services will be priced relatively expensively. This entails less scope for de-familialization via the private market. In this scenario, women will have less time available for paid work. We expect women in such countries to have inferior economic positions in the family relative to their husbands or male partners.

The literature also assesses other labor market factors that affect women's relative position compared with their husbands or male partners. Huber and Stephens (2000) considered the role of government in offering public sector jobs, especially jobs in female-dominated occupations. Many of the cost concerns of private sector employers may not apply to public sector employers. On the basis of Huber and Stephens's insights, we might expect the size of the public sector to positively influence women's economic position in their family.

BACK TO WORK-FAMILY RECONCILIATION POLICIES

As discussed above, the effects of labor market characteristics can be mediated by work-family reconciliation policies. Jacobs and Gornick (2002) examine the number of hours worked by married women and men; they conclude that when more child care is provided publicly, the working hours of dual-earner couples become more egalitarian. In other words, public child care provision is more likely to improve women's economic status within the marriage than private child care (or de-familialization via the market, to use Esping-Andersen's terminology). Therefore, we should expect the provision of public child care to increase wives' share of family earnings. It is important to point out that there is a close affinity between the generosity of public child care and the size of the public sector (Huber and Stephens 2000). We will come back to this issue later in the chapter.

What about paid maternity and parental leaves? Scholars generally find that the gender gap in employment rates is lower in countries that provide paid leaves (Gornick et al. 1997; Gornick and Meyers 2003). Paid maternity and extended parental leaves are known to increase women's labor market attachment (Waldfogel 1997; Ruhm 1998). In particular, generously paid leaves should push otherwise non-career-oriented women into the labor market by offering them "carrots" in the form of earnings-related social wages during their child-rearing years. However, just as with wage inequality, we can also envisage a different scenario. Recent studies find negative effects of long-term maternity and parental leaves on gender parity in the labor market (Ruhm 1998; Moss and Deven 1999; Ondrich, Spiess, and Yang 2002; Stier and Mandel 2003; Edin and Gustavsson 2005; Estévez-Abe 2005, 2006; Datta Gupta, Smith, and Verner 2008; Mandel 2009). The argument is that long leaves increase women's time away from work, thereby lowering women's current and future earnings as well as hindering career promotions. Indeed, Stier and Mandel (2003) reasoned that although paid maternity leaves are likely to push more married women into the labor market, very long leaves might lock them into "feminized sectors" of the economy where wages are lower, thereby reducing women's economic standing in the family compared with their male partners.

The main focus of this chapter is on the effects of social policies and labor market institutions on the wives' contributions to the family earnings.[8] However, as discussed at the beginning of the chapter, countries also vary in terms of how their tax codes treat married couples. When the unit of taxation is the household rather than the individual, the rate of income tax applied to the wife's earnings may become higher. Scholars have found that such tax penalties have negative effects on married women's labor force participation rates (Jaumotte 2004). We therefore include the tax penalty on second earner's earnings as one of our variables.

DATA AND METHODS

We are primarily interested in investigating the effects of strong labor market regulation, public sector size, and wage compression in explaining cross-national variations in wives' contribution to family earnings. To this end, we conduct a multi-level analysis that evaluates the effects of individual-level and institutional characteristics.

We use data from the *LIS Database* from around 2004. Although the *LIS Database* includes 30 countries, following the standard practice in the study of comparative political economy of high-income countries, this study focuses on a subset of relatively homogeneous countries—that is, we exclude former socialist countries. Excluding those countries for which some of the institutional variables of interest were not available, our sample consists of Australia, Austria, Belgium, Canada, Denmark, Finland,

France, Germany, Ireland, Italy, Norway, Netherlands, Spain, Sweden, the United Kingdom, and the United States.

Our causal variables of interest are country-level institutional variables. Nonetheless, we need to control for individual characteristics of wives and their households. The multi-level analysis permits us to simultaneously control for both individual-level and country-level characteristics. Due to the hierarchical structure of our independent variables, we estimate linear multi-level models, including a linear random intercept. The model can be stated as follows:

$$y_{ik} = \beta_{0k} + \beta_1 x_{1ik} + \dots + \beta_n x_{nik} r_{ik},$$

where y_{ik} is the share of family earnings for wife i in country k; β_{0k} is the country-specific random intercept; β_1 to β_n are the fixed coefficients for individual characteristics x_1 to x_n, such as age of wife, education level of wife, and number of children; and r_{ik} is the individual error term for wife i in country k. In contrast to the coefficients of the individual (level-1) characteristics, the intercept is allowed to vary across countries. This variation is modeled in the following way:

$$\beta_{0k} = \gamma_{00} + u_{0k},$$

where γ_{00} is the overall country mean of the dependent variable, and u_{0k} is a country-specific random term. This means that all country intercepts are spread randomly around the overall intercept. In a second step, we introduce the country (level-2) characteristics. A country's deviation from the overall mean is no longer solely due to random variation but depends on observed country characteristics—such as public sector size, for instance— that shift the country mean:

$$\beta_{0k} = \gamma_{00} + \gamma_{01} z_{1k} + \dots + \gamma_{0m} z_{mk} + u_{0k},$$

where γ_{01} to γ_{0m} are the coefficients for country characteristics z_1 to z_m.

This modeling strategy has two advantages. First, multi-level analysis leads to consistent estimates of the standard errors of the coefficients, which would not be the case in a standard OLS regression (Snijders and Bosker 1999). Second, multi-level models can be used to measure how much variation in the data refers to which level. Therefore, model fits can be calculated for each level separately, which helps us better understand what most accounts for the variation in the dependent variable. Of course, multi-level models are only useful if there are country differences in the distribution of our dependent variable. Country means of wife's share of family earnings in our sample do vary significantly across high-income countries.[9] Finally, all models are estimated using the multi-level commands implemented in Stata 9 (xtmixed commands).

As stated earlier, in addition to the *LIS* data from around 2004, we use country-level institutional variables from several different sources. Our principal dependent variable is the wife's share of family earnings. "Family earnings" is calculated as the sum of net wages from dependent employment for the household head and the spouse, plus, for women, maternity and parental leave benefits.[10] (In *LIS* datasets where gross earnings are reported, we constructed net earnings based on reported gross earnings and reported taxes paid; in *LIS* datasets where net earnings are reported, we used the net earnings contained in the microdata. Thus, our earnings measures are as comparable as possible across all of our study countries.) We construct wife's earnings as consisting of her net wages from employment plus any maternity and parental leave benefits that she received. The wife's share of family earnings is calculated by dividing the wife's earnings by the family earnings. The share variable is a two-side censored variable with limited range 0 to 100. Linear models should be applied to variables with restricted ranges. Therefore, we convert the variable into $\ln(y/1 - y)$, a variable ranging from minus infinity to plus infinity.[11]

We include maternity and parental leave benefits to avoid recording parents on leave as not earning anything. Unlike unemployment or pension benefits, maternity and parental leave benefits replace the market earnings usually paid to workers who have jobs. Not counting paid maternity and parental benefits as part of mothers' earnings runs the risk of dramatically understating women's economic contributions to family earnings, especially in countries with high take-up rates of such paid benefits. For this reason, we included the benefits as part of wives' net wages. We did not add paternity benefits to men's net wages. Even in a country such as Sweden, where the take-up rate of paternity leave is high, less than one-fifth of parental leave time claimed was taken by fathers in 2004 (Duvander, Ferrarini, and Thalberg 2005). Given that only mothers receive paid maternity benefits, the actual share of total benefits that are received by fathers is much smaller than one-fifth of all benefits claimed, even in the most generous Nordic countries. Not including fathers' leave benefits as part of their earnings, therefore, may have resulted in our overstating the positive earnings effect for mothers in a country such as Sweden, but it should not lead to substantial overstatement in most of the other countries.

As described in detail below, all our models include the generosity of maternity and parental benefits as one of the independent variables. This, however, does not mean that we have the same variable both in the left-hand and right-hand sides. The paid benefits that are included in the construction of the dependent variable are the actual amount of benefits claimed by mothers for the duration of leave each of them chose to take. On the other hand, the institutional variable we use is a lagged institutional variable that measures generosity in terms of the design of paid leaves in the past. Therefore, these are two distinct variables.

We have two sets of independent variables: individual-level and country-level. We include the following independent variables at the individual level: wife's age (in years), wife's age squared,[12] wife's education level (low, medium, high), wife's relative education level compared to the husband (1 = equal or higher), presence of children under 18 (1 = yes), and the husband's earnings level. *LIS* reports earnings in national currencies. For reason of international comparability, we use the z-standardized values of husband's earnings. All of these variables are present in the *LIS Database.*

Our country-level variables include public child care provision, public sector size, generosity of paid maternity and parental leave benefits, wage inequality, strictness of employment protection, and the tax penalty on wives' earnings. Variables that measure country-level institutional characteristics are taken from several different databases. As a measure of labor market regulation, we use the index of employment protection regulation developed by the OECD (OECD 2004, Table 2.A2.4 version 1). As a measure of government support for public child care, we use national public child care coverage expressed in percentages (Esping-Andersen 1999, Table 4A). We measure the generosity of maternity and extended leave benefits by counting the number of weeks at full-time pay equivalent. We use the data sources compiled by Gornick and colleagues (1997), Gauthier (1999), and Kamerman (2000), and, for reasons explained below, we use the early 1990s as our base period. For measuring wage inequality, we used the ratio of the 90th percentile to the 10th percentile and calculate it using the OECD gross earnings database.[13] Public sector size is based on the ratio of public sector employment as a percentage of total employment (OECD 1997,

Table II.4). The variable capturing the tax penalty measures the ratio of tax rates on second earners in the family who earn 100 percent of average workers' pay compared with single persons who earn the same amount. The larger the ratio, the greater the penalty on second earners' earnings. This ratio captures possible tax disincentives on wives' work. We used the rates calculated by Florence Jaumotte (2004, Table 2).

We use institutional variables that lag significantly from Wave VI (around 2004). We do this for two reasons. The first reason is the age structure of our sample. We assess married and cohabiting couples of different generations—that is, all cohorts younger than 65. For this reason, using the most recent institutional variables for child care and maternity/parental leaves would not be appropriate for our multi-generation sample of women. Even if the child care provision or maternity/parental leaves offered generous paid benefits in 2004, women who raised their children in the 1990s may not have been able to take advantage of them. For this reason, as a compromise, our child-rearing-related institutional variables come from the early 1990s. This strategy makes sense, given that these work-family policies increase mothers' labor market attachment and therefore might have lasting effects on their earnings in later years. The child care variables compiled by Esping-Andersen that we use are based on data from the early 1990s. The base year for the maternity/parental leaves is 1990. Comparable institutional variables are very hard to find and are not available for all years. Our choice of years was, therefore, partly constrained by the availability of comparable data.

The second reason we chose institutional variables that lag significantly from the year 2004 is the dramatic reforms of labor market regulations in a number of European countries in the past ten years. For labor market variables, such as employment regulation and wage dispersion, we use data from the late 1990s and 2000—before these major labor market reforms.[14] Because we use public sector size to compare its effect to the effect of public child care, we use the available data closest in year to the public child care variable. The OECD data on the public sector size ranges from 1993 to 1995. We are aware that social policies and labor market policies have changed dramatically in some countries in the 2000s, but our intent is to capture the effects of the institutional environment in which the majority of our sample lived and made their critical economic and family decisions.

We estimate six models. As previously stated, we include common individual-level attributes, such as wives' education, age, presence of young children, and husbands' earnings. That said, our primary interest lies in the effects of national-level variables. Because we are interested in exploring the effects of labor market variables, in addition to the effects of work-family reconciliation policies, Models I and III include public child care, generosity of leaves, tax penalty on wives' earnings, and either the strictness of employment protection (Model I) or wage inequality (Model III). Model V includes both strictness of employment protection and wage inequality in the same model. Models II, IV, and VI replace our public child care variable with a public sector–size variable. We do not include the public child care variable and the public sector–size variable into the same model due to their being highly correlated (results not shown). Thus, we estimate three models each—one set with the public child care variable and the other set with the public sector–size variable.

We use the model fit (i.e., the R^2 value at the second level) of each model to assess which bests explains cross-national variation in the outcome. All of the models were estimated using data on all working-age married and cohabiting women in couples where the household head is younger than 65 years.

RESULTS

Table 9.1 reports the results from our multi-level analysis. The results for individual-level characteristics are in line with those in earlier studies. As women get older, their contributions to family earnings increase. Yet, as can be seen from the negative sign on the age-squared variable, the relationship is concave: when women get much older, the effect of age becomes negative. Wives' education levels have a positive and significant effect uniformly throughout different specifications of the basic model. Wives' educational level relative to their husbands' (or male partners') has a positive effect as well. When the wife is at least as or more highly educated than her husband, her contribution is larger. The presence of children has a significant negative effect. Husbands' earnings do matter. As already explained, we use z-standardized values of husbands' earnings. This variable has a negative effect on wives' contribution to household earnings, so women married to

TABLE 9.1
Linear multi-level regression of wife's contribution to family earnings (measured as logarithm of percentage of the overall (NET) family earnings)

Variable	Model I	Model II	Model III
	LEVEL 1		
Age	0.58***	0.58***	0.58***
	(0.01)	(0.01)	(0.01)
Age^2	−0.007***	−0.007***	−0.007***
	(0.00)	(0.00)	(0.00)
Education	1.82***	1.82***	1.82***
	(0.04)	(0.04)	(0.04)
Relative education	−0.16***	−0.16***	−0.16***
	(0.05)	(0.05)	(0.05)
Children <18	−1.28***	−1.28***	−1.28***
	(0.12)	(0.12)	(0.12)
Children × education	0.12***	0.12***	0.12***
	(0.05)	(0.05)	(0.05)
Husband's income	−3.22***	−3.22***	−3.22***
	(0.02)	(0.02)	(0.02)
	LEVEL 2		
Public child care	0.003		0.02
	(0.02)		(0.03)
Public sector size		0.03	
		(0.04)	
Wage inequality			−0.09
			(0.49)
Tax penalty	0.44	0.50	0.04
	(1.65)	(1.63)	(2.10)
Employment protection	−0.78**	−0.77**	
	(0.32)	(0.30)	
Paid leaves	0.03**	0.03*	0.01
	(0.01)	(0.01)	(0.01)
Constant	−16.31***	−16.78***	−16.48***
	(2.26)	(2.34)	(3.59)
	MODEL FIT		
R^2 (level 1, %)	19.02	19.02	19.02
R^2 (level 2, %)	61.64	62.91	40.44
N (level 1)	137.561	137.561	137.561
N (level 2)	16	16	16

SOURCE: Authors' calculations from the *LIS Database*, Wave VI.
*$p < 0.1$; **$p < 0.05$; ***$p < 0.01$.

high-earning men contribute less to household earnings than those married to low earners.

The strictness of labor market regulation (i.e., employment protection) has a statistically significant negative effect on wives' earnings share in the models in which it is included. This offers support for our argument that a rigid labor market might also be gender biased. However, we do not

Model IV	Model V	Model VI
0.58***	0.58***	0.58***
(0.01)	(0.01)	(0.01)
−0.007***	−0.007***	−0.007***
(0.00)	(0.00)	(0.00)
1.82***	1.82***	1.82***
(0.04)	(0.04)	(0.04)
−0.16***	−0.16***	−0.16***
(0.05)	(0.05)	(0.05)
−1.28***	−1.28***	−1.28***
(0.12)	(0.12)	(0.12)
0.12***	0.12***	0.12***
(0.05)	(0.05)	(0.05)
−3.22***	−3.22***	−3.22***
(0.02)	(0.02)	(0.02)
	−0.02	
	(0.02)	
0.04		−0.02
(0.06)		(0.05)
−0.004	−0.82**	−0.79*
(0.53)	(0.41)	(0.45)
0.19	−0.15	−0.18
(2.12)	(1.49)	(1.54)
	−1.12***	−1.06***
	(0.33)	(0.32)
0.02	0.03***	0.03***
(0.01)	(0.01)	(0.01)
−17.54***	−12.31***	−12.13***
(4.15)	(2.83)	(3.42)
19.02	19.02	19.02
40.66	70.20	69.19
137.561	137.561	137.561
16	16	16

observe a significant effect of wage inequality in Models II and IV, even though the sign is in the expected negative direction. When the strictness of employment protection and wage inequality are included in the same model (Models V and VI), wage inequality shows a negative and significant effect, as does the strictness of employment protection. Aside from these variables, only the generosity of paid leaves shows a consistently significant effect. Generous leave benefits increase wives' contributions.

Of the six models estimated, Model V has the best model fit, suggesting that variations in the level of wage inequality, strictness of employment protection, and the generosity of paid leaves account for the greatest portion of cross-national variation in the mean value of wives' contribution to the family earnings. (To reiterate, we include paid leave benefits as part of wives' earnings.)

Unexpectedly, public sector size and public child care provision are not statistically significantly associated with wife's earnings share. These variables are typically found to be significant in studies of gender equality in the labor market. However, it should be noted that, although not statistically significant, the signs on these two coefficients are in the expected directions (i.e., positive).

The effect of the tax penalty is also not significant. This may be due to the fact that the variable only captures tax rates and not social security contributions. Some governments exempt married women from social security contributions if their earned income is below certain thresholds. Our tax penalty variable does not capture such institutional differences.

When we conducted the same analysis defining the dependent variable differently—that is, without paid leave benefits—the effects of public sector size and public child care provision were positive and significant, while the generosity of leave benefits was positive but not significant (results not shown here). The effect of strictness of employment protection remained negative and significant (results not shown here; see Estévez-Abe and Hethey 2008). Given our interest in wives' contribution to household earnings, however, we stand by our decision to include the leave benefits as part of net wages. By including these benefits as part of mothers' earnings, we avoid erroneously underestimating their contributions to household resources.

CONCLUSION

This chapter demonstrates that social policies and labor market characteristics both affect women's economic position within the family. Our findings suggest that the generosity of paid leave benefits improves women's economic position relative to their husbands and cohabiting partners, although—somewhat surprisingly—we did not find statistically significant effects of public child care provision. Wage inequality appears to have negative effects on wives' relative economic position within the couple. Although our results do not report consistently significant effects of wage inequality, wage inequality had significant and negative effects in the two models with better model fits. Also, this finding, while preliminary, corroborates those reported in earlier studies on the relationship between wage structure and the gender wage gap (Blau and Kahn 1992; Pettit and Hook 2009). The novel contribution of this chapter is our finding that strict employment protection has negative effects on women's economic position vis-à-vis their male partners. This result was consistent in all models.

As noted at the beginning of this chapter, many scholars argue that long parental leaves disadvantage women in the labor market. The empirical evidence, however, has been mixed, partly due to different measures of maternity/parental leaves used in the analyses. Some studies assessed only the length of paid maternity leaves, while others considered the length of paid and unpaid leaves taken together, for instance. In addition, earlier studies attempted to explain varied aspects of women's economic disadvantages. Scholars who examined the impact of the actual time mothers took off from work on their post-leave earnings consistently found negative effects of taking off long periods of time (Ruhm 1998; Ondrich et al. 2002; Edin and Gustavsson 2005). Other scholars who looked at the impact of national institutions on variables such as women's current earnings relative to men (Mandel 2009), women's economic dependence on their husbands and male partners (Stier and Mandel 2003), and employment status (Pettit and Hook 2009) found more mixed results. The latter group of scholars all find that generously paid leave benefits improve women's economic position compared with their male partners by improving mothers' employment rates but that there are negative wage effects on highly educated women. The finding in this chapter is thus compatible with findings reported in earlier studies that examine institutional effects on women's relative economic position within couples.

Does our main finding suggest that we should eliminate job security for the sake of gender equality? Not necessarily. In less regulated labor markets, women with low education face an especially precarious existence. We can imagine two ways of potentially addressing this problem. The first is to increase labor market flexibility while supplementing it with other safety nets, such as adequate income support for the unemployed or policies to facilitate geographical relocation and skill upgrading. The second is to enact policies aimed at increasing men's engagements in unpaid care work within the family as a way of reducing women's labor market disadvantage due to their traditionally greater domestic role. The so-called "daddy leaves" in place in the Nordic countries represent efforts of this kind. Although our study did not investigate the effects of national institutions on highly educated women as a separate group, if the findings from prior literature about the negative effects of generous leaves on highly educated women are correct, policy makers might aim to implement especially strong incentives for highly educated (and high-earning) men in the private sector to take more time off for parenting as a strategy for leveling the playing fields for mothers.

However, some words of caution are in order. Given the small number of countries we studied and the complexity of institutional variables, our findings remain tentative. Future research into these questions will benefit from including in the analyses an expanded set of countries and could also use policy variation within countries across time.

NOTES

1. Bianchi and colleagues (1996, 1999) explored the gender implications of Esping-Andersen's taxonomy before Esping-Andersen himself did. Their understanding of the gendered effects of the three welfare states is not the same as the argument Esping-Andersen later developed (Esping-Andersen 1999).

2. We also assessed the countries in our sample by selecting only families with small children (below age three). The results were very similar.

3. Esping-Andersen (1999) is his response to the feminist criticisms. For feminist critiques of Esping-Andersen's three worlds of welfare capitalism, see Orloff (1993), Gornick et al. (1997), and Daly and Rake (2003).

4. Folbre (2008) argues that a large share of women's work is unpaid, and she rightly critiques the undervaluing of care provided within the family as a serious flaw in standard economic analyses.

5. O'Connor, Orloff, and Shaver (1999) take a different approach to suggest that anti-discrimination law might be promoting female employment in liberal countries, although they do not provide evidence empirically.

6. It should be pointed out that Esping-Andersen (1999) does not see such a trade-off in his study. For a recent study of possible trade-offs between equality and service sector job growth, see Kenworthy (2004, 2008).

7. In such a context, becoming a housewife and stay-at-home mother is not necessarily a risky choice. As Hakim (2000) points out, women have heterogeneous preferences. Those women who prefer to become housewives might be happy in a system that protects male breadwinners' jobs and earnings. Male labor market

outsiders who do not possess the same ability to become the breadwinner might become losers—compared to male labor market insiders—in the marriage market.

8. By "wives" we also refer to those women in cohabiting couples.

9. The country means in the sample range from 28 percent in Spain to more than 40 percent in the Nordic countries. An ANOVA F-test for group differences finds these differences to be highly significant.

10. The *LIS* household file only reports earnings from non-farm self-employment at the household level. As a result, we have not been able to determine the relative contribution of the spouse. For this reason, earnings from self-employment are recorded as zero earnings. When the two partners report zero earnings, the couple drops from the sample; couples in which one reports zero earnings are included. In a country such as Spain, where close to 20 percent of individuals are self-employed and the majority of them are men, our strategy underestimates men's earnings. Because more men are self-employed in countries with stronger employment protection, our study may have resulted in reporting smaller negative coefficients for strength of employment protection than otherwise.

11. To obtain valid values for the edges $y = 0$ and $y = 100$ instead of minus and plus infinity, we changed them to $y = 0.000001$ and $y = 99.99999$.

12. We add the wife's age squared to the models because the age effect is not linear but is instead concave. This is to say that a wife's share of family earnings is expected to rise with age but only to a certain point, after which it will decline.

13. We have used the OECD earnings data because it uses gross earnings. The numbers are from the late 1990s.

14. As discussed in the section on data and methods, we use the strictness of employment protection regulation measured by OECD for the 1990s (the OECD data source simply lists it as the late 1990s). For wage dispersion, we use OECD wage data for 2000 and the closest earlier year when data for 2000 were missing.

REFERENCES

Bianchi, Suzanne, Lynn Casper, and Pia Peltola. 1996. "A Cross National Look at Married Women's Economic Dependency." *LIS* working paper 143. Luxembourg: LIS.

———. 1999. "A Cross National Look at Married Women's Economic Dependency." *Gender Issues* 17(3): 3–33.

Blau, Francine, and Lawrence Kahn. 1992. "The Gender Earnings Gap: Learning from International Comparisons." *American Economic Review* 82(2): 533–38.

Boeri, Tito, and Jan Van Ours. 2008. *The Economics of Imperfect Labor Market*. Princeton, NJ: Princeton University Press.

Daly, Mary. 2000. "A Fine Balance: Women's Labor Market Participation in International Comparison." In *Welfare and Work in the Open Economy*, edited by Fritz Sharpf and Vivien Schmidt. New York: Oxford University Press.

Daly, Mary, and Katherine Rake. 2003. *Gender and the Welfare State.*
   Cambridge: Polity.
Datta Gupta, Nabanita, Nina Smith, and Metter Verner. 2008. "The Impact of
   Countries' Family Friendly Policies on Employment, Wages, and Children."
   Review of Economics of Household 6: 65–89.
Duvander, Ann-Zofie, Tommy Ferrarini, and Sara Thalberg. 2005. "Swedish
   Parental Leave and Gender Equality: Achievements and Reform Challenges
   in a European Perspective." Working paper 11. Stockholm: Institute for
   Futures Studies.
Edin, Per-Anders, and Magnus Gustavsson. 2005. "Time Out of Work and Skill
   Depreciation." *Industrial and Labor Relations Review* 61(2): 163–80.
Elsmeskov, Jorgen, John P. Martin, and Stefano Scarpetta. 1998. "Key Lesson
   for Labor Market Reforms: Evidence from OECD Countries' Experience."
   Swedish Economic Policy Review 5(2): 205–52.
Esping-Andersen, Gøsta. 1990. *The Three Worlds of Welfare Capitalism.*
   Princeton, NJ: Princeton University Press.
———. 1999. *Social Foundations of Postindustrial Economies.* Princeton, NJ:
   Princeton University Press.
Estévez-Abe, Margarita. 2005. "Gender Bias in Skills and Social Policies: The
   Varieties of Capitalism Perspective on Sex Segregation." *Social Politics* 12(2):
   180–215.
———. 2006. "Gendering the Varieties of Capitalism: A Study of Occupational
   Segregation by Sex in Advanced Industrial Societies." *World Politics* 59(1):
   142–75.
Estévez-Abe, Margarita, and Tanja Hethey. 2008. "How Policies Affect Women's
   Economic Position within the Family: Labor Market Institutions and Wives'
   Contribution to Household Income." *LIS* working paper 505. Luxembourg:
   LIS.
Folbre, Nancy. 2008. *Valuing Children: Rethinking the Economics of the Family.*
   Cambridge, MA: Harvard University Press.
Gauthier, Anne Hélène. 1999. *The State and the Family: A Comparative Study of
   Family Policies in Industrial Countries.* New York: Oxford University
   Press.
Gornick, Janet C. 1999. "Gender Equality in the Labour Market: Women's Em-
   ployment and Earnings." In *Gender and Welfare State Regimes*, edited by
   Diane Sainsbury. Oxford: Oxford University Press.
Gornick, Janet C., and Jerry Jacobs. 1998. "Gender, the Welfare State, and Public
   Sector Employment: A Comparative Study of Seven Industrialized Coun-
   tries." *American Sociological Review* 63(5): 688–710.
Gornick, Janet C., and Marcia K. Meyers. 2003. *Families That Work: Policies
   for Reconciling Parenthood and Employment.* New York: Russell Sage
   Foundation.

Gornick, Janet C., Marcia K. Meyers, and Katherin E. Ross. 1997. "Supporting the Employment of Mothers: Policy Variation across Fourteen Welfare States." *Journal of European Social Policy* 7(1): 45–70.

Hakim, Catherine. 2000. *Work-Life Style Choices in the 21st Century: Preference Theory*. Oxford: Oxford University Press.

Hobson, Barbara. 1990. "No Exit, No Voice: Women's Economic Dependency and the Welfare State." *Acta Sociologica* 33(3): 235–50.

Huber, Evelyn, and John D. Stephens. 2000. "Women's Employment, and the Social Democratic Service State." *American Sociological Review* 65(3): 323–42.

Jacobs, Jerry A., and Janet C. Gornick. 2002. "Hours of Paid Work in Dual-Earner Couples: The United States in Cross-National Perspective." *Sociological Focus* 35(2): 169–87.

Jaumotte, Florence. 2004. "Labour Force Participation of Women: Empirical Evidence on the Role of Policy and Other Determinants in OECD Countries." *Economic Studies* 37, 2003/2. Paris: OECD.

Kamerman, Sheila B. 2000. "Parental Leave Policies: An Essential Ingredient in Early Childhood Education and Care Policies." *Social Policy Report* 14(2): 3–18.

Kenworthy, Lane. 2004. *Egalitarian Capitalism: Jobs, Incomes and Growth in Affluent Countries*. New York: Russell Sage Foundation.

———. 2008. *Jobs with Equality*. New York: Oxford University Press.

Luxembourg Income Study (LIS) Database, http://www.lisdatacenter.org (multiple countries; microdata last accessed in July 2012). Luxembourg: LIS.

Mandel, Hadas. 2009. "Family Policy and Gender Inequality across Classes." Paper presented at the Seventh ESPAnet Conference. Urbino, Italy (September 17–19, 2009).

Morgan, Kimberly J. 2006. *Working Mothers and the Welfare State: Religion and the Politics of Work-Family Policies in Western Europe and the United States*. Stanford, CA: Stanford University Press.

Moss, Peter, and Fred Deven, eds. 1999. *Parental Leave: Progress of Pitfall? Research and Policy Issues in Europe*. Brussels: Centrum voor Bevolkings en Gezinsstudie.

O'Connor, Julia S., Ann Shola Orloff, and Sheila Shaver. 1999. *States, Markets, and Families*. Cambridge: Cambridge University Press.

Ondrich, Jan, C. Katharina Spiess, and Qing Yang. 2002. "The Effect of Maternity Leave on Women's Pay in Germany 1984–1994." Discussion paper 289. Berlin: DIW Berlin.

Organisation for Economic Co-operation and Development (OECD). 1994. *Job Study*. Paris: OECD.

———. 1997. *Public Sector Size: Measuring Public Employment in OECD Countries*. Paris: OECD.

———. 2004. *Employment Outlook*. Paris: OECD.

Orloff, Ann, S. 1993. "Gender and Social Rights of Citizenship: State Policies and Gender Relations in Comparative Research." *American Sociological Review* 58(3): 303–28.

Pettit, Becky, and Jennifer L. Hook. 2009. *Gendered Tradeoffs: Family, Social Policy, and Economic Inequality in Twenty-One Countries.* New York: Russell Sage Foundation.

Rosenfeld, Rachel, and Arne Kallenberg. 1990. "A Cross-National Comparison of the Gender Gap in Income." *American Journal of Sociology* 96(1): 69–106.

Ruhm, Christopher. 1998. "The Economic Consequences of Parental Leave Mandates: Lessons from Europe." *Quarterly Journal of Economics* 113(1): 285–317.

Saint-Paul, Gilles. 2000. *The Political Economy of Labor Market Institutions.* Oxford: Oxford University Press.

Siebert, Horst. 1997. "Labor Market Rigidities: A Root of Unemployment in Europe." *Journal of Economic Perspectives* 11(3): 37–54.

Snijders, Tom A. B., and Roel J. Bosker. 1999. *Multilevel Analysis. An Introduction to Basic and Advanced Multilevel Modelling.* London: Sage.

Sorensen, Annemette, and Sara McLanahan. 1987. "Married Women's Economic Dependency, 1940–1980." *American Journal of Sociology* 93(3): 659–87.

Stier, Haya, and Hadas Mandel. 2003. "Inequality in the Family: The Institutional Aspects of Wives' Earnings Dependency." *LIS* working paper 359. Luxembourg: LIS.

Waldfogel, Jane. 1997. "The Effect of Children on Women's Wages." *American Sociological Review* 62(2): 209–17.

Part V

WEALTH: THE DISTRIBUTION OF ASSETS AND DEBT

CHAPTER TEN

The Distribution of Assets and Debt

*Eva Sierminska, Timothy M. Smeeding,
and Serge Allegrezza*

Income alone may not be sufficient to measure economic well-being. Economic well-being may well depend not only on current income and consumption but also on values, expectations, and aspirations. Income and access to other economic resources, however, can also affect the extent to which these can be realized. One important resource that is often overlooked in analyses of the distribution of economic well-being is wealth. Wealth provides status as well as economic security in the current period and for the future. Wealth can, for instance, be drawn upon to finance current consumption in the case of an adverse income shock such as job loss, allowing a household to maintain its current lifestyle. In this chapter, we examine cross-national evidence on the distribution of wealth and its composition, with an emphasis on variation in wealth across the income distribution—that is, low-, middle-, and high-income groups—and across family types, especially comparing one- and two-parent families.

In considering wealth portfolios, we focus on net worth, financial assets, home ownership, net home value, and debts. We use data for Germany, Italy, Luxembourg, Sweden, the United Kingdom, and the United States from the *Luxembourg Wealth Study (LWS) Database.*

We find that, despite institutional variation across countries, financial assets do not play a very large role in wealth portfolios, in contrast to the important role of owned homes. In all countries except Luxembourg, single parents—that is, parents with a dependent child and without a partner—are about 20 percentage points less likely to own their homes than the rest of the population. They are also just as likely, if not more so, to be in debt. On the other hand, compared to the entire population, couples with children are just as likely to own financial assets and are more likely to own their homes and to be in debt for that home.

In terms of wealth holdings, we find that, on average, single parents hold half of what we find for couples with children. The value of one's home is the largest asset for both types of households. Home value and its affordability vary consistently across countries. Indebtedness is two to three times the annual income in countries with high levels of indebtedness, and it is larger in couple-headed families than for single parents.

LITERATURE REVIEW

We focus our discussion of the literature in two areas: the newer cross-national literature on wealth holdings, with a focus on housing wealth, and research on the wealth holdings of different household types. We also review research on the assets and debt of single parents, as they have not yet been studied in the cross-national literature on wealth.

Wealth in Cross-National Perspective

New studies of comparative wealth holdings, several of which focus on particular wealth components such as owner-occupied housing and pensions, have emerged over the past ten years (Banks, Blundell, and Smith 2003; Kapteyn and Panis 2003; Apgar and Di 2005; Chiuri and Jappelli 2010). Many of these have been limited because of the unavailability of comparable data. Authors typically study two or three countries, harmonizing their own data for the purpose of the comparison at hand. With this method, errors in data and measurement are more likely than with harmonized wealth survey data.

Housing Wealth

Housing wealth is by far the most studied of these components (Claus and Scobie 2001; Doling et al. 2004; Apgar and Di 2005; Banks et al. 2005; Chiuri and Jappelli 2010). While housing is the most widely held real asset in many countries, its effects on consumption of goods other than housing and additional wealth accumulation are less generalizable (Apgar and Di 2005). In the United States, reverse annuity mortgages and home equity loans are used by "home rich but cash poor" elderly to access their savings. Even then, the use of these tools is not widespread, with fewer than 10 percent of the elderly in the United States in the early 2000s using them, and likely even fewer after the 2007 housing value crash (Copeland 2006; Fisher et al. 2007; see also Mitchell and Pigot 2004 on Japan; and Hurst and Stafford 2004 on the United States). At the same time, Apgar and Di (2005) report that low-income families (bottom 20 percent of the elderly ranked by income) in the United States who own their own homes outright may still end up spending 25 percent or more of their income on housing due to property taxes, utilities, and upkeep. Such households are also likely to have very low net worth in their housing (Gornick, Sierminska, and Smeeding 2009). Thus, ownership is not without direct costs, even when the mortgage has been paid off and not all the elderly have large amounts of home equity.

Researchers have examined the joint distribution of housing wealth and income/consumption. The effects of housing on consumption vary over time in the United States (Carroll 2004; Case, Quigley, and Shiller 2005): short-term and long-term estimates of the marginal propensities to consume from wealth are estimated to be in the range of 2 to 8 percent over the past 40 years. Similar propensities are found by Catte and colleagues (2004) for a range of Organisation for Economic Co-operation and Development (OECD) countries. The effects of housing wealth on consumption are smaller than those of financial wealth in some studies (Barrel and Davis 2004), but the results vary with the methods used (see Sierminska and Takhtamanova 2012 for an overview). Others have made forays into the extent of financial wealth holdings and their effect on consumption, claiming that the propensity to hold stocks in the United States is more widespread than in other rich countries (Dvornak and Kohler 2003) and therefore has a larger effect on spending.

Evidence of home ownership and maintenance of housing wealth has been studied by many analysts in specific countries—for instance, by Venti and Wise (2004) and Fisher and colleagues (2007) for the United States; by Crossley and Ostrovsky (2003) for Canada; by Ermisch and Jenkins (1999) for the United Kingdom; by Tatsiramos (2006) for six European countries; and by Chiuri and Jappelli (2010) for countries included in the *LIS Database*. Using the *LIS* data, Chiuri and Jappelli find that housing is held long into retirement, with the exception of in Finland and Canada, where the transition from owning to renting takes place earlier in life. In most other countries, rules of housing finance, borrowing, and other national idiosyncrasies have large effects on renting versus owning across the life cycle (e.g., see Chen 2006; Chiuri and Jappelli 2003; Ortalo-Magné and Rady 2006; Martins and Villanueva 2009).

Wealth and Household Structure: Single Parents versus Couples

So far, no one has produced a complete, cross-national study of wealth and its distribution among single, divorced, and unmarried parents compared with married parents. Of the studies completed, none have targeted the middle class. According to a recent report by the U.S. Department of Commerce (2010), U.S. middle-class families of all types, including single-parent families, aspire to home ownership, owning a car, college education for their children, good health insurance, and retirement security. Public policy can help with many of these needs, supplying guaranteed health insurance and college education subsidies, among other things. Of course, some countries—most of the countries studied here, except the United States—provide guaranteed health insurance and affordable university opportunities for qualified students. But still a large share of the costs of health care (especially long-term care) and education remain the responsibility of the family in all countries. Due to their increased financial security, two-parent families are much more likely to meet these standards than single-parent families. Gender and family wealth gaps for single versus other parents have been studied in the United States (Sedo and Kossoudji 2004; Conley and Ryvicker 2004; Schmidt and Sevak 2006) and in Germany (Frick and Grabka 2010).

Recent studies in the United States on the effect of wealth on marriage and cohabitation suggest that wealth also has powerful effects on family formation, including assortative mating. While adults at all education levels are likely to both form partnerships and bear children, family formation varies markedly across educational levels. For instance, in the United States, young women with a high school degree or less are likely to bear children between the ages of 19 and 21, mainly out of wedlock, and with subsequent post-birth uncertainty for both mother and child. In contrast, college-educated women often have a first child at age 28 after marriage to another college graduate and tend to have smaller and more stable families (Smeeding, Garfinkel, and Mincy 2011). Assortative mating therefore further strengthens the wealth position of more advantaged couples and their children and does exactly the opposite for less educated, younger parents (Schneider 2011).

Cross-national studies on family wealth are limited. Recent papers by Lusardi, Schneider, and Tufano (2011) assess household financial risk in the United States, France, Germany, the United Kingdom, Canada, and Italy, but they do not focus on single parents. For their cross-national analyses, they use a six-country survey of 7,240 households conducted during the summer of 2009 regarding risk exposures, risk-bearing capacity, and coping mechanisms. The limited sample size means that there are insufficient numbers of single mothers in each country to draw firm conclusions about their wealth holdings. While informative, these studies also do not capture the entire wealth distribution.

Bover (2010) studied wealth inequality and household structure in Spain and the United States and found that household structure is an important determinant of overall wealth. Sierminska, Frick, and Grabka (2010) examined gender gaps in wealth in Germany and included unmarried parents in their analysis; they found a sizeable wealth gap between partners within households. Sierminska and Takhtamanova (2012) studied cross-national differences in wealth spending by family structure, controlling for age, education, and family formation and found important age differences.

Other *LWS*-based papers considered the joint distributions of income and wealth across five rich countries, but with no differentiation across family types (Jäntti, Sierminska, and Smeeding 2008). The study discussed in this chapter is the first to examine both income and wealth holdings and their joint distributions for various family types, using the best available cross-national wealth data for such purposes: the *LWS* data.

Poverty and Income in Cross-National Perspective among Older Women and Others

Asset ownership among older women, and asset and income poverty more generally, has been studied recently using the *LWS* data (Gornick et al. 2009; Brandolini, Magri, and Smeeding 2010). In most cross-national research, income is the main indicator on older people's well-being. A number of researchers have used the *Luxembourg Income Study (LIS)* data to analyze a broader range of income disparities among elders. Many of these studies examined the income portfolios of the elderly and found balanced packages of private/occupational pensions, retirement savings, earnings, and public transfers only at the higher-income levels. At median and below-median income, social retirement pensions or income-tested public transfers are the most important income source for the elderly in every country. But wealth is rarely examined in these studies. An exception is Smeeding (2003), who capitalizes interest, rent, and dividend flows to estimate financial wealth, differentiating between home owners and renters in some comparisons. Brandolini and colleagues (2010) conducted a study of asset poverty for all *LWS* countries but without any emphasis on household structure. Few studies have analyzed debt in a cross-national context, using *LWS* or any other comparable data (Crook 2006).

In summary, there is still a lot we do not know about the distribution of wealth across countries. In particular, we know very little about wealth across class and across family type. In this chapter, we attempt to gain a better understanding of how the joint distribution of income *and* wealth varies across family types.

DATA, VARIABLES, METHODS, AND MEASUREMENT ISSUES

Data

This chapter uses comparable microdata on wealth and income from the *Luxembourg Wealth Study (LWS) Database*, which contains harmonized wealth microdatasets from 12 rich countries.[1] We include six countries: Germany, Italy, Luxembourg,[2] Sweden, the United Kingdom, and the United States. The availability of information on housing and financial wealth largely dictated the countries studied, as not all countries in the database contain all the necessary details. In addition, we chose countries representing varying economic environments in order to highlight variation in wealth allocation patterns across relatively diverse countries as of the first decade of the twenty-first century. For example, both Germany and Italy are traditionally low-debt countries as opposed to the Anglo-Saxon countries: the United Kingdom and the United States. Home ownership is encouraged to varying degrees across countries by providing tax incentives, such as mortgage interest deductibility in the United States. Finally, pension systems vary in generosity and structure—for example, pensions are much more generous in Sweden than in the United States—and that creates different incentives for investment behavior.

In this chapter, we use the latest datasets available in the *LWS Database* for years from 2000 to 2007. The original datasets included in the harmonized database that we use here, are for the United States, the Survey of Consumer Finances (SCF) 2007; for Germany, the Socio-Economic Panel (SOEP) 2007; for Italy, the Survey of Household Income and Wealth (SHIW) 2004; for Luxembourg, PSELL-3/EU-SILC 2007; for Sweden, the Wealth Survey 2002; and for the United Kingdom, the British Household Panel Study (BHPS) 2000. These countries are captured at somewhat different stages in the business cycle, but wealth holdings are reasonably stable, so the snapshot of wealth and income that we take in these years of observation is still quite useful.

To reduce the number of missing observations, the data for Germany, Luxembourg, and the United States are multiply imputed, which means that there are five replicates for each original observation.[3] The data for Italy, Sweden, and the United Kingdom do not use multiple imputation.

Income and Wealth: The Aggregate Indicators and Their Components

Our main income variable used in the analyses is household disposable income (DPI). DPI is defined as the sum of total revenues from earnings, capital income, private transfers, and public transfers (social insurance and public social assistance), net of taxes and social security contributions. The income definitions and basic results regarding income inequality and poverty in the *LWS* are very close to those found in *LIS*, as discussed in Niskanen (2006).

In the *LWS* data, these income sources are defined as follows:

1. *Earnings* include wages and salaries, as well as income from self-employment activities.

2. *Capital income* includes interests and dividends, rental income, income from savings plans (including annuities from life insurance and private individual retirement accounts), royalties, and other property income.[4]

3. *Private transfers* include occupational and other pensions (e.g., pensions of unknown type or foreign pensions), alimony, regular transfers from other households/charity/private institutions, and other incomes not elsewhere classifiable.[5]

4. *Public transfers* include *social insurance* (including some universal benefits such as social retirement pensions, unemployment insurance, disability benefits, and family allowances), as well as *public social assistance*, which includes income-tested and means-tested cash and near-cash public income transfers.[6]

5. *Taxes* include all direct taxes on income.

The counterpart of DPI, with respect to wealth, is the concept of net worth (NW1), which consists of financial assets and non-financial assets net of total debt. Financial assets include deposit accounts, stocks, bonds, and mutual funds. Non-financial assets are divided into two areas: owned home and other real estate. Finally, total debt refers to all outstanding loans, both home-secured and non-home-secured. We do not include pension wealth that has not been realized in the form of a pension flow or converted to accessible financial assets. We include business assets, although they are not available for all countries (see net worth definitions at www.lisdatacenter .org/our-data/lws-database/).

Analyzing the Economic Well-Being: The Unit of Analysis

In analyzing economic well-being, we ignore differences in holdings among individuals within households (e.g., between spouses), and because assets are recorded at the household level, we implicitly assume full sharing of all resources among members of the household. The unit of analysis is, therefore, the total household, or all the individuals in such households. We analyze the whole population and also focus on two types of households: single-parent and two-parent. Single-parent households consist of one adult and at least one child; two-parent households consist of two adults and at least one child.

Analyzing Economic Well-Being: Methods and Measurement Issues

After providing an overview of portfolios among all households across the countries, we focus our analysis on the middle class. Although there is an ongoing discussion on what constitutes the middle class (see Chapter 2), and different definitions are explored in this book, we remain faithful to Solow's "middle 60 percent." Thus, we define the "middle class" as consisting of households located in the middle 60 percent of the income distribution. We use DPI and divide the income distribution into three parts. The bottom 20 percent are labeled as the "bottom," the middle 60 percent are the "middle," and the top 20 percent are the "top."

As is standard in research on income, we "equivalize" the income data—meaning we adjust each household's income to account for household size. Incomes are equivalized using the square root scale. Although there is a large literature on income equivalence scales, there is much less consensus on how to equivalize wealth. Sierminska and Smeeding (2005) address this, and their results suggest that equivalizing has only small effects on the wealth distribution. Whether or not wealth should be equivalized depends on the purpose of the analysis. For example, when the goal is to compare wealth level holdings (home values, financial assets, or the level of debt) across household types, as is the case here, equivalizing would suggest that home prices are much lower (housing is cheaper) than they actually are for some household types (couples and singles, for example). On the other hand, when we are conceptualizing wealth as a potential stream of income that can be converted to finance consumption and that contributes to individual well-being in the household (see Chapter 11), the potential for a given level of wealth to generate well-being depends on household size and structure. In that case, we argue that wealth should be equivalized just as income is. In the analyses in this chapter, we do not equivalize wealth because we are comparing wealth holdings across household types. Finally, incomes are bottom-coded at 1 percent of the mean equivalized DPI and top-coded at 10 times the median.

The wealth variables are not bottom-coded or top-coded, and as a result, wealth variables (net worth in particular) can contain both negative and zero values. Because the top and bottom of these wealth distributions may differ across countries depending on the quality of the wealth survey and the sampling practices among the richest sectors of the population, we also rely on medians in our analysis. All observations with missing or zero disposable income or missing net worth are dropped from our analysis sample. Furthermore, when we report actual currency amounts, all amounts are expressed as U.S. dollars adjusted by purchasing power parities (PPPs), using the 2009 OECD actual individual consumption PPPs. Amounts referring to years prior to 2009 are deflated using each country's CPI.

RESULTS

We begin by presenting a set of basic results. Descriptive statistics for the whole population are followed by a more detailed examination of wealth across the income distribution. We examine the portfolio composition, wealth packages, financial asset holdings, and housing values. Next, we examine housing affordability and indebtedness for single parents and for households with children.

Asset Participation and Wealth Holding: All Households

Patterns of asset holding and portfolio composition across these countries differ less in terms of prevalence of assets than in level or composition of those assets (Table 10.1).[7] Germany and Luxembourg have a somewhat narrower definition of financial assets and exclude deposit accounts, and in addition, the data in Luxembourg are bottom-coded. Excluding those two countries, about 80 to 90 percent of households are likely to hold some form of financial assets. In Germany and Luxembourg, savings and other types of investments are held by at least half of the population. Stock and mutual

TABLE 10.1
Characteristics of wealth portfolios

Wealth variable	United States 2007	Germany 2001	Italy 2004	Luxembourg 2007	Sweden 2002	United Kingdom 2000
HOUSEHOLD ASSET PARTICIPATION (%)						
Financial assets	91	50	84	62	83	81
Stocks/mutual funds	34	n/a	23	n/a	74	48
Owned home	71	48	70	70	62	73
Other real estate	20	14	22	27	16	9
Business assets	14	6	22	7	9	n/a
Total debt	82	41	27	n/a	79	69
Home debt	54	27	15	41	74	48
Other debt	72	17	16	n/a	n/a	55
AVERAGE ASSET VALUES ACROSS COUNTRIES (2009 USD)						
Financial assets	115,210	20,956	27,810	42,205	30,702	35,070
Owned home	228,052	127,014	183,484	353,331	81,111	174,482
Other real estate	81,319	42,055	48,505	145,401	13,551	20,377
Total assets	424,581	190,025	259,799	540,937	125,364	229,929
Total debt	124,624	49,741	10,373	n/a	50,001	56,288
Home debt	84,967	27,175	8,806	49,801	44,978	49,870
Net worth	299,957	140,284	249,426	491,136	75,363	173,641
Business equity	144,083	30,744	47,672	21,833	13,161	n/a
Net worth 2	444,040	171,028	297,098	512,969	88,524	n/a
SHARES OF TOTAL ASSETS						
Financial assets	27	11	11	8	24	15
Owned home	54	67	71	65	65	76
Other real estate	19	22	19	27	11	9
Total assets	100	100	100	100	100	100
Total debt	(29)	(26)	(4)	n/a	(40)	(24)
Home debt	(20)	(14)	(3)	(9)	(36)	(22)
Net worth	71	74	96	n/a	60	76

SOURCE: Authors' calculations from the *LWS Database* (2000–2007) and 2007 PSELL-3.

NOTE: Financial assets in Germany and Luxembourg refer to saving accounts, bonds, shares, and investments and do not include deposit accounts.

fund ownership is far less prevalent, but is still high in Sweden (74 percent), followed by the United Kingdom (48 percent), and the United States (34 percent) (see Sierminska, Brandolini, and Smeeding, 2006). Home ownership rates are quite similar across countries, with about two-thirds of the population owning their main residence despite differences in financing options. Germany is an exception, with 48 percent home ownership and a low share of debt holders. Owning a business is most prevalent in Italy (22 percent), and then in the United States (14 percent), followed by Germany, Luxembourg, and Sweden, with a 6 to 9 percent ownership across these three countries.

Although financial asset holdings are widespread, they account for no more than about one-quarter of total assets in any of these countries. In Sweden and in the United States, financial wealth constitutes 24 and 27 percent, respectively, of the total wealth portfolio (see Table 10.1). In the other countries, financial holdings are only 8 to 15 percent of total wealth. (In Sweden, this relatively large share of financial assets is explained in part by the relatively low valuation of real estate that can be seen in Table 10.1.)

Non-financial assets, particularly the main residence, are the most important component of assets in all countries. This is most notable in the United Kingdom (76 percent of total assets) and Italy (71 percent of total assets). Non-financial assets constitute about 65 percent in Germany, Luxembourg, and Sweden, but less than 55 percent in the United States. In Luxembourg, about a quarter of the population owns other real estate, slightly less in Germany, Italy, and the United States. Only in the United Kingdom do fewer than 10 percent of households own other real estate.

Total debt is widespread among the population in Sweden (79 percent), the United States (82 percent), and the United Kingdom (69 percent). Apart from functioning mortgage markets and home loans, which are found in most countries, a country's tax structure may also create incentives to take up loans, as loan interest may be tax deductible. In Luxembourg, 41 percent of households have home-secured debt (home mortgages). In Germany and Italy, an even smaller proportion of households hold such debt: 27 and 15 percent, respectively. The low share of households with debt and the high share of home owners in Italy suggest that many own their homes outright.[8] Unlike in the United States or the United Kingdom, many loans in Sweden use the principal residence as collateral, resulting in a very small share of other than housing loans.

Wealth levels vary across countries and, given that financial assets play only a small role in wealth portfolios, are to a large extent driven by home prices. These vary depending on the valuation methods and local housing market conditions. Luxembourg has the highest values of non-financial assets as well as net worth in our study, due to its high real estate prices. Luxembourg net worth and non-financial assets are followed by those in the United States and Italy. Besides having a large participation rate, the United States also has the highest levels of investments in financial assets. The levels of home debt (for owners who still owe mortgages) hover around $50,000 in Luxembourg, Sweden, and the United Kingdom, but they are lower in Germany and Italy and higher in the United States. Home debt constitutes between 3 percent of total assets in Italy to 36 percent in Sweden. The value of home debt is the highest in the United States ($85,000) and accounts for about one-fifth of the total assets in that country.

Asset Participation and Wealth Holding across the Income Distribution

Next, we focus on the joint distribution of income and wealth by examining the probability of owning assets across the income distribution (Table 10.2). We distinguish between those at the bottom (bottom 20 percent of the distribution), the middle (middle 60 percent), and the top (top 20 percent) of the income distribution for all persons. We focus our analysis on the middle of the distribution and refer to it as the "middle class," but then we compare these outcomes to those at both ends of the distribution.

Among the middle class, the probability of having financial assets remains high (over 82 to 95 percent) in the United States, Italy, Sweden, and the United Kingdom, although in Germany and Luxembourg it is about 55 to 65 percent. Among the middle class, the probability of owning one's home remains close to the average, with a little over two-thirds of the middle class (except in Germany) being home owners. Indebtedness among this group is quite high in the United States, Sweden, and the United Kingdom. It is a bit lower in Germany (44 percent) and Italy (28 percent). Home-secured debt is most prevalent in Sweden, where 77 percent of households report holding household secured debt, followed by the United States (59 percent), the United Kingdom (48 percent), and Luxembourg (45 percent). The lowest probability of having home-secured debt is reported in Germany

TABLE 10.2
Portfolio composition across the income distribution by family type

	UNITED STATES			GERMANY			ITALY			LUXEMBOURG			SWEDEN			UNITED KINGDOM		
	Bottom	Middle	Top	Bottom	Middle	Top	Bottom	Middle	Top	Bottom	Middle	Top	Bottom	Middle	Top	Bottom	Middle	Top
ALL																		
Financial assets	70	95	100	23	53	78	59	89	95	29	64	79	63	85	97	59	82	95
Risky assets	14	36	75	n/a	n/a	n/a	4	20	47	n/a	n/a	n/a	48	75	93	23	44	74
Owned home	44	76	94	28	49	70	55	70	82	40	74	81	32	64	85	56	70	92
Other real estate	10	19	53	5	13	37	15	20	37	11	23	51	6	14	34	6	7	15
Business assets	11	12	37	2	4	19	16	18	40	4	5	14	6	9	12	n/a	n/a	n/a
Total debt	62	87	84	21	44	61	19	28	33	n/a	n/a	n/a	58	81	93	53	69	82
Home debt	25	59	72	11	29	43	9	14	23	23	45	43	44	77	90	24	48	67
Other debt	53	77	52	11	18	20	12	18	15	n/a	n/a	n/a	n/a	n/a	n/a	39	56	62
SINGLE PARENTS																		
Financial assets	52	86	*	7	33	68	50	91	*	52	57	*	59	76	*	47	69	92
Risky assets	10	24	*	n/a	n/a	n/a	6	18	*	n/a	n/a	n/a	53	69	*	8	32	64
Owned home	17	56	*	8	35	52	29	58	*	40	74	*	23	44	*	31	52	93
Other real estate	3	13	*	1	9	30	21	20	*	11	13	*	3	8	*	2	4	10
Business assets	5	7	*	2	1	20	26	7	*	1	6	*	4	3	*	n/a	n/a	n/a
Total debt	56	89	*	21	42	61	14	37	*	n/a	n/a	n/a	80	90	*	64	72	84
Home debt	14	47	*	5	22	36	14	14	*	25	35	*	69	85	*	17	40	56
Other debt	53	84	*	17	20	34	20	26	*	n/a	n/a	n/a	n/a	n/a	n/a	58	63	66
COUPLES WITH CHILDREN																		
Financial assets	74	96	100	20	49	79	63	91	96	22	64	79	63	90	99	55	84	96
Risky assets	16	39	86	n/a	n/a	n/a	3	22	46	n/a	n/a	n/a	52	84	97	26	44	76
Owned home	53	79	98	33	58	77	50	72	84	46	77	83	44	77	93	64	77	96
Other real estate	12	20	59	7	14	42	14	21	39	14	25	55	10	13	41	12	8	15
Business assets	19	15	44	3	5	25	21	26	44	4	7	18	11	10	10	n/a	n/a	n/a
Total debt	73	94	91	36	61	74	26	37	37	n/a	n/a	n/a	86	96	98	76	87	91
Home debt	39	71	85	21	44	57	12	20	29	28	58	47	80	94	96	42	67	77
Other debt	61	84	53	17	23	22	16	22	15	n/a	n/a	n/a	n/a	n/a	n/a	51	70	72

SOURCE: Authors' calculations from the *LWS Database* (2000–2007) and 2007 PSELL-3.

*Results not shown because the number of observations in the cell is less than 20.

and Italy (29 and 14 percent, respectively), owing mainly to high levels of outright home ownership in the latter.

We observe large differences in asset participation between the bottom and middle of the distribution, particularly for home ownership, with differences of 20 to 30 percentage points. There are also differences in debt participation, but they are not as large as for home ownership, indicating that poorer renters sometimes fall into debt to finance their spending. Generally, at the top of the distribution, households are more likely to own financial assets, homes, investment real estate, and their own businesses. Such households are also more likely to hold debt to finance these purchases, which makes them vulnerable in case of unexpected life events.

Asset Participation and Wealth Holding: Single Parents and Couples with Children

As reported in Bover (2010), variation in wealth accumulation across countries exists not only due to institutional differences but also because of variations in household formation and structure. To net out differences due to family demographics and to examine comparable households, we focus on two types of households with children: single parents and couples.[9]

In all of these countries, most single-parent households fall in the middle or bottom of the income distribution. In Germany and Luxembourg, single-parent households are about equally likely to be in the bottom of the distribution as in the middle; in the other countries, most single-parent households fall in the middle of the distribution (see the online appendix, Table 10.A1). There are very few single parents in the top of the distribution in any country, and those who are in the top are less well-to-do than other household types, a finding that is consistent with other studies of the middle class (U.S. Department of Commerce 2010). Households with couples, on the other hand, are more evenly distributed, except in Sweden, where they are more likely to be in the middle of the distribution.

The fact that single parents are more likely to be financially constrained than are other family types can be seen from their lower probability of owning financial assets compared to the entire population in most countries in the study: Germany, Sweden, the United Kingdom, and the United States. They are also approximately 20 percentage points less likely to own their homes in all countries, except Luxembourg, where there is no difference (see Table 10.2). They are just as likely to be in debt as the whole population in Germany, the United Kingdom, and the United States, but more likely in Italy and Sweden.

There are large differences in ownership between single parents in the middle and the bottom of the distribution. Differences in home owner-ship, for example, are in the range of 20 (in Sweden) to 40 (in the United States) percentage points. Differences in financial asset ownership are small in Luxembourg (8 percentage points); 17 to 26 percentage points in Swe-den, the United Kingdom, and Germany; and very high in the United States (34 percentage points) and Italy (41 percentage points). Differences are more striking for home debt (due to differences in home ownership rates) than in other types of debt.

The literature on the well-being of families in the United States has found that couples with children are better off compared to single parents and, in particular, are more likely to be home owners (Sedo and Kossoudji 2004). This pattern is confirmed for other countries and for the middle class. In Table 10.2, we find that couples with children in the middle of the distribution are almost just as likely or more likely to own financial assets and are more likely to own their homes when compared to the whole popu-lation, particularly in Germany and Sweden. They are also more likely to be in debt in Germany (by 17 percentage points), Italy (by 9 percentage points), Sweden (by 15 percentage points), the United Kingdom (by 18 percentage points), and the United States (by 7 percentage points). In Luxembourg, they are 13 percentage points more likely to have a mortgage than the over-all population.

Wealth Packages across the Income Distribution

We compare wealth packages in Table 10.3, which expresses financial as-sets, non-financial assets, and debt as shares of total assets. In the middle of the income distribution, the owned home is about 75 percent of the wealth portfolio of single parents and couples with children, and a slightly larger share in the portfolios of single parents in Sweden and the United Kingdom. In many countries, the main home accounts for a smaller share of the wealth portfolio for those at the bottom of the distribution, where home ownership rates are much lower. Understandably, for these households, financial assets play a larger role in their wealth portfolio. Debt plays an important role in the wealth portfolios of middle-income single-parent families with children in all countries, except in Italy, where it is not very common in general.

TABLE 10.3

Wealth packages across the income distribution by family type

	United States			Germany			Italy			Luxembourg			Sweden			United Kingdom		
	Bottom	Middle	Top	Bottom	Middle	Top	Bottom	Middle	Top	Bottom	Middle	Top	Bottom	Middle	Top	Bottom	Middle	Top
WHOLE POPULATION																		
Financial assets	32	16	43	7	10	13	6	9	13	5	7	10	29	22	28	9	14	18
Owned home	45	67	35	78	75	52	80	77	61	79	78	46	61	70	57	82	79	71
Other real estate	23	17	22	15	14	35	13	14	25	17	15	44	10	8	16	9	7	11
Total assets	100	100	100	100	100	100	100	100	100	100	100	100	100	100	100	100	100	100
(Total debt)	(23)	(39)	(16)	(22)	(25)	(29)	(4)	(4)	(4)	n/a	n/a	n/a	(45)	(43)	(34)	(16)	(27)	(24)
(Home debt)	(13)	(28)	(10)	(11)	(16)	(12)	(3)	(3)	(3)	(15)	(11)	(6)	(34)	(39)	(32)	(14)	(23)	(21)
Net worth	77	61	84	78	75	71	96	96	96	—	—	—	55	57	66	84	73	76
SINGLE PARENTS																		
Financial assets	36	12	*	8	11	13	7	12	*	3	10	*	18	13	*	9	8	10
Owned home	62	72	*	90	77	64	64	72	*	90	79	*	78	81	*	86	88	84
Other real estate	3	17	*	2	13	23	29	16	*	7	11	*	4	5	*	5	4	6
Total assets	100	100	*	100	100	100	100	100	*	100	100	*	100	100	*	100	100	100
(Total debt)	(49)	(42)	*	(29)	(24)	(43)	(11)	(5)	*	n/a	n/a	*	(76)	(58)	*	(21)	(30)	(26)
(Home debt)	(36)	(31)	*	(13)	(20)	(17)	(7)	(4)	*	(21)	(8)	*	(56)	(50)	*	(19)	(26)	(20)
Net worth	51	58	*	71	76	57	89	95	*	n/a	n/a	*	24	42	*	79	70	74
COUPLES WITH CHILDREN																		
Financial assets	31	12	41	5	7	10	7	9	12	3	4	8	16	15	21	4	9	14
Owned home	46	72	36	77	79	55	79	78	63	75	81	52	69	78	63	86	82	73
Other real estate	23	17	22	19	14	35	14	13	25	22	15	40	15	6	16	10	9	12
Total assets	100	100	100	100	100	100	100	100	100	100	100	100	100	100	100	100	100	100
(Total debt)	(29)	(49)	(18)	(36)	(33)	(36)	(5)	(6)	(4)	n/a	n/a	n/a	(70)	(56)	(40)	(24)	(36)	(28)
(Home debt)	(17)	(35)	(11)	(19)	(23)	(16)	(5)	(5)	(4)	(14)	(13)	(7)	(60)	(51)	(38)	(22)	(32)	(25)
Net worth	71	51	82	64	67	64	95	94	96	n/a	n/a	n/a	30	44	60	76	64	72

SOURCE: Authors' calculations from the *LWS Database* (2000–2007) and 2007 PSELL-3.

*United States: 66/5 observations; Italy: 9 observations; Luxembourg: 16 observations; Sweden: 17 observations.

As a share of total assets, it has the highest value in Sweden (58 percent), the United States (42 percent), the United Kingdom (30 percent), Germany (24 percent), and Italy (5 percent). The same ranking and similar shares are observed among couples with children. Hence, regardless of the household structure, debt is most prevalent in Sweden and the United States. Luxembourg does not contain full information on the indebtedness of the population, and home debt represents a rather low share of total assets in the middle of the distribution compared with the other countries.

Financial Assets

Next, we examine in more detail the main components of the wealth portfolio. Financial wealth is the most liquid part of the wealth portfolio and can easily be used to instantaneously smooth consumption or cushion economic hardship. The patterns of financial wealth holdings are examined in the upper panel of Table 10.4, with mean and median values given for single parents and couples with children with positive wealth holdings. Single parents in the middle of the distribution have the largest financial cushion in Luxembourg: about USD87,500. In Italy, Germany, and the United States, among those who own financial assets, the average value is USD30,000. In Sweden and the United Kingdom, the average is only USD12,000. The differences in these values are most likely due to cross-country differences in household formation (Bover 2010). The median values are more compressed, varying between USD2,400 and USD15,500. Average financial assets for couples with children range from USD21,000 in the United Kingdom to USD39,000 in the United States. At the median, the range is from USD5,800 in the United Kingdom to USD16,000 in Germany. By comparing the mean to the median, we get a sense of the inequality within these groups. The highest mean-median difference is in the United States and Luxembourg, followed by the rest of the countries for both household types. The very high difference for the United States is, in part, explained by the fact that the survey oversamples the very wealthy, which may be driving the results at the mean, as can be seen from the "Top" column.

Home Ownership and Value

Wealth accumulated in one's home can also serve as a monetary cushion for families (see Chapter 12). The extent to which, and the ease with which, home ownership can provide income varies cross-nationally with the avail-

TABLE 10.4

Summary statistics of main wealth components conditional on ownership for single parents and couples with children (in USD)

| | FINANCIAL ASSETS | | | | | | | | |
| | UNITED STATES | | | GERMANY | | | ITALY | | |
	Bottom	*Middle*	*Top*	*Bottom*	*Middle*	*Top*	*Bottom*	*Middle*	*Top*
Single parents									
Mean	32,547	31,416	*	19,170	31,880	53,624	9,193	27,771	*
Median	400	3,000	*	9,193	15,278	13,200	5,542	8,674	*
Percentage with assets	52	86	100	7	33	68	50	91	100
n	71	195	13	20	121	23	24	84	9
Couples with children									
Mean	141,599	38,716	1,211,120	20,663	28,373	67,020	12,914	23,550	64,873
Median	1,200	6,130	313,000	13,192	17,195	31,730	5,338	11,182	26,688
Percentage with assets	74	96	100	20	49	79	63	91	96
n	215	859	276	108	1,434	750	365	1,572	706
	PRINCIPAL RESIDENCE								
	Bottom	*Middle*	*Top*	*Bottom*	*Middle*	*Top*	*Bottom*	*Middle*	*Top*
Single parents									
Mean	171,596	246,290	*	170,408	209,392	363,492	149,122	270,460	*
Median	72,000	170,000	*	132,210	205,660	376,064	70,456	240,192	*
Percentage with assets	17	56	98	8	35	52	29	58	89
n	23	120	13	27	113	17	11	52	8
Couples with children									
Mean	303,232	289,884	1,099,216	214,524	253,785	380,734	188,078	251,283	380,127
Median	105,000	230,000	750,000	179,533	235,040	323,180	160,128	200,160	306,912
Percentage with assets	53	79	98	33	58	77	50	72	84
n	185	715	270	177	1,666	738	310	1,273	609

SOURCE: Authors' calculations from the *LWS Database* (2000–2007) and 2007 PSELL-3.
*Results not shown because the number of observations in the cell is less than 20.

ability of home equity loans and ease of transaction. In terms of home values, there is not much cross-country variation for middle-class single parents. The value rankings are similar based on the mean and median. Germany is at the lower end, followed by the United Kingdom, the United States, and Italy, with values between USD209,000 and USD250,000 for the mean and USD165,000 to USD240,000 for the median; the two outliers are Sweden (mean of USD98,000 and median of USD76,000) and Luxembourg (mean of USD535,000 and median of USD452,000). Among couples with children, the home values are about USD50,000 higher in Germany, Sweden, and the United States; similar in the United Kingdom; and lower,

	LUXEMBOURG			SWEDEN			UNITED KINGDOM	
Bottom	*Middle*	*Top*	*Bottom*	*Middle*	*Top*	*Bottom*	*Middle*	*Top*
9,685	87,570	*	6,732	9,573	*	15,017	14,501	36,595
1,358	15,844	*	1,224	2,482	*	145	5,118	16,575
52	57	84	59	76	94	47	69	92
26	65	12	169	384	16	50	127	31
26,010	28,187	114,898	18,347	21,803	82,335	12,990	21,509	66,020
6,790	15,844	33,952	3,209	8,233	33,521	2,839	5,843	27,036
22	64	79	63	90	99	55	84	96
67	457	192	279	2,660	722	81	715	323

Bottom	*Middle*	*Top*	*Bottom*	*Middle*	*Top*	*Bottom*	*Middle*	*Top*
366,216	534,362	*	75,611	98,798	*	226,639	211,787	291,929
362,155	452,694	*	59,968	76,469	*	145,033	165,752	186,471
40	74	70	23	44	76	31	52	93
34	75	12	75	231	13	34	99	31
295,212	487,696	678,722	114,005	130,366	258,582	221,943	209,914	336,236
271,616	452,694	669,986	84,927	106,086	221,461	165,752	171,968	269,347
46	77	83	44	77	93	64	77	96
78	549	188	187	2,234	672	84	653	322

if not the same, in Italy and Luxembourg. In accordance with the literature about the United States, in all countries home ownership rates among parents with children are higher than those for single parents.

Home Affordability

Owning one's home is one of the key aspirations of the middle class (U.S. Department of Commerce 2010). We treat home affordability as an important characteristic of the housing market and examine it based on the relationship between gross housing values and income. We proxy affordability by examining home value–to–income ratios. We again divide the income distribution into bottom, middle, and top, and within these, we calculate

TABLE 10.5
Home value and income ratios for all home owners and by household type

	UNITED STATES			GERMANY			ITALY		
	Bottom	Middle	Top	Bottom	Middle	Top	Bottom	Middle	Top
All									
Mean	32.00	7.93	5.50	20.81	10.71	7.08	20.31	12.84	8.49
Median	14.71	6.68	4.25	16.84	9.70	6.99	15.52	11.30	8.37
Single parents									
Mean	19.12	9.38	*	17.99	9.61	8.28	30.96	14.46	*
Median	8.52	7.27	*	13.17	9.93	8.79	18.29	12.62	*
Couples with children									
Mean	43.84	8.69	7.77	22.74	10.95	7.89	24.67	13.30	9.17
Median	13.28	7.48	6.04	17.28	10.46	7.71	19.46	10.48	9.14

SOURCE: Authors' calculations from the *LWS Database* (2000–2007) and 2007 PSELL-3.
*Results not shown because the number of observations in the cell is less than 20.

mean and median home values and incomes for home owners. The ratios of these values are presented in Table 10.5. First, as expected, we find that the home-value-to-income ratios decline in all countries as we move up the income distribution, except for Sweden (most likely due to the survey's home-valuation method), regardless of the household type. Second, among the middle class, the rankings across countries in terms of the highest home-value-to-income ratios are quite consistent across the income distribution. Luxembourg, Italy, and Germany exhibit the highest ratios (being the least affordable), followed by the United Kingdom, the United States, and Sweden (being the most affordable). The home-value-to-income ratios are quite similar in all countries for the top portion of the income distribution, being in the range of 8 to 10. Conventional wisdom suggests that homes are more affordable for couples with children than for single parents. Our results indicate that this is not necessarily the case in all countries. The home-value-to-income ratios are lower in Germany and Sweden than in other countries. At the bottom of the distribution, they are higher for couples in the United States, Germany, Sweden, and the United Kingdom.

Aside from home values, we also compare outstanding home debt as compared to annual income (Table 10.6). Generally, we find that the indebtedness of those at the bottom of the distribution is larger than the indebtedness of those at the top. Comparing across countries, the largest indebtedness is in the United States, the United Kingdom, and Sweden (in the range of two to three times annual income), and the smallest is in Italy,

LUXEMBOURG			SWEDEN			UNITED KINGDOM		
Bottom	*Middle*	*Top*	*Bottom*	*Middle*	*Top*	*Bottom*	*Middle*	*Top*
22.68	15.75	10.07	7.08	4.72	4.60	21.39	8.44	6.21
17.22	15.33	10.44	4.76	3.76	4.10	14.26	6.76	5.97
25.67	17.96	*	6.99	5.17	*	28.01	8.92	5.98
25.13	16.17	*	4.88	4.21	*	14.77	7.54	4.69
20.19	15.98	10.78	11.91	5.69	6.23	32.83	8.60	7.14
16.43	15.56	11.23	8.09	4.67	5.91	23.60	6.89	6.28

with Germany and Luxembourg in the middle (one to two times annual income). In all countries except for Sweden, the indebtedness ratio is larger for couples with children than for single parents. This suggests, once again, that two-parent families find housing loans more plentiful and much more affordable than do single parents.

CONCLUSION

Based on this descriptive exercise, using harmonized, comparable wealth data from the *LWS Database*, we find similarities and differences in wealth holdings both across and within countries. We find the home to be the most important asset in wealth packages, especially for the middle class; the value of the owned home makes up about 75 percent of total assets across the countries studied here. Consequently, financial assets do not play a very important role in the wealth portfolio in most countries, especially for the bottom income group, although they may play a cushioning role in times of economic hardship.

Understandably, single parents are in the most difficult situation. They are slightly less likely to own financial assets compared with the rest of the population and have lower levels (USD30,000 on average and USD10,000 at the median). They are also about 20 percentage points less likely to own their home in all countries except Luxembourg. At the same time, they are just as likely to be in debt as the whole population in Germany, the

TABLE 10.6

Home debt value and income ratios for all home owners and by household type

	UNITED STATES			GERMANY			ITALY		
	Bottom	Middle	Top	Bottom	Middle	Top	Bottom	Middle	Top
All									
Mean	10.35	3.48	1.80	3.05	2.40	1.74	0.75	0.54	0.46
Median	1.76	2.91	1.37	0.00	1.07	1.12	0.00	0.00	0.00
Single parents									
Mean	14.29	3.96	*	2.59	2.48	2.18	*	0.88	*
Median	5.93	3.39	*	0.30	1.31	2.75	*	0.00	*
Couples with children									
Mean	16.14	4.41	2.52	5.63	3.27	2.40	1.28	0.75	0.52
Median	4.72	3.86	1.82	2.95	2.65	2.12	0.00	0.00	0.00

SOURCE: Authors' calculations from the *LWS Database* (2000–2007) and 2007 PSELL-3.
*Too few observations.

United Kingdom, and the United States; more likely in Italy and Sweden; and less likely in Luxembourg. Couples with children, on the other hand, are just as likely to own financial assets (having on average, USD20,000 to USD28,000 and USD6,000 to USD17,000 at the median), and they are more likely to own their home than the whole population, particularly in Germany and Sweden. They are also more likely to be in debt, but most of the value of that debt is related to owning a home.

The value of one's home is the largest asset; its value varies across countries, and its affordability based on home-value-to-income ratios varies consistently with home values. The indebtedness across countries is in the range of two to three times that of annual income in countries with high indebtedness, and it is larger in couple families than in single-parent households.

While we know that single parents in the middle- and low-income groups are less likely to hold assets, and to hold less next value of these assets, we do not yet understand the driving forces behind these results. For example, what is the role of divorce or out-of-wedlock childbearing? Including additional waves and country-level data in the *LWS Database* will provide new opportunities to study these questions and to examine changes over time as well as policy impacts with the use of policy evaluation methods.

LUXEMBOURG			SWEDEN			UNITED KINGDOM		
Bottom	*Middle*	*Top*	*Bottom*	*Middle*	*Top*	*Bottom*	*Middle*	*Top*
4.39	2.16	1.41	3.57	2.57	2.63	4.07	2.51	1.98
1.43	1.07	0.32	0.16	1.98	2.00	0.00	2.14	1.78
6.09	1.79	*	3.27	2.82	*	5.80	2.64	1.50
4.40	0.00	*	1.95	2.33	*	4.85	2.27	1.48
3.74	2.52	1.56	8.84	0.24	3.74	7.51	3.37	2.45
1.37	1.84	0.76	4.67	0.27	3.30	4.85	3.13	1.97

NOTES

1. See www.lisdatacenter.org for a detailed description of the *Luxembourg Income Study (LIS)*, including both the original *LIS* datasets and the new *LWS* datasets. See also the first methodological paper from LWS by Sierminska and colleagues (2006).

2. The data for Luxembourg come from the original survey, which was carried out in 2008 for the PSELL-3/EU SILC Luxembourg wealth module.

3. Table 10.A1 in the online appendix shows the number of observations, including the replicates.

4. Capital income does not include capital gains/losses, which are both excluded from the concept of DPI.

5. Private transfers do not include irregular incomes such as lottery winnings or any other lump sums, which are excluded from the concept of DPI.

6. Our income measure does not include health care benefits in kind, even though we know they are large (Garfinkel, Rainwater, and Smeeding 2006), nor does it contain in-kind housing benefits in the form of imputed rent. It does include the cash value of having housing allowances, food stamps, and heating allowances.

7. Simply stated, ownership is one way to consider assets; another is valuation.

8. Outright home owner rates (without mortgages) are 63 percent in the United States, 78 percent in Germany, 96 percent in Italy, 87 percent in Luxembourg, 45 percent in Sweden, and 74 percent in the United Kingdom.

9. We do not create a separate category for "other" types of households with children, but we focus exclusively on households that include only parents and children.

For additional results, please see the online appendices by following the link in the listing for Income Inequality *on the Stanford University Press website: http://www.sup.org.*

REFERENCES

Apgar, William C., and Zhu Xiao Di. 2005. "Housing Wealth and Retirement Savings: Enhancing Financial Wealth for Older Americans." Working paper 05-8. Cambridge, MA: Joint Center for Housing Studies, Harvard University.

Banks, James, Richard Blundell, Zoe Oldfield, and James P. Smith. 2005. "House Price Volatility and Housing Ownership over the Life Cycle." *Discussion Papers in Economics* discussion paper 04-09. London: University College London.

Banks, James, Richard Blundell, and James P. Smith. 2003. "Understanding Differences in Household Financial Wealth between the United States and Great Britain." *Journal of Human Resources* 38(2): 241–79.

Barrell, Ray, and E. Philip Davis. 2004. "Consumption, Financial and Real Wealth in the G-5." Discussion paper 232. London: National Institute of Economic and Social Research.

Bover, Olympia. 2010. "Wealth Inequality and Household Structure: U.S. vs. Spain." *Review of Income and Wealth* 56(5): 259–90.

Brandolini, Andrea, Silvia Magri, and Timothy M. Smeeding. 2010. "Asset-Based Measurement of Poverty." *Journal of Policy Analysis and Management* 29(2): 267–84.

Carroll, Christopher. 2004. "Housing Wealth and Consumption Expenditure." Paper presented at the Academic Consultants' Meeting of the Board of Governors of the Federal Reserve System. Washington, DC (February 10, 2004).

Case, Karl, John Quigley, and Robert Shiller. 2005. "Comparing Wealth Effects: The Stock Market versus the Housing Market." Working paper w01-004. Berkeley, CA: Institute of Business and Economic Research.

Catte, Pietro, Nathalie Girouard, Robert Price, and Christopher Andre. 2004. "Housing Markets, Wealth and the Business Cycle." *Economics Department* working paper 394. Paris: OECD.

Chen, Kaiji. 2006. "The Welfare Implications of Social Security for Homeowners." Ph.D. diss., University of Oslo.

Chiuri, Maria Concetta, and Tullio Jappelli. 2003. "Financial Market Imperfections and Home Ownership: A Comparative Study." *European Economic Review* 47(5): 857–75.

———. 2010. "Do the Elderly Reduce Housing Equity? An International Comparison." *Journal of Population Economics* 23(2): 643–63.

Claus, Iris, and Grant Scobie. 2001. "Household Net Wealth: An International Comparison." Working paper 2001/19. Wellington: Treasury of New Zealand.

Conley, Dalton, and Miriam Ryvicker. 2004. "The Price of Female Headship: Gender, Inheritance, and Wealth Accumulation in the United States." *Journal of Income Distribution* 13(3): 41–56.

Copeland, Craig. 2006. "Debt of the Elderly and Near Elderly, 1992–2004." *Employee Benefit Research Institute Notes* 27(9): 2–14.

Crook, Jonathan. 2006. "Household Debt Demand and Supply: A Cross-Country Comparison." In *The Economics of Consumer Credit*, edited by Giuseppe Bertola, Richard Disney, and Charles Grant. Cambridge, MA: MIT Press.

Crossley, Thomas, and Yuri Ostrovsky. 2003. "A Synthetic Cohort Analysis of Canadian Housing Careers." *Social and Economic Dimensions of an Aging Population* research paper 107. Hamilton, Ontario: McMaster University.

Doling, John, Marja Elsinga, Peter Boelhouwer, and Janet Ford. 2004. "Playing Snakes and Ladders: The Gains and Losses for Homeowners." Paper presented at a workshop session on Housing and Risk at the European Network for Housing Researchers Conference. Cambridge (July 2–6, 2004).

Dvornak, Nikola, and Marion Kohler. 2003. "Housing, Wealth, Stock Market Wealth and Consumption: A Panel Analysis for Australia." *Economic Research Department* discussion paper 2003–07. Sydney: Reserve Bank of Australia.

Ermisch, John, and Stephen Jenkins. 1999. "Retirement and Housing Adjustments in Later Life: Evidence for the British Households Panel Study Survey." *Labour Economics* 6(2): 311–33.

Fisher, Jonathan, David Johnson, Joseph Marchand, Timothy M. Smeeding, and Barbara Boyle Torrey. 2007. "No Place like Home: Older Adults, Housing, and Life-Cycle." *The Journals of Gerontology Series B: Psychological Sciences and Social Sciences* 62(2): S120–S128.

Frick, Joachim R., and Markus M. Grabka. 2010. "Alterssicherungsvermögen dämpft Ungleichheit—abergroße Vermögenskonzentration bleibt bestehen." *DIW-Wochenbericht* 77: 2–12.

Garfinkel, Irwin, Lee Rainwater, and Timothy M. Smeeding. 2006. "A Reexamination of Welfare States and Inequality in Rich Countries: How In-Kind Transfers and Indirect Taxes Change the Story." *Journal of Policy Analysis and Management* 25(4): 897–919.

Gornick, Janet C., Eva Sierminska, and Timothy M. Smeeding. 2009. "The Income and Wealth Packages of Older Women in Cross-National Perspective." *Journal of Gerontology: Social Sciences* 64B(3): 402–14.

Hurst, Eric, and Frank Stafford. 2004. "Home Is Where the Equity Is: Mortgage Refinancing and Household Consumption." *Journal of Money, Credit and Banking* 36(6): 985–1014.

Jäntti, Markus, Eva Sierminska, and Timothy M. Smeeding. 2008. "How Are Household Income and Wealth Distributed? Evidence from the Luxembourg Wealth Study." In *Growing Unequal: Income Distribution and Poverty in OECD Countries*. Paris: OECD.

Kapteyn, Arie, and Constantijn Panis. 2003. "The Size and Composition of Wealth Holdings in the United States, Italy, and the Netherlands." Working paper 10182. Cambridge, MA: National Bureau of Economic Research.

Lusardi, Annamaria, Daniel Schneider, and Peter Tufano. 2011. "Financially Fragile Households: Evidence and Implications." Working paper 17072. Cambridge, MA: National Bureau of Economic Research.

Luxembourg Wealth Study (LWS) Database, http://www.lisdatacenter.org (multiple countries; microdata last accessed in July 2011). Luxembourg: LIS.

Martins, Nuno, and Ernesto Villanueva. 2009. "Does Limited Access to Mortgage Debt Explain Why Young Adults Live with Their Parents?" *Journal of the European Economic Association* 7(5): 974–1010.

Mitchell, Olivia S., and John Piggott. 2004. "Unlocking Housing Equity in Japan." Working paper 10340. Cambridge, MA: National Bureau of Economic Research.

Niskanen, Emilia. 2006. *The Luxembourg Wealth Study: Technical Report on LWS Income Variables.* Luxembourg: LIS.

Organisation for Economic Co-operation and Development (OECD). 2009. Economic Outlook Statistical Annex, House Prices, Annex Table 59. http://www.oecd.org/eco/economicoutlookanalysisandforecasts/economicoutlookannextables.htm.

Ortalo-Magné, François, and Sven Rady. 2006. "Housing Market Dynamics: On the Contribution of Income Shocks and Credit Constraints." *Review of Economic Studies* 73(2):459–85.

Schmidt, Lucie, and Purvi Sevak. 2006. "Gender, Marriage, and Asset Accumulation in the United States." *Feminist Economics* 12(1–2): 139–66.

Schneider, Daniel. 2011. "Wealth and the Marital Divide." *American Journal of Sociology* 117(2): 627–67.

Sedo, Stanley A., and Sherrie A. Kossoudji. 2004. "Rooms of One's Own: Gender, Race and Homeownership Wealth Accumulation in the United States." Discussion paper 1397. Bonn, Germany: Institute for the Study of Labor.

Sierminska, Eva, Andrea Brandolini, and Timothy M. Smeeding. 2006. "The Luxembourg Wealth Study—A Cross-Country Database for Household Wealth Research." *Journal of Economic Inequality* 4(3): 323–32.

Sierminska, Eva, Joachim R. Frick, and Markus Grabka. 2010. "Examining the Gender Wealth Gap." *Oxford Economic Papers* 62(4): 669290.

Sierminska, Eva, and Timothy M. Smeeding. 2005. "Measurement Issues: Equivalence Scales, Accounting Framework and Reference Unit." Unpublished paper. Luxembourg: LIS.

Sierminska, Eva, and Yelena Takhtamanova. 2011. "Job Flows, Demographics, and the Great Recession." *Research in Labor Economics* 32: 115–54.

———. 2012. "Financial and Housing Wealth and Consumption Spending: Cross-Country and Age Group Comparisons." *Housing Studies* 27(5): 685–719.

Smeeding, Timothy M. 2003. "Income Maintenance in Old Age: Current Status and Future Prospects for Rich Countries." *Genius* 59(1): 51–83.

Smeeding, Timothy M., Irwin Garfinkel, and Ronald Mincy. 2011. "Young Disadvantaged Men: Fathers, Families, Poverty, and Policy." *Annals of the American Academy of Political and Social Science* 635(1): 1–28.

Tatsiramos, Konstantinos. 2006. "Residential Mobility and Housing Adjustment of Older Households in Europe." IZA Discussion paper 2435. Bonn, Germany: Institute for the Study of Labor.

Venti, Steven F., and David A. Wise. 2004. "Aging and Housing Equity: Another Look." In *Perspectives on the Economics of Aging*, edited by David A. Wise. Chicago: University of Chicago Press.

U.S. Department of Commerce. Economics and Statistics Administration. 2010. *The Middle Class in America*. Washington, DC: U.S. Government Printing Office.

CHAPTER ELEVEN

The Joint Distribution of Income and Wealth

Markus Jäntti, Eva Sierminska, and
Philippe Van Kerm

Chapter 10 examines levels of net worth and household portfolio composition in a subset of the countries included in the *Luxembourg Wealth Study (LWS) Database*. In this chapter, we extend that analysis and examine aspects of the joint distribution of disposable income and net worth.

Social indicators such as the Gini coefficient and quintile shares are routinely computed by researchers and policy analysts to monitor social cohesion, both when looking at progress over time and in cross-national comparisons. They are computed from data on disposable household income and thus capture inequality in the stream of income that people can readily draw on (Jenkins and Van Kerm 2009). Far less is known about other measures of economic well-being such as inequality in consumption expenditure and wealth and asset holdings, which are the subjects of this chapter. However, there should be little dispute that net worth is a relevant measure of living standards and one that is, arguably, able to capture long-term economic resources better than monthly or annual income flows. Perhaps the main factor underlying the imbalance between the use of income-based social indicators and wealth-based indicators is the availability of reliable data, with income being much easier to collect. Some conceptual and measurement issues also make measurement of inequality in wealth somewhat more challenging; these include the presence of a substantial fraction of negative net worth in most sample data on wealth, the strong skewness, and the fat tails of the distributions, all of which make some traditional measures of inequality inadequate (Cowell and Victoria-Feser 1996; Jenkins and Jäntti 2005).

Relatively little is known about the interdependence between income and wealth, especially outside the United States (Jäntti, Sierminska, and Smeeding 2008; Kennickell 2009). While there is an obvious link between income and net worth accumulation through savings and borrowing constraints, the dependency between these two variates cannot be summarized simply. The relationship is mitigated by, for example, wealth-portfolio-allocation choices, life-cycle effects, inter-generational transfers (especially inheritances), past income streams and their volatility, and so on. There is, however, substantial interest in capturing and better understanding how these measures of economic well-being co-vary. This would provide a broader portrait of social inequality than measures focusing on just one or the other variable. It is not entirely clear—empirically and theoretically—if there is some trade-off between them (think of a high earner with no taste for savings, or a mansion owner with no income) or if they tend to be strongly positively associated, thereby reinforcing social inequality overall. Better knowledge about the joint distribution of income and wealth is also relevant for the design of taxation and redistribution policies, as well as for better identification and targeting of vulnerable population groups.

This chapter uses data from the *LWS Database* to examine the joint distribution of wealth and income in Germany, Italy, Luxembourg, Sweden, and the United States. We first discuss the specific data choices we made for this study. We then take a look at the composition and distribution of net worth and its main components. In that section, we start to approach the question of how disposable income and net worth co-vary by also examining the concentration of wealth by income groups. We then examine the joint distribution of net worth and disposable income. We first do so descriptively and then proceed to estimating simple bivariate regressions, accounting for both disposable income and net worth, using age, education, and family structure. After examining the regression coefficients, we analyze the joint distribution of the residuals to assess to what extent the co-variation of income and wealth is accounted for by observable characteristics.

DATA

We rely mainly on the same choices regarding datasets and variables as those reported in Chapter 10 (except we do not examine the UK data).

However, on one specific aspect of the analysis, we decided to proceed differently. That is, we apply an equivalence scale to both disposable income and to net worth.

Which deflator, purchasing power parity (PPP) exchange rate, and equivalence scale to use for income on the one hand and wealth on the other involves judgment calls. It is far from certain that the best choice of, say, a deflator for income is the same as that for wealth. There are reasonably standard choices about how to treat incomes for comparative analyses—for example, the use of a consumer price index to deflate incomes to a common base year and of "standard" PPPs to render incomes comparable in purchasing power terms (Gottschalk and Smeeding 1997). While there are many equivalence scales to choose from, there is little debate as to the appropriateness of using one that takes some kind of household economies of scale into account. For instance, in this volume, the so-called "square root scale," where the number of adult equivalents equals the square root of household size, is used throughout.

Whether or not the same set of choices is appropriate for the distribution of wealth is an open question and depends, among other things, on the purposes for which we think wealth has been accumulated. Suppose, for example, that the bulk of wealth is held to smooth consumption during periods of low income, such as what might occur during spells of unemployment, temporary illness, or maternity. In that case, the purpose is to be able to draw down on wealth to finance present consumption by (more or less) the current household; thus, the same kinds of choices that apply to income are appropriate. That is, the value of wealth is in its capacity to finance the consumption by the current household. In that case, we should treat wealth as we treat income—that is, measure its real value by applying, for example, a consumer price deflator, PPP-adjustment, and an equivalence scale based on the current household. These transformations translate the capacity of a given nominal sum of money to generate well-being across households of different structures, years, and countries into comparable amounts.

On the other hand, suppose wealth is accumulated to finance consumption after retirement. While that wealth is also held to finance consumption, it is consumption not by the current household but by one that will exist at some future point in time. Presumably, for instance, offspring who at this point in time are minors will by then be self-supporting adults in their own households. So using an equivalence scale based on the current household structure may undervalue the capacity of the wealth held now to finance future consumption.

For the super-rich, the purpose of holding wealth is unlikely to be (solely) to finance consumption, but presumably some element of the capacity of wealth to yield status and power to its holder is involved. In that case, cross-country comparisons might reasonably rely on exchange rates, not PPPs. For instance, those on the Forbes list of billionaires from around the world may rely on comparisons of portfolio values based on exchange rates.

Because this chapter concerns the distribution of well-being in a sense closely related to the tradition of income distribution research, we opt to use methods that are quite standard in research on income. In particular, we use the OECD's price deflators for Actual Final Consumption to express national currencies in 2007 prices and convert all currencies to international dollars using PPPs for personal consumption in 2007 as published by the Organisation for Economic Co-operation and Development (OECD) (OECD 2011a, b). All income and wealth components are further adjusted for the current household's economies of scale using the square root scale.

To repeat, we chose to use data for Germany, Italy, Luxembourg, Sweden, and the United States (see Chapter 10 for descriptions of the data, and see *Luxembourg Wealth Study Database*, 2011). These countries were chosen to represent a broad type of welfare state regimes. The datasets used are among the most recent in the *LWS Database*, although they correspond to different years.

The U.S. survey included in the *LWS Database* that we use, the Survey of Consumer Finances (SCF), is exceptionally good at capturing wealth at the very top of the distribution. This, unfortunately, creates some comparability problems, because not all surveys attempt to capture (and are successful in getting) information from the very rich. To increase the comparability of the datasets across countries, we "shave" off both the top and the bottom of the bivariate distribution. Specifically, we include those persons whose adjusted household disposable income and net worth are within the inner 98 percent of both marginal distributions. Table 11.A1 in the online appendix shows the sample sizes pre- and post-applying the "shaving" procedure, and Table 11.A2 shows the estimated percentiles in the pre-shaved data, which show very large variations in wealth values at the top and bottom of the distribution.

We use a simple definition of the middle class by defining it as individuals whose income falls between the 20th and 80th percentiles of adjusted household disposable income; in other words, we define the middle class as consisting of the three middle-income quintile groups.

THE DISTRIBUTION AND COMPOSITION OF NET WORTH

We begin by examining selected quantiles of net worth along those for its main components. We assess the whole population first, and then we condition on being in the middle-income group. We do this to gain initial insights into the extent to which net worth and disposable income co-vary; if the two were independent, then the conditional quantiles would roughly equal the unconditional ones. Table 11.1 reports the 90th percentile and median of net worth and its main components for all persons, and for those who belong to the middle-income classes. Unsurprisingly, the 90th percentile of wealth among the middle classes is lower than that among all persons (suggesting that net worth and disposable income do co-vary positively). There is substantial variation across countries in the size of that gap. For instance, in Luxembourg, the 90th percentile of the net worth of the three middle-income quintile groups is only USD7,000 lower than that for the full distribution, while in the United States, the difference is USD100,000. The big difference in the United States is due both to a gap of about USD56,000 in the 90th percentile of financial assets across the two distributions (all and middle-income classes) and an even larger gap in the distribution of non-financial assets of USD68,000. The difference in the distribution of debt between all earners and middle-income earners is, by contrast, very small in most cases. In Germany, the difference is about USD12,000, and in the United States, it is about USD24,000.

For the median, the net worth of the middle classes is lower in all countries except Luxembourg (where it is about USD10,000 higher for the middle class than for all households). The differences in median net worth across all and middle-class households are relatively small, at least compared to the 90th percentile. At the median, financial asset values are relatively small; the bulk of median wealth is in non-financial assets. Interestingly, the distribution of debt appears to be extremely skewed in Germany, Italy, and Luxembourg. In the first two, even at the median, no debt is held at all, and in Luxembourg, essentially none is held among all households.

TABLE 11.1
Quantiles of wealth and debt—all classes and middle-income classes

A: 90TH PERCENTILE

	Net worth	Financial assets	Non-financial assets	Debt
Germany				
All	243,506	74,566	225,766	63,062
Middle income	203,190	56,961	188,139	50,848
Italy				
All	306,141	28,813	288,343	12,429
Middle income	258,804	23,177	241,319	10,869
Luxembourg				
All	549,267	52,271	530,446	93,662
Middle income	542,008	49,045	523,691	93,013
Sweden				
All	121,199	37,786	119,500	51,513
Middle income	105,695	31,666	100,109	45,402
United States (SCF)				
All	348,597	137,324	313,611	129,090
Middle income	248,138	81,950	245,010	104,800

B: MEDIAN

	Net worth	Financial assets	Non-financial assets	Debt
Germany				
All	35,338	11,391	10,188	0
Middle income	30,264	10,780	5,020	0
Italy				
All	95,412	4,134	91,972	0
Middle income	93,679	4,273	90,686	0
Luxembourg				
All	198,336	2,714	217,721	39
Middle income	210,539	3,143	225,080	1,787
Sweden				
All	16,315	3,652	28,972	11,748
Middle income	14,207	3,011	28,687	12,531
United States (SCF)				
All	43,392	4,172	79,075	23,701
Middle income	38,232	3,724	74,297	25,374

SOURCE: Authors' calculations from the *LWS Database*.

There are strikingly large differences in net worth across these countries. What stands out, in particular, is that net worth in Luxembourg is very high at both the 90th percentile and the median. This is mainly due to high values for non-financial assets, which in turn are mainly in real estate, driven by high house prices there. In Italy, similarly but to a lesser extent, non-financial assets are very high and are likely account for the high levels of net worth.

What, then, of the distribution of net worth? While the presence of substantial but varying proportions of negative net worth makes comparisons based on traditional measures of relative inequality, such as the Gini coefficient, hard to interpret (because the substantively meaningful negative net worth values increase very much the size of the differences), it is still helpful to take a look at the patterns. Table 11.2 shows the estimated Gini coefficients among all classes and the middle classes, again for net worth and its main components. Sweden turns out to have the highest level of net worth inequality thus measured, followed by the United States, Germany, Italy, and Luxembourg with the least (see also Jäntti et al. 2008). Among the middle classes, the order remains, except that now net worth is most equally distributed in Italy rather than Luxembourg. In looking at these estimates, it is useful to bear in mind that Gini coefficients for disposable income vary between 0.23 (Sweden 2005) and 0.38 (United States 2004); see Figure I.1 in the Introduction to this book. The ordering of countries by their Gini coefficients for net worth appears largely unrelated to that by income; Sweden has by far the highest Gini for net worth but the lowest among these countries for disposable income.[1]

TABLE 11.2

Gini coefficients for wealth and debt—all classes and middle-income classes

Gini coefficient	Net worth	Financial assets	Non-financial assets	Debt
Germany				
All	68.5	68.3	70.3	81.3
Middle income	67.3	65.2	69.9	81.3
Italy				
All	52.3	71.0	52.2	89.8
Middle income	48.7	66.0	49.2	89.5
Luxembourg				
All	50.9	78.3	47.6	77.8
Middle income	47.1	77.4	43.4	76.1
Sweden				
All	77.7	73.7	62.4	61.6
Middle income	79.5	74.3	59.9	57.7
United States (SCF)				
All	72.5	83.3	62.5	67.2
Middle income	69.5	81.9	56.6	62.0

SOURCE: Authors' calculations from the *LWS Database*.

To further explore the distribution of net worth and take a first look at its association with disposable income, we next estimate a set of Lorenz and concentration curves. Specifically, we show in Figure 11.1 the Lorenz curves for disposable income and for net worth, as well as the concentration curve for net worth, conditional on disposable income.[2] That is, we order each person in the data by their disposable income, from poorest to richest,

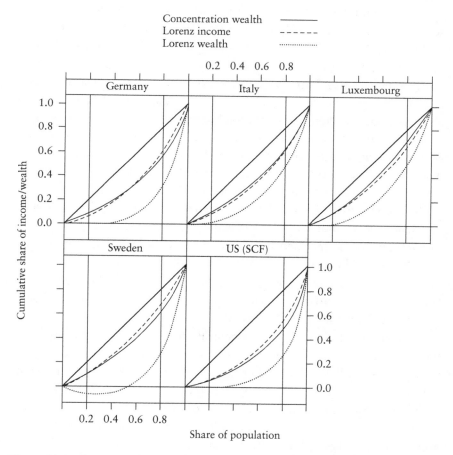

Figure 11.1.   Lorenz and concentration curves for disposable income and net worth

SOURCE: Authors' calculations from the *LWS Database*.

NOTE: "Income" is equivalent disposable income, and "wealth" is equivalent net worth. The concentration curve for net worth is the cumulative fraction of total net worth held by *p* percent of the population ranked by disposable income.

and plot the cumulative sum of their net worth, divided by the sum total of net worth. (The data that underlie the figure are given in the online appendix, Table 11.A3.) Vertical bars are drawn at 20 percent and 80 percent of the population to show where the middle class lies.

In all cases, the Lorenz curve for net worth lies far below that for disposable income. In all cases, for a substantial fraction of the population, net worth is zero or negative, as suggested by Lorenz curves that are either at or below zero. Indeed, for Sweden, the Lorenz curve is substantially below zero and crosses the zero line above 0.5. In Germany, the Lorenz curve becomes positive at about population proportion 0.4; in the United States, at about 0.3; and in Luxembourg and Italy, at or below 0.2. This variation in the extent to which the Lorenz curve for net worth is negative or zero reflects, in part, the fact that very few households hold debt in Italy but also the large variation in the fraction holding negative or zero net worth.[3]

Inspection of the curves suggests that the countries consist of two groups (see the online appendix, Table 11.A3). The Lorenz curves of net worth for Italy and Luxembourg are clearly above those for the other three countries and indicate much less inequality there, but their Lorenz curves cross at approximately population proportion 0.4, suggesting that these two countries cannot be ordered unequivocally by inequality. The curve for Germany lies everywhere above that for Sweden but crosses that for the United States. Thus, Germany has less inequality than Sweden, but it cannot be ordered relative to the United States. The curves for Sweden and the United States also cross (just below 0.8), so these two countries cannot be ordered by the inequality of net worth.

The figure also shows the concentration curve for wealth relative to the distribution of disposable income. These concentration curves lie very close to and (in all cases except for Italy) cross the Lorenz curve for income within the same country. This suggests that, while net worth is very unevenly distributed, it is far less so when considered across the distribution of disposable income. That is, at every level of disposable income, there are households that hold quite different amounts of wealth. Another way of putting this is that, while wealth and income are clearly positively related— the concentration of net worth with respect to disposable income rank is close to the concentration of disposable income with itself (i.e., disposable income's Lorenz curve)—the two are not perfectly correlated. We shall now turn to examining their joint distribution directly.

THE JOINT DISTRIBUTION OF NET WORTH
AND DISPOSABLE INCOME

The Unconditional Joint Distribution

To get a first impression of the shape of the bivariate distribution of income and wealth, we show in Figure 11.2 the cross-tabulation of the quintile groups of both resource variables. The patterns across countries are quite similar, with a few exceptions. The most striking similarity is that for persons in the top quintile group of disposable income (the five bars that are

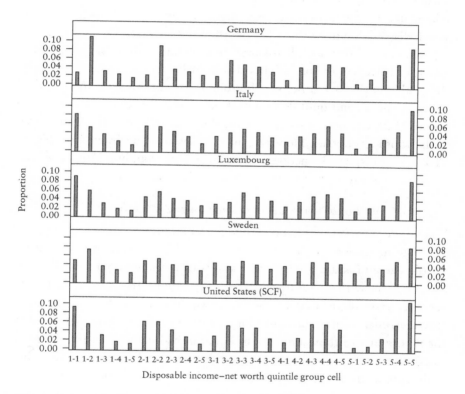

Figure 11.2. Distribution across quintile groups of disposable income and net worth

SOURCE: Authors' calculations from the *LWS Database.*

NOTE: The bars denote the probability that a person falls into the *x-y* cell of the cross-classification of disposable income (*x*) and net worth (*y*) quintile group. If disposable income and net worth were independent of each other, the probability of being in each cell would equal (100/25 = 4 percent).

furthest to the right in the figure), the probability of being in a particular quintile group of net worth increases very quickly, suggesting a heavy concentration at the top of the distribution of both disposable income and net worth. The otherwise perfect monotonicity of this increase is broken by a single exception: in Sweden, the probability of being in cell 5-1 is slightly greater than of being in cell 5-2; that is, it is more likely that a person in the top-income quintile group is also in the lowest-wealth quintile group than in the second. The difference is not very large, but it appears plausible that this anomaly is accounted for by the lack of public pension wealth in our wealth variable, which, because the pension system in Sweden is strongly earnings related and has high coverage, may affect the lower tail of the Swedish net worth distribution more than that of other countries (see Chapter 13).

There are a few notable dissimilarities across countries. In both Germany and Sweden, the probability that a lowest-income quintile group individual is in the lowest net-worth group is lower than such an individual being in the second quintile group of net worth (see cells 1-1 and 1-2 in Figure 11.2). Germany also has a pointedly large spike at cell 2-2 compared with the other countries. However, the main lesson to be drawn from Figure 11.2 is that disposable income and net worth are highly positively associated, particularly at the top and bottom of the distribution.

The Conditional Correlation of Income and Wealth

To explore the nature of the bivariate distribution, we estimate descriptive bivariate regressions of disposable income and net worth, regressing these on the age and educational qualifications of the household head, as well as on a variable that captures differences in family structure. We estimate such bivariate regressions for two reasons. First, by comparing the coefficient estimates for income and for wealth, we hope to gain insights into the nature of wealth accumulation. Longitudinal data on wealth are hard to come by, but by comparing regressions on the flow variable (income) with regressions on the stock variable, we hope to gain insights into differences in accumulation across groups. For instance, suppose wealth is only accumulated to finance consumption in retirement and savings rates vary very little. Then we should observe a steeper age gradient in wealth than in income, reflecting the fact that the main determinant of wealth differences is time to accumulate savings, which is picked up by age. We should also observe larger education gradients for wealth than income, indicating the cumulative advantage that accrues to the better educated from savings behavior. Household structure tends to change across time, but it is likely that those with an economically disadvantaged household structure, such as single parents, need to consume more of their income than, say, childless couples. Second, by comparing the unconditional with the conditional correlations (i.e., the correlation of the residuals from the bivariate regression), we can measure how much of the observed association in disposable income and net worth is driven by the three characteristics that we observe. If much of the correlation is accounted for by observed characteristics, there is little idiosyncratic variation in wealth accumulation. Furthermore, cross-country variation in the extent to which observed characteristics account for the variation may inform us of variations in savings behavior across countries.

Our explanatory variables are defined as follows. Age of household head consists of four groups (less than 30, 30–49, 50–69, and 70+); education of household head consists of three groups (low, medium, and high educational attainment); and family structure includes five categories (couples with no children, couples with children, single childless, single parent, and other, such as multi-generational households or households with unrelated adults).

The descriptive regressions are estimated directly on the levels of disposable income rather than on the log or some other standard transformation.[4] This non-standard procedure has the benefit of allowing for very simple interpretations of the coefficients in terms of 2007 international dollar differences between groups (all co-variates are dummy variables). The intercept case (i.e., the omitted groups) consists of persons in households with a young head (under the age of 30), low education, and a household consisting of a couple without children.

The bivariate regression results are reported in Table 11.3. The coefficient estimates are shown in the first two panels of Table 11.3, first for disposable income (DPI) and then for net worth (NW). The bottom panel shows, apart from sample size and number of coefficient estimates, the estimated residual standard deviations of disposable income and net worth, the estimated residual correlation of the two, and the share of the variance of disposable income and net worth, respectively, that is captured by the explanatory variables in each country.

The proportion of the variance of disposable income and net worth that is captured by the age, education, and household structure variables

TABLE 11.3
Regression results: Net worth and disposable income (GLS estimates)

	Germany	Italy	Luxembourg	Sweden	United States (SCF)
A: DISPOSABLE INCOME					
Intercept (DPI)	15,973.3 (549.3)	14,071.5 (656.9)	28,656.4 (1,038.9)	17,917.7 (256.8)	13,305.3 (2,459.7)
AGE OF HEAD: (OMITTED: BELOW 30)					
30–49	7,195.6 (478.2)	2,389.6 (644.8)	5,822.3 (995.8)	6,607.1 (225.1)	12,211.2 (1,934.9)
50–69	8,690.4 (466.7)	4,740.9 (635.9)	10,581.4 (1,035.9)	7,452.1 (224.2)	19,498.3 (1,976.9)
70–	5,683.8 (507.6)	1,492.5 (653.8)	7,022.1 (1,286.8)	1,051.2 (263.0)	8,937.2 (2,410.8)
EDUCATION OF HEAD: (OMITTED: LOW)					
High	11,847.5 (400.0)	13,960.8 (407.1)	21,777.2 (720.9)	8,429.3 (185.7)	38,683.3 (1,817.6)
Medium	2,455.1 (368.6)	6,554.4 (256.4)	10,161.1 (745.2)	2,925.6 (171.8)	11,186.4 (1,717.9)
FAMILY STRUCTURE: (OMITTED: COUPLE W/O CHILDREN)					
Couple with children	−1,701.5 (349.9)	−786.7 (296.3)	−7,285.5 (756.4)	−5,954.6 (194.3)	−4,816.1 (1,566.8)
Other	−2,769.3 (1,014.9)			−27,595.6 (8,029.4)	
Single, no children	−5,068.5 (329.6)	−1,445.3 (289.4)	−5,649.5 (752.9)	−7,430.1 (152.3)	−12,313.0 (1,500.8)
Single parent	−10,227.8 (568.7)	−6,544.6 (845.2)	−15,422.4 (1,269.0)	−12,623.2 (321.1)	−18,879.1 (2,155.9)
B: NET WORTH					
Intercept (NW)	4,112.8 (6,574.0)	40,411.9 (11,926.5)	39,575.7 (17,183.3)	−4,110.1 (2,328.3)	−73,872.5 (35,051.7)
AGE OF HEAD: (OMITTED: BELOW 30)					
30–49	42,587.7 (5,722.9)	51,307.6 (11,706.6)	124,504.7 (16,470.7)	16,998.3 (2,040.7)	100,597.3 (27,573.2)
50–69	111,470.8 (5,584.8)	121,324.6 (11,545.1)	341,351.7 (17,133.1)	56,859.6 (2,033.2)	341,494.8 (28,171.5)
70–	113,238.2 (6,074.9)	119,656.6 (11,870.7)	423,040.1 (21,283.3)	71,545.3 (2,384.7)	376,275.3 (34,354.7)
EDUCATION OF HEAD: (OMITTED: LOW)					
High	74,128.2 (4,787.1)	177,404.9 (7,391.6)	66,747.8 (11,922.8)	26,164.9 (1,683.9)	444,344.4 (25,901.0)
Medium	20,878.6 (4,411.2)	88,541.9 (4,656.0)	67,530.4 (12,325.6)	9,687.1 (1,557.7)	104,711.4 (24,480.0)
FAMILY STRUCTURE: (OMITTED: COUPLE W/O CHILDREN)					
Couple with children	−6,230.6 (4,187.2)	−24,108.4 (5,379.6)	−73,348.9 (12,510.9)	−14,384.2 (1,762.1)	−60,674.3 (22,327.6)
Other	−30,703.3 (12,145.0)			−52,732.8 (72,805.2)	
Single, no children	−43,926.8 (3,944.8)	−20,348.4 (5,254.3)	−36,809.1 (12,452.7)	−23,454.8 (1,381.2)	−147,232.5 (21,386.2)

TABLE 11.3 (*Continued*)

	Germany	Italy	Luxembourg	Sweden	United States (SCF)
Single parent	−55,079.1	−54,428.2	−117,549.1	−27,383.9	−136,218.0
	(6,805.9)	(15,344.9)	(20,988.4)	(2,911.8)	(30,722.7)
n	11,077	7,702	3,570	16,847	3,493
k	20	18	18	20	18
sd(DPI)	13,270	9,464	16,551	8,026	33,281
	(89)	(76)	(196)	(43)	(398)
sd(NW)	46,629	40,725	67,959	24,490	127,510
	(515)	(542)	(1,339)	(223)	(2,488)
correlation	0.414	0.383	0.345	0.292	0.456
(DPI, NW)	(0.008)	(0.010)	(0.015)	(0.007)	
					(0.013)
R^2 DPI	0.199	0.200	0.274	0.383	0.243
R^2 NW	0.126	0.120	0.235	0.157	0.228

SOURCE: Authors' calculations from the *LWS Database*.

ranges from a low of 0.120 to a high of 0.383. Sweden has the highest R^2 for disposable income (38 percent of the overall variance), followed by Luxembourg at 27 percent. In Germany and Italy, the explanatory variables capture roughly 20 percent of the variance of disposable income, while in the United States, about 24 percent is captured. The share of the variance of net worth that is captured by the explanatory variables is highest for Luxembourg at 24 percent, followed by the United States at 23 percent. It is lowest in Italy at 12 percent, followed by Germany at 13 percent and Sweden at 16 percent. By and large, for cross-sectional regressions, the three sets of explanatory variables capture a reasonable fraction of the variance (although recall that we have "shaved" the data, which as a result omits many outliers whose inclusion would presumably lead to a lower share of variance captured).

We discuss the gradients in age, education, and household structure for disposable income in turn (panel A). We start by discussing the cross-country pattern in the gradient for disposable income, with which we tend to be quite familiar, and then turn to highlighting the differences in the income and wealth gradients.

We start with the age gradient in income, which is similar in all countries in that income increases on moving from the under-30 category (in the intercept) to the 50–69 age range, even if the size of both of these steps varies substantially. For example, a U.S. household with a head in the age range 30–49 earns USD12,211 more per year, on average, than a household headed by a person under the age of 30. In Italy, the corresponding estimate is USD2,390. In all five countries, households headed by a 50- to 69-year-old earn the most, with the United States having the highest advantage at USD19,498 and Italy the lowest at USD4,741. And yet again, in all five countries, incomes decline on moving to the household headed by a person who is older than 70. In the United States, such a household still earns USD8,937 more than a household headed by a person under the age of 30. Sweden has the lowest-point estimate at USD1,051 per year for this category.

The gradient of net worth with respect to age differs from that of income in at least three respects (panel B). First, the country differences in the size of the coefficients are much larger. Second, the differences in net worth held by households headed by persons in the different age categories vary much more than for income and have a steeper gradient, consistent with our expectation that the gradient in wealth reflects wealth accumulation from savings from disposable income. Third, net worth for households headed by a person who is 70 years or older is greater than one headed by a 50- to 69-year-old in all countries except Italy (where the two estimates are statistically indistinguishable from each other, suggesting roughly equal net worth for the two groups). This last difference offers a striking contrast to the familiar age-income profile, with a steep decline in income for the 70 and over category. At least part of the difference is due to differences in home ownership, which is an important part of the wealth portfolio of all groups.[5] It also highlights the varying importance of private savings to finance consumption in retirement. Sweden, with its well-developed pension system, has a quite low age gradient, whereas the U.S. gradient is very high.

There is a sizeable education gradient in disposable income in all countries. Households whose head has medium-level educational qualifications earn between USD2,455 (Germany) and USD11,186 (United States) more than one with low educational qualifications. Households whose head has high educational qualifications—in practice, at least some college education—have between USD8,429 (Sweden) and USD38,683 (United States) more than those in the lowest educational category qualifications. The United States is the outlier here, with a point estimate that is close to twice as high as the next highest, Luxembourg, with a point estimate of USD21,777.

The gradient of net worth with respect to education is, again, similar, but with larger differences across countries and between categories. Medium-level education is now associated with between USD9,687 (Sweden) and USD104,711 (United States) greater net worth than is associated with low education. High-level education is, in turn, associated with between USD26,165 (Sweden) and USD444,344 (United States) more of net worth. The U.S. point estimate is now 2.5 times higher than the next-highest educational premium for this category, in Italy, of USD177,404. Apart from owner-occupied housing and supporting consumption in retirement, an important motive for accumulating wealth is probably the financing of higher education for offspring. To the extent more highly educated parents are more likely to spend more on the education of their offspring, this should be reflected in wealth accumulation by education. Moreover, as higher education is privately most costly in the United States, we would expect to observe exactly what we do: a steep education gradient for wealth in the United States, both relative to the gradient for income in the United States and relative to the gradient for wealth in other countries.

There are sizeable differences across family types in both income and net worth. Single parents, for example, earn between USD6,545 (Italy) and USD18,879 (United States) less than couples without children (the reference category). Couples with children are at a slightly smaller disadvantage, all else equal, with a point estimate that ranges from −787 (Italy) to −5,955 (Sweden). The differences in net worth are much larger, ranging from a −27,384 (Sweden) to −136,218 (United States) for single parents, and −6,231 (Germany) to −73,349 (Luxembourg) for couples with children. This likely reflects large differences in how different types of families are publicly supported across countries (which in turn affects their consumption and thus savings possibilities).

Taken as a whole, the differences across both groups and across countries are substantially larger for net worth than for income. Most likely this reflects the fact that small income differences accumulate over time, through differences across households in amounts saved, to become larger differences in the stock of net worth. The qualitative patterns of inter-group differences are remarkably similar across countries but translate to large absolute differences.

The estimated residual standard deviations of income and net worth order the countries similarly: the United States has the largest standard deviation; followed by Luxembourg, Germany, and Italy; and finally Sweden with the lowest. The residual standard deviation of net worth is much higher in all cases. In Sweden, for instance, the net worth residual standard deviation is three times that for income: 24,490 compared with 8,026. In Italy, the ratio is 4.3: 40,725 compared with 9,464. The U.S. standard deviation of both net worth and disposable income is a little less than twice as high as for Luxembourg: USD127,510 for net worth compared with USD67,959, and USD33,281 for disposable income compared with USD16,551 in the United States and Luxembourg, respectively.

However, instead of looking at cross-country differences in the estimates, we can turn to differences between income and wealth. Given the very large differences in the age, education, and household structure gradient between income and wealth, the differences in residual standard deviations are not strikingly large. For instance, in the United States, a highly educated head of household earns USD38,683 more than one with low education but who holds more than ten times that—USD444,344—in net worth, all else equal. The U.S. residual standard deviation of net worth is not more than roughly four times that for disposable income, suggesting that the observed characteristics do pick up a substantial portion of the difference in wealth accumulation across households.

Finally, we turn to the residual correlation. This is the correlation of disposable income earned in the year and the stock of net worth held after the explanatory variables have been accounted for. The correlation is estimated quite precisely in all five countries, is positive in all cases, and is reasonably, if not overwhelmingly, high. Sweden, with the lowest-point estimate, has an estimated correlation coefficient of 0.292. In the next lowest, Luxembourg, the estimate is 0.345. In Italy, the estimate is 0.383, followed by Germany at 0.414, and the highest in the United States at 0.456. These differences across countries are sizeable, but recalling from Tables 11.1 and 11.2 the very large difference in levels of wealth across countries and the big differences in how net worth changes on moving from the full distribution to the middle-income classes, one may still conclude that countries are remarkably similar in the extent to which income and wealth co-vary *conditional* on observed characteristics.

How do the regression-adjusted correlations compare with the "raw" correlation between income and wealth? We can think of the estimate based on regression residuals as having "netted out" that part of the correlation that is driven by the co-variates. That is, part of the positive association in disposable income and net worth is driven by the fact that the same characteristics are associated with both high income and high wealth, but part of the correlation remains after conditioning on the co-variates. We illustrate this in Figure 11.3, where we plot both the raw correlation and the residual-based estimate from Table 11.3.

The bulk of the positive association remains after the regressions. That is, the residual-based estimates are quite close to the raw estimates, and the ordering of countries is (with one exception) the same. Italy has the second highest raw correlation, right after the United States, but using the regression-adjusted correlation, it is third, now behind rather than ahead of Germany. The difference in the two correlations—before and after regression—is large in Italy at more than 0.10 and sizeable in the United States at close to 0.09. Dividing the residual-based estimate by the raw estimate, we get a measure of how much of the correlation in net worth and disposable income the three sets of explanatory variables—age, education, and family structure—fail to account for. This ratio ranges from 0.786 in Italy, suggesting that the explanatory variables have the most effect there, to 0.948 in Germany, suggesting that they pick up the least amount of the association there.

CONCLUSION

In this chapter, we examine the joint distribution of disposable income and net worth. The real levels of net worth, examined at the outset, vary substantially across countries at both the top (90th percentile) and middle (50th percentile) of the distribution of net worth. The inequality of net worth, as measured by the Gini coefficient, is between two and three times that of disposable income. The Lorenz curves for wealth are, for much of the population, at or below zero, suggesting negative and/or zero net worth for a substantial fraction of the population. However, the concentration of net worth across the distribution of disposable income suggests that, across these countries, even if net worth is positively associated with disposable income, there is, at all income levels, substantial variation in net worth.

Our examination of the joint distribution directly reveals a general pattern of positive association between income and wealth, but with some departures, especially at low levels of income for Germany and Sweden.

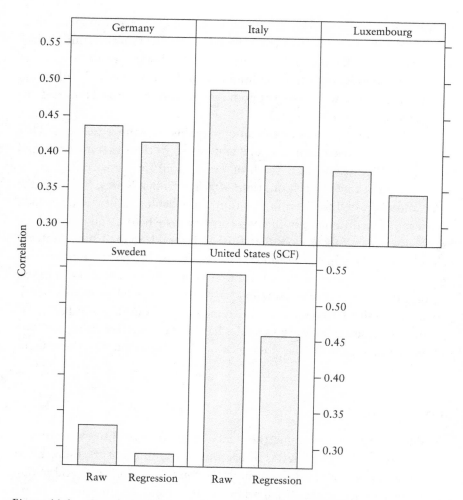

Figure 11.3. Correlation between disposable income and net worth—raw and regression-based estimate

SOURCE: Authors' calculations from the *LWS Database*.

NOTE: The "raw" correlation is the standard correlation coefficient of disposable income and net worth. The "regression" correlation is the correlation coefficient of the bivariate regressions, controlling for age, education, and household structure.

Regressing both disposable income and net worth on a set of age, education, and family structure dummies, we could account for between 12 and 24 percent of the variation in net worth, and between 20 and 38 percent of the variation in disposable income. The qualitative pattern of inter-group differences was quite similar across countries, but the absolute size of the inter-group differences varies substantially. While the regression equations did pick up part of the positive association of disposable income and net worth, between 77 and 95 percent of the estimated correlation between the two remains after controlling for the explanatory variables. This suggests a substantial residual association between income and wealth after the age and education profiles and differences in family structure have been accounted for.

Our findings suggest that, in general, those with higher incomes tend to accumulate more wealth. This association varies across countries, but it remains almost as strong after age, education, and family structure have been taken into account. Our data are cross-sectional, so we cannot tell to what extent those with low disposable incomes have low incomes more or less permanently, and to what extent they are currently suffering from a transitory negative income shock. To the extent that wealth is held to finance temporary declines in income, our results are somewhat mixed. Income and wealth are strongly positively associated, so there is, on average, not much scope to finance consumption out of net worth. On the other hand, our results do suggest that there is some variance in net worth at all income levels, suggesting that at least some low-income households hold relatively high levels of net worth. Whether or not such households are able to finance consumption out of their net worth remains a question for future research.

The strong association of income and wealth suggests the presence of large differences in the ability to support consumption levels in the face of adverse income shocks. It appears likely that the most vulnerable households—those headed by single parents or by those with low education—are least able to accumulate wealth to smooth consumption during adverse times. In many countries, wealth taxes have been eliminated and taxation of capital income is low compared to income, and there is pressure to increase taxes on consumption. To increase tax equity, more focus might be placed on taxing wealth and on income flows from wealth.

Moreover, the results from our bivariate regression do suggest that some of the observed variation in the distribution of net worth across countries can be accounted for by a few observed individual-level characteristics. Further explanations for cross-national variation in wealth holdings may include variation in country-level factors, such as policies that affect home ownership (see Chapter 12), pension systems (see Chapter 13), and the financing of higher education across countries. However, even after controlling for observed characteristics, there are differences across countries in the association of income and wealth. This suggests there may be differences across countries in the importance of unobserved factors that affect the extent to which income accumulates into wealth. Future research into such cross-country variation in wealth accumulation will benefit from microdata on not only income and wealth but also on variables that measure behavioral factors likely associated with savings, such as attitudes to risk and time preferences.

NOTES

1. We should note that an important reason for accumulating wealth is to finance consumption in retirement. In countries with earnings-related pension systems that have high coverage, such as Sweden, the incentives for accumulating other wealth are weaker than in those that are less inclusive and less earnings related. As the German case in Chapter 13 illustrates, including pension rights and examining so-called augmented wealth can have a large equalizing impact on the distribution of net worth. Thus, the fact that our net worth data do not capture pension rights and that this omission varies in importance across countries affects the estimates of both levels and distribution.

2. A Lorenz curve is a graph that plots for the population, ranked by income or wealth, the cumulative proportion of total income or wealth held (see, e.g., Jenkins and Van Kerm 2009). The Lorenz curve lies everywhere on the 45-degree line in the case everyone has the same income, or below it when income is unequally distributed. The further below the 45-degree line the curve is, the greater the inequality of income or wealth. The Gini coefficient equals twice the area between the Lorenz curve and the 45-degree line, with complete inequality being zero and, when one person holds all income or wealth, one. A concentration curve of, say, wealth with respect to income plots the cumulative proportion of wealth held by the population that has been ordered by income.

3. See Cowell (2011) for similar analyses of wealth inequality.

4. The regressions are estimated using the gls function in the package nlme in the statistical package R (Pinheiro and Bates 1999).

5. See Chiuri and Jappelli (2006, 2011) for analyses, using multiple waves of *LIS* data, on the drawing down on home ownership with age.

For additional results, please see the online appendices by following the link in the listing for Income Inequality *on the Stanford University Press website: http:// www.sup.org.*

REFERENCES

Chiuri, Maria, and Tullio Jappelli. 2006. "Do the Elderly Reduce Housing Equity? An International Comparison." *LIS* working paper 436. Luxembourg: LIS Cross-National Data Center.

———. (2010). "Do the Elderly Reduce Housing Equity? An International Comparison." *Journal of Population Economics* 23(2): 643–63.

Cowell, Frank A. 2011. "UK Wealth Inequality in International Context." Unpublished manuscript, London School of Economics.

Cowell, Frank A., and Maria-Pia Victoria-Feser. 1996. "Robustness Properties of Inequality Measures." *Econometrica* 64(1): 77–101.

Gottschalk, Peter, and Timothy M. Smeeding. 1997. "Cross-National Comparisons of Earnings and Income Inequality." *Journal of Economic Literature* 32(2): 633–86.

Jäntti, Markus, Eva Sierminska, and Timothy M. Smeeding. 2008. "How Is Household Wealth Distributed? Evidence from the *Luxembourg Wealth Study*." In *Growing Unequal? Income Distribution and Poverty in OECD Countries*. Paris: OECD.

Jenkins, S. P., and Markus Jäntti. 2005. "Methods for Summarizing and Comparing Wealth Distributions." Working paper 05. Colchester, UK: Institute for Social and Economic Research, University of Essex.

Jenkins, Stephen P., and Philippe Van Kerm. 2009. "The Measurement of Economic Inequality." In *Oxford Handbook of Economic Inequality*, edited by Wiemer Salverda, Brian Nolan, and Timothy M. Smeeding. Oxford: Oxford University Press.

Kennickell, Arthur B. 2009. "Ponds and Streams: Wealth and Income in the United States, 1989 to 2007." *Finance and Economics*, discussion series 13. Board of Governors of the Federal Reserve System: U.S. Federal Reserve.

Luxembourg Wealth Study (LWS) Database, http://www.lisdatacenter.org (multiple countries; microdata last accessed in July 2011). Luxembourg: LIS.

Organisation for Economic Co-operation and Development (OECD). 2011a. "Prices and Price Indices—Consumer Prices." http://stats.oecd.org/Index .aspx?DataSetCode=MEI_PRICES.

———. 2011b. "Purchasing Power Parities (PPP) Statistics: 2008 PPP Benchmark Results." http://stats.oecd.org/Index.aspx?DataSetCode=PPP2008.

Pinheiro, José C., and Douglas M. Bates. 1999. *Mixed-Effects Models in S and S-PLUS*. New York: Springer-Verlag.

CHAPTER TWELVE

The Fourth Retirement Pillar in Rich Countries

Bruce Bradbury

Wealthy countries use a variety of methods to support consumption in old age. Each of these is subject to different economic, political, and social risks while having varying advantages. This multi-pronged approach was summarized by the World Bank in 1994 as a three-pillar model of retirement income support, consisting of public minimum pensions, contributory pensions, and private savings. Since then, there has been a growing interest in the role of "asset-based welfare" in providing social insurance via private accumulation of assets (Doling and Ronald 2010). Additional pillars have been added to the retirement policy model as the contributions of different forms of private savings have been considered. This chapter examines the role of a "fourth pillar" of private home ownership in supporting consumption in old age and considers this in the context of both income transfers and other forms of privately held wealth.

Private home ownership provides direct flows of housing services and increases the money available for non-housing consumption by reducing housing expenditures. In countries with historically high rates of home ownership, it has been a prominent part of the retirement provision discourse.[1] Moreover, it will soon form a major part of the retirement landscape in many other countries as new cohorts with higher rates of home ownership move into retirement (Chiuri and Jappelli 2008).

What lessons can home-ownership leaders such as the United States and Australia provide for other countries as they build this pillar? Does this form of asset-based welfare spread the risks of retirement provision, or does it distort consumption patterns and fail to improve the non-housing consumption of the elderly? Are the implications different for those at the top, middle, and bottom of the income distribution? In particular, is greater home ownership associated with more or less inequality of retirement consumption?

These issues are analyzed using data from the *Luxembourg Wealth Study (LWS) Database* (supplemented by comparable Australian data). The results are presented for Australia, Canada, the United Kingdom, the United States, Germany (limited results), Italy, Finland, and Sweden. These data allow a unique assessment of the varying packages of income, housing, and other wealth holdings that the elderly use to support their living standards in rich countries.

The chapter introduces these issues with a discussion of cross-national variation in the income and wealth holdings of the older population. Both income replacement rates and wealth holding patterns vary significantly across our sample of countries. The role of housing wealth in retirement is particularly variable—ranging from 10 times the annual income in Australia to only 2.4 times in Sweden.

To put these income and wealth patterns on a common footing, the chapter introduces a retirement consumption framework that can be estimated using data from *LWS*. Income minus housing expenditures is used as an indicator of non-housing consumption, and own-home housing wealth is used to impute the housing consumption accruing to home-owning households.

The chapter presents results on the pattern of housing and non-housing consumption among the older population and then examines retirement replacement rates comparing the older and prime age populations. The chapter then turns to consider variations in these outcomes among the top, middle, and bottom of the income distribution. It then considers the lessons that can be drawn from the high-home-ownership countries for the other countries that are expected to increase their home-ownership rates over the coming decades. The recent volatility in housing markets is unlikely to prevent this increase, but it may have important implications for the distribution of home ownership, which in turn will have important implications for retirement living standards in the future.

INCOME AND WEALTH AFTER RETIREMENT:
A FIRST LOOK

We begin with an overview of income and wealth patterns in retirement. Data from seven of the countries in *LWS* are used, covering the period from the late 1990s to the early 2000s. The countries and years are Canada (1999), the United States (2001, PSID version), the United Kingdom (2000), Finland (1998), Sweden (2002), Germany (2002), and Italy (2002). Because of missing housing cost data, only limited results are provided for Germany. In addition, data from a recent Australian survey are assembled in a similar fashion and analyzed alongside the *LWS* data. See the online appendix, Table 12.A1, and the Introduction to this book for more information on the *LWS* surveys.

Across these eight countries, the United States stands out as having considerably higher average national incomes (measured on a price-adjusted common currency basis). This is the case irrespective of whether incomes are measured as gross domestic product per capita or mean disposable income per household (see the online appendix). Using the latter measure, average U.S. incomes were around $50,000, whereas the other countries had average incomes of between $25,000 and $36,000 (2002 USD per annum). Part of this difference reflects the lower personal taxation in the United States, which in turn is associated with a lower level of state-provided services.

Using data from around the turn of the century means we largely avoid the distorting effect of the rapid inflation in house prices in the years leading up to the 2008 global financial crisis. This makes it easier to impute the service flows from home ownership and thus provides a more accurate picture of the long-run impact of housing wealth on consumption in retirement. The main exception is Australia, where house prices had risen sharply in the years prior to the survey and by 2003–2004 were almost 70 percent above their long-run trend (similarly, Sweden was 20 percent above). To compensate for this, when calculating the service flows from owner occupation, house prices are deflated by their deviation from long-run trend values. The adjustments used (small except for Australia and Sweden) are shown in the online appendix.

The starting point for the analysis is the wide variation in retirement wealth holdings across countries (Table 12.1). The retired or, more precisely, the older population is defined in this chapter as households where

TABLE 12.1

Wealth relative to annual disposable income among households with head aged 65+

	Australia	Canada	United Kingdom	United States	Germany	Italy	Finland	Sweden
Main residence	10.4	2.9	5.3	2.9	4.7	5.5	3.2	2.4
(% owners)	(83)	(67)	(64)	(79)	(46)	(74)	(73)	(52)
Other real estate	2.4	0.6	0.4	1.1	1.7	1.4	1.2	0.6
Financial assets	2.9	2.0	2.0	3.0	1.0	1.4	0.9	2.2
Total assets	15.7	5.5	7.5	7.0	7.4	8.3	5.3	5.1
Total debt	0.3	0.2	0.1	0.3		0.0	0.1	0.5
Net worth	15.4	5.3	7.4	6.7		8.3	5.3	4.6
Mean income ($000 USD 2002)	20.1	28.3	20.7	42.0	22.1	21.4	18.1	18.6
Mean income of 65+ relative to 45–59	0.49	0.58	0.53	0.67	0.60	0.59	0.58	0.56

SOURCE: Australia, Australian Bureau of Statistics 2003–04 Household Income and Expenditure Survey, confidentialized unit record file. Other countries, LWS Database. Mean income estimate is adjusted using OECD PPP indexes. See Online Appendix Table 12.6.

NOTE: Over 65 is defined using the age of the male household head where there is one. The top panel of the table shows means for each category of wealth divided by mean disposable income. Wealth items excluded are life insurance and unrealized pension assets, business assets and debt, vehicles, household durables, and collectibles. In Australia, superannuation account balances are included but not entitlements to defined benefit plans or other income streams. Other real estate wealth is net of debt in the United States. Note that UK data do not add up due to some cases that are missing data (although there are no missing data for main residence value).

the age of the household head is 65 or older. Because wealth is most naturally recorded at the household level, the counting units in are households. (In subsequent tables, where we turn our attention to consumption outcomes, individuals are used as the counting unit.)

We are interested in how wealth holdings can finance consumption in retirement, so it is most natural to consider wealth in relation to income. Hence, average wealth levels are expressed relative to average disposable income in the upper panel of the table. The lower panel provides additional information on the incomes of the older population. As for overall income, the average disposable income of the U.S. elderly is much higher than in the other countries, at around $42,000 per annum (in 2002 USD equivalents). Canada is next largest at $28,000, followed by the other countries at around $20,000.

One of the key objectives of retirement income policy is to smooth consumption across the life course. One measure of this is given by the average income replacement rate, defined here as the mean household disposable income for households with head 65 and over relative to the mean for households with "prime age" heads, aged 45 to 59. These ratios are shown in the final row of the table. They vary considerably, ranging from 67 percent in the United States to 49 percent in Australia. The United Kingdom also has a relatively low replacement rate of 53 percent, with the other countries ranging from 56 to 60 percent. The incomes in this table are not adjusted for household size, so the fact that all these ratios are under 100 percent does not directly indicate a fall in living standards after retirement. Nonetheless, the wide variation in rates across countries does suggest either diversity in relative living standards after retirement or an important role for other, non-income methods of supporting consumption in retirement.

One such means, and the focus of this chapter, is wealth, which is shown in the top panel of Table 12.1. The average stock of wealth held by the older population ranges from 4.6 times annual disposable income (Sweden) to 15.4 times (Australia). The country with the lowest income replacement rate (Australia) also has the highest wealth holding relative to income, but otherwise there is no general cross-national correlation in these two variables.

Most of the cross-national variation in wealth holding stems from home ownership. Wealth held in the form of own-home ownership ranges from 2.4 times average annual income in Sweden to 10.4 times in Australia. This partly reflects variations in home-ownership rates. Australia and the United States have very high levels of home ownership among the older population (83 and 79 percent), while only half of the older population in Germany and Sweden are home owners. However, the cohort analysis of Chiuri and Jappelli (2008) suggests that future decades will show a significant catch-up in home ownership among the older population in those countries that currently have lower rates of home ownership.

The variation in own-home wealth also reflects cyclical variation in housing markets. As noted above, the 2003–2004 data in Australia were collected at the end of a 5-year house price boom (and a similar but smaller deviation was evident for Sweden), while the other countries had house prices much closer to the longer-term average of house prices relative to rents. Nonetheless, even if Australian house prices were deflated back to their long-run average level (by dividing the housing wealth estimates in Table 12.1 by 1.7), they would still be higher relative to income than in any other country.

With respect to other forms of wealth, the United States and Australia have the highest level of financial assets relative to disposable income. On average, these are around three times annual income. When real estate other than the main residence is included, the older Australian and U.S. households have 5.3 and 4.1 times their incomes held in potentially income-generating assets, respectively. (Though note that some of the "other real estate" comprises non-income-generating vacation homes.) Excluded from this table is wealth held in business ownership, so this will be an underestimate of income-generating assets held in retirement.

As a picture of overall wealth holdings in retirement, however, the largest shortcoming of Table 12.1 is its non-inclusion of rights to future pensions. These entitlements include both public pension entitlements as well as private pensions that deliver income streams. Though pensions provide rights to future consumption in a similar way to other forms of wealth, they do differ in some respects. In particular, pension holders cannot bequeath future pension entitlements to heirs (except for spouses in some cases). Nonetheless, they should ideally be included if we wish to use wealth information to provide an overall picture of potential living standards in retirement.

Because of this absence in the wealth holdings data, a more comprehensive picture can be obtained if we switch to a consumption perspective.

In particular, because owner-occupied housing constitutes the main component of non-pension wealth in most countries ("Main residence" relative to "Total assets" ranges from 44 to 71 percent in Table 12.1), and because it provides direct consumption services, we focus primarily on the consumption implications of this form of wealth holding. The framework and methods used for this analysis are outlined in the next section.

FRAMEWORK AND METHODS

This section describes a simple framework for considering the impact of housing wealth on retirement consumption. It is closely related to the approach of adding imputed rent to disposable income, as used in the National Accounts, but it has some differences so as to address a consumption rather than an income concept.

The framework is illustrated in Figure 12.1. This describes the role of housing in relation to the economic concepts of disposable income, imputed rent, full income, saving, consumption, and expenditure. The first column shows the allocation of household disposable income to non-housing consumption (purchases of goods and services other than housing), rent, mortgage repayments (interest and principal), and non-housing saving (the increase in value of other assets). Non-housing saving can be negative if people are drawing down on their non-housing assets. In this case, the sum of non-housing consumption, rent, and mortgage repayments will be greater than disposable income.

Unlike most other forms of savings used to support retirement, own-home housing both provides consumption services and is an investment. Imputed rent is the income that the household could receive if it were renting its home to itself. It can be defined as the gross rent that would be obtained for the dwelling, minus the maintenance costs and (inflation-adjusted) interest costs of financing the dwelling. One way of estimating gross rent is as a function of the value of the house and land.[2] Here, it is assumed that 5 percent of the gross value of the dwelling (adjusted for the house price cycle) is a reasonable estimate of rental value. This value has been used in previous Australian and U.S. research[3] and is here assumed to apply also to the other countries.

The "full income" concept shown in Figure 12.1 adds capital gains to disposable income and imputed rent. (It does not include the other

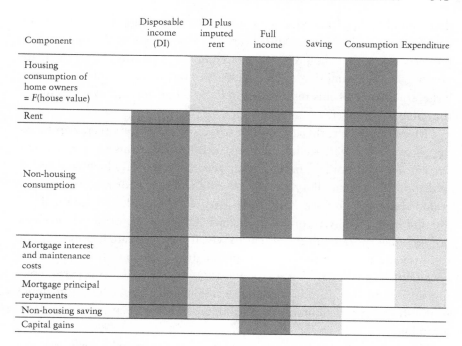

Component	Disposable income (DI)	DI plus imputed rent	Full income	Saving	Consumption	Expenditure
Housing consumption of home owners = *F*(house value)						
Rent						
Non-housing consumption						
Mortgage interest and maintenance costs						
Mortgage principal repayments						
Non-housing saving						
Capital gains						

Figure 12.1.   Housing-related income and consumption concepts

NOTE: Excludes non-housing durables, state and employer-provided non-cash income, value of home production, and value of leisure. Mortgage components assumed to be on an inflation-adjusted basis.

non-housing elements that some might include in such a concept; see the note to the figure.) Saving is defined as those flows that add to the stock of the household's wealth. Here this includes (real) mortgage principal repayments, non-housing saving, and capital gains. Consumption is full income minus saving. It has two components: housing and non-housing consumption. As shown in the final column, this is different from expenditure.

Figure 12.1 shows that non-housing consumption can be estimated from several sources. One approach is to subtract rent, mortgage interest, maintenance, mortgage repayments, and non-housing saving from disposable income. Another is to collect data on non-housing expenditure.[4] We do not have suitable expenditure data, but we can approximate the first approach by deducting rent and mortgage payments from disposable income.

This housing-related income and consumption framework forms the basis for the results below. However, there are several important caveats that should be appreciated when considering the results. First, we do not have data on maintenance expenditures (nor other landlord costs, such as property taxes, that should be considered in the same way). If we calculate non-housing consumption as income minus housing costs, this will be too large, since some of this residual income should be devoted to maintaining the value of the asset.

More important, this approach excludes some of the other, non-housing aspects of private saving for retirement. Some forms of non-housing savings are incorporated because they generate income, which is included in disposable income. For example, wealth held in the form of annuities is included because both the interest return and the capital draw-down of the annuity are typically recorded as income. Other forms of private savings are only incorporated to the extent to which they generate income but not to the extent to which the capital might be drawn down to finance current consumption. Such wealth draw-downs should be included as negative non-housing saving in Figure 12.1. If they were included, they would contribute to non-housing consumption because this is the item that is calculated as a residual.

One approach that has been used by previous researchers is to remove capital income from disposable income and then add the value of an annuity that could be purchased using the current value of all non-housing wealth (Wolff and Zacharias 2003). This gives a measure of total potential consumption. The problem with this is that it describes a behavior that is not often undertaken. Some people might approximate this dis-saving flow via a gradual liquidation of their assets. However, it is probably equally common for people to hold constant the nominal value of assets while consuming the income flow.[5] This income flow will usually be included in the income measure used here. Indeed, in the absence of comprehensive insurance markets to cover longevity and care needs risks, maintaining a substantial level of precautionary savings is a sensible strategy. For these reasons, the main estimates here do not impute any annuity flows to assets.

Finally, the treatment here excludes many other components that some might include in full income, such as the value of home production and leisure and the value of government services used. This exclusion is mainly for data availability reasons but also because of conceptual difficulties in comparing these benefits for people of different ages. In particular, in most countries the elderly receive much more in state-provided health benefits than do the prime-age population, but this is mainly because their health needs are greater. A comparison of the living standards of the two age groups that included health benefits would need to take these differences into account.

Nonetheless, there are substantial cross-national differences in the social provision of health services. Using data from the mid- to late 1980s, Whiteford and Kennedy (1995, Table 5.2) found that health benefits as a proportion of cash income for the older population varied substantially across the countries considered here. In Sweden, average health benefits were valued at 44 percent of disposable income. In Australia, Canada, and the United Kingdom, they ranged from 20 to 27 percent, while in the United States and Germany, they were only 14 to 15 percent. Though the countries with the highest benefits for the elderly also tended to have the highest benefits for the working-age population, the greater importance of health care for the former group means that these benefits should ideally be included in any comprehensive picture of how the relative living standards of the elderly vary across countries. The exclusion of these benefits should be borne in mind when considering the results presented below.

This chapter focuses on the impact of cash disposable income and housing circumstances on living standards in retirement. To do this, the model outlined above is operationalized using the following measurement definitions. Households are classified according to the age of the household head (the male if partnered).[6] Two groups are considered, *prime age*—defined in this chapter as aged 45 to 59—and *old*—aged 65+. In subsequent results (i.e., other than in Table 12.1), all income, expenditure, and consumption variables are presented in adult equivalent units, divided by the square root of the number of people in the household (top-coded to 6 to match the Australian data). In addition, the own-home wealth and housing expenditure values are Winsorized at the 99th percentile within each age group in each country.[7]

Disposable income is total household cash income, minus income tax and compulsory employee social security contributions. Negative incomes are set to zero. Households are defined as *middle income* if their disposable income falls into the middle three quintile groups (middle 60 percent) of the disposable income distribution for their age group (prime age or old). For this calculation, each quintile group is defined to contain the same number of household heads and spouses. This approach is used rather than the more common counting by people, because we are primarily interested in a comparison of the living standard of prime-age adults with that of older adults.[8]

Owner-occupied housing wealth is the market value of the dwelling (usually as estimated by the respondent). It is set to zero where the dwelling is not owned by any household members. For farms, only the value of the dwelling and the land on which it is situated are included. Households with positive owner-occupied housing wealth are defined as home owners.

Own-housing consumption is estimated as 5 percent of owner-occupied housing wealth, after adjustment for the deviation from the long-run house price to rent ratio (i.e., divided by column 8 of Table 12.A1 in the online appendix). This adjustment removes the impact of cyclical variations in house price movements. *Rent* is the annual rent paid for the dwelling. In the United Kingdom, this is gross rent paid before reductions due to housing benefit.[9] Total housing consumption is defined as own-housing consumption plus rent.

Housing expenditures are reported in slightly different ways across the countries. In the United Kingdom, the United States, and Italy, *housing expenditures* are recorded as rent plus mortgage principal and interest payments (housing benefit for renters is deducted in the United Kingdom).[10] In Canada, Finland, and Sweden, mortgage principal repayments are not included, and this is denoted as *housing expenditures excluding mortgage repayments* in the tables that follow. No housing expenditure results are reported for Germany because of the large fraction of missing data. In Australia, both measures are available and are reported. In Australia, at least, the two measures are very similar for the older population, though there are differences among the prime-age population.

One indicator of living standards that is often used in poverty research[11] is *income after housing expenditures* (disposable income minus housing expenditures). If people do not save or dis-save, and we ignore the services from other durables, then this residual will be equal to *non-housing consumption*. On the other hand, if people are dis-saving by drawing down their assets, this will be an underestimate of non-housing consumption. As noted above, some researchers have addressed this issue by calculating potential consumption using an annuitization of wealth holdings. However, given the prevalence of precautionary savings among the elderly, ignoring non-housing saving is likely to lead to estimates that are just as close to the true level of non-housing consumption.

With this caveat about other forms of saving in mind, we then create an index of total *consumption* by adding together housing consumption and income after housing costs (non-housing consumption). Similarly, for those countries where data on mortgage principal repayments are not available, *income after current housing expenditures* can be calculated. Adding this to housing consumption leads to a measure denoted *full income* because it is equal to consumption (as defined in the previous paragraph) plus saving via home loan repayments. The same caveat about saving/dis-saving via non-housing means applies to the interpretation of this measure. This measure is similar to the measure "disposable income plus imputed rent" used in previous research (e.g., Whiteford and Kennedy 1995).

CONSUMPTION PATTERNS IN RETIREMENT

Table 12.2 presents a decomposition of household income, housing expenditures, and consumption, using this framework. This shows the mean levels of the different consumption components for the older population (people in households with aged 65+), all expressed relative to mean disposable income. The components are equivalized, and the counting units are adults (heads and spouses), as described above. The actual PPP-adjusted mean dollar values can be found in the online appendix, Table 12.A2.

In interpreting these numbers, it is important to be cognizant of both the numerator and the denominator. In particular, the Italian pattern is unusual in that the housing consumption to disposable income ratio is high both for the old and prime-age groups (not shown here). For the prime aged, the ratio is 29 percent, compared with 23 percent or lower for all the other countries (see the online appendix, Table 12.A2). This is suggestive, though not conclusive, of a more general under-recording of disposable income in Italy.

Although housing consumption is quite large relative to income in many countries, housing expenditure generally constitutes a much smaller proportion of the disposable income of the older population. Housing expenditure includes rent plus mortgage interest payments and, in some countries, mortgage principal repayments. Data on mortgage payments both with and without principal repayments are available in Australia. The average difference between them is only about 0.3 percent of average disposable income.

TABLE 12.2

Consumption and expenditures relative to disposable income for the older population (%)

	Australia	Canada	United Kingdom	United States	Germany	Italy	Finland	Sweden
(1) Disposable income	100	100	100	100	100	100	100	100
(2) Housing consumption	33	21	32	16	33	34	18	21
Own home	30	13	26	14	24	26	14	10
(3) Housing expenditures	3		6	9				
(4) Housing expenditures excluding mortgage principal	3	19				34	4	24
(5) Income after housing expenditures (non-housing consumption) = (1) – (3)	97		94	91		66		
(6) Income after current housing expenditures (non-housing consumption + mortgage repayments) = (1) – (4)	97	81					96	76
(7) Consumption = (2) + (5)	129		127	108		100		
(8) Full income = (2) + (6)	129	102					114	97
(9) Housing consumption as share of either total consumption or full income = (2)/(7) or (8)	0.25	0.21	0.25	0.15		0.34	0.16	0.22

SOURCE: Australia, Australian Bureau of Statistics 2003–04 Household Income and Expenditure Survey, confidentialized unit record file. Other countries, LWS Database.

NOTE: The table shows the mean consumption or expenditure aggregate relative to mean disposable income. All measures are equivalized, and the mean of each component is calculated across household heads and spouses (where present). Note that UK data do not add up due to missing data on housing expenditures for a small fraction of households.

The primary exception to the low housing expenditure pattern is Italy, where housing expenditures are around one-third of disposable income, which reinforces the suggestion of income under-reporting discussed above. However, housing expenditures are also reasonably large, at almost one-fifth to one-quarter of disposable income, in Canada and Sweden.

The variables "income after housing expenditures" and "income after current housing expenditures" (which are indicators of non-housing consumption) subtract these housing expenditures, so they vary across countries in the opposite fashion. That is, in Italy, non-housing consumption is only two-thirds disposable income; in Sweden and Canada, it is 76 and 81 percent, respectively; and in the other countries, over 90 percent of disposable income is available for non-housing consumption among the older population.

Finally, the "consumption" and "full income" items add housing consumption to the after-housing measures to show total housing-adjusted consumption (or consumption plus mortgage saving in some countries). Among the elderly, Australia has the highest level of total consumption relative to disposable income because of its high level of home ownership and corresponding low housing expenditures. Despite having much less home ownership, the United Kingdom also has a high total consumption relative to income—in this case because of low rental expenditures due to rental subsidies.

The final row of Table 12.2 shows the share of consumption (or full income) devoted to housing consumption. After Italy, Australia and the United Kingdom report the highest shares of consumption devoted to housing (25 percent), followed by Sweden (22 percent) and Canada (21 percent). The United States (15 percent) and Finland (16 percent) have relatively low shares of consumption devoted to housing. The possible data issues associated with the Italian data have already been discussed. However, the variation in the housing share of consumption across the other countries also seems surprising. The United States and Finland in particular seem to be unusual in terms of their low housing consumption shares.

In interpreting these results, it is important to revisit the assumptions on which they are based. Non-housing consumption does not include state-provided benefits or any consumption arising from any asset liquidation. Housing consumption uses a very simple approach for estimating own-housing consumption (a fixed fraction of long-run home value). Similarly, for renters, rent paid is used as an estimate of housing consumption, which will be too small when there are substantial subsidies. These are accounted for in the country where they are most important (the United Kingdom) but not in other countries. Whether any of these reasons can explain the apparently low housing consumption shares in the United States and Finland is a topic for further research.

The impact of these simplifying assumptions is ameliorated if we compare across the life cycle within the same country. Indeed, this is probably the more interesting question when looking at the role of private saving in providing for retirement. How do consumption levels and patterns change between prime age and retirement in these different countries? What is the role of the fourth pillar of home ownership in creating this? Is this picture different for the top, middle, and bottom of the income distribution?

THE TRANSITION FROM PRIME AGE TO RETIREMENT

The overall picture of the retirement transition is presented in Table 12.3. This shows the income and consumption of people in retirement-age households (head 65+) relative to that of prime-age households (head 45–59). Because these ratios are derived from a single cross-section, they do not represent retirement replacement rates for any particular cohort. Indeed, in many countries, increasing home-ownership rates means that the wealth-holding patterns of the current prime-age population will be quite different when they reach retirement. Nonetheless, the cross-sectional results shown here do provide a useful starting point for summarizing the current structure of the retirement income protection package and how this differs across countries. This pattern is indeed quite variable.

The first row of Table 12.3 presents equivalent disposable income replacement rates. The cross-national picture is similar to that shown in Table 12.1, though the replacements rates here are higher because these estimates adjust for the smaller households of the retired population. In the United States and Italy, older households have equivalent incomes around 80 percent of those with prime-age heads. At the other extreme, the Australian elderly have incomes only 62 percent of the prime aged. The remaining countries have intermediate replacement rates of between 67 and 73 percent.

Because these calculations are based on equivalized income, they provide some indication of the relative living standards of the different age

TABLE 12.3

Old relative to prime age (%)

	Australia	Canada	United Kingdom	United States	Germany	Italy	Finland	Sweden
(1) Disposable income	62	73	67	81	73	77	71	68
(2) Own-home consumption	121	98	85	109	108	94	91	72
(3) Housing consumption	113	110	95	106	104	93	94	101
Housing expenditures								
(4) Current (rent + mortgage interest)	29	75					70	97
(5) All (rent + mortgage interest + principal)	19		44	22		78		
(6) Income after housing expenditures (non-housing consumption)	68		70	108		77		
(7) Income after current housing expenditures (non-housing consumption + mortgage repayments)	65	72					71	62
Consumption = (3) + (6)	75		75	108		82		
Full income = (3) + (7)	72	78					74	68
Housing consumption as a percentage of total consumption								
Old	25		25	15		34		
Prime age	17		20	15		30		
Ratio	1.50		1.27	0.98		1.14		
Housing consumption as a percentage of full income								
Old	25						16	22
Prime age	16						12	15
Ratio	1.56						1.28	1.48

NOTE: The table shows the mean consumption or expenditure aggregate for people in "old" households (head aged 65+) relative to the mean for prime-age households (head 45–59). All measures are equivalized, and the mean of each component is calculated across household heads and spouses (where present). Note that UK data do not add up due to missing data on housing expenditures for a small fraction of households.

groups. However, the fact that most of the estimates in this table are below 100 does not necessarily imply that living standards fall after retirement. In particular, there is no consensus on how to take account of different needs associated with aging and retirement. The retired have lower work-related expenditures and more leisure time, but also poorer health and greater health expenditures (even though they also receive greater health subsidies). Finally, all estimates assume the same simple equivalence scale for each commodity, which is unlikely to be appropriate for housing consumption in particular. Nonetheless, in broad terms at least, these caveats with respect to retirement needs apply in all the countries here (though as noted earlier, there are differences in public health expenditures).

Does the fourth pillar of home ownership compensate for the cross-national differences in income replacement rates? Australia is the outlier with the lowest disposable income replacement rates, and it is also a country where home ownership has been a prominent part of the retirement policy discourse (Yates and Bradbury 2010). In this table, we can see that the relatively high rates of home ownership among the Australian elderly do compensate for their relatively low income, but not entirely. In terms of non-housing consumption, the replacement rates of the Australian elderly are above those in Sweden but below those in the remaining countries. Using the consumption/full income measures, the retirement replacement rates are the same as in the United Kingdom but below the other countries.

It is interesting to compare the situation of Australia with that of the United States, two countries where various forms of private saving are important components of retirement provision. In both cases, the equivalent housing consumption of the elderly is higher than that of the prime age (see row 3 of Table 12.3). However, while the consumption/full income replacement rate is low in Australia, it is very high in the United States (by far the highest). This result arises because in the United States, home ownership is a supplement to a strong pension system and other forms of income-generating private savings. In Australia, on the other hand, the fourth pillar is a replacement for a weakly developed pension system, although it is conceivable that Australia might move toward the U.S. model in the future as mandated private pension schemes (superannuation) grow in importance.

The bottom panel of Table 12.3 shows the fraction of either consumption or full income that is allocated to housing consumption among the prime-age and older populations. In all countries, the older population devotes a greater share of its consumption/full income to housing. The post-retirement shift in apparent consumption patterns is greatest in Australia and Sweden and lowest in the United States. In Australia, this result arises because the older population has high home-ownership rates and high home values but low incomes. In Sweden, this arises because the older population has relatively high housing expenditures—particularly rent (see the online appendix, Table 12.A2)—that reduce non-housing consumption. In the United States, this pattern is driven largely by the high disposable incomes in retirement.

Whether these differences imply a problematic pattern of housing consumption by the elderly in some countries cannot be ascertained on this evidence alone. It does suggest, however, the need for further investigation of the possible over-consumption of housing in Australia (because of high home ownership) and in Sweden (because of high housing costs). In the former country at least, this is consistent with an often-stated policy concern that the elderly are housing-asset rich but income poor (e.g., AHURI 2004).

As noted above, it is possible that Table 12.3 might underestimate non-housing consumption because some households are able to liquidate their assets in retirement. Some of this liquidation *is* included (annuities and the income flows from investments, which might thus be declining in real value over time), but other forms, such as the liquidation of financial and non-financial assets and indeed of owner-occupied housing, are not. As discussed above, calculating the maximum potential consumption that could be derived from these goods via an annuitization calculation is arguably not appropriate when estimating consumption, because these assets are unlikely to be fully liquidated before death.[12]

RETIREMENT REPLACEMENT RATES ACROSS THE INCOME DISTRIBUTION

These replacement rates also differ across the income distribution. Table 12.4 summarizes the same calculations reported in Table 12.3, but they are calculated separately for the top 20 percent, middle 60 percent, and bottom 20 percent of the income distribution (within each age group).

The top panel of Table 12.4 shows disposable income and reflects the different models of income support policy in these countries. All of the countries except for the United States have replacement rates that are sig-

TABLE 12.4
Old relative to prime age in top-, middle-, and low-income households (%)

	Australia	Canada	United Kingdom	United States	Germany	Italy	Finland	Sweden
DISPOSABLE INCOME								
Top	69	71	71	91	73	78	81	72
Middle	54	68	63	73	73	74	64	64
Bottom	92	118	80	74	85	98	76	78
OWN-HOME CONSUMPTION								
Top	123	98	93	111	98	88	96	82
Middle	111	98	76	105	103	94	87	64
Bottom	160	99	100	126	161	115	100	83
HOUSING CONSUMPTION								
Top	118	106	96	108	100	89	102	90
Middle	105	110	93	105	102	93	91	107
Bottom	129	112	99	106	120	100	93	99
INCOME AFTER HOUSING EXPENDITURES (+ MORTGAGE PAYMENTS IN SOME COUNTRIES)								
Top	75/72	72	75	115		78	81	70
Middle	59/56	67	64	96		73	63	57
Bottom	107/102	140	91	315		118	75	68
CONSUMPTION OR FULL INCOME								
Top	80/77	75	79	114		80	83	72
Middle	67/64	74	70	97		80	67	64
Bottom	116/112	129	94	197		108	79	77

NOTE: As for Table 12.3, for all outcome measures, people are classed as "top" if they fall in the top 20 percent, middle in the middle 60 percent, and bottom in the lowest 20 percent of household disposable income within each age group. The Australian estimates are for the measures including and excluding principal payments as part of housing expenditures, respectively.

nificantly higher for the bottom than for the middle—reflecting the role of retirement income guarantees. In Australia and Canada, replacement rates are much higher at the bottom—reflecting the impact of flat-rate pensions in Australia and generous minimum pensions in Canada.

Own-home consumption is often higher in retirement than in prime age, reflecting the differing age and income distributions of home-ownership and housing wealth (though not too much should be made of the absolute values due to the simple equivalence scale used). Similarly, total housing consumption is usually similar in retirement to prime age. The exception here is low-income Australians, whose rate of home ownership in retirement is similar to those of higher-income households.

Our proxy for non-housing consumption, income after housing expenditures, generally has a higher replacement rate at the bottom of the income distribution. (The very high replacement rate for low-income persons in the United States, for this and for the consumption measure, is because a few prime-age households have very high mortgage repayments that are probably not representative of long-term housing costs.)

CONSUMPTION INEQUALITY IN RETIREMENT

What, then, are the implications of these transitions for the consumption patterns in high-, middle-, and low-income households after retirement? In particular, what impact do the different mixes of income protection and home ownership have on consumption inequality?

Table 12.5 shows the average values of income and consumption for the top 20 percent relative to the middle three quintile groups, as well as the values for the bottom 20 percent relative to the middle. These estimates can be considered as (partial) indicators of inequality in the top and bottom of the older population—representing the distance in living standards of the top and the bottom from the middle, respectively.[13]

The two outliers in the top half of the figure are the United States and Sweden—in opposite respects. In the United States, the disposable income of the top 20 percent is over three times that of the middle 60 percent, compared to around two times for Sweden and between 2.2 and 2.5 times for the other countries. A similar disparity exists for non-housing consumption (income after housing) and for consumption including housing services. Sweden has more equal housing consumption than the other countries, while the U.S. inequality in housing consumption is similar to that in the other countries.

The lower panel of the table tells a story similar to that found in relative poverty estimates that take account of housing costs (Ritakallio 2003; Yates and Bradbury 2010), even though here the anchor point is the living standards of the middle of the older population rather than the overall population median. The variation in the disposable-income bottom/middle ratio mirrors that for the top of the distribution, with the United States again an outlier, having an average income for the bottom quintile group of only 36 percent that of the middle. Sweden is joined by Finland and Canada in having relatively high incomes for the bottom 20 percent. Australia is not

TABLE 12.5
Older population: The top and bottom vs. the middle

	Australia	Canada	United Kingdom	United States	Germany	Italy	Finland	Sweden
TOP RELATIVE TO THE MIDDLE								
Disposable income	255	225	229	328	220	238	252	197
Own-home consumption	176	168	232	199	209	173	179	244
Housing consumption	164	131	179	177	192	150	157	124
Income after housing expenditures (+ mortgage payments in some countries)	262	253	247	352		281	260	228
Consumption or full income	236	225	228	320		231	242	203
BOTTOM RELATIVE TO THE MIDDLE								
Disposable income	57	60	49	36	51	49	61	63
Own-home consumption	101	55	97	50	76	66	60	63
Housing consumption	106	94	89	63	76	71	93	102
Income after housing expenditures (+ mortgage payments in some countries)	53	49	48	33	—	39	54	50
Consumption or full income	67	60	59	38	—	52	61	62

NOTE: Each cell shows the mean value for the top (or bottom) 20 percent of the older population relative to the value for the middle 60 percent. The Australian results are the same for the two housing cost measures (at this level of precision).

far behind, though this is partly because the average incomes of the middle-income elderly are relatively low.

Turning to the more comprehensive measures of living standards that take account of housing wealth, we find that this improves the relative position of the low-income elderly in some countries but not in others. The consumption/full income measures suggest that the Australian retirement housing model has been generally successful in reducing inequality among the older population, with the bottom quintile group having a consumption level of around two-thirds that of the middle—higher than in any other country. Elsewhere (Yates and Bradbury 2010), we show that this is despite the existence of a doubly disadvantaged (but small) subgroup with low incomes and no housing wealth. However, this result is driven by the high level of own-home consumption at the bottom. In terms of income after housing expenditures (non-housing consumption), the Australian pattern is not that different from Finland, Sweden, Canada, and the United Kingdom. The United Kingdom also appears more equal on the basis of consumption/full income than on a disposable-income basis.

These results make the U.S. result even more striking as an example of how a strong fourth pillar need not reduce the inequality of consumption in retirement. Taking account of housing consumption does not significantly reduce the large gap between the bottom and the middle in the United States (indeed it increases for non-housing consumption). Moreover, the ranking here is on the basis of income rather than consumption or full income. If the latter were used, the inequality would be even more striking.

Though both Australia and the United States have high rates of home ownership among the older population, these different impacts on inequality arise from the very different patterns of own-home wealth holdings. The housing wealth holdings of the bottom income-quintile group in Australia are essentially the same as for the middle group, whereas in the United States, they are about half. To put this another way, the correlation between income and housing wealth is weak in Australia but strong in the United States. The strength of this correlation (and the inequalities in life-cycle wealth accumulation patterns that drive it) is crucial for determining the impact of fourth pillar savings on inequality in retirement. For Australia, a key question is whether the home-ownership patterns of the future will continue to be as equal as those of the past (Yates and Bradbury 2010).

CONCLUSION

These eight countries vary widely in the extent to which home ownership and other forms of private savings are used to support consumption in retirement. These patterns, however, do not have any neat correspondence with the different welfare-state models of retirement income provision that developed during the twentieth century. Two of the English-speaking former colonies, Australia and the United States, stand out as having the highest rates of home ownership in retirement. But these two countries have very different models of retirement pensions. Other English-speaking countries (Canada and the United Kingdom) have middling rates of home ownership—lower than in Italy and Finland—while the other Nordic country in our sample, Sweden, is very different, with a relatively low home-ownership rate (along with Germany).

If the home-ownership rates currently observed among younger cohorts continue into retirement, then we can expect to observe a substantial convergence over future decades as countries with middling rates of home ownership catch up to those where home ownership has been the norm for several generations (though Sweden and Germany will likely retain low rates).[14] In this respect, the Australian and U.S. cases provide interesting alternative examples of the impact of home ownership on retirement living standards.

To a large extent, the Australian housing wealth model is successful in compensating for the low incomes provided via its flat-rate pension system (even though gaps remain). Adding the imputed consumption of housing services to income moves the Australian replacement rate up to levels similar to those found in the other countries. The U.S. model, if anything, seems to over-support the living standards of the average older person (compared to prime age), with home ownership also reinforcing the inequality of pension access in retirement.

In terms of disposable income, Sweden stands out as having the most equal living standards in retirement, while the United States has the most unequal. At the bottom end of the distribution, Sweden is joined by Finland and Canada as countries where the income of the bottom 20 percent is relatively close to that of the middle. When measures of living standards taking account of housing consumption are included, the relative position of the bottom in Australia is now similar to that of the more equal countries, but the U.S. bottom-quintile group remains particularly disadvantaged. This arises from the relatively strong correlation between home ownership and wealth in the latter country.

One potential problem of this fourth pillar of retirement provision is that it might lead to under-consumption of non-housing goods among people who are asset-rich but income-poor after retirement. In all the countries examined here, the older population devotes a greater share of their total consumption to housing than does the prime-age population. However, this increase in the housing share of consumption is particularly large in Australia because of the combination of home ownership and low retirement incomes. But rental markets can also lead to apparently similar consumption patterns, with the older Swedish population also having particularly high housing expenditures.

It is likely that, if home ownership continues to increase, there will be increasing demand in many countries for policies that support the drawing down of housing wealth to finance non-housing consumption. If this is not possible, then much of the wealth value in housing will eventually pass to the next generation via inheritances—lessening its usefulness as an across-life-cycle resource transfer mechanism. However, mechanisms to support wealth draw-downs such as reverse mortgages and equity-sharing arrangements are still relatively undeveloped in most countries. Moreover, they do not, in themselves, cover the longevity and disability risks that encourage many people to hold onto housing wealth.

More generally, how will the further development of this additional retirement pillar complement the existing retirement support pillars? The policy support for the "pillars" model has stemmed from the ability of the different pillars to independently cope with different risks. Public pensions are subject to fiscal and political sustainability risks but relatively insulated from financial market risks, while private pensions and savings have the opposite characteristics.

Housing investments are, of course, subject to substantial risks—as events in 2008 in many countries showed. This experience also showed that such risks are not independent of the risks facing private and public retirement funds. Paradoxically, one of the limitations of housing as a means of saving for retirement—its illiquidity—means that the volatility of housing markets are less important for retirement living standards. Once people own their home, it does not matter if its value plummets; they still can live in it. (The next generation of inheritors will be the ones to bear the burden of lower house values.)

However, housing booms and busts can have important implications for determining who owns their house upon entering retirement. Volatility can drive low- and middle-income prime-age households out of home ownership, or sustained high prices can prevent many from entering. As the comparison of the United States and Australia indicates, the distribution of home ownership is of central importance in understanding the impact of the fourth pillar on retirement living standards. In all the countries considered here, an understanding of housing markets and their distributional outcomes is likely to become increasingly important for predicting future patterns of retirement living standards.

NOTES

I am grateful to the editors, Jean-Pierre Schoder, other conference attendees, and an anonymous referee for comments on earlier drafts. This work has been partly supported by an Australian Research Council grant (DP0878643).

1. This is especially the case in Australia. See Kemeny (1980), Jones (1990), Castles (1998), Ritakallio (2003), and Yates and Bradbury (2010).

2. Other approaches have also been used. See Yates (1991, 1994) and Saunders and Siminski (2005).

3. See Yates (1991, 1994), Saunders and Siminski (2005), and Davis, Lehnert, and Martin (2008).

4. Though it might appear the most direct approach to this question, using expenditure data has some limitations. First, the irregular timing of expenditures related to shopping patterns makes it difficult to estimate distributional characteristics. More importantly for the purposes here, the additional costs associated with the collection of these data mean that they are less readily available in cross-nationally comparable form.

5. With respect to the liquidation of housing equity, in the United States, there is mixed evidence. Haider and colleagues (2000) find some evidence that retirees do tend to move their wealth into non-housing forms. Fisher and colleagues, on the other hand, conclude that home equity increases after retirement, with few retirees leaving home ownership or increasing their housing debt. Across countries, Disney and Whitehouse (2002) find some limited evidence of home-ownership downsizing. Chiuri and Jappelli (2008) find across several countries that within-cohort home ownership rates decline by about 1 percentage point per annum after age 75.

6. Where the household is headed by a couple, the age of the male is used. This coding is to ensure approximate comparability with Canada, where the only information available is the age of the survey-defined household head.

7. Winsorization of variable X means that the value of X_i is replaced with $\min(X_i, X(99))$, where $X(99)$ is the 99th percentile of X. The main motivation for this adjustment is that the U.S. data contain a small number of cases with very high housing expenditures, possibly reflecting some large lump-sum mortgage repayments that are not indicative of average expenditure patterns.

8. Ideally, the analysis would be conducted at the person level. However, we cannot do this using the Canadian dataset that is in the *LIS Database*.

9. The LWS variable RIXP is used (plus NRCBEN for the United Kingdom). Rent is set to zero for home owners because RIXP also includes mortgage payments.

10. LWS variable RIXP (plus NRCBEN for the United Kingdom). Ideally, maintenance expenditures should also be included in such a measure but are not available for any of the countries.

11. Recent examples include Ritakallio (2003) and Yates and Bradbury (2010).

12. An estimate of the maximum additional consumption that could potentially be available from liquidating non-housing wealth can be obtained from the data in Table 12.1. In Australia, for example, non-own-home wealth adds up on average to 5.3 times annual disposable income, compared with 2.2 to 2.9 times in the other countries (other than the United States, which is also high). The additional potential non-housing consumption can be crudely measured by assuming that approximately 3.5 units of annual disposable income were drawn down linearly over a 15-year period. Adding this to the disposable income calculation of Table 12.3 would be sufficient to make the patterns of non-housing consumption in Australia more similar to those in other countries. However, much of this reflects the non-financial wealth of the very wealthy. The same calculation for middle-income households would only increase disposable income by 10 percent, still leaving Australia as an outlier in terms of the increase in housing consumption share after retirement.

13. Because the ranking is always by income, the results for the other consumption measures are more akin to concentration indices than to inequality indices.

14. Bradbury (2010, Figure 12).

For additional results, please see the online appendices by following the link in the listing for Income Inequality *on the Stanford University Press website: http:// www.sup.org.*

REFERENCES

Australian Housing and Urban Research Institute (AHURI). 2004. *Housing Futures for an Ageing Australia*. Melbourne: AHURI.

Bradbury, Bruce. 2010. "Asset Rich, but Income Poor: Australian Housing Wealth and Retirement in an International Context." Social Policy Research paper 41. Canberra: Australian Government Department of Families, Housing, Community Services and Indigenous Affairs.

Castles, Frank. 1998. "The Really Big Trade-Off: Home Ownership and the Welfare State in the New World and the Old." *Acta Politica* 33(1): 5–19.

Chiuri, Maria Concetta, and Tullio Jappelli. 2008. "Do the Elderly Reduce Housing Equity? An International Comparison." *Journal of Population Economics* 23(2): 643–63.

Davis, Morris A., Andreas Lehnert, and Robert F. Martin. 2008. "The Rent-Price Ratio for the Aggregate Stock of Owner-Occupied Housing." *Review of Income and Wealth* 54(2): 279–84.

Disney, Richard, and Edward Whitehouse. 2002. "The Economic Well-Being of Older People in International Perspective: A Critical Review." *LIS* working paper 306. Luxembourg: LIS.

Doling, John, and Richard Ronald. 2010. "Home Ownership and Asset-Based Welfare." *Journal of Housing and the Built Environment* 25: 165–73.

Fisher, Jonathan D., David S. Johnson, Joseph T. Marchand, Timothy M. Smeeding, and Barbara Boyle Torrey. 2007. "No Place like Home: Older Adults and Their Housing." *Journal of Gerontology* 62B(2): 120–28.

Haider, Steven, Michael Hurd, Elaine Reardon, and Stephanie Williamson. 2000. "Patterns of Dissaving In Retirement." *AARP Public Policy Institute* issue paper. Washington, DC: AARP.

Jones, M. A. 1990. *The Australian Welfare State*, 3rd ed. Sydney: Allen and Unwin.

Kemeny, J. 1980. *The Myth of Home Ownership*. London: Routledge and Kegan Paul.

Luxembourg Wealth Study (LWS) Database, http://www.lisdatacenter.org (multiple countries; microdata last accessed in December 2010). Luxembourg: LIS.

Organisation for Economic Co-operation and Development (OECD). 2005. "Recent House Price Developments: The Role of Fundamentals." *Economic Outlook*, Vol. 78. Paris: OECD.

Ritakallio, Veli-Matti. 2003. "The Importance of Housing Costs in Cross-National Comparisons of Welfare (State) Outcomes." *International Social Security Review* 56(2): 81–101.

Saunders, Peter, and Peter Siminski. 2005. "Home Ownership and Inequality: Imputed Rent and Income Distribution in Australia." Discussion paper 144. Sydney: Social Policy Research Centre.

Whiteford, Peter, and Steven Kennedy. 1995. "Incomes and Living Standards of Older People." *Department of Social Security* research report no. 34. London: HMSO.

Wolff, Edward, and Ajit Zacharias. 2003. "The Levy Institute Measure of Economic Well-Being." Working paper 372. Annandale-on-Hudson, NY: Levy Economics Institute of Bard College.

Yates, Judith. 1991. "Australia's Owner-Occupied Housing Wealth and Its Impact on Income Distribution." Reports and proceedings 92, Sydney: Social Policy Research Centre, University of New South Wales.

———. 1994. "Imputed Rent and Income Distribution." *Review of Income and Wealth* 40(1): 43–66.

Yates, Judith, and Bruce Bradbury. 2010. "Home Ownership as a (Crumbling) Fourth Pillar of Social Insurance in Australia." *Journal of Housing and the Built Environment* 25: 193–211.

CHAPTER THIRTEEN

Public Pension Entitlements and the Distribution of Wealth

Joachim R. Frick and Markus M. Grabka

MOTIVATION

Pension entitlements—whether statutory, occupational, or private—represent a considerable source of wealth. But despite the importance of this wealth component—often referred to as public pension wealth[1]—in obtaining unbiased wealth estimates, it has not been adequately investigated in research on wealth distributions (see, e.g., Brugiavini, Maser, and Sundén 2001).

The aim of this chapter is to show the relevance and magnitude of public pension wealth when considered in an augmented wealth measure. Given that such information is not readily available in survey data, we describe how, in the German case, pension entitlements can be determined by means of statistical matching and how the present value can be defined.[2] We analyze the impact of pension entitlements on the distribution of net worth, considering variation in wealth across socio-economic groups defined according to age and occupational status. We refine the analysis by comparing pension wealth levels across income groups and show how pension wealth affects the German middle class. We also discuss the impact of pension wealth on inequality of augmented wealth. Based on our findings for Germany, we strongly recommend the use of an augmented wealth measure such as the one proposed here, with the ultimate goal of taking the present value of pension entitlements fully into account in cross-country comparative research on wealth inequality.

Pension wealth is typically disregarded in wealth analyses based on survey data for two reasons. First, interviewees usually do not know their accumulated pension entitlements (see Johnson, Sambamoorthi, and Crystal 2000), given that in a standard pay-as-you-go (PAYG) old-age security system, contributions are compulsory for both employers and employees. Pension entitlements are based on earnings, but they are also affected by periods of child rearing, education, long-term care, or unemployment, with pension entitlements for each such period being calculated differently. The insured person generally does not know the precise sum of all of these entitlements.[3]

Second, one may argue that pension wealth represents only a "notional" asset (Frick, Grabka, and Hauser 2010). Simply adding this component to financial and material assets is problematic, because such standard assets carry specific functions that pension entitlements largely fail to fulfill. For example, in contrast to interest payments received from savings, no (further) income can be gained from pension entitlements; the latter also lack the usage function of real estate, and the possibility of bequeathing them usually takes only the severely limited form of provision for dependents (in the form of widow/er pensions). The power, socialization, and prestige functions associated with great monetary and material wealth holdings are also not relevant in the case of old-age pension entitlements. Premature liquidation of entitlements—for example, for the purchase of real estate—is barred, as is taking an advance. What remains, then, is merely the security function. But even this function is limited to the phase of life that follows retirement or to cases of occupational disability or provision for dependents. Finally, although pension wealth represents protected private-sector capital stock, the state could change the value of assessment-financed entitlements, making pension entitlements a variable stock of wealth.

Notwithstanding all these arguments, which are similarly valid across countries, conventional analyses using a standard net worth measure also face the problem of major differences between occupational groups *within* a given country in terms of both pension scheme designs and the savings behavior resulting from different incentive structures. In the case of Germany, some occupational groups are exempted from the statutory pension system and therefore have to put away money for retirement on their own (BMAS 2008). This is true for most self-employed people, who typically invest in private insurance plans, real estate, or business assets—that is, the types of assets that are usually adequately captured in a standard measure of net worth. A second important group not covered by the statutory pension system is civil servants, who generally do not contribute a significant percentage of their earnings to their pension scheme but still enjoy fairly high tax-financed benefits after retirement.[4] By contrast, wage earners and salaried employees generally have compulsory pension schemes and in some cases occupational pension schemes as well.[5]

The problem of dissimilarities across occupational groups is considerably larger in the case of cross-national comparisons. Depending on which welfare regime is being examined, the relevance of public pension wealth may differ widely. For countries like Germany with a mature PAYG pension system, pension wealth is clearly more important in quantitative terms than in liberal welfare systems that put more emphasis on private pension provision. Convincing evidence about cross-country differences in the relevance of pension wealth—at least for men—is provided by the Organisation for Economic Co-operation and Development (OECD) (2007). Countries with strong PAYG systems, such as the Scandinavian countries, have above-OECD-average pension wealth levels, the highest being Luxembourg, with almost USD1 million.[6] Liberal welfare regimes, such as the United States or the United Kingdom, only reach 58 percent (USD173,000) to 74 percent (USD224,000) of the OECD average, respectively. Germany is ranked somewhat above the average with USD342,000 between France with USD330,000 and Finland with USD396,000.

In addition to these cross-country differences, these numbers demonstrate the quantitative importance of pension wealth: the mean across all OECD countries is about USD300,000. This wealth component is especially important for middle-income groups, who tend to have rather stable earnings histories with long periods of contributions paid, given the compulsory nature of (public) pensions systems. However, making compulsory contributions also limits the possibilities for accumulating standard net worth.[7] Demographic changes, such as population aging and declining fertility, place public pension systems under pressure to reduce the generosity and implicit returns on accumulated pension assets. One may therefore find a general trend in various countries and welfare regimes toward private pension provision (Bonin 2009). This may affect middle-income earners most severely, given that a large share of total net worth is contained in pension entitlements.

DETERMINING PUBLIC PENSION ENTITLEMENTS

Population surveys in Germany typically do not ask for information about social security wealth because respondents usually do not know their total pension entitlements at any particular point in time. Register data, on the other hand, contain detailed information on pension entitlements but not necessarily information about other wealth components or the individual's socio-economic background or household situation. For the purpose of a comprehensive analysis of the wealth distribution, ideally, survey and administrative data could be directly merged using a unique identifier such as the individual's social security number ("record linkage"). However, at least in Germany, this option is not feasible for data confidentiality reasons; one would have to ask for the social security number and for informed consent (with respect to record linkage), both of which motivate respondents to reject (further) participation. Statistical matching may provide a second-best option to overcome the drawbacks of both data sources and to use their respective merits. Unlike record linkage, statistical matching does not aim at finding the exact same person but links observations that are statistically similar, at least in terms of certain characteristics observed in both datasets ("matching variables").

Statistical Matching of Survey Data and Pension Account Information

In this section, we discuss the double matching approach to determining public pension entitlements. First, we combine standard data on net worth from the representative German Socio-Economic Panel (SOEP) study with data on total pension entitlements accrued over the life course from the German Social Security Administration's sample of active pension accounts (*Versicherungskontenstichprobe*, VSKT). An additional link to data from the "statistics on pension benefits splitting after divorce" (*Versorgungsausgleichsstatistik*), or divorce statistics, provides an effective control of the effects of divorce on pension benefits, which would otherwise be ignored but can have important impacts on divorced people's pension entitlements. The most important outcome measure resulting from this double matching procedure is an estimate of each individual's social security wealth as of 2007.

The German SOEP is a multidisciplinary household panel study (Wagner, Frick, and Schupp 2007). Started in 1984, it covers a representative sample of the total population living in private households in Germany. In 2007, about 12,000 households and 22,000 individuals were interviewed. The microdata provide detailed information on individuals, households, and families, and enable researchers to monitor changes in living conditions over time. The standard components are surveyed annually, whereas certain special topic modules are surveyed at roughly five-year intervals. In 2007, a special wealth module collected detailed data on material and financial wealth at the individual level (Frick, Grabka, and Marcus 2007) but no information on public pension entitlements.[8] This chapter seeks to fill this gap by using data from the VSKT. This is a 1 percent random sample of pension accounts, containing records for approximately 570,000 individuals, both actively insured and already retired. These records are representative of all those individuals who contribute(d) to the public pension scheme. The VSKT collects detailed longitudinal pension-relevant information on monthly earnings, unemployment spells, and periods of child care, as well as long-term care over the course of working life. The third dataset we use, the *Versorgungsausgleichsstatistik*, is designed to aid the administration of the pension system and contains information on the splitting of pension benefits in all relevant divorce settlements—a total of 5.5 million cases since its introduction in 1977. Further, these statistics contain information about marriages and divorces that goes beyond the information provided in the VSKT.

We slice both datasets, SOEP and VSKT, by sex, region, and immigrant status, taking into account pronounced regional and gender differences in pension entitlements. Pensionable earnings and pension-relevant transfer payments (e.g., unemployment benefits, etc.) are the most important determinants of the individual's social security wealth and are our key matching variables. An income measure summarizes all income that qualifies for the accrual of pension benefits (earnings, unemployment benefits, sickness allowances, etc.).[9] For the computation of the distance function, income enters the equation as a three-year moving average to smooth individual income histories for the years 1983–1985, 1984–1986, . . . , 2004–2006.[10] A woman's fertility history is used in the statistical matching as additional information, since it determines the number of child care credits that translate directly into pension entitlements credited to the woman's pension account. In addition, we take various duration variables into account in the computation of the distance metric, reflecting the number of years spent in different activities such as employment, unemployment, education, compulsory military or community service (men only), and long-term care. Finally, the statistical matching includes the age of the respondent as of 2007.

Given the representativeness of the SOEP sample for the German population, we match VSKT information to SOEP data—in other words, the SOEP data provide the *recipient file*. Matching the data in this way enables us to maintain the representative demographic structure of the SOEP population and eliminate potential issues of selectivity inherent to VSKT data.[11]

The statistical matching between the SOEP and the VSKT data uses Mahalanobis distance matching (Kantor 2006), which is frequently used in cluster analysis. For each observation x_i in the SOEP, the Mahalanobis distance d_{ij} from each observation x_j in the VSKT is determined on the basis of the selected matching variables p. The statistical donor chosen is the VSKT observation with the smallest distance from the SOEP case. Unlike the Euclidean distance, the Mahalanobis score incorporates correlations between matching variables and differences in variances. This implies that highly correlated matching variables do not enter the computation of the Mahalanobis distance with the same weight. This property is particularly useful in our application because the individual's annual income at time t is likely to be highly correlated with the annual income at time $t + 1$.[12]

Divorce cannot be adequately considered when matching SOEP data with the administrative pension data provided by the VSKT, so an additional match is required to correct for the splitting of statutory pension benefits between former spouses. For every divorce, the pension rights accrued by husband and wife during their marriage are summed up and split in half at the date of divorce.[13] Information provided in the divorce statistics of the statutory pension insurance is the appropriate data source to correct for this potential bias. To estimate the divorce correction, we combine VSKT and divorce statistics using record linkage. The unique identifier used for the linkage is a combination of the exact amount of the split pension, gender, region, and age. Based on the linked data, we estimate group-wise linear regression models that provide us with the divorce correction, which is then applied to SOEP data.[14]

The Principle of Capitalization of Pension Entitlements

For the following analysis of (augmented) wealth inequality, we use a measure of net worth from SOEP data in conjunction with the present value of pension wealth entitlements accrued so far from statutory and occupational pension plans and pension schemes for occupations in the "liberal professions" (such as architects, physicians, or lawyers). The latter complement the asset information contained in the SOEP data: owner-occupied and other real estate holdings, financial assets, assets from life insurance policies and private pension schemes, building society savings agreements (*Bausparverträge*), business assets, valuables, and consumer and mortgage loans. Total net worth—the relevant criterion when discussing social welfare and the key indicator when analyzing the personal wealth distribution—is determined by subtracting liabilities from gross assets.

The income section of the SOEP questionnaire asks retired people a number of questions about benefit payments from the different types of pension schemes. As a result, pension entitlements—that is, the present value of the future income streams for the already retired—can be derived directly from their answers, assuming these benefits will be paid as an annuity for the remaining lifetime. However, for the insured—people of working age—the information about pension entitlements from the statutory pension insurance is obtained through statistical matching as described above. The SOEP does not contain questions about pension benefits—such as occupational pensions, pensions for liberal professionals, or tradespeople—for the currently insured population because respondents are rarely able to provide good answers. Nor is there external information comparable to the statutory VSKT data that could be used to generate this missing information through statistical matching. For the cohorts prior to entry into retirement, therefore, the entitlements under these old-age pension systems have been underestimated.[15] A crucial exception is data on pension entitlements for non-retired civil servants. For active civil servants, the amount of the entitlements can be reliably approximated based on current pay level and years of service. For each year of service, civil servants are entitled to about 1.80 percent of the level of gross earnings received during the last three years prior to retirement.[16] After 40 years of service, this accumulates to a maximum share of 71.75 percent.

Pension entitlements are assessed through capitalization—that is, by calculating the discounted present value of recurring future payments (see

Formula 1). For the payout period, the average further life expectancy (according to the 2005/2007 mortality charts of the German Federal Office of Statistics, separated by East and West Germany and by sex) is considered. In addition, a retirement entry age that varies between 65 and 67 (according to the Pension Reform Act of 2007), depending on the age cohort, is used as a basis. With the additional assumption that future pension increases and inflation will balance each other out, the calculations are simplified in such a way that the real value of the entitlements is preserved.[17] An interest rate of 2 percent is assumed for discounting purposes.[18] The resulting value is the gross pension entitlement.

Formula 1: Determining the Present Value (PV) of pension entitlements:

$$PV = \frac{C}{i}\left[1 - \frac{1}{(1+i)^n}\right],$$

where C = pension benefit, i = discount rate, and n = further life expectancy in years (payment period).

However, various status groups differ with respect to the tax treatment of retirement income. For example, life annuities and other benefits such as public pensions, agricultural pension funds, or trade association pension funds are not fully taxed; rather, a taxable income share, which varies depending on when one starts receiving the pension, applies (§22 of the German Income Tax Act [*Einkommensteuergesetz*]).[19]

To prevent double counting, no present value is determined for entitlements from private pension plans because the SOEP collects data on these wealth components in the part of the SOEP questionnaire dealing with net financial assets.

THE IMPACT OF PENSION ENTITLEMENTS ON WEALTH INEQUALITY

Individual Net Worth without Pension Entitlements

The aggregated net worth of individuals in private households in Germany amounted to about 5.9 trillion euros in 2007 (Table 13.1), which is about 83,000 euros per capita.[20] However, such mean values can be highly affected by outliers, which appear to be more of an issue for wealth analysis than for income analysis.[21] Additionally, one should keep in mind that net worth can take on negative values. As such, comparing the mean and

TABLE 13.1
Net worth and public pension wealth in Germany, 2007[a]

Basic statistics	Net worth (€) (1)	Public pension wealth[b] (€) (2)	Augmented wealth (€) (3)	Change (%) [(1)/(3)]
Mean	83,077	78,479	161,556	94.5
Median	14,751	46,680	94,675	541.8
Sum in billion euros	5,908	5,581	11,489	94.5
Inequality				
Gini	0.800	0.566	0.604	−24.6
HSCV	6.51	0.73	2.03	−68.9
P90:P50[c]	14.15	4.12	3.83	−72.9
Wealth shares (%)				
Lowest quintile	−1.5	0.9	0.4	−126.7
Second quintile	0.4	5.2	4.5	1,025.0
Third quintile	3.9	12.0	11.8	202.6
Fourth quintile	17.3	24.1	22.4	29.5
Highest quintile	79.9	57.7	60.9	−23.8
Population with zero or negative wealth (%)	28.1	4.5	3.3	−88.3

SOURCE: Authors' calculations from SOEPv25.
[a]Population: persons in private households aged 17 or older (N = 69,321,834).
[b]With a discount rate of 2 percent, without provision for dependents.
[c]Lowest value for the top 10 percent in the wealth distribution in relation to the median (50 percent).

median of the distribution is already very informative: indeed, in the year 2007, the latter takes on a value of less than 15,000 euros, so the mean exceeds the median by a factor of 5.5, which indicates high inequality.

Following the standard life-cycle hypothesis (Modigliani 1988), there is a strong relationship between net worth and age, assuming that with increased age, wealth is typically accumulated until retirement. After leaving the labor force, dis-saving occurs to smooth income gaps. However, there are pronounced deviations in the levels of wealth accumulation between various status groups over the life cycle (Figure 13.1). Not surprisingly, self-employed persons in Germany accumulate the highest levels of net worth. Around retirement age (at 60), their net worth is about 400,000 euros, twice as high as that of civil servants and 3.5 times higher than individuals insured under the public pension scheme. Even for members of the public pension scheme with a continuous occupational history and few to no periods of unemployment, which would have led to a reduced ability to save, net worth adds up to only 140,000 euros around retirement.

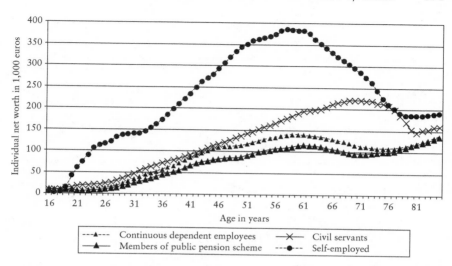

Figure 13.1. Individual net worth by age and status group, Germany 2007
SOURCE: Authors' calculations from SOEPv25.

Individual Net Worth Considering Public Pension Entitlements

The general shape of the age profile of the present value of pension entitlements follows the life-cycle hypothesis: it increases with age up to the
time of retirement, with a somewhat steeper slope in the second half of
working life. Apparently, this is mainly because earnings typically increase
with age, as does the absolute value of the contributions, given that these
are calculated as a fixed percentage of earnings (up to a certain income
threshold). On retirement, contributions are no longer paid into the system;
rather, pensions are paid out, reducing the present value of future pension
income flows until the statistical death occurs. The choice of discount rate,
of course, matters: using a discount rate of 2 percent, the net present value
of all pension entitlements in Germany amounts to about 5.6 trillion euros
(see Table 13.1) in 2007, which nearly doubles aggregate net worth. Across
all adults in Germany, this equals a mean value of 78,500 euros or a median
of roughly 47,000 euros.[22]

    Comparing the age profile of net worth and the augmented wealth
measure, which includes the present value of pension entitlements over the
life course (Figure 13.2), the highest values for augmented wealth can be

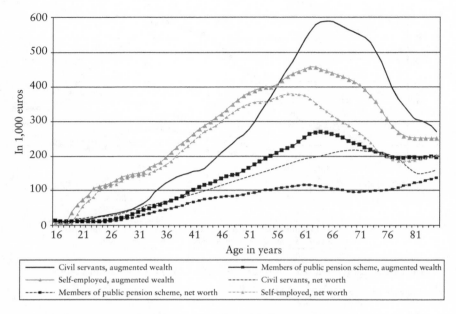

Figure 13.2. Net worth and augmented wealth by age and status group, Germany 2007

SOURCE: Authors' calculations from SOEPv25; public pension wealth using a discount rate of 2 percent.

observed for those around retirement age (about 65 years old). This is true for all groups, but the levels vary substantially. Although the self-employed have the highest levels for net worth, their pension entitlements make up only a minor share of augmented wealth. For civil servants, this picture is clearly different. Their pension entitlements roughly triple their net worth, which amounts to about 600,000 euros around retirement age. Finally, members in the public pension scheme also gain significantly from their pension entitlements, but at retirement age, this accumulates only to less than 270,000 euros.

The Relevance of Public Pension Entitlements by Income Classes

The above kernel regressions present a picture about the accumulation of net worth and pension entitlements over the life course. However, there are significant differences across income classes in the ability for saving and accumulating such economic resources. Thus, we now partition the income hierarchy into several income classes. Contrary to a classification according to quantiles such as deciles or quintiles, we divided the population into eight income classes relative to median equivalent income. We report net worth and pension entitlements at around the median (90 to 110 percent of the median), as well as in three below-average and four above-average income classes. The extreme positions result for persons who have an income of less than 50 percent or more than 200 percent of the median. The middle class is here defined as the population group with a relative income position of 70 to 150 percent of the median (Figure 13.3).[23] In 2007, this middle class makes up about 60 percent of the total population.[24] The concept of a middle class has a long tradition in Germany, not only since the seminal work of Schelsky (1965), who argued that after World War II, modern societies would tend to be more mobile, with more people from the lower-income class moving up and more people from the higher-income class moving down the social ladder. As a result, he predicted that the middle class would gain in importance (*nivellierte Mittelstandsgesellschaft*) and form the most important pillar of the social security system. Although this theory has

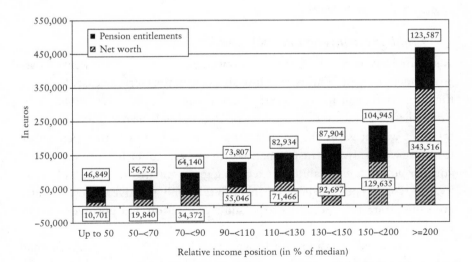

Figure 13.3.   Mean net worth and mean pension wealth by income classes,[a] Germany 2007

SOURCE: Authors' calculations from SOEPv25; public pension wealth using a discount rate of 2 percent.

[a]Relative income position based on the median of equivalent post-government income.

been widely criticized, today's middle-income classes bear a large portion of the financial burden of the welfare systems in many countries worldwide. Due to the statutory nature of the pension scheme, a significant share of wealth is tied to pension entitlements, in particular for the middle class.

Mean net worth of the middle (income) class varies between 34,000 and 93,000 euros (see Figure 13.3). However, adding the present value of public pension entitlements, the net worth of this group more than doubles. For those in the lower middle class (70 to 90 percent of the median), net worth almost triples; for the upper middle class (130 to 150 percent of the median), net worth roughly doubles. Moving up the income distribution, we consistently observe the absolute value of pension entitlements increasing. The relative contribution of pension entitlements to the augmented wealth measure, on the other hand, decreases as we move up. Among those in the poorest-income group (with income below 50 percent of the median), pension entitlements add more than 80 percent to augmented wealth. While the top-income group (with more than twice the median income) enjoys three times as much public pension wealth in absolute terms as the poorer group—124,000 euros versus 47,000 euros—this adds only about 25 percent to augmented wealth.

Wealth Inequality and Pension Entitlements

Net worth is typically far more concentrated than (equivalent) post-government income. This is certainly also true in the German case. In 2007, the Gini coefficient for net worth takes a value of 0.800 (see Table 13.1). The richest 20 percent of the adult population holds nearly 800 percent of total net worth, while the poorest 60 percent owns less than 3 percent of total net worth. In contrast to net worth—where about 8.3 percent of the adult population had liabilities exceeding gross wealth—that is, had negative net worth—pension entitlements can take only positive values.[25] Thus, even the poorest 20 percent of the adult population had positive pension entitlements.

As expected, pension entitlements are less concentrated, given that nearly everyone is insured in at least one old-age pension scheme. More than 28 percent of the population has zero or negative net worth, while less than 5 percent of the population—mostly very young people—has not yet accrued any public pension entitlements at all. Hence, the Gini coefficient of 0.566 for public pension wealth is much lower than for net worth.

Adding pension entitlements to net worth yields a Gini coefficient for augmented wealth of around 0.600, which is a significant decrease in inequality of about one-quarter.

The lower concentration of pension entitlements can also be observed when looking at the top-sensitive half-squared coefficient of variation (HSCV). While this measure takes an extraordinary high value of 6.5 for net worth, the respective outcome for public pension entitlements is only 0.7, which is the result of an upper-contribution ceiling in the public pension scheme. For the resulting augmented wealth measure, the HSCV comes to just 2.0—a decrease in inequality of more than two-thirds. The rationale for the larger reduction for the HSCV than for the Gini coefficient is the extreme top-sensitivity of the wealth data. This result is mirrored for the 90th/50th percentile ratio as well. While the top 10 percent of the net worth distribution owns at least 14 times more wealth than the median, this relationship is "only" 3.8 for augmented wealth—again, a large decrease of 73 percent.

The widespread presence and more even distribution of pension entitlements and their equalizing effect on augmented wealth become apparent when examining entitlements by decile group of net worth (Figure 13.4). The lower part of each bar depicts average net worth, which ranges from a negative 12,000 euros in the lowest tenth to more than 500,000 euros in the top tenth. Keeping the deciles fixed and adding the public pension entitlements yields average augmented wealth per decile group of net worth. In the lower half of the distribution, average pension entitlements vary only slightly between 45,000 and 65,000 euros. However, in this part of the distribution, this wealth component is much more important than net worth. Higher up in the distribution, pension entitlements also increase—which is in line with the principle of equivalence applied in the German pension schemes—but not as much as net worth. For those in the richest tenth of the net worth distribution, average pension entitlements are more than 130,000 euros, but because their average net worth is more than 500,000 euros, it is no more than 20 percent of augmented wealth. This process is also dampened by the top-coding effect in the statutory pension system, resulting from an upper-income threshold.

With respect to wealth composition or portfolio structure, public pension wealth accounts for basically almost all of "augmented wealth" in the lower half of the net worth distribution (see Figure 13.4). In the sixth decile group, public pension entitlements account for some 80 percent, and in the

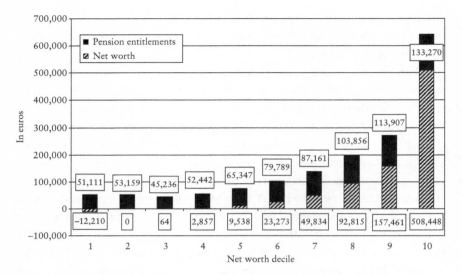

Figure 13.4.   Mean net worth and mean pension wealth by net worth deciles, Germany 2007

SOURCE: Authors' calculations from SOEPv25; public pension wealth using a discount rate of 2 percent.

eighth decile, for about half of augmented wealth. Among the wealthiest 10 percent, only one-fifth consists of public pension wealth.

Inequality Decomposition by Occupational Status

We next focus on the population of employable age (20–65) and examine net worth and augmented wealth by occupational status. Table 13.2 shows average wealth levels before (column B) and after (column C) inclusion of public pension entitlements, along with the relative change (column D). Those who had already retired by the age of 65—a group that includes former public pension employees as well as former civil servants—"profit" considerably from widening the wealth definition. Above and beyond owning a net worth of almost 90,000 euros, this group has more than 214,000 euros in public pension entitlements, yielding an augmented wealth measure of 304,000 euros—an increase of about 240 percent.

Among those currently working, civil servants hold an above-average net worth of 113,000 euros. Their very generous public pension entitlements place them with 240,000 euros in augmented wealth, an increase of more than 110 percent. While employees who are members of the public pension scheme also gain substantially—from 63,000 in net worth to 123,000 euros (an increase of 60,000 euros or 94 percent)—their relative wealth position does not change significantly, staying at just 84 percent of the overall average. Here, the self-employed have clearly lost ground in relative terms: although they have 46,600 euros in public pension entitlements, their relative wealth position has declined from 370 percent to "only" 226 percent of the overall average. While unemployed persons—as expected—have very limited net worth (16,000 euros), they also have significant public pension entitlements, making them clearly much better off in the analyses of augmented wealth: in fact, this group shows an increase of about 340 percent when considering pension entitlements, to about 70,000 euros. This indicates the importance of old-age provisions in stabilizing the individual economic position, even in the case of (short-term) unemployment.

Wealth shares are also influenced substantially by the extension of the wealth definition: retirees double their wealth holdings (up from 8.8 percent to 15.6 percent in columns H through J), while the wealth share contributed by the self-employed drops from more than 25 percent down to roughly 15 percent.

All of this, as expected, reduces inequality substantially. Starting from a value of 0.816 for net worth, the Gini coefficient for the population aged 20 to 65 years decreases by about one-quarter to 0.616 when public pension entitlements are included. Given the group-specific variations described above, this goes hand in hand with massive changes in the inequality decomposition by subgroup.[26] In all groups, we see a pronounced reduction in inequality as shown in columns E through G, based on group-specific Gini coefficients. Not surprisingly, this reduction is smallest among the self-employed (−9 percent) and largest among the already retired (−52 percent). In fact, between-group inequality increases from 14 to 21 percent (columns K and L). The group-specific contribution to overall inequality has reached an above-average level for civil servants (columns O and P), while being considerably reduced for the self-employed and retirees.

CONCLUSION

Entitlements from old-age pension schemes—statutory, occupational, and private—represent a considerable source of wealth. For data-related

TABLE 13.2

Inequality decomposition[a] by subgroup—individuals of working age (20–65 years old in Germany, 2007)

	A	B	C	D	E	F	G
			MEAN			GINI	
Occupational status	Population share (%)	Net worth	Augmented wealth	Percentage change, including PPW[c]	Net worth	Augmented wealth	Percentage change in inequality, including PPW
Not employed	9.5	78,080	135,000	73	0.785	0.620	−21
In education	6.0	7,712	14,100	83	0.931	0.740	−21
Unemployed	8.5	15,680	69,300	342	1.138	0.636	−44
Employed[b]	56.9	63,340	123,000	94	0.771	0.554	−28
Self-employed	6.9	285,400	332,000	16	0.782	0.709	−9
Civil servant	4.6	113,000	240,000	112	0.623	0.504	−19
Early retirees	7.5	89,460	304,000	240	0.754	0.365	−52
Total	100.0	76,855	146,351	90	0.816	0.616	−24

SOURCE: Authors' calculations from SOEPv25, with a discount rate of 2 percent, without provision for dependents.
[a]Decomposition based on the Gini coefficient using ANOGI.
[b]Employee covered by public pension scheme.
[c]PPW: present value of public pension entitlements.

reasons, however, empirical analyses of wealth inequality in Germany, as in most other countries, have not taken this important component into account. This chapter uses statistical matching to combine representative individual net worth information from a major household panel study—the German Socio-Economic Panel (SOEP)—with detailed administrative data about pension entitlements from the statutory pension scheme in Germany. According to our calculations based on 2007 data, the present value of total pension entitlements (not including entitlements to provisions for dependents) amounted to roughly 5.6 trillion euros at a discount rate of 2 percent. This corresponds to an average of 78,500 euros per adult. When this is combined with net worth held in financial and material assets, which amount to an average of 83,000 euros, the result is a more comprehensive measure of augmented wealth, amounting to more than 160,000 euros. The German middle-income class profits to an above-average extent from pension wealth compared with net worth due to the compulsory nature of the public pension system.

H	I	J	K	L	M	N	O	P
WEALTH SHARE (%)			PERCENTAGE CONTRIBUTION TO AGGREGATE INEQUALITY		POPULATION NORMALIZED WEALTH SHARE (%)		POPULATION NORMALIZED CONTRIBUTION TO AGGREGATE INEQUALITY (%)	
Net worth	Augmented wealth	Percentage change in wealth share, including PPW	Net worth	Augmented wealth	Net worth	Augmented wealth	Net worth	Augmented wealth
9.7	8.7	−9	9.4	8.9	101.6	92.0	98.8	93.2
0.6	0.6	−4	0.6	0.6	10.0	9.6	9.9	10.2
1.7	4.0	132	2.7	4.1	20.4	47.3	31.4	47.5
46.9	47.9	2	42.2	39.9	82.4	84.1	74.1	70.1
25.5	15.5	−39	19.3	16.4	371.4	226.2	281.0	238.8
6.8	7.6	11	4.0	5.1	146.9	163.4	85.1	110.7
8.8	15.6	78	7.8	4.4	116.4	207.3	103.8	57.8
100.0	100.0	0	85.9	79.3	100.0	100.0	85.9	79.3
Between-group inequality (%)			14.1	20.7				

The augmented measure of wealth shows considerably (about 25 percent) less inequality than does inequality of only financial and material assets—that is, net worth. This is mainly the result of the substantial and widespread pension entitlements under the various pension schemes for the vast majority of adults in Germany.

There are marked differences in levels of pension entitlements across occupational groups. While civil servants have the highest entitlements, the self-employed, who typically make their own provisions for old age, have below-average public pension entitlements. Such differences likely exist in other countries as well. The large variation in publicly provided pension insurance across welfare regimes—which lead to very different levels of pension wealth, at least for men, such as the average levels of USD173,000 in the United States and about USD342,000 in Germany—should be carefully considered when conducting comparative wealth analyses, such as those based on the *LWS Database* (see Sierminska, Brandolini, and Smeeding 2006).[27] In other words, every effort should be made to include pension entitlements in comparative analyses of wealth data.

Future research in this area should address appropriate means of determining the present value of pension entitlements. Based on the findings presented here, it appears necessary to invest more effort in defining the discount rate, in determining future pension adjustments, and in addressing the problem of selectivity in mortality rates, since high-income earners typically live longer than low-income earners (see Himmelreicher et al. 2008). This should be accompanied by a discussion about the need to consider liabilities to pension schemes. In a pay-as-you-go pension system, there is already an implicit liability with birth, which levels off until middle age, when the entitlements accrued so far are higher than the present value of the future contributions. Adequately dealing with this phenomenon would also mean taking liabilities that lie outside the private household sector into consideration, because employers and the state both make considerable contributions to overall pension expenditures.

In conclusion, this chapter demonstrates that including public pension entitlements in wealth analyses leads to both large increases in levels of wealth and a large drop in the inequality of wealth, as well as changes in the relative position of different socio-economic groups. While data on net worth can be collected successfully in population surveys, respondents' information on pension entitlements appears incomplete at best. This shortcoming can best be overcome by direct record linkage to administrative data, a technique that is often infeasible due to confidentiality concerns. But since this may lead to difficulties, such as substantial and selective increases in non-response rates, statistical matching as used here may be a successful second-best solution.

NOTES

The authors are grateful to Anika Rasner for very valuable comments and to Rainer Siegers for outstanding programming assistance. We also thank the research data center of the German Public Pension Administration (FDZ-RV) for providing microdata.

1. The terms *public pension wealth* and *social security wealth* are defined as the total sum of individual pension rights accrued so far over the life course. These pension rights translate into old-age public pension benefits as the individual retires. Both terms are used interchangeably throughout the chapter and refer only to entitlements in the old-age public pension scheme.

2. We follow the approach by Gruber and Wise (1999) in converting future income flows from old-age pension schemes into a stock measure.

3. In a small pretest of the German Socio-Economic Panel Study (SOEP) in 2002, interviewees were asked for individual social security wealth. The question

generated an extraordinarily high percentage of missing data; the reliability of the information given by the remainder of respondents was questionable. Similarly, a 2009 pilot study tested the willingness of the Survey of Health, Ageing and Retirement in Europe (SHARE) respondents to allow for record linkage with administrative data using their social security number. While 77 percent gave their consent, only 64 percent of these respondents actually provided their number.

4. The replacement rate for civil servants in Germany retiring after 40 years of full-time employment amounts to almost 72 percent of their recent gross earnings. In contrast, the replacement level for the standard public pension system retiree (the so-called "Eckrentner") who worked for 45 years with average earnings is as high as approximately 48 percent of previous earnings (BMAS 2008).

5. The consideration of public pension entitlements in wealth analyses might also be helpful for a better understanding of savings behavior across occupational groups, given that there is still not a fully satisfying theoretical model to explain savings behavior (see Börsch-Supan 2001).

6. Pension wealth is here defined as a multiple of economy-wide average earnings.

7. The above-average relative importance of public pension wealth for the middle-income class is—at least in Germany—also the result of a contribution ceiling, given that for top-income earners, pension entitlements are capped to a certain amount.

8. The SOEP wealth data are included in the *LWS Database*.

9. Both datasets contain earnings and income information for the years 1983 to 2007 for West Germany and 1991 to 2007 for East Germany. Thus, we are covering the entire period since German unification in 1990, when the West German social security system was by and large transferred to East Germany, providing GDR workers with pension entitlements for all years of employment during the existence of the GDR without having paid any contributions.

10. For all 2007 SOEP respondents with incomplete income profiles, missing information was imputed starting in 2007 and going back to 1984 for West Germany and to 1991 for East Germany. The imputation process made maximum use of all available longitudinal income information since the respondent's initial participation in the SOEP.

11. The VSKT is a 1 percent sample of active pension accounts—in other words, individuals who are covered by the compulsory pension scheme. Certain population subgroups are excluded/not eligible for this public pension scheme. These include the self-employed, civil servants, and some groups of craftspeople who have their own pension schemes.

12. In alternative specifications, OLS regression, univariate imputation sampling, and hotdeck imputation were used to combine the two datasets. Using information on actual pension payments received by retired SOEP respondents, we compared imputed results using the different approaches with the observed

amounts. The Mahalanobis distance performed best with respect to absolute differences, distribution, and correlation (see Rasner, Frick, and Grabka 2013).

13. In practice, women are the main beneficiaries of pension splitting because of their weaker labor market attachment. For the majority of divorced couples, the pension is split immediately upon divorce, while bonuses and maluses remain unaffected by the remarriage of either former spouse.

14. For a detailed description of the matching process, the matching variables used, and a simulation to determine the appropriate matching strategy, see Rasner et al. (2013).

15. The figures in this chapter do not include any provisions for dependents (widows or orphans).

16. Using the current pay level most likely leads to an underestimation of the true future pension entitlement of civil servants, given that subsequent earnings increases are not considered.

17. Because of the pension reform act of 2004 and the sustainability factor introduced with it, future pension entitlements will decline from birth cohort to birth cohort for the same number of payment points. For reasons of simplicity, however, this aspect is ignored here.

18. In alternative specifications we vary the interest rate between 1 and 3 percent; the choice of interest rate influences, by definition, the amount of the present value but changes little in the basic relationships according to occupational groups as described here.

19. For example, the taxable share of pensions received for the first time in 2007 is as high as 54 percent. With each additional calendar year, the income share for new pensions increases, reaching 80 percent by the year 2020 and 100 percent by 2040. On the other hand, civil servants' annuities are already fully taxable. To determine the net present value of any pension entitlements, the individual tax rate applicable in 2007 is used here and is also differentiated according to the various status groups. By applying the current individual tax rate, a relatively high tax burden is assumed for insured working persons. The actual tax burden would, however, have to be simulated separately for each age cohort at the time of entry into retirement. Because of the recently introduced deferred taxation, however, such a simulation is combined with major assumptions about the future income situation of the persons in question.

20. See also Frick and Grabka (2009, 2010).

21. The effect of outliers in wealth inequality research has been demonstrated by Frick, Grabka, and Sierminska (2007).

22. The application of a discount rate of about 2 percent is a rather normative decision, which is oriented toward the long-term real interest rate of federal bonds in Germany. In alternative specifications, we apply an interest rate of 1 percent and 3 percent, yielding an aggregated net value of pension wealth of about 6.5 trillion euros and 4.9 trillion euros, respectively. The respective mean values

vary between about 91,000 euros and about 68,000 euros for a discount rate of 1 percent and 3 percent.

23. This comes to about 1,100 and 2,300 euros per month for a one-person household in Germany in 2008. For a detailed development of the middle-income class in Germany, see Grabka and Frick (2008). The modified OECD equivalence scale has been applied.

24. The middle-income class in Germany decreased by more than 6 percentage points between 1997 and 2010 (Burkhardt et al. 2012).

25. A precise quantification of liabilities to PAYG pension schemes is complex. It requires, among other things, simulating cohorts as yet unborn, all of whom would already have negative wealth by the time they are born. Here we refrain from calculating any liabilities—for example, future contributions to pension schemes; thus, the lowest possible value is zero.

26. We run Gini decomposition as suggested by Lerman and Yitzhaki (1985) using the Stata routine ANOGI, provided by Jann (2006). Typically, such decomposition analyses are based on Generalized Entropy Measures such as the Mean Log Deviation (MLD). This was not possible for the analysis at hand, as net worth can take on negative values.

27. In a cross-country comparison of German and Australian retirees (aged 65 and over), Frick and Headey (2009) accounted for the present value of pension wealth in an augmented wealth measure. Comparing the wealth position for augmented wealth yields very similar levels of wealth for these groups in both countries, in contrast to the results based on standard net worth, which clearly favor elderly Australians. Furthermore, while net worth is clearly less equally distributed in Germany than in Australia, taking public pension wealth into consideration in the augmented wealth measure brings inequality down to similar levels in both countries.

REFERENCES

Bonin, Holger. 2009. "15 Years of Pension Reform in Germany: Old Success and New Threats." *The Geneva Papers on Risk and Insurance* 34(4): 548–60.

Börsch-Supan, Axel. 2001. "Das Sparverhalten verstehen." In *Berlin-Brandenburgische Akademie der Wissenschaften: Berichte und Abhandlungen Band 8*, edited by Akademie Verlag.

Brugiavini, Agar, Karen Maser, and Annika Sundén. 2001. "Measuring Pension Wealth." Paper presented at the conference of the Luxembourg Wealth Study. Perugia, Italy (January 27–29, 2001).

Bundesministerium für Arbeit und Soziales (BMAS). 2008. *Ergänzender Bericht der Bundesregierung zum Rentenversicherungsbericht 2008 gemäß §154 Abs. 2 SGB VI.* Berlin: BMAS.

Burkhardt, Christoph, Markus M. Grabka, Olaf Groh-Samberg, Yvonne Lott, and Steffen Mau. 2012. *Mittelschicht unter Druck?* Gütersloh, Germany: Verlag Bertelsmann Stiftung.

Frick, Joachim R., and Markus M. Grabka. 2009. "Wealth Inequality on the Rise in Germany." *DIW Berlin Weekly Report* 5(10): 62–73.

Frick, Joachim R., and Markus M. Grabka. 2010. "Old-Age Pension Entitlements Mitigate Inequality—But Concentration of Wealth Remains High." *DIW Berlin Weekly Report* 6(8): 55–64.

Frick, Joachim R., Markus M. Grabka, and Richard Hauser. 2010. *Die Verteilung der Vermögen in Deutschland. Empirische Analysen für Personen und Haushalte.* Berlin: Edition Sigma.

Frick, Joachim R., Markus M. Grabka, and Jan Marcus. 2007. "Editing and Multiple Imputation of Item-Non-Response in the 2002 Wealth Module of the German Socio-Economic Panel (SOEP)." *Data Documentation* 18. Berlin: DIW Berlin.

Frick, Joachim R., Markus M. Grabka, and Eva Sierminska. 2007. "Representative Wealth Data for Germany from the German SOEP: The Impact of Methodological Decisions around Imputation and the Choice of the Aggregation Unit." *SOEP Papers on Multidisciplinary Panel Data Research* 3. Berlin: DIW Berlin.

Frick, Joachim R., and Bruce Headey. 2009. "Living Standards in Retirement: Accepted International Comparisons Are Misleading." *Schmoller's Jahrbuch Journal of Applied Social Science Studies* 129(2): 309–19.

Grabka, Markus M., and Joachim R. Frick. 2008. "The Shrinking German Middle Class—Signs of Long-Term Polarization in Disposable Income?" *DIW Berlin Weekly Report* 4: 21–27.

Gruber, Jonathan, and David S. Wise, eds. 1999. *Social Security and Retirement around the World.* Chicago: University of Chicago Press.

Himmelreicher, Ralf K., Daniela Sewöster, Rembrandt Scholz, and Anne Schulz. 2008. "Die fernere Lebenserwartung von Rentnern und Pensionären im Vergleich." *WSI Mitteilungen* 5: 274–80.

Jann, Ben. 2006. ANOGI: Stata Module to Generate Analysis of Gini. Statistical Software Components S456730. Boston: Boston College Department of Economics. http://econpapers.repec.org/software/bocbocode/s456730.htm.

Johnson, Richard W., Usha Sambamoorthi, and Stephen Crystal. 2000. "Pension Wealth at Midlife: Comparing Self-Reports with Provider Data." *Review of Income and Wealth* 46(1): 59–83.

Kantor, David. 2006. MAHAPICK: Stata Module to Select Matching Observations Based on a Mahalanobis Distance Measure. Statistical Software Components S456703. Boston: Boston College Department of Economics. http://ideas.repec.org/c/boc/bocode/s456703.html.

Lerman, Robert I., and Shlomo Yitzhaki. 1985. "Income Inequality Effects by Income Source: A New Approach and Applications to the United States." *Review of Economics and Statistics* 67(1): 151–56.

Modigliani, Franco. 1988. "The Role of Intergenerational Transfers and Life Cycle Saving in the Accumulation of Wealth." *Journal of Economic Perspectives* 2: 15–40.

Organisation for Economic Co-operation and Development (OECD). 2007. *Pensions at a Glance: Public Policies across OECD Countries*. Paris: OECD.

Rasner, Anika, Joachim R. Frick, and Markus M. Grabka. 2013. "Statistical Matching of Administrative and Survey Data, an Application to Wealth Inequality Analyses." *Sociological Methods and Research*. Forthcoming.

Schelsky, Helmut. 1965. *Auf der Suche nach Wirklichkeit. Gesammelte Aufsätze.* Düsseldorf, Germany: Diederichs.

Sierminska, Eva, Andrea Brandolini, and Timothy M. Smeeding. 2006. "The Luxembourg Wealth Study—A Cross-Country Comparable Database for Household Wealth Research." *Journal of Economic Inequality* 4(3): 375–83.

Socio-Economic Panel (SOEP). 2008. Data for years 1984–2008, version 25. Statistical Database. http://www.diw.de/sixcms/detail.php?id=diw_01.c.387319.en.

Wagner, Gert G., Joachim R. Frick, and Juergen Schupp. 2007. "The German Socio-Economic Panel Study (SOEP) Scope, Evolution and Enhancements." *Schmollers Jahrbuch Journal of Applied Social Science Studies* 127(1): 139–69.

Part VI

COUNTRY CASE STUDIES: INEQUALITY IN JAPAN, ICELAND, INDIA, AND SOUTH AFRICA

CHAPTER FOURTEEN

Income and Wealth Inequality in Japan

Colin McKenzie

This chapter provides estimates of income inequality, income mobility, and wealth inequality—three complementary indicators of well-being—for Japan. Given an owner-occupied home, the ability to use financial markets to convert assets into income streams, or social security payments subject to only income tests can mean that a sole focus on income may provide a misleading picture of inequality, so it makes sense to look at wealth as well.[1] Inequality at one or several points in time, of course, provides little insight into the probability or frequency of income fluctuations. Therefore, this chapter presents estimates of income mobility to show, for example, how often people fall in and out of poverty and whether mobility changes over time. The meaning of a given level of income inequality will be quite different when income mobility is high, such that the number of people who successively experience a low level of income is low compared with when income mobility is low.

Due to limited data availability and language barriers, Japan is often excluded from cross-country comparisons of inequality. One of the motivations of this chapter is to place Japan in comparative perspective, along with other major industrialized countries—in particular, Germany, the United Kingdom, and the United States. Where possible, this comparison is attempted on several core dimensions, including income mobility and wealth distributions. Data used in this study come from two publicly available sources: the Keio Household Panel Survey (KHPS) and the Japan Household Panel Survey (JHPS). In relation to its analysis of income inequality and income mobility, this chapter closely follows Ohtake's (2008) analysis of income inequality in Japan until 2004. In relation to its analysis of wealth inequality, it closely follows the analysis of the Organisation for Economic Co-operation and Development (OECD 2008).

The OECD provides the most up-to-date cross-national comparison of income inequality, where Japan is compared with other OECD countries. Measuring income inequality by the Gini coefficient of equivalent house-hold disposable income, Japan belongs to a group of countries that includes Korea, Canada, Spain, and the United Kingdom—a group that slightly exceeds the average level of inequality in the OECD countries. Inequality in Japan is lower than that reported for the United States and is slightly higher than in Germany.

Between the mid-1980s and the mid-1990s, the dominant pattern observed among OECD countries was a widening of the income distribution, and this is true for Japan as well. Between the mid-1990s and the mid-2000s, the OECD indicates a diverse pattern of change across the OECD countries, but there was little change in Japan. Although the popular press in Japan attributes much of the recent worsening in income inequality to deregulation, economic reform, and globalization, Ohtake (2005) argues that the aging of the Japanese population and changes in the composition of Japanese households are two important factors explaining the rise in income inequality, measured by the Gini coefficient of pre-tax income using official Japanese statistics. More recently, the combination of continuing economic stagnation and firms switching from hiring full-time regular workers to hiring irregular workers (who can be fired more easily) are argued to have contributed to instability of employment and income.

One measure of poverty in Japan is the proportion of households receiving Livelihood Protection Assistance (*seikatsu hogo*), a social program that provides assistance to households facing reduced or no income due to the breadwinner's death, sickness, or injury.[2] The Ministry of Health, Labor and Welfare (2011) reports that the proportion of households that are receiving this benefit increased from 8.1 percent in 2000 to 12 percent in 2008, 13.1 percent in 2009, and 14.7 percent in 2010. The figures for the same years among persons aged 60 and over (16.6, 21.7, 22.7, and 24.2 percent, respectively) indicate that the needy are concentrated among the aged.[3] In fact, aged households constitute somewhere between 43 and 45 percent of all households receiving Livelihood Protection Assistance. Clearly, poverty in Japan is quite concentrated among the elderly. The current policy discussion in Japan concerning the reform of the national old-age pension system, however, focuses on the burden of the aging population (and future unfunded liabilities of the pension system) and the government debt burden. The solutions proposed aim to increase pension contributions and reduce pension benefits. An increase of the consumption tax from 5 to 10 percent in two stages, passed in 2012, will significantly hit the elderly.

Most of the existing studies of wealth inequality in Japan have used data from the National Survey of Family Income and Expenditure (Zenkoku Shohi Jittai Chosa, NSFIE), conducted by the Statistics Bureau of the Ministry of Internal Affairs and Communications. These studies have sought to uncover the trend of wealth inequality over time and the impact of factors such as home ownership and land prices on this inequality (for example, Takayama et al. 1989; Ohtake 2005; Inaba, Takaoka, and Oka 2008). Using data from the 1984 survey, Takayama and colleagues (1989) found that home ownership plays a large role in explaining wealth inequality. Wealth inequality has been found to increase over the period 1989 to 1999 (Ohtake 2005) and to decrease over the period 1989 to 2004 (Inaba et al. 2008). Decreases in land/housing prices are suggested as being an important reason for the observed decline between 1989 and 2004.

Two studies (published in Japanese) compared Japanese wealth outcomes with those in other countries (Ota 2003; Shikata 2011). Ota (2003) compared Japan with results from a variety of published sources for Canada, Finland, France, Italy, the Netherlands, Sweden, the United Kingdom, the United States, and West Germany. Using data from NSFIE surveys for 1994 and 1999, he found that Japan's wealth inequality in the 1990s was comparatively "small" but that there was large wealth inequality across age groups. Shikata (2011) used data from the JHPS survey to compare wealth outcomes with those in Canada, Germany, Italy, Sweden, the United Kingdom, and the United States, using data from the *Luxembourg Wealth Study (LWS) Database*. He found that wealth inequality in Japan fell somewhere in the middle of the countries included in the *LWS Database*, being neither excessively large nor excessively small. He also found that wealth holdings of the elderly in Japan were relatively large.

The popular press in Japan contains little discussion of income mobility, but given that recipients of Livelihood Protection Assistance are concentrated among the non-working aged, we can easily speculate that aged individuals who start receiving Livelihood Protection Assistance because of the death of a spouse, sickness, or injury find it very difficult to change their income status. That is, their income mobility can be expected to be rather low.

Two studies examined household income mobility in Japan by estimating the probability of transition from one income class to another over a period of time. Ohtake (2008) reported transition probabilities for 1985–1986 and 2000–2001 for income quintile groups and found that income mobility rose between 1986 and 2001. Ishii and Yamada (2007) reported transition probabilities for 2004–2005 and 2005–2006 for income classes based on median bands relative to equivalent gross household income. For three groups with income below the median, they reported that the probability of being in the same class in the following year was just below 50 percent, while the probability of being in the class with income over 1.5 times the median income a year later was over 70 percent. The OECD (2008) reported estimates for three-year transition probabilities using income quintile groups for a group of OECD countries (excluding Japan), as well as the OECD averages. Using the OECD averages, it was found that the probability of remaining in either the bottom or the top quintile group three years later was about 66 to 68 percent and between 44 and 47 percent for the three middle quintile groups. For the lowest three quintile groups, these probabilities were higher than those reported by Ohtake (2008) for *one*-year transitions for both 1985–1986 and 2000–2001.

There are three parts to the analysis presented in this chapter. The first two use only data from the KHPS surveys, and the third uses data from both the KHPS and JHPS datasets. First, I examine income and consumption inequalities that are measured by the Gini coefficient and estimated using data from the KHPS2004–2009[4] surveys. Gini coefficients of yearly pre-tax income suggested there was little change in income inequality in Japan over the period 2004–2008. Second, the panel nature of the KHPS data was used to compute the probability that households stay in the same income quintile group in the short term (one year) and the longer term (four years). This analysis suggested that, compared to estimates of short-run transition probabilities for the 1990s and 2000–2001, the probability of a household staying in the same income quintile group was much higher in 2004–2005 and 2007–2008. Third, using data from the KHPS2004 and JHPS2009 surveys, I examine aspects of the distribution of wealth in Japan and compare them with those of countries included in the *LWS Database*.

KEIO HOUSEHOLD PANEL SURVEY AND JAPAN HOUSEHOLD PANEL SURVEY

Most of the data used in this chapter are drawn from the first six waves of KHPS that has been undertaken in the first quarter of every year since 2004. KHPS is a household survey conducted by Keio University, with financial assistance from the Japanese Ministry of Education, Culture, Sports and Technology. Respondents were limited to Japanese individuals aged 20 to 69 at the time of the first wave of the survey in 2004—that is, born between February 1, 1934, and January 31, 1984. It should be noted that respondents were not limited to household heads and could be any member of the household who satisfied the age restriction. In 2004, this group represented roughly 67 percent of the total Japanese population. KHPS's goal was to investigate various aspects of household behavior, including the labor supply of respondents and, if present, their spouses; various aspects of household behavior in relation to consumption; and the asset holdings of households. Individuals for the initial KHPS survey in 2004 were randomly selected from throughout Japan using a two-stage sampling procedure. The first KHPS survey was conducted during the period January–March 2004 with a sample size of 4,005 households and is referred to as KHPS2004.[5] Subsequent surveys are denoted by the abbreviation KHPSxxxx, where xxxx is the year the survey was conducted. Later waves of KHPS were also conducted from January to March every year. In 2007, because 28 percent of the original sample had been lost to attrition between KHPS2004 and KHPS2006, a supplementary sample of 1,419 randomly selected individuals aged 20 to 69 at the time of the survey in 2007 (people born between February 1, 1937, and January 31, 1987) was added, although this supplementary sample is not used in this chapter.

One key question about KHPS relates to how well its data represent the Japanese population it surveys. Kimura (2005) investigated this issue by comparing descriptive statistics for several variables for KHPS2004 with comparable descriptive statistics from official surveys. The gender composition of the KHPS2004 survey data very closely matched the estimates of the gender composition of the relevant population at the time contained in Population Estimates (Jinko Suikei). While respondents aged 20 to 34 tend to be slightly under-represented, and respondents aged 35 to 69 tend to be over-represented, Kimura found there was no statistically significant difference between the age distribution for the KHPS survey and the national population estimates. Compared to estimates contained in the Labor Force Survey (Rodoryoku Chosa), single-person households are under-represented and three-person households are over-represented, but, again, Kimura found that the differences in the distribution of household size in the two sets of data were not statistically significant.

Kimura found that for households with more than two individuals, KHPS2004's average expenditure was about 20,000 yen (USD250)[6] lower than the average expenditure reported in the Household Expenditure Survey (Kakei Chosa = KC) (KHPS: 279,000 yen (USD3,488); KC: 302,000 yen (USD3,775)). For households with two or more individuals, including at least one who works as an employee, KHPS2004's average income was about 15,000 yen (USD188) lower than the average income reported in the Survey of Family Expenditure (KHPS: 460,000 yen (USD5,750); KC: 445,000 yen (USD5,563)). Kimura (2005) argued that these differences could be largely attributed to differences in survey methods and the match between the two sets of results was rather good. For assets and liabilities, Kimura found there is a relatively close match between KHPS and official surveys in relation to the proportion of people with loans and holdings deposits, but for households with two or more people, the average deposits held by households surveyed in KHPS tended to be slightly lower, and the average amount of loans tended to be slightly higher than official estimates.

With any panel survey dataset, attrition is potentially important. The cumulative attrition rates for the KHPS initial sample were 17.3 percent in 2005, which increased to 28 percent in 2006, 34.2 percent in 2007, 39 percent in 2008, and 42.8 percent in 2009. That is, of the initial sample of 4,005 in 2004, only 2,290 remained by 2009. Although it is possible that attrition could influence the analysis undertaken in this chapter, the impact of attrition is not taken into account. Miyauchi, McKenzie, and Kimura (2006); McKenzie and colleagues (2007); and Naoi (2007) have all studied the importance of attrition for distributional outcomes in the KHPS dataset. McKenzie and colleagues investigated the impact of attrition on different aspects of labor market behavior, using the KHPS2004-2006 data, and they found different results, depending on what aspect of labor market behavior was studied. Analyses of labor market participation do not appear to be affected by the sample selection induced by attrition, whereas analyses of wage rates do appear to suffer from sample selection bias.[7] Using data from KHPS2004-2006, Naoi's examination of the impact of attrition on analyses of household residential mobility suggested that sample attrition leads to a statistically significant bias when residential mobility is examined using KHPS2005, but the impact of this bias is less in KHPS2006.

The second dataset used in this chapter, the Japan Household Panel Survey (JHPS), has been undertaken in the first quarter of every year since 2009. JHPS is a household survey also conducted by Keio University, also with the financial assistance of the Japanese Ministry of Education, Culture, Sports and Technology. One of the key differences between the KHPS and JHPS surveys relates to the choice of respondents for the initial survey. KHPS2004 was limited to respondents aged 20 to 69, while for JHPS2009, respondents had to be aged 20 or over at the time of the first wave of the survey in 2009 (people born before February 1, 1989). In 2009, this group represented roughly 81.5 percent of the total Japanese population. The JHPS sample design, aims, and content were very similar to the KHPS. The first JHPS survey was conducted in the period January–March 2009 with a sample size of 4,022 households and was referred to as JHPS2009. Compared to the early KHPS surveys, JHPS provides far more detailed information on the sources of annual income for the respondent and spouse, but the information relating to housing is not as detailed. Naoi and Yamamoto (2010) reported that for households with two or more individuals, the average amount of deposits and the percentage of households holding deposits estimated using JHPS2009 were slightly lower than those reported in the latest Official Statistics for 2004. They suggest that some of these differences can be attributed to differences in economic conditions between 2004 and 2009.

INCOME INEQUALITY

How does income inequality in Japan compare with income inequality in the other major industrialized countries, such as Germany, the United Kingdom, and the United States? For around 2000, Förster and d'Ercole (2005), who measured inequality using Gini coefficients for household disposable income equivalized with the square root scale, reported Japan's Gini to be 0.314, slightly above the OECD-25 average of 0.308. The Japanese estimate was close to the United Kingdom's of 0.326, higher than Germany's of

0.277, and lower than the United States' of 0.357. In the mid-2000s, OECD (2008) reported Japan's Gini to be 0.321, again slightly above the OECD-24 average of 0.313, close to the United Kingdom's estimate of 0.335, higher than Germany's of 0.298, and lower than the United States' of 0.381.

OECD (2010) reported that Japan's rate of relative poverty (the percentage of households with less than half of median household disposable income) had risen from 12 percent in 1985 to 15 percent in the late 2000s. In addition, OECD (2011) noted that since the mid-1980s, in Japan, the real incomes of those at the bottom of the income ladder had actually fallen, and the Gini coefficient had risen by more than 2 percentage points from just over 0.30 to just under 0.34.

Rather than focusing on "macro" indicators such as the Gini coefficient—which moves slowly and is not published very frequently (depending on the data source)—the focus of poverty/inequality discussions in Japan tends to be on the number of households receiving Livelihood Protection Assistance and on the proportion who are among the "working poor"—that is, those who cannot make ends meet despite having full-time jobs.

This section focuses on what is currently known about income inequality in Japan and how it is changing over the longer term by turning to domestic estimates of income inequality. As mentioned before, the two official sources of estimates of income inequality in Japan are NLS, which is conducted by the Ministry of Health, Labour and Welfare, and NSFIE, which is conducted by the Statistics Bureau of the Ministry of Internal Affairs and Communications.

NSFIE is a nationwide survey conducted every five years, with the latest survey results being available for 2004. In 2004, the NSFIE surveyed nearly 60,000 households—54,372 households with two or more members and 5,002 single-person households. Two types of NLS surveys are conducted, and both are nationwide surveys. A large-scale survey is conducted every three years, with the latest survey results being available for 2007, at which time about 230,000 households were surveyed. Smaller-scale surveys are conducted in other years.

Table 14.1 summarizes estimates of the Gini coefficients computed from various domestic data sources: NSFIE, NLS, and KHPS. According to the NSFIE data, inequality increased between 1979 and 2004, regardless of whether the Gini coefficient was computed using yearly household income[8]

TABLE 14.1

Estimates of Gini coefficients for Japan

Survey	Variable used to compute coefficient	Household type	YEAR								
			1979	1992	2004	2005	2006	2007	2008	2009
NSFIE	Annual household income	All households	0.271		0.308					
NSFIE	Monthly consumption expenditures	All households	0.151		0.163					
NLS	Annual household income	All households		0.377	0.400	0.395	0.398	0.395		
NLS	Annual household income	Aged households		0.452	0.389					
KHPS	Annual pre-tax income	All households			0.326	0.316	0.319	0.325	0.326	
KHPS	Monthly pre-tax income	All households			0.354	0.351	0.347	0.327	0.343	
KHPS	Monthly consumption	All households			0.284	0.298	0.292	0.300	0.293	0.310

SOURCE: For KHPS, author's calculations using data from KHPS2004, KHPS2005, KHPS2006, KHPS2007, KHPS2008, and KHPS2009.

or monthly consumption expenditure. NLS data suggested that inequality rose between 1992 and 2007, but in the four years following 2004, the Gini coefficient was essentially flat. In contrast, for elderly households, inequality declined between 1992 and 2004. For annual income for all households, both the NLS and NSFIE data indicated that income inequality was rising over time in Japan.

As is well known in Japan, the estimates of the Gini coefficients from the NLS and NSFIE data were quite different. According to Ohtake (2008), the estimates of the Gini coefficients computed using the NSFIE data only included households with two or more persons, while the Gini coefficient results based on the NLS data included single-person households. Ohtake argued that estimates of inequality using data excluding single-person households were usually lower than those including single-person households because single-person households tend to have lower incomes than households with two or more members.

Although the proportion of households receiving Livelihood Protection Assistance has increased, estimates of overall inequality, such as the Gini coefficient, did not in this case capture such changes that most likely took place in the lower tail of the income distribution. The Ministry of Health, Labor and Welfare is reported to have begun work on developing new indices to measure economic disparities and poverty in Japan. In particular, this work focuses on incorporating the well-being of people receiving Livelihood Protection Assistance and unemployment insurance. Compared with the current publication frequency of once every three years for the Gini coefficient and the poverty rate, the Ministry hopes to be able to increase the frequency of publication. That will allow finer assessments of economic disparities arising from differences between regular and non-regular workers and of the well-being of people receiving Livelihood Protection Assistance.[9]

Ohtake (2008) offered two key reasons for the observed rise in income inequality in Japan. The first is the aging of the Japanese population. As the NLS estimates of the Gini coefficients for the elderly presented earlier indicate, these coefficients tend to be higher for the elderly. The second reason is changes in the distribution of the number of persons in a household. Between 1980 and 2005, the average number of persons in a household fell from 3.2 to 2.7, and the percentage of single-person households rose from 18 to 24 percent.

Using the KHPS data, estimates of the Gini coefficients were computed over the period 2004–2008 using three different measures: yearly pre-tax income for the household (denoted yearly pre-tax income); monthly consumption of the household (denoted monthly consumption); and monthly pre-tax income of the respondent and his or her spouse, if present (denoted monthly pre-tax income). In computing these estimates, "income" and "consumption" refer to equivalent income and consumption (adjusted by the square root of household size), respectively. Using the three alternative measures suggests that inequality is basically unchanged during the period 2004–2008. Because these estimates also included single-member households, the NLS Gini coefficients were probably the most relevant point of comparison. The KHPS Gini coefficients, based on yearly pre-tax income were slightly lower than those for the NLS, but they show that little change in income inequality was observed between 2004 and 2008. Given that respondents to KHPS2004 were limited to individuals aged 20 to 69, it is likely that households with heads aged 70 and over are significantly under-represented. As the NLS estimates indicate, until quite recently, income inequality tended to be higher for this group. In contrast, the consumption-based inequality estimates show an upward trend over the period between 2004 and 2009.

Using monthly consumption in 2009, the estimated Gini coefficient was 0.310. The Lehman Brothers shock occurred in September 2008. Figures for monthly consumption relate to January in the year of the survey, so the Gini coefficient for monthly consumption for 2009 is a post-shock estimate. The yearly pre-tax income figures relate to income in the relevant calendar year, so the income figure for 2008 includes a mix of both pre-shock and post-shock data. On the basis of these data alone, it is difficult to argue that the Lehman Brothers shock had a significant effect on inequality in Japan.

Inequality estimates based on Japanese official data suggest rising inequality up to 2004, but both NLS and KHPS data suggest that between 2004 and 2008, there was little change. In contrast, the number of households receiving Livelihood Protection Assistance has been steadily increasing.

INCOME MOBILITY

The previous discussion suggests there has been little change in income inequality as measured by the Gini coefficient during the period 2004 to

2008. It is possible that at the same time there have been changes in income mobility such that households in, say, the lowest quintile group are on average staying for longer or shorter periods. Ohtake (2008, 93) argues that "less frequent movements across income classes would result in larger inequality in lifetime income, even if inequalities were unchanged within each age group." To examine whether movements across income classes had changed over time, Ohtake computed one-year transition probabilities for 1985–1986 and 2000–2001. These one-year transition probabilities were estimates of the percentage of households in the ith income quintile group in the initial year that were in the jth quintile group in the subsequent year. Similarly, n-year transition probabilities were estimates of the percentage of households in the ith income quintile group in the initial year that were in the jth income quintile group n years later.

It was possible to estimate these transition probabilities because KHPS is a longitudinal survey that follows the same respondent over time.[10] The results for the one-year transition probabilities showed that the percentage of households in the same quintile groups in 2004 and 2005, and in 2007 and 2008 was essentially the same at around 60 percent. This was about the same as Ohtake's estimate for the 1990s but higher than his estimate for 2000 to 2001, which was 53 percent. This suggests that income mobility may have fallen over the 2000s.

Table 14.2 provides estimates of transition probabilities based on annual pre-tax income for the households between 2004 and 2005 (upper panel), between 2007 and 2008 (middle panel), and between 2004 and 2008 (bottom panel). The upper panel of Table 14.2 shows that 70 percent of households in the first quintile group in 2004 remained there in 2005, and the middle panel shows that about 69 percent of the first group in 2007 remained there in 2008. Both these estimates are higher than Ohtake's estimates for 1985–1986 of 61 percent and 2000–2001 of 56 percent, respectively. This is consistent with falling income mobility. At the top end of the distribution, 74 and 73 percent of households in the top income quintile group in 2004 and 2007 remained in the top income quintile group in 2005 and 2008, respectively.

For households in the second and third income quintile groups in 2004 or 2007, the probability of being in the same group in the following year was about 50 percent, which is about 10 percentage points higher than what Ohtake reported for 2000–2001. That is, with the exception of the top group,

TABLE 14.2
Transition probabilities: 2004–2005, 2007–2008, and 2004–2008

		2005 quintile groups					Total (%)
		1	2	3	4	5	
2004 quintile groups	1	70	18	8	3	1	100
	2	21	53	19	5	2	100
	3	5	19	50	22	4	100
	4	3	7	16	52	22	100
	5	2	3	6	15	74	100
		2008 quintile groups					
		1	2	3	4	5	
2007 quintile groups	1	69	23	5	2	2	100
	2	20	53	17	8	2	100
	3	8	19	51	19	3	100
	4	3	5	22	49	21	100
	5	1	1	4	22	73	100
		2008 quintile groups					
		1	2	3	4	5	
2004 quintile groups	1	58	26	9	5	2	100
	2	24	40	19	12	5	100
	3	10	23	41	20	7	100
	4	3	7	21	37	31	100
	5	5	3	8	24	60	100

SOURCE: Author's calculations using data from KHPS2005, KHPS2006, KHPS2008, and KHPS2009.

there appears to be less income mobility in 2004–2005 and 2007–2008 compared with what Ohtake reported. Consistent with Ohtake's findings, there appears to be much more movement out of the three middle quintile groups. It goes without saying that households in these three groups have the possibility of moving up or down. In these middle groups, around 50 percent of households are in the same group in the following year. The percentages of households moving to a higher and to a lower quintile group are both about 20 percent. This contrasts with Ohtake's findings for the three middle quintile groups for 2000–2001, when the percentage moving to a lower quintile group was more than 10 percentage points higher than the percentage moving to a higher quintile group.

From the 2004–2005 (2007–2008) transition probabilities, we see that 60 percent (59) of households stayed in the same quintile group (two-year immobility rate), while 21 percent (20) entered a higher quintile group, and

19 percent (21) entered a lower quintile group. Similar estimates for the United States using data over the period 1993–2003 show that, depending on the period, 60 to 71 percent of households stayed in the same quintile group, while 15 to 21 percent entered a higher group, and 14 to 20 percent entered a lower group (see Hisnanick 2011). This comparison suggests that income mobility was slightly higher in Japan. Based on a similar analysis for income *decile groups* in Germany, the United Kingdom, the United States, and Canada, Chen (2009) suggested that incomes were the most mobile in the United Kingdom and the least mobile in Canada. Because the two-year mobility rates for the United States were between Germany's and the United Kingdom's, we can speculate that Japan's income mobility was probably closest to the United Kingdom's.

For those households that stayed in the same quintile group for 2004–2005 (2007–2008), 23 percent stayed in the bottom quintile group, 52 percent stayed in the middle quintile groups, and 25 percent stayed in the top quintile group. These are relatively close to the figures reported by Hisnanick (2011) for the United States: 22 to 26 percent for the bottom quintile group, 52 to 54 percent for the middle quintile groups, and 22 to 24 percent for the top quintile group.

The bottom panel of Table 14.2 provides estimates of the four-year transition probabilities from 2004 to 2008. The four-year transition probabilities for staying in the same quintile group were about 10 percent lower than the one-year transition probabilities. As with the one-year transition probabilities, the probability of staying in the bottom or the top quintile group was about 20 percentage points higher than the probabilities of staying in one of the middle three quintile groups. In these three middle quintile groups, about 40 percent of households were in the same quintile group four years later. There are some interesting differences in movements out of the middle three quintile groups. For households in the second and fourth quintile groups in 2004, the probability of moving up over the next four years was about 10 percent higher than for the next one year. For households in the third quintile group in 2004, the probability of moving down over the next four years was about 10 percent higher than for the next one year.

Table 14.3 seeks to identify some of the characteristics of the household heads in each of the five income quintile groups in 2004 and to assess how these characteristics might differ between "stayers" (households in the same

TABLE 14.3
Characteristics of movers and stayers, 2004–2005

Quintile group in 2004		Total	STATUS IN 2005		
			Down movers	Stayers	Up movers
First	Female	21		23	16
	Work 2005	74		72	80
	Work 2006	76		74	80
	Work both	70		67	78
	UE both	20		21	18
	Single	27		29	21
	Age	52		50	54
Second	Female	8	11	5	10
	Work 2005	86	90	85	85
	Work 2006	85	89	82	87
	Work both	82	85	81	81
	UE both	11	5	14	9
	Single	11	12	10	14
	Age	50	51	49	53
Third	Female	8	12	9	4
	Work 2005	90	89	90	93
	Work 2006	90	87	90	91
	Work both	88	84	88	90
	UE both	8	9	8	6
	Single	11	15	11	8
	Age	50	52	49	51
Fourth	Female	6	10	5	5
	Work 2005	91	83	96	90
	Work 2006	90	77	95	91
	Work both	88	74	94	89
	UE both	7	14	2	8
	Single	10	11	9	11
	Age	53	55	50	56
Fifth	Female	5	10	3	
	Work 2005	91	82	94	
	Work 2006	91	81	95	
	Work both	89	75	93	
	UE both	6	12	5	
	Single	7	13	5	
	Age	54	56	54	

SOURCE: Author's calculations using data from KHPS2005 and KHPS2006.

NOTE: The figures in the columns headed "Total," "Down movers," "Stayers," and "Up movers" are the proportions for the relevant quintile group: in total, for households that moved down one or more quintile groups, for households that stayed in the same quintile group, and for households that moved up one or move quintile groups, respectively.

income quintile group in both of the two years), "up movers" (households in a higher-income quintile group in 2005 compared to 2004), and "down movers" (households that were in a lower-income quintile group in 2005 compared to 2004). I looked at both employment and household structure in the proportion of female-headed households (Female), the proportion of households in which the household head reported that he or she was working in early 2005 (Work2005), the proportion of households where the household head reported that he or she was working in early 2006 (Work2006), the proportion of households where the household head reported that he or she was working in both early 2005 and early 2006 (Work Both), the proportion of households where the household head reported that he or she was not working in early 2005 or early 2006 (UE Both), and the proportion of household heads who are single (Single). Age is the age of the household head.[11] With the exception of Age, a comparison of the figures in the Total column for the first quintile group and the other quintile groups suggests large differences between the first and second quintile groups but much smaller differences between the other quintile groups. Households with an unmarried or female head and households with a head who is not working are much more likely to be found in the first quintile group.

WEALTH INEQUALITY

This final section closely follows the analysis presented in Chapter 10 of OECD (2008), which analyzed wealth inequality using the *LWS Database*. KHPS collects data on two broadly defined financial assets, deposits, and securities (which include stocks, bonds, and investment trusts), the total amount of loans that a household has outstanding, and the household's principal residence. Where a residence is owned, respondents are asked to report its acquisition price as well as its current estimated value. KHPS also collects information on real estate (land, buildings, houses, etc.) owned for investment purposes. With the exception of real estate owned for investment purposes, the information collected by JHPS on financial and real assets is essentially the same as by KHPS. JHPS does not collect any information on real estate owned for investment purposes. Total assets are computed as the sum of financial assets (deposits plus securities) and non-financial assets (principal residence plus investment real estate, where available). Net worth is computed as total assets minus debt. In reporting these asset/debt values, no adjustment is made for the number of members in the household.

Panel A of Table 14.4 reports the proportion of households holding various types of assets in 2004 and 2009, both for the sample as a whole and by income quintile group.[12] When interpreting Table 14.3, it is important to bear in mind that the figures reported for 2004 and 2009 come from two different surveys: the KHPS2004 and the JHPS2009, respectively. In the KHPS survey, the age of the survey's respondents is between 20 and 69, while in the JHPS survey, it is 20 and over.[13] The figures in the "All" column of panel A correspond to Table 10.1 in OECD (2008), which reports estimates of household asset participation for countries in the *LWS Database*—namely, Canada, Finland, Germany, Italy, Norway, Sweden, the United Kingdom, and the United States. In both 2004 and 2009, the proportion of Japanese households reporting they owned some type of financial asset, about 80 percent, is similar to that reported for almost all *LWS* countries. For three high-income countries—Germany, the United Kingdom, and the United States—the proportions are 49 percent, 80 percent, and 83 or 91 percent (depending on which of the two alternative sources is used), respectively.[14] The proportion of Japanese households owning some portion of their principal residence—70 percent in the 2004 survey and 74 in the 2009 survey—was slightly higher than the percentages reported in other countries included in the *LWS Database*: Italy (69 percent), the United Kingdom (69 percent), and the United States (64 and 68 percent in the Panel Study of Income Dynamics (PSID) data and the Survey of Consumer Finances (SCF) data, respectively). The Japanese rate was, in contrast, substantially higher than in Germany (48 percent). With respect to household debt, Japan's 43 percent rate fell above the 32 percent seen in Germany but below the 59 percent reported in the United Kingdom and 68 percent (PSID) or 75 percent (SCF) in the United States.

Turning to household asset participation by income quintile group, I found that as income increases, the household participation rate for all assets tends to increase as well—as might be expected. Focusing on the middle three income quintile groups, it is easy to see that with the exception of investment real estate, between the second and fourth groups there is usually at least a 10 percentage point difference in the household asset participation rate for any given asset type. In 2004, there seem to be only

TABLE 14.4
Household asset participation (%) and portfolio composition in 2004 and 2009

A: HOUSEHOLD ASSET PARTICIPATION (%)

Year	Asset	All	First quintile group	Second quintile group	Third quintile group	Fourth quintile group	Fifth quintile group
2004	Non-financial assets	70	65	62	66	74	85
	Principal residence	70	64	62	65	73	84
	Investment real estate	8	4	4	8	7	18
	Financial assets	79	67	70	77	86	94
	Deposit accounts	79	66	70	77	85	94
	Securities	18	9	10	15	19	35
	Total assets						
	Debt	43	36	37	44	47	53
	Net worth						
	Median total assets (10,000 yen)						
2009	Non-financial assets	74 (73)	57	71	77	81	86
	Principal residence	74 (73)	57	71	77	81	86
	Investment real estate	—	—	—	—	—	—
	Financial assets	79 (79)	59	73	82	87	91
	Deposit accounts	78 (78)	59	73	82	85	91
	Securities	25 (24)	12	16	25	32	40
	Total assets						
	Debt	47 (52)	38	49	50	51	50
	Net worth						
	Median total assets (10,000 yen)						

B: PORTFOLIO COMPOSITION (PERCENTAGE SHARE OF TOTAL ASSETS)

Year	Asset	All	First quintile group	Second quintile group	Third quintile group	Fourth quintile group	Fifth quintile group
2004	Non-financial assets	77	78	82	78	78	73
	Principal residence	67	74	72	73	71	55
	Investment real estate	10	4	10	5	7	18
	Financial assets	23	22	18	22	22	27
	Deposit accounts	20	20	16	19	19	22
	Securities	3	2	2	3	3	5
	Total assets	100	100	100	100	100	100
	Debt	18	17	13	18	19	21
	Net worth	82	83	87	82	81	79
	Median total assets (10,000 yen)	2,182	1,500	1,510	1,950	2,500	3,800
2009	Non-financial assets	67 (68)	78	74	68	65	59
	Principal residence	67 (68)	78	74	68	65	59
	Investment real estate	—	—	—	—	—	—
	Financial assets	33 (32)	22	26	32	35	41
	Deposit accounts	27 (27)	19	22	27	28	34
	Securities	6 (5)	3	4	5	7	7
	Total assets	100 (100)	100	100	100	100	100
	Debt	22 (26)	19	28	24	23	20
	Net worth	78 (73)	81	72	76	77	80
	Median total assets (10,000 yen)	2,080 (2,000)	800	1,600	2,100	2,500	3,345

SOURCE: Author's calculations using data from KHPS2004 and JHPS2009.

NOTE: The figures in parentheses for 2009 in the "All" column are for when the sample is restricted to respondents aged 20–69, the same as the 2004 sample. Quintile groups are based on income.

small differences between household asset participation for the first and second quintile groups, but in 2009 there are much larger differences.

Panel B of Table 14.4 reports the composition of household portfolios in 2004 and 2009 for the sample as a whole and by income quintile group. The figures in the "All" column of panel B correspond to Table 10.2 in OECD (2008). In terms of the proportion of the portfolio held in non-financial assets (77 percent) in 2004, Japan seems to fall somewhere between Germany (87 percent) and the United Kingdom (83 percent) on the one hand and the United States (67 percent for both PSID and SCF) on the other hand. In contrast, the portion of debt in the Japanese portfolio (18 percent) in 2004 is lower than the relevant figures for Germany (23 percent), the United Kingdom (21 percent), and the United States (21 percent [PSID] and 22 percent [SCF]). There is a significant decline in the proportion of the household portfolio held in the principal residence between 2004 and 2009. There are also rather large differences in the median total assets held by households in the two periods.

The composition of the household portfolio in 2004 is quite similar for the third and fourth quintile groups, but compared with these, households in the second quintile group tend to have a lower proportion of debt and financial assets and a higher proportion of non-financial assets (especially investment real estate). In 2009, the portfolio compositions of third and fourth quintile group households are quite similar, but those in the second quintile group tend to have a higher proportion of their portfolio as the principal residence and debt and a lower proportion as financial assets. As the income quintile group rises, the share of the principal residence in the household portfolio falls. For 2009, the key impact of excluding households with respondents aged 70 and older is that the average percentage of debt in total assets decreases somewhat.

Panel A of Table 14.5 provides information on the median holdings of various assets in 2004 by income quintile group and age group. The "All" income/age group corresponds to the information represented graphically in Figure 10.1 in OECD (2008). For the "All" income group, the median holdings of the principal residence, financial assets, and net worth all increase with the age of the household head. Debt appears to be concentrated in the 35- to 55-year-old age group, although the median amount of debt is rather small, given that one of the principal reasons for a loan is to purchase a house. Comparing households in the second, third, and fourth

TABLE 14.5

Median wealth holdings by age of household head and distribution of net worth, 2004

		A: MEDIAN WEALTH HOLDINGS BY AGE OF HOUSEHOLD HEAD (VALUES IN 10,000 YEN)				B: DISTRIBUTION OF NET WORTH SHARES OF INDIVIDUALS (%)		
Income group	Age group	Principal residence	Financial assets	Debt	Net worth	Negative net worth	Zero net worth	Positive net worth
All	All	1,600	300	0	1,500	12	7	81
	−24	0	20	0	20	20	16	64
	25–34	0	50	0	100	17	16	67
	35–44	1,200	200	70	500	20	7	73
	45–54	1,700	250	120	1,510	13	5	82
	55–64	2,000	500	0	2,650	7	4	90
	65–	2,500	700	0	3,800	4	4	92
First quintile group	All	1,000	100	0	1,070	14	12	74
	−24	*	*	*	*	*	*	*
	25–34	0	10	0	30	10	24	67
	35–44	0	25	0	100	22	22	56
	45–54	1,200	135	0	950	20	7	74
	55–64	1,500	300	0	2,000	13	7	80
	65–	1,300	300	0	1,706	12	10	78
Second quintile group	All	1,100	120	0	890	13	10	77
	−24	*	*	*	*	*	*	*
	25–34	0	40	0	100	18	14	68
	35–44	1,250	100	30	250	24	11	65
	45–54	1,100	100	0	600	15	12	73
	55–64	1,400	400	0	1,890	3	3	93
	65–	2,000	500	0	2,600	1	8	91

Third quintile group	All	1,400	200	0	1,025	13	6	81
	−24	*	*	*	*	*	*	*
	25–34	0	95	0	95	20	13	67
	35–44	900	150	90	400	21	7	72
	45–54	1,583	200	150	1,500	13	4	84
	55–64	2,128	500	0	3,000	2	5	93
	65–	2,850	1,130	0	4,200	2	0	98
Fourth quintile group	All	1,900	300	0	1,600	12	5	83
	−24	*	*	*	*	*	*	*
	25–34	0	150	0	220	15	18	67
	35–44	1,600	300	130	600	17	4	80
	45–54	2,000	245	195	1,740	13	3	84
	55–64	2,000	500	0	2,730	7	2	91
	65–	2,800	1,000	0	4,081	4	0	96
Fifth quintile group	All	2,500	800	95	2,635	8	1	91
	−24	*	*	*	*	*	*	*
	25–34	0	225	95	260	27	4	69
	35–44	2,000	380	350	1,450	17	0	83
	45–54	2,400	500	600	2,200	8	2	90
	55–64	2,400	1,120	0	3,550	4	1	95
	65–	4,000	2,500	0	6,930	0	0	100

SOURCE: Author's calculations using data from KHPS2004.
*The results for this entry are not reported because of the small size of the relevant sample.

income quintile groups, there are quite large differences in the median value of the principal residence. Within each income quintile group, the general tendency is for the median holdings of the principal residence, financial assets, and net worth to increase with the age of the household head. In all quintile groups, for households with a household head aged 55 and older, the median holding of debt is zero.

Panel B of Table 14.5 shows the distribution of net worth overall, in each age group, and in each income quintile group in 2004. The row for "all" income and "all" age groups corresponds to Table 10.3 in OECD (2008). The proportion of Japanese households reporting positive net worth (81 percent) is close to the value for the United Kingdom (82 percent) and Finland (83 percent), but above the values for Germany (63 percent) and the United States (77 percent in both the PSID and SCF data). For the "all" income group, as the age of the household head increases (especially aged 35 or over), the proportion of households with negative net worth tends to fall, and the proportion of households with positive net worth tends to rise. Compared with the other groups, a larger percentage of older households in (55 years and over) in the lowest quintile group report having negative net worth.

CONCLUSION

Using data for individual households in Japan collected in the Keio Household Panel Survey (KHPS) and the Japan Household Panel Survey (JHPS), this chapter examines trends in household income inequality in the mid- to late 2000s, income mobility, and asset holdings—making cross-national comparisons where possible. During the period 2004–2009, there was little change in inequality of annual household income, as measured by the Gini coefficient. Short-term income mobility in the mid- to late 2000s is lower than it was in 2000–2001 for all income quintile groups, except the top group. Thus, even if income inequality has not changed much, other indicators may turn up evidence of increasing hardship—for example, the duration of poverty spells in Japan is likely to be getting longer. Even after four years, nearly 60 percent of households in the lowest-income quintile group remain in that group.

One of the key motivations of this chapter has been to place Japan in comparative perspective—especially with respect to three major industrialized countries: Germany, the United Kingdom, and the United States. Where possible, this comparison is attempted on multiple dimensions, including income mobility and wealth distributions. A comparison of quintile group income mobility suggests there is more income mobility in Japan compared with the United States. Relative to these three comparison countries, Japan's asset holdings generally fall between those of the United States and Germany. The principal residence forms the largest component of Japanese household's wealth portfolios for all quintile groups. Debt appears to be most concentrated in the 35- to 54-year-old age group. The proportion of Japanese households reporting positive net worth is close to the values for the United Kingdom. The main exception is the portion of debt in the portfolio, which in Japan is the lowest of the four countries.

One key issue that has not been addressed in this chapter and that should be the subject of future research is the joint distribution of income and assets. Official estimates of income inequality for the aged show that they tend to exhibit higher income inequality than in the whole population. In contrast, on average, aged households tend to have much larger asset holdings, both financial and real, than do younger households, but again there are likely to be wide inequalities across aged households here also. Another important topic for future research is the adequacy of using standard measures of income inequality in Japan, something that has been highlighted by the rising number of households receiving Livelihood Protection Assistance, even though income inequality measures do not appear to be changing.

NOTES

The author thanks Janet Gornick, Markus Jäntti, Hubert Strauss, the designated discussant, and participants at the conference on "Inequality and the Status of the Middle Class: Lessons from the *Luxembourg Income Study*" held in Luxembourg in July 2010 for their helpful comments and suggestions; and Tamaki Miyauchi and Michio Naoi for their assistance with the Keio Household Panel Survey and Japanese Household Panel Survey data. The financial and research assistance provided by the Japanese Ministry of Education, Culture, Sports and Technology's 21st Century Center of Excellence awarded to Keio University (2003–2008) on the theme of "Development of a Theory of Market Quality and an Empirical Analysis Using Panel Data" and the Japanese Ministry of Education, Culture, Sports and Technology's Global Center of Excellence awarded to Keio University

(2008–) on the theme of "Improving Markets and the Comprehensive Design of Market Infrastructure" are gratefully acknowledged.

1. In this chapter, I do not attempt to solve the difficult problem of how to combine information on income and assets (particularly real estate, which is the principal residence).

2. There are four eligibility criteria imposed on those applying for Likelihood Protection Assistance: an income test; an assets test (applicants are required to have sold any land or housing they own); a work test (applicants who can work must demonstrate that they are working to their limit); and a reliance test (applicants must have exhausted the possibilities of relying on their immediate family (children, parents, brothers, and sisters)). These have been deemed to be quite strict, so many people with low levels of income are thought to be ineligible. It is often suggested that there is some degree of variability in the application of eligibility rules across Japan, with Osaka (with a high number of recipients) perceived as an area in which local government officials apply eligibility rules rather laxly. The recent case of the mother of a famous TV entertainer, Junichi Kawamoto, receiving Livelihood Protection Assistance benefits was viewed by many as indicating that the eligibility rules, especially those related to relying on relatives, have not been properly enforced.

3. The number of households receiving Livelihood Protection Assistance has been steadily rising from 0.75 (1.07) million households (individuals) in fiscal year 2000 to 1.04 (1.48) million households (individuals) in fiscal year 2005 and slightly over 1.40 (1.95) million households (individuals) in fiscal year 2010. In 2010, of the 1.40 million households, there were no earners in 1.2 million of the households. Even though single-person households make up only 24 to 25 percent of Japanese households, 75 percent of the households receiving Livelihood Protection Assistance are single-person households (see Ministry of Health, Labour and Welfare (Japan) (2011)).

4. KHPSxxxx refers to the KHPS dataset collected in the year xxxx, so, for example, KHPS2004 refers to the KHPS dataset collected in 2004. References to the JHPS data follow the same pattern.

5. Some of the data in KHPS2004 are now available in the *LWS Database*.

6. An exchange rate of 80 yen to one U.S. dollar is used throughout this chapter.

7. Although McKenzie and colleagues (2007) did not do so, it would be worth assessing how attrition affected the dispersion of wages.

8. In the NSFIE survey, household income is defined as including income from employment, rents, public and private pensions, interest and dividends, and some payments in kind.

9. See "Getting a Grip on the Real State of Economic Disparities and Poverty, Ministry of Health, Labor and Welfare to Make an Index and Use It for Countermeasures (Kakusa ya Hinkon no jittai wo haaku, Koryosho. shihyou tsukri taisaku ni katsuyo)," Nihon Keizai Shinbun, January 12, 2012.

10. Ishii and Yamada (2007) use data from KHPS2004–2006 to compute one-year income class transition probabilities between 2004 and 2005, and between 2005 and 2006. Rather than using income quintile groups, Ishii and Yamada use classes based on median equivalent income—for example, less than 0.50 of median income and 0.50 to 0.75 of median income. As a result, their analysis is not strictly comparable with Ohtake's (2008).

11. When the household head is the survey respondent or the respondent's spouse, a great deal more information is available.

12. For the 2004 results, income refers to the monthly income of the respondent (and the respondent's spouse, if there is one), and for the 2009 results, income refers to annual income for the household. In both cases, this income refers to income adjusted by the square root of household size equivalence scale.

13. It would be possible to restrict the age of respondents in the JHPS to between 20 and 69 so the KHPS2004 and JHPS2007 would be directly comparable. The key impact of excluding Japanese households with respondents aged 70 or more is that the proportion of households with debt increases by 5 percentage points—that is, aged households tend not to hold debt.

14. In these comparisons, it should be noted that in the German data most financial assets and non-housing debt are recorded only for values exceeding 2500 euros. For the United States, the data sources are the 2001 Panel Study of Income Dynamics (PSID) and the 2001 Survey of Consumer Finances (SCF), respectively.

REFERENCES

Chen, Wen-Hao, 2009. "Cross-National Differences in Income Mobility: Evidence from Canada, the U.S., Great Britain, and Germany." *Review of Income and Wealth* 55(1): 75–100.

Förster, Michael, and Marco Mira d'Ercole. 2005. "Income Distribution and Poverty in OECD Countries in the Second Half of the 1990s." *OECD Social, Employment and Migration*. Working paper 22.

Hisnanick, John J. 2011. "Who Are the Winners and the Losers? Transitions in the U.S. Household Income Distribution." *Review of Radical Economics* 43(4): 467–87.

Inaba, Yoshiyuki, Nobuyuki Takaoka, and Ayuko Oka. 2008. "The Trend of Household Asset Differentials and a Breakdown of Causes (Kakei Shisan Kakusa no Suii to Yoin Bunkai)." *Tokyo: Statistical Research and Training Institute, Ministry of Internal Affairs and Communications* (in Japanese). Research paper 14.

Ishii, Kayoko, and Atsuhiro Yamada. 2007. "An Analysis of Poverty—The Actual Situation in 3 Years Based on KHPS and an International Comparison (Hinkon no Jittai Bunseki—KHPS ni Motozuku 3 Nenkan no Jittai oyobi

Sono Kokusai Hikaku)." In *Dynamism of Household Behavior in Japan [II]* (*Nihon no Kakei Kodo no Dainamizumu [III]*), edited by Yoshio Higuchi and Miki Seko. Tokyo: Keio University Press (in Japanese).

Kimura, Masakazu. 2005. "The Sample Characteristics of the 2004 Keio Household Panel Survey (2004nen Keio Gijuku Kakei Paneru Chosa no Hyohon Tokusei)" In *Dynamism of Household Behavior in Japan [I]* (*Nihon no Kakei Kodo no Dainamizumu [I]*), edited by Yoshio Higuchi. Tokyo: Keio University Press (in Japanese).

McKenzie, Colin R., Tamaki Miyauchi, Michio Naoi, and Kensuke Kiso. 2007. "Individual Behaviour and the Attrition Problem in the Labour Market (Rodo Shijo ni okeru Kojin Kodo to Datsuraku Mondai)." In *Dynamism of Household Behavior in Japan [II]* (*Nihon no Kakei Kodo no Dainamizumu [III]*), edited by Yoshio Higuchi and Miki Seko. Tokyo: Keio University Press (in Japanese).

Ministry of Health, Labour and Welfare (Japan). Statistics and Information Department, Minister's Secretariat. 2011. *Handbook of Health and Welfare Statistics 2011* (*Kosei Tokei Yoran Heisei 23nen*). Tokyo: Health and Welfare Statistics Association (in Japanese). http://www.mhlw.go.jp/toukei/youran/indexyk_3_1.html.

Miyauchi, Tamaki, Colin R. McKenzie, and Masakazu Kimura. 2006. "An Analysis of Panel Data Continuation and Responses (Paneru Deta Keizoku to Kaito Bunseki)." In *Dynamism of Household Behavior in Japan [II]* (*Nihon no Kakei Kodo no Dainamizumu [II]*), edited by Yoshio Higuchi. Tokyo: Keio University Press (in Japanese).

Naoi, Michio. 2007. "Residential Mobility and Panel Attrition: Using the Interview Process As Identifying Instruments." *Keio Economic Studies* 44(1): 37–47.

Naoi, Michio, and Koji Yamamoto. 2010. "The Sample Design and Representativeness of the Japan Household Panel Survey (Nihon Kakei Paneru Chosa no Hyohon Sekkei to Daihyousei)." In *The Dynamism of Poverty: Japan's Tax and Social Welfare and Employment Policies and Houshould Behaviour (Hinkon no Dainamizumu: Nihon no Zeishakai Hosho-Koyo Seisaku to Kaei Kodo)*, edited by Yoshio Higuchi, Tamaki Miyauchi, and Colin R. McKenzie. Tokyo: Keio University Press (in Japanese).

Ohtake, Fumio. 2005. *Japanese Inequality—The Mirage and Future of the Unequal Society (Nihon no Fuboudo–Kakusa Shakai no Genso to Mirai)*. Tokyo: Nihon Keizai Shibunsha (in Japanese).

———. 2008. "Inequality in Japan." *Asian Economic Policy Review* 3(1): 87–109.

Organisation for Economic Co-operation and Development (OECD). 2008. *Growing Unequal? Income Distribution and Poverty in OECD Countries.* Paris: OECD.

————. 2010. *OECD Factbook 2010: Economic, Environmental and Social Statistics.* Paris: OECD.

————. 2011. *Divided We Stand. Why Inequality Keeps Rising.* Paris: OECD.

Ota, Kiyoshi. 2003. "Asset Differentials in Japan (Nihon ni okeru Shisan Kakusa)." In *The Japanese Income Differential and Social Classes (Nihon no Shotoku Kakusa to Shakai Kaiso)*, edited by Yoshio Higuchi. Tokyo: Nihon Hyoronsha (in Japanese).

Shikata, Masato. 2011. "Asset Differentials in Japan—An International Comparison Using JHPS and the Luxembourg Wealth Study (Nihon no Shisan Kakusa—JHPS to Lukusenburuku Shisan Chosa ni yoru Kokusai Hikaku)." In *The Dynamism of Education, Health and Poverty: The Impact on Income Differentials of the Tax and Social Welfare System (Kyoiku–Kenko to Hinkon no Dainamizumu: Shotoku Kakusa ni Ataeru Zeishakai Hosho Seido no Kokka)*, edited by Yoshio Higuchi, Tamaki Miyauchi, and Colin R. McKenzie. Tokyo: Keio University Press (in Japanese).

Takayama, Noriyuki, Fumio Funaoka, Fumio Ohtake, Masahiko Seikiguchi, and Tokiyuki Shibuya. 1989. "Japanese Household Assets and the Savings Rate (Nihon no Kakei Shisan to Chochikuritsu)." *Keizai Bunseki*, 116. Tokyo, Japan: Economic Research Institute Economic Planning Agency (in Japanese).

CHAPTER FIFTEEN

Income Inequality in Boom and Bust

A Tale from Iceland's Bubble Economy

Stefán Ólafsson and Arnaldur Sölvi Kristjánsson

From the 1990s, Iceland became the subject of an unusual neoliberal experiment that produced an excessive bubble economy that reached its height between 2002 and 2008. Neoliberalism had started to gain ground in politics and economic policy from the early 1980s, as it had in many other affluent countries. This involved a strong reliance on the virtues of unfettered markets, privatization, reservations about the role of government in the economy, favorable tax treatment of firms and investors, and a laissez-faire attitude in finance and the economy in general.

Iceland's entry into the European Economic Area (EEA) in 1995 introduced the four freedoms of the European Union into the Icelandic political economy, with full freedom for the flow of capital across borders being the most novel and consequential aspect.[1] The privatization of the main state banks, which was started in 1998, proved to be a major turning point. When the banks were fully privatized at the beginning of 2003, the new owners turned them on the spot into aggressive investment banks. They greatly increased their participation in leveraged mergers and acquisitions, first within Iceland but then to a greater extent in the neighboring countries. They also promoted an extensive use of tax havens among Icelandic businesspersons and financiers.

External debt escalated, and excessive risk behavior became predominant in the Icelandic financial and business environment, driven by the quest for accumulation of assets, profits, and bonuses (PIC 2010). With the easy flow of borrowed foreign capital at low interest rates, the economy had ample resources for rapid growth, which soon turned into an excessive speculation bubble (Kindleberger and Aliber 2005; Minsky 2008/1986).

Already by the end of 2004, Iceland had become the world's most heavily indebted economy, measured as gross external debt as a share of GDP. Before the collapse of the banks in October 2008, foreign debt had grown to about eight times GDP, a high-risk situation and totally unsustainable once growth slowed down (Buiter and Sibert 2008; Ólafsson 2008, 2011a; Aliber and Zoega 2011; Halldórsson and Zoega 2010; PIC 2010). The size of the bubble and the collapse were indeed extreme by all accounts.

Iceland is thus an interesting case for studying societal correlates of an excessive bubble economy and financial crisis. Income distribution is certainly an important topic for such a study. This chapter examines how the bubble economy affected income inequality in Iceland. The primary data source consists of public tax data for the period from 1992 to 2010. These data provide comparability from year to year, though they are not fully comparable to income distribution data in other countries (Atkinson and Piketty 2007).

Iceland has been included in the European Union Statistics on Income and Living Conditions (EU-SILC) data from 2003 to 2010, and the Organisation for Economic Co-operation and Development (OECD) has published inequality and poverty estimates for Iceland for the mid- and late 2000s. However, the OECD and EU-SILC data exclude capital gains, which were a major factor in the Icelandic bubble economy.[2] Therefore, the data that the OECD and Eurostat use underestimate income inequality as measured using Icelandic tax data, as we will see later in this chapter.

The EU-SILC data indicate that income inequality in Iceland was similar to that in the other Nordic countries in 2003 (Statistics Iceland 2009, 2012). The Nordic countries—especially Finland, Sweden, and Norway—experienced increased income inequality from the early 1990s. The tax data also suggest that income inequality in Iceland increased rapidly after 1995. Fritzell, Bäckman, and Ritakallio (2012) compare trends in inequality in the five Nordic countries from 1995 to 2008, measured by the Gini coefficient of disposable income, including capital gains. Their estimates also show income inequality increasing rapidly from 1995 in all the Nordic countries. By 2001, inequality in Iceland had outpaced that in the other Nordic countries, a lead it increased greatly up to 2007 (Fritzell et al. 2012).

When capital gains are excluded, as in estimates based on the EU-SILC, the Gini coefficient in Iceland in 2003 was close to the Nordic average. But it then increased from 0.24 in that year to 0.30 in 2008 (Statistics Iceland

2009, 2012). That is a large increase by any standard. But since these data do not include capital gains, both the level and change in inequality are underestimated, as we show later in this chapter.

Thus, Fritzell and colleagues show that inequality in the other Nordic countries increased during and after the so-called ICT bubble—referring to information and communication technologies—of 1995–2000. In Norway, a particularly large increase in inequality in 2004–2005 was associated with increased financial earnings (see also Atkinson, Piketty, and Saez 2011).[3] The OECD (2011) finds that the income inequality, starting from the most egalitarian position, increased more in the Nordic countries than the OECD average from 1995 onward. Although the OECD estimates exclude capital gains, they conclude that other financial earnings were a relatively large and growing income component in all Nordic countries. As it is likely that financial earnings are a key driver of inequality during financial bubbles, we need a more complete measure of financial earnings, including capital gains, to assess the effect of a financial bubble on income distribution. For Iceland, we can use tax data that include capital gains so we are in a better position to assess the impact of the financial bubble on the income distribution.

The study of income distribution during the bubble economy period is obviously of great interest from an Icelandic perspective, but it is also of general interest as a case study of income distribution and economic bubbles. Periods of financial speculation and overheating have become a prominent feature of modern economies since the increased liberalization of global financial markets after the early 1980s (Reinhart and Rogoff 2009; Stiglitz 2010; Wolf 2010). Information technology has contributed to financial volatility by expanding globalization in this area. An increased understanding of the effects of financial markets, speculation, and overheating on income distribution is thus of wider relevance.

The role of government policy is also important, especially how governments do and do not counter market-driven changes in inequality (Kenworthy and Pontusson 2005; Brandolini and Smeeding 2009; OECD 2011). How taxation and welfare systems fare can be of great importance for inequality. The Icelandic case is instructive in this regard.

In what follows, we analyze the evolution of the income distribution in Iceland in the period leading up to the crisis, when the bubble burst in the autumn of 2008, and in the years following the crash. Inequality increased substantially during the bubble but decreased again during the ensuing recession.

THE DATA

Icelandic tax data cover the whole population and include all taxable incomes. They allow for a disaggregation of different income components (such as labor market earnings, pensions, other public benefits, and financial earnings), and they also make possible an assessment of the effects of taxation on the distribution. The data also facilitate analysis by family type (households with couples and single persons), age group, and income group. The data cover the years 1992 to 2009 and some of 2010—a period that is relatively short but includes the bubble and the aftermath of its bursting.

We have worked with the Icelandic tax authorities to modify the tax data to make it more amenable to conventional income distribution analysis. Most importantly, this involved equivalizing the incomes (by dividing by the square root of household size). This chapter reports the first use of these modified data. In previous studies, we used unequivalized data for couples and singles separately (see, for example, Ólafsson 2006a, 2006b; Kristjánsson and Ólafsson 2009). A comparison shows that estimates for couples obtained using unequivalized incomes are quite similar to those using equivalized incomes for all households.

There is little reason to expect that the black economy in Iceland is significantly larger than that in other Nordic countries, so under-reporting in general should be of no more concern in Iceland than in the other Nordic countries (Olsen et al. 2004). However, under-reporting of financial earnings during the financial bubble may be an issue because of international links of Icelandic banks and businesses and, in particular, widespread use of foreign tax havens. For the vast majority of the population, the data should be reasonably reliable and thus a good gauge of distributional trends, as whatever problems exist in the data are likely to have remained roughly constant throughout the period.

MAJOR SHIFTS IN THE INCOME STRUCTURE

Examinations of the long-run trend in income distribution in Iceland suggest that changes were relatively small during the period of rapid economic growth from the 1960s to the early 1980s.[4] During the 1980s and early 1990s, income inequality in Iceland was at about the same level as in the other Nordic countries. Thus, Iceland was a very egalitarian society from the 1960s through 1980 (Ólafsson 1999; Jónsson et al. 2001). A high rate of economic growth was achieved while maintaining a high degree of equality.

During the 1980s, earnings inequality increased, but from 1988 to 1993, the distribution of disposable income became slightly more equal. This was due to an increased equalizing effect of taxation and benefits, following tax changes implemented in 1988.[5] The tax data suggest that inequality started to increase rapidly after 1995 (Jónsson et al. 2001; Ólafsson 2006a, 2006b; Baldursson et al. 2008; Kristjánsson and Ólafsson 2009, 2010). Figure 15.1 shows the Gini coefficient for households consisting of couples from 1993 to 2010 and for two income concepts: disposable earnings with and without capital gains (non-equivalized income; see note 4).

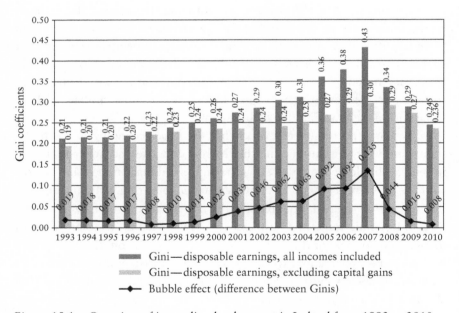

Figure 15.1. Overview of inequality development in Iceland from 1993 to 2010. Gini coefficients for two income concepts: Disposable earnings with and without capital gains and indication of bubble effects on inequality

SOURCE: Authors' calculations from Icelandic tax data.
NOTE: The incomes are not equivalized, and the population consists of married and cohabiting couples.

The large increase in inequality during this period was due to both the effect of the bubble economy, especially through capital gains—as suggested by the much more rapid increase in inequality when they are included—and to changing government tax and benefit policies.

The Gini coefficient of disposable income including capital gains increased from 0.21 in 1993 to 0.43 in 2007, before coming down again to about 0.25 in 2010. The Gini coefficient thus more than doubled between 1993 and 2007, a gigantic increase by any standard. The Gini coefficient of disposable income excluding capital gains increases less, by one half, increasing from 0.19 in 1993 up to 0.30 in 2007, before decreasing to just under 0.24 in 2010. Even this change in the Gini coefficient exceeds what the OECD calls a "strong increase" in inequality (Förster and d'Ercole 2005; see also OECD 2008).

The difference between the two sets of Ginis indicates a significant bubble economy effect on income distribution, mediated in particular through capital gains (see the line at the bottom of the figure). The growing contribution of capital gains reflects increasing asset prices and intensifying speculation on financial markets. Capital gains increased rapidly during the bubble, and financial earnings were taxed at a lower level than other incomes. Since they accrued disproportionately to the highest income groups, the effect on inequality was large. This effect was growing during the 2000s and reached its peak in 2007. After the bubble burst in 2008, the bubble effect disappears along with the capital gains. At that time, interest earnings increased substantially because many transferred their assets into savings accounts prior to the crash (Ólafsson and Kristjánsson, 2012).

Our Gini coefficients for disposable income excluding capital gains are comparable to survey-based income distribution data such as those published by the OECD, LIS, and EU-SILC, except that top incomes may be under-represented in survey-based data, unlike in our universal tax data (Atkinson et al. 2011). While inequality using this measure increased substantially during the height of the bubble, from 2003 to 2007, the increase is very much larger when capital gains are included. This suggests not only that the financial bubble in Iceland increased inequality substantially but that inequality measures that exclude capital gains may substantially underestimate inequality in other countries that are experiencing overheating and economic bubbles, phenomena that have increasingly affected high-income economies after the early 1980s.

As Table 15.1 shows, the income shares of all decile groups, except the top tenth, declined after 1995.[6] The lowest decile group's share decreased from 3.0 percent in 1996 to 2.1 percent in 2007, while the share of the fifth decile group declined from 8.6 percent in 1995 to 6.5 percent in 2007. Interestingly, the decline in the share of the ninth decile group was proportionally smaller, from 14.3 percent to 12.3 percent. The top decile group, by contrast, gained—its share increased from 21.3 percent in 1995 to 38.4 percent in 2007—and then decreased to 27.5 percent by 2009, after the bust. We also show the income share of the top 1 percent, the development of which is by far the most dramatic. Their share increased from 3.8 percent in 1995 to 10.8 percent by 2003, and onwards up to 19.8 percent by 2007, before decreasing to 8.5 percent in 2009. The influence of the bubble economy was thus largest on top earners, with financial earnings playing a decisive role, as we show below.

The Gini index in the last column summarizes the overall development for the equivalized incomes, increasing from 0.26 percent in 1994 to 0.44 percent at the height of the bubble in 2007, before decreasing to

TABLE 15.1

Decile group shares, top 1 percent share and the Gini coefficient of equivalent disposable income, 1992–2009

Year	I	II	III	IV	V	VI	VII	VIII	IX	X	Top 1%	Gini coefficient
1992	2.6	5.7	6.7	7.7	8.6	9.6	10.8	12.3	14.4	21.6	4.1	0.28
1993	2.8	5.8	6.8	7.7	8.6	9.6	10.8	12.2	14.4	21.2	3.8	0.27
1994	3.0	5.9	6.8	7.7	8.6	9.5	10.7	12.2	14.3	21.2	3.8	0.26
1995	3.0	5.8	6.8	7.7	8.6	9.5	10.7	12.2	14.3	21.3	3.8	0.27
1996	3.0	5.7	6.6	7.5	8.5	9.5	10.7	12.2	14.5	21.8	4.1	0.28
1997	2.9	5.6	6.5	7.4	8.4	9.4	10.7	12.2	14.5	22.5	4.6	0.29
1998	2.8	5.4	6.3	7.3	8.3	9.4	10.7	12.3	14.7	22.7	4.5	0.29
1999	2.8	5.2	6.1	7.1	8.2	9.3	10.6	12.2	14.6	23.8	5.2	0.30
2000	2.8	5.1	6.0	7.0	8.1	9.2	10.5	12.2	14.6	24.5	6.0	0.31
2001	2.7	4.9	5.9	6.9	8.0	9.1	10.4	12.0	14.3	25.7	7.7	0.32
2002	2.7	4.9	5.8	6.8	7.9	9.0	10.3	11.9	14.3	26.4	8.3	0.33
2003	2.5	4.8	5.6	6.6	7.6	8.7	10.0	11.6	13.9	28.6	10.8	0.35
2004	2.5	4.8	5.7	6.6	7.6	8.7	10.0	11.6	14.0	28.6	9.8	0.35
2005	2.3	4.5	5.3	6.2	7.2	8.3	9.5	11.0	13.2	32.6	14.2	0.39
2006	2.3	4.3	5.1	6.0	7.0	8.1	9.2	10.7	13.1	34.0	14.8	0.40
2007	2.1	4.1	4.8	5.7	6.5	7.5	8.6	10.0	12.3	38.4	19.8	0.44
2008	2.4	4.6	5.5	6.4	7.4	8.4	9.6	11.2	13.7	30.9	10.8	0.37
2009	2.5	5.0	5.9	6.8	7.7	8.8	10.1	11.7	14.1	27.5	8.5	0.34

SOURCE: Authors' calculations from Icelandic tax data.

NOTE: Incomes are equivalent disposable income, including capital gains.

0.34 in 2009. Changes of this magnitude are indeed rare, if not unique, in Western countries, at least in the last five or six decades (Atkinson et al. 2011; OECD 2011). The Gini coefficient increased by 52 percent from 1997 to 2007, while in the ten years before the stock market boom—from 1992 to 2002—it increased by 18 percent. The OECD defines a 12 percent or larger increase in the Gini coefficient across ten years as a "strong increase" (Förster and d'Ercole 2005; also OECD 2008). By that standard, the increase in income inequality in Iceland after 1995 clearly lives up to the description of "a very strong increase." The decrease after the bubble burst is, on the other hand, "a very strong reduction" in inequality.

FATE OF DIFFERENT INCOME CLASSES

But how did these changes affect different income classes? We have already seen that the overall income share of the lower and middle decile groups decreased during the bubble years, a decline that started in 1995. As we show below, the real disposable income of all income groups increased after 1995, although the increase was more rapid for the higher-income groups. We therefore analyze further the dynamics of the changes by income groups, looking both at relative and absolute changes.

The changing shape of the income distribution can be analyzed in three ways: by examining the changing income shares of different groups, by taking various income ranges relative to the median (and studying how their size changes), and by assessing changes in real disposable income across income groups. In what follows, we use the latter two to shed light on income changes across the distribution during the boom and bust experienced in Iceland in the last decades (see Chapter 2; also see Atkinson, Rainwater, and Smeeding 1995; Foster and Wolfson 2010).

Even though the people/space measure—the share of total income accruing to a defined part of the population—is popular in the literature, it has some drawbacks. Foster and Wolfson show that the people space is primarily a measure of the *skewness* of the distribution. Although undoubtedly an important aspect of the changing Icelandic income distribution, as we showed above, it is not the whole story. We use the approach developed by Foster and Wolfson to assess how the size distribution of different income classes, defined relative to the median changed in the period in question, reported in Table 15.2 (see also Duclos, Esteban, and Ray 2004).

TABLE 15.2

Percentage of population in various income groups and the Foster-Wolfson index of polarization. Income groups defined as proportions of the median

Year	Below poverty line (<50%)	Lower class (50%–75%)	Middle class (75%–125%)	Upper class (125%–200%)	Very rich (200%+)	Foster-Wolfson index
1992	9	17	43	25	6	0.108
1993	8	16	45	25	6	0.106
1994	7	17	45	25	6	0.104
1995	7	18	45	24	6	0.105
1996	7	19	42	25	7	0.112
1997	7	20	41	25	7	0.114
1998	8	21	39	24	8	0.119
1999	8	21	38	25	8	0.123
2000	8	22	37	25	8	0.125
2001	9	21	37	25	8	0.126
2002	8	22	37	25	8	0.127
2003	9	21	37	24	9	0.129
2004	10	20	37	24	9	0.130
2005	10	21	36	24	9	0.133
2006	10	21	35	24	10	0.136
2007	9	21	36	24	10	0.136
2008	10	19	38	23	10	0.132
2009	9	19	39	24	9	0.126

SOURCE: Authors' calculations from Icelandic tax data.
NOTE: Incomes are equivalent disposable income, including capital gains.

The middle class is defined as those with disposable income between 75 and 125 percent of the median. The lower class is defined as those with 50 to 75 percent of the median, and below poverty line are those with less than 50 percent of the median. Similarly, we get an upper class (125 to 200 percent of the median) and the very rich (200 percent+ of the median). In the last column, we also show the Foster-Wolfson index of polarization.[7]

The fraction of the population with incomes under the relative poverty line increased from about 7 percent in 1994 to 9 to 10 percent from 2001 onward. The lower class (50 to 75 percent of median) moves from 16 percent in 1993 to 21 to 22 percent between 1998 and 2007, before decreasing to 19 percent during the crisis in 2008. The middle class, however, is significantly reduced in size, from about 45 percent to 35 percent at its lowest in 2006, to increase to 39 percent by 2009.

The upper class (125 to 200 percent of median) remains more or less with the same proportion of population, while the size of the group of the "very rich" (200 percent+) increases substantially, from 6 to 10 percent. In

2009 that group still remains at around 9 percent of the population. So we clearly see an increasing number of very high-income earners.

The Icelandic income distribution shows clear signs of increased spread and increased polarization as evidenced by the declining middle class and increases in the sizes of the bottom and top groups. The Foster-Wolfson index of polarization increases from 0.104 in 1994 to 0.136 in 2007, and after the bubble it decreases to 0.126 in 2009. Thus, the Icelandic bubble economy was an extreme affair, as were the changes in the income distribution in the same period.

Real Income Growth Disaggregated by Boom and Bust Periods

One drawback of the above analyses is that they are all based on relative distributions. Taken at face value, they might indicate the fortunes of the lower and middle classes declined during the bubble period. That is, however, misleading. In fact, the real disposable incomes of the Icelandic middle class increased throughout the bubble period, although at a slower pace than those of the higher-income groups. The disposable incomes of the lowest groups also increased, but at the slowest pace of all (Ólafsson 2006a, 2011b; Kristjánsson and Ólafsson 2009; Ólafsson and Kristjánsson 2012). We examine real incomes further in this section.

Table 15.3 shows real income growth for different income groups through the main periods of expansion, recession, boom, and bust. Looking first at the last column, we see the figures for cumulated growth of real disposable income (including capital gains) for the whole period in each income group. This is the net outcome for the whole 15-year period, and the pattern is clear. Income growth is lowest for the three lowest decile groups and increases as one moves up the income ladder. Members of the top decile group outrun all others by far, with a growth rate that is almost six times that of the lowest three decile groups. The top 5 percent further outperforms the top decile group, as does the top 1 percent to a much greater extent still, as we already saw in Table 15.1.

We divide the whole period into four sub-periods. From 1994 to 2000, there was first an expansion period, with economic growth above the OECD average and yearly average real income growth ranging from 3.4 percent (decile group 2) to 8.6 percent (top tenth) and 9.9 percent for the top 5 percent. So the pattern then has a profile that is similar to the total period. The middle 60 percent captured about 47 percent of overall income

TABLE 15.3

Real income growth by income groups, in differing boom and bust periods, 1994–2009. Annual changes by periods (%)

Income groups	1994–2000 expansion	2000–2002 minor recession	2002–2007 boom	2007–2009 bust	Total period 1994–2007
I	4.3	2.3	2.5	−5.3	52
II	3.4	1.2	3.5	−2.7	49
III	3.8	1.3	3.7	−2.9	53
IV	4.3	1.4	3.7	−3.9	59
V	4.9	1.5	3.8	−4.6	65
VI	5.4	1.7	3.8	−4.8	71
VII	5.7	1.6	3.9	−4.9	74
VIII	6.0	1.6	4.1	−5.2	78
IX	6.3	1.8	4.5	−5.8	86
X	8.6	6.7	16.5	−25.8	294
Mean income	6.0	2.9	7.8	−12.3	117
Bottom 20%	3.7	1.6	3.2	−3.6	50
Middle 60%	5.2	1.5	3.9	−4.5	68
Top 20%	7.7	4.9	12.8	−20.6	210
Top 5%	9.9	9.4	20.9	−31.3	426
Income changes captured by bottom 20%	5.2	4.2	2.9	1.9[a]	3.8
Income changes captured by middle 60%	47.2	28.1	23.9	17.0[a]	32.5
Income changes captured by top 20%	47.6	67.6	73.2	81.1[a]	63.7
Income changes captured by top 5%	22.8	52.3	59.0	69.8[a]	45.7

SOURCE: Authors' calculations from Icelandic tax data.

NOTE: Incomes are equivalent disposable income, including capital gains.

[a]These figures refer to declines in real earnings falling on the specified group. The other figures refer to shares of growth captured by the relevant groups.

growth, while the top 20 percent captured 48 percent of growth. The top 5 percent captured about 23 percent of the growth.

The minor recession after the bursting of the high-tech bubble, in 2001–2002, still saw some growth in real earnings in Iceland, in the region of 1 to 2 percent per year for most and nearly 7 percent for the top tenth. The top 20 percent captured about two-thirds of the income growth in those years. Then we enter the height of the bubble economy, from 2002 through 2007. The pattern of growth of real earnings was similar to the 1994–2000 period but more extreme—that is, less marked in the lowest groups and by far the highest among the top 20 percent (12.8 percent compared with 7.7 percent in the former period) and more so among the top 5 percent (20.9 percent compared with 9.9 percent). The top 20 percent captured about 73 percent of the total real income growth in that period compared with 24 percent running to the middle 60 percent and only 2.9 percent going to the bottom 20 percent. The top-income groups were the prime gainers of the bubble period.

As we see from the bust period, 2007–2009, the contraction of real earnings indicated a reversed pattern, with the earnings of the lower groups losing proportionally less than the higher-income groups. The top 20 percent captured over 81 percent of the decline in real equivalized earnings. This was due to both the rapid decline of financial earnings with the collapse of the stock market and the banks, and changed government tax and benefit policy that aimed to shelter the lower-income groups against the vagaries of the crisis (Kristjánsson and Ólafsson 2010; Ólafsson 2011b).

So while we see a significantly larger spread of earnings in Iceland and indeed increased polarization, we also see a significant but differential increase of real disposable earnings for all groups on the upswing. This is interesting, for example, in the context of the increasing inequality in the United States after the early 1980s. In that case, large groups in the lower and middle rungs of the income ladder experienced no or only small increases in their real earnings (Bernstein, Mishel, and Allegretto 2006; Bartels 2008; Krugman 2009). The Icelandic case is thus more favorable to the lower and middle classes, while the top-income groups in Iceland were rapidly approaching the earnings level of the top 10 percent in the United States during the height of the bubble. With continued growth for only a few more years after 2007, Iceland would have reached the same level of inequality as the United States, a notable deviation for a Nordic welfare state (Ólafsson 1999; Kristjánsson and Ólafsson 2009, 2012). With the bursting of the bubble, however, inequality ceased to increase and indeed declined, although it has not returned to the level it was at in 1995, before the ascent of the neoliberal policies and the bubble economy.

THE ROLE OF FINANCIAL EARNINGS

In a bubble economy, financial earnings—interest, rent, dividends, and capital gains—increase and affect the distributions of both income and wealth.

Much of the action is in capital gains, so fewer traces of the bubble are seen in income data that omit capital gains, such as data from the *Luxembourg Income Study (LIS) Database*, the EU-SILC, and the OECD, than in data that include all income sources, such as the tax data used in this chapter. This makes our data well suited to gauge the influence of the bubble on inequality—for example, as we demonstrate in Figure 15.1. The only significant aspect missing is earnings exported to offshore tax havens. That was, apparently, quite common among Icelandic top-income earners during the bubble economy period (PIC 2010). Thus, our data almost certainly understate both the level and inequality of disposable income in the years leading up to the collapse of the financial sector. However, even acknowledging that we underestimate inequality, the changes that we observed were quite dramatic.

In this section, we take a closer look at the role of financial earnings in the whole affair. Table 15.4 shows the share of financial earnings in the gross income of each decile group, in the top 1 percent, and in average income. We thus see both how the share of financial earnings changed over time and how both the share and its change differ across income groups.

TABLE 15.4
*Share of financial earnings in gross income, by deciles, the top 1 percent,
and at the mean income level*

Year	I	II	III	IV	V	VI	VII	VIII	IX	X	Top 1%	Mean
1992	3.3	1.6	2.1	2.1	2.3	2.2	2.0	2.0	2.1	6.6	18.2	3.2
1993	3.0	1.5	2.0	2.2	2.3	2.2	2.0	1.9	2.2	6.3	17.7	3.1
1994	2.3	1.3	1.6	1.7	1.8	1.6	1.6	1.4	1.5	4.6	12.2	2.3
1995	2.6	1.3	1.8	1.8	1.7	1.8	1.6	1.6	1.8	5.1	13.9	2.5
1996	2.6	1.5	1.9	2.1	2.2	2.0	1.8	1.7	2.0	6.8	19.2	3.1
1997	4.0	2.0	2.5	3.1	3.1	2.7	2.4	2.4	2.9	12.0	34.5	5.1
1998	3.5	2.2	2.8	3.3	3.2	2.6	2.3	2.3	2.6	10.2	28.5	4.6
1999	3.6	2.8	3.4	4.3	3.8	3.2	3.2	3.4	3.9	16.2	41.3	6.8
2000	3.7	2.9	3.9	4.6	4.1	3.7	3.4	3.6	4.6	19.2	49.0	8.0
2001	3.9	2.7	4.0	4.6	4.0	3.5	3.4	3.6	3.9	23.7	63.1	9.2
2002	3.9	2.6	3.8	4.0	3.6	3.2	2.9	2.9	3.8	24.1	64.6	9.2
2003	3.6	2.6	3.4	3.9	3.7	3.4	3.2	3.6	4.4	31.3	72.9	11.9
2004	4.3	2.4	3.2	3.9	3.8	3.6	3.8	3.9	5.4	32.0	71.5	12.4
2005	4.7	2.7	3.9	4.4	4.1	3.6	3.7	4.4	5.6	42.3	81.7	16.9
2006	5.1	3.0	4.3	5.3	4.7	4.2	4.4	5.3	7.4	46.3	83.2	19.3
2007	5.1	3.0	4.4	5.5	5.2	5.1	4.9	6.1	8.3	54.0	85.3	24.4
2008	8.8	5.7	7.7	8.7	8.4	8.4	8.5	9.3	11.8	41.8	75.4	19.5
2009	8.8	5.5	7.3	7.9	7.6	7.1	6.9	7.4	8.6	31.4	67.8	14.5

SOURCE: Authors' calculations from Icelandic tax data.
NOTE: Incomes are equivalent disposable income, including capital gains.

The main pattern is that, before 2002, the share of financial earnings was similar across the middle eight decile groups. It was by far the highest in the top tenth, but also higher in the bottom tenth than among the middle 80 percent. The reason for that is probably a rather high proportion of elderly individuals in decile I, who have savings and earn interest income on them. The share of financial earnings in general started to rise modestly beginning in 1996 and gathered speed after 2002. The share of financial earnings rose rapidly in the top tenth from 1996 onward, accelerating markedly at the height of the bubble before collapsing in October 2008. It is also interesting that the share of financial earnings was quite large after the collapse in 2008 and 2009. This was in part due to higher inflation and interest rates during the recession, which raised interest earnings. So the role of financial earnings in the total income among the top tenth is quite marked throughout the years we examine and was especially pronounced during the bubble.

The role of financial earnings for the top 1 percent of income receivers is the most dramatic part of the story. Their financial earnings share was as high as 85 percent of total earnings in 2007, up from 12 percent in 1994. The collapse brought their share down to about 68 percent, the same level as in 2002 and 2003. Despite the extensive financial collapse, the richest in Iceland clearly still own assets that earn financial earnings, which leads us to ask if anything is going to be different in the next upswing. Inequality might increase rapidly again, because financial earnings play such a large role in increasing the earnings of the highest-income groups.

The main lesson of this section is that financial speculation during the bubble economy produced enormous financial earnings that played a very large role in increasing income inequality. The prime beneficiaries of that were the top 10 to 20 percent and especially the top 1 percent. The middle and lower classes, however defined, did not benefit very much from this development. Finally, we examine the role of government policy in inequality changes and particularly in shaping the fate of the middle class through these tumultuous times in Iceland.

GOVERNMENT POLICY—SHIFT OF TAX BURDEN FROM HIGHER- TO LOWER-INCOME GROUPS

A part of the policy programs of successive governments from 1995 to 2007 was to lower the tax burden of firms and investors and to lower marginal income tax rates, as well as the estate duty and property tax. The stated aim was to increase incentives to investors and entrepreneurs and to increase labor supply. In 1997, the government implemented a dual-income tax system with a rate of only 10 percent on financial earnings, which was much lower than the tax on labor and pension incomes and was, in fact, one of the lowest in the OECD (OECD 2010). While lower marginal tax rates on personal incomes were decreased, the main personal income deductions—the personal tax allowance, child benefits, and interest rebates on mortgages—decline in value, thus significantly raising the net tax burden of lower-income households (Ólafsson 2006a, 2007; Baldursson et al. 2008; Kristjánsson 2011a).[8] The policy model from 1995 to 2007 seems to have been moving toward a flat-tax model without any deductions—a model that, if fully implemented, would have raised the tax burden of lower-income groups drastically and lowered the tax burden of the higher-income groups (Hall and Rabushka 1995; Icelandic Chamber of Commerce 2006). The tax system did, indeed, move in this direction, but it was not the stated official policy. The reduced deductions, a form of fiscal drag and bracket creep, went largely unnoticed by both the general public and, for example, unions up until 2006 (Ólafsson 2006a, 2007; Thorláksson 2007).

The effects of these changes of taxation can be seen in Table 15.5, which shows how the net effective tax burden changed from 1996 to 2010 in each income decile group (the estimates are for non-equivalized tax data for couple households). The table also shows the tax burden of the top 1 percent, along with that at average income. We see that the tax burden of the lower- and middle-income groups increased drastically, while the tax burden of the higher-income groups decreased. The reduced tax burden of the top tenth, as well as in the top 1 percent, is the most pronounced change in the net tax burden. Indeed, from 1996 to 2004, the tax burden increased for all groups except the richest tenth. The net tax burden in the highest-income decile decreased from 30.3 percent in 1996 to 23.4 percent in 2004 and 17.1 percent in 2007. The decrease was even larger for the top 1 percent, whose effective tax burden declined from 32.2 percent in 1996 to 13 percent in 2007, before increasing to 20.2 percent in 2009 and 33.3 percent in 2010.

The causes of the changes shown in Table 15.5 are threefold (Kristjánsson 2011a, 2011b). First, the value of the personal allowance as well as child benefits and tax rebates on mortgage interest payments lagged greatly

TABLE 15.5

Net effective tax burden by income groups, 1996–2010

Year	I	II	III	IV	V	VI	VII	VIII	IX	X	Top 1%	Mean income
1996	−6.0	1.1	7.4	12.4	16.4	19.4	21.7	23.9	26.2	30.3	32.2	20.3
1997	−6.0	2.4	8.0	12.4	16.4	19.4	21.9	24.2	26.4	29.0	27.8	20.3
1998	−4.2	4.6	9.9	14.2	17.7	20.3	22.6	24.4	26.3	29.0	27.7	21.1
1999	−1.9	7.2	12.1	15.8	18.8	21.0	23.0	24.6	26.3	27.7	24.5	21.5
2000	−1.4	7.8	12.8	16.6	19.4	21.6	23.3	24.7	26.5	27.2	22.0	21.8
2001	0.8	10.1	14.9	18.3	20.9	22.8	24.4	25.8	27.2	25.9	17.4	22.5
2002	0.4	9.7	14.0	17.4	20.1	22.2	23.9	25.4	26.9	25.1	16.5	21.9
2003	2.2	10.6	14.6	18.0	20.4	22.3	23.9	25.3	26.8	23.5	15.3	21.7
2004	4.1	12.2	15.8	18.8	21.2	23.0	24.5	25.9	27.2	23.4	15.8	22.2
2005	3.1	11.4	15.1	18.4	20.6	22.6	24.2	25.2	26.3	20.2	13.3	20.9
2006	3.3	11.3	14.7	17.9	20.2	22.1	23.5	24.6	25.3	18.8	13.1	20.1
2007	3.0	10.5	13.8	16.7	18.8	20.5	22.2	23.4	24.3	17.1	13.0	18.6
2008	2.1	10.1	13.4	16.1	18.3	20.0	21.6	23.0	23.8	19.5	14.7	19.1
2009	−0.3	8.3	11.9	15.0	17.5	19.5	21.5	23.3	25.0	24.2	20.2	20.1
2010	−3.0	7.0	11.0	14.6	17.5	20.2	22.4	24.5	26.5	30.6	33.3	21.7

SOURCE: Authors' calculations from Icelandic tax data. Total direct taxes paid, net of benefits, as a proportion of gross earnings before tax. Non-equivalized data, all incomes counted. Couples and cohabiting households.

NOTE: Figures show total direct taxes net of benefits received as a proportion of gross income, including capital gains.

behind labor income. That caused an increase in the tax burden for lower- and middle-income groups—the more, the lower the incomes. This happens because a lower personal allowance means a larger portion of earnings is taxed. Child benefits and tax rebates on mortgage interest payments are directly subtracted from calculated income tax. All these subtractions have more weight for lower-income groups—hence their relatively large distributional effect. Second, the marginal tax rate on labor income was lowered, which caused a reduction in the tax burden primarily for higher-income groups. Third, a lower tax rate on financial earnings was particularly important: when the share of financial earnings increased, the tax burden decreased. Because the share increased most for higher-income groups, their tax burden decreased the most.[9]

The reduction in tax burden in higher-income groups was caused both by direct effects (changes in the tax code) and indirect effects (change in the composition of income—that is, the increased share of financial earnings in the highest-income groups). The reason for changes in the latter part of the period is that, in 2006, a public discussion about the roles of the reduced personal tax allowance, child benefits, and mortgage interest rebates led to a change of policy in the Federation of Labour, which then affected the government from the latter part of 2006 (taking effect in 2007). The entry into government of the Social Democratic Alliance in the spring of 2007 also facilitated a change of tax policy in this respect (Ólafsson 2007; Kristjánsson 2011a). The left government that came into power in 2009 further increased the redistributive effect of the tax system by raising the personal tax allowance and benefits as well as increasing the top marginal tax rate in 2010. Thus, major tax policy changes in the direction of greater redistribution were implemented during the crisis.

CONCLUSION

Iceland provides a very interesting test case for examining the effects of an extreme bubble economy on the income distribution. We base our analysis on extensive tax data, covering most of the adult population in Iceland from 1992 to 2010. The bubble economy period reached its height between 2002 and 2007, but the impact of neoliberal policies had begun to be felt starting in 1995. Our data cover the period of growing neoliberal policies, the height of the bubble, and the collapse in 2008 and the crisis in 2009 and 2010.

Income inequality, starting from among the most egalitarian Nordic levels in the early 1990s, increased from 1995 at an unprecedented rate, reaching its peak from 2004 to 2007 and then decreasing from 2008 through 2010 after the bubble had burst. In the early part of the neoliberal period, 1995 to 2002, slower growth of lower incomes, including Social Security benefits, and an increased tax burden at the lower end of the income ladder were the main drivers of increased inequality.

After 1997, when the introduction of the dual-income tax lowered the tax rate on financial earnings to 10 percent and with increased liberalization of the financial market, financial earnings played a rapidly growing role in increasing income inequality. Lower marginal tax rates also contributed to higher inequality before the crisis. By 2007, the Gini coefficient for total disposable equivalized income, including capital gains, had increased to 0.44 percent from 0.26 percent in 1994. Iceland was rapidly approaching U.S. levels of inequality before the bubble burst (Atkinson et al. 2011). In 2008, the year of the banking collapse, the Gini index came down again to 0.37 percent, mainly due to lower financial earnings and also a changed tax and benefit policy. That development continued in the following two years.

Thus, we show that financial earnings, including capital gains, played a particularly large role in the Icelandic financial bubble. Our results suggest that the financial earnings of the higher-income groups should be taken into account when economies are overheated and during large speculative bubbles. Most income distribution data are based on surveys that exclude capital gains, as well as other financial earnings that may grow particularly quickly during bubbles. This applies to data such as those from OECD, Eurostat, and *LIS*. Tax data, however, may allow analysts to measure financial earnings more fully, as is the case in Iceland (see also Atkinson and Piketty 2007, 2010). With the increased frequency of bubbles and financial crises after 1980, financial earnings in general and capital gains in particular may have contributed to much higher inequality than is typically acknowledged in this period of financial globalization (Reinhart and Rogoff 2009; OECD 2011).

Thus, some accounts of inequality trends may have understated inequality increases during the buildup of economic bubbles. Inequality decline may similarly be understated during contractions, as the decline in financial earnings contribute to decreasing inequality. Differences between regulatory regimes may affect inequality and its change differently. It is, for example, interesting to note that income inequality in Ireland does not seem to have increased as much as that in Iceland, even though their respective bubbles shared some characteristics, at least in terms of overheating and excessive debt accumulations (Nolan and Smeeding 2005; Nolan 2007).

One difference between Ireland and Iceland is that from 1995 to 2006, the Icelandic governments contributed to increased inequality significantly by reducing the personal tax allowance, which greatly increased the tax burden of lower-income groups, as well as having Social Security benefits lag behind pay in the labor market, particularly between 1995 and 2003. Judging from OECD's tax and benefits data, this was not the case in Ireland (Ólafsson 2007).

The lower and middle classes were not significant beneficiaries of the bubble economy development compared with higher-income groups. Financial earnings as a share of their total income did not increase decisively. The top 10 percent, and more so the top 1 percent, reaped by far the most. The top groups also received favorable tax treatment from the reigning governments between 1995 and 2006, lowering their effective tax burden drastically. The very low tax on financial earnings of 10 percent is an example of that. At the same time, the tax burden of the middle class, as well as lower classes, was increased.

Government policy thus amplified the trend toward increased inequality beyond what the unrestrained financial market was already achieving. The top-income groups were the main beneficiaries of tax privileges rather than the lower and middle classes.

Iceland's extreme bubble economy thus changed the income distribution in a radical way. The bursting of the bubble in 2008–2009 shifted the distribution again significantly toward more equality. It remains to be seen how the distribution will fare during the next upswing.

NOTES

1. The other three freedoms consist of movement of goods, persons, and services.

2. The reason for the exclusion of capital gains in *LIS*, OECD, and Eurostat data seems to be difficulties in obtaining comparable measures, due, for example, to different taxation rules for treatment of capital gains (cf. The Canberra Group—Expert Group on Household Income Statistics). Some countries do, however, produce income distribution data including capital gains, such as the Nordic nations (Fritzell et al. 2012) and the United States (Atkinson and Piketty 2007, 2010).

3. This chapter uses the term *financial earnings* to denote what is generally called "capital income," and "disposable earnings" to denote what is more often known as "disposable income." This slightly non-standard terminology corresponds closely to Icelandic naming conventions.

4. Figures from Geirsson (1977), Snævarr (1988), and the National Economic Institute (1994–2001) indicate that the Gini coefficient was quite stable in the period from 1960 to 1985. However, these figures are not comparable to the more recent data we are using. See also Jónsson et al. (2001).

5. The Gini coefficient for market income increased marginally from 1988 to 1994, while disposable income decreased significantly (Jónsson et al. 2001).

6. The data in Table 15.1 and other tables in the chapter (except Table 15.5) refer to the equivalized data, while the data in Figure 15.1 refer to couples' households only. These data are presently available to 2010, but the equivalized data are only available up to 2009.

7. The Foster-Wolfson index measures the size of the middle class, which is related to the particular definitions for cutoffs chosen for the middle class.

8. The tax on labor income is a linear one above a tax threshold, from 1993 to 2006, and from 2009 an upper income bracket was reintroduced, which while

in effect in the former period was only paid by the top 15 percent of households. Therefore, the tax threshold is an important factor of the tax system, dictating the equalization effects along with the family benefits.

9. This can be stated formally. The tax burden of a dual income tax is:

$$g = \alpha_L g_L + \alpha_K g_K,$$

where g is the total tax burden and g_L and g_K are the tax burdens of labor and financial earnings, respectively. a_L and a_K are the ratios of labor and financial earnings of gross income. In a dual-income tax system, the tax burden of financial earnings is typically lower than that of a labor income—namely, $g_L > g_K$. So when the share of financial earnings increases, the total tax burden (g) decreases, keeping all else equal. Formally it can be stated as:

$$\frac{\partial g}{\partial \alpha_K} = \alpha_K' [g_K - g_L] < 0, \quad \text{if } g_K < g_L,$$

observing that $-\partial \alpha_L / \partial \alpha_K = \alpha_K'$.

REFERENCES

Aliber, Robert Z., and Gylfi Zoega, eds. 2011. *Preludes to the Icelandic Financial Crisis*. New York: Palgrave Macmillan.

Atkinson, Anthony B., and Thomas Piketty. 2007. *Top Incomes over the Twentieth Century: A Contrast between European and English-Speaking Countries*. Oxford: Oxford University Press.

———. 2010. *Top Incomes: A Global Perspective*. Oxford: Oxford University Press.

Atkinson, Anthony B., Thomas Piketty, and Emmanuel Saez. 2011. "Top Incomes in the Long Run of History." *Journal of Economics Literature* 49(1): 3–71.

Atkinson, Anthony B., Lee Rainwater, and Timothy M. Smeeding 1995. "Income Distribution in European Countries." In *Incomes and the Welfare State*, edited by Anthony B. Atkinson. Cambridge: Cambridge University Press.

Baldursson, Friðrik Már et al. 2008. "Íslenska skattkerfið: Samkeppnishæfni og skilvirkni" (Report on the Icelandic Taxation System—Its Competitiveness and Efficiency). Reykjavík, Iceland: Ministry of Finance.

Bartels, Larry M. 2008. *Unequal Democracy—The Political Economy of the New Gilded Age*. Princeton, NJ: Princeton University Press.

Bernstein, Jared, Lawrence Mishel, and Sylvia A. Allegretto. 2006. *The State of Working America 2006–2007*. Ithaca, NY: Cornell University Press.

Brandolini, Andrea, and Timothy Smeeding. 2009. "Income Inequality in Richer and OECD Countries." In *The Oxford Handbook of Economic Inequality*, edited by Wiemer Salverda, Brian Nolan, and Timothy M. Smeeding. Oxford: Oxford University Press.

Buiter, Willem, and Anne Sibert. 2008. "The Icelandic Banking Crisis and What to Do about It: The Lender of Last Resort Theory of Optimal Currency Areas." Policy Insight 26. London: Center for Economic Policy Research.

Duclos, Jean Yves, Joan Esteban, and Debraj Ray. 2004. "Polarization: Concepts, Measurement, Estimation." *Econometrica* 72(6): 1737–72.

Foster, James, and Michael Wolfson. 2010. "Polarization and the Decline of the Middle Class: Canada and the U.S." *Journal of Economic Inequality* 8(2): 247–73.

Förster, Michael, and Marco Mira d'Ercole. 2005. "Income Distribution and Poverty in OECD Countries in the Second Half of the 1990s." OECD Social, Employment and Migration working paper 22. Paris: OECD.

Fritzell, Johan, Olof Bäckman, and Veli-Matti Ritakallio. 2012. "Income Inequality and Poverty: Do Nordic Countries Still Constitute a Family of Their Own?" In *Changing Social Equality: The Nordic Welfare Model in the 21st Century*, edited by Jon Kvist, Johan Fritzell, Bjørn Hvinden, and Olli Kangas. Bristol, UK: Policy Press.

Geirsson, Finnur. 1977. "Tekjudreifing meðal manna" (Income Distribution amongst Individuals). Occasional report. Reykjavík, Iceland: National Economic Institute (Þjóðhagsstofnun).

Hall, Robert, and Alvin E. Rabushka. 1995. *The Flat Tax*. Stanford, CA: Hoover Institution Press.

Halldórsson, Ólafur G., and Gylfi G. Zoega. 2010. "Iceland's Financial Crisis in an International Perspective." Working paper W10:02. Reykjavík, Iceland: University of Iceland, Institute of Economic Studies.

Icelandic Chamber of Commerce (Viðskiptaráð). 2006. "15% landið Ísland" (Iceland—"the 15% Country"). Occassional report. Reykjavík, Iceland: Viðskiptaráð.

Jónsson, Ásgeir, Ásta H. Hall, Gylfi Zoëga, Marta Skúladóttir, and Tryggvi Þór Herbertsson. 2001. *Tekjuskipting á Íslandi—Þróun og ákvörðunarvaldar (Income Distribution in Iceland—Development and Determinants)*. Reykjavík, Iceland: University of Iceland, Institute of Economic Studies.

Kenworthy, Lane, and Jonas Pontusson. 2005. "Rising Inequality and the Politics of Redistribution in Affluent Countries." *Perspectives on Politics* 3(3): 449–71.

Kindleberger, Charles P., and Robert Z. Aliber. 2005. *Manias, Panics and Crashes: A History of Financial Crises*. London: Palgrave Macmillan.

Kristjánsson, Arnaldur Sölvi. 2011a. "Áhrif breytinga skattkerfisins á skatttekjur, skattbyrði og tekjuskiptingu 1992–2009" (Influence of Changes in the Taxation System on Tax Revenues, Tax Burden and Income Distribution). MSc thesis in economics. Reykjavík, Iceland: University of Iceland.

———. 2011b. "Income Redistribution in Iceland: Development and International Comparisons." *European Journal of Social Security* 13(4): 392–423.

Kristjánsson, Arnaldur Sölvi, and Stefán Ólafsson. 2009. "Heimur hátekjuhó-panna—Um þróun tekjuskiptingar á Íslandi 1993–2007" (Top Incomes—On the Development of Income Distribution in Iceland 1993–2007). *Stjórnmál og Stjórnsýsla* 5(1): 93–121.

———. 2010. "Aukinn ójöfnuður tekna 1995–2007 og umskiptin 2008–9: Greining á þróun tekjuskiptingarinnar" (Increased Inequality of Incomes 1995–2007 and the Conversion 2008–9). *Newsletter* 11: 2010. Reykjavík, Iceland: Social Research Center, University of Iceland.

Krugman, Paul. 2009. *Conscience of a Liberal*. New York: Norton.

Minsky, Hyman Philip. 2008/1986. *Stabilizing an Unstable Economy*. New York: McGraw-Hill. First published 1986 by Yale University Press.

National Economic Institute. 1994–2001. "Tekjur og eignir" (Yearly Reports on Income Distibution and Wealth). Reykjavík, Iceland: National Economic Institute (Þjóðhagsstofnun).

Nolan, Brian. 2007. "Long-Term Trends in Top Income Shares in Ireland, in Atkinson and Piketty." In *Top Incomes over the Twentieth Century: A Contrast between European and English-Speaking Countries*, edited by Anthony B. Atkinson and Thomas Piketty. New York: Oxford University Press.

Nolan, Brian, and Timothy M. Smeeding. 2005. "Ireland's Income Distribution in Comparative Perspective." *Review of Income and Wealth* 51(4): 537–60.

Ólafsson, Stefán. 1999. Íslenska leiðin (The Icelandic Welfare Model). Reykjavík, Iceland: University Press and Social Security Administration.

———. 2006a. "Aukinn ójöfnuður á Íslandi: Áhrif stjórnmála og markaðar í fjölþjóðlegum samanburði" (Increased Inequality in Iceland: Influence of Politics and Markets in a Comparative Perspective). *Stjórnmál og stjórnsýsla* 2(2): 129–56.

———. 2006b. "Breytt tekjuskipting Íslendinga: Greining á þróun fjölsky-ldutekna 1996–2004" (Changing Income Distribution: Analyzing Family Incomes 1996 to 2004). In *Rannsóknir í Félagsvísindum VII*, edited by Úlfar Hauksson. Reykjavík, Iceland: Félagsvísindastofnun/Social Science Research Institute.

———. 2007. "Skattastefna Íslendinga" (Taxation Policy in Iceland). *Stjórnmál og stjórnsýsla* 3(2): 231–63.

———. 2008. "Íslenska efnahagsundrið—Frá hagsæld til frjálshyggju og fjár-málahruns" (The "Economic Miracle" in Iceland). *Stjórnmál og stjórnsýsla* 4(2): 231–56.

———. 2011a. "Icelandic Capitalism: From Statism to Neoliberalism and Finan-cial Collapse." In *Nordic Varieties of Capitalism. Special Edition of Comparative Social Research*, edited by Lars Mjöset. Bingley, UK: Emerald Group Publishing Limited.

———. 2011b. "Iceland's Financial Crisis and Level of Living Consequences." Working paper 3: 2011. Reykjavík, Iceland: Social Research Centre, University of Iceland.

Ólafsson, Stefán and Kristjánsson, Arnaldur Sölvi. 2012. "Áhrif hrunsins á lífskjör þjóðarinnar I" (Effects of Iceland's Financial Collapse on the Nation's Well-Being). Reykjavík, Iceland: Social Research Centre, University of Iceland.

Olsen, Snorri et al. 2004. "Skýrsla nefndar um umfang skattsvika á Íslandi" (Report of a Public Committee into Tax Fraud in Iceland). Reykjavík, Iceland: Ministry of Finance.

Organisation for Economic Co-operation and Development (OECD). 2008. *Growing Unequal?* Paris: OECD.

———. 2010. *OECD Tax Database.* Paris: OECD

———. 2011. *Divided We Stand: Why Inequality Keeps Rising.* Paris: OECD.

Parliamentary Investigation Committee (PIC) into the Collapse of the Icelandic Banks. 2010. Volumes 1–8. Reykjavík, Iceland: Alþingi.

Reinhart, Carmen M., and Kenneth S. Rogoff. 2009. *This Time Is Different— Eight Centuries of Financial Folly.* Princeton, NJ: Princeton University Press.

Snævarr, Sigurður. 1988. "Dreifing atvinnutekna á 9. Áratugnum" (Income distribution during the 1980s). *BHMR tíðindi.* Reykjavík, Iceland: BHM.

Statistics Iceland. 2009. Lágtekjumörk og tekjudreifing 2003–2006. Hagtíðindi (Economic Bulletin) 27(94). Reykjavík, Iceland: Hagstofa Íslands.

———. 2012. Lágtekjumörk og tekjudreifing 2011. Hagtíðindi (Economic Bulletin) 11(97). Reykjavík, Iceland: Hagstofa Íslands.

Stiglitz, Joseph. 2010. *Freefall—America, Free Markets and the Sinking of the World Economy.* New York: Norton.

The Canberra Report. 2001. Expert Group on Household Income Statistics— Final Report and Recommendatins. Ottawa (available at www.lisproject .org).

Thorláksson, Indriði H. 2007. "Skattapólitík: Er skattkerfið sanngjarnt og hvernig nýtast ívilnanir þess?" (Tax Policy). *Stjórnmál og Stjórnsýsla* 3(1): 11–33.

Wolf, Martin. 2010. *Fixing Global Finance.* New Haven, CT: Yale University Press.

CHAPTER SIXTEEN

Horizontal and Vertical Inequalities in India

Reeve Vanneman and Amaresh Dubey

Using the first nationally representative detailed income data for India from the 2005 India Human Development Survey (IHDS), Desai and colleagues (2010) reported Indian income inequality to have the high levels typical for low- and middle-income countries. The IHDS Gini of 0.52 puts India at a similar level as Brazil (0.49) and well above the levels observed even in the most unequal high-income countries included in the *Luxembourg Income Study (LIS) Database*, such as the United States at 0.37 (LIS 2011).

This high level of inequality may have come as a surprise to researchers accustomed to the moderate levels often reported for India. Dreze and Sen (2002) report Ginis for rural areas hovering around 0.30 and for urban areas around the mid-0.30s in the last decades of the twentieth century. Concern has been raised as those coefficients rose recently. Datt and Ravallion (2009), for instance, reported urban Ginis rising to the high 0.30s by the end of the first decade of the century. Compared to those results, a coefficient above 0.50 is startling.

The main international databases have also included Ginis for India in the low to mid-0.30s. Deininger and Squire (1996) report a mean Gini of 0.32 for 31 annual observations between 1951 and 1992. The World Inequality Data Base updates this for India in 2004 to 0.37. But all of these earlier calculations depended on expenditure-based data that usually provide results well below those for income. Deininger and Squire suggest adding 6.6 percentage points to expenditure-based Ginis to provide better comparability with income-based measures. But Atkinson and Brandolini (2001) are skeptical that a uniform additive fix will suffice—a stance that the IHDS results support. Galbraith and Kum (2005) adjust for the

439

downward bias of expenditure surveys and re-estimate Indian Ginis based on projections from consistent UN data on industrial wage inequality. Their mean estimate of 0.48 is thus much closer to the IHDS estimate of 0.52.

Whatever the reason for the discrepancies among the estimates, the lack of income data for India has prevented useful cross-national comparisons. The IHDS data, therefore, come as a welcome addition to available sources. This chapter reports a more detailed examination of Indian income inequality as revealed by the IHDS income data.

India is a widely diverse country of over a billion people, in many ways more comparable to the diversity of Europe than to any single country in Europe. Many Indian states have larger populations than the typical rich country, and one, Uttar Pradesh, would have the second largest population in the *LIS Database* if it were an independent country. In this chapter, we focus on this regional diversity in Indian incomes. State-level variation in incomes is one example of what we call "horizontal inequalities" that can be distinguished from the "vertical inequalities" observed in state economies. Like national differences across high-income *LIS* countries, these horizontal inequalities within India are substantial and have attracted widespread interest.

The IHDS data confirm that the states of India vary widely in levels of development and levels of income inequality. The range of inequality indices lies well within what is usual for low- and middle-income economies, but all Indian states have more inequality than any high-income *LIS* country. Although average incomes vary widely across states, state income levels are not correlated with state levels of inequality, nor do state differences in average incomes account for much of the total income inequality in India. Most inequality is found within states, but there are two distinct types of inequalities: gaps between the middle and the bottom, and gaps between the middle and the top. Across Indian states, the two types are virtually uncorrelated.

DATA

Sample

In 2005, the University of Maryland and the National Council of Applied Economic Research in Delhi fielded a survey of 41,554 households in 1,503 villages and 971 urban neighborhoods across India (Desai et al. 2010). These households included 215,754 people. The sample encompasses 33 states and union territories of India, excluding only the small populations living in the island states of the Andaman and Nicobar Islands and Lakshadweep. One male and one female interviewer administered two questionnaires in 13 local languages, using face-to-face interviews. The respondents included a knowledgeable person regarding the household economic situation (typically but not always the male head of the household). In addition to income, the interview included modules on household employment, consumption expenditure, social networks, education, gender relations, marriage, health, and fertility.

Income

Obtaining accurate household income data in a developing economy such as India's entails well-known difficulties. The IHDS household income measure is derived from over 50 separate survey questions. The amount of income from sources such as monthly salaries is relatively easy to collect. Income from self-employment, either in agriculture or family businesses, is more difficult to measure and yet is quite common in India, far more so than in high-income countries. The IHDS reported that the majority (53 percent) of Indian households received some agricultural income, and 20 percent received income from non-farm businesses and self-employment. Most Indian households receive income from more than one source. Farm households often supplement their incomes with wage labor, both in agricultural and non-agricultural employment. Even non-farm households often keep some animals in rural areas. The variety of income sources and household economic strategies presents a much greater challenge for income measurement in India than is typical in rich-country data. Nevertheless, we believe that these difficulties can be addressed with careful survey methods, and the resulting data, while perhaps not as precise as those for high-income countries, will more than justify the additional effort. Moreover, as this chapter demonstrates, the expansion of the *LIS Database* to countries such as India expands the range of possible comparisons so not only will our research conclusions change, but our research questions will as well.

The IHDS income data used in this chapter are net, equivalized, after-tax annual incomes. Direct taxes in India are only collected from a small proportion of relatively high-income salaried earners who typically report after-tax incomes. In addition to total household income, we include subtotals for the following:

- Wages, including monthly salaries or daily wages, which we further divide into agricultural and non-agricultural daily wages; bonuses and the value of meals or housing received as part of employment are added to the wage totals.
- Agricultural output either marketed or consumed by the household (valued at prevailing local selling prices) or fed to animals owned by the household, less farm operating expenses
- Net non-farm business income after expenses
- Remittances from family members living outside the household
- Dividends and rents received from property (including from agricultural equipment)
- Pensions
- Government transfers, including school scholarships and the major programs operative in 2004–2005: National Old Age Pensions, Widows' Pension Scheme, National Maternity Scheme, National Disability Pension, and Annapurna

Imputed housing rents are not included because rental homes are so uncommon in rural India that it is not possible to calculate meaningful estimates for imputed rents. We also do not include government subsidies for food and kerosene distributed through the Public Distribution System.

We have adjusted all incomes for the official regional price index used for calculating poverty levels across Indian states. This index varies from 0.72 to 1.62 and is particularly important for distinguishing urban and rural areas. The index averages 1.33 for towns and cities and 0.88 for rural areas. State-wise variance is also substantial, from a low of 0.87 in Andhra Pradesh to a high of 1.46 in Delhi (although the next highest state, Maharashtra, averages only 1.19).

Income is aggregated across all household members to define total household income. Households are defined in the IHDS as all individuals who "live under the same roof and share the same kitchen for 6+ months." Extended families are common in India. Over half of all households include at least one member who is not a spouse or child of the household head. Household sizes can therefore be quite large, with a median size of six. Ten percent of Indian households have ten or more persons. We equivalize income across household size by dividing total income by the square root of the number of persons in the household. It is more common in India to use per capita income, so we also provide results using per capita income in the online appendix tables.

Self-employment income will be negative when annual expenses exceed gross income. This is particularly common for farm households when crops fail in a given year. In the IHDS, 8.7 percent of households report negative farm incomes. These households often had positive non-farm income as well, so only 1.3 percent of all households reported negative total income for the previous year. Households with negative income appear substantially better off than other low-income households on long-term measures of economic standing, such as counts of household assets. Because they are so unlike other low-income households, we have omitted these negative-income households from the analyses.

The IHDS also included a modified expenditure module, modeled on a short form from the Indian National Sample Survey (NSS). This module asked for monthly consumption or annual expenditures on 47 types of goods designed to cover all household expenditures and consumption. Poverty estimates derived from these data compare well with the official poverty estimates from the NSS (Desai et al. 2010).

Income measures based on consumption expenditures are often thought to be better measures of economic position because they are less volatile than actual income and because expenditures can be more reliably measured than income. However, survey measures of expenditures have their own measurement problems (for example, respondent fatigue) and volatility (marriages, debts, and health crises can create unrepresentative spikes for some households). But the advantage of the IHDS is that it includes measures of both income and expenditures.

Middle-Income Households

This chapter defines middle-income households as those whose equivalized income is above half and below twice the all-India median. Individuals in households below half the median are defined as poor; those in households with income higher than twice the median are defined as affluent. In practice, this definition is close to defining middle-income as the middle 60 percent of households, because 18 percent of individuals are in households with less than half the median income (i.e., are relatively poor) and 22 percent are in households with more than twice the median income (i.e., are relatively affluent). When comparing inequalities across Indian states, we also repeat for each state the same method for defining poor, middle, and affluent households.

Although this is a conventional definition of relative poverty and affluence, this middle-income group is not what would be considered middle
class in any global sense. Their equivalized annual income ranges from Rs.
(rupees) 6,809 to 27,235; this translates to between USD518 and USD2,071,
using the recent (7.0) revisions of purchasing power parities (PPPs) (Heston,
Summers, and Aten 2011). Most of these households depend on small farms
or wage labor for their living. A more recognizable "middle class" would be
the households identified as "affluent" with incomes more than twice the
Indian median. These households enjoy an average equivalized income of
Rs. 54,451 annually (USD4,141), hardly well-off by OECD standards but
comfortable in the Indian context. Most of these households are based on
income from relatively secure, salaried positions, and most own or aspire
to an array of consumer goods that make them targets for modern marketing. When commentators refer to an emerging market of the Indian middle
classes, it is this "affluent" group that they are thinking of, not the group
we identify as middle-income households for this chapter.

RESULTS

Overall Inequality

Table 16.1 reports the shares of annual equivalized income by the three income classes—poor, middle class, and affluent—and by ten decile groups.
As can be readily seen, incomes are quite concentrated in India. Households
with more than twice the median income, the affluent, receive 61 percent of
income but constitute only 22 percent of all households. The middle-income
group receives only 36 percent of household income in spite of constituting
60 percent of all households. The 90/50 and 50/10 ratios also confirm the
high inequality in India. An individual at the 90th percentile is 3.2 times
better off than the median. And that median individual is 2.7 times better
off than one at the 10th percentile.

The Gini coefficient for these income data is 0.48. This is about average
for other middle-income countries included in *LIS*. It is slightly below Peru
(0.51) and Colombia (0.51), about the same as Brazil (0.49), and slightly
above Mexico (0.46). But these small differences among middle-income
countries are minor compared to the gap between them and the high-income *LIS* countries where the Gini ranges from a low of 0.24 for Sweden
only up to 0.37 for the United States. What is striking in the cross-national

TABLE 16.1
Indian incomes by income class and decile groups

	Maximum	Percentage of population	Percentage of income
By income classes			
Poor	6,807	18	3
Middle	27,235	60	36
Affluent	2,168,054	22	61
By decile groups			
Lowest	5,024	10	1
Second	7,235	10	2
Third	9,162	10	3
Fourth	11,187	10	4
Fifth	13,618	10	5
Sixth	16,880	10	6
Seventh	21,495	10	8
Eighth	29,016	10	11
Ninth	43,672	10	17
Highest	2,168,054	10	41

SOURCE: Authors' calculations from the India Human Development Survey, 2005.

NOTE: Sample is individuals in households with annual income greater than Rs. 1,000 ($N = 211,811$).

comparisons is the stark discontinuity in inequality between the high-income and middle-income countries. The differences among all high-income countries or among all middle-income countries, while interesting, are not nearly as large as the gap between the most unequal high-income country and the most equal middle-income country. Only Russia and Uruguay, officially middle-income countries but with European heritages, have Ginis of 0.43, which partially bridge the gap between the two clusters of inequality results. Nevertheless, even with these somewhat more equal middle-income countries included, there is still no overlap with the greater equality observed in every high-income country. Variation in inequality among high-income countries—and change over time within these countries—has generated an enormous literature. However, that variation seems rather constricted compared with the gap between the equality in rich countries and the inequality in middle-income countries—especially in middle-income countries classified as "lower-middle," such as India.

This discontinuity in income inequality across the world has been observed before. Korzeniewicz and Moran (2009) highlighted it to call for more attention to the ways in which between-country levels of income inequality are linked to between-country levels of income and to histories of linkages among countries in the global system. Galbraith and Kum (2005) used this discontinuity to validate their new calculations of household income inequality based on more internationally comparable UN wage data. We show it is also consistent with variation in inequality across Indian states.

While high by rich-country standards, our estimated Gini coefficient of 0.48 for income is below the IHDS estimate of 0.52 reported at the start of this chapter. The difference between our estimate and the IHDS report derives from our adjustment for regional price differences, which reduces the Gini by 2.7 percentage points, and our use of equivalized rather than per capita income, which reduces the index by another 1.3 points. Moreover, including the negative income households would have increased the Gini by a further 1.5 points. So a Gini of 0.48 is a lower bound of alternative options for calculating Indian income inequality.

We also estimated Gini coefficients using the expenditure data in the IHDS. These expenditure data are equivalized and adjusted for price differences, as were the income measures. As expected, this expenditure Gini index is considerably lower, 0.35, and is comparable to the estimates of Indian income inequality available from most earlier sources based on expenditure data from the National Sample Survey. The large difference between the IHDS income and expenditure Ginis derived from the same sample suggests that income and expenditure Ginis may be even less comparable for middle-income than for high-income countries, perhaps because of the greater volatility of farm, self-employment, and daily wage incomes that predominate in low- and middle-income economies. Once data from the second wave of the IHDS (fielded in 2011–2012) are available, we will be able to study this volatility directly.

Income Sources

The widely disbursed structure of income sources in India is described in Table 16.2. While almost three-quarters of Indian households have some employment on a daily wage or monthly basis, half of all households have some agricultural income, and another fifth of households derive income from their own family business.

Not surprisingly, poor households are over-represented in income sources that typically contribute less income, and affluent households are well represented in income sources that are more generous. Fifty-seven

TABLE 16.2
Structure of Indian household incomes

| | PROPORTION OF HOUSEHOLDS RECEIVING ANY INCOME | | | | |
	Total	*Poor*	*Middle*	*Affluent*	*Median for household with income*	*Gini for household with income*
Wages and salaries	72	68	75	68	21,957	0.488
Salaries (monthly)	29	10	24	57	37,920	0.477
Agricultural wages	29	41	34	7	10,557	0.435
Non-agricultural wages	28	28	34	10	15,749	0.406
Business	20	12	21	27	25,135	0.548
Own farm	52	64	51	45	7,108	0.661
Crops	38	50	36	33	7,596	0.680
Animals	42	51	42	33	1,086	0.581
Remittances	5	5	5	7	11,372	0.555
Rents and pensions	10	5	7	23	13,362	0.583
Government	13	17	13	8	814	0.627

SOURCE: Authors' calculations from the India Human Development Survey, 2005.
NOTE: Sample is all households with annual income greater than Rs. 1,000 ($N = 40,717$).

percent of affluent households, but only 10 percent of the poor, receive monthly salary income; the median salary income for households with any salary income is Rs. 37,920. In contrast, 41 percent of poor families have income from agricultural wages, while only 7 percent of the affluent do, but the average household with such income earns only Rs. 10,557.

Government assistance is primarily useful for the poor, as it should be; 17 percent of poor households receive some form of direct government assistance. Nevertheless, some middle-income (13 percent) and even affluent (8 percent) households also benefit from government payments. These are typically quite modest, however; the average recipient gets only Rs. 814.

Not all income sources show such large differences between the poor and the affluent. Farm incomes are more common among the poor (64 percent of poor households), but neither are they uncommon among the affluent (45 percent), even though farm incomes are typically quite low (Rs. 7108). And incomes from businesses are more common among the affluent (27 percent) but still significant among the poor (12 percent), even though they typically pay quite well (Rs. 25,135).

Private transfers (remittances) from other family members, while received by only 5 percent of all households, benefit Indians at all income levels. Seven percent of the affluent receive remittances, as do 5 percent of the poor and the middle-income households. Although uncommon, when they are present, private transfers can be substantial. The average household that receives any remittances receives Rs. 11,372.

For the most part, middle-income households fall somewhere between the poor and the affluent in their income sources. They are better represented than the poor in high-income sources (e.g., salaries and own businesses) and more common than the affluent among low-income sources (e.g., agricultural wages and farm incomes).

Non-agricultural wages are the one interesting exception to this linear pattern of steadily rising or falling proportions of income sources by income levels. Thirty-four percent of middle-income households have some non-agricultural wages, more than for either the poor (28 percent) or the affluent (10 percent). Accordingly, non-agricultural work pays typically moderate levels of income (Rs. 15,749), more than farm incomes and agricultural wages, but less than own businesses and salaries.

This association of non-agricultural wages with middle-income households is consistent with the usual perception of the skilled working class becoming the foundation for large concentrations of middle-income earners. In higher-income economies, a broad middle-income cluster of households is often based on well-paid steel- and autoworkers, on the skilled construction trades, and on white-collar administrative and clerical workers. This process is only beginning in India, but as more workers move out of farming and agricultural labor into non-agricultural labor, one possible consequence is an expansion of the middle-income groups and an eventual decline in overall inequality. Because most recent trends in Indian inequality statistics, albeit expenditure based, show increasing rather than decreasing inequality, the growth of the middle-income working class must have been offset by other forces that are creating greater inequality.

Income Levels by State

Income varies widely across India. Figure 16.1 shows this range at the district level. IHDS samples are quite small at the district level, and districts without data were estimated by interpolation, so caution must be used in interpreting any individual district estimate.[1] But the general pattern is clear, and the results are familiar: high income in the northwest (Punjab, Haryana, Delhi, and Himachal Pradesh) and along the west coast (Gujarat,

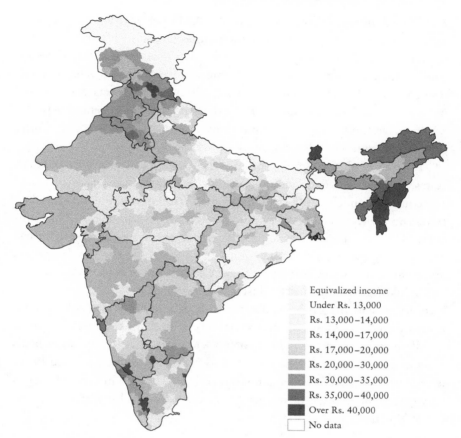

Figure 16.1.   Income levels by Indian districts, 2004

SOURCE: Authors' calculations from the India Human Development Survey, 2005.

coastal Maharashtra, Goa, and Kerala). Perhaps somewhat more surprising are the high incomes in the Northeast, but this is consistent with the high levels of education and government employment there. Lower incomes characterize central India: eastern Uttar Pradesh, Bihar, Orissa, and much of Madhya Pradesh.

More reliable income estimates can be calculated at the state level. In 2005, India had 35 states and territories, but many of these are quite small, as are the IHDS samples. For the purposes of these analyses, we merge small states with larger neighboring states to calculate incomes across 22 "state-like" regions.[2] The range in median incomes is substantial: from Orissa with a median equivalized income of Rs. 9,315 per year to the Northeast states at Rs. 31,812 per year, over three times Orissa's level. The rankings of average state incomes have been reasonably stable for decades. There are some notable exceptions, such as the impressive rise of Himachal Pradesh over the last half century (Dreze and Sen 2002) and the recent good performance of Rajasthan and Madhya Pradesh in the post-reform era (Ahluwalia 2000). Nevertheless, the relative positions of most states have changed little since India achieved independence.

In spite of this threefold variation in average incomes across Indian states, there is no overlap with median incomes from other middle-income *LIS* countries, much less with high-income *LIS* countries. Figure 16.2 illustrates this consistent gap between India and other middle-income *LIS* countries. While the addition of middle-income Latin American countries has dramatically extended the range of average incomes in the *LIS Database*, all Indian states are at notably lower levels than any other *LIS* country.

While Figure 16.2 clearly illustrates how the discontinuities in average incomes extend the range of income comparisons now available in *LIS*, it also demonstrates substantial variability within India and even within middle-income countries. The income variation across Indian states is almost as great as across high-income *LIS* countries, only at a much lower level. The difference between a household in Poland and in Luxembourg is very great, but so is the difference between a household in Orissa and one in the Northeast.

Inequality by State

Our main interest, however, is in the levels of income inequality across Indian states. There is again significant variation, comparable to the variation among high-income *LIS* countries. Those comparisons are illustrated in Figure 16.3, where Indian states and *LIS* countries are organized from low to high incomes as in Figure 16.2. Within India, Gini coefficients extend from Chhattisgarh (0.38) and Delhi (0.39) to Karnataka (0.52) and Kerala (0.54). This range is even greater than for the differences between Sweden (0.24) and the United States (0.37). But, again, what is most obvious in Figure 16.3 is that while the range of inequality across Indian states may be comparable to the range of inequality across high-income *LIS* countries, the entire range for high-income countries is at a much lower level of inequality. Thus, there is variation in inequality within the Indian states (and within

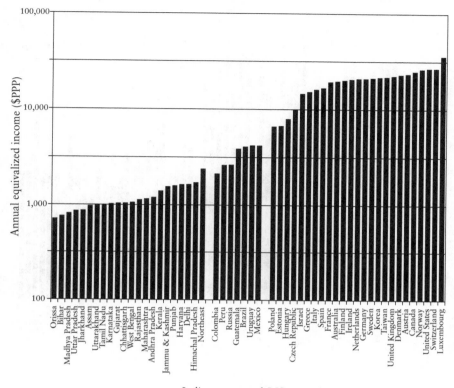

Figure 16.2. Income levels across Indian states and *LIS* countries, around 2004

SOURCE: *LIS* Key Figures, Wave VI, and authors' calculations from the India Human Development Survey, 2005.

high-income *LIS* countries), but this variation is dwarfed by the variation between the rich countries as a group and the Indian states as a group (and indeed between high-income and middle-income countries in general).

Despite the dramatic association between low income level and high income inequality when comparing India with high-income countries, within India or within high-income countries, there is almost no relationship. Within India, higher-income states have almost the same average levels of inequality as lower-income states ($r = -0.04$). This is even weaker than the slightly negative correlation found among high-income countries ($r = -0.19$). But if we were to combine all the Indian states with all the

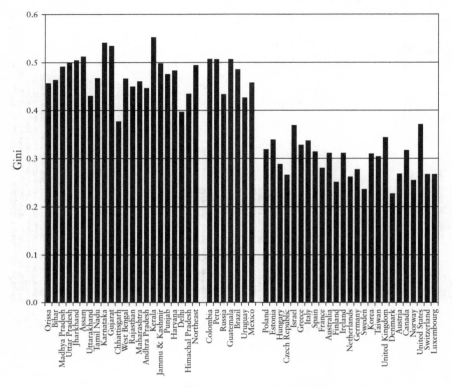

Indian states and *LIS* countries

Figure 16.3.   Income inequality across Indian states and *LIS* countries, around 2004

SOURCE: *LIS* Key Figures, Wave VI, and authors' calculations from the India Human Development Survey, 2005.

middle-income and high-income *LIS* countries, the relationship between median incomes and income inequality jumps to –0.83!

Figure 16.4 illustrates the problems of investigating variation within India or within high-income *LIS* countries. The dramatic difference between the two groups of observations and the lack of any discernible difference within each group demonstrate how discontinuous the relationship is between average income levels and income inequality. And the figure also illustrates how different a perspective there is now that the *LIS Database* has expanded to include middle-income countries.

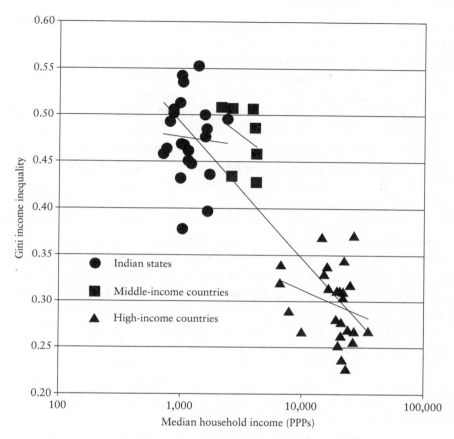

Figure 16.4. Income levels and income inequality across Indian states and *LIS* countries, around 2004

SOURCE: *LIS* Key Figures, Wave VI, and authors' calculations from the India Human Development Survey, 2005.

The Proportion of Middle-Income Households across States

Within India, more unequal states with higher Ginis have, by definition, fewer middle-income households and more poor and affluent households (as defined separately in each state). Across the 22 states, the correlation of the Gini index and the proportion of households that fall in the middle-income group is predictably negative ($r = -0.62$). But a larger middle-income group can arise from either fewer poor or fewer affluent households. Interestingly, there is almost no relationship between concentrations at the two ends of the income spectrum. States with many poor households may or may not have many affluent households. The correlation is weak ($r = +0.20$). A similar conclusion is drawn by comparing 90/50 ratios with 50/10 ratios across Indian states; that correlation is a negligible ($r = -0.03$). States with a large gap at the top of the income distribution (between the middle and the affluent above them) may or may not show a large gap between the middle and the poor below them. The low correlation suggests that the social and economic processes that generate inequality at the top seem to be different from the processes that generate inequality at the bottom.

In fact, a small proportion of *relatively* poor households is not always a blessing. For example, in states where a majority of households engage in landless labor, that concentration of low paid labor reduces even median incomes because even "average" households must depend on this low-income source. But a lower median income means fewer households will fall below half the median, our definition of relatively poor. If half of all households are landless, the average (median) household is not doing very well, even though there are smaller differences among the bottom half. This is exactly what happens across Indian states: the correlation of how many households have agricultural wage income with the proportion of relatively poor households is strongly *negative*, $r = -0.73$. The 50/10 income gap is also *lower* in these states with much landless labor ($r = -0.59$) because the 50th percentile is pulled down even more than the 10th percentile when the majority of households perform low paid agricultural labor.

A similar process works at the top of the income spectrum, with contrasting results. In states where many households secure well-paid monthly salaries, those household incomes raise the median level, making it less common for households to earn more than double this higher median, our definition of relatively affluent. So the proportion of salaried households in a state is somewhat negatively correlated with the proportion of affluent ($r = -0.15$) and with the 90/50 ratio ($r = -0.48$).

Thus, what drives up inequality at the top is a *small* proportion of relatively well-off households earning good salaries from steady public and private sector jobs, while almost everybody else has to make do with low-paid daily wages or low-income farm production. What drives up inequality at the bottom is a *small* proportion of landless laborers concentrated at the bottom of the income spectrum, most of whom earn less than half the median income. As the proportion of landless labor increases, their low absolute income levels become relatively more common, so there is less inequality.

Conversely, low-income households are more common if there are either many salaried or many landless labor households. While it may be more desirable to have more salaried than more landless households, the effect on inequality is similar. Because the economic and social forces that drive up landlessness are quite different from those that increase salaried positions, there is no consistent relationship between inequality in the top half of the income distribution and inequality in the bottom half.

The practical lesson for analyses of Indian income inequality is that we must analyze inequality at the top separately from inequality at the bottom. The two are quite distinct. And, of course, we must pay attention to absolute levels of income while we are comparing relative levels.

Nevertheless, it bears repeating that from a global perspective, all Indian states have low average incomes, and all are highly unequal. While we need to understand the differences in inequality among India's regions (as well as the changes over recent years in inequality and whether the recent increases are related to the recent growth in average levels), within the context of global inequality, the Indian differences are relatively minor. Of course, the same can be said for analyzing the differences in inequality across high-income *LIS* countries. From a global perspective, such analyses are investigating only a small range of global inequality.

Finally, given the large state differences in average incomes shown in Figure 16.2, one might expect that this regional inequality accounts for a substantial part of total Indian income inequality. However, the large state-specific inequality indices shown in Figure 16.3 are about as large as overall, national income inequality, implying that most Indian inequality is within states. Decomposing inequality indices such as the Theil index confirms this. For India as a whole, the Theil index is 0.455, but the between-states inequality accounts for only 5.5 percent of the total Indian inequality.

CONCLUSION

The expansion of the *LIS Database* to include India and several other middle-income countries around the world introduces a global perspective that will profoundly affect the types of questions that can be asked and the kinds of answers that will result. Indian income inequality is an order of magnitude greater than in high-income *LIS* countries and is more similar to inequality in the Latin American *LIS* countries, such as Brazil and Peru. There are regional variations in income inequality within India as there are within the high-income *LIS* countries, but the principal fact to be explained is not the inequality variation within these groups of economically similar countries but the enormous gap in inequality between high-income countries on the one hand and low- and middle-income countries on the other.

While from this global perspective, income inequality is fundamentally shaped by country income levels (and, undoubtedly, vice versa) within India, there is little systematic relationship between state levels of income and the extent of income inequality within the state. Some of the wealthier states have high inequality, and some have low inequality. Some poor states have high inequality, and some have low.

Moreover, we need to distinguish at least two distinct types of inequality across India. Some states have more inequality and a smaller middle-income cluster because of a large gap between the middle and the bottom; others have a smaller middle-income cluster because of a larger gap between the middle and the top. A large gap between the middle and the bottom implies a larger group of *relatively* poor households receiving less than half the median income. Somewhat paradoxically, these are states with relatively small proportions of households who depend on agricultural labor. As the proportion of households with agricultural wage income expands to a majority of households, the state's median income declines, and there is more consistency of low incomes across the entire bottom half of the income distribution. Similarly, a smaller proportion of prosperous salaried-income households creates a large gap between them and the average household and, thus, more inequality at the top. As the proportion of salaried households increases, there is a wider spread of good incomes across the top of the spectrum and, thus, less inequality at the top. But the size of the two sectors, the landless and the salaried, are quite independent of each other; thus, across Indian states, inequalities at the top are uncorrelated with inequalities at the bottom.

Regional variation in income levels within India is also substantial. The higher-income states have three times the income of the lower-income states. Nevertheless, these state differences in income levels account for only a minor proportion of national income inequality. Most income inequality in India is within states. In other words, horizontal inequalities are substantial but are still small relative to vertical inequalities within states. And even the threefold variation in state incomes across India covers only a small portion of the global variation in household incomes.

The expansion of *LIS* to India and other middle-income countries in general will force a global perspective on researchers who have been constrained in the past to investigate differences only among high-income countries. And the availability now of income data for India removes the illusion based on expenditure data that India has only moderate levels of inequality. There is literally a world of new questions waiting to be asked.

NOTES

1. IHDS sampled approximately half the districts in India. Moreover, the rural and urban samples used different sampling frames. Income levels were calculated separately for urban and rural samples, and estimates for districts without data were calculated by interpolating from the mean of neighboring districts. An estimate for the total district was calculated from a weighted average of the urban and rural estimates, using Census 2001 urban proportions.

2. Seven smaller northeastern states are collapsed into a single "Northeast." Goa is included with Maharashtra, Daman, and Diu, as well as Dadra and Nagar Haveli with Gujarat, Chandigarh with Punjab, and Pondicherry with Tamil Nadu. Lakshadweep and the Andaman and Nicobar Islands are not included in the IHDS.

For additional results, please see the online appendices by following the link in the listing for Income Inequality *on the Stanford University Press website: http:// www.sup.org.*

REFERENCES

Ahluwalia, Montek S. 2000. "Economic Performance of States in Post-Reforms Period." *Economic and Political Weekly* 35(17): 1637–48.

Atkinson, Anthony, and Andrea Brandolini. 2001. "Promise and Pitfalls in the Use of Secondary Data-Sets: Income Inequality in OECD Countries as a Case Study." *Journal of Economic Literature* 39(3): 771–99.

Datt, Gaurav, and Martin Ravallion. 2009. "Has India's Economic Growth Become More Pro-Poor in the Wake of Economic Reforms?" Policy research working paper 5103. Washington, DC: World Bank.

Deininger, Klaus, and Lyn Squire. 1996. "A New Data Set Measuring Income Inequality." *World Bank Economic Review* 10 (3): 65–91.

Desai, Sonalde B., Amaresh Dubey, Brij Lal Joshi, Mitali Sen, Abusaleh Shariff, and Reeve Vanneman. 2010. *Human Development in India: Challenges for a Society in Transition.* New Delhi: Oxford University Press.

Dreze, Jean, and Amartya Sen. 2002. *India: Development and Participation.* New Delhi: Oxford University Press.

Galbraith, James K., and Hyunsub Kum. 2005. "Estimating the Inequality of Household Incomes: A Statistical Approach to the Creation of a Dense and Consistent Global Data Set." *Review of Income and Wealth* 51(1): 115–43.

Heston, Alan, Robert Summers, and Bettina Aten. 2011. Penn World Table Version 7.0. Philadelphia: Center for International Comparisons of Production, Income and Prices at the University of Pennsylvania. http://pwt.econ.upenn .edu/php_site/pwt_index.php.

Korzeniewicz, Roberto Patricio, and Timothy Patrick Moran. 2009. *Unveiling Inequality: A World-Historical Perspective.* New York: Russell Sage Foundation.

LIS Inequality and Poverty Key Figures. 2011. http://www.lisdatacenter.org (multiple countries; microdata last accessed in July 2011). Luxembourg: LIS.

CHAPTER SEVENTEEN

Post-Apartheid Changes in South African Inequality

Murray Leibbrandt, Arden Finn, and Ingrid Woolard

A prominent stylized fact to emerge from cross-national studies of income distribution is that South Africa is one of the most unequal countries in the world. This is especially true when measures of the country's income disparity are compared to high-income countries; South Africa's Gini coefficient in the late 2000s stood at close to 0.70, compared to the Organisation for Economic Co-operation and Development (OECD) average of about 0.32 (OECD 2011). However, inequality in the country is also higher than in other middle-income countries such as Brazil, China, and India, with Gini coefficients of around 0.55, 0.41, and 0.38, respectively (OECD 2011).

This chapter maps out the key dimensions of income inequality in South Africa over the post-Apartheid era. It does this using data from the first wave of the National Income Dynamics Study (NIDS) in 2008[1] and benchmarking this contemporary picture with the situation as it was in 1993, as measured using data from the Project for Statistics on Living Standards and Development (PSLSD).[2] Both are regular living standards measurement instruments with similar income and expenditure modules. Wherever possible, we use both the income and the expenditure data from these two sources to examine whether these two measures provide a consistent picture.

The chapter then presents an assessment of data comparability. After we clearly define the nature of the 1993 and 2008 datasets that are to form the basis of the comparison, we present, in the third section, an overview of income and expenditure inequality in the two years. Our results indicate conclusively that inequality has increased over the post-Apartheid period, both overall and within each racial group. We also show significant

459

increases in the shares of income coming from social grants for individuals in the lower-income decile groups. Given this, in the fourth section, we use an income source decomposition of the Gini coefficient to examine the importance of different income sources in driving inequality in each of the two years. This shows that unequal access to labor market incomes and inequality of these labor market incomes were the key drivers of aggregate inequality in 1993 and remain so in 2008.

While there are many ways in which to decompose and analyze inequality, it is understandable that the most common feature of post-Apartheid studies is the focus on changes in inequality by racial group. We maintain this tradition in the analysis, the fifth section, using new methods to ensure that measured between-group contributions are comparable over time. This exercise shows that the between-race component of inequality has fallen. Finally, we focus on the middle class in South African society, where middle class is simply shorthand for those in decile groups three through eight. This focus allows us to examine some of the key factors determining entry and exit from the middle groups into the top and bottom decile groups, in both 1993 and 2008. This is useful in highlighting how key factors that allocate individuals across the income distribution—such as race, education, and location—changed over time.

THE CONSTRUCTION OF INCOME AND EXPENDITURE MEASURES

Quantitative comparisons of well-being over time are useful only to the extent that they are based on data that are comparable, an issue addressed in this section. A comprehensive overview of the sampling and fieldwork, and the construction of the income and expenditure variables in the 1993 data are described in PSLSD (1994). The sampling and fieldwork for the 2008 data are described in Woolard, Leibbrandt, and Villiers (2010). The derivation of the 2008 summary income and expenditure variables are described, respectively, in Argent (2009) and Finn and colleagues (2009). Here, we discuss some of the key factors that could confound comparisons over time and explain how the income and expenditure variables were adjusted to make them consistent. This is not a trivial exercise. Although the 1993 and 2008 datasets have income and expenditure modules that are broadly consistent with each other, the fact that we are comparing different cross-sectional datasets over a 15-year period means that methodological differences could cloud a naive comparison of income and expenditure measures.

Starting with the measurement of income and expenditures, the questionnaires in both 1993 and 2008 asked respondents to report on incomes that they received during the 30 days preceding the interview and about expenditures during "last month." The advantage of measuring incomes and expenditures in this way is that it mitigates the recall bias associated with asking for annual figures. The main drawback to this approach is that it may mask large one-off incomes or expenditures—for example, inheritance income or funeral expenses—that affect household welfare dramatically. In this regard, individual incomes and expenditures are smoothed before being aggregated to a household-level figure.

In both 1993 and 2008, a single individual answered all of the questions pertaining to expenditures. However, the same is not true for incomes. In the 1993 survey, a single individual answered all questions relating to the income of all members of the household, whereas in 2008 each member of the household answered individual income questions. The result is that the 2008 data are likely to provide a superior measure of income due to less measurement error. However, it is difficult (if not impossible) to determine the size and direction of the biases arising from these different approaches without designing a survey explicitly for this purpose. There is more room to actively promote comparability by carefully assessing the comparability of all the component variables that are aggregated into total income and expenditure. The two most important variables in this regard are implied rental income and income from agricultural sources.

The treatment of implied rental income and expenditure is always challenging (Deaton 1997; Deaton and Zaidi 1999), and this difficulty is enhanced when comparing the 1993 and 2008 datasets. Individuals who occupy homes that they own (or, more precisely, do not rent) enjoy an implicit income stream from this that roughly equals the difference in the market rent of the home and the costs associated with owning it. The inclusion of implied rental income is important to ensure that the household income of owner-occupiers does not understate their economic well-being. However, the implied rental incomes in the 1993 data were imputed using a rule-based approach, combining a set rate of return with the price of the house, while the 2008 figures were calculated by using a regression-based approach that tried to more broadly capture the true opportunity cost of living in one's own house (Argent 2009). Unfortunately, it is not possible to apply a uniform method to estimate the implied rental income across both datasets, and including these figures as they currently stand would lead to significant differences that are driven by differences in methods.[3] For this reason, we omit the implied rental income from both the income and expenditure analyses in this chapter.

As far as income from agricultural sources is concerned, the 1993 data contain a number of very high household-level agricultural incomes that clearly belong to commercial farmers. In the 2008 survey, commercial farmers were not included in the agricultural income module. The consequence of this is that the distributions and summary statistics of agricultural income for the two datasets are not comparable in any meaningful way, and these are also excluded from the analysis of inequality in this chapter. For a more comprehensive overview of the comparison of the 1993 and 2008 agricultural income variables, see Leibbrandt and colleagues (2010).

Given the exclusion of these two factors, aggregate household income was defined as the sum of five broad components: income gained through the labor market (for both wage earners and the self-employed) net of tax, income received in the form of various government grants, remittance income received, income of a capital nature, and all "other" income.

Although income is by far the most common basis for measures of inequality, it is also instructive to analyze the distribution of household expenditures. Abstracting from measurement error, income and expenditures should generally be consistent in the data and should capture approximately the same level of household welfare.

Once implied rental and subsistence agriculture figures are removed from total household expenditures, the 1993 and 2008 datasets are broadly comparable. In both cases, total household expenditure is made up of the sum of food and non-food expenditures, which themselves are divided into smaller sections in the questionnaires in both years.

A DESCRIPTIVE COMPARISON OF 1993 AND 2008 INCOME AND EXPENDITURE INEQUALITY

Having settled on comparable data for the comparison of well-being over time, in this section, we provide initial summary statistics of the key changes in incomes and expenditures. Throughout the chapter, to measure each household member's well-being, we assign to each member the household's income and expenditures, equivalized using the square root of household size. All estimates are weighted using sampling weights.[4]

Mean and median real incomes and expenditures by racial group between 1993 and 2008 are shown in Table 17.1. Mean real equivalized household income increased over the 15-year period, as did mean expenditures. For both income and expenditures, however, the real equivalized median decreased—and quite substantially in the case of expenditures. In fact, a comparison of the distributions of expenditures between 1993 and 2008 reveals a leftward shift at the lower end of the expenditure distribution and a rightward shift at the top. That is, the 2008 expenditure distribution is not as narrow as the one in 1993, which explains how the mean increased over the time period but the median did not. This dynamic is not mirrored in the distributions of income (see Figure 17.A1 in the online appendix), which overlap to a greater extent and reveal clear rightward shifts at the bottom of the income distribution and a leftward shift at the top.

The deep racial disparities of South African society are evidenced once again by the data, with African mean equivalized income increasing from R1,173 to R1,537 in real terms, while the corresponding figures for whites are R8,149 and R10,685. For Africans, the ratio of the share of income to the share of the population increased over the 15-year period from 0.52 to 0.58. We return to a more detailed analysis of the role of race in South African inequality later in the chapter when we conduct within-race and between-race decompositions.

We provide breakdowns of the components of aggregate household income in South Africa by income decile group for 1993 and 2008, respectively (see Figure 17.1, panels A and B). This is an important part of identifying what the differences are in the composition of household income at both extremes of the distribution, and, as is clear in the figures, this changed significantly over time. The main driver of the compositional change was the increasing share of government grants in household income for those in the lowest decile groups. It appears that income from these grants has crowded out remittances to a certain extent. For the poorest tenth, the share of government grants increased from 7 percent in 1993 to about 64 percent in 2008. The importance of earnings for the highest decile groups is obvious, and it is interesting to note the nearly linear increase in the share of labor market earnings from decile groups one to nine in 2008.

TABLE 17.1

Income and expenditure summary statistics overall and by racial group, 1993 and 2008

	1993 mean income	2008 mean income	1993 median income	2008 median income	1993 mean expenditures	2008 mean expenditures	1993 median expenditures	2008 median expenditures
African	1,173	1,537	762	843	1,140	1,242	893	620
Colored	2,346	2,780	1,919	1,682	1,878	2,659	1,590	1,453
Asian/Indian	4,435	8,195	3,061	4,205	3,701	6,811	2,809	4,300
White	8,149	10,685	6,519	7,072	5,986	9,125	5,147	6,141
Overall	2,244	2,659	1,037	1,021	1,880	2,236	1,108	780

SOURCE: Authors' calculations from 1993 PSLSD data and 2008 NIDS data.

NOTE: Figures are in 2008 rands and are based on equivalized income and expenditure data.

A

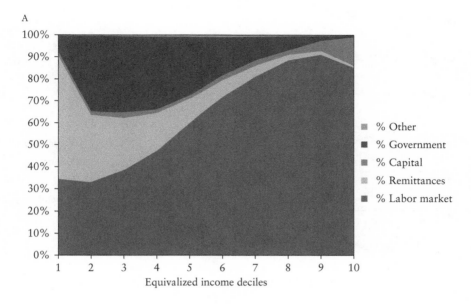

B

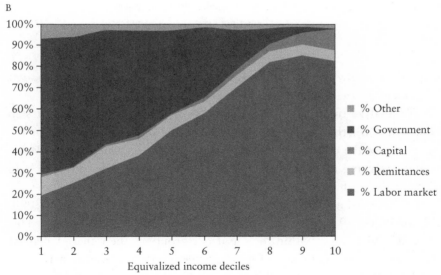

Figure 17.1. Composition of income by decile group, 1993 and 2008

SOURCE: Panel A: authors' calculations from 1993 PSLSD data. Panel B: authors' calculations from 2008 NIDS data.

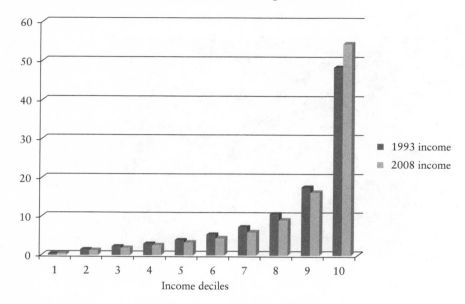

Figure 17.2.   Shares of total income by decile, 1993 and 2008
SOURCE: Authors' calculations from 1993 PSLSD data and 2008 NIDS data.

Capital income was a small component in both years, although it stood at 10 percent for the wealthiest tenth in 2008.

To analyze the dynamics of inequality more finely, a good first step is to assess whether or not income has become more concentrated at the upper end of the distribution. We do this by reporting the share of overall income accruing to each decile group and then comparing the figures in 1993 to those of 2008 (Figure 17.2). The results indicate that income has become increasingly concentrated in the wealthiest tenth. In fact, in 2008, the wealthiest 10 percent accounted for 54 percent of total income. This trend is evident even within the top decile group, as the richest 5 percent maintain a 40 percent share of total income, up from about 33 percent in 1993. Furthermore, the cumulative share of income accruing to the poorest 50 percent dropped from 10.78 percent in 1993 to 9.79 percent in 2008. These findings are consistent with Bhorat, Westhuizen, and Jacobs (2009), who used data from the Income and Expenditure surveys of 1995 and 2005.

To examine whether income inequality in South Africa increased across the board between 1993 and 2008, we show in Figure 17.3 the Lorenz

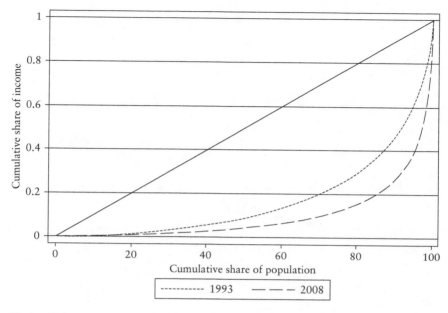

Figure 17.3.   Income Lorenz curves for total income, 1993 and 2008

SOURCE: Authors' calculations from 1993 PSLSD data and 2008 NIDS data.

curves for both years (Fields 2001). The closer a curve is to the 45-degree line of perfect equality, the more equal the income distribution. The Lorenz curves do not cross one another anywhere, and the 2008 curve is further away from the 45-degree line, thus confirming that the income distribution in 2008 was strictly more unequal than that in 1993.

The Lorenz curves for each racial group in 2008 are shown in Figure 17.4. Inequality is highest amongst Africans, followed by coloreds, and then whites.[5] As the Asian/Indian Lorenz curve crosses all the others, we cannot say much about overall Asian/Indian inequality relative to the other groups, based on this analysis. Leibbrandt, Woolard, and Woolard (2009) show that this was the inequality ranking in 1993 as well.

Lorenz curves can become unwieldy in studying changes in inequality by race between 1993 and 2008. We now estimate the Gini coefficients of both incomes and expenditures in 1993 and 2008 for each racial group and for the country as a whole (Table 17.2). The overall Gini coefficient of income rose from 0.61 to an extremely high 0.65 between 1993 and 2008.

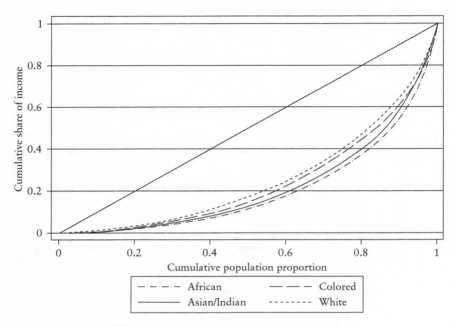

Figure 17.4. Income Lorenz curves by race, 2008
SOURCE: Authors' calculations from 2008 NIDS data.

As expected from the Lorenz curves, inequality is in most instances highest among Africans and lowest among whites, which complements the findings of Bhorat and colleagues (2009), who used data from different years for South Africa.

The 2008 income and expenditure measures are more consistent with each other than were those from 1993. In fact, the 1993 measures of equivalized expenditure inequality are very low (comparatively). This is not unusual in a developing country context. For example, as shown in Chapter 16, the expenditure Gini coefficient is far lower than the income Gini coefficient, based on the 2005 Indian data. However, the fact that this was the case in South Africa in 1993 but not in 2008 makes the measured *increase* in expenditure inequality over time much larger than that in incomes. As discussed above, this may be because the expenditure measure in 1993 was not as accurate as it was 15 years later, but this is conjecture.[6]

TABLE 17.2
Inequality measures overall and by racial group, 1993 and 2008

GINI COEFFICIENTS

	INCOME		EXPENDITURES	
	1993	2008	1993	2008
African	0.49	0.56	0.37	0.57
Colored	0.40	0.51	0.35	0.55
Asian/Indian	0.45	0.58	0.34	0.54
White	0.40	0.49	0.30	0.46
Overall	0.61	0.65	0.51	0.66

GENERALIZED ENTROPY MEASURES

	INCOME				EXPENDITURES			
	1993 GE(0)	2008 GE(0)	1993 GE(1)	2008 GE(1)	1993 GE(0)	2008 GE(0)	1993 GE(1)	2008 GE(1)
Overall	0.73	0.83	0.75	0.89	0.44	0.84	0.47	0.91
African	0.46	0.58	0.44	0.64	0.24	0.57	0.24	0.66
Colored	0.31	0.47	0.27	0.49	0.22	0.54	0.22	0.57
Asian/Indian	0.38	0.66	0.47	0.60	0.19	0.57	0.22	0.51
White	0.31	0.46	0.32	0.42	0.15	0.39	0.16	0.40
Within	0.43	0.56	0.37	0.54	0.23	0.55	0.21	0.54
	57.86%	67.48%	49.68%	60.61%	50.76%	65.24%	43.32%	59.23%
Between	0.31	0.27	0.38	0.35	0.22	0.29	0.27	0.37
	42.14%	32.52%	50.32%	39.39%	49.24%	34.76%	56.68%	40.77%

SOURCE: Authors' calculations from 1993 PSLSD data and 2008 NIDS data.

AN INCOME SOURCE DECOMPOSITION OF SOUTH
AFRICAN INEQUALITY

As we have seen, there have been large changes in the income packages in 2008 compared with 1993 across decile groups. This analysis can be extended to unpack how the relative importance of these sources has changed in driving the aggregate increase in inequality. One of the strengths of the Gini coefficient is that it allows for the assessment of the importance of different income sources in determining overall inequality. Although this exercise can be conducted on expenditure components, too, the usefulness of this approach is not as readily apparent as that using income sources, and we do not undertake this exercise here.

As described in Leibbrandt and colleagues (2009), the key aspects of the method can be summarized as follows. If South African society is represented as n households deriving income from K different sources or components, then Shorrocks (1983) shows that the Gini coefficient (G) for the distribution of total income can be derived as:

$$G = \sum_{k=1}^{K} R_k G_k S_k,$$

where S_k is the share of source k income in total income (i.e., $S_k = m_k/m$); G_k is the Gini coefficient measuring the inequality in the distribution of income component k; and R_k is the Gini correlation coefficient of income from source k with total income.[7]

The larger the product of these three components, the greater the contribution of income from source k to total income inequality. While S_k and G_k are always positive and less than 1, R_k can fall anywhere on the interval $[-1, 1]$. When R_k is less than zero, income from source k is negatively correlated with total income and thus serves to lower the overall Gini measure for the sample.

The results of this decomposition for 1993 and 2008 are presented in Table 17.3, and they suggest that it is the labor market that is the driving force behind inequality. The proportion of households receiving income from the labor market hovered at just over 70 percent in 1993 and 2008, while the real mean monthly household income from this source was largely unchanged. The share of labor market income in the overall Gini coefficient is very high at between 85 and 88 percent. Relating back to the decomposi-

TABLE 17.3
Decomposing the Gini coefficient by income source, 1993 and 2008

Income source	Percentage of HHs receiving income source	Mean HH monthly income from source	Percentage share in total income	Gini for income source for HHs receiving source	Gini for income source for all HHs	Gini correlation with total income rankings	Contribution to Gini of total income	Percentage share in overall Gini
1993								
Remittances	24.2	157	3.1	0.52	0.88	-0.10	0.00	-0.5
Capital income	9.7	437	8.7	0.72	0.97	0.83	0.07	11.6
State transfers	21.9	273	5.4	0.28	0.84	0.03	0.00	0.2
Labor market	73.4	4,154	82.4	0.56	0.68	0.95	0.53	88.3
Total		5,043	100.0		0.60		0.60	99.7
2008								
Remittances	14.0	287	5.4	0.75	0.96	0.65	0.03	5.2
Capital income	7.8	416	7.9	0.61	0.97	0.83	0.06	9.7
State transfers	46.8	386	7.3	0.43	0.73	-0.03	0.00	-0.2
Labor market	71.9	4,148	78.8	0.64	0.74	0.95	0.56	84.9
Total		5,263	100.0		0.65		0.65	99.5

SOURCE: Authors' calculations from 1993 PSLSD data and 2008 NIDS data.

tion formula, the reasons for this are twofold. First, income from the labor market is the most significant contributor to total household income—that is, the S_k for earnings is high. Second, even if members of a household have paid employment, the distribution of income within the labor market is very unequal—that is, its G_k if high.

The biggest change in the composition of household income has been the fact that the share of households receiving income from state grants more than doubled between 1993 and 2008. Income from this source increased as a share of total household income from 5.4 percent to 7.3 percent and also increased significantly in real terms. As shown in earlier figures, it was households in the lowest decile groups that experienced a surge in income from government grants. However, despite income from government grants generally accruing to the poor in South Africa, the increasing level of income from the state has not changed this factor's importance in overall inequality. The very weak correlation between state transfers and total household income seems to suggest that these transfers are effectively reaching poorer households as grant recipients. Despite this, it appears that state grants had a neutral impact on overall inequality in the country (see final column). The most plausible explanation for this is that many of those receiving grants are, through receipt of the grant, shifted up from the bottom of the income distribution and into the lower-middle sections. This would explain the non-negative correlation between state grants and aggregate household income.

As shown by Lerman and Yitzhaki (1994), the Gini coefficient for a particular income source (G_k) is driven by the inequality among those earning income from that source (G_A) and the proportion of households who have positive income from that source (P_k), or, more accurately, *the proportion of households with no access* to a particular income source $(1 - P_k)$. Explaining this with respect to the 1993 situation, it can be seen that:

$$G_{\text{wage}} = P_{\text{wage}}G_A + (1 - P_{\text{wage}}) = (0.73)(0.56) + (1 - 0.73) = 0.41 + 0.27 = 0.68.$$

In this case, 40 percent of the contribution of wage inequality is due to the fact that 27 percent of households have zero wage income, and 60 percent of the wage inequality is due to the inequality among the 73 percent of households that do have access to some wage income.

By 2008 this same decomposition is as follows:

$$G_{\text{wage}} = P_{\text{wage}}G_A + (1 - P_{\text{wage}}) = (0.72)(0.64) + (1 - 0.72) = 0.46 + 0.28 = 0.74.$$

The aggregate wage income Gini coefficient has increased. This outcome reflects both the increase in the share of zero wage income households (to 28 percent) and an increase in inequality among the 72 percent of households that do have access to wage income. The net shares of these two components of wage income inequality are similar in the two years at 38 percent and 62 percent, respectively.

A BETWEEN-RACE AND WITHIN-RACE DECOMPOSITION OF SOUTH AFRICAN INEQUALITY

Although the Gini coefficient is decomposable by income sources, it is not additively decomposable across population groups, which is an advantage of the generalized entropy (GE) class of inequality indices. A population-group decomposition is illuminating in assessing how much inequality is due to differences between groups as opposed to within groups. The GE measures range from 0 (perfect equality) to any higher number representing increasing inequality (Duclos and Araar 2006). Different members of the class are distinguished by the parameters α, which captures varying degrees of inequality sensitivity. A low value of α implies greater inequality sensitivity to income changes at the bottom end of the distribution, while a high value is more sensitive to changes at the top. For the purposes of this chapter, as in most work on the subject, α is 0 (also known as the Theil L Index or the mean log deviation) or 1 (also known as the Theil T Index).

The estimates for both income and expenditure, shown below the Gini coefficients in Table 17.2, also suggest that inequality in South Africa increased between 1993 and 2008. It is also noteworthy that the 2008 GE(0) and GE(1) measures for income and expenditures are very close to each other, which is not the case for the 1993 data, but is what we found for the Gini coefficient.

Inequality within racial groups increased, by all measures, with African income inequality displaying the strongest upward trend. As noted above, the GE measures are additively decomposable into within- and between-group components. The latter is interpreted as what inequality would be if everyone were assigned the mean income of their group, and the former as the inequality that would remain if differences between groups were eliminated (Cowell and Jenkins 1995). Such a decomposition is particularly interesting for an analysis of the changing contribution of race in South African inequality.

We see that, in both years, inequality within each racial group is most often a larger contributor to overall inequality than inequality between the groups, but that within-group inequality increased between 1993 and 2008. For example, looking at the GE(1) measure for income, we see that inequality within racial groups accounted for about 50 percent of overall inequality in 1993 and that this had increased to almost 61 percent by 2008.

Comparing between- and within-group changes in inequality over time, as in Table 17.2, is a standard technique in the academic literature. However, a recent paper by Elbers and colleagues (2008) suggests that conventional methods need to be extended to get a more accurate understanding of how between-group inequality changes over time. The authors argue that varying underlying population structures confound the ability to compare traditional between-group inequality measures. That is to say, traditional between-group measures are implicitly not unit free because they are based on the number and relative sizes of the selected groups (in our case, race). Another way of thinking about this is that in Table 17.2 we calculate the contribution of between-group inequality to total inequality by taking the ratio of between-group inequality to total inequality (0.31/0.73, as in column 1, for example).

Total inequality can be thought of as "the between-group inequality that would be observed if every [individual] in the population constituted a separate group" (Elbers et al. 2008). Elbers and colleagues argued that comparing measured between-group inequality for a small number of groups (four in this chapter) against a much larger benchmark (about 40,000 and 28,000 for 1993 and 2008 data, respectively) biases the conventional measures downward.

The new proposed measure complements the traditional approach by assessing what the ratio is between measured between-group inequality and the maximum possible level of between-group inequality that can be counterfactually constructed from the data while retaining the same number of observations, the same number of groups, and the same relative sizes of the different groups. The advantage of this measure is that it allows for a more natural comparison of inequality across different times and settings because the measure itself is normalized by parameters that are present (and changing) in the data.

Calculating the denominator of the measure involves reassigning individuals to four non-overlapping groups that maintain the relative sizes of the original racial groups. So, for example, in the 2008 data, the population shares were approximately 79 percent, 9 percent, 3 percent, and 9 percent for Africans, coloreds, Asians/Indians, and whites, respectively. The household per capita income data are then sorted and assigned to groups A, B, C, and D, where group A receives the lowest 79 percent of the sorted data, group B the next 9 percent, and so on. Inequality is then decomposed into within- and between-group components for this new distribution, and the new "maximum possible" level of between-group inequality is recorded and compared to the "measured" level present in the data. This implies that, when comparing 1993 with 2008, we interpret the measured level of inequality relative to the maximum possible level that could be achieved at each point in time, while keeping the number of groups, their sizes, and the distribution of income constant.

As shown in Table 17.4, between 1993 and 2008, there was a significant decline in the measured between-group income inequality as a proportion of the maximum possible. However, the figures remain very high and serve to temper the results in Table 17.2. While one might be tempted to say that "only" 39 percent of overall income inequality was made up of between-group dynamics in 2008, according to the GE(1) measure in Table 17.2, the new measure shows that the income distribution in South Africa in 2008 was almost 50 percent of the maximum possible level of inequality, given the conditions outlined earlier. Nevertheless, the findings using this new method complement those using the traditional method qualitatively by providing some evidence that inequality between racial groups is less pervasive than it was in 1993, even though it is still very high. The conclusion, then, is that inequality change in South Africa is being driven by growing inequality within racial groups in general and within the African population specifically.

Mean and median expenditures in Table 17.1 show much more modest increases than those for income do between 1993 and 2008. The 2008 expenditure figures are roughly consistent with the corresponding income figures at between 47 and 51 percent. Therefore, the source of the difference is the fact that the 1993 expenditure figures differ substantially from the 1993 income figures, with a much lower contribution of between-group inequality according to this new measure.

TABLE 17.4

Measured "between inequality" as a percentage of maximum possible, 1993 and 2008

ALL RACIAL GROUPS

INCOME				EXPENDITURES			
1993 GE(0)	2008 GE(0)	1993 GE(1)	2008 GE(1)	1993 GE(0)	2008 GE(0)	1993 GE(1)	2008 GE(1)
64.16	45.90	68.42	49.30	70.05	47.22	72.27	50.57

WHITE/NON-WHITE GROUPS ONLY

INCOME

1993 GE(0)	2008 GE(0)	1993 GE(1)	2008 GE(1)
69.99	47.42	70.78	46.93

SOURCE: Authors' calculations from 1993 PSLSD data and 2008 NIDS data.

Perhaps the key schism in South African society lies along the white/non-white line, rather than between each population group. Elbers and colleagues (2008) used data from the South African Income and Expenditure Survey of 2000 and found that taking a broader partition of only two groups (white and non-white) raised the inequality observed as a proportion of maximum possible to 80 percent. This is far higher than the 56 percent they found when the division is made according to four population groups.

Our findings, using data from 1993 and 2008, show that the white/non-white division is starker than the division into four population groups (see Table 17.4). However, the increase in observed between-group inequality is not as significant as that found in Elbers and colleagues (2008). White/non-white between-group inequality as a percentage of the maximum possible decreased substantially between 1993 and 2008. This suggests that the white/non-white division may have been the key division along which to analyze racial inequality in the past, but its ability to provide a distinctly different dynamic to a four-way population group division has decreased markedly over time.

INEQUALITY AND THE MIDDLE CLASS

Operationalizing the concept of the "middle class" in the South African context is a challenging task and is worthy of a separate study in itself. The heavily skewed nature of the income distribution toward the richest tenth means there is not much difference between the income accruing to households in what could loosely be defined as "poor" decile groups and that accruing to households in the "middle" decile groups.[8] To tease out some of the drivers allocating the population into these middle decile groups, rather than the bottom or the top tenths, we use household income per capita as the variable of interest in defining who falls into the middle of the income distribution. Rather than taking different cutoff points relative to the overall median of the distribution,[9] we divide households into decile groups and define the middle class as consisting of the middle 60 percent. In the ordered probit discussion at the end of this section, we adjust this definition to include households in quintile groups (rather than decile groups) two, three, and four. Given our definition of the middle class, this section discusses how middle-class inequality changed between 1993 and 2008 and then analyzes some key characteristics of middle-class households through the use of an ordered probit model.

As discussed earlier, the equivalized household income distribution shifted slightly rightward for much of the bottom and a small part of the top. The relationship between the middle and the two ends of the distribution between 1993 and 2008 shows the very top of the distribution moving farther away from the median, as the 90/50 ratio increased, while the 50/10 ratio decreased. The share of total income among the middle class decreased from 32 percent in 1993 to 27 percent in 2008. This is reflected in Figure 17.2, which shows that all decile groups, except for the very richest, received declining shares of total income over the relevant time period.

The broad characteristics of those in the middle class in both 1993 and 2008 differed significantly from the rest of the population but were fairly consistent over the 15-year period. Africans are over-represented, and all other races are under-represented relative to overall population shares. In fact, in 1993, over 91 percent of households in the middle class were African, while under 1 percent were white. By 2008, the share of Africans in the middle class had dropped slightly but was still above the African population share. The urban-rural divide in the middle class was fairly evenly split in 1993. By 2008, urban households dominated the composition of the middle class at 64 percent of this group. This reflects both a distribution neutral increase in the urban population share, as well as the fact that urban areas contributed more heavily to both the top and bottom ends of the income distribution. Leibbrandt and colleagues (2010) showed that rural-urban migration resulted in an increasing urban share of South African poverty over time. This is consistent with these developments in the lower tail of the middle class. The education shares of those in the middle class remained consistent over time. Individuals with little or no education are over-represented in the middle class, while individuals with a matric or tertiary education are far less likely to be found in decile groups three to eight.[10] The male-female shares in the middle class closely reflect those of the population at large, as expected.

So far, the discussion of the middle class has focused only on the unconditional shares of various groups in each decile group. However, there is extensive overlap in these unconditional statistics on race, space, and education. For example, relatively poorly educated Africans are over-represented in rural areas. Given this, it is informative to control for other features and look instead at the probabilities of falling into the middle-class category, given certain individual and household characteristics. We apply a similar procedure to that of Diamond, Simon, and Warner (1990)[11] by examining the changing relationship between household characteristics and the probability of being in a particular income quintile group over time. This enables us to describe how the correlates of being in the middle class—income quintile groups two, three, and four—changed between 1993 and 2008.

The probabilities of interest are generated from an ordered probit model that was run with the five income quintile groups as the dependent variable. Controls included household size; province; an urban dummy variable; a dummy variable for whether at least one household member was employed; and the household head's age, race, gender, and level of education.[12]

The results of the ordered probit model can be presented in a variety of ways. We have chosen to report the predicted probability of a household being in the middle class, given certain characteristics. To this end, we construct a measure of the predicted probabilities of being in quintile groups two, three, and four by the household head's race, the household head's education, and whether the household is in a rural or an urban area. This is predicted on the basis of the ordered probit results while holding all other control variables constant at their means.

Table 17.5 presents the results of this analysis. At the level of household head's education, we see a consistent decline in the probability of being in the middle class for all levels of education. This increased spread operates in a downward direction for those households headed by an individual with 12 or fewer years of education. However, for households headed by a person with tertiary education, the probability of migration away from being in the middle class tends strongly upward, toward the richest fifth. In fact, in calculations not shown, the probability of one of these households being in the top quintile group increased from 22 percent in 1993 to 52 percent in 2008. This is striking, particularly given that all of the other variables are held constant.

For African, colored, and white households, the probability of being in the middle class remained the same. For Asian/Indian-headed households, there was a decrease in the probability of being in the middle class, with most of the movement into the top fifth. These relatively stagnant conditional probabilities on the basis of race reflect the fact that inter-racial inequality is highly persistent even when controlling for other factors. For

TABLE 17.5
*Predicted probabilities of being in the
middle class, 1993 and 2008*

	1993	2008
Education		
No education	76.41	73.79
Primary	77.72	76.26
Incomplete secondary	81.67	81.01
Matric	82.22	78.55
Tertiary	75.38	47.85
Race		
African	78.49	78.63
Colored	82.20	81.60
Asian/Indian	78.33	74.91
White	65.45	66.18
Geotype		
Urban	82.26	81.59

SOURCE: Authors' calculations from 1993 PSLSD
data and 2008 NIDS data.
NOTE: Predicted probabilities from an ordered
probit model while holding all other control variables
constant at their means.

urban households, the probability of being in the middle class remained at
about 82 percent during the time period under study.

CONCLUSION

An inter-temporal comparison of economic inequality is only useful if it is
based on accurate and comparable data. Both the 1993 PSLSD survey and
the 2008 NIDS survey were explicitly designed to measure economic well-
being, and there is much about these surveys that makes them useful for
comparative analysis of inequality. Nonetheless, the second section of the
chapter details a number of specific assumptions that were made to increase
the comparability of these datasets. Even after these changes, we noted that
2008 incomes and expenditures were closer to each other than the respective 1993 figures.

Having defined the data, we then focused on measuring the changes in
aggregate income inequality between 1993 and 2008. These data show that
South Africa's high aggregate level of income inequality increased between
1993 and 2008. The same is true of inequality within each of South Africa's
four major racial groups. A major driver of this increasing inequality is the

increased share of income (and expenditure) going to the top tenth. This agrees with our decompositions that show a declining between-race component of inequality over the post-Apartheid period.

From a policy point of view, it is important to flag the fact that intra-race—and in particular intra-African—inequality trends play an increasingly influential role in driving aggregate inequality in South Africa. The majority of the population is beginning to exert majority influence, and we must pay increasing attention to policies that stem and reverse the increasing inequality within each racial group and especially within the African group. For example, we showed that the contemporary South African labor market operates in a way that is not facilitating the equalization of incomes either across racial groups or within racial groups. Indeed, rising inequality within the labor market—due both to rising unemployment and rising earnings inequality—lies behind these rising levels of aggregate and within-group inequality. On the other hand, we showed how important social grants (mainly the child support grant and the old-age pension) have become to those in the bottom half of the income distribution. Our income source decompositions suggest that access to these grants shifts many South Africans away from the bottom of the distribution into the lower-middle decile groups.

That said, the between-race component of South African inequality is still at world-record levels and a stark reminder of the lingering footprint of Apartheid. In addition, these between-group and within-group decompositions are at best indicative, as is well illustrated by the fact that our decomposition analysis using expenditures implies a more muted increase in within-race inequality than that suggested by our income data.[13] The key point to note is that the direction of these between-group and within-group changes is not inexorable but is the product of actual socio-economic developments in the post-Apartheid period.

We highlighted the negative role of the labor market and the positive role of social grants in this regard. We conclude by estimating an ordered probit model to highlight changes over time in the factors allocating individuals into or out of the middle class. This complements the existing analysis by showing that, even conditionally, rising within-race inequality makes race a poorer predictor of being in the middle class in 2008 compared with 1993. In 2008, all racial groups except the white group have members with increased probabilities of moving up and out of the middle class and other members with increased probabilities of moving down and out of the middle class. Education has a similar bifurcating effect in 2008 relative to the 1993 situation, with tertiary education being shown to unambiguously push people out of the middle class to the top of the distribution and all other levels of education pushing people below the middle class.

NOTES

The authors acknowledge financial support for this chapter from the National Income Dynamics Study in the South African Presidency and from the Social Policy Division of the OECD. Murray Leibbrandt acknowledges the Research Chairs Initiative of the Department of Science and Technology and National Research Foundation for funding his work as the Research Chair in Poverty and Inequality. The authors are particularly grateful to the editors of this book, to Michael Förster of the OECD Social Policy Division, and to Charles Meth of the Southern Africa Labour and Development Research Unit (SALDRU) for detailed written comments.

1. This dataset is now included in the *Luxembourg Income Study (LIS) Database*.

2. The chapter draws heavily on the working paper by Leibbrandt and colleagues (2010).

3. If we include this component in each wave, inequality of equivalized household income rises from 0.61 to 0.62 in 1993 and remains at 0.65 in 2008.

4. See Project for Statistics on Living Standards and Development (1994) for a description of the derivation of weights in the 1993 survey, and Wittenberg (2009) for a description of the weights in the 2008 survey.

5. Respondents are classified by racial groups according to Statistics South Africa guidelines. In South Africa in general, "black" refers to all people who were classified as "non-white" under Apartheid. This can be further broken down into three groups: African, colored, and Asian/Indian.

6. To assess the robustness of these coefficients, we derived bootstrapped standard error for these Gini coefficients (not reported here). The standard errors are very small relative to the Gini coefficients and relative to the change in the Gini coefficients. This implies that we are confident that the sample data imply significant increases in overall inequality as well as within each racial group between 1993 and 2008. See Duclos and Araar (2006) for a description of the derivation and use of these standard errors.

7. R_k is a form of rank correlation coefficient, since it measures the extent to which the relationship between Y_k (the income from source k) and the cumulative rank distribution of total income coincides with the relationship between Y_k and its own cumulative rank distribution.

8. For example, in the 2008 data, the proportion of total income lying in the second decile group is 1 percent, while the corresponding proportion for the fifth decile group is 3.4 percent. The percentage difference in mean household per capita between decile groups two and five is about the same as between decile groups nine and ten.

9. For example, using the commonly cited definition of the middle class as those households with incomes falling within the range of 75 and 125 percent of the overall median would limit our "middle class" to between 15 and 20 percent of the overall population. Such is the extent of income disparity.

10. "Matric" refers to the final (12th) year of schooling in South Africa.

11. However, we address the question using an ordered probit rather than a multinomial logit model.

12. All regressions were weighted using census-raised weights (1993) and post-stratification weights (2008) and report robust standard errors.

13. The analysis of Bhorat and colleagues (2009) suggests that this increase may actually have stalled.

For additional results, please see the online appendices by following the link in the listing for Income Inequality *on the Stanford University Press website:* http://www.sup.org.

REFERENCES

Argent, Jonathan. 2009. "Household Income: Report On NIDS Wave 1." *NIDS* technical paper. Cape Town, South Africa: University of Cape Town, Southern Africa Labor and Development Research Unit.

Bhorat, Haroon, Carlene Van Der Westhuizen, and Tougheda Jacobs. 2009. "Income and Non-Income Inequality in Post-Apartheid South Africa: What Are the Drivers and Possible Policy Interventions?" *Development Policy Research Unit* working paper 09/138. Cape Town, South Africa: University of Cape Town.

Cowell, Frank, and Stephen Jenkins. 1995. "How Much Inequality Can We Explain? A Methodology and an Application to the United States." *Economic Journal* 105(429): 421–30.

Deaton, Angus. 1997. *The Analysis of Household Surveys: A Microeconometric Approach to Development Policy.* Baltimore: Johns Hopkins University Press.

Deaton, Angus, and Salman Zaidi. 1999. *Guidelines for Constructing Consumption Aggregates for Welfare Analysis (Living Standards Measurement Study Working Paper).* Princeton, NJ: Princeton University Press.

Diamond, Charles, Curtis Simon, and John Warner. 1990. "A Multinomial Probability Model of Size Income Distribution." *Journal of Econometrics* 43(1–2): 43–61.

Duclos, Jean-Yves, and Abdelkrim Araar. 2006. *Poverty and Equity: Measurement, Policy and Estimation with DAD.* New York: Springer.

Elbers, Chris, Peter Lanjouw, Johan Mistiaen, and Berk Özler. 2008. "Reinterpreting Between-Group Inequality." *Journal of Economic Inequality* 6: 231–45.

Fields, Gary S. 2001. *Distribution and Development, A New Look At the Developing World.* Cambridge, MA: MIT Press.

Finn, Arden, Simon Franklin, Malcolm Keswell, Murray Leibbrandt, and James Levinsohn. 2009. "Expenditure: Report on NIDS Wave 1." *NIDS* technical paper. Cape Town, South Africa: University of Cape Town, Southern Africa Labor and Development Research Unit.

Leibbrandt, Murray, Ingrid Woolard, Arden Finn, and Johnathan Argent. 2010. "Trends in South African Income Distribution and Poverty since the Fall of Apartheid." *Social, Employment and Migration* working paper 101. Paris: OECD.

Leibbrandt, Murray, Chris Woolard, and Ingrid Woolard. 2009. "Poverty and Inequality Dynamics in South Africa: Post-Apartheid Developments in the Light of the Long-Run Legacy." In *South African Economic Policy under Democracy,* edited by Janine Aron, Brian Kahn, and Geeta Kingdon. Oxford: Oxford University Press.

Lerman, Robert, and Shlomo Yitzhaki. 1994. "Effect of Marginal Changes in Income Sources on U.S. Income Inequality." *Public Finance Review* 22(4): 403–17.

Luxembourg Income Study (LIS) Database, http://www.lisdatacenter.org (multiple countries; microdata last accessed in July 2011). Luxembourg: LIS.

Organisation for Economic Co-operation and Development (OECD). 2011. *Divided We Stand: Why Inequality Keeps Rising.* Paris: OECD.

Project for Statistics on Living Standards and Development. 1994. *South Africans Rich and Poor: Baseline Household Statistics.* Cape Town, South Africa: University of Cape Town, Southern Africa Labor and Development Research Unit.

Shorrocks, Anthony. 1983. "The Impact of Income Components on the Distribution of Family Incomes." *Quarterly Journal of Economics* 98(2): 311–26.

University of Cape Town, Southern Africa Labor and Development Research Unit. National Income Dynamics Study (NIDS). 2008. Wave 1 dataset. http://www.nids.uct.ac.za/home/.

University of Cape Town, Southern Africa Labor and Development Research Unit. Project for Statistics on Living Standards and Development. 1993.

Statistical dataset. http://www.datafirst.uct.ac.za/catalogue3/index.php/
catalog/5.

Wittenberg, Martin. 2009. "Weights: Report on NIDS Wave 1." *NIDS* technical
paper. Cape Town, South Africa: University of Cape Town National Income
Dynamics, Southern Africa Labor and Development Research Unit.

Woolard, Ingrid, Murray Leibbrandt, and Louise De Villiers. 2010. "The South
African National Income Dynamics Study: Design and Methodological Issues." *Studies in Economics and Econometrics* 34(3): 7–24.

Conclusion

Janet C. Gornick and Markus Jäntti

In this Conclusion, we highlight key lessons learned regarding the substantive issues addressed as well as the adequacy of available data. We suggest some extensions to the research reported in this book, and we offer ideas for future research.

WHAT HAVE WE LEARNED—SUBSTANTIVELY?

Income Inequality and the Middle Class

The first key lesson that emerged from this book is that it is crucial to "look inside" aggregate changes in inequality to clarify where in the distribution changes have been located. Multiple countries could display similar aggregate changes, but those changes may have come about in diverse ways. Across countries, increased (or decreased) overall inequality could be due to varying patterns of "upgrading" (households moving up), "downgrading" (households moving down), or both. This type of disaggregation is especially meaningful in the context of policy making, as increases in inequality located in the bottom of the distribution, for example, may be viewed as of greater concern than increases closer to the top.

Other key lessons concern the interplay between inequality and the economic status of households in the middle of the income distribution. First, it is important to recognize that the answer to the question "How is the middle class doing?" depends on which definition of the middle class is used. Conclusions drawn from income-based definitions may differ from those drawn from classifications based on occupation, wealth, and/or other

487

non-income factors. Second, we learned that it is not self-evident that increased income inequality, within a country, is associated with adverse effects on the real income level of the middle class—as is sometimes assumed. Third, we learned that the relative economic prospects of different birth cohorts vary substantially across countries—and that this variation seems to have institutional roots.

Overall, we learned from Parts I and II that cross-national variation in the shape of inequality change suggests that, despite many countries being subject to broadly similar technological changes and economic shocks, some of the factors that drive inequality shifts are clearly country-specific. This means that, apart from worldwide changes that affect labor markets and macro-economies, within-country changes in institutions, demography, and other factors play important roles in shaping inequality outcomes. Identifying which factors are driving inequality levels and trends is, of course, crucial for understanding how high and/or rising inequality can be mitigated.

Politics

Politics influence income inequality, and inequality, in turn, influences politics, as reported in the studies in Part III. The findings reported in this book suggest, specifically, that different forms of participation affect inequality in different parts of the distribution. By examining redistribution over a period of decades, the findings also suggest that redistribution has almost, but not quite, kept up with increases in pre-tax and pre-transfer inequality across the *LIS* countries. Both electoral turnout and, in particular, union density, appear to be important channels through which the position of the middle class can be affected. Examination of the reverse question—how preferences for redistribution at the individual level are formed—suggests that individuals' own expectations and income positions, as well as overall patterns of inequality, affect preferences for redistribution in complex and sometimes unexpected ways, depending on country-specific circumstances.

Gender, Employment, and Household Income

The studies in Part IV suggest that, across the *LIS* countries, rising employment and/or earnings by wives—and female partners more generally—tend to *decrease* inter-household inequality of labor income. That finding, supported by the decompositions and counterfactual analyses reported here, is at odds with what is often assumed: that women's rising engagement in the labor market *increases* inter-household inequality.

In addition, the research presented in this section underscores that institutions matter, and in intricate ways, with respect to women's employment outcomes. Specifically, the final study in Part IV finds that strict labor market regulation (i.e., employment protections) has a downward effect on wives' contributions to household income, suggesting that women workers may be over-represented among labor market "outsiders"—most likely as an indirect result of their disproportionate responsibility for unpaid work at home.

Wealth

Income alone provides an incomplete picture of living standards, as is demonstrated in Part V. Other important components of economic well-being include living arrangements and their financing; the extent to which income is maintained following retirement; and how current disposable income is allocated to finance housing, savings for future expenditures (such as children's higher education and retirement income), and current consumption. The study of wealth levels and portfolio compositions, as well as the joint distribution of income and wealth, illuminates an expanded picture of economic well-being.

The study that addresses how the living standards of the elderly vary within and across countries, when housing expenditures are examined, demonstrates that richer measurement of economic standards than enabled by disposable income alone is crucial for a fuller understanding of the distribution of well-being across diverse institutional contexts—in this case, the prevalence of owner-occupied housing. In addition, in the study focused on Germany, the inclusion of pension entitlements (through statistical matching) demonstrates the importance of filling out the picture of household net worth by incorporating pension entitlements. In most countries, but to varying degrees, first-, second-, and third-pillar pension incomes are substantial parts of household income, and thus implied current wealth holdings (which include the implied stock value of future pension income streams) are large relative to actually held net worth. In Germany, estimated net worth roughly doubles by including the current value of pension entitlements. Making the parallel adjustment in other countries may substantially change our assessment of how countries vary with respect to wealth levels and disparities.

Country Cases

The case studies of the two high-income countries, Japan and Iceland, allow us to take a look at two countries for which comparable data are rarely available for cross-national research. Because they use national datasets rather than harmonized *LIS* microdata, these chapters are also able to provide a partial glimpse of some post-crisis years, especially in the Icelandic case.

The case studies from the two middle-income countries, India and South Africa, highlight some of the complex issues related to integrating research on high- and middle-income countries. These chapters, for example, bring into relief classic questions about the extent to which income is an appropriate measure of well-being in middle-income countries. Results in the latter two chapters in Part VI also suggest that levels of inequality are higher in these middle-income countries than in most high-income countries and that the distributions take a different shape. Indeed, the qualitative differences between the South African and Indian income distributions, relative to those that we observe in higher-income countries, help to underscore the challenge of meaningfully defining the middle class in comparative perspective.

WHAT HAVE WE LEARNED ABOUT DATA NEEDS?

Several chapters combine data sources in innovative ways to extend the research capacity of the *LIS* and *LWS* microdata. Two of the studies use statistical matching techniques to impute values from other microdata *into* the *LIS* microdata; one matches on income quintiles and one matches on family/employment characteristics. Two studies estimate multi-level models that combine macro-level indicators with micro-level data. When existing data sources do not contain all information that is required to assess a given question, these sorts of innovative combinations of data (both micro-micro and macro-micro) provide valuable pathways forward.

We argue, however, that many of the studies in this book point to the need for more comprehensive and more multi-dimensional microdata collection. A fuller picture of economic well-being would benefit from having more microdatasets that include household disposable income, consumption expenditures, and wealth—within a common dataset and recorded for the same household units. Income, consumption, and wealth are all closely related, yet few datasets provide data on all three. The Haig-Simons income definition corresponds to what can be consumed during a time period with no change in net worth (Haig 1921; Simons 1938); capturing that would, in fact, require researchers to have income, consumption, and wealth within in a single dataset or to have wealth in two consecutive years (at the end of the preceding year and of the current year), as well as income in the intervening year. This is in line with the recommendations for national accounts-based measurement of household disposable income in the report of the authoritative Stiglitz-Sen-Fitoussi Commission on the *Measurement of Economic Performance and Social Progress* (Stiglitz, Sen, and Fitoussi 2009).

Including other non-income dimensions of economic well-being on a systematic and comparable basis in datasets with detailed income information would also be highly useful. These might include, ideally at both the person and household levels, information on the use and value of publicly provided services (i.e., non-cash transfers), data on time use, and indicators of subjective well-being. Furthermore, in light of the findings in Part III, more information on political preferences and civic behavior (especially in the form of microdata that could be linked to income microdata) would contribute considerably to deepening our understanding of the changing politics of redistribution.

We would emphasize that there are many cases where the requisite data do exist in an integrated dataset, but often for only a single country and/or time period. Increasing our understanding of what drives inequality in different countries at different points in time would require that these types of datasets be available for multiple countries and across time. Gathering microdata is costly, and the public sectors in high- and middle-income countries all face considerable budgetary pressures. However, it is important to bear in mind that the cost of collecting more adequate data pales compared with the government expenditures devoted to supporting the living standards of national populations.

FUTURE RESEARCH ON INEQUALITY USING *LIS* AND *LWS* DATA

Extending the Research Questions Addressed in This Book

The studies reported in this book could be extended in several ways. Accounts of the factors underlying changes in overall inequality and in the distribution of economic well-being would benefit from drawing on the rich approach to measuring distributional change that is applied in Part I. As reported there, aggregate measures of distributional change mask important variation in how distributions change; the hypothesized explanations for distributional change imply varied patterns of change. Relative distribution methods constitute one of several powerful approaches to exploring such change because they allow for differentiating among alternative accounts. In our view, much more work needs to be done in analyzing (relative and absolute) changes in real income in different parts of the income distribution.

In addition, the interplay between distributional patterns/trends and analyses of the status of the middle class remains an essential area of future research. What is needed is a more multi-dimensional portrait of the middle class, based on middle-class definitions that draw on indicators of well-being other than income. Such extensions might draw not only on wealth and occupation/labor market position, as in this book, but also, for example, on education and/or family structure.

To better understand economic well-being and its distribution, a promising area of research is the further exploration of alternative, or more complete, resource packages that extend income in the spirit of the recent recommendations by Stiglitz, Sen, and Fitoussi (2009). The analysis in this collection that combines money income from paid work (using the *LIS* microdata) with the value of unpaid work (based on other microdata) should be extended to include a broader set of countries and more time periods. Time-use data, used in combination with income data, could also provide an opportunity to expand measures of economic well-being to include the value of time spent in leisure and in unpaid civic activities, elements that have not been explored in this book.

Clearly, income and wealth are closely but imperfectly correlated. With the emerging availability of more comparable datasets that contain both income and wealth, and that cover an increasing number of countries and time periods, it will be possible to assess, more comprehensively, the overall evolution of economic well-being across countries.

Both the results presented in this book and recent research in the United States suggest that "politics matters" for both inequality and for the living standards of the middle classes. Evidence from the United States that indicates that political decision making is almost totally insensitive to the preferences of the poor and is much less sensitive to the preferences of the middle-income classes than of the affluent is particularly striking and worrisome (Bartels 2009; Gilens 2009). Careful cross-national studies of the nature of political decision making and its responsiveness to different parts of the income distribution constitute, we believe, a crucial area of future research.

New Lines of Inquiry and Emerging Areas of Research

Several crucial research questions that have not been explored in this book deserve attention. Although this book includes an assessment of the economic fortunes of different birth cohorts, it does not examine, in detail, the importance of alterations in the population age structure for changes in inequality or for the position of the middle class. Clearly, populations are aging in many countries, and changing age structures may have consequential effects on income distributions. With the addition of more and later waves to the *LIS* and *LWS Databases*, researchers will be able to more fully explore at least two dimensions of the importance of age—that is, how income and wealth distributions change as age structures change, and how the income and wealth gradients (by age) change across time. Moreover, age structure transformations are driven simultaneously (to different degrees across countries and over time) by shifts in fertility, life expectancy, and immigration; future research exploring changing age structures is a promising avenue for assessing changes in economic well-being.

This book does not address the role or status of immigration or racial or ethnic minorities. Many high-income countries contain substantial populations of foreign-born residents, and they often face income disadvantages. In many of the *LIS* countries, certain racial/ethnic groups are also at a significant disadvantage. Unfortunately, across countries, data on immigrant and race/ethnicity status are highly diverse—capturing and combining indicators of legal status, the country of origin, years since arrival, linguistic grouping, skin color, and so on—reflecting to a large degree the diversity of country-specific situations. Thus, while systematic study of the effects of immigrant/racial/ethnic status will always be a challenge, researchers would do well to push this line of inquiry forward.

In addition, this book also does not systematically explore the drivers of changing earning distributions across countries. Labor market income constitutes, on average, the lion's share of household disposable income, so changes to the distribution of employment and wages are consequential drivers of inter-household income inequality. While it is crucial to recognize that there are many other factors that affect inequality, including household structure, the functioning of capital markets, and public taxes and transfers (Atkinson 1997), developments in labor markets are always important. Across the periods and countries included in *LIS*, globalization and technological change, as well as institutional reforms such as shifts in unionization and labor market regulations, have likely had large effects on both employment and earnings. Much more work is necessary to identify and assess factors that affect earnings distributions across countries and over time.

LIS recently expanded by adding several Latin American countries and China, and is now in the process of adding 10 to 15 additional middle-income countries, at multiple time points. Two of these middle-income countries are India and South Africa, whose data provide the basis of two chapters in this book. After these additional datasets have been harmonized and included in the *LIS Database*, countless new areas of research will be enabled. *LIS* researchers will be able to explore, for example, inter- as well as intra-regional disparities—especially vis-à-vis Europe and Latin America. The inclusion of comprehensive consumption expenditure data in many of the new datasets will allow a thorough assessment of the relationship between income disparities and consumption inequality. Researchers will also have access to harmonized data that allow examination of important phenomena that are less prevalent in high-income countries, such as production for own consumption, the interplay of formal and informal labor markets, and the importance of transnational remittances for household income.

Finally, at the end of 2007, the global financial crisis hit many countries, albeit to varying degrees. In many cases, the crisis sparked severe recessions, setting off perhaps the greatest economic downturn to hit high-income countries since the 1930s. Studying the effects of this downturn on income inequality and on the size and status of the middle class constitutes a major opportunity for future research. Early results using non-harmonized microdata suggest both that the recession itself played out differently across countries and that its immediate effects on income distribution were in many cases relatively, and surprisingly, modest (Jenkins et al. 2011). However, as we saw in the study focused on Iceland, in some cases the effects on income distribution were dramatic (even if the Icelandic crash was a special case and can, to some extent, be considered as independent of the Great Recession itself). However, the Great Recession has left many, but not all, high-income countries with large budget deficits and sizeable stocks of public debt; it has also left the private sector, including private households, with large debts and insufficient savings (Senior Budget Officials 2011). The medium- to long-term effects of the Great Recession may thus come through governments' decisions to cut spending on social programs, including transfers, and/or to increase taxes. Furthermore, given the importance of women's employment in equalizing household income, the distribution of the incidence of non-employment across households and the extent to which it is correlated within households will be a crucial area for future research.

All in all, this book emphasizes that cross-national and over-time analyses of inequality call for the adoption of multi-dimensional and multi-faceted approaches and that country-level patterns and trends should be disaggregated into their underlying components. The studies reported here have used the rich microdata available from LIS—sometimes in conjunction with external datasets—to assess diverse aspects of inequality levels and trends—across 28 countries, in some cases—at multiple time points. These analyses lay the groundwork for countless future studies that would extend the findings reported here, and they hint at an array of research questions not yet tackled in this book or, in some cases, in the inequality literature more generally. We began this book by observing that few social and economic conditions are more compelling or more vexing than inequality. Our ultimate hope is that this collection sheds some light on crucial aspects of inequality and that it motivates new and innovative lines of future research.

REFERENCES

Atkinson, Anthony B. 1997. "Bringing Income Distribution In from the Cold." *Economic Journal* 107(441): 297–321.

Bartels, Larry M. 2009. "Economic Inequality and Political Representation." In *The Unsustainable American State*, edited by Lawrence R. Jacobs. Oxford: Oxford University Press.

Gilens, Martin. 2009. "Preference Gaps and Inequality in Representation." *Political Science and Politics* 42(2): 335–41.

Haig, Robert M. 1921. *The Federal Income Tax*. New York: Columbia University Press.

Jenkins, Stephen P. et al., eds. 2011. "The Great Recession and the Distribution of Household Income." A report prepared for, and with the financial assistance of, the Fondazione Rodolfo Debenedetti, Milan for presentation at "Incomes Across the Great Recession," XIII European Conference of the Fondazione Rodolfo Debenedetti. Palermo. Milan: FRDB.

Senior Budget Officials, Organisation for Economic Co-operation and Development Working Party. 2011. *Restoring Public Finances*. Paris: OECD.

Simons, Henry. 1938. *Personal Income Taxation: The Definition of Income as a Problem of Fiscal Policy*. Chicago: University of Chicago Press.

Stiglitz, Joseph E., Amartya K. Sen, and Jean-Paul Fitoussi, eds. 2009. Report by the Commission on the Measurement of Economic Performance and Social Progress. www.stiglitz-sen-fitoussi.fr.

The Kuyper Center Review

New Essays in Reformed Theology and Public Life

The Kuyper Center Review publishes substantial essays of a historical or critical kind that relate the tradition of Reformed theology to issues of public life. Although it will take a special interest in the writings of Abraham Kuyper (1837-1920) and in the neo-Calvinist style of thought that he initiated, the aim is also to provide a vehicle for the widest-ranging exploration of the history and contemporary relevance of Reformed theology to important topics in politics, economics, and culture. Contributions from a variety of disciplines—history, philosophy, the humanities, and social sciences, as well as theology—are warmly welcomed.

The Kuyper Center Review

VOLUME 4   *Calvinism and Democracy*

Edited by

John Bowlin

WILLIAM B. EERDMANS PUBLISHING COMPANY

GRAND RAPIDS, MICHIGAN / CAMBRIDGE, U.K.

Published 2014 by

Wm. B. Eerdmans Publishing Co.

2140 Oak Industrial Drive N.E., Grand Rapids, Michigan 49505 /

P.O. Box 163, Cambridge CB3 9PU U.K.

Printed in the United States of America

20 19 18 17 16 15 14   7 6 5 4 3 2 1

Library of Congress Cataloging-in-Publication Data

ISBN 978-0-8028-7115-2

www.eerdmans.com

Contents

Contents

Editorial Introduction

This volume is the fourth issue of the *Kuyper Center Review*, and it includes papers presented at a conference on Neo-Calvinism and Democracy sponsored by the Abraham Kuyper Center for Public Theology at Princeton Theological Seminary in April 2012.

Abraham Kuyper (1837-1920) — pastor, theologian, journalist, and politician — was a principal force, both practical and intellectual, behind the democratization of politics and public life that occurred in the Netherlands at the close of the nineteenth century. The purpose of the conference, and so too this volume, is to reflect on this legacy, to explore its theological roots and historical context, but also to assess democracy's prospects in our own day and to consider the ways in which Reformed theology might provide resources for democratic criticism and renewal.

In his contribution to this volume, George Harinck considers Kuyper's complicated response to democracy. On the one hand, Kuyper's theological anthropology is democratic in both substance and consequence. Calvinism, Kuyper insists, "places our entire human life immediately before God." It regards us "as equals before God, and consequently equal as man to man."[1] It resists every claim of natural authority, every rule or lordship justified on appeal to the nature of things.

> Hence Calvinism condemns not merely all open slavery and systems of caste, but also all covert slavery of woman and of the poor; it is opposed

---

1. Abraham Kuyper, *Calvinism: Six Stone Lectures* (New York: Fleming H. Revell, 1899), pp. 26-27.

to all hierarchy among men; it tolerates no aristocracy save such as is able, either in person or in family, by the grace of God, to exhibit superiority of character or talent, and to show that it does not claim this superiority for self-aggrandizement or ambitious pride, but for the sake of spending it in the service of God. So Calvinism was bound to find its utterance in the democratic interpretation of life.[2]

On the other hand — and for precisely these same reasons — Kuyper opposes the idea of popular sovereignty that emerged in the French Revolution. Authority to rule does not come from the people. Rather, all legitimate temporal authority, democratic or otherwise, begins in the recognition of God's sovereignty and arrives by divine delegation.

Kuyper's contribution to democratic theory emerges at precisely this point. In response to the leveling and unifying effects of popular sovereignty, he offers a social ontology of sovereign spheres. This social ontology offers two distinct benefits. It helps Kuyper account for the differentiation that distinguishes modern life, in which family, work, school, and religion have a relative autonomy of their own, and it enables him to mark the boundaries of legitimate authority and action. God delegates authority to certain roles and offices within each sphere, and this authority is ordered to the tasks and purposes of each. It extends no further.

In a democracy, then, the authority of a people to rule comes from God and is limited to the mechanical tasks of politics and restrained by the reality and sovereignty of the spheres that God has created. Accountability is thus both vertical and horizontal, and on the horizontal axis it not only abides *among* the citizens of a democratic community but also *between* that community and the other spheres. It's these multiple orders of accountability and authority that distinguish Kuyper's political vision and that determine the contours of a democratic politics that he can actually endorse.

As I write, the citizens of Istanbul, Cairo, and São Paulo have taken their discontent to the streets and public places, protesting rule that refuses to be held accountable, arbitrary hierarchies of rank and position, and the covert enslavement of women and the poor. The Kuyper Center was created, in part, to stimulate new work and interest in the traditional concerns of the Reformed tradition and the emerging discourses of public theology. Our hope is that these efforts will help sustain a new and lively conversation,

---

2. Kuyper, *Calvinism*, p. 27.

not just about Kuyper and his intellectual progeny, but also about the most pressing issues of the day in theology and public life. Such is our hope for this volume.

JOHN R. BOWLIN

Contributors

GEORGE HARINCK is professor of the history of neo-Calvinism and director of the Historical Documentation Center at the Free University Amsterdam, and special professor of history at the Theological University Kampen. He has published widely on the history of Dutch Protestantism in its international context.

DAVID LITTLE is a fellow of the Berkley Center for Religion, Peace, and International Affairs, Georgetown University. He has taught at the University of Virginia and at Yale and Harvard Divinity Schools, among other places, and was a distinguished fellow at the United States Institute of Peace. His major publications include titles in the history of Calvinism, comparative ethics, and religion and human rights, nationalism, and peace.

JEFFREY STOUT is a professor of religion at Princeton University, where he has taught since 1975. He is a member of the American Academy of Arts and Sciences and is the author of *Blessed Are the Organized: Grassroots Democracy in America* (Princeton, 2010).

CLIFFORD B. ANDERSON is the Director for Scholarly Communications at Vanderbilt University. He was formerly the Curator for Special Collections at Princeton Theological Seminary.

MICHAEL BRÄUTIGAM is a doctoral candidate at the University of Edinburgh. His research focuses on the Christology of Adolf Schlatter. He holds degrees in psychology (University of Trier) and theology (University of Glasgow) and he was the 2012 visiting Puchinger Scholar at Princeton Theological Seminary.

CLAY COOKE is a Ph.D. candidate at the Free University Amsterdam in theology and a Ph.D. candidate at Fuller Theological Seminary in Christian ethics. He has written numerous articles for *Capital Commentary* and *Comment Magazine* on the topics of political theology and Christianity and culture.

MICHAEL DeMOOR is an assistant professor of social philosophy in politics, history, and economics at The King's University College, Edmonton, Alberta.

JAMES EGLINTON is research fellow in systematic and historical theology at the Theologische Universiteit Kampen. He holds a Ph.D. in systematic theology from the University of Edinburgh and is the author of *Trinity and Organism: Towards a New Reading of Herman Bavinck's Organic Motif* (T&T Clark, 2012).

BRANT HIMES holds a Th.M. from Princeton Theological Seminary and is a Ph.D. in Theology candidate at Fuller Theological Seminary. His published work on theology and discipleship includes "Discipleship as Theological Praxis: Dietrich Bonhoeffer as a Resource for Educational Ministry" in *Christian Education Journal*.

HARRY VAN DYKE attended Calvin College, where he was involved in the Groen van Prinsterer Society, and was awarded a Woodrow Wilson Fellowship. He is a professor emeritus of history at Redeemer College, Ancaster, Ontario, Canada.

Neo-Calvinism and Democracy: An Overview from the Mid-Nineteenth Century till the Second World War

George Harinck

The notion of democracy has accompanied neo-Calvinism from its early start. Insiders and outsiders labeled the neo-Calvinist movement as democratic. But the relationship between the two is more complex than it may seem at first sight. In order to shed some light on this relationship, I distinguish between three levels of discourse on democracy. The first is the meta-level, the level of worldviews. The second is the meso-level, the level I roughly define as that of political theory. And then there is a third level, the micro-level of politics, canvassing, elections, and coalitions. It is not always easy to distinguish which argument belongs to what level, but in general I hope these distinctions will be helpful in clarifying some of the complexities in the relationship between neo-Calvinism and democracy.

I

I don't think we have to pay a lot of attention to the notion that the neo-Calvinist worldview is democratic. Neo-Calvinists themselves have not been very hesitant on this issue. Abraham Kuyper (1837-1920) put it famously in the first of his Stone lectures that he delivered in 1898 in Miller Chapel at Princeton Theological Seminary:

> Calvinism has derived from its fundamental relation to God a peculiar interpretation of man's relation to man. . . . If Calvinism places our entire human life immediately before God, then it follows that all men or women,

1

rich or poor, weak or strong, dull or talented, as creatures of God, and as
lost sinners, have no claim whatsoever to lord over one another, and that
we stand as equals before God, and consequently equal as man to man. . . .
So Calvinism was bound to find its utterance in the democratic interpretation of life.[1]

This qualification of the democratic nature of Calvinism was formulated in
1898, but it is already present in Kuyper's early works. It has found its expression on the micro-level of church organization and politics. This does
not mean it has never been disputed, but supporters who disagreed on the
democratic character of neo-Calvinism (Ph. J. Hoedemaker) or in the implications of this character (A. F. De Savornin Lohman) sooner or later distanced
themselves from this movement.

I won't pay much attention to the micro-level of the relationship between neo-Calvinism and democracy, either. It is beyond doubt that the neo-
Calvinists were democratic in their policies. At about 1870 they presented
themselves in Dutch politics with a demand for the same rights for all, thereby
criticizing the underdeveloped democratic character of Dutch politics and the
institutionalized dominance of the liberals. In 1871 Kuyper asked for political
recognition of the different worldviews among the Dutch people and to make
room not only for the liberal worldview, but for of all of them, "In order to
take away the root of bitterness, to clear the political atmosphere, and give to
the Christian and to the catholic and to the liberal parts of the Dutch people
the same domain and full freedom to develop. Then a battle of moral powers
will take the place of factitious bickering that worries and harasses us without
bringing the issue to a solution."[2] In 1872 Kuyper founded his political daily *De
Standaard,* using it to inform people on political issues who did not yet have
the right to vote. In 1879 the neo-Calvinists founded the first political party in
the Netherlands. By its practice of plurality and publicity the Antirevolutionary Party reached out to the people behind the voters and made a decisive step
in developing Dutch democracy. This view is undisputed among historians.

But when we deal with democracy at the meso-level and consider neo-
Calvinist political theory, then difficulties arise. When it comes to the use of

---

1. Abraham Kuyper, *Calvinism: Six Lectures Delivered in the Theological Seminary at
Princeton* (New York: Fleming H. Revell, 1899), pp. 26, 27.

2. *De Heraut,* 6 January 1871, quoted in *Gedenkboek. Opgedragen door het feestcomité aan
prof. dr. A. Kuyper, bij zijn vijf en twintigjarig jubileum als hoofdredacteur van 'De Standaard,'
1872–1 April–1897* (Amsterdam: G. J. C. Herdes, 1897), p. 10. Unless indicated, translations are
by the author.

the word "democracy" in this context, neo-Calvinists have been hesitant. This needs a historical explanation.

II

France is the nation where the idea of democracy originated that dominated Dutch politics in the nineteenth century. Until the end of the eighteenth century authority in France was with the king, who had absolute power according to a *droit divin*. People suffered from this absolute power and felt restricted in their freedom. Philosophers reflected on the possibility of a different relationship of power and freedom in society, for example about the idea of a contract between individuals that would guarantee a certain degree of safety and freedom to each of them.

This was theory, but then in 1789 the French Revolution against the abuse of power occurred. A National Assembly took the lead. It implemented a constitution and the National Convention in 1792 put King Louis XVI (1754-1793) on trial for treason. He died on the guillotine, and an episode of the Terror followed. Abolishing absolute power is one thing; creating a new political system with checks on power is something else. In France the power shifted abruptly from the king to the people, which resulted in a time of chaos until one man, Napoleon Bonaparte (1769-1821), stood up and concluded that millions of citizens could not rule a country. Therefore he grabbed the executive power in the name of the people. In his function as French emperor he absorbed the sovereignty of the people. He was the nation, and as such he was godly, like God. From him came all authority, right, and justice, and whoever would offend him offended the nation. There was no freedom without Napoleon's consent: no freedom of print and no freedom of association, whether in commerce, literature, or religion. In this way he restored order, unified the French nation, and ruled for some time most of Western Europe.

When in 1815 Europe defeated Napoleon at Waterloo, his political theory was not considered obsolete; on the contrary, it was copied, for example in the Netherlands. The Kingdom of the Netherlands had been created in 1813 after decades of French occupation, and the first Dutch king, William the First of Orange-Nassau (1772-1843), intended to unify the nation and ruled in a Napoleonic way. This unification was a very welcome goal for many, because one of the main reasons the Dutch Republic had collapsed at the end of the eighteenth century was the very fact that the Republic had been so divided that federal power had become impotent. The Dutch constitution delegated almost all authority to the king. There was no freedom of press and in general there was no freedom outside of William the First, who, like Napoleon, absorbed the sovereignty of the people. The Netherlands had been liberated from French rule, but it implemented Napoleonic ideas.

Still, this implementation was mitigated in some ways. The liberals would take the lead in developing the political structure of the Dutch nation. Now that the monarch was bound to a constitution, their real challenge was to design this new kind of state. They had learned from the French Revolution that theories of the state could have disastrous consequences, so they were historically oriented and practical. But the liberals stuck to the idea that the state was the expression of the will of the people, and they supported the expansion of the state. The authority of the state was rooted more firmly than any theory of the divine rights of kings could ever have been.[3]

There was not much room for citizen political involvement under the constitution of 1814. Members of Parliament were elected indirectly by a small electorate, and the king could act independently of Parliament. This changed with the liberal constitution of 1848; in this constitution, freedom of press and freedom of association were embedded, and Parliament got a stronger position over against the king. Still, this did not mean that full democracy had arrived. The liberals were quite reluctant to grant the people direct political influence. They relied on rationality and free debate, and they did not trust the ability of the average Dutch citizen to argue in a reasonable way. They were also averse to religious elements in political debate. They defined Parliament as the place where reasonable men would debate in a reasonable way and come to reasonable decisions in favor of the public good. This meant that liberalism mainly appealed to the educated. Still, even if nothing like full democracy arrived with the 1848 constitution, it established a framework for democracy to emerge in later years.

III

It is against this background that the neo-Calvinists' understanding of democracy developed. I point to two defining historical moments. First, in the Dutch state of Napoleonic design, no association was allowed without the consent of the king. William I granted freedom of religion to existing churches, but new

---

3. So Frank Ankersmit, "Het liberalisme en de 21ste eeuwse staat," http://www.liberales .be/essays/ankersmit, consulted on July 18, 2013.

denominations had to apply for recognition. And all churches had to accept a church order designed by the government. When a group of orthodox believers organized themselves outside of the Reformed Church in the so-called Secession of 1834, they came into conflict with the government. They did not apply for recognition of their church from the king for an obvious reason: one of their complaints was that the church had accepted a church order from the government that violated the Reformed church order. They expressly wanted to be independent of the king's will. The small Seceder church did not fit with the ideals of the unified nation-state of William I. The Seceders were fined, put into prison, and had soldiers quartered in their houses, but they did not give in. This situation lasted until the early 1840s and was the last instance of religious persecution in Dutch history.

From a democratic point of view, the Secession was a first sign in the Netherlands that the French ideal of the sovereignty of the people imposed uniformity in the public domain that violated the *freedom* of the people. The Seceders stated that the source of their freedom was not grounded in the constitution, nor in the King as executer of the will of the people, but in the Calvinist religion of election by grace. The certainty of their total dependence on God made these Seceders independent of the state.[4] This experience from the first half of the nineteenth century made the next generation of neo-Calvinists suspicious of the modern state's defense of the liberties of the people.

The second historical moment was the implementation of the Constitution of 1848 in laws on primary education. At stake was the character of the public school. Guillaume Groen van Prinsterer (1801-1876) was the first political leader of the orthodox Christians in the Dutch parliament. He was the only significant opponent of the liberals. He claimed that the Netherlands was a Protestant nation and therefore its public institutions — for example, church and school — should be Protestant. Against him in Parliament was the liberal Jan Rudolf Thorbecke (1798-1872), the prime minister who had been the architect of the 1848 Constitution. Defending the separation of church and state, he favored a non-religious public school. According to the constitution, Catholics, Protestants, and Jews were allowed to create their own free schools, but these schools would not be funded by public money. In short, Thorbecke defended the liberal character of the public domain, and Groen its Protestant character.[5]

4. C. Gerretson, "De fonte libertatis: De Afscheiding van 1834 en haar nationale betekenis," in C. Gerretson, *Verzamelde werken III* (Baarn: Bosch en Keuning, 1974), p. 68.
5. See George Harinck, "Een leefbare oplossing Katholieke en protestantse tradities en de

Their conflict culminated in the parliamentary debates on a new law for primary education. In 1857 a law was adopted that excluded confessional religion from the public school. Parliament did this at a time when more than 95 percent of the population adhered to a confessional religion.[6] Groen concluded that the liberties of the people could not be defended by parliamentary means and gave up his seat. At that time only 58 out of 3,422 primary schools were free Christian schools.[7] What he did next was create and lead a free Christian school association (1860). Most Dutch citizens did not have the right to vote for Parliament at that time, but they did have the right to found free schools. If this Christian school movement would grow stronger, Groen reasoned, it might put pressure on Parliament to reconsider the law of 1857. In this way, a separate school system, financed with private money, developed alongside the public school system. This experience made the neo-Calvinists suspicious of the uniform character of the public domain.

These were the two defining moments for the neo-Calvinist idea of democracy: the defense of freedom of religion in a unified state, and the opposition to liberal hegemony in the public domain.

IV

It was clear that a non-public alternative such as independent schools might avoid collisions with the liberal state, but would not end liberal hegemony. This is where Abraham Kuyper stepped in. In 1869 the Christian school association adopted his motion to call upon Christian parents to remove their children from the public school because of its anti-Christian character. He had two reasons for this: he wanted to make the cause of Christian schools more urgent among parents, and he believed that Christians should not avoid but oppose the liberals.[8]

Kuyper's intervention on behalf of the Christian schools led to a split in

---

scheiding van kerk en staat," in Marcel ten Hooven & Theo de Wit, eds., *Ongewenste goden: De publieke rol van religie in Nederland* (Amsterdam: SUN, 2006), pp. 106-30.

6. Census, 1849.

7. A. C. Rosendaal, *Naar een school voor de gereformeerde gezindte. Het christelijke onderwijsconcept van het Gereformeerd School Verband (1868-1971)* (Hilversum: Verloren, 2006), p. 28. In 1889, when Christian schools received government funding, a third of the children attended a non-public school. Gert van Klinken, *Actieve burgers. Nederlanders en hun politieke partijen 1870-1918* (Amsterdam: Wereldbibliotheek, 2003), p. 231.

8. Jeroen Koch, *Abraham Kuyper: Een biografie* (Amsterdam: Boom, 2006), pp. 88-89.

the association. Some members did not want to give up on the many Christians who sent their children to public schools, and they did not want the Dutch nation to be divided between Christians and non-Christians. But Kuyper favored this divide, not just for tactical reasons, but because he believed that liberalism was in the end nothing but anti-Christian. That is why he called himself antirevolutionary — in opposition, not just against this or that law, but against the French revolutionary spirit of the liberals that was embodied in the Dutch laws.

V

It was Kuyper, and before him Groen, who appealed to the parents and to the people behind the voters and made room for the democratic element in the neo-Calvinist political movement. In the 1870s he organized public opinion, founded a political party, and presented a complete political alternative to liberal politics. But in all this, he hardly ever used the word "democratic." A liberal commentator wrote about Groen that "he belonged to those who were most averse toward democracy, but propagated it at the same time."[9]

Kuyper's attitude toward the political concept of democracy was rather indifferent, as had been John Calvin's.[10] In 1874 he wrote, "The issue is not whether the people rule or a king but whether both, when they rule, do so in recognition of Him." In the founding twenty-one articles of the Antirevolutionary Party that he organized in 1879, Kuyper articulated no preference for any political system. In Article Six he accepted the present Dutch situation of the constitutional monarchy as fitting for the Netherlands.[11] But the word "democracy" is absent from these articles, and in his more than 1300 pages

9. L., "Democratie en constitutionele monarchie," *De Gids* 35 (April 1871): 81: "De heer Groen is geen voorstander van het imperatieve mandaat, maar hij behoort m.i. onder hen, die ik in het begin heb genoemd als onbewust, en zelfs afkeerig en tegen hun zin, tot de zegepraal der, democratie het hardst mede te werken."

10. Abraham Kuyper, *Het Calvinisme oorsprong en waarborg onzer constitutioneele vrijheden: Een Nederlandsche gedachte* (Amsterdam: B. van der Land, 1874), p. 47. Translation: "Calvin regarded the form of government as a product of history that was to be respected. In a monarchy one should honor the king, in a democracy the 'ephori,' in a commonwealth the 'proceres.' God can entrust sovereignty as well to the one, the many, or to all." From "Calvinism: Source and Stronghold of Our Constitutional Liberties," in James D. Bratt, ed., *Abraham Kuyper. A Centennial Reader* (Grand Rapids: Eerdmans, 1998), p. 305.

11. Kuyper, *Ons program* (Met bijlagen) (Amsterdam: J. H. Kruyt, 1879), p. 2.

of commentary on them he hardly paid attention to the political concept of democracy.

To Kuyper the word "democracy" referred to authority, not to participation or representation. Who has the authority in a state to execute power, and what relationship obtains between institutions and citizens in regard to that authority? Neo-Calvinism's view of democracy was rooted in the notion of God's sovereignty. Kuyper agreed that there was a contradiction in his argument that civic liberties were basically dependent on recognizing the absolute sovereignty of God.[12] But this contradiction was only apparent, or so he argued. Since God is the absolute sovereign, there is no natural sovereignty on earth: "One creature cannot have authority over another unless God gives it."[13] This goes for a family, as well as for a business or for a state. But this insight did not lead to a preference for a political democracy on principle. To God, Kuyper wrote, "a democracy, as in America, is just as useful for his sovereign glory as is Russian absolutism."[14]

VI

Did Kuyper not speak out more positively on democracy? In April 1871 a liberal complimented the neo-Calvinists in *De Gids* for their balanced democratic view of authority and freedom.[15] This compliment implied that according to the liberals the neo-Calvinists were on the right track by embracing democracy. The liberals believed that God's plan for this world was revealed in the victory of democratic principles.[16] But, as the Trojans said: fear the Greeks, even those bearing gifts.[17] When Kuyper accepted the compliment, he felt the need to explain the antirevolutionary position towards democracy. He wrote that the origin of state authority lay in God, and therefore the neo-Calvinists obeyed the state and its Constitution. But this also meant that the state had to respect God's authority as revealed to the conscience of citizens.[18] The au-

---

12. Kuyper, "Calvinism: Source and Stronghold," p. 307.

13. Kuyper, "Calvinism: Source and Stronghold," p. 307.

14. Kuyper, "Calvinism: Source and Stronghold," p. 307.

15. L., "Democratie en constitutionele monarchie," pp. 81-82.

16. L., "Democratie en constitutionele monarchie," p. 83: the author states, "dat Gods wereldorde nu reeds duidelijk wijst op de toekomstige volledige zegepraal der demokratische beginselen."

17. Virgil, *Aeneid*, II, 49: "Timeo Danaos et dona ferentes."

18. Kuyper, *Ons program*, p. 1114.

thority of a government is subjected to God's laws, and the will of the people is bound to God's Word.[19] So, the ultimate authority was neither the state nor the people, but the Word of God.

Democracy therefore could not be an end in itself for neo-Calvinists; it was a means, and nothing more. To make this clear Kuyper compared the French idea of democracy with the American. He qualified the French democracy as anti-religious. At the end of the eighteenth century the French people had not only stood against the abuse of authority by French kings and aristocrats, "but against *all* power and authority." It was a democracy "that wanted to derive its right from nothing else but the will of the majority, the will of the sovereign people."[20] Kuyper showed sympathy for the immediate cause of resistance against the French authorities, but not for what he saw as the aim of this resistance: the replacement of God's order by the revolutionary order of freedom, equality, and liberty. The rejection of God's order had an immediate impact on authority and freedom, as Kuyper illustrated with the practical consequences of the concept of equality. The will of the people would always to be understood as the will of the majority of the people. This concept did not leave room for the dissenting opinions of minorities, and could only result in the reign of a new Napoleon. In this example the history of the school struggle and the Secession resonated.

But this did not mean a rejection of democracy all over. American democracy, Kuyper went on to explain, originated in religion. "It was born out of the resistance of the Christian conscience against the illicit aim of a lawful authority to suppress that conscience violently. It was the successful attempt . . . to put the lawful authority, which had gone astray, on the right track again and ground it anew in the revealed will of God."[21] That is why, continued Kuyper, the American institutions of the state respect the liberties of the people and Americans show a strong preference for the law and the authority of the government. By this Christian view of democracy, derived from Calvin, "despotism was banned, lust of power bridled, arbitrariness restricted and our civil liberties were granted."[22] It was not a rejection or takeover of authority, but a restoration of its proper use. In this context authority in the state would stay with the government. "The idea that each person . . . is entitled to a share in political authority," Kuyper wrote in 1874, "limits God's freedom, places the

19. *De Heraut*, 28 April 1871.

20. *De Heraut*, 5 May 1871. For a broader comparison between the American and the French state, see Kuyper, "Calvinism: Source and Stronghold," pp. 286-92.

21. Kuyper, *Ons program*, p. 1115.

22. Kuyper, *Het Calvinisme oorsprong en waarborg*, p. 49.

source of sovereignty in man." In order to stay as far away from revolutionary ideas as he could, Kuyper found refuge in the Calvinist notion of God's
sovereignty. He quoted approvingly Alexander Hamilton (1755/57-1804), who
considered "the French Revolution to be no more akin to the American Revolution, than the faithless wife in a French novel is like the Puritan matron in
New-England."[23]

Kuyper referred to the American situation, but the United States was far
away. It was the Netherlands and the dominance of the liberals that the Antirevolutionary Party had to deal with. For this reason one will search in vain for
an exposition on or defense of the Christian roots of the idea of democracy.
In the Dutch political context the association of the word "democracy" with
the French Revolution was simply too strong.

Instead, Kuyper gave a central position to the word "sovereignty" in his
view of politics and society. Later on, the word would return when he introduced the concept of sphere sovereignty. "Sovereignty" has the connotations
of unassailability and of a direct relationship between God and the people
or institutions that are endowed with his sovereignty. This emphasis on sovereignty kept the Antirevolutionaries from having a more open approach to
shifts in authority within society.

VII

Another aspect of the Antirevolutionaries' reluctance to use the word "democracy" was that to a certain degree their party was a liberal party. In his early
days as a politician, Kuyper described himself as a Christian liberal.[24] Indeed,
with his plea to liberate the public domain he even radicalized liberal ideas.
However, Kuyper soon dropped the name Christian liberal, because it was too
confusing: the main Antirevolutionary opponents were themselves liberals.
But in the 1890s he again gave in to the liberal nomenclature when he defended
a qualified use of the term "democracy" and spoke of Christian democracy. As
more people got involved in politics after suffrage was extended in the Netherlands from the late 1880s on, and as the word "democracy" became more
acceptable over these same years, the more the word lost its connotations of
revolution or radicalism. Neo-Calvinists now used new arguments to make
clear their view of democracy. Their main opponents were no longer the lib-

23. Kuyper, *Calvinism*, p. 111.
24. Kuyper, "Calvinism: Source and Stronghold," p. 307.

erals. In 1888 the constitution had been changed: the liberals now accepted the plural character of the public domain in principle, and in exchange the Antirevolutionaries agreed with the extension of the suffrage. From that year about a quarter of the adult males (about 292,000) had the right to vote. By the parliamentary elections of 1897 the suffrage had been doubled to about 50 percent of the adult males (515,000).[25] As a result, the Antirevolutionary Party became the largest party in Parliament with 27 out of 100 seats, while at the same time the first Socialist was elected.

Now that democracy had become broadly accepted and the Netherlands was on its way to general suffrage (implemented in 1918; for women in 1922), the Antirevolutionaries had to accommodate their organization and their program to this new context. At the same time, Kuyper had to deal with a conservative opposition within his own party that in the mid-1890s opposed the tendency in Parliament to extend the suffrage. This conservative wing considered democracy in conflict with the order of society as created by God: the working class should not bear political responsibility, and government should not give in to their social demands, as these were not the government's responsibility. Kuyper defended democracy just as he had defended the monarchy before: this was the actual political reality and it should be accepted so long as the freedom for the people on the one hand and the authority of the state on the other would be regarded in accordance with God's ordinances. To make the word "democracy" more acceptable, he added the adjective "Christian." Being Christian-democratic meant that Christ not only saved souls, but also reigned over and redeemed nature — that is, our natural life, including politics.[26] But to the conservative wing this was not convincing, and they left the Antirevolutionary Party in 1894.[27]

The departure of the conservatives gave the Antirevolutionary Party a stronger democratic image. But again the neo-Calvinists were reluctant to use the word "democracy" breezily, because of the claim the socialist movement now laid on the word. Again they felt the need to emphasize the difference with a concurrent political movement: "Even though our demands sometimes resemble those of the most active radicals, they grow from different roots. . . . We expect everything, and they nothing, from the faith! *From the faith!* That demand we cannot surrender."[28] The Social Democrats were blamed for de-

---

25. Van Klinken, *Actieve burgers,* pp. 255, 375.

26. Abraham Kuyper, *De Christus en de sociale nooden en democratische klippen* (Amsterdam: J. A. Wormser, 1895), pp. 92, 93.

27. Koch, *Kuyper,* pp. 364-76.

28. Kuyper, "Calvinism: Source and Stronghold," p. 316.

manding equality by denying the authorities that were ordained by God in this world, for asking for material progress as if this was the aim of life. Kuyper wrote in 1895, "The Social Democrat is right when he accuses the inequality in our society that is not according to the will of God, but he is not right when he tries to replace this by an equality that has not been wanted by God either."[29]

The neo-Calvinists also wanted to keep distance from the Social Democrats when they demanded general suffrage. Therefore Kuyper presented an alternative to check the revolutionary connotations of the developing democracy. General suffrage according to the one-man one-vote system was blamed as a revolutionary idea, for it denied the organic character of a people. A people was not just a bunch of individuals, but consisted of groups, platoons, and, its smallest entity, the family. A vote therefore should not be given to each individual citizen, but to the head of a household. The Second Chamber (Lower House) would represent the families, while the First Chamber would represent commercial and other interests. This was an attempt to moderate the revolutionary ideas, but basically it was individualistic as well. Kuyper's household voting right was a solution that turned out to be unfeasible and was rejected by the Antirevolutionary Party in the 1910s.[30] The party accepted general suffrage for both men and women alike.

When in 1901 Kuyper became prime minister, many hoped that he would make social laws and in this way would show himself a social-minded democrat. But after the Antirevolutionaries had kept distance from the liberals, they now stressed the difference between their politics and those of the Social Democrats, who were the rising political power in the early twentieth century.

In 1902, Anne Anema (1872-1966), a law professor at the Free University, defended in a public lecture the Christian character of democracy over against the Social Democrats. Christian democrats also have social demands, Anema said. The working class should be able to participate in social and political life, and therefore social rights and voting rights should gradually be granted to them. But, said Anema, the Social Democrat idea of democracy differs from the Antirevolutionary idea. What arouses Antirevolutionary anger in any social injustice first of all is that God's justice and majesty are violated. The foundation for social relations is Leviticus 19:18: "Thou shalt love thy neighbor, for I am the Lord."[31] And last but not least: even if a government does not

29. Kuyper, *Democratische klippen*, pp. 75, 76.

30. George Harinck, Roel Kuiper, and Peter Bak, eds., *De Antirevolutionaire Partij 1829-1980* (Hilversum: Verloren, 2001) pp. 129-34, 152-54.

31. Anne Anema, *Tweeërlei democratie: Rede gehouden op den antirevolutionairen partij-*

follow the social-democratic agenda, government has been ordained by God and should be obeyed regardless.[32] The Social Democrats put their material demands first and expect that social justice will generate ethical progress, but, Anema said, the neo-Calvinists first ask for obedience to God's ordinances, and on that ground plead for the material well-being of the people.[33] Anema also stressed that democracy was not just about material demands, but required a public spirit first. Kuyper had warned in 1879 that the public spirit of the Dutch people was weak. Anyone who dreamt of a democratic political order, he wrote, should know that a public spirit for politics ran counter to the character of the Dutch people.[34] But, according to Anema, Christians develop such a public spirit in church, where they learn to be members of a body. The Antirevolutionary Party had to transfer that spirit to the political sphere. This sphere could only be developed in a democratic way, when citizens felt a moral obligation for the public good. As Herman Bavinck warned in 1916: "When the influence of the citizens on the lawmaking process grows, this moral obligation shouldn't become weaker, but stronger. The more the citizen participates in national affairs, the more his sense of responsibility should grow. If political education does not keep pace with the influence of the people on government, democracy will lead to revolution and anarchy."[35]

The Antirevolutionaries favored a public spirit that felt responsible for the right relationship of freedom and authority in the first place, instead of focusing on the interests of their group of voters only. But although Anema, like Kuyper, distinguished between two kinds of democracies and claimed democracy for the Antirevolutionary tradition as well, the word never became customary among Antirevolutionaries.

VIII

Time and time again the Antirevolutionary Party was reluctant to use the word "democratic." As soon as the word became accepted in Dutch politics,

---

dag voor de provincie Gelderland te Arnhem op 12 mei 1902 (Amsterdam: W. Kirchner, 1902), p. 24.

32. Anema, *Tweeërlei democratie*, p. 17.

33. Anema, *Tweeërlei democratie*, p. 21.

34. Kuyper, *Ons program*, p. 243.

35. H. Bavinck, *De opvoeding der rijpere jeugd* (Kampen: J. H. Kok, 1916), p. 199. Bavinck referred to L. P. Jacks, "Democracy and Discipline," *The Hibbert Journal* (October 1912): 1-24, and Georg Kerschensteiner, *Der Begriff der staatsbürgerlichen Erziehung* (Leipzig: Teubner, 1914).

Socialists presented themselves as Social Democrats in parties that had the word "democratic" in their name. Some progressive Antirevolutionaries, who were disappointed in Kuyper's social policies as prime minister, left the party in 1905 and founded a Christian-Democratic Party. This party did not attract many voters. Still, through the 1930s there were a number of small left-wing defections from the Antirevolutionary Party; clearly the reluctance towards democracy was not self-evident in orthodox Protestant circles.[36] And some progressive liberals founded a Liberal-Democratic Federation. But the Antirevolutionary Party never laid a strong claim on the word.

This is all the more remarkable when we realize that, when Kuyper spoke not of politics but of the church, he candidly related God's sovereignty to democracy. The doctrine of election was foundational for his concept of the church, and this doctrine was closely related to the recognition of God's sovereignty, to the confession that all honor belongs to God. When a church confesses election as the "cor ecclesiae," then a church cannot be priestly, he wrote, "but is bound to find its power in the elect, i.e. in the church members. Thus the democratic form of church government sprang from this confession."[37] However, Kuyper did not use the same argument for the state, although he wrote that "election creates a dynamic sense of public responsibility"[38] — the same argument that was used by Anema in 1902 — and noted that the doctrine of election had led to the civic liberties of the Netherlands and of the United States. He did not take the next step, though: he did not claim that from the confession of the equality of all people before God sprang representation and participation in state government — in short, sprang democracy.

IX

When the Antirevolutionaries wrote about democracy, their starting point was not representation or checking the government, but the sovereignty of God. They considered this confession their stronghold, and starting there they chose God's point of view in political issues: to God there was no real difference between absolutism and democracy; God created the poor and the wealthy;

36. See H. J. Langeveld, "Horzels rond het antirevolutionaire paard. Progressieve dissidenten in de protestantse politiek tussen 1900 en 1940," in *Een land nog niet in kaart gebracht: Aspecten van het protestants-christelijk leven in Nederland in de jaren 1880-1940*, ed. J. de Bruijn (Amsterdam, 1987), pp. 91-112.

37. Kuyper, "Calvinism: Source and Stronghold," p. 310.

38. Kuyper, "Calvinism: Source and Stronghold," p. 310.

humans should not violate God's ordinances. Neo-Calvinists' reflection on democracy was underdeveloped not because there was no potential, but because in the Netherlands the idea of democracy originated in the French Revolution. By positing God's sovereignty over against the anti-Christian features of this revolution, they locked themselves in, and were not able to reflect on the character of democracy. They could only regard democracy with indifference.

There seemed to be a gradual development among the Antirevolutionaries towards accepting democracy, from Groen to Anema. In the 1930s, however, even in the wake of the rise of totalitarian states in Europe, the Antirevolutionary Party still showed a remarkable indifference towards democracy. Yet something had changed in their political theory. In the nineteenth century, the accent was on limiting the state's authority in favor of civic liberties, but now the state was called to actively protect these liberties. In response to totalitarianism, they stressed the necessity of government, of its protection of the sovereignty of spheres. "The life of state and society rest on two pillars," to quote an Antirevolutionary pamphlet in 1933: "the sovereignty of God and sphere sovereignty."[39] This implementing of sphere sovereignty in neo-Calvinist political theory was a new aspect. Kuyper had formulated this idea in 1880 to support and encourage an orthodox Protestant minority in Dutch society that was neglected by the ruling class. He referred to it only now and then, and the concept was not implemented in politics until the 1930s.[40]

Even in the context of emerging totalitarian regimes it was hard for neo-Calvinists to separate democracy from its connotations of revolution, people's sovereignty, and anarchy. Antirevolutionary Party leader and five-time prime minister Hendrik Colijn (1869-1944) complained in 1922 that modern democracy denied the authority of the husband, the teacher, the employer, and the government, and he repeated the classic Antirevolutionary mantra against democracy: "The tendency of revolutionary democracy to destroy all authority in all spheres of life, is in essence the denial of God's authority."[41]

The Antirevolutionary objection to Fascism and National Socialism was

39. W. J. Kolkert Jr., *Democratie* (Aalten: De Graafschap, 1933), pp. 22, 23. *De Heraut,* 29 September 1918: A real democracy combines "de grootst mogelijke kracht en vrijheid van het centraal bewind (. . .) aan de grootst denkbare mate van souvereiniteit in eigen kring." Translation: "A real democracy combines the largest power and freedom of a central government with the largest sphere sovereignty."

40. See George Harinck, "A Historian's Comment on the Use of Abraham Kuyper's Idea of Sphere Sovereignty," *Journal of Markets and Morality* 5:1 (Spring 2002): 277-84.

41. H. Colijn, *Om de bewaring van het pand. Rede ter opening van de deputatenvergadering, gehouden te Utrecht op 23 april 1925* (Amsterdam: De Standaard, 1925), p. 14.

not so much that these movements were anti-democratic. Instead their stress on God's sovereignty made some Antirevolutionaries sensitive to governments or political theories that would enlarge the responsibilities and claims of a state. Colijn had some sympathy for the Italian Fascist dictator Benito Mussolini (1883-1945) and as a prime minister was frustrated with the hardly adroit role of the Dutch Parliament.[42] Even after the war had broken out in May 1940, Colijn in a widely read pamphlet stated that the prewar democracy had been rooted in principles that were alien to Calvinism.[43] But on the other hand, the Antirevolutionaries were also sensitive to political ideas and politicians that violated the freedom of the different spheres and of society as a whole. In arguing against the German National Socialist dictator Adolf Hitler (1889-1945) they did not defend democracy, but the constitutional liberties of the people. The Dutch prime minister during the war was a neo-Calvinist, Pieter S. Gerbrandy (1885-1961). In his radio talks from London, where the Dutch government in exile was stationed in wartime, Gerbrandy once again did not explicitly defend democracy. It was not the constitution but the religious conviction it rested on that ignited his strong resistance against National Socialism.[44]

Still, some Antirevolutionaries could embrace democracy more wholeheartedly. In the late 1930s Klaas Schilder (1890-1952), professor at Kampen Theological Seminary, departed from the tradition of indifference to democracy[45] and provided an argument as to why a democratic political system should be preferred over a totalitarian one. Schilder saw it as typical for authoritarian and totalitarian states not to be able to wait until the harvest, but to want to gather and separate the wheat and the chaff here and now.[46] The quality of a democracy is that such a state shows patience towards differences. Democracy means postponement of judgment. It acknowledges the limitations of its authority. In such a political structure, Christians retain the possi-

---

42. On Colijn, Mussolini, and democracy see Herman Langeveld, *Schipper naast God. Hendrikus Colijn 1869-1944. Deel twee 1933-1944* (Amsterdam: Balans, 2004), pp. 15-52.

43. H. Colijn, *Op de grens van twee werelden* (Amsterdam: De Standaard, 1940), p. 37.

44. P. S. Gerbrandy, *Landgenoten! De radiotoespraken van minister-president prof. mr. P. S. Gerbrandy in de jaren 1940-1945 gehouden voor Radio Oranje en De Brandaris* (Franeker: Wever, 1985), p. 25.

45. In an anti-National-Socialist pamphlet Schilder wrote in 1937 for the Antirevolutionary Party, the word "democracy" is still absent. See *Geen stem voor de N.S.B.* ('s-Gravenhage: Centraal Comité van Antirevolutionaire Kiesvereenigingen, 1937).

46. K. Schilder, *Bezet bezit: Artikelen van de hand van prof. dr. K. Schilder, opgenomen in de nummers van De Reformatie uit de eerste maanden na de bezetting van Nederland — juni-augustus 1940* (Goes: Oosterbaan & Le Cointre, 1945), p. 88.

bility to proclaim God's Word.[47] Confronted with totalitarianism (he studied in Germany at the time of Hitler's *Machtübernahme*), Schilder could no longer stay indifferent to opposing political systems, but favored democracy as a political structure that would leave room for public Christian witness. For in a democracy both wheat and chaff would be protected until the Lord himself would come to his field to harvest.[48] In reaction to Colijn's critique of the prewar Dutch democracy, he suggested that a distinction should be made between the weaknesses of democrats and democracy as such. His contributions formed the first explicitly positive Antirevolutionary stance on democracy.

Conclusion

Neo-Calvinism and democracy offer a more complicated combination than it seems at first glance. Neo-Calvinism's reflection on democracy started in a situation of opposition, and that fact has accompanied neo-Calvinist reflection on democracy for a long time. It not only made neo-Calvinists hesitant to use the word "democracy," but it also hindered reflection on democracy's Christian character. Because they linked God's sovereignty directly to societal order, they were indifferent to the concept of democracy and did not support general suffrage wholeheartedly. And if we look at the history of neo-Calvinism through the present day, the idea of democracy has never drawn much attention from neo-Calvinist political thinkers.

Though the neo-Calvinists only used the word "democracy" hesitantly, it is undeniable that they influenced the Dutch character of democracy. In the first place, they relativized the value of democracy as such, and of the Enlightenment values it represents. Democracy is not the solution to any issue of freedom or authority, as we see today, a year after the Arab Spring.

Second, the stress on God's sovereignty sheds light on the need for an authority outside of citizens and governments, one that can identify civic liberties and secure respect for governmental authority. The issue of authority and its foundation still vexes political theory and practice, and the rule of law as such is no guarantee for the protection of the rights of citizens and governments. Religious and ideological convictions are more deeply rooted and often stron-

47. Schilder, *Bezet bezit,* p. 90.

48. Jac. Schaeffer, review of Harmjan Dam, *De NSB en de kerken: De opstelling van de Nationaal Socialistische Beweging in Nederland ten opzichte van het christendom en met name de Gereformeerde Kerken 1931-1940* (Kampen: Kok, 1986), *Radix* (July 1987): 179-83.

ger than the law. In Europe, for example, the public domain is defined more and more by the ideology of the majority. Separation of church and state now, for the most part, means the exclusion of religion from the public domain. It is unlikely that there will be a reference to God in a European constitution, and several countries have discussed laws directed against Jews or Muslims. Some countries have even adopted them. The litmus test for the quality of a democracy is the protection of minority opinions. This quality is not guaranteed when left to the opinion of the majority. The Netherlands Seceders experienced this in the nineteenth century, and the plea for a plural public domain was constant among Antirevolutionary politicians.

Third, the Antirevolutionaries stressed the need for a public spirit. In the end democracy is not dependent on the rule of law, but on citizens taking responsibility for the public good. Politics is not just about material demands of certain groups. It is not about the economy, no matter how many voters that issue may influence. Antirevolutionaries started by linking worldview to politics and defending the same rights for all groups, and they have avoided becoming a single-issue party, a pitfall that is well known in the fragmented landscape of Dutch politics. A democratic party does not represent group interests but rather an elaborate view of the common good.

And last, democracy needs an independent and active society. The government should promote such a society and protect each sphere from all that hinders its functioning. One of the weaknesses of contemporary Dutch democracy is that it plays on emotion, but does not activate the people, or speak to their responsibilities. Few citizens are members of a political party, and some parties even exclude the possibility of membership. The only thing that government asks in reaction to this emotion-driven political climate is what you can read on the posters of New Jersey transit trains: speak softly, be considerate, keep feet off seats. All other things are taken care of by government officials, from neighborhood watch to childcare and social security. But that is not enough for a sustainable society. Antirevolutionaries have always been strongly rooted in an active civil society, and they have always had a keen eye for the different responsibilities of each sphere. These commitments were made explicit during the Christian school movement in the nineteenth century. Without them, democracy will not work.

Neo-Calvinists never offered an elaborate view of democracy, and they always viewed it in context. At the same time, three aspects of their political theory stand out as promising for today's reflection on Christianity and democracy: the sovereignty of God over all, a focus on the common good, and a defense of civil society.

Bibliography

Anema, Anne. *Tweeërlei democratie: Rede gehouden op den antirevolutionairen partijdag voor de provincie Gelderland te Arnhem op 12 mei 1902.* Amsterdam: W. Kirchner, 1902.

Ankersmit, Frank. http://liberalekerk.nl/wordpress/achtergrond/frank-ankersmit -het-liberalisme-en-de-21ste-eeuwse-staat.

Bavinck, H. *De opvoeding der rijpere jeugd.* Kampen: J. H. Kok, 1916.

Bratt, James D., ed. *Abraham Kuyper: A Centennial Reader.* Grand Rapids: Eerdmans, 1998.

Colijn, H. *Om de bewaring van het pand. Rede ter opening van de deputatenverga- dering, gehouden te Utrecht op 23 april 1925.* Amsterdam: De Standaard, 1925.

———. *Op de grens van twee werelden.* Amsterdam: De Standaard, 1940.

Gedenkboek: Opgedragen door het feestcomité aan prof. dr. A. Kuyper, bij zijn vijf en twintigjarig jubileum als hoofdredacteur van 'De Standaard,' 1872–1 April–1897. Amsterdam: G. J. C. Herdes, 1897.

Gerbrandy, P. S. *Landgenoten! De radiotoespraken van minister-president prof. mr. P. S. Gerbrandy in de jaren 1940–1945 gehouden voor Radio Oranje en De Brandaris.* Franeker: Wever, 1985.

Gerretson, C. "De fonte libertatis: De Afscheiding van 1834 en haar nationale betek- enis." *Verzamelde werken III.* Baarn: Bosch en Keuning, 1974.

Harinck, George. "A Historian's Comment on the Use of Abraham Kuyper's Idea of Sphere Sovereignty." *Journal of Markets and Morality* 5:1 (Spring 2002): 277-84.

———. "Een leefbare oplossing Katholieke en protestantse tradities en de scheiding van kerk en staat." In *Ongewenste goden: De publieke rol van religie in Nederland*, 106-30. Edited by Marcel ten Hooven & Theo de Wit. Amsterdam: SUN, 2006.

Harinck, George, Roel Kuiper, and Peter Bak, eds. *De Antirevolutionaire Partij 1829 1980.* Hilversum: Verloren, 2001.

Jacks, L. P. "Democracy and Discipline." *The Hibbert Journal* (October 1912): 1-24.

Georg Kerschensteiner. *Der Begriff der staatsbürgerlichen Erziehung.* Leipzig: Teub- ner, 1914.

Koch, Jeroen. *Abraham Kuyper: Een biografie.* Amsterdam: Boom, 2006.

Kolkert, W. J., Jr. *Democratie.* Aalten: De Graafschap, 1933.

Kuyper, Abraham. *Het Calvinisme oorsprong en waarborg onzer constitutioneele vrij- heden: Een Nederlandsche gedachte.* Amsterdam: B. van der Land, 1874.

———. *Ons program* (Met bijlagen). Amsterdam: J. H. Kruyt, 1879.

———. *De Christus en de sociale nooden en democratische klippen.* Amsterdam: J. A. Wormser, 1895.

———. *Calvinism: Six Lectures Delivered in the Theological Seminary at Princeton.* New York: Fleming H. Revell, 1899.

L., "Democratie en constitutionele monarchie." *De Gids* 35 (April 1871).

Langeveld, H. J. "Horzels rond het antirevolutionaire paard. Progressieve dissidenten in de protestantse politiek tussen 1900 en 1940." In *Een land nog niet in kaart gebracht: Aspecten van het protestants-christelijk leven in Nederland in de jaren 1880-1940*, 91-112. Edited by J. de Bruijn. Amsterdam, 1987.

Langeveld, Herman. *Schipper naast God. Hendrikus Colijn 1869-1944. Deel twee 1933-1944.* Amsterdam: Balans, 2004.

Rosendaal, A. C. *Naar een school voor de gereformeerde gezindte: Het christelijke onderwijsconcept van het Gereformeerd School Verband (1868-1971).* Hilversum: Verloren, 2006.

Schaeffer, Jac. Review of Harmjan Dam, *De NSB en de kerken: De opstelling van de Nationaal Socialistische Beweging in Nederland ten opzichte van het Christendom en met name de Gereformeerde Kerken 1931-1940.* Kampen: Kok, 1986. *Radix* (July 1987): 179-83.

Schilder, Klaas. *Geen stem voor de N.S.B.* 's-Gravenhage: Centraal Comité van Anti-revolutionaire Kiesvereenigingen, 1937.

————. *Bezet bezit: Artikelen van de hand van prof. dr. K. Schilder, opgenomen in de nummers van De Reformatie uit de eerste maanden na de bezetting van Nederland — juni-augustus 1940.* Goes: Oosterbaan & Le Cointre, 1945.

Van Klinken, Gert. *Actieve burgers: Nederlanders en hun politieke partijen 1870-1918.* Amsterdam: Wereldbibliotheek, 2003.

Calvinism, Constitutionalism, and the Ingredients of Peace

David Little

Constitutional Democracy and the "Liberal Peace"

Considerable empirical evidence supports a strong connection between constitutional democracy and peace. Defenders of the connection advocate something called the "liberal peace."[1] They maintain that the orderly and properly sequenced development of robust liberal political and economic institutions is a critical condition of national and international peace,[2] while the presence

---

1. Jack Snyder, *From Voting to Violence: Democratization and Nationalist Conflict* (New York: W. W. Norton & Co., 2000); Edward D. Mansfield and Jack Snyder, *Electing to Fight: Why Emerging Democracies Go to War* (Cambridge: MIT Press, 2005), and cf. Edward D. Mansfield and Jack Snyder, "Democratic Transitions and War: From Napoleon to the Millennium's End," in *Turbulent Peace: The Challenges of Managing International Conflict*, ed. Chester A. Crocker, Fen Osler Hampson, and Pamela Aall (Washington, D.C.: United States Institute of Peace Press, 2001), ch. 8; Ted Robert Gurr, *Peoples versus States: Minorities at Risk in the New Century* (Washington, D.C.: United States Institute of Peace Press, 2000); Gurr and Barbara Harff, *Ethnic Conflict in Global Politics* (Boulder, Colo.: Westview Press, 2004); Michael W. Doyle and Nicholas Sambanis, *Making War and Building Peace: United Nations Peace Operations* (Princeton: Princeton University Press, 2006); Larry Diamond, *The Spirit of Democracy: The Struggle to Build Free Societies throughout the World* (New York: Times Books, 2008); Roland Paris, *At War's End: Building Peace after Civil Conflict* (New York: Cambridge University Press, 2004); R. J. Rummel, *Power Kills: Democracy as a Model of Nonviolence* (New Brunswick, N.J.: Transaction, 2004); Morton H. Halperin, Joseph T. Siegle, and Michael M. Weinstein, *The Democracy Advantage: How Democracies Promote Prosperity and Peace* (New York: Routledge, 2005).

2. Scholars like Snyder, Mansfield, Gurr, and Paris, among others, emphasize the importance of "orderly and properly sequenced development" in the creation of liberal institutions. A disorderly transition from authoritarianism to democracy, where, for example, elections

of illiberal institutions, namely those that are seriously fractured ethnically, economically, or in other ways, promise a high probability of violence.

Representative are the views of political scientist Jack Snyder, who argues that violence is restrained by means of "thick versions of liberal or constitutional democracy," consisting "of an ample set of preconditions" for "a stable, productive, peaceful society." There is "a certain degree of wealth, the development of a knowledgeable citizenry, the support of powerful elites, and the establishment of a whole panoply of institutions to insure the rule of law and [equal] civic rights."[3] Similarly, Michael Doyle and Nicholas Sambanis, on the basis of their scrupulous study of the ways of resolving civil war, conclude that "the rule of law and constitutional consent," including "a basic framework of rights and duties of citizens," are crucial foundations for durable peace.[4] By contrast, illiberal or predatory regimes with weak to nonexistent constitutional protections that permit extensive ethnic, religious, economic, and other forms of discrimination are prone to violence, of either an institutionalized sort, as in authoritarian systems, or outside of institutional control, as in insurgencies and civil wars.[5]

A particularly important recent study highlights the urgency of protecting "a basic framework of rights and duties of citizens," and especially freedom of conscience, for the sake of peace. The study is by Brian J. Grim and Roger Finke and called *The Price of Freedom Denied: Religious Persecution and Conflict in the Twenty-First Century*.[6] On the strength of a broad and rigorous empirical survey, the book reflects strong support for the liberal peace. It concludes: "to the extent that governments and societies restrict religious

---

precede the creation of stable political, civil, and economic institutions, can greatly increase the likelihood of violence. "The rule seems to be: Go fully democratic, or don't go at all." Edward D. Mansfield and Jack Snyder, "Democratic Transitions and War," in Crocker, Hampson, and Aall, eds., *Turbulent Peace*, p. 124.

3. Snyder, *From Voting to Violence*, pp. 316-17.

4. Doyle and Sambanis, *Making War and Building Peace*, p. 340.

5. Snyder, *From Voting to Violence*, p. 24 and pp. 352-53. There is controversy among scholars over how important political, economic, and social grievances are in causing civil wars. One dissenter is Paul Collier, "Economic Causes of Civil Conflict and Their Implications for Policy," in Crocker, Hampson, and Aall, eds., *Turbulent Peace*, where he defends his now-famous aphorism, "greed not grievance" (see pp. 144ff.). For a critique of Collier's views and the similar views of other social scientists, see comments in the Introduction to David Little and Donald K. Swearer, eds., *Religion and Nationalism in Iraq: A Comparative Perspective* (Cambridge: Harvard University Press, 2006), pp. 5-7.

6. Brian J. Grim and Roger Finke, *The Price of Freedom Denied: Religious Persecution and Conflict in the Twenty-First Century* (New York: Cambridge University Press, 2011).

freedoms, physical persecution and conflict increase."[7] The authors declare that their findings match the conclusions of similar studies, to the effect that

> religious freedom in a country is strongly associated with other freedoms (including civil and political liberty, press freedom, and economic freedom) and with multiple measures of well-being. . . . [W]herever the level of religious freedom is high, there [tend] to be fewer incidents of armed conflict, better health outcomes, higher levels of earned income, prolonged democracy, and better educational opportunities for women.[8]

To be sure, there are criticisms of the liberal peace. One complaint regards the neglect or distortion of the role of religion because of a one-sided secularist perspective deriving from the Enlightenment.[9] As a matter of fact, such a complaint does seem to apply to the study of Grim and Finke. Their "religious economies" approach, holding that deregulated religion is beneficial in the same way as a deregulated market, relies on three Enlightenment figures: Voltaire, David Hume, and Adam Smith.[10] Grim and Finke take these thinkers to believe that religions characteristically seek to dominate by repressing competitors, and the best way to prevent that is to increase the number of competitors, making it hard for any one religion to take control. Accordingly, Grim and Finke assert that to believe in the superiority of one's religion is necessarily to regard competitors as "dangerous and wrong," warranting repression. While American Puritans, on Grim and Finke's account, sought "religious freedoms and an escape from persecution" for themselves, not one of them had any intention "of granting religious freedoms to all."[11] Such claims, of course, disregard many radical English and American Puritans, not to mention many Anabaptists, who help constitute the "free church" tradition in Western Christianity. Members of that tradition regularly believe in the superiority of their religion, and yet favor — often at great cost — the universal protection of the freedom of conscience.

---

7. Grim and Finke, *Price of Freedom Denied*, p. 222.

8. Grim and Finke, *Price of Freedom Denied*, p. 206.

9. Daniel Philpott, "Introduction: Searching for Strategy in an Age of Peacebuilding," p. 4, and Philpott, "Reconciliation: An Ethic for Peacebuilding," pp. 98-102, and Gerard F. Powers, "Religion and Peacebuilding," pp. 319-22, in Daniel Philpott and Gerard F. Powers, eds., *Strategies of Peace: Transforming Conflict in a Violent World* (New York: Oxford University Press, 2010). Cf. Daniel Philpott, *Just and Unjust Peace: An Ethic of Reconciliation* (New York: Oxford University Press, 2012), pp. 2, 9, 70-73, 176-77, 207, 209.

10. Grim and Finke, *Price of Freedom Denied*, pp. 3-6.

11. Grim and Finke, *Price of Freedom Denied*, pp. 46-47.

A second criticism charges that the idea of a liberal peace is too closely associated with a neo-liberal economic order. Free-market strategies may contribute to short-term stability of a kind, but there is considerable evidence that they also help generate "rising inequality within and between countries."[12] Growing inequality fuels grievances and resentment, with an ominous potential for violent conflict and for undermining stable and equitable democratic institutions.[13] Might the liberal peace be reconceived in order better to address the threat of global economic inequality?

The Calvinist Background

To rectify a large gap in understanding the history of the liberal peace, and then, in the light of that history, to reconsider its basic characteristics, I want to take up the Calvinist contribution. Such an effort is, among other things, a response to the two aforementioned criticisms: the widespread neglect of religion, and the lack of imagination regarding economic justice. My central thesis is this: Calvinism played a critical role in the rise of modern constitutionalism, particularly by way of American Puritanism. That role included a significant, if sometimes very ambivalent, contribution to the protection of rights, both civic and economic. Given space constraints, I will limit myself to American Puritanism.

I must start with a note of reassurance. While it once was acceptable among scholars of Puritanism to argue for the influence of English and Colonial Puritans on the rise of modern liberal institutions, such efforts were widely rejected in the later twentieth century by a committed circle of historical revisionists.[14] Such claims, it was said, are anachronistic — they read modern liberal values back into an age where they do not belong; accordingly, they distort the peculiarly religious concerns of the people in question by reducing recondite matters of theology and piety to unrelated political issues like "egalitarianism, individual liberty and tolerance."[15] Moreover, they illicitly ascribe to a congeries of Puritan doctrines and commitments, and to

12. Jackie Smith, "Economic Globalization and Strategic Peacebuilding," in Philpott and Powers, eds., *Stategies of Peace*, p. 353. See also Joseph E. Stiglitz, *Globalization and Its Discontents* (New York: Norton & Co., 2003), esp. ch. 2.

13. Smith, "Economic Globalization and Strategic Peacebuilding," p. 362.

14. See John Coffey and Paul C. H. Lim, "Introduction," in *Cambridge Companion to Puritanism*, ed. John Coffey and Paul C. H. Lim (Cambridge: Cambridge University Press, 2008).

15. Cited in Coffey, "Puritan Legacies," in *Cambridge Companion to Puritanism*, p. 332.

wild fluctuations in membership and allegiance, the attributes of a coherent and continuous movement that never existed. Some scholars even proposed dispensing altogether with the term "Puritan."

Fortunately, students of Puritanism seem of late to have regained their bearings and recovered a more balanced and sensible perspective.[16] In an important new book on the New England Puritans, entitled *A Reforming People*, David Hall, a prominent scholar previously under the influence of revisionism, is now prepared to apply the term "Puritanism" to what he himself calls a "movement" among English and American Protestants in the sixteenth and seventeenth centuries. Its members, whatever their differences, "aimed," he declares, "at taking over a national church and improving it," and they regularly invoked "conscience and divine law" "even when doing so made for tensions with civil rulers and the state church."[17]

Despite the undoubted diversity among them as to theological, ecclesiastical, and political beliefs, as well as substantial ups and downs in the number of adherents, what held all Puritans together was *a common preoccupation with religious and political reform*. They were, precisely, one in being "a reforming people" — a term, as we shall see, with very rich connotations. And while Hall strongly resists turning even the more radical Puritans "into nineteenth-century liberals or twentieth-century social gospelers or democrats," he pronounces that "some aspects" of "the premises of liberalism or democratic theory can be found in what they did and said."[18]

My view is that Hall's conclusions are profoundly correct, and, furthermore, that an important source of this reforming zeal, sometimes expressed in radical political terms, is the Calvinist background, beginning with John Calvin himself. One does not need to turn Calvin and his followers into modern constitutional democrats to appreciate their part in the development of modern constitutional democracy.

We may describe the basic features of modern constitutionalism, or what is sometimes referred to as the "rule of law," in the following way: A writ-

16. Peter Lake, "The Historiography of Puritanism," in *Cambridge Companion to Puritanism*, pp. 356, 359, and 364.

17. David D. Hall, *A Reforming People: Puritanism and the Transformation of Public Life* (New York: Alfred A. Knopf, 2011), p. 194.

18. Hall, *A Reforming People*, p. xii. Similarly, another recovering revisionist acknowledges revisionism went too far. It likely overlooked, he says, the vital Puritan contribution to "an unprecedented surge of radical political thought" in the 1640s, which pushed English Protestantism "in new directions, preparing the ground for the radical Whig politics of eighteenth-century dissent." Coffey, "Puritan Legacies," in *Cambridge Companion to Puritanism*, p. 331.

ten code understood as fundamental law antecedent to the government and based on a "self-conscious," "direct and express" act by "the people" whom the government is taken to represent, in part by means of regular elections; attribution of political and legal authority, including limits on and division of power, such that any act of government outside the enumerated limits is an exercise of "power without right" and properly subject, if need be, to coercive restraint; an independent judiciary responsible to interpret statutory law and to evaluate its constitutionality; and the codification of a set of inalienable individual rights, whose enforcement is regarded as a critical condition of legitimate government.[19]

Over the course of his career, Calvin worked out views that to a greater or lesser degree approximated our present understanding of these basic features. In a fine new biography, Bruce Gordon states that Calvin's "rigorous legal training . . . taught [him] to frame legislation, write constitutions, and offer legal opinions, all of which would loom large in his Geneva career."[20] Along with his legal education in the Humanist tradition at the Universities of Orleans and Breuges from 1528 to 1530, Calvin was exposed earlier to the ideas of John Major, an eminent Scottish Conciliarist, who was teaching at the University of Paris when Calvin was a theological student there. Conciliarism, a late-medieval reform movement favoring government by representative councils in place of monarchy, had a decisive impact on Calvin's ideas.[21]

Calvin drew on the Conciliar tradition in elaborating his interpretations of constitutional government for both state and church. As to the state, he held the following:

- "Every commonwealth rests upon laws and agreements," preferably written,[22] that are regarded as fundamental to the protection of the "freedom of the people,"[23] a term he frequently invoked. Written law is "nothing but

19. Charles Howard McIlwain, *Constitutionalism: Ancient and Modern* (Ithaca: Cornell University Press, 1966), pp. 9, 14, 21, 76, 81, 117, 139-40.

20. Bruce Gordon, *Calvin* (New Haven: Yale University Press, 2009), p. 22.

21. See Quentin Skinner, *Foundations of Modern Political Thought*, vol. 2 (Cambridge: Cambridge University Press, 1979), pp. 114-23, for a good summary of Conciliar political thought. The connection between Conciliarism and Calvinism is, unfortunately, a neglected subject.

22. Calvin's *Homilies on I Samuel*, 10, cited in Herbert D. Foster, "Political Theories of Calvinists," *Collected Papers of Herbert D. Foster* (privately printed, 1929), p. 82.

23. John Calvin, *Institutes of the Christian Religion* (2 vols.), ed. John T. McNeill, trans. Ford Lewis Battles, Library of Christian Classics, vols. XX-XXI (Philadelphia: Westminster Press, 1960), bk. 4, ch. XX, para. 31, p. 1519.

an attestation of the [natural law], whereby God brings back to memory what has already been imprinted in our hearts."[24]

- The structure of government should be polyarchic rather than monarchic, "a system compounded of aristocracy and democracy." For "it is very rare for kings so to control themselves that their will never disagrees with what is just and right, or for them to have been endowed with such great keenness and prudence, that each knows how much is enough. Therefore, men's fault or failing causes it to be safer and more bearable for a number to exercise government."[25]

- "Certain remedies against tyranny are allowable, for example when magistrates and estates have been constituted, to whom has been committed the care of the commonwealth; they shall have power to keep the prince to his duty and even to coerce him if he attempt anything unlawful."[26] Especially toward the end of his life, and facing the Huguenot revolt in France, Calvin welcomed duly authorized redress on the part of "constitutional magistrates," as he called them, countenancing armed rebellion under their authority in extreme cases.[27] Shortly before he died, Calvin even went so far as to condone acts of individual resistance against tyrannical rulers.[28]

- A set of basic rights and freedoms are taken to undergird the founding agreement, and to comprise an imprescriptible limit on governmental power. They are a collection of what are best described as the "original natural rights of freedom," "associated with the second table of the Decalogue," and stressing especially the protection of "personal liberty and property," as well as the rights of conscience.[29]

A few comments on the rights of liberty and property, as well as of conscience, are in order. Underlying Calvin's commitment to constitutional government, as with the Conciliarists and others of the same persuasion, was an abhorrence of arbitrary power. Gradually, he came to support constitutionally authorized armed rebellion aimed at resisting "the fierce licentiousness of

---

24. Calvin's *Commentary on the Psalms* ch. 119, cited in Foster, *Collected Papers*, p. 82.

25. Calvin, *Institutes*, bk. 4, ch. XX, para. 8, p. 1493.

26. Calvin, *Opera Quae Supersunt Omnia*, vol. 29 (Brunsvigae, 1985), p. 552, cited in Foster, *Collected Papers*, p. 82.

27. Calvin, *Institutes*, bk. 4, ch XX, para. 31, pp. 1518-19, and fn. 54.

28. See Calvin, *Opera*, vol. 29, pp. 552-63.

29. Josef Bohatec, *Calvins Lehre von Staat und Kirche mit besonderer Berucksichtigung des Organismusgedankens* (Scientia Aalen, 1961), pp. 94-95 (translations are mine).

kings" "who violently fall upon and assault the lowly common folk,"[30] or as he puts it elsewhere, exercise "sheer robbery, plundering houses, raping virgins and matrons, and slaughtering the innocent."[31] To tolerate such atrocities is both to violate the natural "inborn feeling" "to hate and curse tyrants," and to "betray the freedom of the people."[32]

It is, then, the fundamental purpose of constitutions, and the basic rights they protect, to restrain arbitrary power. Arbitrary power may in part be defined as taking life, inflicting severe pain and suffering, expropriating property, and inhibiting thought and action basically for self-serving purposes. Such behavior is taken to be both wrong in itself and likely to provoke violent resistance. Accordingly, restraining the impulse to act that way — an impulse believed to be endemic to human experience — is the primary justification for constitutional government.

While particular constitutions may vary in certain ways, all have as their ultimate purpose to limit power by "equally press[ing] toward the same goal," namely, what Calvin calls "equity." It is "equity alone," he says, that "must be the goal and rule of all laws."[33] As the essence of the moral law "God has engraved upon the [human mind]," the idea consists of two rules: firstly, "that everyone's rights should be safely preserved,"[34] and, secondly, that everyone "be beneficent to neighbors" and "helpful to the necessities of others," relieving indigence with abundance.[35]

Civilly and politically, Calvin labored during his career in Geneva to expand the rules of due process[36] and to enlarge substantially the civil franchise,[37] and eventually, as mentioned above, he supported armed rebellion abroad aimed at restraining tyrannical power. As to economic justice, he embraced a theory of property rights going back to monastic theologians and developed by the Conciliarists.[38] It involved drawing a distinction between "inclusive rights,"

---

30. Calvin, *Institutes*, bk. 4, ch. XX, para. 31, p. 1519.

31. Calvin, *Institutes*, bk. 4, ch. XX, para. 24, p. 1512.

32. Calvin, *Institutes*, bk. 4, ch. XX, para. 24, p. 1512.

33. Calvin, *Institutes*, bk. 4, ch. XX, para. 16, p. 1504.

34. Calvin, *Commentaries on the Four Last Books of the Pentateuch*, vol. 3, trans. Charles William Bingham (Grand Rapids: Eerdmans, 1950), pp. 110-11.

35. Calvin, *Commentary on II Thessalonians, Calvin's Commentaries*, vol. 21 (Grand Rapids: Baker Books, 2009), p. 358.

36. John Witte Jr., *The Reformation of Rights: Law, Religion, and Human Rights in Early Modern Calvinism* (Cambridge: Cambridge University Press, 2007), p. 52.

37. Foster, "Calvin's Programme for a Puritan State," in *Collected Papers*, p. 65.

38. Brian Tierney, *Idea of Natural Rights: Studies on Natural Rights, Natural Law and Church Law, 1150-1625* (Atlanta: Scholars Press, 1997).

which naturally entitle all human beings to adequate sustenance and health, and "exclusive rights," which protect private property, but only so long as the inclusive rights are provided for. While Calvin nowhere spelled out specific state obligations, he defined "a just and well-regulated government" as one that upholds "the rights of the poor and afflicted," "who are exposed as easy prey to the cruelty and wrongs of the rich,"[39] and he favored and supported in practice welfare efforts in Geneva, both public and private.[40]

Calvin's ideas on the rights of conscience are tied to his theory of the church, and, it turns out, to a deep and pervasive ambivalence concerning constitutional government. On the one hand, he defended a very high doctrine of the sovereignty of conscience, which depends on a critical distinction between the "internal" and "external" forum. The first concerns personal, inward deliberation regarding fundamental belief and practice regulated by "spiritual power," meaning reliance on reasons and argument. The second concerns "external" or public deliberation regarding "outward behavior" — the needs of "the present life," such as food, clothing, and the laws of social cooperation — that are regulated by the "power of the sword," something that limits sovereignty of conscience.

Expositing Romans 13 early in his career, Calvin declared that the proper jurisdiction of a well-ordered government is exclusively that "part of the law that refers to human society," or the second table of the Decalogue, whose basic principle is that "all individuals should preserve their rights." "There is no allusion at all," he asserts, "to the first table of the law, which deals with the worship of God." Since "the whole of [Paul's] discussion [only] concerns civil government," "those who bear rule over consciences attempt to establish their blasphemous tyranny . . . in vain."[41] In short, the subject matter of the first table is the province of conscience, which, except when it threatens to subvert the civil and economic rights of others, ought to be entirely free from state regulation.

In keeping with this line of thought, the church, for Calvin, is the locus of what he calls "liberated consciences." Its members comprehend more fully than non-Christians the "goal and rule of all laws" — the principle of equity (respect for the rights of all supplemented by special concern for the deprived

39. Calvin, *Commentary on the Psalms, Calvin's Commentaries*, vol. 5, pp. 331-32.

40. Robert M. Kingdon, "Social Welfare in Calvin's Geneva," in *Church and Society in Reformation Europe* (London: Variorum Reprints, 1985); and Jennine E. Olson, *Calvin and Social Welfare: Deacons and the Bourse Francaise* (London: Associated University Presses, 1989).

41. Calvin, *Epistles of Paul the Apostle to the Romans and to the Thessalonians*, trans. Ross Mackenzie (Grand Rapids: Eerdmans, 1976), p. 284.

and vulnerable), and they are endowed with a new capacity to embrace and act upon its requirements by means of "spiritual power," *not* the "right of the sword."[42] For this reason, Calvin is particularly emphatic about constitutionalizing the church, about carefully defining and separating the powers of church government so as to maximize the opportunity for voluntary participation by "the people," thereby protecting their fundamental rights, including, above all, their right to conduct their affairs free of state interference. It was, of course, regarding just such issues that Calvin was expelled from Geneva in 1538 by town fathers jealous of their authority over church life. That he was invited back in 1541 marked a certain concession on their part to his belief in an independent church.

It should be stressed that this more liberal side of Calvin's thought presupposed the existence of a natural moral law that is universally both accessible and obligatory. Otherwise, it would not be possible to hold non-Christians accountable, and therefore legitimately subject to coercion, for violations of the restrictions on arbitrary power. It is clear that Calvin held such a view, but he held it only some of the time.[43]

That brings us to the "other side" of Calvin's thought regarding the proper shape of constitutional government. While, in my view, he was always ambivalent about the natural moral capability of human beings, he became increasingly skeptical toward the end of his life, perhaps sometime around 1553 with the trial and execution of Michael Servetus, as John Witte suggests.[44] It is after that event that he specifically reversed himself in regards to limiting the jurisdiction of the state to the second table of the Decalogue, now calling upon civil magistrates to enforce "the outward worship of God" as well as "sound doctrine of piety and the position of the Church."[45] Obviously, such prescriptions radically restricted the right to freedom of conscience, and, by implication, the exercise and enjoyment of other rights as well. To establish religion, to bring both tables of the Decalogue more directly under the control of the state, is to limit the opportunities of citizens not only religiously, but also politically, civilly, and economically. While Geneva during Calvin's career was never free of such regulation, it appears to have intensified after 1555 when Calvin reached his full powers of influence.

Calvin's growing skepticism about natural moral capabilities appears

---

42. Calvin, *Institutes*, bk. 4, ch. XI, para. 4, p. 1217.
43. See David Little, "Calvin and Natural Rights," *Political Theology* 10:3 (2009): 411-30.
44. Witte, *Reformation of Rights*, p. 56.
45. Calvin, *Institutes*, bk. 4, ch. XX, para. 2, p. 1487.

also to have colored his constitutional preferences in both church and state. While at pains to expand democratic participation in both places, he was undoubtedly biased, in the final analysis, toward the "aristocratic" side of his constitutional proposals. What he said about the administration of the church could also go for civil order: Special deference to officials is required in elections, as in the general conduct of affairs, because of the natural disposition of the multitudes to fickleness, shortsightedness, or perversity. Moreover, his deepening suspicion of natural moral capabilities also strengthened in his mind the indispensability of the Reformed church as the locus of true righteousness, and therefore as the exclusive foundation of state authority and practice.

While Calvin made considerable room theoretically for a "liberal" interpretation of constitutional government, based on an expansive understanding of the right to freedom of conscience, both inside and outside the church, he very much qualified that interpretation in practice — increasingly, in the latter years of his tenure in Geneva.

The American Puritan Connection

It is this deep ambivalence toward constitutional government, focused on the understanding of the right to freedom of conscience, but with critical implications for the protection of all rights, that best characterizes the "American branch" of Calvinism, as we might describe the Puritan movement in colonial America. Thanks to our examination of Calvin, we can now see more clearly the roots of the reforming zeal that bound Puritans together, as well as some of the reasons for the abiding fractiousness of the movement. All Puritans wanted constitutional reform of both church and state, but they divided sharply and variously over what sort of reform that should be.

While they by no means agreed on everything, American Puritans, "in their covenanted towns and congregations," as David Hall puts it, *were* of one mind that the "crucial feature of all covenants" is "a people's willing consent," that "covenant [is an] instrument and expression of popular decision-making."[46] That common conviction underlay their commitment to constitutional government, and, in fact, explains their pioneering role in the rise of modern constitutionalism.

According to a leading authority, the Charter of Massachusetts Bay of 1629

46. Hall, *A Reforming People*, p. 157.

"was not strictly a popular constitution, because it was in form and legal effect a royal grant, but in its practical operation after the transfer, it approximated a popular constitution more closely than any other instrument of government in actual use up to that time in America or elsewhere in modern times."[47] Moreover, Massachusetts Bay authorities went well beyond the original wording, claiming that their charter permitted an astounding degree of political independence. As early as 1641, they refused help from the English Parliament because the colony might "then be subject to all such laws as [the Parliament] should make or at least such as [it] might impose upon us."[48] When in 1646 the authorities were criticized for considering themselves "rather a free state than a colony or corporation of England," they agreed! Parliament might have authority in England, but "the highest authority here is in [our legislature], *both by our charter and by our own positive laws. . . . [O]ur allegiance binds us not to the laws of England any longer than we live in England.*"[49] This same interpretation applied to the charters of the other colonies as well. Though American Puritans were slow to admit it, it was not a large step to the eventual replacement of the authority of the English crown, as well as of Parliament, with the will of "the people" who inhabited the colonies.[50]

Of greatest importance was the impulse in Massachusetts Bay and other colonies to adopt declarations of rights as an important feature of their early constitutions. The Body of Liberties was adopted by the Massachusetts Bay legislature in 1641, and amounted to an exceptionally lengthy list of fundamental rights.[51] Though it incorporated provisions from English statutes and precedents, it went well beyond them. It redefined and restructured the traditional rights of English subjects in the light of Puritan Christianity, adding modified portions of Biblical law and some "daring rights proposals"[52] from left-wing English Puritan pamphleteers.

The document opens, significantly, by referring to "such liberties, immunities, and privileges" that "humanity, civility, and Christianity call for as due

47. C. H. McIlwain, *Constitutionalism and Its Changing World* (Cambridge: Cambridge University Press, 1939), p. 241.

48. From *Winthrop's Journal*, cited in McIlwain, *Constitutionalism and Its Changing World*, p. 234.

49. McIlwain, *Constitutionalism and Its Changing World*, p. 235, emphasis added.

50. Donald S. Lutz, *Origins of American Constitutionalism* (Baton Rouge: Louisiana State University Press, 1988), p. 37.

51. Edmund S. Morgan, *Puritan Political Ideas, 1558-1794* (Indianapolis: Bobbs-Merrill Co., 1965), pp. 171-97.

52. Witte, *Reformation of Rights*, p. 280.

to every man in his place and proportion without impeachment or infringement," highlighting the several grounds, religious *and* natural, that rights were believed to rest on.[53] In the first article, the document goes on to enumerate certain fundamental protections against taking life or property, or imposing penalties and burdens, "unless it be by some virtue or equity of some express law . . . established by the [legislature] and sufficiently published. . . ."[54] David Hall makes much of the idea of equity in Puritan New England, echoing what it meant for Calvin (respect for the rights of all supplemented by a special concern for the deprived and vulnerable). Equity "may best be understood," he says, "as expressing strong hopes for even-handedness in a world where 'unrighteousness and iniquity were visibly present in the workings of English politics, civil society, ecclesiastical governance, and the law, each of which was aligned with structures of privilege and power.'"[55]

Hall mentions several kinds of legal reform present in the Body of Liberties aimed at creating a more "equitable society." One was "a cluster of rights and privileges for plaintiffs and defendants with virtually no equivalent in English law," including a "more impartial method of selecting juries than was the norm in England."[56] Another was significantly limiting capital punishment, and abolishing what the code calls "revolting barbarities of the English law." Still another was the abolition of monopolies, which in England had been arbitrarily dispensed to favorites of the Crown, and abolishing as well the practice of primogeniture. In its place was established (though not always observed) a more equitable system of inheritance, including provisions for female children. In that way and others, according to Hall, "the colonists eliminated all but a few traces of the social privileges that pervaded the English system and remade justice into a matter of equal treatment before the law."[57] Incidentally, in respect to the distribution of wealth, Hall stresses that Puritan rhetoric was fervently and repeatedly addressed to the obligations of the affluent for the indigent, accompanied by efforts to make tax policy more equitable than was the case in England,[58] and in places to guarantee "each adult male" "some land, free and clear."[59]

---

53. Morgan, *Puritan Political Ideas,* pp. 172-73. I have modernized and here and there "translated" some of the archaic words and forms of speech in the Body of Liberties, and in some of the subsequent citations from Puritan writings.

54. Morgan, *Puritan Political Ideas,* p. 173.

55. Hall, *A Reforming People,* p. 147.

56. Hall, *A Reforming People,* p. 150.

57. Hall, *A Reforming People,* p. 152.

58. Hall, *A Reforming People,* pp. 67-70.

59. Hall, *A Reforming People,* pp. 64-65.

There was, however, one part of the Body of Liberties that generated a particularly strong division of opinion: the rights pertaining to religious belief and practice, namely, section 95, articles 1 through 11, identified as "A Declaration of the Liberties the Lord Jesus hath given to the Churches." According to these articles, all members of the colony had "full liberty" to practice religion according to conscience, though only so long as they "be orthodox in judgment," and, "every church has full liberty to elect church officers," "provided they be able, pious and orthodox."

This was of course the basis of what John Cotton, a prominent clergyman in the colony, referred to as the "theocratic" character of Massachusetts Bay, namely, a state governed by officials regarded as divinely guided.[60] It is true, Cotton and other leaders believed that church and state should not be "confounded," meaning that magistrates were precluded from holding church office, and church officials from holding civil office. At the same time, he and his associates affirmed with equal resolution that only church members should vote in civil elections, that churches and clergymen should receive direct public support through taxes and other donations, and that religious beliefs and practices should be extensively and severely regulated by laws covering blasphemy, irreverence, profanity, idolatry, and "schismatic" activity.

Although the position was widely shared, by no means did all Puritans agree with the official Massachusetts Bay policy concerning the meaning of "full liberty" of religious belief and practice, or with the commitment to established religion. Roger Williams, a controversial figure from the time he set foot in the New World in 1631, and himself evicted from the colony for unorthodox beliefs five years later, strongly opposed the Massachusetts Bay establishment, and, from his new-found perch in Rhode Island, took up the case against it in a lengthy and heated dispute in print with none other than John Cotton himself.

In essence, the conflict between Cotton and Williams personified dramatically the two sides of the Calvinist background. Both figures were staunch constitutionalists, favoring limited government, and most of the protections enunciated in the Body of Liberties — though they differed, of course, on the *degree* of limits and the *range* of protections. Both were committed to Reformed doctrine and use of scripture in guiding faith and morals, though Williams, it is true, was increasingly skeptical, as Cotton was not, of Reformed ecclesiology. He seemed to take to extremes the motto "the church reformed, always reforming."

---

60. Cotton actually uses the term to describe what in his mind is "the best form of government in the commonwealth, as well as the church," in Morgan, *Puritan Political Ideas*, p. 163.

What divided them most fundamentally was the right to the freedom of conscience and the implications of that difference for the organization of church-state relations, and the enjoyment of civil and political rights. Williams put the issue between them as sharply as possible, quoting passages that pitted Calvin against himself. When Calvin declared that Romans 13 restricts the jurisdiction of the state exclusively to the second table, he was an "excellent servant of God," as Williams writes in *The Bloody Tenent of Persecution,* published in 1644.[61] But when Calvin assigned "Christ's ordinances and administrations of worship . . . to a civil state, town or city, as [in] the instance of Geneva," Williams rejected that practice unconditionally as a contradiction of Calvinist principles.[62]

Williams proceeded to develop his case against Massachusetts Bay very much within the framework of Calvin's "liberal" side. There is the same reliance on the distinction between the "inward" and the "outward" forum, and the accompanying distinction between "spirit" and "sword," and between the two tables of the Decalogue, that Calvin presupposed. There is the same belief that human beings are, within limits, naturally capable of recognizing violations of "second table crimes" prior to and independent of special religious enlightenment, and insofar as they do not violate those prohibitions, they may — and should — be left free to determine their religious convictions as their consciences dictate. It is important to emphasize that in constructing his position, Williams (like Calvin) invoked several separate arguments, some based explicitly on reason and experience, others derived from scripture and doctrine. To his mind, these arguments all worked together. In particular, he repeatedly emphasized, in keeping with the conclusions of Grim and Finke, that the persecution of conscience "fills the streams and rivers with blood."

It is, of course, on these grounds, taken together, that Williams opposed so fervently all forms of established, or what he called "National," religion so prevalent at his time. He was very clear: Given forms of political "power, might or authority [are] not religious, Christian, etc., but natural, humane, and civil."[63] His commitment to the principle of non-establishment was based on a belief in an independent natural moral law accessible to and obligatory upon all people, and it led to a remarkable expansion not only of the rights of conscience but of

61. Roger Williams, *A Bloody Tenent of Persecution,* in *Complete Writings of Roger Williams,* 7 vols. (New York: Russell & Russell, 1963), vol. 3, p. 153.

62. *Complete Writings of Roger Williams,* 7 vols. (New York: Russell & Russell, 1963), vol. 3, p. 225.

63. *Complete Writings of Roger Williams,* 7 vols. (New York: Russell & Russell, 1963), vol. 3, p. 398.

civil, political, and economic rights as well, as expressed in the Rhode Island Civil Code of 1647 and the Rhode Island Charter of 1663.

Martha Nussbaum has demonstrated convincingly in her book, *Liberty of Conscience*,[64] that it is Roger Williams, not John Locke, Thomas Jefferson, or James Madison, who provided the intellectual foundations for the expansive constitutional protection of conscience, that, she believes, Jefferson and Madison intended.

> Many Americans who have a hard time identifying with Jefferson's rather smug disdain for religiosity can find their own concerns well represented in Williams's fervent spiritual quest. His arguments show us clearly that one may be a deeply committed religious person while yet believing that fairness, and the worth of the individual conscience, require a wide and equal religious liberty and a ban on religious orthodoxies in state government.[65]

The only serious shortcoming in Nussbaum's otherwise excellent book is the failure to appreciate the Calvinist background, or at least one side of it. She mistakenly invokes the Stoics as the basis for Williams's approach and thereby neglects the tradition of constitutionalism and natural rights that Calvin and many of his followers so clearly, if sometimes so ambivalently, represented.

Conclusion

We have assumed, following the advocates of "the liberal peace," that "the rule of law and constitutional consent," including "a basic framework of rights and duties of citizens," are crucial foundations for durable peace. But we have questioned some of the presuppositions of those advocates, such as the disregard or "smug disdain" for religion, and certain neoliberal convictions about economic justice. Accordingly, we have offered a fresh historical narrative that does two things: It highlights the critical role of religious thought and action in establishing some of the grounds of the liberal peace, and it reveals some intellectual resources for reevaluating our understanding of the protection of the rights of free conscience, as well as of civil, political, and economic rights.

I certainly do not mean to suggest that the Calvinist background, together with its connections to American Puritanism and thus to one interpretation,

64. Martha C. Nussbaum, *Liberty of Conscience: In Defense of America's Tradition of Religious Equality* (New York: Basic Books, 2008).
65. Nussbaum, *Liberty of Conscience*, p. 70.

at least, of American constitutional protection of conscience, is the exclusive source of such an outcome, or that it is an infallible or exhaustive guide for reevaluation. But I do think the background contains some principles, such as the idea of equity David Hall makes so much of, that introduce moral considerations concerning assistance to the deprived and vulnerable that have too often been ignored in discussions of the liberal peace.

Above all, I would like to state as my last word how much this Calvinist background, starting in part with Calvin himself, anticipated what Judith Shklar called "liberalism of fear" in her classic essay by that name.[66] When Calvin stated that pervasive human "fault or failing causes it to be safer and more bearable for a number [of authorities, rather than one] to exercise government," he was summarizing Shklar's basic point. The heart of liberalism, understood as constitutional democracy, "is freedom from the abuse of power and intimidation of the defenseless that [inequality] invites."[67]

Bibliography

Bohatec, Josef. *Calvins Lehre von Staat und Kirche mit besonderer Berucksichtingung des Organismusgedankens.* Scientia Aalen, 1961.

Calvin, John. *Calvin's Commentaries.* 23 vols. Grand Rapids: Baker Books, 2009.

———. *Commentaries on the Four Last Books of the Pentateuch.* Vol. 3. Translated by Charles William Bingham. Grand Rapids: Wm. B. Eerdmans, 1950.

———. *Epistles of Paul the Apostle to the Romans and to the Thessalonians.* Translated by Ross Mackenzie. Grand Rapids: Eerdmans, 1976.

———. *Institutes of the Christian Religion.* 2 vols. Edited by John T. McNeill. Translated by Ford Lewis Battles. Library of Christian Classics, vols. XX-XXI. Philadelphia: Westminster Press, 1960.

———. *Opera Quae Supersunt Omnia.* 59 vols. Brunsvigae, 1985.

Coffey, John. "Puritan Legacies." In *Cambridge Companion to Puritanism,* 327-45. Edited by John Coffey and Paul C. H. Lim. Cambridge: Cambridge University Press, 2008.

Coffey, John, and Paul C. H. Lim. "Introduction." In *Cambridge Companion to Puritanism,* 1-18. Edited by John Coffey and Paul C. H. Lim. Cambridge: Cambridge University Press, 2008.

Collier, Paul. "Economic Causes of Civil Conflict and Their Implications for Policy." In *Turbulent Peace: The Challenges of Managing International Conflict,* 143-62.

66. Judith N. Shklar, "Liberalism of Fear," in *Liberalism and the Moral Life,* ed. Nancy L. Rosenblum (Cambridge: Harvard University Press, 1989).

67. Shklar, "Liberalism of Fear," p. 27.

Edited by Chester A. Crocker, Fen Osler Hampson, and Pamela Aall. Washington, D.C.: United States Institute of Peace Press, 2001.

Diamond, Larry. *The Spirit of Democracy: The Struggle to Build Free Societies throughout the World*. New York: Times Books, 2008.

Doyle, Michael W., and Nicholas Sambanis. *Making War and Building Peace: United Nations Peace Operations*. Princeton: Princeton University Press, 2006.

Foster, Herbert D. "Political Theories of Calvinists." *Collected Papers of Herbert D. Foster*. Privately printed, 1929.

Gordon, Bruce. *Calvin*. New Haven: Yale University Press, 2009.

Grim, Brian J., and Roger Finke. *The Price of Freedom Denied: Religious Persecution and Conflict in the Twenty-First Century*. New York: Cambridge University Press, 2011.

Gurr, Ted Robert. *Peoples versus States: Minorities at Risk in the New Century*. Washington, D.C.: United States Institute of Peace Press, 2000.

Gurr, Ted Robert, and Barbara Harff. *Ethnic Conflict in Global Politics*. Boulder, Colo.: Westview Press, 2004.

Hall, David D. *A Reforming People: Puritanism and the Transformation of Public Life*. New York: Alfred A. Knopf, 2011.

Halperin, Morton H., Joseph T. Siegle, and Michael M. Weinstein. *The Democracy Advantage: How Democracies Promote Prosperity and Peace*. New York: Routledge, 2004.

Kingdon, Robert M. "Social Welfare in Calvin's Geneva." In *Church and Society in Reformation Europe*. London: Variorum Reprints, 1985.

Lake, Peter. "The Historiography of Puritanism." In *Cambridge Companion to Puritanism*, 346-72. Edited by John Coffey and Paul C. H. Lim. Cambridge: Cambridge University Press, 2008.

Little, David. "Calvin and Natural Rights." *Political Theology* 10:3 (2009): 411-30.

Little, David, and Donald K. Swearer, eds. *Religion and Nationalism in Iraq: A Comparative Perspective*. Cambridge: Harvard University Press, 2006.

Lutz, Donald S. *Origins of American Constitutionalism*. Baton Rouge: Louisiana State University Press, 1988.

Mansfield, Edward D., and Jack Snyder. "Democratic Transitions and War: From Napoleon to the Millennium's End." In *Turbulent Peace: The Challenges of Managing International Conflict*, 113-26. Edited by Chester A. Crocker, Fen Osler Hampson, and Pamela Aall. Washington, D.C.: United States Institute of Peace Press, 2001.

———. *Electing to Fight: Why Emerging Democracies Go to War*. Cambridge: MIT Press, 2005.

McIlwain, Charles Howard. *Constitutionalism and Its Changing World*. Cambridge: Cambridge University Press, 1939.

———. *Constitutionalism: Ancient and Modern*. Ithaca: Cornell University Press, 1966.

Morgan, Edmund S. *Puritan Political Ideas, 1558-1794.* Indianapolis: Bobbs-Merrill Co., 1965.

Nussbaum, Martha C. *Liberty of Conscience: In Defense of America's Tradition of Religious Equality.* New York: Basic Books, 2008.

Olson, Jennine E. *Calvin and Social Welfare: Deacons and the Bourse Francaise.* London: Associated University Presses, 1989.

Paris, Roland. *At War's End: Building Peace after Civil Conflict.* New York: Cambridge University Press, 2004.

Philpott, Daniel. "Introduction: Searching for Strategy in an Age of Peacebuilding." In *Strategies of Peace: Transforming Conflict in a Violent World,* 3-18. Edited by Daniel Philpott and Gerard F. Powers. New York: Oxford University Press, 2010.

———. "Reconciliation: An Ethic for Peacebuilding." In *Strategies of Peace: Transforming Conflict in a Violent World,* 91-118. Edited by Daniel Philpott and Gerard F. Powers. New York: Oxford University Press, 2010.

———. *Just and Unjust Peace: An Ethic of Reconciliation.* New York: Oxford University Press, 2012.

Powers, Gerard F. "Religion and Peacebuilding." In *Strategies of Peace: Transforming Conflict in a Violent World,* 317-52. Edited by Daniel Philpott and Gerard F. Powers. New York: Oxford University Press, 2010.

Rummel, R. J. *Power Kills: Democracy as a Model of Nonviolence.* New Brunswick, N.J.: Transaction, 2004.

Shklar, Judith N. "Liberalism of Fear." In *Liberalism and the Moral Life.* Edited by Nancy L. Rosenblum. Cambridge: Harvard University Press, 1989.

Skinner, Quentin. *Foundations of Modern Political Thought.* Cambridge: Cambridge University Press, 1979.

Smith, Jackie. "Economic Globalization and Strategic Peacebuilding." In *Strategies of Peace: Transforming Conflict in a Violent World,* 247-70. Edited by Daniel Philpott and Gerald F. Powers. New York: Oxford University Press, 2010.

Stiglitz, Joseph E. *Globalization and Its Discontents.* New York: Norton & Co., 2003.

Snyder, Jack. *From Voting to Violence: Democratization and Nationalist Conflict.* New York: W. W. Norton & Co., 2000.

Tierney, Brian. *Idea of Natural Rights: Studies on Natural Rights, Natural Law and Church Law, 1150-1625.* Atlanta: Scholars Press, 1997.

Williams, Roger. *A Bloody Tenent of Persecution.* In *Complete Writings of Roger Williams.* 7 vols. New York: Russell & Russell, 1963.

Witte, John, Jr. *The Reformation of Rights: Law, Religion, and Human Rights in Early Modern Calvinism.* Cambridge: Cambridge University Press, 2007.

Christianity and the Class Struggle

Jeffrey Stout

The title of my lecture comes from Dirk Jellema's 1950 translation of a short book by Abraham Kuyper, based on a lecture he delivered in 1891 to the first Christian Social Congress in the Netherlands. James Skillen retranslated Kuyper's book in 1991 under the title *The Problem of Poverty*.[1] You may be forgiven for thinking, as I did before beginning my research for this presentation, that Jellema and Skillen had translated different works on separate topics.

A literal translation of the Dutch title would be "The Social Problem and the Christian Religion." It is easy to see why our two translators, or perhaps their publishers, didn't want to go with that. A "social problem" sounds like an affliction Mel Gibson or a fractious theology department might have. But by *the social problem,* Kuyper simply means a grave disordering of relationships among groups in the society of his time and place.

He claims that the "untenability of the present state of affairs" must be accounted for "not by incidental causes but by a fault in the very foundation of our society's organization" (44). The book has four sections, for which Skillen supplies titles and Jellema does not. Skillen's section titles reinforce his theme of poverty.[2] But poverty is only one important feature of the disordering

1. Abraham Kuyper, *Het sociale Vraagstuk en de Christelijke Religie* (Amsterdam, Netherlands: Wormser, 1891). Abraham Kuyper, *Christianity and the Class Struggle,* trans. Dirk Jellema (Grand Rapids: Piet Hut, 1950). Abraham Kuyper, *The Problem of Poverty,* trans. James W. Skillen (Sioux Center, Iowa: Dordt College Press, 2011), originally published in 1991 by Baker Book House. I shall be quoting from Skillen's translation, and citing his pages parenthetically in the text.

2. See also Richard J. Mouw, *Abraham Kuyper: A Short and Personal Introduction* (Grand

Kuyper is describing. With his help, I want to tease some of these features apart and consider how they are related to one another in our situation.

The first section of the book argues that Kuyper's socialist contemporaries are right to declare existing societal relationships severely out of whack. The second section gives biblical grounds, derived from the teachings of Jesus, for taking "a stand against such an evil state of affairs" (29). The third section criticizes various modern responses to the social disorder of the era: the French Revolution, nihilism, anarchism, social democracy, state socialism, and "cynical pessimism." The fourth section sketches a neo-Calvinist alternative.

Kuyper acknowledges that the Dutch Congress is tardy in addressing the social problem, as compared with other Christian groups in Europe, including British Protestants inspired by Maurice and Kingsley and Catholics instructed by Pope Leo XIII. After chastising himself and his Dutch audience, Kuyper cites his political mentor Guillaume Groen van Prinsterer and the poets Willem Bilderdijk and Isaac Da Costa as precedents for the sort of stance that needs to be taken. He moves directly from shaming his audience to invoking a tradition with which he identifies and wants his audience to identify.

Why have Dutch Calvinists been tardy in addressing the social problem? Perhaps they hate the false remedies of socialism more than they love justice. "It will do no good," Kuyper declares, "to scoff at 'justice for all' . . . and to let the stupid crowd sing about all the 'socialists in a herring barrel'" (47). Groen was right to chastise the upper classes for the "moral corruption and pseudo-science" that have inflicted harm on the people (19). Society is out of whack, disfigured by sin. The purpose of government, by Kuyper's Calvinist lights, is to constrain sin.

Kuyper's book does not use the expression *class struggle,* but section three does speak of a "struggle for money" on the part of classes unequal in "experience and insight, ability and association, available money and available influence." The result, Kuyper explains, is a "social scale" with "millionaires" at one end and "ant-poor drudges" at the other. The problem is not simply that the millionaires are rich and drudges poor, but that a "well-to-do bourgeoisie *rules over* an impoverished working class, which *exists to increase the wealth* of the ruling class" (italics added). He claims that workers are thereby reduced to "instruments for nourishing capital," while all wealth not strictly required for maintaining the instrumental value of workers is absorbed "by the smaller and larger capitalists" (39-40).

Rapids: Eerdmans, 2011), pp. 35-37, which, despite quoting from the Jellema translation, describes Kuyper's book as "addressing issues of poverty."

The Jellema title, with its reference to class struggle, was meant to make the book seem relevant to a generation that had lived through the Great Depression, endured the horrors of World War II, and then found itself wondering what sort of society it had been fighting for. In the U.S., this was the generation that would shortly end legal segregation and raise the tax rate for top earners to about 91 percent.

By the time Skillen published *The Problem of Poverty* in 1991, the expression *class struggle* might have seemed too divisive, and too indebted to Marxism, to be well received by an American church audience. The Soviet Union was formally dissolved by the end of that year. The income share of the top one percent had climbed by a factor of about half during the presidencies of Ronald Reagan and George Bush the elder. Reagan had taken the top bracket's tax rate down to 28 percent in 1988, and the percentage of Americans living in poverty was rising, as Skillen must have noticed.

In an address to the Conservative Political Action Conference in 1982, Reagan had reframed the social problem in the following questions: "Since when do we in America believe that our society is made up of two diametrically opposed classes — one rich, one poor — both in a permanent state of conflict and neither able to get ahead except at the expense of the other? Since when do we in America accept this alien and discredited theory of social and class warfare?" The remedy Reagan proposed involved not only lower taxes for the wealthy, but also deregulation of corporations, restriction of unions, a monetary policy aimed more at lowering inflation than at lowering unemployment, and repeal of minimum-wage laws.

The benefits were supposed to trickle down. Reagan defended *direct* benefits for the wealthy executives of major corporations on the *theory* that nearly everyone else who *deserved* to benefit would do so, albeit *indirectly*. In the same speech to CPAC, he referred proudly to having excluded "the cheaters and undeserving" from the welfare rolls in California when he was governor. There are diametrically opposed groups in America, according to Reagan, but they are not rich and poor. They are the deserving and the undeserving. The disincentives of poverty and imprisonment could be trusted to set the undeserving on the right path. In the meantime, the deserving would rise in the tide lifting all boats, and faith-based charity — what Bush the elder later christened the "thousand points of light" — would suffice to rescue anyone who had accidentally fallen overboard.

The results, as we now know, included the largest transfer of wealth from the middle class to the top managerial class in American history. Between the inauguration of Reagan and the financial crisis of 2008, the share of the income distribution going to the top 1 percent rose to 23.5 percent, up from 8.9 percent under Carter, and just short of the previous high since 1913, which was in 1928, immediately before the Great Depression. Between 1980 and 2008, the income of the top 1 percent after taxes grew by 281 percent, which is well more than ten times the rate of increase for the middle 20 percent. By 2009, the CEOs of major corporations took home 263 times the compensation of the average worker, with the greatest benefits going to the CEOs who slashed jobs the most.[3]

Why did so many people on the losing end of these outcomes expect anything else? In part, I suspect, because they wanted to believe that creativity, hard work, and niceness were enough, in a relatively unconstrained economy, to bring prosperity to the deserving. As for the direct beneficiaries of Reaganite policies, including Christians among the top CEOs, the theory of indirect benefits meant not needing to think of oneself as corrupted by greed. In what is believed to be a win-win economic situation for everyone who deserves to benefit, the real moral danger is envy down low, not greed on high.

The idea that all boats would rise together if the yachts, ocean liners, oil tankers, drilling stations, and offshore tax shelters were permitted to grow neglected certain manifest facts about what causes small boats to sink and oceans to darken, but it was a nice thing for nice people to believe. Niceness, when combined with unrealistic faith in economic pseudoscience, is pseudo virtue.

By the summer of 2011, Tavis Smiley and Cornel West were touring America, drawing attention to what the problem of poverty had become in the wake of the Great Recession, and by mid-autumn the Occupy Movement had put the rhetoric of class struggle back into circulation. Is it time to reissue the Jellema translation of Kuyper? Perhaps Eerdmans will soon commission yet another translation, this one to be entitled "Christianity and Economic Inequality." *Inequality* is, after all, the concept most often invoked across the political spectrum as a name for the issue now agitating the young. I would advise Eerdmans against using it. *Inequality* is not an apt name for what ails our political economy, at least when used to refer to differences in wealth or income.

Libertarians hold that inequality of wealth or income isn't a problem in itself and that a society of economic equals would lack both liberty and an acceptable standard of living. It might surprise you to hear that I consider libertarians correct on both points. The trouble with these points is not that they are false, but rather their function as red herrings. Worse, the libertarian

3. I am using statistics from http://inequality.org/income-inequality/, consulted on April 16, 2012.

interpretation of their significance gets the nature of liberty wrong. This will take some explaining.

Equality, strictly speaking, is a dichotomous rather than a scalar concept. Two incomes are either equal or not. Inequality does not come in degrees. If Buffett's income equals Gates's, then the two incomes are *the same.* If the two incomes differ *at all,* then they are not equal, period. They do not become less equal if the difference grows. There is therefore no such thing as growing inequality of income or wealth, at least for someone who cares about precision in the use of English. There is, of course, a yawning *gap* in income and wealth, but we need some way of clarifying what ethical significance it might have.

If inequality of income were, strictly speaking, important, then it ought to matter to us whether Buffett's income differs even slightly from Gates's. Our concern for equality would then be a reason for us to keep the state interfering with the professional labor market until Buffett and Gates made the same amount. And every time the market shifted a little, we would have to call on the state again.

A state of that sort would indeed be a threat to liberty, on *any* reasonable definition of liberty, and it would also inhibit many of the activities that produce the wealth being distributed. So when the issue is framed in terms of inequality of income or wealth, and we commit ourselves to using the concept precisely, it becomes hard to deny that libertarians are correct in making the two points I conceded a moment ago. Moreover, those conclusions appear to provide adequate reason for opposing the call for equality as pernicious. If that is what democracy calls for in economics, it is wrong.

I don't care whether Buffett's income equals Gates's, and if one of *them* cares, he probably *is* guilty of envy. Equality of income, strictly speaking, isn't important. Neither is equality of wealth. But the conflict between liberty and these forms of equality is a red herring. The people now complaining about "inequality" aren't really committed to the goal of equal distribution, so they aren't really calling for a state that could achieve that end. The cost of speaking imprecisely is to make their cause vulnerable to libertarian rebuttal. The rhetoric of economic inequality obfuscates the issue.

In a characteristically well-wrought article on why equality of income and wealth isn't important, my colleague Harry Frankfurt writes: "what *is* important from the point of view of morality is not that everyone should have *the same* but that each should have *enough.*" He calls the latter idea "the doctrine of sufficiency."[4] But what does this mean, that each should have enough?

---

4. Harry Frankfurt, "Equality as a Moral Ideal," in *The Importance of What We Care About* (Cambridge: Cambridge University Press, 1988), pp. 134-35.

Enough of *what*? And enough *for* what? If the answer is "enough income for survival" or "enough for a minimally acceptable life," then we are back to discussing what Skillen calls the problem of poverty, in which case we had better sharpen up our terms for discussing it.[5]

I doubt, however, that the issue of economic justice boils down to a concern with poverty. About 15 percent of the U.S. population — which is to say, around 46 million people — have incomes below the official poverty level. That's a lot of people, in many different degrees and types of woe, all of which are worthy of concern and causal explanation. But why be concerned about the condition of the rest of the population? Why speak of the 99 percent and the 1 percent? Why not speak instead of the 15 percent and the 85 percent? What is it that ought to trouble us about the relationship between the top earning American family and, say, a family just above the median in income, assuming that the latter has enough to provide for such necessities as shelter, food, and medical care?

Perhaps Kuyper can help us answer these questions. He is not concerned merely with *poverty*, but also with certain other features of the social problem, the most important of which are what I shall call *domination* and *exploitation*. He appears to think that poverty, domination, and exploitation are distinct but intertwined. He doesn't delineate the differences and relations systematically, but we can learn from what he says.

Poverty designates what Kuyper calls the "misery," "material need," or "wretched condition of the lower classes" (55, 56, 19) — the vague and ambiguous, but important, problem of insufficiency. *Domination* is Kuyper's concern when he rejects plutocracy, in Da Costa's terms, as "the rule of money" (19), or when he describes the bourgeoisie as *ruling over* the lower classes (40). When one group rules over others unchecked, it is in a position to exercise power

---

5. Gordon Graham points out that the concept of poverty is "a *relative* notion twice over," first because it involves implicit reference to one or more respects in which someone is poor, and second because it involves implicit reference to some standard. See *The Idea of Christian Charity: A Critique of Some Contemporary Conceptions* (Notre Dame: University of Notre Dame Press, 1990), pp. 118-22; italics in original. I agree with Graham that this double relativity is important to keep in mind, but not with his conclusion that "The whole conception of 'the poor' as a social or political class is misguided" (p. 120). What is misguided is speaking of the poor without specifying what respects of deficiency and what standards for appraising them one has in mind. In many social circumstances, there is a discernable class of people who lack the material resources required to survive, or to have adequate shelter, or to afford medical care. We all know roughly what we mean by referring to such people as "the poor." We also know that the poor in spirit include lots of people with ample material resources.

arbitrarily over them.[6] *Exploitation* is Kuyper's topic when he refers, with Da Costa, to "the work that gives no bread" (19), with Bilderdijk, to the luxury that "feasts on the hands" of the poor (18), and in his own voice, to the reduction of workers to instruments (40).[7]

The struggle over money, Kuyper holds, has become a conflict between a dominant economic group and those dominated by it. A dominant group benefits from a power imbalance severe enough to permit it to *rule over* others in the sense of being in a position to exercise power *arbitrarily over them*. Economic domination is often at the root of the other two evils, because it permits one class to escape accountability for mistreating others. Exploitation is one kind of mistreatment, and destitution can be its result, its instrument, or both.

Still, these three evils are not always intertwined. There are many causes of material destitution, some of which, such as natural catastrophe, would be likely to remain even if domination and exploitation were overcome. One does not need to be poor to be dominated or exploited. Wealthy women in Kuyper's day were clearly dominated economically, as well as politically, even when their benevolent husbands did not exploit them. One can also be exploited without being dominated or poor. If a dentist charges an outrageously exorbitant fee for relief of my pain during my vacation in a remote place, he exploits me, regardless of my social or financial standing, because he takes unjust advantage of my lack of alternatives.

Although few medical residents are poor, many are both dominated and exploited. Quite a few of my former students who now work on Wall Street are earning high incomes, while rightly regarding their working hours as exploitative and wishing they had some way to check the arbitrariness of their boss's orders. Many adjunct college teachers appear to suffer all three evils simultaneously.

The material destitution of the underclass is not, for Kuyper, a natural fact. It is often, he thinks, either an intended product or an unintended byproduct of human arrangements disordered by sin and error. Either way, citizens have the responsibility to correct it and are complicit in it if they do not. If Kuyper had seen material destitution as the tolerable but regrettable collateral damage of just economic transactions in properly regulated markets, he would neither

6. See Jeffrey Stout, *Blessed Are the Organized: Grassroots Democracy in America* (Princeton: Princeton University Press, 2010), chapter 5 and *passim*. Philip Pettit, *Republicanism: A Theory of Freedom and Government* (Oxford: Oxford University Press, 1997), chapters 2 and 3.

7. For a helpful analysis, to which I am indebted, see Alan Wertheimer, *Exploitation* (Princeton: Princeton University Press, 1996).

be charging the plutocrats with greed and lust for power, nor charging his audience with tardiness.

It is not hard to guess what made him suspect the dominant class of greed and lust for power. If you were a factory owner in Amsterdam in 1891, one way to keep the cost of labor low, and thus to maximize your own profits, would have been to keep an impoverished underclass in the wings. This thought played a major role in Marx's thinking, but it also lay behind Kuyper's charge that "the daily need for food [has] forced men to accept any condition, no matter how unjust" (40). That is how exploitation works under the cover of what Kuyper calls "the mercantile gospel of laissez faire" (39) and Americans call libertarianism.

Employers set wages by trying to maximize their profits in a labor market. A labor market can be distorted by coercion, lack of competition, asymmetries of information, or debt. Markets distorted in these ways are hospitable to exploitation and in some cases slavery, abuse, discrimination, and fraud. The libertarian gospel excuses the distortions by depicting lawful regulation as liberty's enemy rather than its protector. Kuyper regards this gospel as evidence of either "moral corruption" or "pseudoscience," "sin" or "error." If lots of potential workers face a choice between extremely low wages and no income at all, the bargaining situation is skewed so heavily in favor of employers that the resulting wages are bound to be exploitative. Similar coercive distortions arise in the relationship between lenders and debtors.

According to libertarians, minimum wage laws are an assault on liberty. It is true that if you abstract from the distortions of actual economies into the realm of pure economic theory, minimum wage laws look counterproductive. If, however, you examine what happens in actual economies when minimum wage laws are enacted, the advantages of such laws become evident.[8] The point of establishing a floor for wages is to remove a *coercive* distortion from labor markets, just as antitrust laws help keep markets *competitive* and consumer protection laws help safeguard markets from *asymmetries of information*.

In our day, as in Kuyper's, lower income groups are forced to bargain over wages on the edge of an abyss. This turns out to be significant for a surprisingly large percentage of the population. While it is true, as I have said, that roughly 15 percent of the population was classified as impoverished by the U.S. Census Bureau in 2010, nearly 60 percent had spent at least one year

---

8. See David Card and Alan B. Krueger, *Myth and Measurement: The Economics of the Minimum Wage* (Princeton: Princeton University Press, 1995), especially pp. 1-19.

in poverty between the ages of 25 and 75. The chances of falling into poverty are much greater for people in the bottom 90 percent than for people in the top 10 percent. The vast majority of the population lives in fear of plunging suddenly into poverty — often through no fault of their own and at the whim of a corporate manager or lender. Libertarian talk show hosts often ask, rhetorically, how anyone with a television can qualify as poor. But the question neglects what it is like to plunge. When you lose your job and default on your mortgage, there's not much value in selling your toys.

The presence of the abyss explains why Americans are so anxious about getting themselves and their offspring into the top 10 percent. The welfare reforms of the 1990s have exacerbated these anxieties. Social mobility now includes a lot of movement from the middle down into poverty and not much from the middle up into the top 10 percent. The top CEOs are not only essentially secure from the risk of material want, but also in a vastly more powerful negotiating position than the rest of the population. The money you acquire affects what you can do and what you can get away with doing. Money can be used as an incentive to get other people to lend their efforts and resources to your economic and political projects.

It is the power differential, not the gap in income or wealth, taken independently, that matters. The massive transfer of wealth initiated during the Reagan presidency has, crucially, also brought with it an equally massive transfer of political power. The two developments have reinforced one another in a rising, spiraling double movement, with each upward economic step for the privileged few accompanied by another upward step in political power. Thanks to *Citizens United,* the top economic class is now able to transform economic power, as if by alchemical magic, into political power and back again. It can then use both forms of power at will, which is to say, *arbitrarily,* without effective legal regulation or accountability.

As the helix rises, it lifts the fortunate 400 — the top 1 percent of the top 1 percent — above Babylon. No one knows how long a tower so tall can withstand the tremors that have begun to shake its foundations from below. If the height of the tower signifies the income of the billionaires, the problem is not best described as inequality, and the solution is not to equalize what everybody makes. The fundamental problem is an imbalance of power that has mutually reinforcing economic and political aspects. In such a situation, some forms of exploitation and material destitution are likely to last, symbiotically, until the deeper disorder of class domination is resolved.

Because the deeper disorder is a matter of domination, not of mere economic difference, the remedy is to be sought in checks on the arbitrary exercise of economic and political power, not in a quest for economic sameness. No society is free without security from domination. No society enjoys liberty in Kuyper's sense without justly legislated and justly enforced laws that regulate the accumulation, exercise, and interplay of economic and political power. As he says, "there has never been a government in any country of the world that did not in various ways govern the course of social life and its relationship to material wealth" (24).

The question, for Kuyper, is whether the arrangements will establish an order that is free from domination, exploitation, and material destitution, not whether there will be arrangements. In an important footnote, he quotes a long passage from Bilderdijk on the need to "restore the citizen-state" (54-55, n. 2), by which I take him to mean a republic governed by and for citizens, rather than by and for a plutocratic elite. In his 1898 Stone lectures, Kuyper contrasts the revolutions born of Calvin's republicanism, of which he approves, and the French Revolution, which he abhors.[9] Kuyper's habit of blaming anything he can on the French Revolution diminishes the value that his 1891 address can have for us. Had he instead explained his conception of the citizen-state, he could have made salient the positive political tradition in which Kuyperians and American democrats stand.

What Americans, in the midst of the struggle to abolish slavery, began calling *democracy* is a version of republicanism modified by a relatively inclusive conception of citizenship. Because the term *democracy* is used in different ways in Europe and America, there is apt to be some semantic slippage when comparing Kuyper's neo-Calvinism to our way of extending the heritage of Emerson and Lincoln. But it is clear that Kuyper shares with his American cousins a republican quest for security from domination. Otherwise, he wouldn't be reaching for a term like *plutocracy* to name what he opposes.

The classical republican definition of *liberty* is security from domination. This definition is at odds with a libertarian conception of liberty as absence of constraint or independence from governmental interference. Kuyper mocks the gospel of laissez faire because it gets liberty wrong, because it neglects the role of law in checking the arbitrary exercise of both economic and political power. He is not trying to get government off the backs of plutocrats, any more than Frederick Douglass was trying to get government off the backs of slaveholders. While Kuyper rejects a role for the state in providing direct relief for the poor (69), except perhaps as a last resort, his list of appropriate governmental implements for regulating the economy includes inheritance laws,

---

9. Abraham Kuyper, *Lectures on Calvinism* (New York: Cosimo Classics, 2007), pp. 78-109.

taxation, codes of purchase and rent, and more (25). The state he envisions will never be small enough to be drowned in a bathtub.

What, then, is Kuyper calling his Christian audience *to do* about the social problem, with its exploited workers, its materially destitute underclass, and its plutocrats? Compassionate benevolence for everyone in need is always incumbent on Christians. His reason for holding that "deeds of love are indispensable" is, interestingly, that "the poor man cannot wait until the restoration of our social structure has been completed" (69). Benevolent aid to the poor is a necessary but insufficient response to the social problem, according to Kuyper. Benevolence for everyone in need is always incumbent on us. But for reasons I have already touched on, it is not enough, and it has dangers of its own.

The term *benevolence* comes from the Latin words for *good* and *will*. One's will is a cluster of dispositions infused with commitments. Right now your will consists in how you are behaving and how you would behave if the circumstances were different in one or another respect. A person can have good will for others, in the sense of wishing them well, without having a truly good will, in the sense of a will determined by virtue. A truly good will seeks what justice requires. It is shaped by the virtue of justice and motivated by the love that seeks fellowship in virtue.

A person's will is truly good insofar as he or she *does* and *would* treat others well, taking the demands of just relation appropriately into account. Justice demands security from drastic imbalances of power in our basic relationships. Benevolence, when disconnected from justice, ignores this demand. The tipping point in power relations comes when one person or group is in a position to exercise power arbitrarily — that is, at will, without effective accountability — over another. When that tipping point is reached in our basic economic relationships, the result can be plutocracy, monopoly, or even slavery.

The acquired virtues perfect the relevant behavioral dispositions. If we were all perfectly virtuous, we would all have good wills. Benevolence on the part of individuals would then suffice to make our social relationships excellent in themselves and good for us to have and to hold. But none of us is perfectly virtuous. We are sinful and our basic relationships are corrupted by sin. Benevolence alone, as expressed in what we call charitable giving, does not provide adequate security from imbalances of power in those relationships, let alone from the social effects of greed and lust for power. Whenever severe power imbalances obtain, one person or group can be in a position to exercise power arbitrarily over another. In a world shot through with sin, the outcome is domination.

The positional superiority of the dominant need not involve actually showing ill will with regard to the dominated. To be dominant, in the sense I have in mind, is a matter of what one could do, not a matter of what one has done. Warren Buffett and Bill Gates appear to wish us well, just as Thorvald in Ibsen's *A Doll's House* wishes Nora well. Yet in the absence of change in the social structure, no benevolence on the part of Buffett, Gates, or Thorvald suffices to secure liberty for the people they are able to treat as they wish.[10]

The dominated deserve more than acts of good will. They deserve protection against *arbitrary changes of will*, against the possibility or likelihood that especially powerful people on whom they depend will turn out not to be steadily benevolent after all. Short of *ending* slavery, no amount of benevolence was able to correct its fundamental flaw. The same holds for other forms of domination.

It is sometimes possible to lift people out of poverty, or to mitigate exploitation they have suffered, simply by transferring goods to them. Yet charitable giving, as we have come to call it, typically fails to address whatever form of domination might obtain between the richer and the poorer parties. Indeed, when channeled through large-scale bureaucratic agencies, it typically reinforces domination. The giver and the receiver of charity often remain bound in unjust asymmetries of dependence. The gift often reduces its recipients to objects of pity. By undermining their agency and voice, the gift creates a need for more gifts. Charity becomes the gift that goes on taking.

Meanwhile, the giver's sense of her benevolence so fills her heart with love and her life with meaning that the evil of domination recedes from consciousness. Recall the niceness of which I was complaining earlier. It is not nice merely to believe that there is no struggle underway. It is also not nice to believe that *more niceness* will suffice as a remedy. If we are the world, then all you need is love.

Am I saying that we should revive a Marxist conception of class struggle? I am not. It was no accident that the Leninist avant-garde became the dominant class of a post-revolutionary state. State ownership of the means of production exchanged one sort of domination for another. The dictatorship of the proletariat was just a gang of thugs dominating the rest of the population, including the proletariat. Now the thugs are gone, and good riddance. Marxism was wrong about the means for overcoming domination.

It was also wrong about the ends to be sought. Never in this life shall there be a classless society. Kuyper, not Marx, had that right. Our society will go on producing differentials of income, wealth, knowledge, excellence, and

---

10. I owe the Ibsen reference and the point about benevolence and liberty to Philip Pettit.

power. Just arrangements would keep those differentials from morphing into domination, while also providing security against such related ills as poverty and exploitation. Churches, Kuyper argued, have a responsibility to help shape the structure of society. Right again. Why would the churches not have a share in responsibility for the basic relationships of society? They did not sit out the fight to abolish slavery or establish civil rights. If there be prophets in the pulpits, let there be citizens in the pews. The citizen-state needs citizen-congregations.

In many American churches these days, the crucial choice is whether some of the money traditionally budgeted for charitable giving should be used to pay the dues required to join a nonpartisan citizens' organization. If the decision is to join, members of the congregation begin talking with one another. They cultivate their own leaders, discover what concerns are arising in the surrounding communities, research the issues, and learn how to develop and exert their institution's power. Nonpartisan organizing preserves the boundaries of the spheres without relinquishing pastoral and prophetic responsibility for society. One of its goals is to hold public officials and corporate executives accountable. Accountability, backed by organized strength, is domination's antidote. So my informants tell me.[11]

Congregations that do all these things are treating themselves, their allies, and their opponents as stakeholders in a broader community. They recognize that domination rarely crumbles unless an organized opposition calls it to account. They fight when necessary and reconcile later. They are aiming for a beloved community, but are not shy about using power, relational power, to get there.

Other congregations would rather be nice, first and last. Talk of power makes them nervous. They want reconciliation on the cheap: hold the agon, hold the accountability. Their pastors preach benevolence — their ministries enact it — without ever mussing their hair. Conservatives, liberals, and radicals alike pour sugar water over the rotting carcass of laissez faire. Some libertarians wear wing tips; others wear sandals. Niceness is love that has forgotten captivity in Egypt and torture on an empire's cross. The money changers in the temple are unperturbed.

11. Stout, *Blessed Are the Organized.*

Bibliography

Card, David, and Alan B. Krueger. *Myth and Measurement: The Economics of the Minimum Wage.* Princeton: Princeton University Press, 1995.

Graham, Gordon. *The Idea of Christian Charity: A Critique of Some Contemporary Conceptions.* Notre Dame: University of Notre Dame Press, 1990.

Frankfurt, Harry. "Equality as a Moral Ideal." In *The Importance of What We Care About.* Cambridge: Cambridge University Press, 1988.

Kuyper, Abraham. *Christianity and the Class Struggle.* Translated by Dirk Jellema. Grand Rapids, Michigan: Piet Hut, 1950.

———. *Het sociale Vraagstuk en de Christelijke Religie.* Amsterdam, Netherlands: Wormser, 1891.

———. *Lectures on Calvinism.* New York: Cosimo Classics, 2007.

———. *The Problem of Poverty.* Translated by James W. Skillen. Sioux Center, Iowa: Dordt College Press, 2011.

Mouw, Richard J. *Abraham Kuyper: A Short and Personal Introduction.* Grand Rapids: Eerdmans, 2011.

Pettit, Philip. *Republicanism: A Theory of Freedom and Government.* Oxford: Oxford University Press, 1997.

Stout, Jeffrey. *Blessed Are the Organized: Grassroots Democracy in America.* Princeton: Princeton University Press, 2010.

Wertheimer, Alan. *Exploitation.* Princeton: Princeton University Press, 1996.

Liberalism versus Democracy? Abraham Kuyper and Carl Schmitt as Critics of Liberalism

Clifford B. Anderson

I. Introduction

What is the relation between liberalism and democracy? Might liberalism act as a barrier to democracy? If so, are there alternative models for democracy beyond liberalism? Should Christians eschew liberalism in favor of "Christian democracy," for example? What is at stake in the theological critique of liberalism?

These questions suggest, if nothing else, that liberalism and democracy are not coextensive. As Gordon Graham argues in "Liberalism and Democracy," "there is indeed a necessary tension between the fundamental ideas of liberalism and those of democracy."[1] The tension is between the rights of individuals on the one hand and the will of the majority on the other. The point of liberalism is to place limits on popular sovereignty, which is why liberal democracies sometimes face legitimation crises. What Graham calls a "tension," Chantal Mouffe, professor in the Centre for the Study of Democracy at the University of Westminster, describes as a "paradox." In a fashion analogous to Graham's essay, Mouffe contends that liberalism and democracy have "different logics."[2] As Mouffe writes, "it is vital for democratic politics to understand that liberal democracy results from the articulation of two logics which are incompatible in the last instance and that there is no way they could

---

1. Gordon Graham, "Liberalism and Democracy," *Journal of Applied Philosophy* 9:2 (1992): 149.
2. Chantal Mouffe, *The Democratic Paradox* (London: Verso, 2009), p. 4.

be perfectly reconciled."[3] Mouffe holds that the paradox is too strong for consensus to emerge among citizens of a polity. The best that citizens of a polity can hope for is what she terms " 'agonistic confrontation' between conflicting interpretations of the constitutive liberal-democratic values."[4] The point is not to reconcile these logics, but to acknowledge them and exist politically in the tension between them.

In what follows, I address this "tension" or "paradox" in liberal democratic polities by comparing the Dutch theologian and statesman Abraham Kuyper (1837-1920) with the German political philosopher Carl Schmitt (1888-1985). Scholars have not frequently linked the names Abraham Kuyper and Carl Schmitt. This is not surprising given that they lived in different nations, wrote in different genres, belonged to different strands of the Christian church, and had careers that scarcely overlapped in time. Kuyper's major period of political influence was in the decades between the founding of the Antirevolutionary Party in 1879 and 1909. After the so-called *Lintjesaffaire* of 1909, Kuyper's effect on the Dutch political scene was limited.[5] By contrast, Carl Schmitt began publishing in the 1910s but came into prominence only in the early 1920s.[6] He was a major intellectual figure during the Weimar period and also during the early years of the Third Reich. After 1935, however, Schmitt more or less withdrew from the political scene. While he continued publishing during the war and after, his works from the twenties and early thirties have proved most enduring among commentators.

Why did Kuyper's critique of liberalism lead to a flourishing multiparty democracy that continues to endure while Schmitt's critique, in many ways so parallel, led to dictatorship? Among the few who have asked this question is Ido de Haan, professor of political history at Utrecht University in the Netherlands.[7] The key difference according to Haan was their distinct ways of conceptualizing the "people" in a democracy. For Schmitt, the critique of liberalism proceeded hand-in-hand with an essentialist concept of the *demos*.

3. Mouffe, *The Democratic Paradox*, p. 5.

4. Mouffe, *The Democratic Paradox*, p. 9.

5. See Jan de Bruijn, *Het Boetekleed Ontsiert de Man Niet: Abraham Kuyper en de Lintjesaffaire (1909-1910)* (Amsterdam: Bert Bakker, 2005).

6. For an intellectual biography of Carl Schmitt, see Gopal Balakrishnan, *The Enemy: An Intellectual Portrait of Carl Schmitt* (London: Verso, 2000).

7. Ido De Haan, "Democracy, Ethnicity, and the Nation: Nineteenth-Century France and the Netherlands," in *Political Democracy and Ethnic Diversity in Modern European History*, ed. André Gerrits and Dirk Jan Wolffram (Palo Alto: Stanford University Press, 2005).

Kuyper, by contrast, "pleaded for the sovereignty of the separate parts within the nation."[8]

While Kuyper's acceptance of internal heterogeneity undoubtedly set him apart from Schmitt, Haan misses the dynamic in the development of Kuyper's thinking about liberalism and democracy. Kuyper experimented early in his political career with an essentialist understanding of the Dutch nation that equated orthodox Calvinism with the concept of "Dutchness." His acceptance of the pluralism of the Dutch nation came only in the wake of an unsuccessful democratic assault on liberalism. The practical acquiescence to a heterogeneous nation — begrudging perhaps, at first — rescued Kuyper from the excesses of Carl Schmitt's critique of liberalism, but his commitment to the liberal political system remained provisional. His ultimate hope was that liberal democratic politics might pave the way to the restoration of the lost connection between the Dutch people and orthodox Calvinism.

The best way to get at the nearness and distance between Kuyper and Schmitt is, I argue, to explore a nearly forgotten text by Kuyper titled *Liberalisten en Joden*.[9] This unsavory bit of pamphleteering will help us to see how Kuyper's critique of liberalism might have become mired in nationalism had his political aspirations not pushed him toward a practical acceptance of democratic heterogeneity.

II. Carl Schmitt's Critique of Liberalism

Carl Schmitt's criticism of liberal democracy remains controversial. In *The Crisis of Parliamentary Democracy*, Schmitt argued against the identification of parliamentary (or liberal) democracy with the concept of democracy per se. "Democracy can exist without what one today calls parliamentarism and parliamentarism without democracy," wrote Schmitt. "[A]nd dictatorship is just as little the definitive antithesis of democracy as democracy is of dictatorship."[10] More strongly, he suggested that liberal constraints on the popular will were essentially undemocratic. In certain circumstances, a dictator might better represent the popular will than representatives of a liberal democratic

---

8. De Haan, "Democracy, Ethnicity, and the Nation," p. 50.

9. Abraham Kuyper, *Liberalisten en Joden* (Amsterdam: Kruyt, 1878).

10. Carl Schmitt, *The Crisis of Parliamentary Democracy*, trans. Ellen Kennedy (Cambridge: MIT Press, 1985), p. 32.

government, particularly when those representatives had become captured by special interests.

Schmitt disliked political parties with their "special interests" not simply because he regarded the social process of party formation as undermining the rational basis of liberalism, but primarily because he considered pluralism a threat to the unity of the state. This disdain for the pluralism of political parties may perhaps be explained against the background of the late Weimar Republic, in which divisions between political parties on the right and the left had brought the activity of government to a standstill. But Schmitt's disdain for party pluralism has deeper roots. For Schmitt, the domain of politics is international, not national. If the "friend-enemy" binary constitutes the essential structure of politics,[11] its proper sphere of application is between states — not within the state. Of course, a state may identify an "internal enemy," but states divided between "friends" and "enemies" are weak and subject to dissolution. As Richard Wolin notes, Schmitt emphasized the significance of "homogeneity" for the constitution of a political polity. "In Schmitt's framework," he writes, " 'homogeneity' plays the role in democratic theory formerly played by 'equality' — a concept Schmitt dismisses outright as part of the conceptual baggage of the liberal mentality."[12] Schmitt's dismissal of liberal checks on the popular will becomes understandable in this light. After all, why do we need to separate powers if the political body is fundamentally united? But the pursuit of political homogeneity is more elusive — and far more destructive — than the search for political equality. Wolin rightly characterizes Schmitt's remark from the second edition of *The Concept of the Political* about the *"elimination or eradication of heterogeneity"* as "chilling."[13]

For Schmitt, the advent of political parties marked the downfall of classical liberalism. Liberalism aimed to give rational expression to the will of the people. Classical liberalism eschews party politics because parliamentary discussion is supposed to take place in open forums without external pressures. "According to the *Contrat social*," wrote Schmitt, "there can be no parties in the state, no special interests, no religious differences, nothing that can divide persons, not even a public financial concern."[14] By forming political parties

11. Carl Schmitt, *The Concept of the Political*, trans. George Schwab, expanded ed. (Chicago: University of Chicago Press, 2007), p. 26.

12. Richard Wolin, "Carl Schmitt, Political Existentialism, and the Total State," *Theory and Society* 19:4 (1990): 403.

13. Wolin, "Carl Schmitt, Political Existentialism, and the Total State," p. 403.

14. Schmitt, *Crisis*, p. 13.

and by brokering agreements in closed committees, parliamentary liberalism was undermining its raison d'être. As Schmitt argued, by displacing public deliberation, "parliamentarism thus abandons its intellectual foundation and the whole system of freedom of speech, assembly, and the press, of public meetings, parliamentary immunities and privileges, is losing its rationale."[15] The formation of political parties poses a threat not only to liberalism but also to the state as a whole. The alignment of the people with parties divides the nation and, if unchecked, may lead to civil war.

After the founding of the Anti-Revolutionary Party in 1879, Kuyper was accused of fostering the kind of degradation of parliamentary liberalism that Schmitt described in *The Crisis of Parliamentary Democracy*. Whether or not Kuyper shrewdly perceived that political parties are inimical to classical liberalism, he advocated their formation as a way to overcome the false pretenses of liberal neutrality about the character of the Dutch nation. While we credit him today as a leading innovator of Christian democracy, in his early career he had the reputation of being a dangerous populist rather than a democratic statesman.

III. Abraham Kuyper on National Sovereignty

The question of sovereignty was of crucial significance to both Kuyper and Schmitt. Both struck at the nerve of classical liberalism, which claimed to represent the popular will but effectively disenfranchised a majority of the nation. Schmitt's proposal was to locate sovereignty away from constitutional law or the republican assemblies toward whoever decides on the "exception" to the laws.[16] Kuyper, by contrast, upheld the sovereignty of God in opposition to the theory of popular sovereignty. While their critiques moved in different directions, both raised the question of how the theory of popular sovereignty could support liberal elitism. In other words, how could liberalism claim to represent the will of the nation when so few participated in parliamentary elections? In a parliamentary speech delivered on December 7, 1875, Kuyper objected to a liberal representative's claim that the Dutch nation had voted for "neutral schools." "What does the speaker understand by *the nation*?" he

---

15. Schmitt, *Crisis*, p. 49.
16. See Carl Schmitt, *Political Theology: Four Chapters on the Concept of Sovereignty* (Cambridge: MIT Press, 1985).

inquired.[17] This question — "What is the nation?" — became the subject of a nearly forgotten pamphlet written a few years later.

In 1878, Abraham Kuyper published a series of articles in *De Standaard* under the title *Liberalisten en Joden* [Liberals and Jews]. He subsequently collected the articles as an eponymously titled pamphlet.[18] The purpose of this pamphlet was to expose the influence of Jews on the ruling liberals of the Netherlands. In a tired line of argument, Kuyper contended that Jews controlled the press and the economy, exercising an untoward influence over public life in the Netherlands. A small excerpt conveys the tone of the articles. After noting how small the population of Jews were in Western Europe, Kuyper complained, "And yet, this group — almost vanishingly imperceptible — undeniably calls the tune in Europe; is master of its political terrain; controls the development of public ideas; and has the fate of Europe in its hand."[19] The publication occasioned a flood of protest from journals. The *Handelsblad* accused Kuyper of inciting his followers to a modern pogrom against the Jews.[20] For his part, Kuyper complained that he had been misunderstood. He was not advocating that Jews be denied their civil rights.[21] He contended that some of his best friends from his earliest days were Jews.[22] His quarrel was not with Jews, but with liberals. For the underlying purpose of the pamphlet was not so much to expose Jewish influence on the economy, media, and politics of the Netherlands, but to unmask the liberals as Jews in spirit.[23]

Kuyper published these articles during a particularly discouraging time in his political career. Early in 1878, Kuyper had organized the so-called "Popular Petition" [*Volkspetitionnement*] to protest against pending changes to the funding and governance of the school system in the Netherlands. "The Popular Petition was signed by more than 305,000 people while a similar petition by the Roman Catholics received 164,000 signatures," explains Jan de Bruijn. "These figures are all the more evocative when one considers that the number of enfranchised [voters] for the Second Chamber numbered approximately

17. Abraham Kuyper, *Eenige Kameradviezen uit de Jaren 1874 en 1875* (Amsterdam: Wormser, 1890), p. 313; my translation.
18. Kuyper, *Liberalisten en Joden*.
19. Kuyper, *Liberalisten en Joden*, p. 9; my translation.
20. Kuyper, *Liberalisten en Joden*, pp. 17f.; my translation.
21. Kuyper, *Liberalisten en Joden*, p. 3; my translation.
22. Kuyper, *Liberalisten en Joden*, p. 4; my translation.
23. See Kuyper, *Liberalisten en Joden*, p. 36; my translation.

122,000."[24] The petition was formally presented to King William III — an appeal to the sovereign to make an exception to the Parliament and thus demonstrate its lack of popular support. However, the king signed the new school law on August 17, 1878.[25] The Popular Petition was an attempt to circumvent the liberal constitution by direct democratic appeal. Had the king rejected the law, the Popular Petition would have caused a constitutional crisis in the Netherlands. As it was, liberalism seemingly triumphed against the expressed wishes of the Dutch people.

The problem of nationhood animated Kuyper's thoughts throughout his life, but especially in this period. What constituted the Dutch nation? The contemporary boundaries of the Netherlands do not reflect demographic divisions between peoples so much as lines of conflict. The Spanish Netherlands included both present-day Belgium and the Netherlands. After the 1568 revolt against the Spanish, a line of demarcation came into existence between the Protestant North and the Catholic South. But the distinction was never absolute — a sizable number of Catholics continued to live in the North even as most Protestants fled from the South.[26] The question of what constituted the people of the Netherlands persisted through the nineteenth century. While the attempt in 1815 to re-forge a common identity between South and North failed in 1830, the failure did not produce a positive solution to the question, just left it open. For Kuyper, of course, the question of national identity could be solved theologically. The essential identity of the Dutch people was constituted by their Reformed faith. "While every nation is subject to the deep truth that it strikes itself from the roster of nations by devaluing its piety," asserted Kuyper in 1869, "this applies all the more to the national existence of the Netherlands, which owes its origin to a religion movement."[27]

Of course, the claim that the Dutch nation has a religious origin begged the question of the status of Catholics, liberal Protestants, and Jews in the modern Netherlands. As Jeroen Koch has shown in his biography, Kuyper asserted

---

24. Jan de Bruijn, *Abraham Kuyper: Een Beeldbiografie* (Amsterdam: Prometheus-Bert Bakker, 2008), p. 119; my translation.

25. See de Bruijn, *Abraham Kuyper*, p. 120.

26. Joris van Eijnatten and Frederik Angenietus van Lieburg, *Nederlandse Religiegeschiedenis* (Hilversum: Uitgeverij Verloren, 2006), p. 208. The authors claim that roughly 37 percent of the population between 1650 and 1850 was Roman Catholic, though the percentage varied widely between provinces.

27. Abraham Kuyper, "Uniformity: The Curse of Modern Life," in *Abraham Kuyper: A Centennial Reader*, ed. James D. Bratt, trans. John Vriend (Grand Rapids: Eerdmans, 1998), p. 43.

in his early writings from the 1870s that orthodox Calvinists constituted the genuine Dutch nation while others presented "special interests."

> He formulated a Dutch identity in religiously exclusive terms. And while he reproached the other parties, most especially the liberals, of representing special interests under the banner of the general interest, he considered himself to speak and to advocate for the nation as a whole.[28]

This slippery assumption provides the background to Kuyper's charge that Dutch liberals had become Judaized. Kuyper charged that whatever the divisions between Orthodox and Reform Jews, all Jews belonged to a single nation. Their nationhood persisted despite their dispersion among other nations: "the Jews in all corners and extremities of our part of the world have still remained a nation in a much stronger sense than any European people have ever been a nation."[29] While the French Revolution granted Jews civil rights, it was naïve to think that liberalism simply privatized differences of religion. Kuyper perceived something far more insidious taking place under the cover of liberalism — namely, the conversion of the Dutch people to the Jewish nation. He argued that the Jews were actively converting people away from Dutchness to Judaism. He could thus estimate that the "Jewish population here at home is perhaps *a million* strong, consisting of 70,000 Semites *plus* 900,000 Caucasian Jews, differing in their origin, but one in both their spiritual confession and in their aversion to the Christ of God."[30] In other words, Jews and liberals were in the process of forming a different nation within the borders of the Netherlands. The conflict between liberalism and Calvinism was therefore not so much a civil struggle as a struggle between two sovereign nations occupying the same land. On this point, Kuyper was explicit:

> . . . the question whether a nation can tolerate as an equal in its midst another nation that does not identify with it is a question *of the numbers,* and as soon as fear comes of *over the top growth,* nobody can speak about struggle over rights, but only about struggle over *life-existence.*[31]

Chilling words, ameliorated perhaps by Kuyper's reassurance that he was not

---

28. Jeroen Koch, *Abraham Kuyper: Een Biografie* (Amsterdam: Boom, 2006), p. 107.
29. Kuyper, *Liberalisten en Joden,* p.14.
30. Kuyper, *Liberalisten en Joden,* p. 28; my translation.
31. Kuyper, *Liberalisten en Joden,* p. 32; my translation.

aiming to take away the civil rights of Jews (or liberals). His selected method of struggle was mission and conversion. Still, we can now understand how Kuyper conceived of himself as the spokesperson of the Dutch nation while disregarding the voice of the liberals. Liberals represented the perspective of a hostile, occupying nation. There was no possibility of coming to terms with them — only tolerating them in small numbers and deploying spiritual force to retard their growth.

The problem of democracy without liberalism comes to the fore here. As we have already seen with Schmitt, demagogic politicians can easily make the rhetorical assertion that the government does not represent the will of the people. Schmitt, writing in the Weimar era, did not have to press his case to convince readers that the Parliament did not represent the German people. The people themselves had fractured with Communists and Nazi "brown shirts" battling in the streets of Berlin. Schmitt's contention was that the principled neutrality of liberal democracy could not be maintained in such situations of internal emergency. In *Legality and Legitimacy,* a treatise on the Weimar constitution that Schmitt published in 1932, he asserted that liberalism could not afford to remain neutral among contending parties when the social fabric was being rent. In a prescient comment, he complained about a prominent liberal's interpretation, writing of his view that "value neutrality here is pushed to the point of system suicide."[32] A system of rights cannot sustain a political system, let alone a people. For Schmitt, a democracy requires a form of "homogeneity" that bridges the gap between parties: "Every democracy, even the parliamentary variety, fundamentally rests on a presupposed homogeneity that is thorough and indivisible."[33] Schmitt rejected the notion that liberalism could provide common ground among intractably opposed parties. As Gopal Balakrishnan explains, for Schmitt " 'homogeneity' indicates the minimal threshold of political unity beneath which 'the people' dissolves into warring parties, each claiming to represent the whole."[34]

An important distinction between Kuyper and Schmitt was that the former glorified spiritual warfare against Jews and liberals whereas the latter would eventually join the National Socialist party and defend the political legitimacy of Hitler's purges. Still, the difference is only relative. Like Schmitt's writings, Kuyper's criticisms of Jewish influence on the Netherlands also con-

---

32. Carl Schmitt, *Legality and Legitimacy,* ed. Jeffrey Seitzer (Durham: Duke University Press, 2004), p. 48.

33. Schmitt, *Legality and Legitimacy,* p. 41.

34. Balakrishnan, *The Enemy,* p. 263.

cern the question of national sovereignty. He contended, for instance, that the Dutch constitution of 1848 — with its "negation of Christendom" — was composed during the "Jewish phase" of liberalism's revolt against Calvinism.[35] By this, he meant that liberalism was sliding from the highest phase of religion — Calvinism — to Judaism (i.e. monotheism) on the way to heathenism and bestiality.[36] That the constitution was established during the "Jewish phase" of this liberal slide into bestiality meant that the law accorded Jews more privileges than warranted. "Imperceptibly, the people thus came to stand *above* the law who had once been placed *outside* the law."[37] In other words, the people whose relation to the law took shape only in the form of a ban (what Giorgio Agamben calls the *Homo Sacer*[38]) have now become the sovereigns, those who stand above the law. As Jacques Derrida commented on Carl Schmitt in *The Beast and the Sovereign,* both positions have significant points in common with the violator of the law. "Both of them, all three of them, the animal, the criminal, and the sovereign, are outside the law, at a distance from or above the laws: criminal, beast, and sovereign strangely resemble each other while seeming to be situated at antipodes, at each other's antipodes."[39] In his way, Kuyper made the same point about liberalism. The liberal attempt to substitute popular sovereignty for divine sovereignty had started a slide into bestiality — precisely because liberals had placed themselves apart from and above the divine law. The Jewish influence on liberalism had alienated them from the laws of the Dutch people — ultimately derived from the sovereign will of God — but liberals were in mortal peril because Jews still adhered to an antiquated form of divine law that prevented their slide down the spiritual ladder. Liberals, by contrast, would soon prove living witness to the identification between beast and sovereign. Or so Kuyper asserted in 1878.

IV. Conclusion

Ido de Haan juxtaposed Kuyper and Schmitt more than compared them. In his analysis, the main difference between them concerned the homogeneity

35. Kuyper, *Liberalisten en Joden,* p. 25; my translation.

36. Kuyper, *Liberalisten en Joden,* p. 25; my translation.

37. Kuyper, *Liberalisten en Joden,* pp. 6f.; my translation.

38. Giorgio Agamben, *Homo Sacer: Sovereign Power and Bare Life,* trans. Daniel Heller-Roazen (Stanford: Stanford University Press, 1998).

39. Jacques Derrida, *The Beast and the Sovereign,* trans. Geoffrey Bennington, vol. 1 (Chicago: University of Chicago Press, 2009), p. 17.

of the people. Put succinctly, Kuyper rejected the idea that homogeneity was a prerequisite to politics, whereas Schmitt required it. "The dangerous message [Kuyper] presented was that the Dutch nation did not need to be unified," contends Haan. "He argued that his fellow antirevolutionary Protestants were entitled to an independent place within the Dutch nation, to be sovereign within their own sphere of life."[40] Haan credits Kuyper with fostering the system of pillarization that flourished in the mid-twentieth century. Schmitt, by contrast, erred in his assumption that democracy requires homogeneity.[41] I agree that at least after 1879 Kuyper embraced a more pluralistic conception of society and politics. But I consider this endogenous to Kuyper's development as a politician rather than as a consequence of exogenous cultural forces. That is, whereas Haan presents Kuyper as exemplifying distinctive historical trends in Dutch culture and politics, I consider Kuyper's acquiescence to national heterogeneity as the outcome of his early years of wrestling with the question, "What is the Dutch nation?"

Jeroen Koch's charge that Kuyper equivocated especially after the mid-1880s between considering orthodox Calvinists as the essence of the Dutch nation or as a part of the nation similarly misses the dynamism of Kuyper's thought.[42] Rather than temporizing, Kuyper held the part and the whole in dialectical tension. He came to accept after 1878 that his orthodox Calvinists had to form coalitions and work with other parties to gain political power. In other words, he acquiesced to national heterogeneity as a political fact of life. But he never gave up his view that Calvinism expressed the authentic Dutch nation. This dialectical tension permitted him to participate in a fundamentally liberal form of government (suitably adjusted to accommodate political parties) while still holding to the claim that orthodox Calvinists represented the genuine Dutch nation.

In short, Kuyper managed to develop what today is called "agonistic" political theory *avant la lettre*.[43] Whereas Schmitt asserted that genuine politics takes place between nations, not within nations, Kuyper adapted the framework of liberalism to foster domestic party politics. His politics — to use

40. De Haan, "Democracy, Ethnicity, and the Nation," p. 49.

41. De Haan, "Democracy, Ethnicity, and the Nation," pp. 62f.

42. Koch, *Abraham Kuyper*, p. 107.

43. See Mouffe, *The Democratic Paradox;* for a Christian interpretation, see Ashley Wood-iwiss, "Deliberation or Agony? Toward a Post-liberal Christian Democratic Theory," in *The Re-Enchantment of Political Science: Christian Scholars Engage Their Discipline*, ed. Thomas W. Heilke and Ashley Woodiwiss (Lanham: Lexington Books, 2000).

the terminology of Chantal Mouffe[44] — moved from Schmitt's antagonism of friend/enemy to an agonistic rivalry of adversaries. By adapting liberalism to accept agonistic rivalries among democratic parties — where every party seeks to speak for the whole while accepting that they represent only a part — Kuyper sparked a vibrant and flourishing democracy, whereas Schmitt led to the dead end of totalitarianism.

Bibliography

Agamben, Giorgio. *Homo Sacer: Sovereign Power and Bare Life.* Translated by Daniel Heller-Roazen. Stanford: Stanford University Press, 1998.

Balakrishnan, Gopal. *The Enemy: An Intellectual Portrait of Carl Schmitt.* London: Verso, 2000.

De Bruijn, J. *Abraham Kuyper: Een Beeldbiografie.* Amsterdam: Prometheus-Bert Bakker, 2008.

————. *Het Boetekleed Ontsiert de Man Niet: Abraham Kuyper en de Lintjesaffaire (1909-1910).* Amsterdam: Bert Bakker, 2005.

De Haan, Ido. "Democracy, Ethnicity, and the Nation: Nineteenth-Century France and the Netherlands." In *Political Democracy and Ethnic Diversity in Modern European History.* Edited by André Gerrits and Dirk Jan Wolffram. Palo Alto: Stanford University Press, 2005.

Derrida, Jacques. *The Beast and the Sovereign.* Translated by Geoffrey Bennington. Vol. 1. Chicago: University of Chicago Press, 2009.

Graham, Gordon. "Liberalism and Democracy." *Journal of Applied Philosophy* 9:2 (1992): 149-60.

Koch, Jeroen. *Abraham Kuyper: Een Biografie.* Amsterdam: Boom, 2006.

Kuyper, Abraham. *Liberalisten en Joden.* Amsterdam: Kruyt, 1878.

————. *Eenige Kameradviezen uit de Jaren 1874 en 1875.* Amsterdam: Wormser, 1890.

————. "Uniformity: The Curse of Modern Life." In *Abraham Kuyper: A Centennial Reader.* Edited by James D. Bratt. Translated by John Vriend. Grand Rapids: Eerdmans, 1998.

Mouffe, Chantal. *The Democratic Paradox.* London: Verso, 2009.

Schmitt, Carl. *The Crisis of Parliamentary Democracy.* Translated by Ellen Kennedy. Cambridge: MIT Press, 1985.

————. *Political Theology: Four Chapters on the Concept of Sovereignty.* Cambridge: MIT Press, 1985.

————. *Legality and Legitimacy.* Edited by Jeffrey Seitzer. Durham: Duke University Press, 2004.

44. Mouffe, *The Democratic Paradox*, pp. 102f.

————. *The Concept of the Political.* Translated by George Schwab. Expanded edition. Chicago: University of Chicago Press, 2007.

Van Eijnatten, Joris, and Frederik Angenietus van Lieburg. *Nederlandse Religiegeschiedenis.* Hilversum: Uitgeverij Verloren, 2006.

Wolin, Richard. "Carl Schmitt, Political Existentialism, and the Total State." *Theory and Society* 19:4 (1990): 389-416.

Woodiwiss, Ashley. "Deliberation or Agony? Toward a Post-liberal Christian Democratic Theory." In *The Re-Enchantment of Political Science: Christian Scholars Engage Their Discipline.* Edited by Thomas W. Heilke and Ashley Woodiwiss. Lanham: Lexington Books, 2000.

The Christian as *homo politicus:* Abraham Kuyper and Democratic Imbalance in Post-Democratic Times

Michael Bräutigam

Liberal democracy in the West is in a critical condition — not only in democracy's country of birth, Greece, where the people protest against the tough austerity measures imposed on them, but also in the post-Kuyper Netherlands, where the liberal de-pillarization of society has created more difficulties than solutions; and also in Germany, where the "Pirates" are trying to capture the *Bundestag,* collecting votes from an electorate that is frustrated with the political class.[1] On the other side of the Atlantic, the Democratic president is faced with his own challenge of governing a nation that is "democratically unbalanced," as two scholars at Yale University recently observed.[2] Western liberal democracy is in a crisis.

I believe that Abraham Kuyper (1837-1920), though a figure from the past, provides vital insights into responding to this democratic crisis today. In this essay, I will make the case that Abraham Kuyper's Calvinist *Weltanschauung,* and in particular his distinction between the church as institute and as organism, provides a significant motif for Christian political involvement that addresses our contemporary democratic crisis.

This essay will proceed in three steps. At the first two stages we shall analyze the present democratic crisis and at the third stage look at this crisis from

---

1. Gareth Jones, "Germany's Pirates Surge in Poll after Local Election," *Reuters Online,* April 3, 2012, http://www.reuters.com/article/2012/04/03/us-germany-pirates-poll -idUSBRE83207R20120403 (accessed April 23, 2012).

2. Jacob S. Hacker and Oona A. Hathaway, "Our Unbalanced Democracy," *The New York Times,* August 1, 2011, http://www.nytimes.com/2011/08/01/opinion/our-unbalanced -democracy.html (accessed April 23, 2012).

Abraham Kuyper's vantage point. The line of argument goes like this: *First,* British sociologist Colin Crouch has suggested that we live in a *post-democratic era.* Crouch argues that the political elite tends to be more and more removed and estranged from the people it is supposed to represent. A growing influence of the business lobby, increasing corruption, and lack of political transparency and vision are just some of the many factors that contribute to empty ballot boxes in major elections.

Still, and this is the *second* point, social scientists observe an increase of new democratic forms of participation, what they describe as a *new participatory revolution.* Citizens more often organize themselves in independent pressure and cause groups, human rights groups, and the like. This democratic revolution, however, is spearheaded almost exclusively by the rich and well-educated who are able and eloquent enough to articulate their concerns and thus to influence political decisions. Left behind are the less educated and the disadvantaged. What we have here is a serious democratic crisis, what I call a severe *democratic imbalance.*

Thirdly, in my opinion, Abraham Kuyper's life, his theology, and his policy provide relevant ways of tackling this democratic imbalance. It is in particular his view on the *church as institute and as organism* which offers not only a coherent theoretical foundation but also a practical moral motivation to address this democratic imbalance from a Christian perspective.

I. Democratic Fatigue in Post-Democratic Times

With this we move to our first point: the seeming decline of Western traditional democratic culture.[3] What seems to be the problem with liberal democracy in the West? Some ten years ago, Colin Crouch coined the expression

---

3. It might be helpful to clarify some terminology first. Democracy literally means the "rule of the people" (*dēmos* meaning "people" and *kratia* "power"). The most common form of rule is parliamentary or representative democracy, where the voting public elects politicians to represent them in a parliament, an assembly, a *Bundestag,* the Commons, etc. In the West, one sometimes adds the label "liberal" to democracy in order to underline foundational rights such as equality before the law, the freedom to vote, civil liberties, and human rights. When we talk about "democracy," we refer to a form of rule, a system of governance (what we in German call *Herrschaftsform*). What we do *not* refer to is the form of a specific state (*Staatsform*), which can be a republic, a constitutional monarchy, or a dictatorship, for example. In combining the two, various options are possible: we find a democracy in a constitutional monarchy (United Kingdom), in a federal parliamentary republic (Germany), or a presidential republic (USA).

"post-democracy."[4] We have certainly witnessed an inflationary use of the prefix "post" in recent years. We speak for example of post-materialism, post-modernism, post-industrialization, and, now, post-democracy. It is worthwhile, though, to discuss whether the way in which Crouch uses this term could correctly capture the current socio-political status quo.

Crouch bemoans an "an entropy of democracy," particularly evident in the Western liberal democratic countries.[5] At least compared to our (from my European perspective) Arab neighbors, this seems to be true. While the Near East is currently experiencing a democratic spring — with the recent revolutions in Tunisia,[6] in Egypt,[7] Libya,[8] and Syria,[9] the West seems to be suffering from a severe form of democratic hibernation. Over the last four decades, voter turnout has been steadily declining in the established democracies.[10] Western citizens seem to be passive and apathetic rather than keen on actively participating in the traditional democratic decision process. Colin Crouch and others have identified several reasons for this democratic lethargy in the West. It is worthwhile taking a brief look at some of these factors.

One major factor is a growing *political elitism.* The political class in Western liberal democracies seems more and more uncoupled from the electorate. Colin Crouch argues that "politics and government are increasingly slipping back into the control of privileged elites in the manner characteristic of pre-democratic times."[11] This obviously leads to frustration on the part of the constituents. Sociologists and pollsters observe a growing general disenchantment with politics and classic forms of democratic participation.[12] German phi-

4. Colin Crouch, *Post-Democracy* (Cambridge: Polity, 2004).

5. Crouch, *Post-Democracy,* p. 12.

6. This revolution began in December 2010. It resulted in the ousting of President Zine El Abidine Ben Ali in January 2011, giving rise to the democratization of the country.

7. The Egyptian revolution, starting in January 2011, was influenced by the Tunisian uprising and made an end to the regime of Hosni Mubarak.

8. The popular movements in Tunisia and Egypt led to the revolt in Libya (beginning in February 2011). With the support of allied forces, Muammar Gaddafi was overthrown, making way for a democratic change, headed by the National Transitional Council.

9. The revolution in Syria began with mass protests in the spring of 2011, leading to a civil war still ongoing at this writing.

10. Richard G. Niemi and Herbert F. Weisberg, eds., *Controversies in Voting Behavior* (Washington, D.C.: CQ Press, 2001), p. 31.

11. Crouch, *Post-Democracy,* p. 6.

12. For some figures and statistics see Colin Hay, *Why We Hate Politics* (Cambridge: Polity, 2007), pp. 1-60. Kees van Kersbergen of the Vrije Universiteit Amsterdam warns of the dangers resulting from a disenchantment with politics in Western democracies: "Currently, I see no project or mission on the horizon, which could be interpreted as comparably enchanting,

losopher Jürgen Habermas recently wrote an article in the British newspaper *The Guardian* entitled "Europe's Post-Democratic Era."[13] Habermas contends that political actors not only make their decisions "far away" in Brussels but they are also not capable of communicating their actions in a transparent and coherent way. This, argues Habermas, is responsible for an undermining of the civic solidarity so central to the European project. "A dangerous asymmetry has developed," writes Habermas, "because to date the European Union has been sustained and monopolised only by political elites — an asymmetry between the democratic participation of the peoples in what their governments obtain for them on the subjectively remote Brussels stage and the indifference, even apathy, of the citizens of the union regarding the decisions of their parliament in Strasbourg."[14] Yet a political lack of transparency is not the only problem. Beyond this, the rather remote political elites are increasingly influenced by *lobbyists*. Political actors in a post-democracy, argues Colin Crouch, lose their legitimacy as they are increasingly under the influence of business lobbyists, spin doctors, and private interest groups, instead of being what they should be: elected representatives who are responsible to their constituents and who act for the common good. Crouch identifies the powerful business lobby of global enterprises in particular as a significant threat to democracy: "Under the conditions of a post-democracy that increasingly cedes power to business lobbies," writes Crouch, "there is little hope for an agenda of strong egalitarian policies for the redistribution of power and wealth, or for the restraint of powerful interests."[15]

---

sagacious, yet still cautious, as the projects of the Nation-State, Democracy, the Welfare State and European Integration. On the contrary, the political enterprises that are filling the void seem to be endangering democracy and are, ultimately and in their effects, endangering the integration of society." Kees van Kersbergen, "The Disenchantment of Politics," paper presented at the *Kollegiat am Kulturwissenschaftlichen Kolleg Konstanz*, Germany, May 2008, 18; http://nbn-resolving.de/urn:nbn:de:bsz:352-opus-54991 (accessed February 16, 2012).

13. Jürgen Habermas, "Europe's Post-Democratic Era," *The Guardian*, November 10, 2011, http://www.guardian.co.uk/commentisfree/2011/nov/10/jurgen-habermas-europe-post-democratic (accessed January 24, 2012).

14. Habermas, "Europe's Post-Democratic Era."

15. Crouch, *Post-Democracy*, p. 4. This negative trend is even intensified in a climate of accelerated globalism. "Democracy," writes Colin Crouch, "has simply not kept pace with capitalism's rush to the global" (p. 29). That is, if today a global firm feels it does not benefit enough from the fiscal system in country A, it threatens the government of this country to move (or at least to outsource key elements) to country B if A does not comply with their fiscal preferences. As a result, Crouch notes that "taxation becomes less redistributive; politicians respond primarily to the concerns of a handful of business leaders whose special interests are allowed to be translated into public policy" (p. 23).

In this context, one also observes an increasing merger of politics with economic interests and media power. This leads, in many cases, to an unhealthy *conflict of interests* that damages democratic culture and contributes to a general disenchantment with politics among citizens. Let us consider a few examples, beginning in Germany. In December 2011 former German President Christian Wulff stumbled over a private loan affair. He managed to get a mortgage from a German bank for over 500,000 Euros for a flexible interest rate varying between 0.9 and 2.1 percent.[16] Surely not a bad deal at all. In February 2012, the public prosecution department in Hannover decided to file for a withdrawal of Wulff's immunity so that a legal inquiry for corruption could be taken up. A day after this news broke, Wulff was forced to resign from the highest public office in Germany, an office he had considerably damaged in the months of his lingering affair.[17] In Great Britain, Tony Blair, Gordon Brown, and David Cameron all had good relations with media tycoon Rupert Murdoch and his News Corporation. David Cameron recently had a rough time as his Conservative party's communications manager Andy Coulson, a former editor of one of Murdoch's newspapers, had to resign and was arrested in connection with allegations of corruption and the phone hacking scandal.[18] Further south in Europe, owning a prosperous business empire as well as controlling major TV channels (through his media company, Mediaset), billionaire Silvio Berlusconi has been able to rule in Italy for almost the past ten years. Berlusconi repeatedly faced charges for corruption and abuse of office.[19]

In light of these scandals and embroilments, it is perhaps understandable when citizens not only lose respect *for* but also confidence *in* their political representatives. When the political actor is perceived to be more concerned

16. Lutz Meier and Jörn Petring, "Wulffs rätselhafte Umschuldungen," *Financial Times Deutschland,* December 28, 2011, http://www.ftd.de/politik/deutschland/:privatkredit-wulffs -raetselhafte-umschuldungen/60147207.html (accessed February 15, 2012).

17. To make matters worse, President Wulff had earlier tried to prevent the press from spreading background information about this loan. See Ralf Wiegand, "Enthüllung — Wulff drohte 'Bild'-Journalisten mit Strafanzeige," *Süddeutsche Zeitung,* January 2, 2012, http://www. sueddeutsche.de/politik/bundespraesident-in-not-wulff-drohte-mit-strafanzeige-gegen-bild -journalisten-1.1248384 (accessed February 15, 2012).

18. Amelia Hill, "Andy Coulson to Be Arrested over Phone Hacking Tomorrow," *The Guardian* (UK), July 7, 2011, http://www.guardian.co.uk/media/2011/jul/07/andy-coulson -arrest-phone-hacking (accessed February 15, 2012).

19. Rachel Sanderson, "Berlusconi Faces Another Court Case," *The Financial Times* (Milan), February 7, 2012, http://www.ft.com/cms/s/0/33dac7ca-51a8-11e1-a30c-00144feabdc0 .html#axzz1lz9nZK2s (accessed February 15, 2012).

with his or her own profit or media influence than in affairs of state, the resulting general distrust in representative liberal democracy is easy to understand.

Yet this is not the full picture. While the classic model of representative democracy has been suffering for want of civic support, more direct participatory approaches have been making an appearance on the democratic stage. Not everything seems to be unwell with democracy.

II. The New Participatory Revolution and Democratic Imbalance

Sociologists, historians, and political scientists are observing new forms of direct participation flourishing within Western democracies.[20] They describe a surge of cause and pressure groups, such as the Occupy movement, human rights movements, environmental groups, and nongovernmental organizations (NGOs). At a more local level, one witnesses the increasing formation of panels and roundtables in local communities, and the increasing importance of town hall meetings. Participatory movements are, as Paul Nolte, professor of history at the Freie Universität Berlin, suggests, the "most important innovation in the history of democracy in the past half a century."[21] Dirk Jörke of the University of Greifswald speaks of a recurrence of the "participatory revolution" of the 1960s and 1970s, obviously under new conditions.[22]

Two factors seem to be responsible for the genesis and expansion of this new participatory revolution. It is, on the one hand, a result of the general public's frustration with the (often corrupt) political elites, noted earlier. On the other hand, these developments could also be said to be fueled by our climate of post-materialism. Ronald Inglehart, who coined this expression, argues that, as in the past few decades citizens of Western societies became somewhat economically saturated, post-materialistic values, such as human rights, freedom, and self-determination, came more and more to the fore.[23] The pursuit of these "higher" motives[24] is then channeled into the formation of human rights

20. See for example Nancy C. Roberts, ed., *The Age of Direct Citizen Participation* (Armonk, N.Y.: M. E. Sharpe, 2008).

21. Paul Nolte, "Von der repräsentativen zur multiplen Demokratie," *Aus Politik und Zeitgeschichte* 1-2 (2011): 9.

22. Dirk Jörke, "Bürgerbeteiligung in der Postdemokratie," *Aus Politik und Zeitgeschichte* 1-2 (2011): 14.

23. See Ronald Inglehart, "Changing Values among Western Publics from 1970 to 2006," *West European Politics* 31 (1-2): 130-46.

24. This term is derived from Abraham Maslow's "hierarchy of needs." See his classic

groups and related organizations. This expansion of new (and sometimes very unconventional) forms of civic participation is certainly a positive democratic trend. Democracy thus seems less "post" democratic than Colin Crouch has suggested. Paul Nolte points out that these new participatory forms do not substitute for but rather complement the classic representative model of democracy.[25] In fact, what we now have, Nolte says, is a "multiple democracy."[26]

What then seems to be the problem? Is this not satisfactory? Democracy is alive and well; maybe not in its classic form, but in new, multiple, and exciting ways. Yet there clearly is a problem. I alluded to it earlier when I mentioned the problem of *democratic imbalance.* Indeed, this is a serious problem. For not everyone is taking part in these new and creative forms of democracy. Those who successfully use these new participatory options are predominantly the well-educated white-collar workers and the socially privileged. They are able and eloquent enough to raise their concerns and to influence political decisions. Political participation, then, is in danger of degenerating into a playing field solely for the winners of modernization.[27] Left behind are the less well-educated and the socially disadvantaged who do not have the essential resources to take part in this new democratic participatory process.[28] This is a serious participatory gap, a severe democratic imbalance. What is more, the lower income groups fail to make an appearance not only in the new democratic groups, but also in the "classic" representative forms of democratic participation. It is particularly this group at the lower end of the socio-economic spectrum that tends not to appear at the ballot boxes at major elections.[29] This is what Wolfgang Merkel, political scientist at the Humboldt University in Berlin, calls a "social selection."[30]

While the degree of democratic imbalance and social injustice at Abra-

---

paper, "A Theory of Human Motivation," *Psychological Review* 50:4 (1943): 370-96. Ronald Inglehart explicitly drew upon Maslow's theory in his argument for post-materialism. See Inglehart, *The Silent Revolution: Changing Values and Political Styles Among Western Publics* (Princeton, N.J.: Princeton University Press, 1977), pp. 22, 41, 55.

25. Nolte, "Von der repräsentativen zur multiplen Demokratie," pp. 9-10.

26. Nolte, "Von der repräsentativen zur multiplen Demokratie," p. 10.

27. As Dirk Jörke put it in "Bürgerbeteiligung in der Postdemokratie," p. 16.

28. As Paul Nolte shows in "Von der repräsentativen zur multiplen Demokratie," pp. 11-12.

29. See Dirk Jörke, "Bürgerbeteiligung in der Postdemokratie," 15. The growing (surely legitimate) exercise of these citizens' right to abstain from voting certainly expresses their dissatisfaction with political institutions and somewhat seems to indicate that they have "given up" the hope that their vote could change things for the better.

30. Wolfgang Merkel, "Volksabstimmungen: Illusion und Realität," *Aus Politik und Zeitgeschichte* 44-45 (2011): 50.

Michael Bräutigam

ham Kuyper's time was certainly different from ours, the underlying reasons for them are still the same today: laissez-faire capitalism, political elitism, economics driven by greed of gain, a strong business lobby, and so forth.[31] All this was well known to Kuyper. And he took up the "fight of faith"[32] because he was convinced that Christianity must not remain silent in face of social and democratic imbalance.

III. Kuyper's Vision of the Christian as *Homo Politicus*

If Abraham Kuyper were alive today, how would he tackle the problem of democratic imbalance? Kuyper, I think, would first of all provide a firm theoretical foundation for Christian political engagement before moving to the more practical question of how to counter democratic imbalance *in situ*. Kuyper had, as Nicholas Wolterstorff describes it, the "endemic habit of mind . . . of digging beneath the surface of whatever religious, social, cultural, or intellectual development he was dealing with to discover its fundamental principles."[33] So one is well advised *first* to look at Kuyper's *fundamental principles* for Christian democratic participation before one turns, *secondly,* to his distinction between the *church as an institute and as an organism,* which leads, *thirdly,* to the *concrete application of Kuyper's vision* to the present challenge of democratic imbalance.

1. Kuyper's Fundamental Principles for Christian Democratic Participation

In terms of fundamental principles, then, Kuyper offers nothing less than an overall *wereldbeschouwing (Weltanschauung)* that entails the theoretical foundations for practical Christian political engagement. For Kuyper, this overall

31. See Nicholas P. Wolterstorff, "Abraham Kuyper (1837-1920) Commentary," in John Witte Jr. and Frank S. Alexander, eds., *The Teachings of Modern Protestantism: On Law, Politics, and Human Nature* (New York: Columbia University Press, 2007), pp. 38-39.

32. Kuyper writes, "Therefore in the affairs of the nation, as well as in all other spheres of life, the Christian is called upon to fight the fight of faith, to be a soldier of Jesus Christ. If we fail to obey the command of God, if we fail to defend the right, we shall suffer the downfall of the church and of the nation." Kuyper in McKendree R. Langley, *The Practice of Political Spirituality: Episodes from the Public Career of Abraham Kuyper, 1879-1918* (Jordan Station, Ontario: Paideia Press, 1984), p. 175.

33. Wolterstorff, "Abraham Kuyper (1837-1920) Commentary," p. 30.

worldview was Calvinism, and Kuyper's particular translation of Calvinism into real-life situations is still relevant today and deserves analysis. "The sociopolitical vision that Kuyper developed," argues Wolterstorff, "has proven to be the most influential appropriation and elaboration of the sociopolitical dimension of the Calvinist tradition in the past two centuries." What, then, was the basis of Kuyper's Calvinist-driven thought and action?

This basis clearly was Holy Scripture. And the scriptures introduced Kuyper not only to a God who is righteous and who executes justice,[34] but also to a sovereign Lord who demands from the human beings created in his image the enactment of justice on earth. The Dutch Reformed minister knew that the divine code required not only the vertical love of God but also the horizontal love of neighbor. Just as the Word of God reflects a significant concern for the disadvantaged, such as the mandate of "remembering the poor" (Galatians 2:10), or of caring for the widows and orphans (1 Timothy 5:3; James 1:27; Deuteronomy 10:18), so does Kuyper's policy and his whole life's work.[35] Kuyper took the biblical social imperatives seriously. In his address, "The Social Question and the Christian Religion,"[36] delivered at the First Christian Social Congress in the Netherlands in November 1891, Kuyper points to the Christ-centered, theological roots of his concern for social action:[37]

---

34. "The Lord is righteous [saddîq] in all his ways and kind in all his works" (Psalm 145:17). "I know that the LORD will maintain the cause of the afflicted, and justice [mishpat] for the poor" (Psalm 140:12). All Bible translations are from the *English Standard Version* (Wheaton, Ill.: Crossway Bibles, 2001).

35. See Frank Vanden Berg, *Abraham Kuyper: A Biography* (St. Catharines, Ontario: Paideia Press, 1978), p. 223. With regard to this social emphasis, Kuyper was also decidedly influenced by German Catholic philosopher, physician, engineer, and social reformer Franz von Baader (1765-1841). See Glenn Friesen, "The Mystical Dooyeweerd Once Again: Kuyper's Use of Franz von Baader," *Ars Disputandi* 3 (2003), http://www.ArsDisputandi.org, section 1). In 1835, Baader published a work on "The Situation of the Proletariat" *(Die Lage des Proletariats),* whereby he established himself as one of the earliest nineteenth-century social reformers (long before the era of Marx and Engels). The complete title of his work is: *Über das dermalige Mißverhältnis der Vermögenslosen oder Proletairs zu den Vermögen besitzenden Klassen der Sozietät in betreff ihres Auskommens, sowohl in materieller Hinsicht, aus dem Standpunkte des Rechts betrachtet.* In Baader, *Sämmtliche Werke,* ed. Franz Hoffmann et al. (Leipzig: Bethmann, 1854), pp. 125-44.

36. Abraham Kuyper, "The Social Question and the Christian Religion [Het Sociale Vraagstuk en de Christelijke Religie, 1891]," in *The Problem of Poverty,* ed. and trans. James W. Skillen (Sioux Center, Iowa: Dordt College Press, 2011), pp. 17-71.

37. Wolterstorff comments on this address that "whole paragraphs read as if they had been written by a late-twentieth-century liberation theologian." "Abraham Kuyper (1837-1920) Commentary," p. 38.

> You do not honor God's Word if . . . you ever forget how the Christ (just as
> his prophets before him and his apostles after him) invariably took sides
> *against* those who were powerful and living in luxury, and *for* the suffering
> and oppressed [. . .] The question on which the whole social problem really
> pivots is whether you recognize in the less fortunate, even in the poorest,
> not merely a creature, a person in wretched circumstances, but one of your
> own flesh and blood: for the sake of Christ, *your brother.*[38]

Throughout his life Kuyper showed a special concern for the little people,
the "kleine luyden,"[39] as he called them, and to whom his contemporary the
Scottish preacher, theologian, and social reformer Thomas Chalmers (1780-
1847) referred as the "ground-floor" of the society he wanted to see elevated.[40]
Abraham Kuyper continually pointed to the inalienable rights of those who,
one could say in our context, were affected by democratic imbalances and
social selection.[41] Those who were increasingly marginalized in the course
of the industrial revolution, who were left speechless as a result of injustice,
suffering and exploitation, Kuyper intended to give a voice.[42] His sermons,
newspaper articles, political speeches in Parliament,[43] and his decisions later
as prime minister of the Netherlands, bear witness to his constant passion to

---

38. Kuyper, "The Social Question and the Christian Religion," pp. 56, 67.

39. "The Little People" is the title of a speech the eighty-year-old Kuyper delivered on November 23, 1917, as the leader of the Anti-Revolutionary Party.

40. William Hanna, *Memoirs of Thomas Chalmers,* 2 vols. (Edinburgh: Constable, 1854), 2:705.

41. Kuyper's biographer writes: "In the dreary social-economic wilderness of the 1870s, Kuyper's was the most magnetic voice that spoke — in the national interest, for social justice and economic security. His keen sense of social responsibility, his sympathy for the labouring classes, and his love for the great multitude of the common people made him a pioneer on the social frontiers early in his career." Vanden Berg, *Abraham Kuyper: A Biography,* p. 77.

42. One needs to point out that the term "kleine luyden" does primarily refer to the "spine" of society, the working people, who had only little influence due to their limited possibilities of representation both in the ecclesial system (before 1867) and in the Dutch political system of the nineteenth century. Kuyper's intention was to strengthen the democratic right of the "kleine luyden," while also lobbying for the rights of the economically and socially disadvantaged, the widows, orphans and slaves.

43. In a speech delivered on October 25, 1899, in the Second Chamber of the Dutch Parliament, Kuyper based his argument for the introduction of insurance for workers (Workmen's Compensation Law) on biblical principles: "I wish to declare openly in this Chamber that I deem the battling against all human misfortunes a divinely decreed duty for all men, and that we are to recognize the system of insurance as a good gift from God." In Vanden Berg, *Abraham Kuyper: A Biography,* p. 191.

voice the concerns of the "kleine luyden" and the socially and economically disadvantaged.[44]

In addition to the biblical imperative, Kuyper, wearing his Calvinist spectacles, was also strongly motivated by the Reformed doctrine of *common grace*. As divine grace is "operating outside the church" in the form of common grace, argues Kuyper, Christians are "duty-bound to honor [this] operation of divine grace in human civic life by which the curse of sin, and sin itself, is restrained even though the link with salvation is lacking."[45] The doctrine of common grace thus underpins Kuyper's argument for the Christian's role of a *homo politicus*. In his Stone Lectures he explains that common grace is the reason why

> The Calvinist cannot shut himself up in his church and abandon the world to its fate. He feels, rather, in his high calling to push the development of this world to an even higher stage, and to do this in constant accordance with God's ordinance, for the sake of God, upholding, in the midst of so much painful corruption, everything that is honorable, lovely, and of good report among men.[46]

2. Contra Democratic Imbalance: *The Church as Institute and as Organism*

This distinction between institute and organism is significant for an understanding of Kuyper's view of the Christian's role as a political being, a *zoon politikon*. Kuyper make the distinction:

> [T]he Ecclesia visibilis has a *twofold* form of existence, firstly as *organism* and secondly as *institute*. As organism, where you can observe its organic

44. In 1905, when Kuyper was still prime minister, he not only drafted a three-volume social reform proposal, but the cabinet under his leadership also proposed a whole range of socio-economic bills to be submitted to Parliament. Among these suggestions were provisions for labor contracts, the creation of Chambers of Labor, increased protection of women and young persons in the industry, and the establishment of an insurance system covering sickness, disability, and old age, widows included. Vanden Berg, *Abraham Kuyper: A Biography*, p. 223.

45. Abraham Kuyper, "Common Grace," in *Abraham Kuyper: A Centennial Reader*, ed. James D. Bratt (Grand Rapids: Wm. B. Eerdmans, 1998), p. 193.

46. Abraham Kuyper, *Lectures on Calvinism* (Grand Rapids: Wm. B. Eerdmans, 1931), p. 73.

workings in the people and in the relationships among them, and as institute, in as far as it has, through independent organization, developed into a specific form.[47]

The role of the *church as institute,* according to Kuyper, is to focus on its core mission: the preaching of the word of God and the administration of the sacraments.[48] In this role, and in the activities that are involved, the church is unique, very different from the world. In fact, the church as an institute needs to be different from the world; it needs to be pure and holy, set apart for God.[49] In this sense, Kuyper clearly distinguishes between church and state, between the sacred and the profane. Nonetheless, the church beyond doubt exerts an influence on society. According to Kuyper, Dekker and Harinck observe, it "should be oriented toward society, not as an institute, but through the people."[50] The primary means through which Christians work towards the eradication of democratic imbalance is then *not* via the church as institute, but

47. Abraham Kuyper, *Encyclopedie der Heilige Godgeleerdheid,* part three (Kampen: Kok, 1908/09), p. 204; in Gerard Dekker and George Harinck, "The Position of the Church as Institute in Society: A Comparison between Bonhoeffer and Kuyper," *The Princeton Seminary Bulletin* 28:1 (2007): 91. For Kuyper, the Christian church is "neither exclusively an *institute,* nor only an *organism,* but both" (p. 92).

48. See Dekker and Harinck, "The Position of the Church as Institute in Society," p. 93.

49. Abraham Kuyper was clearly aware that the church, if it does not focus on its core role, is in danger of losing its true identity. In that sense, there is a fascinating ecumenical overlap between Abraham Kuyper and Pope Benedict XVI. Abraham Kuyper might have welcomed the pontiff's address delivered in Freiburg during his last visit to his native Germany in September 2011. The Bishop of Rome fears that the church "becomes self-satisfied, settles down in this world, becomes self-sufficient and adapts herself to the standards of the world." For that reason, argues the head of the Catholic Church, "it is time once again to discover the right form of detachment from the world [*Entweltlichung*], to move resolutely away from the Church's worldliness. This does not, of course, mean withdrawing from the world: quite the contrary. A Church relieved of the burden of worldliness is in a position, not least through her charitable activities, to mediate the life-giving strength of the Christian faith to those in need, to sufferers and to their carers." Speech delivered at the meeting with Catholics engaged in the life of the Church and society (Freiburg im Breisgau, Concert Hall, September 15, 2011), http://www.vatican.va/holy_father/benedict_xvi/speeches/2011/september/documents/hf_ben-xvi_spe_20110925_catholics-freiburg_en.html (accessed March 6, 2012).

50. Dekker and Harinck, "The Position of the Church as Institute in Society," p. 96. In Kuyper's view, "Christian social, cultural, and political action does not flow *directly* from the structures and authorities of the church," notes John Bolt, "but comes to expression *organically* in the various spheres of life as believers live out the faith and spirituality that develops and is nurtured in the church's worship and discipline." John Bolt, *A Free Church, a Holy Nation: Abraham Kuyper's American Public Theology* (Grand Rapids: Eerdmans, 2001), p. 429.

in an organic way, through the *church as organism*. It is worthwhile to quote Kuyper at length on this point:

> The church as institute exists through the offices which Christ established, and hence exclusively serves the preaching of the word, the administration of the Sacraments, the collection, and furthermore church discipline. . . . As things stand now, of course, the Church does not come into contact with public life, is completely separated from it and stands opposite from it. However, if one realizes that the Church is not merely institute, but is also an organism, and as such consists of believers . . . then of course it's an entirely different matter. Then those believers are the same people who in their families act as parents and children, in their businesses as patrons and workers, in society as citizens, and who, as such, make the powers of the kingdom felt in their domestic lives, in their education, in their businesses and in all contacts with people, and also as citizens in society. Whereas the Church as institute is removed from the world and therefore stands opposite to it, the Church as organism enters into the life of the world in exactly the opposite way, turns it around, gives it another form, raises it, and sanctifies it.[51]

So when Jürgen Habermas argues that the "Christian churches must meet the challenges of globalization by drawing more deeply on their own normative sources,"[52] Kuyper would answer: Yes, but this is primarily *not* the task of the church as an institute but a task of the church as an organism. The Christian as *homo politicus* is called to transform this world in an organic, non-confessional way. Christian effectiveness as salt and light in this world does not work primarily by going *to* church, but, while being part of the church, by going *out* into the world, as organic church members, and transforming it. Based on Kuyper's insights, New York Presbyterian minister Tim Keller warns us that "Churches that, against Kuyper's advice, try to take on all the levels of doing justice often find that the work of community renewal and social justice overwhelms the work of preaching, teaching, and nurturing the congregation."[53] The church as institute, then, must retain its spiritual core mission and at the

---

51. Kuyper, *De gemeene gratie,* part three, 424-25; in Dekker and Harinck, "The Position of the Church as Institute in Society," p. 96.

52. Jürgen Habermas, "A Conversation about God and the World," in *Time of Transitions* (Cambridge: Polity Press, 2006), p. 151.

53. Timothy Keller, *Generous Justice: How God's Grace Makes Us Just* (London: Hodder & Stoughton, 2010), p. 146.

same time equip its members to be active agents in a fallen world, contributing to the flourishing of human communities. "[I]f we apply Kuyper's view," Tim Keller writes, "then when we get to the more ambitious work of social reform and the addressing of social structure, believers should work through associations and organizations rather than through the local church."[54] With this organic emphasis, Kuyper's approach is far away from any tendency towards Fundamentalist imperialism.[55] Kuyper never argued for a "clericalization of life."[56] His vision was not of a confessional, Calvinist Reformed society.[57] This would have been a contradiction to his principle of "sphere sovereignty." The Dutch Christian democrat[58] rather argued for a pluralist, liberal, even secular,[59] democratic society where Christians enter the public space in confidence and raise their concerns humbly, yet with coherence and conviction.[60] At any rate, Kuyper, ever the energetic politician, emphasizes that Christian political lethargy or apathy is no option. Christians, as part of the organic church, are by nature political beings and need to act according to their intrinsic disposition. In short, Christians need to become what they are, namely "political disciples," as Graham Ward put it.[61]

54. Timothy Keller, *Generous Justice*, pp. 145-46. "Christian action" from a Kuyperian viewpoint, McKendree Langley points out, "is not to be carried out by churches but by various types of Christian citizens' groups organized to deal with specific matters such as public policy, newscasting, research on Christian politics and controversial issues of the day." McKendree R. Langley, *The Practice of Political Spirituality*, p. 169.

55. John Bolt argues that Kuyper is "opposed to 'church-sponsored' social and political action, and even speaks approvingly of a Calvinist note of 'secularization.'" Bolt, *A Free Church, A Holy Nation*, pp. 428-29.

56. Kuyper in Dekker and Harinck, "The Position of the Church as Institute in Society," pp. 95; 98.

57. Kuyper was for a "strong confessional church but *not* a confessional civil society *nor* a confessional state. This secularization of state and society is one of the most basic ideas of Calvinism." Kuyper, "Common Grace," p. 197.

58. Kuyper once declared in the Second Chamber of the Dutch Parliament, "I have always been a democrat and I hope to die a Christian democrat." Kuyper in Vanden Berg, *Abraham Kuyper: A Biography*, p. 224. One must be careful in evaluating this statement. For when Kuyper refers to himself as a Christian democrat, he does so as a European (and not as an American Democrat). See Peter S. Heslam, "Prophet of a Third Way: The Shape of Kuyper's Socio-Political Vision," *Journal of Markets & Morality* 5:1 (2002): 12-13. There remains, however, a certain ambiguity as to Kuyper's real position on democracy. See Heslam, "Prophet of a Third Way," pp. 12-14.

59. Cf. Bolt, *A Free Church, A Holy Nation*, p. 429n35.

60. Wolterstorff, "Abraham Kuyper (1837-1920) Commentary," pp. 40-41.

61. Graham Ward talks about the "call to political discipleship for Christians." In Ward, *The Politics of Discipleship: Becoming Postmaterial Citizens* (London: SCM Press, 2009), p. 39.

3. Applying Kuyper's Vision: Remedial and Preventative Action

This leaves us with our final and very practical question: How do political disciples act in real-life situations? How shall one concretely apply Kuyper's vision of the Christian as *homo politicus* to today's problem of democratic imbalance? As far as I see it, there are basically two options: one is *remedial action,* and the other option is *preventative action.*

By *remedial action* I refer to a kind of ambulance service in the here-and-now for those left behind by the new participatory revolution. The concrete task of the political disciple here is to make sure that the concerns of the "kleine luyden" are being heard, that their interests are not only included in the democratic decision process but are also translated into political action. This can happen in a classic way, by becoming a member of a political party, through lobbying or petitioning for a referendum and the like. In the context of the present participatory revolution, though, our options to voice the concerns of the less privileged are even greater, namely by means of direct democratic instruments at the grassroots level, such as through the formation of pressure and cause groups.[62] Christian political engagement is vital not only on the larger political scene but also, and more importantly, at a smaller and more local level. Kuyper himself continually emphasized the importance of the small political entities (in particular the family) as core pillars of society. This is where political discipleship begins, where it becomes tangible, for example, through a neighborhood group that takes action on homelessness, through the organization of town hall meetings on relief ministry options for the community, through the formation of local cause groups that support single parents, asylum seekers, or the long-term unemployed, through the establishment of a local group that offers debt counseling, or by simply offering language courses for migrants.

All these activities demonstrate that there are no limits for direct democratic Christian creativity. What is more, the new media with their social network options (Facebook, Twitter, etc.) certainly facilitate the establishment, organization, and development of these groups (Kuyper, who knew well how to use the media in his own context, is a role model). Again, for the Kuyperian, this is not the task of the church as an institute but the task of active political organisms, individual Christian political disciples who work together toward

---

62. As Colin Crouch writes, "Democratic politics therefore needs a vigorous, chaotic, noisy context of movements and groups. They are the seedbeds of future democratic vitality." *Post-Democracy,* p. 120.

democratic equality. This aspect of "togetherness" is very important. Abraham Kuyper did not endorse individualism. The Christian as political being is therefore never a hermit, but always a part of a group, part of a team.

The second option, then, is *preventative action*. And this is, in a long-term view, perhaps the more important method of addressing the problem. By preventative action I mean the empowerment of the democratically disadvantaged so that they will be able to participate independently in the public space and speak up for themselves in the future. It entails equipping, educating, and mobilizing those who are left behind by modernization so that they are, more and more, enabled to pursue the betterment of their own environments; so that they may become independent, mature participants in the new participatory revolution.[63] In order to achieve this ambitious goal, one could assemble citizens' action committees in the manifold ways already described, which would assist and empower those who are not currently participating in the political process. Again, direct democratic creativity at the communal level is the key. And clearly, both the remedial and the preventive approaches can and must be combined. From a Kuyperian viewpoint, the Christian as *zoon politikon,* as part of the church as organism, is called to take concrete remedial and preventive action against the present de-politicization of large parts of the population.

Conclusion

For Abraham Kuyper there was no room for political quietism. Abraham Kuyper's socio-political vision was and still is a wake-up call for lethargic Christians who are suffering from democratic fatigue in post-democratic times. Contra the Pietistic quietism of his German Protestant neighbors, Kuyper called for a Dutch Calvinist political activism, for the Christian's *Practice of Political Spirituality.*[64] Of course, our challenges today are different from Kuyper's. However, Abraham Kuyper has, I think, with his Scripture-based and common grace–driven agenda, and with his distinction between the church as institute and as organism, provided a unique framework for positive political Christian engagement that is applicable to the challenges of democratic imbal-

63. I am aware of the seeming paradox of using Kuyper, as a former leader of an "Anti-Revolutionary Party," as a role model of mobilizing people to get involved in the new participatory *revolution*. However, Kuyper's anti-revolutionary attitude is primarily to do with his critique of the French Revolution. Thus, I assume he would be quite happy to support what we, in our context, refer to as a participatory revolution.

64. As McKendree R. Langley put it in *The Practice of Political Spirituality.*

ance today. Moreover, Kuyper has, with the example of his own life and work, bequeathed us a role model that we can both admire and emulate.

Kuyper has left a significant legacy in that he, with his Calvinist *Weltanschauung,* theoretically and emphatically affirmed the church's right to participate in the political process within the context of a confessionally pluralist society. This is perhaps his most important contribution. Of course, one might disagree with the concrete application of his agenda, namely his distinction between the church as institute and the church as organism. Donald Macleod, for example, fears that this draws "too sharp a distinction between the sacred and the secular."[65] What is more, "[p]rotest against an intellectually bankrupt penal system," Macleod writes, "or against the inhumane treatment of immigrants cannot be left to either individual Christians or to voluntary associations."[66]

Ultimately, Christians are continually faced with the paradox of dual citizenship which entails dual responsibilities. This world is in dire need of Christians who do not (only) retreat to the safe haven of the church, but who go out into the world and contribute to the flourishing of democracy. As world-affirming Christians, living in this world, we are called to "seek the welfare of the city" (Jeremiah 29:7), to pray and to work for what is just, good, true, and beautiful, using all the democratic means available, while always keeping in mind that we are heading toward the world to come, where our liberal democracy will be replaced by the eternal theocracy in the New Jerusalem where "God may be all in all" (1 Corinthians 15:28).

Bibliography

Benedict XVI. Speech delivered at the meeting with Catholics engaged in the life of the Church and society. Freiburg im Breisgau, Concert Hall, September 15, 2011. http://www.vatican.va/holy_father/benedict_xvi/speeches/2011/september/documents/hf_ben-xvi_spe_20110925_catholics-freiburg_en.html

Bolt, John. *A Free Church, a Holy Nation: Abraham Kuyper's American Public Theology.* Grand Rapids: Eerdmans, 2001.

Crouch, Colin. *Post-Democracy.* Cambridge: Polity, 2004.

Dekker, Gerard, and George Harinck. "The Position of the Church as Institute in Society: A Comparison between Bonhoeffer and Kuyper." *The Princeton Seminary Bulletin* 28:1 (2007): 86-98.

65. Donald Macleod, "The Influence of Calvinism on Politics," *Theology in Scotland* 16:2 (2009): 17.

66. Macleod, "The Influence of Calvinism on Politics," p. 17.

Friesen, Glenn. "The Mystical Dooyeweerd Once Again: Kuyper's Use of Franz von Baader." *Ars Disputandi* 3 (2003), section 1. http://www.ArsDisputandi.org

Habermas, Jürgen. "A Conversation about God and the World." In *Time of Transitions.* Cambridge: Polity Press, 2006.

————. "Europe's Post-Democratic Era." *The Guardian.* November 10, 2011. http://www.guardian.co.uk/commentisfree/2011/nov/10/jurgen-habermas-europe-post-democratic

Hacker, Jacob S., and Oona A. Hathaway. "Our Unbalanced Democracy." *The New York Times.* August 1, 2011. http://www.nytimes.com/2011/08/01/opinion/our-unbalanced-democracy.html

Hanna, William. *Memoirs of Thomas Chalmers.* 2 vols. Edinburgh: Constable, 1854.

Heslam, Peter S. "Prophet of a Third Way: The Shape of Kuyper's Socio-Political Vision." *Journal of Markets & Morality* 5:1 (2002): 11-33.

Hill, Amelia. "Andy Coulson to be arrested over phone hacking tomorrow." *The Guardian.* July 7, 2011. http://www.guardian.co.uk/media/2011/jul/07/andy-coulson-arrest-phone-hacking

Inglehart, Ronald. *The Silent Revolution: Changing Values and Political Styles Among Western Publics.* Princeton, N.J.: Princeton University Press, 1977.

————. "Changing Values among Western Publics from 1970 to 2006." *West European Politics* 31 (1-2): 130-46.

Jones, Gareth. "Germany's Pirates Surge in Poll after Local Election." *Reuters Online.* April 3, 2012. http://www.reuters.com/article/2012/04/03/us-germany-pirates-poll-idUSBRE83207R20120403

Jörke, Dirk. "Bürgerbeteiligung in der Postdemokratie." *Aus Politik und Zeitgeschichte* 1:2 (2011): 13-18.

Keller, Timothy. *Generous Justice: How God's Grace Makes Us Just.* London: Hodder & Stoughton, 2010.

Kuyper, Abraham. *Encyclopedie der Heilige Godgeleerdheid.* Part III. Kampen: Kok, 1908/09.

————. *Lectures on Calvinism.* Grand Rapids: Eerdmans, 1931.

————. "Common Grace." In *Abraham Kuyper: A Centennial Reader.* Edited by James D. Bratt. Grand Rapids: Eerdmans, 1998.

————. "The Social Question and the Christian Religion." In *The Problem of Poverty.* Edited and translated by James W. Skillen. Sioux Center, Iowa: Dordt College Press, 2011.

Langley, McKendree R. *The Practice of Political Spirituality: Episodes from the Public Career of Abraham Kuyper, 1879-1918.* Jordan Station, Ontario: Paideia Press, 1984.

Macleod, Donald. "The Influence of Calvinism on Politics." *Theology in Scotland* 16:2 (2009): 5-22.

Maslow, Abraham. "A Theory of Human Motivation." *Psychological Review* 50:4 (1943): 370-96.

Meier, Lutz, and Jörn Petring. "Wulffs rätselhafte Umschuldungen." *Financial Times Deutschland.* December 28, 2011. http://www.ftd.de/politik/deutschland/:privatkredit-wulffs-raetselhafte-umschuldungen/60147207.html

Merkel, Wolfgang. "Volksabstimmungen: Illusion und Realität." *Aus Politik und Zeitgeschichte* 44-45 (2011): 47-55.

Niemi, Richard G., and Herbert F. Weisberg, eds. *Controversies in Voting Behavior.* Washington, D.C.: CQ Press, 2001.

Nolte, Paul. "Von der repräsentativen zur multiplen Demokratie." *Aus Politik und Zeitgeschichte* 1-2 (2011): 5-12.

Roberts, Nancy C., ed. *The Age of Direct Citizen Participation.* Armonk, N.Y.: M. E. Sharpe, 2008.

Sanderson, Rachel. "Berlusconi Faces Another Court Case." *The Financial Times.* February 7, 2012. http://www.ft.com/cms/s/0/33dac7ca-51a8-11e1-a30c00144feabdc0.html#axzz1lz9nZK2s

Van Kersbergen, Kees. "The Disenchantment of Politics." Paper presented at the *Kollegiat am Kulturwissenschaftlichen Kolleg Konstanz,* Germany. May 2008.

Vanden Berg, Frank. *Abraham Kuyper: A Biography.* St. Catharines, Ontario: Paideia Press, 1978.

Von Baader, Franz. *Über das dermalige Mißverhältnis der Vermögenslosen oder Proltairs zu den Vermögen besitzenden Klassen der Sozietät in betreff ihres Auskommens, sowohl in materieller Hinsicht, aus dem Standpunkte des Rechts betrachtet.* In Baader, *Sämmtliche Werke.* Edited by Franz Hoffmann et al. Leipzig: Bethmann, 1854.

Ward, Graham. *The Politics of Discipleship: Becoming Postmaterial Citizens.* London: SCM Press, 2009.

Wiegand, Ralf. "Enthüllung — Wulff drohte 'Bild'-Journalisten mit Strafanzeige." *Süddeutsche Zeitung.* January 2, 2012. http://www.sueddeutsche.de/politik/bundespraesident-in-not-wulff-drohte-mit-strafanzeige-gegen-bild-journalisten-1.1248384

Wolterstorff, Nicholas P. "Abraham Kuyper (1837-1920) Commentary." In *The Teachings of Modern Protestantism: On Law, Politics, and Human Nature.* Edited by John Witte Jr. and Frank S. Alexander. New York: Columbia University Press, 2007.

Distinctively Common: Advancing Herman Bavinck's Theology to Pressure Liberal Democratic Ideals

Clay Cooke

Introduction

What posture should Christians take toward liberal democratic ideals? Historically, the tendencies have been to either dilute the Christian confession in order to participate in liberal democratic structures for the common good, or take an oppositional stance toward these structures in order to maintain Christian distinctiveness. Yet when Christians adopt these approaches, it is arguable that their disposition in public life becomes oriented toward the wrong ends. For instance, many would contend that the "Christian Right"[1] assumes a form of civil religion as it engages in American politics, thus watering down Christianity by too closely linking it with "American values." In turn, this group is said to confuse Christian discipleship with political partisanship, often leading to a politicized gospel.[2] The concern is that because the Christian Right does not hold on to their particularity *as Christians,* their primary orientation toward liberalism becomes one of *accommodation.* On the opposite end of the spectrum are those with a separatist mindset. John Milbank, for example, attests that liberal democracies are "a continuous horror almost as grave as the Holocaust, and a more troublingly sustainable mode of nihilism, appropriately disguised by an unparalleled reign of

1. The Christian Right is the expansion of Jerry Falwell's Moral Majority and Pat Robertson's Christian Coalition. Since the 1980s, it has sought to recover moral uprightness in the United States as the solution to saving American democracy.
2. Charles Marsh, *Wayward Christian Soldiers: Freeing the Gospel from Political Captivity* (New York: Oxford University Press, 2007), pp. 2, 10, 76.

kitsch."[3] To put it mildly, Milbank's goal is to purge the Christian church of liberal contamination by upholding the distinctiveness of the Body of Christ. He, and others, take an *oppositional* stance, as they are unwilling to use liberal democratic structures for advancement of the public good.

In light of these Christian proclivities in politics, the goal of this essay is to utilize the thought of Herman Bavinck to develop a "distinctively common" public ethic — one that holds together both Christian peculiarity and the common good — and in turn, articulate a faithful posture that puts *pressure* on liberal democracies like the United States.[4] In contrast to accommodation and opposition, "pressure" enables a nuanced understanding of liberal democratic ideals — not simple acquiescence or wholesale denunciation — and ultimate loyalty to another worldview, namely, Christianity. This approach permits both rejection of liberalism as an ideology and gratitude for the benefits and blessings that modern democracies provide; it is a critical appreciation.[5] The question that remains, then, is which of Bavinck's theological resources can serve as building blocks for developing a "distinctively common" posture — a posture, as it were, that puts pressure on liberal democratic societies to steer them towards the target of the public good?

In what follows, I suggest that Bavinck's notions of creation and virtue provide a suitable answer to this question. By integrating these theological concepts I utilize Bavinck to move beyond Bavinck, extending his theology for twenty-first-century democratic citizens. I have organized this argument into two parts. The first will investigate how liberalism and Bavinck envisage the common good. While the former views this "good" through the aperture of individual liberty, the latter perceives it through the lens of a robust theology of creation. The second will examine how liberalism and Herman Bavinck conceive of religious distinctiveness in public life. Although liberal ideals have a penchant to privatize religion, Bavinck's emphasis on Christian virtue illustrates the importance of maintaining a full Christian identity in politics. Using these two approaches, my ultimate goal is to demonstrate how Christ "holds all things together" — the highest good and common good —

---

3. John Milbank, *Being Reconciled: Ontology and Pardon* (New York: Routledge, 2003), p. 5.

4. I am appropriating this notion of "pressuring" liberalism from John Stuart Mill, who considered it imperative to exert persistent "intellectual pressure" on this political philosophy. Although Mill was a committed liberal, he also thought that liberalism functioned best when its deficiencies were challenged. (See Lionel Trilling's *The Liberal Imagination: Essays on Literature and Society,* Preface).

5. Clay Cooke, "Liberalism, Democracy, and Sphere Sovereignty," in *Capital Commentary,* a publication for the Center for Public Justice, December 9, 2011.

and in turn, apply Bavinck's thought to effectively pressuring liberal democratic principles.

I. Liberalism and Bavinck on the Common Good

Like so many other realities in life, liberal democracies include both positive and negative characteristics. On the positive side, modern democratic citizens experience higher living standards, longer life spans, and freedoms of self-determination; they possess rights to free assembly, fair treatment under the law, equal participation in the political process, and protection and integrity for the person; and they have rights to freedom of speech and religion — rare liberties for anyone in the world prior to 1800.[6] Given this substantial list of rights and freedoms, one can contend that liberal democracies provide genuine "goods" that Christians can appreciate. Nonetheless, one can also make the case that liberalism entails various idolatries that can distort a distinctly Christian view of the common good. One such idolatry, which ironically constitutes one of liberalism's genuine blessings as well, is that of individual liberty.

A. Liberalism's "Individualistic" View of the Common Good

In his seminal work, *The Leviathan,* Thomas Hobbes insists, "A free man is he that, in those things which by his strength and wit he is able to do, is not hindered to do what he has a will to."[7] Hobbes's observation highlights the primary concern of liberalism, namely, individual liberty. Individual liberty is not inherently wrong; it is a wonderful blessing that citizens of modern democracies can enjoy. Yet just like any other created entity or good, it can become an idol when given too much value. As political theologian David Koyzis suggests, liberalism on its own tends toward this misguided valuation; it gravitates, that is, toward a "soteriology of freedom," where the whole of existence is viewed through the perspective of maximizing personal liberty.[8] This perspective is constructed by the fact that the lone person — not the state, community, or family — is the principal ontological unit and building block of the liberal

---

6. Michael Novak, *The Spirit of Democratic Capitalism* (New York: Simon and Schuster, 1982), p. 17.

7. Thomas Hobbes, *The Leviathan* (Whitefish, Mt.: Kessinger Publishing, 2004), p. 88.

8. David T. Koyzis, *Political Visions and Illusions: A Survey and Christian Critique of Contemporary Ideologies* (Downers Grove, Ill.: InterVarsity Press, 2003), p. 70.

society.[9] Whether Christians consciously recognize it or not, this worldview shapes the political and economic frameworks of modern democratic states, and in turn, indelibly forms their understandings of the public good.

Politically and economically, then, what framework is in fact being "formed" by liberalism? Or how is this political philosophy shaping Christians' views of the common good? To understand these questions politically is to recognize that liberalism envisions the individual as sovereign. The individual is like a queen who rules herself by what laws she elects to live by. The state still exists and has a significant role to play, but its actions are authorized by the consent of sole persons, or what is otherwise known as social contract theory. In the social contract, it is because lone persons are willing to relinquish their authority, and by choice enter into contract with other persons, that the state has any legitimacy at all. In this picture, the state becomes more or less inferior to the individual, and its main purpose is to attend to the needs of individuals.[10]

Economically, social contract theory's emphasis on personal choice typically takes the form of capitalism in liberal democratic settings.[11] Capitalism, too, cannot be deemed simply good or evil, but rather profoundly complex. On the one hand it generates innumerable benefits, such as an expanded middle class that now lives more comfortably than most kings and queens throughout history. On the other hand, it also entails great risks and costs. Many worry, for example, that because of its reliance on competing forces to produce results, capitalism necessitates "winners" and "losers." The fear is that this model stacks the deck in such a way that the rich — or those who win — keep getting richer while the poor — or those who lose — keep getting poorer. What's more, in the United States many fret that consumerism has perniciously invaded most spheres of society to the point where these spheres inadvertently operate on market-based priorities.[12] One could argue, for instance, that higher education institutions now have to worry as much about raising money as they worry about students' learning; artists may have to prioritize selling their art instead of making it beautiful; and news organizations may feel pressured to focus on attention-getting headlines instead of journalism. While not all higher education institutions, artists, and news organizations function in this way, they are nonetheless all subject to the norms and temptations of a market-infused

9. Koyzis, *Political Visions and Illusions*, pp. 67-68, 70.

10. Koyzis, *Political Visions and Illusions*, pp. 47-51.

11. Koyzis, *Political Visions and Illusions*, p. 70.

12. Charles Mathewes, *The Republic of Grace: Augustinian Thoughts for Dark Times* (Grand Rapids: Eerdmans, 2010), pp. 115.

culture. In order to survive this climate they must be competitive, meaning that they must appeal to consumers — to the individuals who choose which cultural good to "buy."

These liberal characteristics, both political and economic, undoubtedly shape citizens' perspectives of the public good. In fact, they are impossible to escape and are usually so ingrained that they operate on an unconscious level. As philosopher Charles Taylor asserts, this unconscious, liberal "social imaginary" is indelibly shaped by a concern for individuals, whereby the "underlying idea of mutual benefit of individuals and the defense of their rights takes on more and more importance."[13] Taylor's point is that liberalism's view of the common good is not so "common" after all; it is instead about the lone person, and whether, for instance, she has the freedom to choose who and what she wants to be. Thus by way of aggregating and offsetting individual interests, liberalism actually possesses its own view of the common good. From a Christian standpoint, though, this perspective is inadequate; it both distorts a fully distinctive Christian public ethic and arguably undermines the real "goods" that liberal democracies generate. So while Christians have to look beyond liberalism for a faithful public ethic, liberalism also has to look beyond its own ideology for proper sustenance. Liberalism, that is, needs *pressure* from a Christian perspective in order to best facilitate the "shalom of the city."[14] Herman Bavinck's robust theology of creation is up to this task.

B. How Bavinck's Theology of Creation Informs the Common Good

Like so many of his fellow Christians within the neo-Calvinist tradition, Herman Bavinck possesses a rich theology of creation. He insists that Christianity not only shows the way to salvation, but also reveals the way to abundant life in the here-and-now.[15] Moreover, it is not only relevant inside the walls of the church, but in light of God's sovereignty, Christianity is also germane to every corner and crease of creation — politics, business, education, art, technology,

---

13. Charles Taylor, *Modern Social Imaginaries* (Durham, N.C.: Duke University Press Books, 2003), p. 4.

14. Jeremiah 29:7. In this verse Jeremiah says, "But seek the welfare (shalom) of the city where I have sent you into exile, and pray to the Lord on its behalf, for in its welfare you will find your welfare." Jeremiah's remarks offer a wonderful biblical example of the importance of seeking the common good, or the welfare of the city.

15. Herman Bavinck, "The Future of Calvinism," in *The Presbyterian and Reformed Review* 5:17 (1894): 3.

etc.[16] To employ Bavinck's doctrine of creation to seek the common good, it is imperative to grasp how his creational theology informs his notions of *common grace* and *sphere sovereignty*.

With regard to common grace, in the majority of his writings and especially in his article "Common Grace," Bavinck derives a philosophy of "commonness" from what he sees as God's manifold purposes in creation. As Bavinck contests, "Common grace enables us to acknowledge the importance of creation and human culture as good gifts of God that not only form the arena of his redemptive activity but are themselves subject to redemption."[17] His claim is that the sovereign Lord not only yearns to redeem individuals, but also desires the entire creation to be a reflection of God's wondrous glory, thereby leading God to offer creation common grace.[18] One of the functions of this grace is to restrain sin, for if sin were left untouched, Bavinck suggests that it would ravage creation to the point of utter chaos. Although sin still curses and imbues the entire cosmos, God's common grace ensures that his "good creation" is not destroyed.[19] But common grace is not only a restraining grace; it also enables non-redeemed individuals and communities to do legitimately good works.[20] A non-Christian husband can thus love his wife, a non-Christian citizen can treat a hostile neighbor with civility and respect, and a non-Christian government can seek and establish justice. Unbelievers are able to perform these genuinely good deeds because "[t]here is thus a rich revelation of God even among the heathen — not only in nature but also in their heart and conscience, in their life and history, among their statesmen and artists, their philosophers and reformers."[21] In other words, non-Christians are able to *know* the good because God actively reveals it to them; God pours forth virtues even throughout the "world of the heathen."[22] For Bavinck, then, non-Christian acts of common grace fill the greater theatre of God's glory that Christians can affirm and delight in.

In addition to common grace, Bavinck further clarifies his theology of creation with the doctrine of *sphere sovereignty*. In the approximately 150

---

16. Herman Bavinck, *Our Reasonable Faith* (Grand Rapids: Eerdmans, 1956), p. 550. See also Herman Bavinck, *The Sacrifice of Praise, Meditations Before and After Receiving Access to the Table of the Lord,* trans. Gilbert Zekveld (1922), 12. http://spindleworks.com/library/bavink/TheSacrificeOfPraise.pdf

17. Herman Bavinck, "Common Grace," in *Calvin Theological Journal* 1:24 (April 1989): 37.

18. Bavinck, "Common Grace," pp. 40, 60, 64.

19. Bavinck, "Common Grace," p. 61.

20. Bavinck, "Common Grace," pp. 40, 51.

21. Bavinck, "Common Grace," p. 41.

22. Bavinck, "Common Grace," p. 41.

years that neo-Calvinism has existed as a theological tradition (the tradition of which Bavinck is a part), sphere sovereignty has arguably been its most noteworthy doctrinal contribution. Bavinck's predecessor, Abraham Kuyper, was the first to fully articulate and make this idea well known in his 1880 inaugural address at the Free University of Amsterdam, "Souvereiniteit in Eigen Kring."[23] For all practical purposes, Bavinck and Kuyper fall closely in line on this idea, concurring that the "spheres" are undergirded by the Bible's robust theology of creation. It is interesting to note, however, that while Bavinck upholds Kuyper's doctrine of sphere sovereignty, he does not use Kuyper's terminology when communicating this perspective. Instead of "sphere sovereignty," he prefers to speak of a sphere's "essence" and "calling."[24] Furthermore, Bavinck never directly appeals to Kuyper to theologically justify this precept. Rather, he references Augustine's teaching on the order of creation for its defense, suggesting that he considers Augustine more of a theological authority. Bavinck's delineation of sphere sovereignty generally opens with some version of the following:

> It is God's omnipresent and eternal power that upholds and governs all things. In him, in his plan and also in his rule, originated the unity or harmony that holds together and unites all things over the entire range of their diversity and leads them to a single goal. Consequently, as Augustine keeps saying, there is unity, measure, order, number, mode, degree, and kind of creatures. "To some things he gave more of being and to others less and, in this way, arranged an order of nature in a hierarchy of being." God is present in all things. In him all things live and move and have their being.[25]

In this remark, Bavinck mentions two themes that are fundamental to his broader doctrine of sphere sovereignty, namely, that there is a *unified diversity* and *divine ordering* present within creation. In nearly all of his writings, whenever he speaks of these two creational aspects (and especially when he

---

23. Abraham Kuyper, "Sphere Sovereignty," in *Abraham Kuyper: A Centennial Reader*, ed. James D. Bratt (Grand Rapids: Eerdmans, 1998), pp. 460-61.

24. Herman Bavinck, "Ethics and Politics," in *Essays on Religion, Science, and Society*, ed. John Bolt, trans. Harry Boonstra and Gerrit Sheeres (Grand Rapids: Baker Academic, 2008), p. 264. For purposes of clarity, I will simply use the term "sphere sovereignty" even though Bavinck does not employ this term.

25. Herman Bavinck, *Reformed Dogmatics: Prolegomena*, vol. 1, ed. John Bolt, trans. John Vriend (Grand Rapids: Baker Academic, 2003), p. 370.

mentions them alongside Augustine), he proceeds with an elaboration of "sphere sovereignty."[26]

As to sphere sovereignty's first characteristic, the unified diversity of creation, Bavinck affirms that because human beings are image-bearers of God, they have the need to express themselves in innumerable ways and thereby unfold the rich cultural potential that God has implanted in creation.[27] It is in this process that the spheres — politics, business, art, technology — arise. With regard to these spheres, Bavinck contends that God loves diversity: "In the one world there is room for several kinds of beings."[28] Mere variety, however, is not the final goal of sphere sovereignty. Rather, the aim is a unified diversity, whereby the plurality of spheres works in aggregate for God's glory. This conception paints a picture of society not fundamentally characterized by chaos, but by an organic connection between all of creation's spheres under Christ, who holds all things together.[29]

Furthermore, when Bavinck refers to sphere sovereignty he affirms the presence of a divine ordering within creation. Although this ordering denotes the organic nature of how the spheres function together as a whole, it also indicates how the spheres are internally ordered to operate "after their own kind." Bavinck arrives at this conclusion by extending the divinely implanted order he sees within nature to include the manifold ways in which humans associate themselves — family, art, education, politics, etc. Just as "[s]un, moon, and stars have their own unique task," so too "[e]verything was created with a nature of its own and rests in ordinances established by God."[30] In light of this cosmic order, Bavinck considers it of vital importance to uphold the boundaries between the spheres. A sports team is not designed to function as a family, nor is a school's purpose the same as that of a business. As to the specific ordering of the political sphere, in his article "Ethics and Politics," Bavinck states, "The power of the state is and remains in its essence at the service of righteousness."[31] Righteousness and justice are interchangeable terms

---

26. See Bavinck, *Our Reasonable Faith*, pp. 67-69. See also Bavinck, "Common Grace," p. 64; Herman Bavinck, *Reformed Dogmatics: God and Creation*, vol. 2, ed. John Bolt, trans. John Vriend (Grand Rapids: Baker Academic, 2004), p. 436.

27. Herman Bavinck, *The Origin, Essence, and Purpose of Man*. http://www.the-highway.com/origin_Bavinck.html.

28. Bavinck, *Our Reasonable Faith*, p. 68.

29. Bavinck, *Reformed Dogmatics: God and Creation*, pp. 392, 422, 436. See also Bavinck, *Our Reasonable Faith*, pp. 68-69.

30. Bavinck, *Reformed Dogmatics: God and Creation*, p. 436.

31. Bavinck, "Ethics and Politics," p. 273.

in this article; they signify that the function of the state is to afford each person his or her due.[32] By grasping and maintaining this sphere mode, Christians honor the divinely instilled order of creation, which is essential to individual and societal flourishing.

In the end, are Bavinck's notions of common grace and sphere sovereignty merely philosophical, abstract concepts with no pertinence to the everyday affairs of human life? Not at all. Through their rich accounts of creation these constructs inform how we see reality, which necessarily affects how we inhabit and organize our lives in the world. For those who presently seek to inhabit the world faithfully, Bavinck's theology of creation demonstrates that they are not first and foremost citizens of liberal democracies, but of another republic — the Kingdom of God. As citizens of this republic, they possess a worldview that can more thoroughly inform political imaginations and actions. Christians possess, as it were, a different political language — a language of common grace and sphere sovereignty that conceives of the public good not in terms of maximizing individual liberty, but in terms of shalom. Shalom imagines society as a cosmic symphony, one that is simultaneously diverse and harmonious, and that is guided by the sovereign hand of the Master Conductor. When political life is perceived through this Bavinckian prism, we are able to reject the individualistic ideology of liberalism while also affirming the benefits that a democratic society provides. Moreover, we are afforded a disposition that keeps individual liberty in its proper place — as a "good" and not an idol. This perspective helps articulate an approach to democratic citizenship that more faithfully envisages the common good.

Yet this approach is not yet fully distinctive. For although it applies a theology of creation to political involvement, it is still in need of integration with a uniquely Christian notion of virtue to cultivate properly formed citizens. Only then may we articulate a "distinctly common" public ethic, and in turn, put appropriate pressure on liberal democratic principles. As will become evident in the next section, by rightly combining Bavinck's thoughts on creation and virtue we can advance this public posture.

II. Liberalism and Bavinck on Christian Distinctiveness

Whereas in our families, communities of membership, and leisure activities we frequently encounter persons who are essentially "like" us, in political life

32. Bavinck, "Ethics and Politics," pp. 273, 276.

we experience "otherness" in a more acute form. We come across individuals and groups who do not share our worldviews, convictions, ethnicities, interests, and priorities. Yet because we live within the same geopolitical boundaries, we must construct some kind of common life together. As we build that shared life with one another, a key question is what we should do with our confessional commitments — with those beliefs and loyalties that form the most basic parts of our identities. Do we keep these loyalties private, dilute them in order to find shared public language, or boldly insert them into public life in their unadulterated forms? The liberal and Bavinckian answers to these questions are quite different.

A. Liberalism and the Privatization of Religion

Suspicions about the divisive consequences of religion have imbued the liberal imagination since its beginnings. Thus for many secular thinkers (and even religious devotees), religion poses a grave threat to constructing a common political life together because of its inherent divisiveness. Generally, skeptics have found that religion exacerbates the challenge of engaging "the other" in public life. In liberal democratic societies, then, a gnawing anxiety often surrounds religion's presence in the public square. In his book *The Social Contract,* Jean-Jacques Rousseau reinforces this notion when he argues that it is unfeasible to "live in peace with people one regards as damned."[33] Rousseau, along with other thinkers such as John Locke and Thomas Hobbes, worries that the presence of "thick" religious faith in public life will inevitably lead to horrors such as the religious wars of the sixteenth and seventeenth centuries. Hence for each of these men, religion is appropriate in public life only insofar as it is "thinned down" into rational terms that can be agreed upon. In essence, they contend that if religion is kept private, and the public domain remains religiously "naked," the threat of otherness (or what many refer to as pluralism) can be contained.[34]

One of the most influential contemporary political theorists to demonstrate these liberal apprehensions is John Rawls. Rawls's basic uneasiness con-

---

33. Jean-Jacques Rousseau, *The Social Contract,* trans. Willmoore Kendall (Chicago: Henry Regnery, 1954), p. 160.

34. Nicholas Wolterstorff, "From Liberal to Plural," in *Christian Philosophy at the Close of the Twentieth Century: Assessment and Perspective,* ed. Sander Griffioen and Bert M. Balk (Kampen: Uitgeverij Kok, 1995), pp. 206-209. Here Wolterstorff criticizes the liberal tendency to exclude religion from public life.

cerns how a religiously pluralistic polity might debate and determine issues of public justice — issues such as healthcare, education, and gay rights. He realizes that these issues generate enormous passion in public debate, especially when coupled with religious justifications for certain political positions. For this reason, he too wants to "thin down" religious distinctiveness in political life so that, for instance, democratic citizens do not appeal to their core confessional commitments in a debate on gay marriage. Rawls suggests that liberal citizens instead appeal to "public reason" — a form of discourse typified as exercising rational, secular, and universal claims in political debate.[35] As political theologian Eric Gregory notes, public reason defines Rawls's conception of political virtue; it means that in order to be a virtuous liberal citizen, one must restrict one's deepest convictions to the private sector, and seek a religiously neutral, shared public language in political dialogue. Rawls seems to think that without this neutrality — without an appeal to public reason by those with multifarious ultimate commitments — political life will ineluctably slip into chaos. Religious particularity, then, winds up being a threat to political stability.[36]

From a Christian point of view, Rawls's liberal perspective is problematic.[37] For in his effort to pursue civic peace through religious neutrality, he ends up totalizing his own secular point of view. Although it may seem that Rawls's effort to exclude religion from public life makes this space neutral, in fact it does not. It instead orients public life toward the religion of secularism, wherein secular ideals replace other faith commitments with notions of what is good, right, and valuable. Often in very furtive ways, therefore, the liberal imagination tends to encroach upon civic identity with its very own "thick" worldview. In this view liberalism becomes the only acceptable public "religion," which is pernicious not only for Christian faith, but for liberal democracies as well. For democratic societies are bolstered not when their strengths are affirmed, but when their deficiencies are challenged. They are enhanced, that is, when pressured by "distinctively common" perspectives other than their own.

---

35. John Rawls, *Political Liberalism* (New York: Columbia University Press, 1996), p. 217.

36. Eric Gregory, *Politics and the Order of Love: An Augustinian Ethic of Democratic Citizenship* (Chicago: The University of Chicago Press, 2008), pp. 61-63.

37. Even so, Christians can still praise Rawls's theoretical efforts to establish political justice and peace.

B. Herman Bavinck and Virtue

Although Bavinck's theology of creation helps put pressure on liberalism, this pressure is inadequate because it is not yet fully, or distinctly, Christian. To obtain this uniquely Christian type of pressure, Bavinck's creational theology needs to be integrated with his conception of virtue — an issue he discusses in his article "Ethics and Politics." Here he affirms that one's duty in political life is to work for justice.[38] Nevertheless, he also states that a mere cognitive understanding of this truth is insufficient, for it does not form the dispositions, motives, and character traits that are essential to discerning and actualizing this justice. He also makes this point in *The Philosophy of Revelation,* where he avers, "Beneath consciousness there is a world of instincts and habits, notions and inclinations, abilities and capacities, which continually sets on fire the course of nature. Beneath the head lies the heart, out of which are the issues of life."[39] As these remarks suggest, Bavinck spends considerable energy arguing for what many refer to today as "virtue ethics." More specifically, he sees virtue in Christ as the fundamental link between the highest good and the common good — a perspective that enables him to defend the right and significance of speaking and acting particularly *as Christians* in public life.[40]

It is at this point where Bavinck's notion of virtue differs significantly from the well-known Christian virtue ethicist Stanley Hauerwas. For while Hauerwas also stresses the significance of virtue ethics for the Christian social task,[41] in his view the goal of Christian virtue is not to seek justice or the common good.[42] Instead, virtue's purpose is to enable the church to serve as a "contrast model" to the world, or to "clash" with the world.[43] Virtue, then, necessarily forms a church community that concerns itself with "being the church" (i.e., faithfully embodying the story of Jesus) rather than healing or restoring worldly structures and institutions.[44] When shaped by this brand

---

38. Bavinck, "Ethics and Politics," pp. 264, 272.

39. Herman Bavinck, *The Philosophy of Revelation* (New York: Longmans, Green, and Co., 1909), p. 215.

40. Bavinck, "Ethics and Politics," p. 273. For instance, Bavinck says that "morality involves both the will and character and acts and deeds" and that "justice is not satisfied with only the mere external obedience to the law but is certainly also interested in motives" (p. 273).

41. Stanley Hauerwas, *A Community of Character* (Notre Dame: University of Notre Dame Press, 1981), p. 3.

42. Hauerwas, *A Community of Character,* pp. 92, 109-10.

43. Hauerwas, *A Community of Character,* pp. 49, 84.

44. Hauerwas, *A Community of Character,* pp. 49-50, 176.

of ecclesiology, Hauerwas avers, Christians should become "uninvolved" in worldly politics — even liberal democratic politics.[45]

In contrast, Bavinck depicts virtue as a tool that can help Christians utilize liberal democratic structures to seek the common good. In "Ethics and Politics," for instance, Bavinck accentuates this point in his discussion of politics as *praxis*. The main issue in the praxis of politics, he suggests, concerns the judgment and ability to do what is needed for the welfare of the polity in a certain situation. Or as Bavinck defines it, praxis is that aspect of political discipleship that prepares the politician or citizen to "hit the right mark" in often ambiguous political circumstances.[46] "Hitting the right mark" does not focus simply on being instructed to do justice, but in being properly formed to desire and perceive justice in a given situation. This emphasis is especially pertinent given the context of Bavinck's article, namely, World War I Europe.[47] The "Great War," as it is called, was an exceedingly complex time in the Netherlands, in which right and wrong were often nebulous, so for Bavinck to tell his audience to "do justice" would have been insufficient instruction. Instead, he suggests that in order to discern and establish justice in the convoluted context of the war, one had to first be properly shaped as a moral agent. In the end, his argument is not for a particular stance on the war, but instead for his fellow Christian citizens to take the cultivation of virtue, and its relationship to the pursuit of justice, seriously.[48]

In addition to "Ethics and Politics," Bavinck more precisely addresses

---

45. Hauerwas, *A Community of Character*, p. 74.

46. Bavinck, "Ethics and Politics," p. 264. Bavinck says that the politician or citizen "is like a hunter or fisherman; with fishing or hunting, nearly everything depends on patient waiting, the correct observation, and then the sudden use of the right moment" (p. 264). Political "praxis" in Bavinck's thought could be an analogue to phronesis in Aristotelian conceptions. As I will note below, however, in contrast to Aristotle, Bavinck says that humans do not *achieve* virtue; it is always the result of God's grace.

47. Bavinck's "Ethics and Politics" was initially a speech he delivered at the Dutch Royal Academy of Sciences in 1915. When Bavinck delivered this speech, his context was World War I Europe, a period filled with colossal anxiety and bloodshed throughout the continent. The war had erased the optimism of previous decades, making people feel as if the world was spinning out of control. In the Netherlands during this time, most political conversations focused on what role the country should play in the war. Bavinck's goal, as indicated in the title of his speech, was to communicate the relationship between ethics and politics during a time when the war had shaken the foundations of justice and morality. In order to grasp the full meaning and purpose of Bavinck's "Ethics and Politics," it is imperative to take these conditions into account.

48. Bavinck, "Ethics and Politics," pp. 264, 268, 272-74.

virtue in his lectures on philosophical ethics.[49] Jelle Michiels de Jong, one of Bavinck's students in Kampen, took detailed notes on these lectures.[50] De Jong notes Bavinck's instructions that Reformed ethics has much to learn from philosophical ethics. In fact, Bavinck asserts, "We can profit from Aristotelian thought, and without doubt Aristotle's ethics is basically the best philosophical ethics."[51] Bavinck conveys in these comments his fervent support for the second-order discourse of virtue ethics, namely, its categories and concepts such as feeling, character, and moral formation. He deems these categories essential for any holistic view of moral development, and even affirms that Christians can obtain virtues through practical exercises, or through Christian practices.[52] Nonetheless, he is at the same time a critic of virtue ethics. He expressly rejects the Aristotelian claim that people can achieve the ethical ideal (i.e., the human *telos*) by means of their own agency, or that people can form moral virtues in accordance with their own natures. Rather, in line with his Reformed theology he asserts that virtues are acquired through grace.[53] Moral formation, then, is a process of growing in grace — a process that focuses not on Aristotelian achievement but on Christ-like cruciformity.

Although Bavinck does not expressly link virtue ethics with cruciformity in his lectures on philosophical ethics, this connection seems like a logical progression. For example, in his second article on the imitation of Christ, "The Imitation of Christ in the Modern World" (1918), Bavinck uses the word "virtue" twenty times. Furthermore, it is arguable that one of Bavinck's main purposes in this article is to clarify what comprises cruciform virtue. He makes two key points in this regard: First, in contrast to merely copying Jesus' New Testament ethic, he states that cruciformity in the modern world will "emphasize those virtues which Jesus exhibited in his life of obedience to the Father's will" — virtues such as humility, suffering, meekness, righteous-

---

49. I was led to these lectures by Dirk Van Keulen's article on Bavinck's unpublished works on ethics. See Dirk Van Keulen, "Herman Bavinck's *Reformed Ethics*: Some Remarks About Unpublished Manuscripts in the Libraries of Amsterdam and Kampen," *The Bavinck Review* 1 (2010): 41.

50. These notes are preserved in the historical archives at the Free University of Amsterdam.

51. *Gereformeerde Ethiek van Profess. Dr. H. Bavinck,* notes by Jelle Michiels de Jong, Bavinck Archives, box 26/32 (HB Diktaten), 36. "Ook met de gedachten van Arist[oteles] kunnen we onze winst doen en zonder twijfel is de Ethiek van Aristoteles de beste philos[ophische] Ethiek in hoofdzaak." Noted in Van Keulen, "Herman Bavinck's *Reformed Ethics*," pp. 46-47.

52. *Gereformeerde Ethiek van Profess. Dr. H. Bavinck,* pp. 3, 32.

53. *Gereformeerde Ethiek van Profess. Dr. H. Bavinck,* p. 36.

ness, willingness to forgive, and especially love.[54] Second, the application of these virtues will vary based on historical circumstances. For instance, cruciformity on a World War I battlefield (which Bavinck definitively believes is possible) will look different than it will for a twenty-first-century United States citizen.[55]

Whether in war or in another domain, Bavinck's ultimate goal in examining cruciform virtue is to answer the following questions: "Is there even room in the cultural life of the present for [the imitation of Christ]? Can it still be taken seriously by people in the state, industry, business, marketplace, stock-exchange, office or factory, in science and art, in war, even at the front?"[56] Bavinck's queries are essentially the same as those of this essay; namely, is the heart of the Christian faith — following Christ crucified — relevant to the whole of life, especially life in liberal democratic societies? More specifically, when integrated with a rich theology of creation, does the virtue of cruciformity enable Christians to remain "distinctly common" in public life? With Bavinck's assistance, we can answer these questions with a resounding yes. For the central dynamics of his thought, when combined and advanced within the overall framework of his theology, help defend the need for bold Christian particularity in public life. In contrast to liberal ideals that encourage a religion-free public domain, Bavinck's creational and cruciform approach may better shape us for political agency. This approach may help, that is, form our character so that we can more faithfully live alongside others — those with whom we disagree, are dissimilar from, and perhaps even dislike — and enable them to genuinely thrive as persons. This posture not only makes us better Christians but better citizens as well.

Conclusion

By utilizing Bavinck in order to move beyond Bavinck, I have attempted to articulate a unique posture for inhabiting twenty-first-century liberal democratic societies — one that overcomes some of the typical weaknesses of lone creation-based or virtue-based theories. For example, lone creational approaches to Christian political theology (which are predominant among

---

54. Herman Bavinck, "De Navolging van Christus en het Moderne Leven," no. 3 in the series *Schild en Pijl* (Kampen: Kok, 1918), unpublished translation by John Bolt.

55. Bavinck, "De Navolging van Christus en het Moderne Leven," unpublished translation by John Bolt.

56. Bavinck, "De Navolging van Christus en het Moderne Leven."

Bavinck's neo-Calvinist heirs) often rely on overly cognitive, worldview-based methodologies. Not only do these approaches sometimes struggle to remain distinctly Christian, they also operate under the false assumption that if one thinks correctly, one will automatically inhabit political life correctly. Little emphasis is placed on properly formed emotions, desires, motivations, and character. At the same time, solely virtue-based political theologies have problems of their own. As noted above, for thinkers such as Stanley Hauerwas, virtue divides Christians from their fellow citizens by precluding any form of shared ethical language in the public square.[57] On the other hand, for natural law proponents such as John Finnis and Germain Grisez, virtue provides shared ground between Christians and their fellow citizens apart from explicit confession. The downfall of each of these positions is the inability to communicate how Christian particularity can invigorate and sustain the pursuit of the common good.

Bavinck, in contrast, holds together both Christian distinctiveness and the common good. In doing so, he overcomes the weaknesses of merely creation-based and virtue-based political theologies, and he transcends liberal ideals that idolize individual liberty and privatized religion. Hence, Bavinck ultimately offers a unique take — a "distinctively common" take — on the deeply complex issue of relating Christian faith to liberal democratic politics. The strength of this "distinctively common" ethic is that it is good both for the individual soul and the flourishing of society. As Christians we can therefore uphold the Bavinckian approach of pressuring liberal democracies, for by challenging them we can make them stronger.[58] In the end, however, this posture will not produce simple and straightforward solutions to political enigmas this side of the eschaton. More likely, it will make political engagement even more fraught with complexity. For as we integrate creation and virtue as a way of faithfully living as political disciples, we will not receive answers; we will instead receive a calling that requires us to be relationally open to Christ and to our fellow citizens. This calling may look much more like losing, or suffering, than it does winning. Perhaps this is the message that Bavinck leaves us with. Politics is not about winning; it is about finding in our Christian distinctiveness the ability to love creation and others as God loves them — *via crucis*, by Way of the Cross.

---

57. Hauerwas, *Community of Character*, pp. 54, 91, 95, 100.

58. As underscored in note 4, this claim draws on the thought of John Stuart Mill. Mill argued that liberal democracies function best when thoughtful citizens challenge their deficiencies.

Bibliography

Bavinck, Herman. "Common Grace." *Calvin Theological Journal* 1:24 (April 1989): 35-65.

———. "Ethics and Politics." In *Essays on Religion, Science, and Society,* 261-78. Edited by John Bolt. Translated by Harry Boonstra and Gerrit Sheeres. Grand Rapids: Baker Academic, 2008.

———. "The Future of Calvinism." *The Presbyterian and Reformed Review* 5:17 (1894): 1-24.

———. *The Origin, Essence, and Purpose of Man.* http://www.the-highway.com/ origin_Bavinck.html

———. *Our Reasonable Faith.* Grand Rapids: Eerdmans, 1956.

———. *The Philosophy of Revelation.* New York: Longmans, Green, and Co., 1909.

———. *Reformed Dogmatics.* Vol. 1.: *Prolegomena.* Edited by John Bolt. Translated by John Vriend. Grand Rapids: Baker Academic, 2003.

———. *Reformed Dogmatics.* Vol. 2: *God and Creation.* Edited by John Bolt. Translated by John Vriend. Grand Rapids: Baker Academic, 2004.

———. *The Sacrifice of Praise, Meditations Before and After Receiving Access to the Table of the Lord* (1922). Translated by Gilbert Zekveld. http://spindleworks .com/library/bavink/TheSacrificeOfPraise.pdf

———. *Gereformeerde Ethiek van Profess. Dr. H. Bavinck.* Notes by Jelle Michiels de Jong. Bavinck Archives, box 26/32 (HB Diktaten).

———. "De Navolging van Christus en het Moderne Leven." No. 3 in the series *Schild en Pijl.* Kampen: Kok, 1918.

Cooke, Clay. "Liberalism, Democracy, and Sphere Sovereignty." In *Capital Commentary.* A publication for the Center for Public Justice, December 9, 2011. http:// www.capitalcommentary.org/abraham-kuyper/do-justice-and-love-mercy-why-common-good-depends-sphere-sovereignty-and-virtue

Gregory, Eric. *Politics and the Order of Love: An Augustinian Ethic of Democratic Citizenship.* Chicago: University of Chicago Press, 2008.

Hauerwas, Stanley. *A Community of Character.* Notre Dame: University of Notre Dame Press, 1981.

Hobbes, Thomas. *The Leviathan.* Whitefish, Mt.: Kessinger Publishing, 2004.

Koyzis, David. *Political Visions and Illusions: A Survey and Christian Critique of Contemporary Ideologies.* Downers Grove, Ill.: InterVarsity Press, 2003.

Kuyper, Abraham. "Sphere Sovereignty." In *Abraham Kuyper: A Centennial Reader.* Edited by James D. Bratt. Grand Rapids: Eerdmans, 1998.

Marsh, Charles. *Wayward Christian Soldiers: Freeing the Gospel from Political Captivity.* New York: Oxford University Press, 2007.

Mathewes, Charles. *The Republic of Grace: Augustinian Thoughts for Dark Times.* Grand Rapids: Eerdmans, 2010.

Milbank, John. *Being Reconciled: Ontology and Pardon.* New York: Routledge, 2003.

Novak, Michael. *The Spirit of Democratic Capitalism.* New York: Simon and Schuster, 1982.

Rawls, John. *Political Liberalism.* New York: Columbia University Press, 1996.

Rousseau, Jean-Jacques. *The Social Contract.* Translated by Willmoore Kendall. Chicago: Henry Regnery, 1954.

Taylor, Charles. *Modern Social Imaginaries.* Durham, N.C.: Duke University Press Books, 2003.

Van Keulen, Dirk. "Herman Bavinck's *Reformed Ethics:* Some Remarks About Unpublished Manuscripts in the Libraries of Amsterdam and Kampen." *The Bavinck Review* 1 (2010): 25-56. http://bavinck.calvinseminary.edu/wp-content/uploads/2010/04/TBR1.pdf

Wolterstorff, Nicholas. "From Liberal to Plural." In *Christian Philosophy at the Close of the Twentieth Century: Assessment and Perspective.* Edited by Sander Griffioen and Bert M. Balk. Kampen: Uitgeverij Kok, 1995.

Legitimacy, Public Justice, and Deliberative Democracy

Michael DeMoor

The neo-Calvinist tradition has had an ambivalent relation with democracy from its founding. On the one hand, the central claim made by the tradition is that God — and not human beings — is sovereign, even in the realm of politics. This would seem, at least, to undermine the central tenet of democratic governance, namely, that the people are the source of political authority and hence can be considered to be sovereign in politics. On the other hand, the tradition affirmed and practiced democratic politics right from the outset. Unless this is just a vicious contradiction at the heart of the tradition, there must be a way of reconciling democratic politics with the rejection of popular sovereignty, and it is this that I intend to explore in this paper.[1]

Rejecting popular sovereignty and affirming divine sovereignty means that the *principles of justice* that will direct and legitimate public policy cannot be derived from human decision (whether individual or collective) but rather from the creation ordinances of God, revealed in both special and general revelation. In other words, it is God's will for the state, not ours, that should, for neo-Calvinists, serve as the foundation of just governance. The tradition has come to call this conception "public justice" — an account of the enduring, God-given role for the state in human social life and amongst the plethora of other social practices, institutions, and communities, each of which respond to God's ordinances for the full flourishing of human life.[2] It thus includes

---

1. Fred Van Geest gives an excellent account of the sources of this ambivalence in "Democracy and the Neo-Calvinist Tradition," *Christian Scholar's Review* 37, no. 1 (2007): 47-76.
2. On the meaning and place of the idea of public justice, see Jonathan Chaplin, "Defin-

the concept of "sphere sovereignty"; i.e., the principle that human social life is properly differentiated into a variety of "spheres" (e.g., scholarship, family, business, sport, etc.), each bearing its own creational mandate and governed by creational ordinances, none of which are entitled to dominate or replace the others.

In his *Lectures on Calvinism,* Kuyper articulates the conception of public justice in terms of the three fundamental duties of the state:

> 1. Whenever different spheres clash, to compel mutual regard for the boundary-lines of each; 2. To defend individuals and the weak ones in those spheres against the abuse of power of the rest; and 3. To coerce all together to bear *personal* and *financial* burdens for the maintenance of the natural unity of the State.[3]

In other words, the state is entrusted with legally protecting the harmonious interrelationship between different spheres of human activity and with guaranteeing the (public legal) rights, duties, and competencies of individuals within them. It is important to note that there is no reference — at least no direct reference — to democracy in this conception of the fundamental role of the state. It is quite possible on these terms to imagine a law or policy that is *just* (in that it accords with the principle of public justice) but not *democratic.*[4] Given the fact that public justice is the fundamental principle of legitimate governance, if the ideal is going to be linked to democracy, the latter must be derived in some way from the former.[5]

This task is made more formidable by the fact that the idea of public justice as articulated by Kuyper is not merely a *procedural* ideal but one that relies upon a *substantive* vision of the human good and of a flourishing society. The state cannot "compel mutual regard for the boundary-lines" of each sphere

---

ing 'Public Justice' in a Pluralistic Society: Probing a Key Neo-Calvinist Insight," *Pro Rege* 32 (March 2004): 1-11.

3. Abraham Kuyper, *Lectures on Calvinism* (Grand Rapids: Eerdmans, 1961), p. 97.

4. For evidence that various neo-Calvinist thinkers have been willing to prefer (public) justice to democracy, see Van Geest's discussion of Paul Marshall in "Democracy and the Neo-Calvinist Tradition," p. 69; and Jonathan Chaplin on Dooyeweerd's approach to democracy in *Herman Dooyeweerd: Christian Philosopher of State and Civil Society* (Notre Dame: University of Notre Dame Press, 2011), pp. 212-13.

5. Therefore, as we shall see, neo-Calvinists cannot accept Joshua Cohen's suggestion that the principle of (deliberative) democracy is a "fundamental political ideal" in "Deliberation and Democratic Legitimacy," in *The Good Polity: Normative Analysis of the State,* ed. Alan Hamlin and Philip Pettit (Oxford: Basil Blackwell, 1989), p. 17.

without working with a substantive notion of what the enduring identity, task, and competency of each sphere is. This notion in turn depends upon a certain conception of God's creational ordinances and hence of God's will for human social life. Public justice cannot consist simply of a procedural conception of fair social play in the contest between competing "comprehensive"[6] conceptions of the human good; it depends upon such a thing itself. Neo-Calvinists need to show how the (substantive) principle of public justice implies or requires democratic procedures to produce "just" and legitimate policy outcomes.

In this paper, I will focus in particular on a particular model of democracy: "deliberative democracy." I will try to show how its considerations should give neo-Calvinists pause before endorsing existing articulations of deliberative democracy, but also how we might go about articulating a viable ideal of deliberative democracy on the basis of a sophisticated interpretation of the concept of public justice. I focus on this case for two reasons: first, deliberative democracy has been endorsed in two important articles by neo-Calvinist thinkers as the most viable model of democracy for neo-Calvinists; second, in my estimation it is superior to other such models, particularly utilitarian or aggregationist (social choice) models of democracy.[7] Since I do not have the time to argue that latter claim here, I will turn first to discussing Wolterstorff's treatment of deliberative democracy and neo-Calvinism.

I. Wolterstorff

Nicholas Wolterstorff's attraction to deliberative democracy emerges from his consideration of the limitations and failures of "political liberalism" (of which the later Rawls is the best representative) in creating conditions of equitable treatment of diverse religious claims in a pluralistic society. To make a long story short, Wolterstorff identifies a number of theses central to the political liberal view, the crucial one being what he calls the "independent basis" thesis:

> Citizens must be prepared to conduct their public debates concerning the scheme of constitutional and legal rights, and to make their decisions con-

---

6. John Rawls coined the term "comprehensive doctrines" to describe moral views that are embedded in thick religious or philosophical views of God, nature, humanity, and so on. Cf. John Rawls, *Political Liberalism* (New York: Columbia University Press, 1993), pp. xviiiff.

7. For some important arguments against aggregative conceptions of democracy see Amy Gutmann and Dennis Thompson, *Why Deliberative Democracy?* (Princeton: Princeton University Press, 2004), pp. 13-21.

cerning that scheme, on the basis of the deliverances of some source of relevant principles which is not only independent of all the comprehensive religious and philosophical perspectives to be found in society, but is one to which all normal adult citizens (or prospective citizens in the case of constitutional debates) can be rightly required to appeal for this purpose.[8]

This thesis crucially treats any religious or other comprehensive doctrine as "a dispensable add-on" to the universally acceptable political conception of justice.[9]

For Wolterstorff, there are three fundamental problems with this view. First, the closest political liberals get to offering an argument for the independent basis principle is that following it is a requirement of *respect* for one's interlocutors, particularly since the stakes are the legitimacy of coercive legislation. But Wolterstorff asserts that "I know of no liberal who has fleshed out this 'respect' argument in anything like a satisfactory way."[10] Secondly, this principle contradicts (or at least sits uncomfortably with) "the most basic theses of contemporary liberalism" which "tell us that the fundamental business of government is to establish and implement a scheme of constitutional and legal rights which guarantees the pre-legal right of all normal adult citizens to liberty of conscience and of non-harming action."[11] These theses not only do not directly imply limits on the kinds of reasons that citizens may appeal to in justifying this business of government, but the principles of respect for liberty of conscience, the priority of autonomy amongst political values, and the harm-criterion as the primary basis of legal restriction on freedom seem rather to imply that it is illiberal to set such limits on the political discourse amongst a democratic citizenry. Third, the independent-basis principle misconceives the nature of religion in treating it as a "dispensable add-on" to a universally acceptable political conception of justice. Moreover, it violates the conscience of those, like Kuyper, for whom — even if religious belief *could* function merely as an add-on — "that's not how it *ought to function* for those who embrace the Christian religion." Religion is in fact — or at least it ought to be — "not a separable part of life, but a holistic orientation to life."[12] In sum,

8. Nicholas Wolterstorff, "Abraham Kuyper's Model of a Democratic Polity with a Religiously Diverse Citizenry," in *Kuyper Reconsidered: Aspects of His Life and Work*, ed. C. Van der Kooi and J. de Bruijn (Amsterdam: Free University Press, 1999), p. 191.

9. Wolterstorff, "Kuyper's Model of a Democratic Polity," p. 194.

10. Wolterstorff, "Kuyper's Model of a Democratic Polity," p. 195.

11. Wolterstorff, "Kuyper's Model of a Democratic Polity," pp. 194-5.

12. Wolterstorff, "Kuyper's Model of a Democratic Polity," p. 197.

the principle at stake asserts that the basic commitments of liberalism require a *separation* between religious commitment and political governance (including the justification of coercive legislation) whereas what is in fact required is merely the *impartiality* of government with respect to the variety of particular religious and other comprehensive doctrines within the polity.

Wolterstorff then advocates for a deliberative — rather than a political liberal — model of democracy as being more consistent with both the basic principles of liberal governance and the Kuyperian insight about the holistic nature of religious commitment. He characterizes deliberative democracy as understanding "self-governance" (the heart of democracy in general) in line with five principles:

> First, the heart of self-governance is deliberative assemblies of a variety of different sorts and at a variety of different levels and venues, open to the people and to their fairly-chosen representatives. Secondly, the basic topic of discussion in these assemblies is what justice and the common good require. . . . Third, in these assemblies people are free to offer whatever reasons they wish for and against the policies under consideration. . . . Fourth, people enter these assemblies not to cast their pre-determined vote but to participate in the deliberations. . . . And lastly, the decision of the group is whatever may be the outcome of a fair vote.[13]

So characterized, deliberative democracy does not violate the freedom of citizens to engage in public political action in accordance with their holistic, comprehensive religious commitments, since no kinds of reasons are barred from inclusion in the deliberative process. Nevertheless it does not treat any comprehensive doctrine as being foundational or particularly determinative within the process; thus it practices impartiality without separation.[14]

I think that Wolterstorff is right about this but that, left at this, the dialogue between neo-Calvinist political philosophy and deliberative democracy remains superficial. A deeper confrontation is needed, since deliberative democracy is not a monolithic theory and differences within that tradition make a difference for how and to what extent neo-Calvinists should endorse it. The fundamental reason for this "superficiality" is that Wolterstorff treats deliberative democracy as a *model* of democracy and not as a *theory* or *conception*

---

13. Wolterstorff, "Kuyper's Model of a Democratic Polity," p. 200.

14. Van Geest makes a similar case in "Democracy and the Neo-Calvinist Tradition," pp. 65-74.

of democratic *legitimacy* (i.e., as a theory of justice).[15] I want to argue now that it is inescapably the latter and that different accounts of how deliberation yields democratic legitimacy lead to substantially different accounts of what the conditions and consequences of deliberation should be (i.e., to different models of deliberation, the public sphere, and civil society). Given that both of the major streams in deliberative democratic theory have problematic assumptions and consequences from a neo-Calvinist perspective, I will argue that what is needed is a distinctively neo-Calvinist theory and model of deliberative democracy, and that for this it is necessary to show how the norm of public justice can yield an account of how democratic deliberation is a legitimating condition of governance. I will conclude by sketching a version of such an account.

II. Deliberation and Legitimacy

Deliberation in politics is demanding, difficult, and time-consuming work. Deliberative democrats ask a lot of citizens and policy-makers. It is not sufficient, they argue, that citizens have preferences and express them by voting, but rather they must subject these preferences to the give and take of public reasoning. Furthermore, it makes moral demands, since the ideal of deliberative democracy requires that citizens' preferences should be premised on a considered conception of the *common good* rather than a calculation of *their own interests,* a distinction that takes moral as well as intellectual effort to be clear about and to act upon. Policy makers are subject to the same sets of intellectual and moral demands as citizens. They cannot justify policy simply by counting heads; they must offer arguments in support of it and defend it in robust debate in open forums. They cannot simply broker deals with various interest groups in order to build a majority, but must always direct their policy efforts toward the common good, and be responsive primarily to public opinion rather than the interests of various constituencies.[16]

The reason that deliberative democrats make these demands is that they think that mere aggregation of preferences or brokering of interests is not suf-

15. The same might be said of Van Geest's article, in which he compares three different models of democracy (consociational, communitarian, and deliberative) with an eye to how well they fit the fundamental features of neo-Calvinist political theory.

16. John Dryzek helpfully analyzes the components necessary for a genuinely deliberative system in *Foundations and Frontiers of Deliberative Governance* (Oxford: Oxford University Press, 2011), pp. 11-12.

ficient to *legitimate* outcomes in a democratic political process. Rather "delib-erative democrats generally believe that legitimacy is achieved by deliberative participation on the part of those subject to a collective decision" and that "this participation should have substantial influence on the content of the deci-sion."[17] Democracy, on this view, is a process of collective will-formation. The process works when individuals participate together in forming a common will and forging cooperative action such that our institutions can be directed by the *cooperative* self-rule of a *people,* our leaders can be responsive to a genuinely *public* opinion, and social actions can make genuinely *common cause.* The formation of a will, though, must be directed and informed by *reasons,* not by arbitrary aggregations of preferences based on numerical preponderance of one set of preferences. In other words, aggregation may be a process of collec-tive decision-making (it may yield a determinate "yes" or "no" to this or that course of action) but it is not a process of collective *will-formation.* If the latter is essential to the ideal of democracy (as a form of collective self-rule), then, say deliberative democrats, public deliberation is a basic criterion of legitimacy in democracies; it alone gives people *moral reasons* to accept a coercive policy.

This much almost all deliberative democrats share. However, articulating these commitments requires going into greater philosophical depths, and it is here that one can see two fundamentally different sources of the ideal of deliberative legitimacy, which in turn lead to different accounts of how the process of deliberation and its social and institutional structure ought to be laid out.[18] Though these two different conceptions of deliberation and legit-imacy overlap and intertwine in various ways, it is important to distinguish them for the purposes of making a neo-Calvinist assessment of deliberative democracy both in theory and practice.

III. Kantian Universalism

Probably the preponderant philosophical and moral source of deliberative conceptions of legitimacy is what I will call "Kantian Universalism." The fun-damental goal of this conception is to derive a set of universally valid political norms without essential reference to either divine commands or an objective natural law. Rather, it seeks the source of political rights and obligations within

17. Dryzek, *Foundations and Frontiers,* pp. 21-22.
18. I do not intend for this typology of deliberative democratic theories to be exhaustive but largely representative.

the formal requirements of the practical reason of autonomous rational agents. The key feature of this account is the way in which it imbricates reason and autonomy: political right derives from the conditions for autonomous judgment rather than from a transcendent norm imposed by either God or nature. For a judgment to be autonomous it must issue from the pure practical *reason* of an agent; judgments premised on fear, force, or a calculation of self-interest (with respect to the consequences of actions) do not measure up since they are based on considerations outside of oneself. Reciprocally, if an agent is not free (i.e., autonomous) to base her political judgment on considerations other than these, then she cannot be said to have acted rationally. In other words, autonomous judgment must be based on reason, and rational judgment must be exercised autonomously. Since the conditions for autonomous rational judgment are the same for all rational agents, there are certain norms that bind all such judgments, which in the realm of morals take the form of duties (the categorical imperative being the most obvious one) and rights, which apply unconditionally and hence universally to all rational agents.

The "Kantian" case for deliberative democracy emerges from this combination of reason and autonomy in the grounding of moral and political right. Any political norm that binds an agent without his rational assent prohibits autonomy and hence violates fundamental rights *qua* rational agent. This means that such norms must — as a condition of their legitimacy — be justified in such a way that those subject to them are given *reason* to assent to them on the basis of their *moral* merits rather than on the basis of threats or enticements. Coercive political policies must appeal to the reason and respect the autonomy of those whom they affect: "claims for and against collective decisions need to be justified to those subject to these decisions in terms that, given the chance to reflect, these individuals can accept."[19]

Kant himself gives a version of such a principle in the second appendix to *Perpetual Peace*,[20] but in the contemporary conversation, the primary expositor

19. Dryzek, *Foundations and Frontiers*, p. 23. Cf. Cohen, "Deliberation and Democratic Legitimacy": "outcomes are democratically legitimate if and only if they could be the object of a free and reasoned agreement among equals," p. 22; and Gutmann and Thompson, *Why Deliberative Democracy?*: "reasons given in this process should be *accessible* to all the citizens to whom they are addressed. To justify their imposing their will on you, your fellow citizens must give reasons that are comprehensible to you," p. 4.

20. Just as in morality the fundamental principle of practical reason (the categorical imperative) is a *formal* condition for autonomous action, the fundamental principle of public right is "the formal attribute of publicness." From this Kant derives his "transcendental formula of public right: 'All maxims affecting the rights of other human beings are wrong if their

of this view is Jürgen Habermas. For Habermas, what bars Kant's fundamental principle of public right from being a fully deliberative conception of legitimacy is the fact that the unity of reason and autonomy that grounds all "Kantian" conceptions happens, for Kant, only in the individual agent *qua* transcendental logical ego. The crucial development that Habermas makes is the claim that the rational self-determination that founds legitimacy must be a *social* or *communicative* process. Kant's conception "miss[es] the legitimating force of a discursive process of opinion- and will-formation in which the illocutionary binding forces of a use of language oriented to mutual understanding serve to bring reason and will together — and lead to convincing positions to which all individuals can agree without coercion."[21] As long as Kant is right that the fundamental principle of public right is a formal feature of individual rational action and reflection, then no ongoing communicative activity of deliberation is necessary to satisfy the requirements that respect for rational autonomy imposes. If, however, practical reason is necessarily *socially* articulated, then the source of political legitimacy must be a formal feature of that social activity. Legitimacy is derived from the intrinsic requirements of *communicative* rationality, in other words from a "principle that merely expresses the meaning of postconventional requirements of justification" (107) of action norms, whether moral or political. Habermas calls this principle the "discourse principle" and formulates it thus: "Just those action norms are valid to which all possibly affected persons could agree as participants in rational discourses" (107).

For Habermas, all communicative action — as distinct from strategic action predicated on instrumental (i.e., amoral) rationality — depends upon participants aiming at reaching mutual understanding through the raising of contestable (i.e., rational) validity claims. Thus the practical use of reason is directed toward consensus, and consensus must be predicated on the force of the better reason rather than on non-rational enticements and threats. This is the "social" equivalent to the fundamental Kantian correlation between autonomy and practical rationality. Thus it is a formal feature of all communicative (moral) action that it proposes action norms in such a way that action in accordance with them is motivated by a shared understanding of the norms and rational assent by all affected parties to what they require. This formal feature requires, then, a social practice of ongoing deliberation in which reasons are

---

maxim is not compatible with their being made public.' " Immanuel Kant, "Perpetual Peace: A Philosophical Sketch," in *Kant: Political Writings*, 2nd ed., ed. Hans Reiss, trans. H. B. Nisbet (Cambridge: Cambridge University Press, 1991), p. 126.

21. Jürgen Habermas, *Between Facts and Norms: Contributions to a Discourse Theory of Law and Democracy*, trans. William Rehg (Cambridge: MIT Press, 1996), p. 103.

given for proposed action norms and aimed at the generation of rationally-motivated consensus (or mutual understanding). I will discuss below what this conception requires with respect to the terms of this deliberation and its location in "public space."

IV. Civic Republicanism

The "Kantian Universalist" approach I have been describing requires inclusive deliberation as a condition of legitimacy because of the requirements of political *right* rather than as an expression of a view of the substantive human *good;* it sees deliberation as a procedural requirement that allows people who accept different (even incompatible) views of the good life to arrive at collective decisions in a fair process that does not subject anyone arbitrarily to the will of others. In other words, it preserves Rawls's famous prioritizing of the *right* over the *good.*²² The civic republican view, on the other hand, is grounded in a substantive view of the human good, and hence endorses deliberative democracy because it is a component of a higher, better, and more dignified form of life than one in which one is subjected to laws that one had no part in forming and which one has not reflectively endorsed.

Naturally, not all proponents of this approach would articulate things in the same way, but generally they espouse something like an Aristotelian understanding of the good life. On this view, human beings are by nature political animals and at the same time rational animals. "By nature" does not indicate merely a set of ingrained habits or preferences, but a *telos;* human beings live a fully human life — a life befitting a rational animal rather than any other lower creature — when the rational capacities that they have are employed in the creation and maintenance of a harmonious political community. Human beings who either cannot or will not live this way live a diminished existence, one lacking in the special dignity that active citizenship conveys and expresses.

On this view, any form of political life that discourages or disempowers citizens from actively employing their reason for the common good of the *polis* is one that prevents the full flourishing of human nature. Thus one may say that it is *unjust* in the sense that prevents the full expression of virtue by citizens with respect to others and that it fails to give political authority to those to whom it is due in virtue of their merit as rational beings exercising civic

---

22. Cf. John Rawls, *A Theory of Justice* (Cambridge: Harvard University Press, 1971), pp. 31ff.

virtue.[23] In fact, according to Cicero, it is justice in this sense that constitutes the state as a *res publica:*

> Well then, a republic is the property of the public. But a public is not every kind of human gathering, congregating in any manner, but a numerous gathering brought together by legal consent and community of interest. The primary reason of this coming together is not so much weakness as a sort of innate desire on the part of human beings to form communities. For our species is not made up of solitary individuals or lonely wanderers. . . . [Fragment of text lost]. . . . [Without] certain seeds, as it were, [of that kind] no means could be discovered of establishing other virtues or even the community itself.[24]

A republic (a people's common concern) only exists when people bond together and seek a common good — meaning a kind of virtuous living — not possible outside of that community, and it remains a republic only as long as it remains a community in which these common goods can be cooperatively pursued. This requires active citizenship, motivated by a civic virtue that places the common good above individual interest. There can be other forms of rule than a republic, but they are merely forms of subjugation, ruled as they are not in accordance with the common concerns, but the individual interest and caprices of a tyrant. In such a regime there is no justice and hence no *res publica.*

This being the case, a republic must be held together by a bond beyond merely overlapping self-interest or the power of a ruler. A just regime is premised on a kind of *moral solidarity* between free and equal citizens in which each recognizes the others as partners in a virtuous endeavor that cannot be pursued alone; Aristotle calls this a kind of friendship.[25] This means that citizens bear certain fundamental responsibilities toward one another, at minimum to treat one another as they are: free and equal and capable of conducting their public affairs in accordance with reason. Without this bond of civic friendship and the willingness of citizens to abide by what it requires of them in their shared political life, there is no justice, no public concern, only the tyrannical domination of the private wills of some over those of others.

Charles Taylor offers a more contemporary articulation of this ideal, start-

---

23. I put these two sources of injustice in these terms to connect them to the two senses of justice as a virtue that Aristotle distinguishes in *Nicomachean Ethics,* Book V, chapters 1 and 2.

24. Marcus Tullius Cicero, *The Republic* and *The Laws,* trans. Niall Rudd (Oxford: Oxford University Press, 1998), p. 19.

25. Cf. Aristotle, *Nicomachean Ethics,* Book VIII, chapters 9-12.

ing with a different definition of "freedom" than is offered in classical liberal theory:

> "Free" is to be understood here not in the modern sense of negative liberty, but more as the antonym to "despotic." . . . In a despotism, a regime where the mass of citizens are subject to the rule of a single master or a clique, the requisite disciplines are maintained by coercion. In order to have a free society, one has to replace this coercion with something else. This can only be a willing identification with the polis on the part of the citizen, a sense that the political institutions in which they live are an expression of themselves. The "laws" have to be seen as reflecting and entrenching their dignity as citizens, and hence to be in a sense extensions of themselves. This understanding . . . transcends egoism in the sense that people are really attached to the common good, to general liberty.[26]

The key here is that "freedom" in the republican sense is put forward not so much as a pre-political right, but rather as attaching to the moral status ("dignity") of citizens participating in a common good. Correspondingly the moral solidarity (the "friendship" if you will) that binds citizens together is not merely "respect" for the abstract (because strictly universal) rights of others *qua* autonomous human agents. If it includes this, it transcends it by attaching that moral solidarity to the joint participation of citizens in a concrete, particular endeavor in pursuit of the best and most excellent form of life. In this sense, civic friendship and its attendant duties is joined to a kind of "patriotism" where loyalty to concrete others is wrapped up with common dedication to "a common political entity."[27]

This civic-republican ideal, then, funds a way of grounding the necessity of deliberation for democratic legitimacy. The authentic expression of our freedom — and our full flourishing as rational, political animals — requires us to pursue a common life with others and hence forge of a bond of moral solidarity (civic friendship) with them. The means by which this bond is forged and maintained must likewise be in keeping with our nature as rational animals and our dignity as free and equal citizens. This means that I cannot arbitrarily coerce my fellow citizens, but must pursue common ends through persuasion befitting their and my status as rational beings, i.e., through the giving and asking of reasons, deliberation. No other means of conducting

26. Charles Taylor, "Cross Purposes: The Liberal-Communitarian Debate," in *Philosophical Arguments* (Cambridge: Harvard University Press, 1995), p. 187.

27. Taylor, "Cross Purposes," p. 188.

political affairs accords with our dignity as citizens or contributes to the living of a flourishing (good) life. Correspondingly, as Philip Pettit argues, republican freedom requires that those in power offer contestable *reasons* to those subject to them; otherwise

> They will not be able to take a stand in relation to public decisions, if those decisions are the outcome of interest-group bargaining or of voting on the basis of naked, unargued preference. Such non-deliberatively generated decisions would have the profile of dictates or fiats from on high, where the products of deliberative-democratic procedure would present themselves as reasoned — well reasoned or badly reasoned — judgments that people are in a position to examine, assess and, if necessary, challenge.[28]

In both the Kantian Universalist and the Civic Republican traditions, the moral necessity of deliberative democracy is connected to the necessity of arriving at communal decisions in a just way. The fundamental difference is that, whereas the Kantian view stipulates that deliberative procedures are necessary to arrive at such decisions in a way that respects the individual rights of those affected, the republican view insists that need for deliberative procedures derives from the fact that making such decisions is an indispensable part of the good life, which means that they must be made in such a way that they achieve and maintain a thick moral solidarity between citizens without which the good life could not be fully enjoyed. To put it more simply, the Kantian position depends upon the universal moral norm of respect, whereas the republic position depends upon the ethical[29] attachment to civic friendship within a particular political community.

V. Deliberation, the Public Sphere, and Civil Society

With these contrasting approaches to the question of deliberative legitimacy in hand, I want to turn to the practical, structural, and institutional repercussions of these views. Specifically, I want to argue that, given their differences with respect to why and how deliberation is constitutive for democratic legitimacy, Kantian Universalism and Civic Republicanism offer different prescriptions for how this kind of deliberating is to be realized. Crucial to these descriptions

---

28. Philip Pettit, "Deliberative Democracy, the Discursive Dilemma, and Republican Theory," *Philosophy, Politics, and Society* 7 (2003): 153.

29. I use "moral" and "ethical" here in Habermas's sense (see below).

is the account they offer of the "public sphere" and its relationship to civil society, both of which, I shall go on to argue, stand in tension with the neo-Calvinist account of these implicit in the ideal of public justice.

The Kantian Universalist approach is a *proceduralist* account of deliberation. Deliberation is a procedure that allows (or rather requires) local, particular, and comprehensive views of the common good to be transformed into universally valid reasons that can justify coercive policies in terms that all subject to them are in a position to accept or endorse. Although this procedure will work differently in different situations insofar as its contents will vary depending on the different views of the good and the concrete needs and expectations of a particular citizenry, it is possible to describe the essential *form* of this procedure in a universal, albeit, abstract way. It is a condition of its legitimacy that any concrete political deliberation accords with this form. Joshua Cohen offers an influential account of the primary characteristics of this "ideal deliberative procedure":

> I.1. Ideal deliberation is *free* in that it satisfies two conditions. First, the participants regard themselves as bound only by the results of their deliberation and by the preconditions for that deliberation. . . . Second, the participants suppose that they can act from the results, taking the fact that a certain decision is arrived at through their deliberation as a sufficient reason for complying with it.

> I.2. Deliberation is *reasoned* in that the parties are required to state their reasons for advancing proposals. . . . Reasons are offered with the aim of bringing others to accept the proposal, given their disparate ends and their commitment to settling the conditions of their association through free deliberation among equals. Proposals may be rejected because they are not defended with acceptable reasons, even if they could be so defended.

> I.3. In ideal deliberation parties are both formally and substantively *equal*. They are formally equal in that the rules regulating the procedures do not single out individuals. . . . The participants are substantively equal in that the existing distribution of power and resources does not shape their chances to contribute to deliberation. . . .

> I.4. Finally, ideal deliberation aims to arrive at rationally motivated *consensus*. . . .[30]

30. Cohen, "Deliberation and Democratic Legitimacy," pp. 22-23.

Thus this procedure stipulates both what is required in the process of deliberation but also (I.3) what is required as a precondition of deliberation. In both cases, the ideal deliberative procedure is "a model for institutions to mirror."[31] If our practical collective decision-making is going to abide by the requirements of this procedure — i.e., if those decisions are to be legitimate — then it requires substantive institutional reforms: "And so, in seeking to embody the ideal deliberative procedure in institutions, we seek, *inter alia*, to design institutions that focus political debate on the common good, that shape the identity and interests of citizens in ways that contribute to an attachment to the common good, and that provide favourable conditions for the exercise of deliberative powers that are required for autonomy."[32] It is crucial to note, here, that Cohen does not stipulate these as requirements only for *political* institutions and office-bearers, but rather generalizes it to include any and all institutions within which potentially coercive rules are made or justified and hence within which deliberative legitimacy is required. Put differently, this view does not constrain these requirements and ideals to parliaments and courtrooms but to any place where public deliberation aims to promote and justify such policies — i.e., to the public sphere as a whole.

Furthermore, there is an implicit restriction on the kinds of reasons that the ideal deliberative procedure allows in all of these forums. The first requirement (I.1) — that ideal deliberation is *free* — requires of participants that "their consideration of proposals is not constrained by the authority of prior norms or requirements."[33] Cohen intends here that the outcome of a *free* deliberation cannot be constrained by any considerations, preferences, or reasons that are not thematized within the process of deliberation. In other words, the outcome must depend only upon the quality of the reasons given to one another by the various parties.

We can further understand what the ruled-out "prior norms or requirements" include, then, by examining what kinds of reasons the procedure allows and disallows. In I.2 these parameters are delimited in terms of the aims of deliberation: "Reasons are offered with the aim of bringing others to accept the proposal, given their disparate ends [their "diverse preferences, convictions, and ideals concerning the conduct of their own lives"]. . . . Proposals may be rejected because they are not defended with acceptable reasons, even if they

---

31. Cohen, "Deliberation and Democratic Legitimacy," p. 22.
32. Cohen, "Deliberation and Democratic Legitimacy," p. 26.
33. Cohen, "Deliberation and Democratic Legitimacy," p. 22.

could be so defended."[34] Such allowable reasons, then, cannot depend for their persuasive force on having one's interlocutor change their mind about their preferences, convictions, and ideals in favor of one's own, and hence must appeal only to considerations that are shared or neutral. This would, it seems to me, rule out reasons essentially rooted in religious, philosophical, or other "comprehensive" commitments.

The fact that Cohen does not limit these considerations to decision-making political bodies implies that all of these institutions ought to be reformed in such a way that they can be modeled on the ideal deliberative procedure and hence that they "shape the identity and interests of citizens" in such a way that they are inclined to offer only reasons that are neutral between the divergent comprehensive ends of other citizens. This would, in effect, rule out religious voices and institutions (what you might call "religious civil society") from the public square unless they reform their practices such that they accord with these required ways of shaping citizens.

Jürgen Habermas, for his part, offers a similar principle of exclusion, though he insists that his requirements allow for greater freedom and diversity within the public sphere than Cohen's. I want to argue that, notwithstanding this advance on Cohen's view, Habermas also recommends a conception of public deliberation that is unduly restrictive of the public role of religious civil society. As mentioned above, a legitimate piece of legislation is valid only in the case that it would be agreed to by every participant in an ideal communication situation (i.e., one in which every affected person is included and given equal consideration — Habermas's parallel idealization of the form of legitimizing deliberation to Cohen's ideal deliberative procedure). Since public reasoning means raising claims to inter-subjective validity, arguing for the adoption of an action norm (say, a law) means appealing to this standard: that the position I am advocating can be agreed to by everyone in an ideal communication situation. This means that only appeals to what is *right* (i.e., normatively valid of a shared social world — what Habermas calls a "moral" claim) are admissible. Any appeal to one's idea of the *good* (the kind of life that is best to lead — what Habermas calls an "ethical" position) is illegitimate, since such an appeal is tied to an ethical worldview that cannot be expected to be shared by all, since it strives not for moral *validity* but for expressive *authenticity* (i.e., has reference to a subjective world).[35]

34. Cohen, "Deliberation and Democratic Legitimacy," p. 22.

35. Cf. Jürgen Habermas, "Reconciliation through the Public Use of Reason: Remarks on John Rawls' Political Liberalism," *Journal of Philosophy* 92, no. 3 (1995): 124-26.

Though he offers a version of Cohen's argument for restricting comprehensive or "ethical" reasons from legitimating deliberation, Habermas nevertheless chides Cohen for having "still not completely shaken off the idea of a society that is deliberatively steered *as a whole* and is thus politically constituted."[36] In other words, Cohen's view imposes norms for political or legal discourse onto all discursive interactions in the public sphere thereby suggesting that all institutions that partake in the public sphere ought to be remade in the image of the (ideal, deliberative) state. For his part, Habermas "would like to understand the procedure from which procedurally correct decisions draw their legitimacy . . . as the core structure in a separate, constitutionally organized political system, but not as a model for all social institutions."[37] This means that a distinction must be drawn between two different locations of public deliberation playing two different functions with respect to the legitimation of coercive law:

> The publics of parliamentary bodies [which are strictly regulated by the ideal deliberative procedure] are structured predominantly as a *context of justification*. These bodies rely not only upon the administration's preparatory work and further processing, but also on the *context of discovery* provided by a procedurally unregulated public sphere that is borne by the general public of citizens.[38]

What is discovered by citizens in the public sphere — in the unregulated give and take of reasons of all sorts, whether moral or ethical — are the principles of conduct that can be made into legitimate law by governments, but only if they can justify them in strictly moral terms (i.e., in terms that all those affected by them can accept given their differences with respect to ethical ideals).

Habermas's view gives much more space for "religious civil society" to play an active public role and thus, viewed from the standpoint of the neo-Calvinist principle of public justice (including the idea of sphere sovereignty) it constitutes real progress over Cohen's account. However, it is still unduly restrictive given basic neo-Calvinist commitments about the nature of religious commitment and its relationship to political action. This is because Habermas continues to insist on the possibility that deliberative procedures can be *neutral* between ethical worldviews and that, moreover, at least law-

---

36. Habermas, *Between Facts and Norms*, p. 305.
37. Habermas, *Between Facts and Norms*, p. 305.
38. Habermas, *Between Facts and Norms*, p. 307.

makers are obliged to adhere strictly to those procedures and hence to justify laws in these neutral terms.

He responds to the "radical" "communitarian" objection that "standards for an impartial judgment of practical questions in general cannot be separated from the context of specific worldviews and life projects: on this view, no presumptively neutral principle can ever be neutral in fact. Every apparently neutral procedure reflects a specific . . . conception of the good life."[39] If this were so, he argues, genuine argumentation would be impossible, since the neutrality of procedures of argumentation (i.e., their being shared between disputants regardless of their disagreements) is a "universal rule of argumentation" and hence is "unavoidable."[40] Even if people cannot *articulate* these basic rules of argumentation in ways that are ethically neutral, it nevertheless remains the case, he argues, that

> In all languages and in every language community, such concepts as truth, rationality, justification, and consensus, even if interpreted differently and applied according to different criteria, play *the same grammatical role*. At any rate, this is true for modern societies that, with positive law, secularized politics, and a principled morality, have made the shift to a postconventional level of justification and expect their members to take a reflexive attitude toward their own respective cultural traditions.[41]

In other words, a "neutral dialogue" in which an ethical disagreement can "transition to a higher level of abstraction characteristic of justice [i.e., moral] discourses" is possible in societies — or social communities and institutions — that meet the requirements of a postconventional society (including positive law, secularized politics, etc.). Given this possibility, it is not unreasonable to expect that the language of justification used by lawmakers be "neutral" with respect to ethical worldviews.

The implications of this, however, are (1) that the language used to justify coercive legislation by lawmakers cannot be that of non-postconventional societies, and (2) that no one who only has a non-postconventional vocabulary at their disposal can participate in the making of legitimate law, at least not as a public official. In other words, lawmakers at least — and anyone else who wants to participate in public debate according to the terms of the ideal procedure — must be comfortable with a secularized politics, a principled

---

39. Habermas, *Between Facts and Norms*, p. 310.
40. Habermas, *Between Facts and Norms*, p. 310.
41. Habermas, *Between Facts and Norms*, pp. 311-12.

morality (as opposed to one predicated on traditional or divinely ordained norms), and so on. Social communities that do not meet this requirement are barred from anything but relatively marginal participation in the public sphere — they are accepted into the context of discovery, but barred from the context of justification.[42]

Though neo-Calvinism certainly accepts the rule of positive law (within divinely imposed limits) and even a degree of "secularized politics," it is characteristic of the tradition that it endorses something like the "radical" "communitarian" thesis that Habermas argues against. As Wolterstorff puts it: "Devotion to God in Christ is to *transform* one's life, not merely serve as an add-on to a shared human nature or a shared liberal democratic way of life. . . . Religion is not a separable part of life but a holistic orientation of life."[43] This means that both public discourse and public conduct are "unavoidably perspectival."[44] There are certainly common moral states of affairs — for example, a kind of natural law — but "epistemologically, [Kuyper] expects abiding disagreement about the content of natural law."[45] This abiding disagreement requires that discussion not only in the public sphere but also in parliament and the courts be open to disclosing the basic roots of these disagreements, including different fundamental religious commitments, and hence also to the representatives even of non-postconventional communities and institutions within civil society.

In the Civic Republican tradition, the appeal of deliberative democracy is grounded in the shared moral commitment of citizens to a common good realized in political life. Out of this common commitment comes a kind of moral solidarity between citizens which imposes the requirement that we treat our fellow citizens as political friends, and hence as free and equal rational creations. As mentioned, this ideal depends upon a kind of patriotism: we are not morally bound to everyone in the world by some requirement of cosmopolitan right — at least not in the sense relevant to republican conceptions of deliberative democracy — but rather to a particular group of citizens in a particular place, hence to a particular country. Therefore, whereas for Kantian

---

42. Of course, it is probably a good thing for religious communities to exemplify at least some of the characteristics of postconventional societies — at least the capacities of its members to take a reflexive stand. The problem with Habermas's view is that, rather than this being *recommended* as a *good* development, it is an unconditional *requirement* of public right (at least if members of these religions want any significant public clout).

43. Wolterstorff, "Kuyper's Model of a Democratic Polity," p. 197.

44. Wolterstorff, "Kuyper's Model of a Democratic Polity," p. 197.

45. Wolterstorff, "Kuyper's Model of a Democratic Polity," p. 198.

Universalists the concrete model for legitimating deliberation (the ideal deliberative procedure) emerges from the formal requirements of any free and reasoned discourse, for Civic Republicans this model will emerge from the particular character, values, mores, and commitments of a particular people uniting for the common good.

This fact implies that the nature of the deliberation and the concrete forms that it will take cannot be specified formally and hence universally as Cohen and Habermas do. This means that there can be no a priori grounds for rejecting particular kinds of voices or reasons from the public sphere and hence no similar version of the tendency to either marginalize non-deliberative (non-postconventional) bodies in civil society or to reshape them in the mold of the ideal deliberative procedure and thus of a deliberative state. However, the Civic-Republican approach to discursive democracy has its own ways in which it can come into conflict with a "public justice" approach to civil society and the public sphere.

The key to these conflicts emerges from the tradition's insistence on viewing the state as a moral community, held together by thick bonds of moral solidarity and requiring patriotic allegiance and even sacrifice (sacrifice at least of one's private interests for the sake of the common good). These values themselves do not necessarily conflict with a neo-Calvinist view of the state and the status of citizens within it,[46] but they do lend themselves thereto. Primarily, the legitimate interest of the state in ensuring the moral solidarity of citizens can imply distrust, even hostility, toward other less inclusive moral communities. Strong moral commitment to a community other than the state can be seen as fragmenting the political community and introducing new kinds of private interest (the private interest of "sectarian" groups) that militate against their members' willingness to exercise civic virtue and hence to subordinate their private or sectional interests to the common good. In terms of the requirements on the form and content of public deliberation, such a view may take the form of a demand that, in public deliberations, participants must only present themselves *qua* citizens, and hence to couch their arguments only in terms of the shared national values, character, history, etc.

The most obvious historical example of such a view is that of Rousseau. Reflecting on the obstacles to people's recognition of and submission to the general will, he identifies in particular the role of "sectional associations":

46. Or so I have argued in "Kuyper, Sphere Sovereignty, and the Possibility of Political Friendship," in *The Kuyper Center Review, Volume 1: Politics, Religion, and Sphere Sovereignty,* ed. Gordon Graham (Grand Rapids: Eerdmans, 2010), pp. 61-82.

> But if groups, sectional associations are formed at the expense of the larger association, the will of each of these groups will become general in relation to its own members and private in relation to the state; we might then say that there are no longer as many votes as there are men but only as many votes as there are groups. . . . Finally, when one of these groups becomes so large that it can outweigh the rest, the result is no longer the sum of many small differences [which can produce a general will], but one great divisive difference; then there ceases to be a general will, and the opinion which prevails is no more than a private opinion. Thus if the general will is to be clearly expressed, it is imperative that there should be no sectional associations in the state and that every citizen should make up his own mind for himself. . . . But if there are sectional associations, it is wise to multiply their number and to prevent inequality among them. . . . These are the only precautions which can ensure that the general will is always enlightened and the people protected from error.[47]

This is more than a moral requirement that people appear in the public sphere as citizens first and foremost. It is a call for state intervention in associational life in order to either, at worst, eradicate associations that may make moral demands that conflict with those of the state or to, at best, reduce the social power and authority of such associations to the level of all other groups. Such interventions are, needless to say, direct contraventions of the principle of sphere sovereignty.

Of course, not all Civic Republican views are as radical as Rousseau's. Alexis de Tocqueville, for example, famously champions associational life on the grounds that it equips citizens with the skills and virtues necessary to practice genuinely democratic, cooperative self-rule.[48] However, even this endorsement of civil society as a boon for (proto-deliberative) democracy does not measure up to the principled requirements of the neo-Calvinist model of civil society as expressed in the concept of sphere sovereignty. As Jonathan Chaplin argues, such Tocquevillian arguments for a free and flourishing associational life — though commendable in general from a neo-Calvinist perspective — often lead to "a common tendency in civil society thinking to view particular social institutions largely from an instrumental point of view" insofar as the

---

47. J. J. Rousseau, *The Social Contract*, trans. Maurice Cranston (Harmondsworth, U. K.: Penguin, 1968), pp. 73-74.

48. For a variety of "neo-Tocquevillian" approaches to civil society, see Don Eberly, ed., *The Essential Civil Society Reader: Classic Essays in the American Civil Society Debate* (Lanham, Md.: Rowman & Littlefield, 2000).

real benefit of associational life is an enriched and properly democratic public political life.[49] This view, then, tends to ignore the "irreducible identities" of institutions in civil society and can lead to public neglect of the distinctive role that different kinds of institutions can play in the common social life of a (political) community. If it is merely associational life in general that bestows a generic benefit on the political community (say, the fostering of "social capital" and civic virtue), then that political community has no particular responsibility to exercise care for or recognition of particular *kinds* of institutions given their particular social roles or tasks, which is what the principle of public justice requires.

I conclude from all of this that, despite the fact that deliberative democratic theories appear as — and, as a rule, are indeed — friends of civil society and an inclusive public sphere, many of these theories nevertheless present models of deliberation that conflict with neo-Calvinist convictions about these issues. As a result, these sorts of theories can end up being a threat to civil society institutions that are non-deliberative or appear as threats to the kinds of deliberation that they favor. This particularly singles out what I have called non-postconventional communities, i.e., those that are rooted in traditional forms of discursive authority, those that abide by traditional moralities and those that have difficulties accepting a "secularized" politics. These conflicts emerge, I have argued, from varying conceptions of why and how rational deliberation legitimates public decision-making in democratic societies. What this situation requires, if neo-Calvinists are to endorse a version of discursive democracy, is an alternative account of discursive legitimation that accords with the principles of public justice and sphere sovereignty.

VI. Public Justice, Moral Solidarity, and Deliberation

As discussed at the beginning of this paper, a neo-Calvinist version of discursive democracy would have to derive the requirement of discursive legitimation from the principle of public justice, since it details the fundamental nature and task of the state. Public justice is, furthermore, a substantive conception of justice, and is grounded in a comprehensive idea of the human good rather than a religiously neutral attempt to articulate a fair procedure for making universally acceptable policy in a pluralistic context. These facts orient the neo-Calvinist justification of discursive democracy more toward

49. Chaplin, "The Concept of 'Civil Society' and Christian Social Pluralism," p. 17.

the Civic Republican approach than the Kantian Universalist one. I have argued elsewhere that there is some substantial affinity between elements of the republican tradition and Kuyper's understanding of the relationship between citizens, government, and civil society, so there are historical links between the two traditions as well.[50] For my argument here, though, I need to examine a more sophisticated conception of the norm of public justice than Kuyper offers in order to show the internal connection between public justice and discursive legitimation. Thus I will examine the political thought of Herman Dooyeweerd, or, more precisely, Jonathan Chaplin's take on it. I will argue that Chaplin's rethinking of some of Dooyeweerd's fundamental commitments stands in some continuity with the republican line of thought and can provide a distinctively neo-Calvinist approach to the issues at hand.

The first key in Chaplin's reconstruction of Dooyeweerd's social philosophy for my argument is his attempt to ground the enduring and irreducible identity of social structures not in the essentialist manner that Dooyeweerd himself does, but in "a normative conception of the human person."[51] On such a view, human flourishing involves the development and expression of a variety of modally qualified capacities, each of which requires particular kinds of social contexts in which it can be disclosed. Social structures that are developed to provide these contexts may vary significantly over time, but have a continued identity based on the irreducibility and stability of these aspects of the good life. What is particularly important here, for my purposes, is that this view simultaneously underwrites an enduring and irreducible normative identity for various social structures and allows for significantly varying expressions of that identity given different historical realities.

Furthermore, these social structures gain their normative principles from their particular contributions to human flourishing. Chaplin's account would "indicate how these social structures need to be designed in certain ways and that if this design is distorted, human fulfillment is curtailed."[52] One might say that this view is a neo-Calvinist turn on the republican grounding of the necessity of a certain type of politics in the requirements of human flourishing described in the "Aristotelian" terms I articulated above. The distinctive neo-Calvinist turn would be the insistence that human flourishing is, first, grounded in God's will and pleasure for his creation, and second, articulated

---

50. DeMoor, "Kuyper, Sphere Sovereignty, and the Possibility of Political Friendship," pp. 73-75.

51. Chaplin, *Herman Dooyeweerd*, p. 106.

52. Chaplin, *Herman Dooyeweerd*, p. 106.

into a variety of irreducible capacities and practices of which politics and the cultivation of our rationality are merely two among others rather than the fulfillment and perfection of our other ends. It is, however, politics and reason that primarily concern me, given that the topic at hand is deliberative democracy.

For Dooyeweerd, as for Chaplin, the norm of public justice is grounded in the irreducible institutional identity of the state. As just discussed, on Chaplin's view, it emerges from some part(s) of a normative account of human flourishing which this irreducible identity is meant to structure and secure. Now, in Dooyeweerd's social ontology, social institutions have both a qualifying function and a founding function. The qualifying function expresses its "intrinsic destination," meaning that it qualifies or leads "by guaranteeing the coherence of its internal structure and by guiding its other functions as they contribute in their own ways to its proper functioning."[53] For the state, this qualifying function is the juridical (hence the centrality of *law* in the identity and functioning of states) and its intrinsic destination is public justice, which is "a harmoniously balanced complex of juridical relationships among a multiplicity of judicial interests," or, put less abstractly, when the state pursues public justice, it does so by "*justly interrelating* different individuals and communities."[54]

A founding function, on the other hand, "furnishes the indispensable support making such a [intrinsic] destination realizable."[55] The founding function of a social structure does not define its irreducible identity, but rather provides the necessary conditions upon which that identity can be expressed. If the state's qualifying function is its public-legal character, and thus if its intrinsic destination is public justice, then its qualifying function is that apart from which public justice could not be realized. For Dooyeweerd, this function is the state's monopoly on the legitimate use of coercive force; without this, the state could not do the things that make the state the state. Chaplin, however, argues that coercive force cannot be the founding function of the state, and one of his suggestions for what it might be instead is the second crucial feature of his reconstruction for my argument.

Though in the end he concludes that "the state . . . has no founding function,"[56] Chaplin also entertains the possibility that the functional *sine qua*

---

53. Chaplin, *Herman Dooyeweerd*, p. 88.
54. Chaplin, *Herman Dooyeweerd*, p. 201.
55. Chaplin, *Herman Dooyeweerd*, p. 67.
56. Chaplin, *Herman Dooyeweerd*, p. 185.

non of effective public governance is not coercive force, but rather "the moral principles of the citizenry."[57] This cannot be just their general moral beliefs, but rather their shared "convictions about normative political order: the rule of law, civil rights, just distribution, and so on."[58] These moral convictions make the administration of public justice possible by constituting the basis of "subjective legitimacy," meaning citizens' *recognition* of the right of governments to exercise political power (in particular ways) and their own corresponding duty to obey or to be governed.[59] Without a substantial degree of subjective legitimacy, even coercive force would not be sufficient to make public governance effective. The goal of doing public justice — which is the *objective* condition of legitimacy for neo-Calvinists — cannot, then, be achieved without the achievement of subjective legitimacy.

I would want to add to this that implicit in this public recognition on the part of citizens of the right of governments to administer public justice is a certain moral stance taken by citizens also with respect to one another. Subjective legitimacy is not conferred upon governments person by person, or at least not merely so. It is not as if each citizen individually assesses the right of public officials to govern himself or herself as an individual; rather the question at stake is whether and how those officials have the right to govern *us* and the extent of the duty *we* have to obey their justly formulated laws. The attitudes constitutive of subjective legitimacy are not merely specifiable in the first-person singular, but also the first-person plural. This presupposes an understanding on the part of citizens that they together form a *moral community,* that their rights, duties, and competencies *as citizens* are held *together* and in turn hold them together in a morally substantial social bond. Thus, subjective legitimacy — understood as the founding function of the state — depends upon a kind of political friendship or moral solidarity between citizens without which it would lack the force sufficient to make public governance effective.[60]

In different historical circumstances this moral solidarity may be underwritten by different things — a shared religion, ethnic nationality, commitment to a goal, or a shared sense of victimization — but, if my suggestion is correct, no state can exist without it; that is the character of a founding function. I want now to suggest that, given the historical conditions of modern political

57. Chaplin, *Herman Dooyeweerd*, p. 183.
58. Chaplin, *Herman Dooyeweerd*, p. 183.
59. Chaplin, *Herman Dooyeweerd*, p. 183.
60. I've discussed these matters at greater length in "Kuyper, Sphere Sovereignty, and the Possibility of Political Friendship."

societies, the best — perhaps the only — way of achieving and maintaining this moral solidarity is through the practice of public deliberation. Given the post-national, post-Christian (but also post-secular), substantially rationalized and differentiated character of many modern states, we cannot premise political friendship on identification grounded in religion, ethnicity, national history, or the like. However, it is not unreasonable to expect modern citizens to recognize and value the moral status of "citizenship" and the moral ideals it entails, particularly the rational participation in the public life of one's own political community. This leaves us in the sphere of modern forms of Civic Republicanism. As discussed above, this implies the necessity of deliberation as the fundamental means by which citizens engage in public life and by which, in turn, governments address and respond to citizens, since anything less would be a denial of their dignity *qua* citizens.

The conclusion I want to draw from all of this is that deliberation is an *intrinsic requirement of the principle of public justice* (at least in modern political societies) because it is related to the practice of public justice as a founding function to a qualifying function of a societal structure. Without its founding function, the activities that constitute the qualifying function of a societal structure are not possible. Correspondingly, the activities that constitute the founding function are led, directed, and shaped by the qualifying function. In keeping with the latter point, this implies that the moral solidarity — grounded in practices of democratic deliberation — that is the founding function of the state is given its particular *public political* character by its orientation toward public justice. This explains why the content of the moral principles and the object of deliberation must always be the *common* good of the *political* community, not the interests of particular stakeholders therein or even the unspecified common good of "society as a whole." Thus the scope and content of public deliberation (and the norms according to which it is conducted) are shaped by its public legal/political character, i.e., by the ideal of public justice. Reciprocally, the ideal of public justice is simultaneously enabled and constrained by practices of democratic deliberation. There are things that those entrusted with administering public justice (i.e., officeholders in the state) are empowered to do as a result of democratic deliberation (and thus the formation of public opinion),[61] but this practice simultaneously limits these powers and holds them accountable for their exer-

---

61. This accounts for the necessity of what Dryzek describes in his analysis of deliberative system as "public space," "empowered space," and "transmission." See Dryzek, *Foundations and Frontiers*, p. 11.

cise. Understanding the relationship between deliberation and public justice in terms of the founding and qualifying functions of the state allows us to see their internal connection and the ways in which this shapes our conception of the normative character of each.

This in turn will shape our understanding of the normative relationship of a deliberative democratic state, the public sphere, and civil society. Space does not permit me to work this out at any length, but the normative social ontology that underlies this neo-Calvinist version of a republican conception of deliberative democracy also underwrites a distinctive conception of the public sphere, one that does not fall into the trap of arbitrarily restricting the place of certain parts of civil society (especially religious civil society) from equal participation in democratic deliberation in the public sphere. On this view, the "public sphere" is neither identical with "civil society" — since it is "the arena in which the free citizenry of a political community exist independently from any other community"[62] — nor is it exclusive of any part of civil society. It is "a realm in which all persons and structures necessarily participate but which by no means exhausts the entirety of the interests of such persons or structures."[63]

If the public sphere were identical with civil society (as in their own ways both Cohen and the neo-Tocquevillian views tend to suggest), then either it would lose its character as a site of specifically public legal/political deliberation or the institutions and communities of civil society would lose their identities as being pre- or supra-political (that is, their "irreducible institutional identities" would be subsumed by their political function). If the public sphere excluded any part of civil society (as both Cohen and Habermas as well as Rousseau suggest), then although their irreducible identity may be protected, the fact that that community/institution/tradition has a bona fide interest in the public realm and a bona fide contribution to make to public deliberation would be effaced (and this would be a failure of public justice). Within a genuinely neo-Calvinist model of deliberative democracy, on the other hand, civil society and its constituent communities would be liberated to play their protective, integrative, and transformative roles that simultaneously seek the common good and safeguard their irreducible identities.[64]

---

62. Chaplin, *Herman Dooyeweerd*, p. 228.
63. Chaplin, *Herman Dooyeweerd*, p. 228.
64. On this three-fold role of civil society, see Chaplin, *Herman Dooyeweerd*, chapter 11.

VII. Conclusion

In their defense and articulation of deliberative democracy, Gutmann and Thompson distinguish between two orders of moral theories. First-order moral theories "seek to resolve moral disagreement by demonstrating that alternative theories and principles should be rejected. The aim of each is to be the lone theory capable of resolving moral disagreement."[65] Among these they identify utilitarianism, libertarianism, liberal egalitarianism, and communitarianism. Deliberative democracy, on their view, is none of these. It is instead of those "second-order" theories that "are *about* other theories in the sense that they provide ways of dealing with the claims of conflicting first-order theories. They make room for continuing moral conflict that first-order theories purport to eliminate. They can be held consistently without rejecting a wide range of moral principles expressed by first-order theories."[66]

My point in this paper has been to suggest that, this distinction notwithstanding, the articulation and application of second-order theories cannot be done independently of first-order theories. In other words, when we try to hash out just *why* moral disagreement in modern societies should be addressed through democratic deliberation, *how* that deliberation ought to work, and *who* will be included in these deliberations and on what terms, we will inescapably draw upon first-order moral and political theories, particularly first-order convictions about democratic *legitimacy*. This is why I have urged that neo-Calvinists need to articulate their own conception of deliberative democracy grounded in the principle of public justice and the normative social ontology that articulates the principle of sphere sovereignty.

Deliberative democracy thus cannot be a neutral procedure; it always brings with it certain substantive commitments and conceptions that are themselves objects of moral disagreement. For Habermas, this would render the ideal of deliberative democracy moot since it would undermine the prospect of rational argument moving toward consensus or at least robust mutual understanding. My case regarding the inescapable connection between first- and second-order theories runs the risk, then, of making nonsense out of the possibility of deliberation as a means of managing deep moral disagreement. How can deliberation be non-neutral but also a way of dealing fairly with deep disagreement? How can we look to deliberative political institutions to bring us out of our sectarian or personal interests and point us to the genuine

---

65. Gutmann and Thompson, *Why Deliberative Democracy?* p. 13.
66. Gutmann and Thompson, *Why Deliberative Democracy?* p. 13.

public good if our conceptions of the public and its good that will shape those very institutions are not shared by all involved? It would take another paper to answer this question adequately, but for now I would merely suggest that the fact that normative conceptions of deliberation are themselves the object of disagreements points to the necessity of institutionalizing practices of "meta-deliberation" that would allow us to constantly revisit and revise the ways in which deliberation is used to manage first-order moral disagreement. Even here, of course, neutrality is not possible, but non-neutrality should not be assumed to imply the impossibility of mutual understanding and engagement.

Bibliography

Chaplin, Jonathan. "Defining 'Public Justice' in a Pluralistic Society: Probing a Key Neo Calvinist Insight." *Pro Rege*, March 2004.
———. "The Concept of 'Civil Society' and Christian Social Pluralism." In *The Kuyper Center Review, Volume One: Politics, Religion, and Sphere Sovereignty*, 14-33. Edited by Gordon Graham. Grand Rapids: Eerdmans, 2010.
———. *Herman Dooyeweerd: Christian Philosopher of State and Civil Society.* Notre Dame: University of Notre Dame Press, 2011.
Cicero, Marcus Tullius. *The Republic* and *The Laws*. Translated by Niall Rudd. Oxford: Oxford University Press, 1998.
Cohen, Joshua. "Deliberation and Democratic Legitimacy." In *The Good Polity: Normative Analysis of the State*, 17-34. Edited by Alan Hamlin and Philip Pettit. Oxford: Basil Blackwell, 1989.
DeMoor, Michael J. "Kuyper, Sphere Sovereignty, and the Possibility of Political Friendship." In *The Kuyper Center Review, Volume One: Politics, Religion, and Sphere Sovereignty*, 61-82. Edited by Gordon Graham. Grand Rapids: Eerdmans, 2010.
Dryzek, John. *Foundations and Frontiers of Deliberative Governance.* Oxford: Oxford University Press, 2011.
Eberly, Don, ed. *The Essential Civil Society Reader: Classic Essays in the American Civil Society Debate.* Lanham, Md.: Rowman & Littlefield, 2000.
Gutmann, Amy, and Dennis Thompson. *Why Deliberative Democracy?* Princeton: Princeton University Press, 2004.
Habermas, Jürgen. "Reconciliation Through the Public Use of Reason: Remarks on John Rawls' Political Liberalism." *Journal of Philosophy* 92, no. 3 (1995): 109-31.
———. *Between Facts and Norms: Contributions to a Discourse Theory of Law and Democracy.* Translated by William Rehg. Cambridge: MIT Press, 1996.
Kant, Immanuel. "Perpetual Peace: A Philosophical Sketch." In *Kant: Political Writings*, 2nd edition, 93-130. Edited by Hans Reiss. Translated by H. B. Nisbet. Cambridge: Cambridge University Press, 1991.

Kuyper, Abraham. *Lectures on Calvinism.* Grand Rapids: Eerdmans, 1961.

Pettit, Philip. "Deliberative Democracy, the Discursive Dilemma, and Republican Theory." *Philosophy, Politics, and Society* 7 (2003): 138-62.

Rawls, John. *A Theory of Justice.* Cambridge: Harvard University Press, 1971.

———. *Political Liberalism.* New York: Columbia University Press, 1993.

Rousseau, J. J. *The Social Contract.* Translated by Maurice Cranston. Harmondsworth: Penguin, 1968.

Taylor, Charles. "Cross Purposes: The Liberal-Communitarian Debate." In *Philosophical Arguments.* Cambridge: Harvard University Press, 1995.

Van Geest, Fred. "Democracy and the Neo-Calvinist Tradition." *Christian Scholar's Review* 37, no. 1 (2007): 47-76.

Wolterstorff, Nicholas. "Abraham Kuyper's Model of a Democratic Polity with a Religiously Diverse Citizenry." In *Kuyper Reconsidered: Aspects of His Life and Work,* 190-205. Edited by C. Van der Kooi and J. de Bruijn. Amsterdam: Free University Press, 1999.

Democracy and Ecclesiology:
An Aristocratic Church for a Democratic Age?

James Eglinton

Introduction

The Dutch neo-Calvinist movement spanning the end of the nineteenth and the beginning of the twentieth centuries is interesting for a variety of reasons. At its center was a renewed interest in the theology of John Calvin, and in that context it saw a new appropriation of Calvinism in the modern world.[1] One of the most interesting areas of that Calvinist renewal movement was its fresh engagement between theology and politics. This paper will focus on that area of neo-Calvinism, particularly in the reception of democratic ideas in neo-Calvinist thought. The central focus therein is the neo-Calvinist handling of the extent to which church government should accept democratic values on political enfranchisement. Its engagement will pay particular attention to the thought of Herman Bavinck, arguably the movement's leading theological mouthpiece and also a keen participant in the political scene of his day. The paper will reach its conclusion by engaging constructively with Bavinck on the relationship between democracy and ecclesiology.

In short, it will show that Bavinck was cautiously supportive of democratic development in the civil state, but that he nonetheless articulated an ecclesi-

---

1. James Eglinton, *Trinity and Organism: Towards a New Reading of Herman Bavinck's Organic Motif* (New York: T&T Clark, 2012), pp. 13-26. See also Herman Bavinck, *Johannes Calvijn: Eene lezing ter gelegenheid van den vierhonderdsten gedenkdag zijner geboorte, 10 Juli 1509-1909* (Kampen: J. H. Kok, 1909). For the English translation, see Herman Bavinck, "John Calvin: A Lecture on the Occasion of his 400th Birthday, July 10th, 1509-1909," *The Bavinck Review* 1 (2010): 57-85.

ology maintaining that the church should not be run like the state. Although Bavinck supported the idea of a democratic state, he also defended the idea of ecclesiastical rule by a (spiritual) aristocracy. Thus, according to Bavinck, while the state should be democratic, the church should not follow suit. Stated otherwise, his argument suggests that Christians can approve a particular form of civil government while nonetheless insisting that their churches be otherwise organized. By way of critical engagement with Bavinck, this paper will propose that the model used by Bavinck as the basis of his reconciliation of democratic social values and non-democratic ecclesiastical ideals requires further thought, particularly in post-Christian secular contexts.

Suffrage in Nineteenth-Century Europe

In writing on neo-Calvinism in relation to democracy, it is useful to acknowledge that one is discussing a series of ideas developing across generations. In handling concepts like *democracy, suffrage,* or *enfranchisement* in this period, it is necessary to acknowledge such as concepts in flux. Throughout the nineteenth century they, as the focus of much debate, remained political ideas in a state of transformation. In this paper, the aspect of democracy in focus is suffrage: who has the right to vote? What influences our decisions as to who should be able to vote? A basic awareness of the fact that suffrage, as a political notion, underwent considerable change in nineteenth-century Europe necessitates that one study Bavinck's response to movements in the relevant debates.

Neo-Calvinist history is far from replete with outright support for, or at least a resounding sense of self-understanding using the language of, "democracy." As a form of political Calvinism, its roots in the antirevolutionary politics of Groen van Prinsterer *et al.* linked democracy to the godless values of the French Revolution. In their context, neo-Calvinism's forerunners felt no great desire to self-identify as "democratic." In the current-day Netherlands, it is interesting to note that the party (arguably) most influenced by neo-Calvinist theology, the *ChristianUnie,* while obviously a Christian democratic party and as such a full player in modern Dutch democracy, nonetheless does not make its most basic political self-identification in "democratic" terms (as does the mainstream *Christen-Democratisch Appèl*).[2]

---

2. Klei has argued provocatively that the *Gereformeerd Politiek Verbond,* the party that merged with the *Reformatorische Politieke Federatie* in 2000 to form the *ChristenUnie,* was anti-democratic in its core political identity. See Ewout Klei, *"Klein maar krachtig, dat maakt*

Neo-Calvinists — even when practicing democracy — are not noted for the regular, bold invocation of its nomenclature. That having been said, information can more easily be found on neo-Calvinist politics and suffrage. With that in mind, this paper thus focuses on the issue of suffrage as a useful aspect of democracy, within which its relationship to neo-Calvinism can be probed somewhat.

We begin, then, with the battle of values between the French Revolution, on one hand, and the Dutch historian and statesman Guillaume Groen van Prinsterer (1801-1876), on the other. In the Revolution, old distinctions of class and power were cast away as power was redistributed along the lines of *liberté, égalité,* and *fraternité.* In van Prinsterer, one finds an engagement with the Revolution's ideals that fought to maintain the place of the monarchy in Dutch society, and that argued against unlimited sovereignty belonging to the people. In the place of *liberté, égalité, fraternité,* van Prinsterer insisted on *God, the Netherlands,* and *the House of Orange.* Van Prinsterer explicitly connected the Revolution to the rejection of Christian theism. His work *Ongeloof en revolutie (Unbelief and the Revolution)* makes this particularly clear.[3]

> Groen's relationship with France was defined in an important sense by his principled rejection of the French Revolution as a spiritual upheaval, and in his objections to French influence in continental Europe which had often posed a threat to the very existence of the Dutch nation.[4]

In this context, one finds van Prinsterer battling against the liberal political theorist (and eventual framer of the new Dutch Constitution) Johan Rudolph Thorbecke over the extent to which the Revolution's new values should be incorporated into Dutch culture. It is interesting, however, to note that van Prinsterer and Thorbecke were friends prior to the former's conversion to

---

ons uniek": Een geschiedenis van het Gereformeerd Politiek Verbond, 1948-2003 (Amsterdam: Uitgeverij Bert Bakker, 2011). Van Geest has also argued that the neo-Calvinist tradition has an underdeveloped account of democracy; see Fred Van Geest, "Democracy and the Neo-Calvinist Tradition," *Christian Scholar's Review* 37:1 (2007): 48.

3. Guillaume Groen van Prinsterer, *Ongeloof en revolutie. Eene reeks van historische voorlezingen* (Leiden: S. en J. Luchtmans, 1847).

4. Jan de Bruijn, "Groen van Prinsterer in internationale context," in *Groen van Prinsterer in Europese context,* ed. Jan de Bruijn and George Harinck (Hilversum: Verloren, 2004), p. 13. "Groens verhouding tot Frankrijk werd in belangrijke mate bepaald door zijn principiële afwijzing van de Franse revolutie als geestelijke omwenteling en zijn bezwaren tegen de Franse invloed op het Europese continent, die in het verleden zo vaak bedreigend was geweest voor het Nederlandse volksbestaan."

the Reformed faith. This friendship endured, despite their eventual arrival at considerably different views on theology and politics.[5] This is all the more noteworthy given that prior to van Prinsterer's Reformed conversion, they had corresponded extensively on the French Revolution.[6]

In attempting to trace the fledgling steps of what later became neo-Calvinism in its response to democracy, it is important to see that van Prinsterer's thought in this regard also underwent a process of development. He moved from the belief that the Netherlands should be a Protestant country within which a degree of tolerance should be extended to Roman Catholics and Jews, to the later belief that Dutch society should be pluralistic, within which there should be a Protestant subculture. In that sense, van Prinsterer was an early advocate of what would eventually become the pillar-model society *(verzuiling)*.

In van Prinsterer's ideological inheritors, the neo-Calvinists Abraham Kuyper and Herman Bavinck, further engagement with the Revolution's democratic values comes to the fore. Under Kuyper's direction, the Antirevolutionary Party, the first modern political party in the Netherlands, came into existence. When one tries to trace the relationship between the Antirevolutionary Party and parliamentary democracy — particularly with regard to themes such as the extent to which suffrage should be extended across a population — the changing relationship of neo-Calvinism to democracy becomes slightly clearer.

It is worth noting that although attempts had been made to separate the right to vote from the necessity that voters own property, Revolutionary France did not succeed in implementing a more egalitarian set of voting rights until the mid-nineteenth century. Indeed, as was typical of that century, Revolutionary France introduced a system of universal *male* suffrage in 1848. The right to vote was only extended to French women in 1945. In the Netherlands, the 1887 Constitution enfranchised male citizens, with unlimited suffrage for Dutch women being granted in 1919. (In that light, it is interesting that the inheritors of van Prinsterer, Kuyper and Bavinck, extended suffrage to women decades before Napoleon's inheritors.)

In examining the attitudes of Bavinck and Kuyper in the extension of voting rights to Dutch citizens, we can see something of their relationship to a democratic concept of civil society. This then has interesting consequences for their ecclesiology.

5. G. J. Hooykaas, "Groen van Prinsterer en Thorbecke," in *Groen van Prinsterer in Europese context*, p. 61.

6. Thorbecke and van Prinsterer corresponded extensively in 1815 on the French Revolution. See Hooykaas, "Groen van Prinsterer en Thorbecke," p. 61.

James Eglinton

Bavinck and Suffrage

When Bavinck joined the Antirevolutionary Party's Central Committee in 1897, he was obliged to explain his convictions on suffrage and democracy. In that context, he affirmed the Party's rejection of the French Revolution's individualistic conception of the citizen. As such, Bavinck underlined his rejection of Revolutionary *égalité* whereby the political participant is the individual, whose social identity is separate from that of any fellow social actors.[7]

Instead, Bavinck affirmed that society is an organism composed of family units. His argument was that people belong together, and that the family unit (rather than the individual), as the most basic building block for society, should also be the most basic democratic participant. Accordingly, he argued that suffrage should be extended to those family units. Within that context, he argued, the responsibility to vote rested with the father as head of the family. This is a view of democracy that Bavinck reaffirmed in 1907 while serving as head of the Antirevolutionary Party Central Committee.[8]

In 1916, three years before universal suffrage was extended to Dutch women, Bavinck's party restated its opposition to an individualistic approach to voting rights. In so doing, it stated once again that it was not in support of universal suffrage for women. However, it did voice approval for suffrage being extended to widows who functioned as family heads. The context of this statement was that the Dutch government had agreed to implement universal, individual suffrage to all male citizens, and to give women passive suffrage: although they still could not vote, they could be voted for. This puzzling situation caused further problems for the Christian political parties — in this case the Calvinistic Antirevolutionary Party and the Roman Catholic *Rooms Katholieke Staatspartij.*[9]

Bavinck's response to the extension of suffrage along individualistic lines

7. Niels van Driel, "The Status of Women in Contemporary Society: Principles and Practice in Herman Bavinck's Socio-Political Thought," in *Five Studies in the Thought of Herman Bavinck, a Creator of Modern Dutch Thought*, ed. John Bolt (Lewiston: The Edwin Mellen Press, 2011), p. 174. See also Bernard Groethuysen and Alix Gullian, *Philosophie de la Révolution française* (Paris: Gallimard, 1982), pp. 252, 280. On the centrality of a radical concept of *l'individu* in the French Revolution's political values, see Edgar Quinet, *La Révolution* (Paris: Librairie Internationale, 1869), p. 43.

8. See van Driel, "The Status of Women in Contemporary Society," p. 174.

9. Elsbeth Locher-Scholten, *Women and the Colonial State: Essays on Gender and Modernity in the Netherlands Indies 1900-1942* (Amsterdam: Amsterdam University Press, 2000), p. 155.

was to restate his belief in an organic model of society. Within that context, his ideal was that human beings should find their place in coherent family units which would function as the basic building blocks of civil society. However, he also affirmed a complementarian view of gender wherein men and women have different social functions, but where women are no less skilled or capable of exercising political prudence than men.[10] Bavinck also recognized the inevitability of individualistic, universal suffrage for men and women. Although his ideal was that people be associated in families as democratic units, he argued that Scripture gave no clear, decisive judgment on whether families or individuals have the power to vote. It was not a hill on which to die (a sentiment which drew much displeasure from Kuyper, who saw this as a compromise on a fundamental antirevolutionary principle).[11]

In 1919, Bavinck — as a member of the First Chamber — voted *for* the introduction of general suffrage for women. Although Bavinck's ideal was that people would be grouped together in family units, and that these family units would function as participants in democracy, he recognized that the influence of the Revolution — in terms of an individualistic concept of the human being as political participant — was just too great: this was the direction in which democracy was moving. Furthermore, he believed that Scripture gave no clear guidance on voting rights.

How did Bavinck handle himself in such a context? It should be said that Bavinck saw cultural development as occurring through the action of God's providence, which in turn works on the basis of common grace. For Bavinck, the only thing faith opposes is sin itself:[12] thus, if a cultural development occurs in God's providence, and that development is not actually condemned by Scripture as sinful, Christianity must grant that cultural development a degree of independence. In this context, Bavinck also explained that he saw the core of modern culture, within which attitudes to suffrage were changing, as essentially Christian. Regarding an issue like individual suffrage, when an essentially Christian culture changes its attitudes to something not dealt with

10. Herman Bavinck, *De Vrouw in Hedendaagsche Maatschappij* (Kampen: Kok, 1918), pp. 17-20.

11. See van Driel, "The Status of Women in Contemporary Society," p. 178.

12. This is closely related to Bavinck's belief that "Christianity does not introduce a single substantial foreign element into the creation. It creates no new cosmos but rather makes the cosmos new. It restores what was corrupted by sin. It atones the guilty and cures what is sick; the wounded it heals." Herman Bavinck, "Common Grace," trans. Raymond Van Leeuwen, *Calvin Theological Journal* 24 (1989): 60-61. See also van Driel, "The Status of Women in Contemporary Society," pp. 164-68.

by Scripture (according to Bavinck), Christians should not be afraid to accept this development.

This approach, of course, presented Bavinck with considerable problems. Although he regarded cultural development as occurring within God's providence, and modern Western culture as being essentially Christian at its core, he did not regard modern culture as something that was always good or that should always be uncritically accepted. Bavinck proposed a two-pronged approach to cultural development: (i) it should be respected, because he thought that the gospel itself required it, and (ii) it should be critically examined.[13] Following this path is very difficult.

In this instance, Kuyper, for example, was for a time very critical of how Bavinck used these two principles in relation to universal suffrage. Furthermore, he was especially critical of Bavinck's conclusion that Christians could assent to universal, individual suffrage: although Kuyper also recognized that universal suffrage was inevitable, he nonetheless maintained that the restriction of voting rights to the heads of families was a principle on which there should be no compromise.[14]

In providing a brief sketch of Bavinck's response to suffrage as an aspect of democratic development, I hope that the following stands clear: as a theologian and politician, Bavinck was open to and ultimately supportive of universal individual suffrage within a democratic system of *government*. We will return later in the paper to the theological model used by Bavinck to move from his early opposition to universal suffrage to a later support of the same. At this point, the most important point is that he, for one reason or another, came to regard a democratic system of universal suffrage as a good thing.

This paper does not concern itself with the fact that Bavinck ultimately came to support democracy in the state. Rather, it focuses on whether that can be reconciled to his refusal to allow the democratization of his ecclesiology.

Bavinck, Suffrage, and the Church

In *Reformed Dogmatics*, Bavinck makes two interesting statements on the church and democracy:

13. Herman Bavinck, "Christian Principles and Social Relations," in *Essays on Religion, Science and Society*, ed. John Bolt, trans. Harry Boonstra and Gerrit Sheeres (Grand Rapids: Baker, 2008), pp. 142-43.
14. Van Driel, "The Status of Women in Contemporary Society," p. 178.

For the church is not a society called into being by the will of human beings but a creation of Christ. All power belonging to the local church therefore has been granted by Christ; it is not a right but a gift. *The church is not a democracy in which a people governs itself.* Christ rules in it, and the choice of the local church [to ordain elders] has no other meaning than that it notes the gifts and designates the persons whom Christ has destined for office.[15]

Following this, one also finds that

On the visible side of the church, [Christ's] *government is not democratic, nor monarchical, not oligarchic, but aristocratic and presbyterial.* These office bearers are the "aristoi," the best, not in money and possessions but in spiritual gifts, whom he himself equips and allows the church to set apart for his service.[16]

At one level, there is very little that is surprising in this aspect of Bavinck's ecclesiology. In essence, he describes a presbyterian form of church government, whereby the church is ruled by Christ as King, who in turn exercises his kingly government by bestowing gifts appropriate to servant leadership upon elders. What is particularly interesting, however, is that Bavinck's standard presbyterian description of church government uses such deliberately anti-democratic language. Why does someone who would go on to vote for universal suffrage in civil society nonetheless articulate such a vividly anti-democratic ecclesiology?

There are two probable ways in which the anti-democratic language used in Bavinck's ecclesiology can be explained. First, this must — in a certain sense at least — reflect the neo-Calvinist unease with "democracy" as mentioned earlier in this paper. Contextually, neo-Calvinists and their antirevolutionary antecedents simply were not comfortable in talking of "democracy" or in using that word in a self-identifying way. Although they were eventually open to extending universal suffrage, the word "democracy" (especially in the nineteenth-century Netherlands) had a string of connotations that the neo-Calvinists wanted to avoid. This factor was no doubt significant in how deliberately Bavinck attempted to show that Christ's church is governed in a way quite unlike the new civic models emanating from Revolutionary France.

The second issue deals with chronology: Bavinck's strongly anti-

---

15. Herman Bavinck, *Reformed Dogmatics,* vol. 4, *Holy Spirit, Church and New Creation,* ed. John Bolt, trans. John Vriend (Grand Rapids: Baker, 2008), p. 379. Emphasis mine.

16. Bavinck, *Reformed Dogmatics,* vol. 4, p. 388. Emphasis mine.

democratic ecclesiology is found, of course, in his *Reformed Dogmatics*. These sentiments take shape in the work completed towards the end of the nineteenth century, while he was still working in Kampen. This distinctive set of anti-democratic ecclesiastical emphases was formed before Bavinck moved to Amsterdam, before he became so involved with the Antirevolutionary Party, before his own position of suffrage and democracy became a major issue in his own thought (as one of the live issues of his day as a politician), and before his own daughter (born in 1894) had entered adulthood in a world very different from that into which her father was born.

It seems likely that there is a sense in which the strongly anti-democratic accent in Bavinck's ecclesiology is particularly bound to the context in which he wrote *Reformed Dogmatics*. The accent reflects the issues he was facing in Kampen at that time. His support of an "aristocratic-presbyterial" form of church government already is clear in the first edition of his *Dogmatiek*.[17] The aforementioned openly anti-democratic ecclesiastical formulation is also found in this first edition: *In het zichtbare is zijne regeering niet democratish noch monarchaal noch oligarchish, maar aristocratish-presbyteraal. Het zijn de ἄριστοι, de besten, niet in geld en goed maar in geestelijke gaven, die Hij zelf bekwaamt en door de gemeente voor zijnen dienst aanwijzen laat.*[18]

However, it is perhaps interesting to query whether Bavinck, if he were rewriting the ecclesiological section of *Reformed Dogmatics* at a later date — for example, after 1919, when he voted *for* unlimited female suffrage — would retain this strongly anti-democratic language. It would be a great surprise if his support for church government by the spiritual *aristoi* should change. However, it does not seem improbable to suspect that the strongly anti-democratic flavor might be lessened somewhat.

Bavinck's Non-democratic Church

Bavinck's ecclesiology, typical of his Reformed tradition, operates along the lines of the church being both visible and invisible.[19] The invisible church is the true catholic church of all ages. Its composition is known only to God, its members are all elect. In explaining the form of government used in the invisible church, Bavinck favors the motif of monarchy: this is a church ruled

---

17. Herman Bavinck, *Gereformeerde Dogmatiek*, 4e Deel (Kampen: J. H. Bos, 1901), p. 82.
18. Bavinck, *Gereformeerde Dogmatiek*, p. 131.
19. Eglinton, *Trinity and Organism*, pp. 187-95.

by a King. The visible church, though, is the church as organism and institute. Bavinck believes that the visible church is under a form of government, but this government is not democratic. As such, the visible church is not a self-governing, self-defining group. By way of its creation, it does not call itself into being; and by way of its ongoing government, the fact that its believers share in a common priesthood does not mean that leaders consult every member.

The visible church's government is also distinguished from that of a monarchy: in asserting that its government is not headed by one individual, Bavinck opposes the monarchy-like ecclesiologies of Erastianism and Roman Catholicism. Furthermore, the visible church's government is not an oligarchy. Bavinck argues against the idea of the church as a vast global organization whose power is wielded by a small, non-representative group. Rather, he maintains, the church is *aristocratic* (the meaning of which should be qualified in terms of spiritual gifts, rather than pre-Revolution ties to property ownership), and *presbyterian* (meaning church government by a plurality of elders in local congregations within a wider ecclesiastical structure).

For Presbyterians (at least) there is little surprise in the substance of Bavinck's ecclesiology. The surprising factor, it seems, is simply that the tone in the *Reformed Dogmatics* is so emphatically anti-democratic. However, as has already been noted, it is interesting to ponder whether that tone would remain the same if Bavinck were to rearticulate his ecclesiology in his later life.

Bavinck's Dilemma: Different Standards for Church and Civil Society

In closing this essay, it is worth saying something about the tension that exists between Bavinck's willingness to vote *for* democratic universal suffrage in civil society, and his opposition to the same in the church. Bavinck's approach to this, of course, rests upon a basic awareness that church and civil society are different contexts, and that he — as a participant in both — should bring a different set of expectations to each.

Bavinck's way of doing so, which is based on his view of Christianity's host culture in his era as essentially Christian, was to create a dialogue between Scripture and God's providential leading of "Christian" Western culture. Although questions of how the Christian faith should be applied in the modern world were difficult for Bavinck, it seems reasonable to suppose that those difficulties are eased somewhat if one's basic conviction is that "God is doing great things"[20] in what is already a "Christian" culture. A reliance on providence and the idea of a "Christian" culture function together as a safety net in those questions.

However, Bavinck's way of doing this becomes much harder to replicate if one no longer believes that one's host culture is essentially Christian. Those reading Bavinck in the context of twenty-first-century secular, post-Christian Europe, and who attempt to participate in democratic politics within that context, may well find it harder to interpret God's providence positively in relation to cultural development.

In such a post-Christian cultural context, Bavinck's work is very useful in helping one see that the church and the civil society are different contexts. Furthermore, his thought (to a certain extent) provides helpful tools in understanding why the church is different: he helps one articulate, for example, why a Christian would vote for a particular political representative while believing that the same person would be wholly unsuitable for leadership within the church. However, in order to make Bavinck more helpful in a post-Christian context, this paper tentatively suggests that two changes need to be more clearly accented in his model. These changes are closely related and depend on each other.

First, his model of Christian participation in democratic politics needs to be more self-consciously grounded in Calvin's principle of accommodation.[21] The kernel of this idea is that it is better to participate in democracy than to withdraw from it, but in participating the best one can often do is to tolerate what one does not condone. Interaction within political process based on an attitude of accommodation, taking into account the fallenness of one's host culture, seems more promising (at least initially) to those unable to presuppose said host culture's Christian character.

Second, and closely tied to the accommodation factor: the distinction between church (as a society undergoing redemption through the gospel) and civil society (as a society ravaged by sin) should be seen more clearly as the distinction between, respectively, societies of *special* and *common* grace. In

20. Herman Bavinck, *Modernisme en Orthodoxie* (Kampen: J. H. Kok, 1911), p. 11. "God is bezig, groote dingen in deze tijden te doen."

21. Ford Lewis Battles, "Was God Accommodating Himself to Human Capacity?" *Interpretation* 31 (1977): 19-38; David Wright, "Calvin's 'Accommodation' Revisited," in *Calvin as Exegete: Papers and Responses Presented at the Ninth Colloquium on Calvin and Calvin Studies* (Grand Rapids: Calvin Studies Society, 1995), pp. 171-90; Jon Balserak, "The God of Love and Weakness: Calvin's Understanding of God's Accommodating Relationship with His People," *Westminster Theological Journal* 62:2 (2000): 178-95.

looking at participation in politics or wider culture through the lens of accommodation, the participant must take into account a realistic picture of that context's fallenness. It is an environment in which the ideals of the Christian faith are often absent: it is a broken social reality whose collapse is prevented by common grace alone.

However, in so doing, the participant must also look to the church as the space wherein the gospel itself is engaged in *recreation:* where the church can become a place in which glimpses of Eden and the New Jerusalem can be seen, and within which glimpses of creation ordinances and pointers to glorification appear from time to time. The distinction between common and special grace has obvious relevance to the sense in which Christians participate in democracy and the church as separate spheres: it seems necessary as one grapples with the reality of the Christian's distinct expectations in both spheres. While the common/special grace distinction forms a major feature in Bavinck's worldview, one wonders whether it should assume a more prominent place in discussions of neo-Calvinist participation in democracy and the church.

The closing question, of course, is whether Bavinck in his later years, having put his neo-Calvinism to much practice in political engagement in his post-Kampen, post-*Reformed Dogmatics* work, would agree.

Bibliography

Balserak, Jon. "The God of Love and Weakness: Calvin's Understanding of God's Accommodating Relationship with His People." *Westminster Theological Journal* 62:2 (2000): 178-95.

Battles, Ford Lewis. "Was God Accommodating Himself to Human Capacity?" *Interpretation* 31 (1977): 19-38.

Bavinck, Herman. "Christian Principles and Social Relations." In *Essays on Religion, Science and Society.* Edited by John Bolt. Translated by Harry Boonstra and Gerrit Sheeres. Grand Rapids: Baker, 2008.

———. "Common Grace." Translated by Raymond Van Leeuwen. *Calvin Theological Journal* 24 (1989): 35-65.

———. *De Vrouw in Hedendaagsche Maatschappij.* Kampen: Kok, 1918.

———. *Gereformeerde Dogmatiek,* 4e Deel. Kampen: J. H. Bos, 1901.

———. *Johannes Calvijn: Eene lezing ter gelegenheid van den vierhonderdsten gedenkdag zijner geboorte, 10 Juli 1509-1909.* Kampen: J. H. Kok, 1909.

———. "John Calvin: A Lecture on the Occassion of his 400th Birthday, July 10th, 1509-1909." *The Bavinck Review* 1 (2010): 57-85.

———. *Modernisme en Orthodoxie.* Kampen: J. H. Kok, 1911.

————. *Reformed Dogmatics*. Vol. 4: *Holy Spirit, Church and New Creation*. Edited by John Bolt. Translated by John Vriend. Grand Rapids: Baker, 2008.

De Bruijn, Jan. "Groen van Prinsterer in internationale context." In *Groen van Prinsterer in Europese context*. Edited by Jan de Bruijn and George Harinck. Hilversum: Verloren, 2004.

Eglinton, James. *Trinity and Organism: Towards a New Reading of Herman Bavinck's Organic Motif*. New York: T&T Clark, 2012.

Groethuysen, Bernard, and Alix Gullian. *Philosophie de la Révolution française*. Paris: Gallimard, 1982.

Hooykaas, G. J. "Groen van Prinsterer en Thorbecke." In *Groen van Prinsterer in Europese context*. Edited by Jan de Bruijn and George Harinck. Hilversum: Verloren, 2004.

Klei, Ewout. *"Klein maar krachtig, dat maakt ons uniek": Een geschiedenis van het Gereformeerd Politiek Verbond, 1948-2003*. Amsterdam: Uitgeverij Bert Bakker, 2011.

Locher-Scholten, Elsbeth. *Women and the Colonial State: Essays on Gender and Modernity in the Netherlands Indies, 1900-1942*. Amsterdam: Amsterdam University Press, 2000.

Quinet, Edgar. *La Révolution*. Paris: Librairie Internationale, 1869.

Van Driel, Niels. "The Status of Women in Contemporary Society: Principles and Practice in Herman Bavinck's Socio-Political Thought." In *Five Studies in the Thought of Herman Bavinck, a Creator of Modern Dutch Thought*. Edited by John Bolt. Lewiston: The Edwin Mellen Press, 2011.

Van Geest, Fred. "Democracy and the Neo-Calvinist Tradition." *Christian Scholar's Review* 37:1 (2007): 47-76.

Van Prinsterer, Guillaume Groen. *Ongeloof en revolutie. Eene reeks van historische voorlezingen*. Leiden: S. en J. Luchtmans, 1847.

Wright, David. "Calvin's 'Accommodation' Revisited." In *Calvin as Exegete: Papers and Responses Presented at the Ninth Colloquium on Calvin and Calvin Studies*, 171-190. Grand Rapids: Calvin Studies Society, 1995.

Distinct Discipleship: Abraham Kuyper, Dietrich Bonhoeffer, and Christian Engagement in Public Life

Brant Himes

For All Their Differences . . .

Abraham Kuyper and Dietrich Bonhoeffer were two very different historical and theological figures. Kuyper (1837-1920) was the son of a Dutch Reformed minister and spent his life building and advocating a Calvinistic worldview in the Netherlands. Bonhoeffer (1906-1945) was born into the old Prussian aristocracy and chose the life of a Lutheran pastor, theologian, and resistance fighter against the Nazi regime. Kuyper died after a long and successful career; he founded several institutions, including the Free University, the Antirevolutionary Party (the first modern, organized popular political party in the Netherlands), and two newspapers, and at the height of his career he was elected prime minister of the Netherlands. Bonhoeffer died at the young age of thirty-nine; he was killed in a Nazi concentration camp for his role in the *Valkyrie* assassination attempt on Hitler. His short life was incredibly productive, though, and some of his theological writings on discipleship, ethics, and the nature of the church have become spiritual classics. Kuyper would never have known of Bonhoeffer, and Bonhoeffer's interaction with Reformed writings seems to lack any direct connection to Kuyper.[1]

For all their differences, however, the outlooks of Kuyper and Bonhoeffer

1. John De Gruchy gives an example of Reformed influence on Bonhoeffer by making the case that Bonhoeffer found himself outside his Lutheran heritage and embracing notions of the Reformed tradition in the decision to participate in the conspiracy against Hitler. See John De Gruchy, *Bonhoeffer and South Africa: Theology in Dialogue* (Grand Rapids: William B. Eerdmans, 1984), pp. 98ff.

were markedly similar, especially in their commitment to Christian engagement with the world. While they employed different methods, emphasized different dogmas, and advocated for different outcomes, Kuyper and Bonhoeffer were really after the same thing. Both were convinced that the nature of the Christian faith demanded clear and direct action in the public arena. As a result, they both sought to build a theology that could make sense of — and meaningfully engage with — the pressing issues in their respective historical circumstances. Kuyper looked to the roots of the Reformed faith in Calvin and worked to construct a theology that was both faithful to its foundations and relevant for the time. Bonhoeffer, too, sought to refine and re-imagine the Lutheran theological tradition in order to articulate a biblical way forward in the context of the rise of National Socialism and the outbreak of war. Their different historical contexts nevertheless led them to a strikingly similar conviction: Christian disciples are called to bear essential witness to the reality of Jesus Christ in the world. Kuyper and Bonhoeffer are therefore excellent resources for exploring the very public nature of Christian discipleship.

Personal discipleship demands public engagement because the reality of life in Christ is public, in that it infuses all aspects of life.[2] Kuyper and Bonhoeffer constructed theologies of discipleship that spoke to the mandate of Christian involvement in and for the world. Their conclusions were both general and specific; they interacted with the world from a set of theological convictions, and yet allowed their unique situation to inform the outworking of that theology. As such, this article will explore the specific historical context and theological implications of concepts from select writings from Kuyper and Bonhoeffer. Investigations of Kuyper's writings on sphere sovereignty, common grace, and worldview coupled with Bonhoeffer's work on church/state authority, Christological ethics, and divine mandates (which culminate in Christonomy) will provide a compelling notion of public discipleship. Kuyper and Bonhoeffer both constructed a theology of engagement that operated from — and bore witness to — the gracious reality of Jesus Christ in the world. This provides a unique opportunity to explore the implications of this witness in the context of present-day public engagement in democracy.[3]

2. Note that the use of "public" throughout the paper is not limited to "politics" but rather signifies a theological orientation to all aspects of our interconnected society and life, including occupations, societies, economics, family, etc.

3. The benefits of placing Kuyper and Bonhoeffer in conversation remain largely undiscovered in academic scholarship. The only direct comparison in English seems to be a recent article by the Dutch historian George Harinck and his colleague in theology Gerard Dekker on the similarities between Kuyper's and Bonhoeffer's ecclesiology. See George Harinck and

Basic Questions of Public Theology: By What Authority?

On October 20, 1880, Kuyper delivered the inaugural address at the opening of the Free University in Amsterdam. His address, "Sphere Sovereignty," set out the institutional implications for a fundamental belief in the glory and reign of God. The concept of sphere sovereignty, for Kuyper, expressed the Reformed view of God's ultimate rule over all creation, and thus affirmed that God's sovereignty alone was the basis for the founding of the Free University. "Sphere sovereignty," he proclaimed, "[is] the hallmark of our institution,"[4] and in its distinctly Reformed character the university affirmed — from the beginning — that the sovereignty of God was above all spheres of life. This, it was argued, was why the Free University — the first university in the Netherlands to exist apart from state or church control — was able to exist and flourish.[5] God's sovereignty, expressed in the very order of creation, affirmed the divine right of this new institution to exist apart from the state. God's rule preceded state sovereignty, or that of any other sphere; all spheres were thus ultimately under God alone.

In Kuyper's Reformed doctrine, creation bore witness to the sovereignty of God over all things. In the beginning, God established a well-ordered creation by his Word. God continually called this creation to order with permanent, universal, and normative structures. Through this order, God manifested his sovereign love and care for all of creation, and the structures of life — such as family, state, and church — became real spheres, each existing in its own do-

---

Gerard Dekker, "The Position of the Church Institute in Society: A Comparison between Bonhoeffer and Kuyper," *The Princeton Seminary Bulletin* 28, no. 1 (2007): 86-98. Otherwise, Bonhoeffer scholars, including Georg Huntemann and John De Gruchy, have made only passing remarks on the two men. Huntemann makes some preliminary connections between Kuyper's concept of common grace and Bonhoeffer's concept of coming of age in *The Other Bonhoeffer: An Evangelical Reassessment of Dietrich Bonhoeffer* (Grand Rapids: Baker Books, 1993), p. 98, and De Gruchy comments mostly on the historical applications of Neo-Calvinism in South Africa and Lutheranism in Nazi Germany in *Bonhoeffer and South Africa*, pp. 105ff. This article aims to demonstrate the theological productivity of looking to Kuyper and Bonhoeffer for constructive and compelling theologies of discipleship for public life.

4. Abraham Kuyper, "Sphere Sovereignty (1880)," in *Abraham Kuyper: A Centennial Reader*, ed. James Bratt (Grand Rapids: William B. Eerdmans, 1998), p. 464.

5. See John Wood, "Covenant Theology for a Secular Society: Abraham Kuyper's *De Leer der Verbonden* (1880) as an Experiment in Modern Theology," in *The Kuyper Center Review* 1 (2010): pp. 85ff. for further discussion of the significance of the concept of sphere sovereignty for the Free University.

main, "and each [having] its own Sovereign within its bounds."[6] God, whether acknowledged or not, was sovereign over all creation, and Christ, in whom "all things hold together" (Col. 1:15-20), was the mediator of all creation. In this way, Christology was more than soteriology. The order of creation was established before the fall, and so God's sovereignty over creation was emphasized before Christ's act of salvation.[7]

Here, explained Kuyper, "is the glorious principle of Freedom! This perfect Sovereignty of the *sinless* Messiah at the same time directly denies and challenges all absolute Sovereignty among *sinful* men on earth, and does so by dividing life into *separate spheres,* each with its own sovereignty."[8] Human life was a complex organism, made up of countless parts; Kuyper referred to these parts as "cogwheels" or " 'spheres,' each animated with its own spirit."[9] These spheres are in constant interaction, and some, like the state, hold more authority or responsibility. But no sphere could claim absolute sovereignty over others; the fact remained that Christ reigns and is ultimately sovereign over all. Scholarship, in this instance for example, was then affirmed in its own sphere, outside of absolute state or church control. The establishment of the Free University stood for Kuyper as a decisive claim for this principle of freedom.[10]

Kuyper was careful, however, to recognize and affirm the unique features of the state's sphere. The state had to acknowledge the authority that came directly from God as power to protect the other spheres. The state "gives stability to the land by justice (Prov. 29:4)"[11] and, he noted, protected those in the other spheres from internal tyranny. Indeed, "The State is the *sphere of spheres,* which encircles the whole extent of human life," and on behalf of others, "it seeks to strengthen its arm and with that outstretched arm to resist, to try to break, any sphere's drive to expand and dominate a wider domain."[12] The state ultimately guarded each sphere against the suppression of life and the limiting of freedom. What the state could not do, however, was infringe upon the unique

---

6. Kuyper, "Sphere Sovereignty," p. 467.

7. See Gordon Spykman, *Reformational Theology: A New Paradigm for Doing Dogmatics* (Grand Rapids: William B. Eerdmans, 1992), pp. 178ff.

8. Kuyper, "Sphere Sovereignty," p. 467.

9. Kuyper, "Sphere Sovereignty," p. 467.

10. See Wood, "Covenant Theology for a Secular Society," pp. 85ff., for the significance of the 1876 education law for establishing the possibility of a free university.

11. Kuyper, "Sphere Sovereignty," p. 468.

12. Kuyper, "Sphere Sovereignty," p. 472.

sovereignty inherent in each separate sphere, for God's absolute sovereignty was conferred only upon Christ, and Christ reigned supreme over all of life.

Bonhoeffer too, early in his career, began working through the responsibility and limits of the state. His explanation of state sovereignty was derived initially from the Lutheran doctrine of the two kingdoms, though the rapid rise of the Nazi regime was cause for deep reflection. Hitler had come to power early in 1933, and on April 17 the Law for Reconstitution of the Civil Service was passed, effectively barring those of Jewish descent from working in any part of the government, including the church. Bonhoeffer leveled his response to this new law in an essay, entitled "The Church and the Jewish Question."

In this essay, Bonhoeffer challenged the Lutheran understanding of the two kingdoms. Around this same time, in his lecture series *Creation and Fall,* delivered in the winter semester of 1932-33, Bonhoeffer had replaced the traditional Lutheran notion of orders of creation with the idea of orders of preservation. Since the fall, Bonhoeffer argued, humans do not have access to the primal creation and liberation except through Jesus Christ, the mediator. God's orders "have no value in and of themselves; instead they find their meaning only through Christ. God's new action with humankind is to uphold and preserve humankind in its fallen world, in its fallen orders, for death — for the resurrection, for the new creation, for Christ."[13] Bonhoeffer's Christocentric interpretation of the orders was quite deliberate. With Karl Barth, Bonhoeffer rejected any hint of natural theology that could legitimize the Nazi religious mythology and its claim of divine right through creation.[14] By demanding Christ's mediation with the orders of preservation, Bonhoeffer placed Christ's mediating sovereignty over both the realms of church and state. He worked out the implications for this order of preservation in his article, "The Church and the Jewish Question."

The beginning of this essay sounded the typical conservative Lutheran explanation of the two kingdoms: "There is no doubt that the church of the Reformation is not encouraged to get involved directly in specific political actions of the state. The church has neither to praise nor censure the laws of the state. Instead, it has to affirm the state as God's order of preservation in this godless world."[15] But it soon became clear that Bonhoeffer was after

---

13. Dietrich Bonhoeffer, *Creation and Fall,* vol. 3 of *Dietrich Bonhoeffer Works,* ed. John De Gruchy (Minneapolis: Fortress Press, 1997), p. 140.

14. See Clifford Green, *Bonhoeffer: A Theology of Sociality,* rev. ed. (Grand Rapids: William B. Eerdmans, 1999), pp. 203ff.

15. Dietrich Bonhoeffer, "The Church and the Jewish Question," in *Berlin: 1932-1933,* vol. 12 of *Dietrich Bonhoeffer Works,* ed. Larry Rasmussen (Minneapolis: Fortress Press, 2009), p. 362.

something quite new, even radical, provided by the doctrine of God's order of preservation. True, the church could not "praise nor censure" the laws of the state, but the church was called to keep asking whether the government's actions could be justified as legitimate, that is, were they "actions that create law and order, not lack of rights and disorder."[16] The church could then be called upon to question the very character of the state. If the state was failing in its responsibility to create law and order by force, the church must intervene. For Bonhoeffer, the so-called Aryan paragraph in the April 17 law effectively delegitimized the Nazi government. His discussion throughout the remainder of the essay was thus not the typical conservative Lutheran stance of separation and distance; instead, he grappled with the church's responsibility in working to re-establish the true state.

After the church questioned the state as to the legitimacy of its actions, it was next called to serve the victims of the state's misdeeds. The church, in its freedom, served the interest of a free state by "binding up the wounds" of those wronged by the state. "The church has an unconditional obligation toward the victims of any societal order, even if they do not belong to the Christian community,"[17] explained Bonhoeffer. Even the deprivation of rights of one group of citizens was enough to call the church to action. Any act of creating either too much or too little law led the state to the act of self-negation, and the church was called to intervene.

In such a case, the church had the possibility of exercising a third option, "[to] not just bind up the wounds of the victims beneath the wheel but to seize the wheel itself."[18] Bonhoeffer envisioned an "evangelical council" that would make such a decision for direct political action on the part of the church. Moreover, the call to seize the wheel itself eventually became a personal mandate through his participation in the conspiracy against Hitler. From the beginnings of Nazi power, then, Bonhoeffer had a heightened awareness of the fragile balance between the realms of church and state, and he was particularly quick to call on the church to be ready for political action against the state.[19]

---

16. Bonhoeffer, "The Church and the Jewish Question," p. 364.

17. Bonhoeffer, "The Church and the Jewish Question," p. 365.

18. Bonhoeffer, "The Church and the Jewish Question," p. 365.

19. Notably, Bonhoeffer recognized that the Nazi law which removed baptized Jews from Christian congregations placed the church in *status confessionis* — "a state of confessional protest in which such matters as church membership and rules are no longer matters of convenience and doctrinal indifference. Rather, they are matters in which the 'very truth of the gospel and Christian freedom are at stake.'" See Bonhoeffer, "The Church and the Jewish Question," p. 366, editor's footnote 14.

Now, it is clear that both Kuyper and Bonhoeffer were working in their respective theological and historical traditions to articulate the implications of God's sovereignty through the revelation of Jesus Christ. As such, there are some significant differences in each of their doctrines of revelation that should be highlighted. Kuyper's concept of sphere sovereignty was based on the Reformed doctrine of creation. The cultural mandate that he saw in Genesis 1 (to be fruitful and multiply, to have dominion, and to fill the earth) was rooted in the sovereign act of creation.[20] Jesus Christ's role in creation was as Sovereign, and so Jesus Christ ruled over the mandate to create culture. Kuyper could then affirm Christ's rule over all of the spheres of life while also encouraging the creative development of each of the various cultural spheres, from church and education to media and politics. Bonhoeffer, for his part, lived and worked in a time that was marked by the emerging abuse by some theologians of the doctrine of creation.[21] Theologians in Hitler's Germany, like Paul Althaus and Emanuel Hirsch, had corrupted the biblical notion of creation ordinances to justify and support the pagan ideology of Nazism. The concept of the creation order was wrongly used by some theologians to argue that the Aryan race in Germany was chosen to usher in the new millennium. The result of such thinking was the atrocity of the Holocaust. Dissenting theologians like Barth and Bonhoeffer saw how the doctrine of creation was being twisted by Nazi ideology and thus reacted very strongly against any idea of natural theology and creation orders.[22] The emergence of Bonhoeffer's orders of preservation was an attempt to salvage the Lutheran doctrine of creation. He argued — from a Christ-centered redemptive framework — that creation orders and mandates were to be understood as a means of God's preserving work, which occurred distinctly through redemption and reconciliation in Jesus Christ. For Bonhoeffer, creation was Christological in its connection to redemption; for Kuyper, Christ was Sovereign first and foremost in creation. These were, to be sure, significant theological differences and should not be glossed over in comparisons between Kuyper and Bonhoeffer.

However, while recognizing the importance of these doctrinal and historical differences, it is important to note that both Kuyper and Bonhoeffer came independently to a similar conclusion about the implication of God's

---

20. See Richard Mouw, *Abraham Kuyper: A Short and Personal Introduction* (Grand Rapids: William B. Eerdmans, 2011), pp. 6-7.

21. See Spykman, *Reformational Theology,* pp. 179-80.

22. See, for example, Emil Brunner and Karl Barth, *Natural Theology: Comprising "Nature and Grace" by Emil Brunner and the Reply "No!" by Karl Barth* (Eugene, Ore.: Wipf and Stock, 2002).

sovereignty: while the state is a vital sphere of God's order, God, through Jesus Christ, is definitively sovereign over all. In Kuyper's booming words, "no single piece of our mental world is to be hermetically sealed off from the rest, and there is not a square inch in the whole domain of our human existence over which Christ, who is Sovereign over *all*, does not cry: 'Mine!' "[23] For Kuyper, this meant that the sphere of scholarship was free to flourish apart from state or ecclesial control. For Bonhoeffer, this meant that the individual and the Christian community had a mandate to respect and hold the state to its responsibility. For both, this meant that Christians were called upon to participate in the very public realm of social engagement and political critique. This public theology does not end here, however. "Sphere Sovereignty" and "The Church and the Jewish Question" lead to much greater theological and practical implications.

Discipleship in and for the World:
Common Grace and Reality in Jesus Christ

Kuyper's concept of common grace emerged naturally and immediately out of the idea of sphere sovereignty. Kuyper spent six years developing and bringing a high degree of nuanced argument to the doctrine of common grace in the pages of his weekly periodical, *De Heraut,* and he published the compiled constructions in book form as *De Gemeene Gratie* in three volumes in 1902, 1903, and 1904. Despite the cries from his conservative opponents that he was inventing a new teaching, Kuyper insisted he was only expanding and systematizing "what earlier Reformed theologians have left as hints and pieces."[24] Additionally, the development of Kuyper's theology of common grace played a practical purpose. At its core, common grace enabled a very public theology, reaching out to the larger society and culture, and so was an excellent political tool. Kuyper completed the series on common grace at the height of his political career: his election as prime minister to the Netherlands.[25]

Kuyper developed the significance of common grace in light of the fall of human history described in the first chapters of Genesis. Before *and* after the fall, he explained, grace abounds: "To every rational creature, grace is the

23. Kuyper, "Sphere Sovereignty," p. 488.
24. James Bratt, "Editor's Introduction to 'Common Grace,'" in *Abraham Kuyper: A Centennial Reader,* ed. James Bratt (Grand Rapids: William B. Eerdmans, 1998), p. 165.
25. See Bratt, "Editor's Introduction to 'Common Grace,'" p. 165.

air he breathes."[26] Yet, since the fall, death, in its full effect, had not set in. Thus, he observed, "Reformed theologians have consistently pointed out how in this non-arrival of what was prophesied for ill we see the emergence of a saving and long-suffering grace."[27] God, solely in his sovereignty and majesty, extended this grace through restraining, blocking, or redirecting the consequences of sin. This grace was both saving and restraining, and distinguished itself in two manifestations. First, there was a *saving* grace, "which in the end abolishes sin and completely undoes its consequences." Second, there was a *temporal restraining* grace, "which holds back and blocks the effect of sin" in the wider world. These manifestations of God's grace flow from his sovereignty and election: "The former," explained Kuyper, "that is saving grace, is in the nature of the case *special* and restricted to God's elect. The second, that is *common* grace, is extended to the whole of our human life."[28] It was this second expression of God's grace, common grace, that had such a profound impact on public theology, for without common grace history could not have developed for God's purposes.

The connection between God's saving, special grace and restraining, common grace was of vital importance. Had the full effects of sin set in at the fall of Adam and Eve, contended Kuyper, Seth would not have been born, and thus humanity and society would not have been established and developed. Further, had hell been released on earth at the time of the fall, the church simply could not have existed; "it would be massacred in less than no time."[29] Without common grace, special grace simply could not function. But Kuyper was also clear that common grace did not simply exist solely for the salvation of the elect. With such an assumption, "people focus more on *their own salvation* instead of on the *glory of God*."[30]

In reality, it was for God's glory when societies developed, creative arts flourished, and science magnified God's truth. As a result, there was in common grace a call to Christian action in political and cultural affairs. Since, Kuyper explained, there was grace operating outside the church, and grace even where it did not lead to eternal salvation, one was duty bound to honor the operation of divine grace in civic life.[31] Here, then, lay the heart of Kuyper's

26. Abraham Kuyper, "Common Grace (1902-1904)," in *Abraham Kuyper: A Centennial Reader,* ed. James Bratt (Grand Rapids: William B. Eerdmans, 1998), p. 167.

27. Kuyper, "Common Grace," p. 167.

28. Kuyper, "Common Grace," p. 168.

29. Kuyper, "Common Grace," p. 169.

30. Kuyper, "Common Grace," p. 169.

31. See Nicholas Wolterstorff, "Abraham Kuyper (1873-1920): Commentary," in *The*

theological basis for engagement in education, politics, and public debate. God was glorified in the quest for truth in the academic halls, in the building of civic society, and in the free and open communication of ideas. To focus all one's attention in the church was not only short-sighted, it denied the existence of God's grace beyond the walls of the church.[32]

The church, therefore, held a special and unique place in the manifestation of God's glory and grace. The church remained true to itself by recognizing and living by special grace in distinction from common grace. The lamp of the Christian religion that burned within the walls of the church "shines out through its windows to areas far beyond, illuminating all the sectors and associations that appear across the wide range of human life and activity." As Kuyper argued in more detail,

> Justice, law, the home and family, business, vocation, public opinion and literature, art and science, and so much more are illuminated by that light, and that illumination will be stronger and more penetrating as the lamp of the gospel is allowed to shine more brightly and clearly in the church institute.[33]

A strong confessional church, therefore, did not and could not make for a confessional state. Rather than co-opt, the church aimed to influence. The Christian character of society was only gained as the light of the gospel shone through the church into all segments of society. Common grace allowed Kuyper the confidence not only to engage directly with all aspects of modern society, but also to affirm its pluriform existence.

As such, it was Kuyper's broad Christological understanding that enabled his deliberate theology of public engagement. Contrary to those who would focus on their own salvation before the glory of God, Kuyper denied that Christ was exclusively the expiator of sin: "No: Christ, by whom all things exist including ourselves, is before all things."[34] The *savior* of the world, he emphasized, was first the *creator* of the world. This creator was also the re-creator, by the mediation of the Son through the Spirit, and would continue to bestow grace upon history until the world reached its consummation and fulfillment. Common grace emphasized what special grace simply could not:

Teachings of Modern Protestantism on Law, Politics, and Human Nature, ed. John Witte Jr. and Frank S. Alexander (New York: Columbia University Press, 2007), p. 53.

32. See Wolterstorff, "Abraham Kuyper," p. 53.

33. See Wolterstorff, "Abraham Kuyper," p. 54 for these particular quotes from Kuyper in *Common Grace*.

34. Kuyper, "Common Grace," p. 170.

God worked in every fiber of history for his glory. Special election was a vital aspect of God's plan, but God also elected to be glorified through the manifold manifestation of his grace in all of cosmic history.

Interestingly, Bonhoeffer took up many of these same themes in two of his later writings, *Ethics* and *Letters and Papers from Prison*. Although he did not write in the same Kuyperian or Reformed terms, he was very much interested in explicating the issues at the heart of Kuyper's notion of common grace. In *Ethics,* Bonhoeffer affirmed the sovereignty of God in the revelation of Jesus Christ with his understanding of the nature of reality. Christ's presence for the world, as described in *Ethics,* in turn made possible a kind of "common grace" that was explored in his theological reflections from Tegel prison.

Ethics remains Bonhoeffer's great unfinished work. His working manuscripts were left mid-thought on his desk when he was arrested on April 5, 1943, by the Nazi military legal branch with the help of the Gestapo. In the manuscript "Christ, Reality, and Good," Bonhoeffer continued the work that he had begun ten years earlier in "The Church and the Jewish Question": to redefine a notion of reality that was over and against the traditional Lutheran doctrine of the two kingdoms. He pointedly described the fallacy of the contemporary understanding of Luther's sacred and secular realms:

> This division of the whole reality into sacred and profane, or Christian and worldly, sectors creates the possibility of existence in only one of these sectors: for instance a spiritual existence that takes no part in a worldly existence, and a worldly existence that can make good its claim to autonomy over against the sacred sector.[35]

Such a bifurcated understanding of reality was detrimental to the call and possibility of Christian engagement with the world. What is more, the division of life into these conflicting realms signaled a forfeited view of reality. Bonhoeffer commented that we have given up on reality when we place ourselves in one of the two realms, "wanting Christ without the world or the world without Christ." Or, worse yet, we try and stand in the two realms at the same time, "thereby becoming people in eternal conflict."[36]

These views, however, bypassed both biblical and Reformation Christian thought. With images reminiscent of those employed by Kuyper, Bonhoeffer explained that the whole reality of the world has already been drawn into and

---

35. Dietrich Bonhoeffer, *Ethics*, vol. 6 of *Dietrich Bonhoeffer Works*, ed. Clifford Green (Minneapolis: Fortress Press, 2005), p. 57.

36. Bonhoeffer, *Ethics*, p. 58.

is held together in Christ. The theme of two realms was foreign to the biblical concern for "the realization of the Christ-reality in the contemporary world." This was a reality that embraced and inhabited the entirety of the world. Indeed, "history moves only from this center and towards this center."[37] There were thus not two realities, the sacred and the secular, "but *only one reality, and that is God's reality revealed in Christ in the reality of the world.*"[38] Reality existed only in and through Jesus Christ, and it was from this center of all reality that Bonhoeffer was equipped to engage fully in and for the world.

In *Letters and Papers from Prison*, Bonhoeffer offered compelling theological implications for this radically Christocentric understanding of reality. Like Kuyper, he was convinced of the serious call for direct Christian engagement with society. In a May 29, 1944, letter to Eberhard Bethge, Bonhoeffer lamented how traditional religious thought had reduced God to a stopgap measure. Rather than allowing God to be pushed ever further into retreat every time science offered a new explanation of the natural world, "we should find God in what we know, not in what we don't know."[39] There was no need to fear the discoveries of science or the cultural expressions of society; God did not forfeit sovereignty when scientific knowledge could replace faith. "God wants to be grasped by us not in unsolved questions but in those that have been solved," including "the universal questions about death, suffering, and guilt."[40] Echoing his conclusions from *Ethics*, Bonhoeffer explained that the ground for this "lies in the revelation of God in Jesus Christ. God is the center of life and doesn't just 'turn up' when we have unsolved problems to be solved."[41] God was present in the very midst of all of life, and in this way, God's revelation in Jesus Christ affected much more than our personal salvation.

Bonhoeffer took up this matter in a May 5, 1944, letter to Bethge. Here, Bonhoeffer began to explicate his emerging concept of "religionless" Christianity. The danger of thinking religiously, as in a religious realm and a secular realm, was that concepts were limited to either the metaphysical or the individualistic. When Christ was only the Lord of the sacred and not at the center of the entire world, his work in the world was merely a matter of personal

---

37. Bonhoeffer, *Ethics*, p. 58. See also Bonhoeffer's development of this concept in the Christology lectures of 1933 in *Berlin: 1932-1933*, vol. 12 of *Dietrich Bonhoeffer Works*, pp. 299-360.

38. Bonhoeffer, *Ethics*, p. 58.

39. Bonhoeffer, *Letters and Papers from Prison*, vol. 8 of *Dietrich Bonhoeffer Works*, ed. John De Gruchy (Minneapolis: Fortress Press, 2009), p. 406.

40. Bonhoeffer, *Letters and Papers from Prison*, p. 406.

41. Bonhoeffer, *Letters and Papers from Prison*, p. 406.

salvation. But Bonhoeffer recognized the practical and biblical limits of such a perception. As he wrote, "Hasn't the individualistic question of saving our personal souls almost faded away for most of us? Isn't it our impression that there are really more important things than this question (— perhaps not more important than this *matter,* but certainly more important than the *question!?*)?"[42] Bonhoeffer was convinced that the question of saving one's soul was not by any means the central concern of the biblical message. Rather, the Bible seemed to proclaim constantly God's righteousness and coming kingdom on earth. "What matters," he continued, "is not the beyond but this world, how it is created and preserved"; and "what is beyond this world is meant, in the gospel, to be there *for* this world — not in the anthropomorphic sense [. . .] but in the biblical sense of the creation and the incarnation, crucifixion, and resurrection of Jesus Christ."[43] To be there *for* this world was a central concern of Bonhoeffer's theology, and it was grounded in the place of Jesus Christ as the center of all reality.

Kuyper and Bonhoeffer both staked their claims for direct engagement with the world on the cosmic centrality of Jesus Christ. To be sure, however, there were important and significant theological differences in how they understood this reality. For Kuyper, the common grace that resulted from God's sovereignty bore witness to the work of Jesus Christ in all aspects of human life and endeavor. But Kuyper was careful to distinguish between the particular, saving grace of salvation and the temporal, restraining grace that was common to all. Bonhoeffer, on the other hand, would not have used Kuyper's language of "common" and "special" grace because he was intent on emphasizing the one reality of Jesus Christ. There were not different manifestations of God's grace for Bonhoeffer. To combat the traditional Lutheran two-kingdoms view, Bonhoeffer stressed that Jesus Christ alone was the center of all reality, and he spoke of God's grace in terms of this one reality of Jesus Christ. So, while Bonhoeffer's Christological understanding of reality certainly resonates with the Kuyperian view, his understanding is a distinct critique and re-orientation of a traditional Lutheran doctrine; it is a distinction that is quite unique in its own way apart from the Reformed tradition.

Despite these theological differences, it does remain that both Kuyper and Bonhoeffer worked from a Christ-centered view of reality to correct the short-sightedness that fixation on personal salvation can breed. Kuyper, looking to the biblical record, illustrated how common grace must precede special grace,

42. Bonhoeffer, *Letters and Papers from Prison,* p. 372.
43. Bonhoeffer, *Letters and Papers from Prison,* p. 373.

concluding that God's purposes are much bigger than individual salvation. God is concerned with God's glory, and will usher in glory through the consummation of all history in Jesus Christ. Similarly, Bonhoeffer argued that there were much more important questions than personal salvation. Because Christ is ultimately for the world, the church must bear witness to the reality of Jesus Christ to all areas of human life. Kuyper's image of the lamp of the gospel shining through the windows of the church out into the world could be an appropriate symbol for Bonhoeffer's thought as well. As Bonhoeffer wrote in *Discipleship,* the church holds the pearl of great mystery, but shines its light as a city on a hill.[44]

Possibilities for Christian Influence: Worldview and Divine Mandates

The implications for Kuyper's concepts of sphere sovereignty and common grace are perhaps most clearly seen in his *Lectures on Calvinism.* Delivered at the annual Stone Lectures at Princeton Seminary in October 1898, the *Lectures* represent one of the most systematic and complete applications of Kuyper's constructive theology. Here, he presented Calvinism as an all-encompassing worldview and demonstrated its superior insights into topics as varied as religion, politics, science, art, and the future. His opening lecture, "Calvinism a Life-system," provided a framework for the rest of the series and is especially useful for approaching his understanding of the ordering of society.

Kuyper began his first lecture with a lively comparison of the two competing worldviews of the time: modernism and Calvinism. The two life systems, he explained, "are wrestling with one another, in mortal combat."[45] On the one hand, modernism sought to build a world that was solely oriented from and toward the natural human. On the other hand, Calvinism worked from and toward the glory of God, and advocated for the continuation of a Christian heritage. Each life system was based on a set of core principles which had far-reaching effects, touching all aspects of life and society, and was therefore fundamentally opposed to the other.

Modernism operated from the principles of atheism and individualism found in the French Revolution, the pantheism of German philosophy, and

---

44. See Dietrich Bonhoeffer, *Discipleship,* vol. 4 of *Dietrich Bonhoeffer Works,* ed. Geffrey Kelly and John Godsey (Minneapolis: Fortress Press, 2001), pp. 110-14 ("The Visible Church-Community") and pp. 146-52 ("Matthew 6: On the Hidden Nature of the Christian Life").

45. Abraham Kuyper, *Lectures on Calvinism* (New York: Cosimo, 2007), p. 11.

Darwinian evolution. The rampant unbelief advanced by the Revolution was seen as a particular threat that Kuyper consistently battled throughout his career.[46] Although Kuyper allowed that God may have used the Revolution to destroy the tyranny of the Bourbons, he contended that its goal of eliminating God from the church, state, society, and science left nothing but self-seeking individuals whose only concern was their personal independence.[47] Despite any advantages to Western civilization brought about by the Revolution, Kuyper abhorred the accompanying and dramatic shift in society from a God-centered to a human-centered worldview. This flood of humanism soon swept into Germany, where it took the form of pantheism. For Kuyper, pantheism represented the trend towards a modern Paganism that found its concrete expression in Darwin's theory of evolution. Pantheism identified God with human progress and thus removed the distinction between God and the world.[48] Calvinism was Kuyper's response to this fatal worldview.

Kuyper took great efforts in his opening lecture to define Calvinism by first explaining how it was a scientific movement, and not merely an ecclesiastical or dogmatic movement. In his historical context, the term "Calvinism" held three distinct connotations — none of which adequately revealed its scientific definition. First, Calvinism could not merely refer to those constantly stigmatized "Calvinists" who bore the derision of the majority press in official Roman Catholic countries like Hungary and France. Second, Calvinism was not just a confessional label for the outspoken subscriber to the dogma of fore-ordination. The Calvinist, third, was not solely one who affixed the name to a denomination or church (as some Baptists and Methodists were doing). Instead, Calvinism must be understood in the *scientific* sense — of history, philosophy, and politics. As he explained:

> Historically, the name of Calvinism indicates the channel in which the Reformation moved, so far as it was neither Lutheran, nor Anabaptist, nor Socinian. In the philosophical sense, we understand by it that system of conceptions which, under the influence of the master-mind of Calvin, raised itself to dominance in the several spheres of life. And as a political name, Calvinism indicates that political movement which has guaranteed

46. Kuyper was so opposed to these principles, particularly the atheism of the French Revolution, that he named his political party the Anti-Revolutionary Party.

47. See Peter Heslam, *Creating a Christian Worldview: Abraham Kuyper's Lectures on Calvinism* (Grand Rapids: William B. Eerdmans, 1998), p. 98.

48. See Heslam, *Creating a Christian Worldview,* pp. 101ff.

the liberty of nations in constitutional statesmanship; first in Holland, then in England, and since the close of the last century in the United States.[49]

Kuyper leaned on this scientific understanding of Calvinism to formulate his ideas of a life system that could combat the false notions of modernism. This highest form of Christian understanding, claimed Kuyper, was the most effective bulwark for an all-encompassing challenge to the prevailing modernistic worldview.[50]

The Calvinistic worldview redefined our fundamental relation to God, to humankind, and to the world. The re-orienting of these relationships in light of the scientific principles of Calvinism fundamentally altered how the Christian understood the ordering of society. For our relation to God, Calvinism offered an immediate fellowship of humans with the divine, apart from the mediation of priest or church. For the relation to our fellow humans, Calvinism affirmed the equality of all in God's creation and recognized the inherent value and worth of each individual. And for our relation to the world, Kuyper returned to the notion of common grace, recognizing that the curse upon the world was under restraint, and thus we must "discover the treasures and develop the potencies hidden by God in nature and in life."[51] For Kuyper, then, all of life was affirmed and must be scoured and engaged with the application of these fundamentally Christian principles. With this commitment, Kuyper constructed a Calvinistic theology of religion, politics, science, art, and the future in his five remaining Stone Lectures. Since space does not permit in-depth treatment of his thoughts on each of these issues, a short summary of his understanding of the arts will provide a compelling hint that indeed Kuyper largely succeeded in creating a comprehensive Christian worldview in which God was sovereign over all, and Jesus Christ's claim of lordship over all was realized.

Kuyper's fifth lecture on Calvinism focused on the arts, and here the full creativity of the concepts of sphere sovereignty and common grace came into

49. Kuyper, *Lectures on Calvinism*, p. 14.

50. Interestingly, Kuyper looks to the inherent structures of modernism as a model for the construction of his Calvinistic worldview. Although the contents of Calvinism are antithetical to modern secularism, Peter Heslam notes that their forms bear a strong resemblance: Like modernism, "[Calvinism] was to be derived from a single unifying principle [the sovereignty of God]; it was to provide answers to the same fundamental questions of human existence; and it was to be comprehensive and internally consistent." See Heslam, *Creating a Christian Worldview*, p. 111.

51. Kuyper, *Lectures on Calvinism*, p. 31.

view. Kuyper, though not an artist himself, nevertheless teased out the Calvinistic implications for painting, architecture, music, poetry, and drama. He did not advocate art for art's sake, but argued instead:

> When I plead the significance of Calvinism in the domain of art, I am not in the least induced to do so by the vulgarization of art, but rather keep my eyes fixed upon the Beautiful and the Sublime in its eternal significance, and upon art as one of the richest gifts of God to mankind.[52]

Art was one of the clearest manifestations of God's work of common grace in the world. As such, Kuyper lamented the artistic poverty of the Calvinist tradition. In the realm of architecture, he thought that Calvinism ought to have boasted the fullness of its ideal in a structure equal to that of the Parthenon in Athens, the Saint Sophia at Byzantium, or Saint Peter's at the Vatican. Historically, explained Kuyper, Calvinism did not develop an artistic style of its own because art was thought to represent a lower level of religious life and expression. Ultimately, however, Calvinism offered a new base of interpretation, and now it could encourage the progress and principle of artistic development. Such a move toward the religious affirmation of the arts was a rarity at the time. Kuyper's discussion was a challenge to the prevailing prejudice against the arts, and his appeal to discovering the beauty of the Creator in art displayed the potential for the Calvinistic worldview to permeate the vast and unique contours of culture and society.

While Kuyper's *Lectures on Calvinism* offered a compelling application of his concepts of sphere sovereignty and common grace, Bonhoeffer aimed to work out some of the implications of his Christological understanding of reality with a structure of divine mandates. Bonhoeffer's *Ethics* contains the manuscript "The Concrete Commandment and the Divine Mandates." Here, Bonhoeffer offered an alternative to the prevailing pseudo-Lutheran doctrines that seemed to legitimize Nazi ideology: the orders of creation, the three estates, and the two kingdoms.[53] His goal was to revise and reclaim these ideas with the doctrine of divine mandates, which "depend solely on God's *one* commandment as it is revealed in Jesus Christ."[54] Although the text remained incomplete due to arrest and imprisonment, Bonhoeffer nevertheless presented his understanding of a Christian ordering of society that took seriously the ultimate reality of Jesus Christ.

52. Kuyper, *Lectures on Calvinism*, p. 143.
53. See Clifford Green, "Editor's Introduction," in Bonhoeffer, *Ethics*, pp. 18-20.
54. Bonhoeffer, *Ethics*, p. 390.

Bonhoeffer approached the concept of social order with four divine mandates: church, state, marriage and family, and culture (also called "work" in some writings). These mandates were key social structures and were given from above, and yet they did not encompass the entirety of human life (friendship, for example, was not a mandate, but was in a realm of freedom).[55] These four divine mandates gave structure and boundaries to human existence, and were regulated by the commandment of God in Jesus Christ. Bonhoeffer would have agreed with Kuyper that society was not a collection of freewheeling individualists. Instead, it found its form as mandates that were with-one-another, for-one-another, and over-against-one-another.

The commandment of God revealed in Jesus Christ found concrete expression in the divine mandates. This commandment was all-encompassing, and embraced the entirety of the world through and in Jesus Christ. However, God's commandment was not found everywhere — it was not in theoretical speculation, private enlightenment, historical forces, or compelling ideas — but only where God had authorized it.[56] The divine mandates of marriage and family, culture, church, and state were concrete commissions of God's revelation in Jesus Christ and Scripture. These institutions did not gain their authority from the primacy of creation, but were conferred authority by divine command. It was for this particular reason that Bonhoeffer preferred the term "mandates" to that of "orders" — a mandate avoided the inherent danger of "focusing more strongly on the static element of order rather than on the divine authorizing, legitimizing, and sanctioning, which are its sole foundation."[57]

The four mandates were implanted from above as organizing structures of the reality of Christ. They were not an outgrowth of history, or an expression of human power, but expressed "the reality of God's love for the world and for human beings that has been revealed in Jesus Christ."[58] Regardless of the particular historical circumstance of a church, family, or government, God had commissioned these ordering structures, and the bearers of these mandates were God's representatives. In this sense, God's commandment recognized the influence of those below, and so the mandates required earthly relationships and organizing structures. But Bonhoeffer was clear: "Even a master has a Master. [. . .] Master and servant owe one another the respect that springs from their respective participation in God's mandate."[59]

55. See Green, "Editor's Introduction," in Bonhoeffer, *Ethics*, p. 18.
56. See Bonhoeffer, *Ethics*, p. 388.
57. Bonhoeffer, *Ethics*, p. 389.
58. Bonhoeffer, *Ethics*, p. 390.
59. Bonhoeffer, *Ethics*, p. 391.

This respect came solely in their being with-one-another, for-one-another, and over-against-one-another. Only in these ways, Bonhoeffer explained, "do the mandates of church, marriage and family, culture, and government communicate the commandment of God as it is revealed in Jesus Christ."[60] For Bonhoeffer, the four mandates must be with, for, and over-against-one-another because they existed in the reality of Jesus Christ — the one who was ultimately with, for, and over-against the world. It becomes clear now how Bonhoeffer's Christocentric theology informed his concept of the mandates. Jesus Christ, as the revelation of God, was the ultimate man-for-others. His life, death, resurrection, and ascension bore witness to his mission of being-for-others, and this defined reality. As God commissioned the structures of society, they were ordered around the for-others reality. The mandates each had their own boundaries and limits, and they only existed in actuality when they appropriately engaged and interacted. A mandate was not self-sufficient; neither could one claim to replace the others, or exist in isolation or separation. Further, in being-with and for-others, the mandates were also limited by the others, by being-over-against-one-another. This three-fold interaction both safeguarded and limited a divine mandate. In this place, a mandate was set free to fulfill its own law; "that is the law inherent in it from its origin, essence, and goal in Jesus Christ."[61]

The crux of Bonhoeffer's theological ethics came together here, when he introduced the concept of Christonomy. Although this particular term appears only once in *Ethics,* it encompassed his Christocentric understanding of reality and provided the basis for the concrete expression of God's commandment in the divine mandates. With Christonomy, Bonhoeffer navigated the complex waters of autonomous existence and individualistic societal structures, explaining that the commandment of Jesus Christ set each of the mandates free to exercise their respective functions. Speaking of the mandate of the church, he explained, "Jesus Christ's claim to rule as it is proclaimed by the church simultaneously means that family, culture, and government are set free to be what they are in their own nature as grounded in Christ." At this point, he inserted a footnote: "Here the antagonism between heteronomy and autonomy is overcome and taken into a higher unity, which we could call Christonomy." He then continued: "Only through this liberation, which springs from the proclaimed rule of Christ, can the divine mandates be properly with-one-

60. Bonhoeffer, *Ethics*, p. 393.
61. Bonhoeffer, *Ethics*, p. 402.

another, for-one-another, and against-one-another[.]"[62] This footnoted concept of Christonomy provided Bonhoeffer with a key hermeneutic.

Christonomy, at its base, was a way to overcome the conflicting pressures of autonomy and heteronomy. An autonomous view of reality, as Kuyper would also have contended with, found its triumph as each individual acted on his or her own free will. On the other hand, heteronomy understood that actions were based upon external forces and obligations, like a principled Christian ethic. Neither of these worldviews was, for Bonhoeffer, an accurate interpretation of reality. Rather, reality was in Jesus Christ, and so individuals and societies were finally liberated and free to be with-one-another, for-one-another, and over-against-one-another. The divine mandates existed to manifest this reality of freedom.

Ulrich Nissen provides helpful commentary here. He reminds us that throughout *Ethics* Bonhoeffer was critical of any attempt to establish a moral reality apart from the will of God. Indeed, ethics for Bonhoeffer *is* following the will of God.[63] Any attempt to follow a strictly autonomous will denied the actual reality of life in Jesus Christ. Yet an equal danger occurred when the "profane" was ignored in favor of a limited Christian ethic; principles in and of themselves could not communicate the will of God. Bonhoeffer's notion of Christonomy as the source of ethics was "an attempt to move beyond both an 'autonomous' ethic and a specific 'Christian' ethic,"[64] toward a higher unity in Jesus Christ.

Freedom, which had its source outside of the autonomous self and was not found in some specific Christian principle, was being in accordance with the will of God. Christonomy was a way to understand that the basic reality of Jesus Christ was in fact what moved and motivated Christian ethical actions. It affirmed that, just as Christ exists-for-others, the divine mandates operated in their potential when they existed with- and for-one-another. Christonomy was then not just a personal ethical principle, but was a vision for God's ordering of society. There was freedom and liberation for the church when it existed with, for, and over-against the state. Likewise, the state flourished when it could support culture, be in culture, and yet receive and incorporate culture's critique. All four mandates — church, state, family, and culture — and thus the major structures of society, reached their full

---

62. Bonhoeffer, *Ethics*, p. 402.
63. Bonhoeffer, *Ethics*, p. 47.
64. Ulrich Nissen, "Disbelief and Christonomy of the World," *Studia Theologica* 60 (2006): 95.

potential when they operated in the reality of Jesus Christ, who was with, for, and over-against the world.

Both Kuyper and Bonhoeffer recognized a positive potential for the structure and ordering of society based on Christian convictions. Kuyper, with his *Lectures on Calvinism,* drew on the implications of sphere sovereignty and common grace in Reformed thought to offer a Christian worldview that was radically in and for the world. Likewise, Bonhoeffer came to the concept of Christonomy in order to communicate the freedom that existed in a society that lived into the reality of Jesus Christ. Both Kuyper and Bonhoeffer realized that the individualistic autonomy inherent in modernism, while promoting certain forms of freedom, in actuality only isolated and constrained. God's sovereignty and reign in Jesus Christ alone offered true liberation. This reality and mode of interaction within and between the various spheres of life set the Christian, and society as a whole, free to experience the fullness of God's grace.

It must also be noted that, for all of these similarities, Kuyper and Bonhoeffer did make significantly different practical choices in their lives — choices that were, at least to some extent, the result of the key differences in their theology and in their historical contexts. For example, Kuyper's Calvinism equipped him not only for life as a Christian minister, but also was the driving force in his involvement in politics, education, and news media. Bonhoeffer, on the other hand, struggled in his defined role as a theologian and pastor to enact effective resistance against the Nazi state. In many ways, his Lutheran heritage proved a liability because, practically speaking, the church relied on the state for its legitimate existence. Interestingly, it was only when Bonhoeffer finally released himself from participation as a pastor in the Confessing Church that he felt able to join the conspiracy to overthrow Hitler. While Bonhoeffer worked to explicate theologically the relationship between the church and the state in new and Christ-centered ways, the Lutheran church remained too wedded to its German national identity for Bonhoeffer's theology to spark widespread resistance against the Nazi regime. In some ways, like the Barmen Declaration (penned largely by the Reformed theologian Karl Barth), the Reformed church could speak much more directly than the Lutheran church to Nazi Germany about the Lordship of Jesus Christ. It may well have been these Reformed cues that helped Bonhoeffer articulate (but not simply repeat) an emerging theology of the reality of Christ's sovereignty. Bonhoeffer's theology, in turn, would have challenged Kuyper to keep Christ's cross at the center of the notion of sovereignty. Christ is indeed Sovereign over creation, but the character of Christ's sovereignty is in how he is with, for, and over-against the world.[65]

Conclusion: Distinct Discipleship

Kuyper and Bonhoeffer provide hope for a way forward in Christian public discourse, which is one of the most pressing issues in our democracy today. Based on their similar, though not dogmatically identical, Christological foundations, both offer a profound mediating perspective. The polar extremes of either releasing the world to modernistic autonomy or Christian-principled flight from the world need not be the only options. Instead, there is hope for the world because of God's very presence and grace in the world through Jesus Christ. Kuyper's Christology, which reaches its height in sphere sovereignty and common (and particular) grace, affirms the continuing work of God in all areas of human life and recognizes the inherent beauty and potential of God's good creation. Bonhoeffer's Christology identifies Jesus Christ as the central defining factor of reality, and thus the affirmation of humanity. There is a common foundation for human life because all of humanity comes to itself in Christ and is affirmed in the reconciliation of Christ.[66] In the broadest sense, Kuyper and Bonhoeffer both recognize that God is reconciling all things to himself through Jesus Christ (Col. 1:15-20), and so they seek to affirm structures and orders in society that mediate this reality. Kuyper's spheres and Bonhoeffer's mandates, while different theological concepts, both speak to God's work and grace in all areas of human life. They offer the call of Christian discipleship to each unique sector of human endeavor, and they provide creative, productive, and promising possibilities for Christian influence and witness that is in and for the world.

Bibliography

Bonhoeffer, Dietrich. *Creation and Fall*. Vol. 3 of *Dietrich Bonhoeffer Works,* English edition. Edited by John De Gruchy. Minneapolis: Fortress Press, 1997.

65. Repentance and the decision to enter into another's place of suffering is a particular aspect of Bonhoeffer's theology of the cross that could provide a balance to Kuyper's emphasis on creation. Glen Stassen provides an important treatment of Bonhoeffer's understanding of the cross as "incarnational representation" in *A Thicker Jesus: Incarnational Discipleship in a Secular Age* (Louisville: Westminster John Knox, 2012), pp. 150-53.
66. See Nissen, "Disbelief and Christonomy of the World," p. 103.

————. *Discipleship.* Vol. 4 of *Dietrich Bonhoeffer Works,* English edition. Edited by Geffrey Kelly and John Godsey. Minneapolis: Fortress Press, 2001.

————. *Ethics.* Vol. 6 of *Dietrich Bonhoeffer Works,* English edition. Edited by Clifford Green. Minneapolis: Fortress Press, 2005.

————. *Letters and Papers from Prison.* Vol. 8 of *Dietrich Bonhoeffer Works,* English edition. Edited by John De Gruchy. Minneapolis: Fortress Press, 2009.

————. "The Church and the Jewish Question." In *Berlin: 1932-1933.* Vol. 12 of *Dietrich Bonhoeffer Works,* English edition. Edited by Larry Rasmussen, 361-70. Minneapolis: Fortress Press, 2009.

Bratt, James. "Editor's Introduction to 'Common Grace.'" In *Abraham Kuyper: A Centennial Reader.* Edited by James Bratt, 165-66. Grand Rapids: William B. Eerdmans, 1998.

Brunner, Emil, and Karl Barth. *Natural Theology: Comprising "Nature and Grace" by Emil Brunner and the Reply "No!" by Karl Barth.* Eugene, Ore.: Wipf and Stock, 2002.

De Gruchy, John. *Bonhoeffer and South Africa: Theology in Dialogue.* Grand Rapids: William B. Eerdmans, 1984.

Green, Clifford. *Bonhoeffer: A Theology of Sociality.* Revised edition. Grand Rapids: William B. Eerdmans, 1999.

————. "Editor's Introduction." In *Ethics.* Vol. 6 of *Dietrich Bonhoeffer Works,* English edition. Edited by Clifford Green, 1-44. Minneapolis: Fortress Press, 2005.

Harinck, George, and Gerard Dekker. "The Position of the Church Institute in Society: A Comparison Between Bonhoeffer and Kuyper." *The Princeton Seminary Bulletin* 28, no. 1 (2007): 86-98.

Heslam, Peter. *Creating a Christian Worldview: Abraham Kuyper's Lectures on Calvinism.* Grand Rapids: William B. Eerdmans, 1998.

Huntemann, Georg. *The Other Bonhoeffer: An Evangelical Reassessment of Dietrich Bonhoeffer.* Grand Rapids: Baker Books, 1993.

Kuyper, Abraham. "Common Grace (1902-1904)." In *Abraham Kuyper: A Centennial Reader.* Edited by James Bratt, 165-201. Grand Rapids: William B. Eerdmans, 1998.

Kuyper, Abraham. "Sphere Sovereignty (1880)." In *Abraham Kuyper: A Centennial Reader.* Edited by James Bratt, 461-90. Grand Rapids: William B. Eerdmans, 1998.

————. *Lectures on Calvinism.* New York: Cosimo, 2007.

Mouw, Richard. *Abraham Kuyper: A Short and Personal Introduction.* Grand Rapids: William B. Eerdmans, 2011.

Nissen, Ulrich. "Disbelief and Christonomy of the World." *Studia Theologica* 60 (2006): 91-110.

Spykman, Gordon. *Reformational Theology: A New Paradigm for Doing Dogmatics.* Grand Rapids: William B. Eerdmans, 1992.

Stassen, Glen. *A Thicker Jesus: Incarnational Discipleship in a Secular Age.* Louisville: Westminster John Knox, 2012.

Wolterstorff, Nicholas. "Abraham Kuyper (1873-1920): Commentary." In *The Teachings of Modern Protestantism on Law, Politics, and Human Nature.* Edited by John Witte Jr. and Frank Alexander, 29-69. New York: Columbia University Press, 2007.

Wood, John. "Covenant Theology for a Secular Society: Abraham Kuyper's *De Leer der Verbonden* (1880) as an Experiment in Modern Theology." In *The Kuyper Center Review* 1 (2010): 83-92.

Abraham Kuyper between Parsonage and Parliament

Harry Van Dyke

The following extract is taken from the correspondence between Willem Groen van Prinsterer (1801-76) and his disciple Abraham Kuyper. It dates from the winter months of 1874 and lets us in on the difficulty that the thirty-six-year-old Kuyper seems to have had in deciding whether he should accept the seat in Parliament to which he had been elected. At the same time it reveals how Groen, the seventy-two-year-old informal leader of the Antirevolutionary Party, quietly encouraged him to accept.[1]

The electoral debacle of 1871 was still fresh in people's minds. Late in the campaign Groen had definitively broken with his aristocratic, conservative friends by suddenly recommending only three candidates: a schoolteacher, a former civil servant from the colonies, and Kuyper, a controversial pastor. These men, Groen knew, would, if elected, push the schools question back on to the agenda of the Chamber, just as he himself had tried to do so often, though to no avail. Groen's recommendations at this late date sowed confusion in the ranks of the Antirevolutionary voters and resulted in defeats for all three men. Groen's reaction was almost laconic: at least we have vindicated our principled stance, it's a moral victory. Kuyper's reaction was different. In between sermon preparation and home visitations in his Amsterdam ward, he pored over the election results, district by district, tallying the votes for each party and marking the districts where the vote was close. His conclusion? Now we know our real strength; the constituency we can

---

1. Excerpted from G. Groen van Prinsterer, *Briefwisseling,* vol. 6 (The Hague: Nijhoff and Instituut voor Nederlandse Geschiedenis, 1925-1992), pp. 488-508, 735-38.

count on is extremely small but loyal — and could grow if we had a national organization.[2]

The following year, 1872, saw the launch of a national newspaper, *De Standaard,* with Kuyper as editor-in-chief. His daily editorials and occasional asterisms began to tell readers in plain language what Christian political action should look like and which developments needed to be assessed and opposed. Groen, a man of considerable wealth, supported the venture financially. He and Kuyper also started the habit of "passing the ball" to each other. The two commented and expanded on each other's printed statements, Kuyper in his daily and Groen in his *Nederlandsche Gedachten,* a political pamphlet that appeared at irregular intervals. In this collaboration, Kuyper relied on Groen's prestige as the country's grand old man of confessional politics, and Groen in turn relied on Kuyper's talent as an effective popular communicator.

The correspondence reproduced below began when the anti-revolutionary voters' club in District Gouda nominated Kuyper for a seat in the Second Chamber. As happened frequently in those days, the nominee was apprised after the fact. Yet Kuyper could not have been all that surprised; after all, he had been publishing critical commentary on the country's politics on a daily basis for almost two years. But how to respond?

Kuyper became very uneasy. If he agreed to serve if elected, what was he to do awaiting the election? Campaigning "on the hustings" was out of the question; besides, it was rarely done except by way of leaflets and posters. But should he agree to serve at all? The consequences stared him in the face. For example, would he be able to combine the editorship of his Amsterdam-based paper with parliamentary duties in The Hague? And were there any non-negotiables on which to base his contribution to the parliamentary debates? Beset by doubts, Kuyper sought Groen's advice. He realized that the father of the Antirevolutionary party in the Netherlands needed to be "on side" before he could venture to represent it and begin organizing it into a battle-ready party with an explicit program.

The election took place in two rounds. After two conservative candidates were eliminated in the first round, Groen encouraged Kuyper to think positively about the whole exercise. In the second round the "ultramontanist" (Catholic) voters in the district switched to Kuyper, who now edged out the liberal candidate and was declared elected.

Was this God's hand? Kuyper felt inadequate. Moreover, he began to distrust his personal motivation. In addition, he was subjected to pressure from

---

2. Groen van Prinsterer, *Briefwisseling,* vol. 6, pp. 249-55.

his parishioners. His loyal followers in the Amsterdam church feared they might lose their beloved pastor. Letters arrived begging him to stay, a petition to that effect was circulating, and an advertisement appeared inviting "all who love church and state to a prayer meeting for Dr. Kuyper." The beleaguered man's father, Rev. Jan Frederik Kuyper, wrote his son: "Bethink yourself seven times, and another seven times, before you trade in your high, sacred and blessed position as a minister of the gospel. . . ."[3] Tensions mounted in the Kuyper household.

Meanwhile the correspondence shows that Groen now began to gently prod Kuyper to put his doubts aside and accept the seat to which he had been elected. At this point in their exchange we are fortunate to have access to a document in which Kuyper spelled out a political "program." He did so in a memorandum of "loose thoughts," as he called them, which he submitted to Groen. He wanted to know whether he was on the right track strategically and ideologically, and whether, if he accepted the seat, Groen would throw his full support behind him with his prestigious name and in other ways.

The memorandum is fascinating in several respects. If the letters show Kuyper as alternately tender and assertive, courtly and brusque, the memo shows him in all his flamboyant, creative, visionary self. His reading, in the circumstances, of the state of the nation's political future is prescient. He confidently predicts the demise of the conservatives and the hemorrhaging of the liberal forces to the left and to the right. It is a diagnosis that emboldens him to suggest to Groen that the time is ripe for his party to "seize the initiative." Antirevolutionaries, once mobilized, could stem the rising tide of revolutionary socialism, he argues, and at the same time prepare their party for eventually moving from Opposition to Government.

Informed by nearly a century of "anti-Revolutionary" thought, the memo is rife with concrete policy proposals. Small wonder that the ever-cautious and battle-scarred Groen shrank back from giving Kuyper a blanket endorsement of all his ideas. Still, he seems to have decided that this was the opportune time to pilot the brilliant Amsterdam pastor into the Second Chamber of Parliament and at the same time to pass the marshal's baton over to the younger man. However, as Kuyper teetered on the threshold, Groen van Prinsterer, being a lifelong master of the "guarded statement" and often accused of being a peddler of principles but rarely of concrete legislative proposals, cautioned Kuyper that upon his entrance in the Chamber he should not to be too explicit, too detailed.

---

3. Quoted in Jeroen Koch, *Abraham Kuyper, een biografie* (Amsterdam: Boom, 2007), p. 114.

Apart from all its explicit details, a key element in Kuyper's "loose thoughts" is a noticeable spirit of accommodation. He holds forth that any Antirevolutionary program must "offer a modus vivendi also to the opponent." Any policy proposal he may want to advocate as a member of Parliament must endeavor to be palatable to those of other minds and must avoid being needlessly adversarial. The program he wants to offer the country should be acceptable to all liberal-minded men solely on its merits. Kuyper has the confidence of the believer who is sure that "Christian-historical" proposals and policies will ultimately be found attractive and sound by many, perhaps by a majority. He has the hope of the zealous evangelist that his message will fall on welcome ears.

The tone of accommodation and cooperation, precisely at what would prove to be a critical turning point in Dutch parliamentary history, would have far-reaching effect. Clearly, Kuyper's goal as a Christian politician was not some kind of theocracy, nor a revived Calvinist state, but a pluralist country in which every persuasion would be free to compete on a level playing field for the votes of the people. But that was exactly why liberalism's monopoly of power, entrenched by an elitist electoral system, had to be broken. The new power relations in the land would have to lead to power sharing. Power sharing would become a marked feature of twentieth-century Dutch politics. Toward the end of Kuyper's life, in 1917, when a revision of the Constitution brought a peaceful ending to both the schools struggle and the franchise question, one could say that his career was crowned with success. Of course, not all liberals had by then come to accept the Antirevolutionary program from the heart, but they were forced to do so by the political leverage wielded by those Dutch Christians, Catholics and Protestants alike, whom Kuyper had helped mobilize.

In 1874 that future was still far off. Kuyper duly resigned as pastor, and after being sworn in, took his seat in the Chamber. While continuing to write for *De Standaard* and the Sunday paper *De Heraut,* he threw himself into the work of a parliamentarian. He scrutinized the documents, studied the issues deep into the night, and delivered himself of his maiden speech with an oratorical flourish at which he excelled (at least as a pulpiteer). He criticized a new child labor bill because it did not go far enough and proceeded from a "false principle." He condemned the "imperialist" war against Achin in the Dutch East Indies. In general, contemporaries agreed that Kuyper conducted himself too brashly for a novice. Halfway through his term he collapsed from complete exhaustion. Seeking restoration, he traveled to southern France, soon to be joined by his wife and family. They would not return to Holland until thirteen months later. Kuyper then resigned his seat, to return to the Second Chamber only after an interval of seventeen years.

Let us now turn to the Groen-Kuyper correspondence.[4]

Groen to Kuyper, January 6, 1874

. . . I consider your election to the Second Chamber almost certain. I shall not be so bold as to give you advice. You seek that from Above. You yourself have excellent insight into our muddled situation.

The timing was more favorable in September than now. Someone like you should preferably make his appearance in the Chamber at the beginning of a session or at the moment when a fundamental issue of crucial importance is drawing the attention of the public. . . .

I know you will agree that the vocation of pastor is incompatible with that of leader of a political party. Your present position is exceptional and cannot in the long run be maintained. In addition, even your strength will fail you in controlling the possibly wholesome storm you have incited in the church.[5] Very well, as an elder you can retain at least the same influence in the Amsterdam church and so nullify an objection [that could be] used against you.[6]

One last point. You wrote about the danger to my party if *De Standaard* would have to be discontinued. Our party: to that I should have no objection. But as soon as we begin to specify, it is not my but your party that would be endangered. You were the *leader*[7] after me to my delight, but in your own right, needing neither my permission nor mandate. Naturally you have subjected yourself to my leadership as little as I have to yours. We are like-minded, but independent.

---

4. Abraham Kuyper, *Groen van Prinsterer. Schriftelijke Nalatenschap,* ed. L. J. van Essen, Deel 7: *Briefwisseling,* Deel 6 (The Hague: Instituut voor Nederlandse Geschiedenis, 1992).

5. As one of the more orthodox pastors of the Reformed Church of Amsterdam, Kuyper was giving strong leadership to the forces for church reform in opposition to the latitudinarianism of the denomination's ruling bodies. He enjoyed a large following in the capital; worship services led by the Rev. Dr. Kuyper were regularly filled to overflowing.

6. Groen is alluding to the fact that Kuyper, if he accepted a seat in parliament, would not be able to continue to give leadership to the church question raised in Amsterdam from a position as pastor, since members of parliament by law could not be members of the clergy.

7. This word is in English in the original.

Kuyper to Groen, January 7, 1874

. . . You are the head of our party and will remain so. You have entrusted me with a flotilla, and have made ample use of the freedom granted me as a "minister plenipotentiary." But my role was, and is, to minister, called only to assist in winning support for your cause among the lower middle classes, where I am at home and whose language I speak.

It was you who founded our party. I can drop out, but you remain. You can retire, but abdicate never. I could. The song I sing to the people comes from you. If I sang falsely, it was unavoidable, but that does not change your song. This in reaction to your contention that the anti-revolutionary party consists of two factions: yours, and as you want to call it, mine. I do not make that claim. I have recruited only for you, though in a way different from the one followed thus far. That the result added more to the ranks than ever before filled me with joy and gratitude for the sake of the principle and for your sake. In any case, if elected I shall visit you after January 21 to consult with you. . . .

The results of the Gouda election[8] have reinforced my view on three points: (1) the Conservatives are finished: without the support of the Catholics they are sinking to a level of impotence, relieving us of opposing them any further; (2) north of the rivers the Catholics are weaker than we are; (3) our party, if maintained, will take giant steps forward. . . . From this I conclude that the day is fast approaching when our party will be charged with the responsibility of being the only large opposition party in the country and the Chamber. Whether the men for that role are available, however, is doubtful. That holds for the press as well as for Chamber and government. After all, if the tide continues like this the possibility of having to assume the government of the country can no longer be dismissed as an absurd illusion. I am confident, however, that this shortage of men will improve.

Our rising influence, resulting from the mobilization of minds, must in turn result in the rehabilitation of our persuasion with people of intellect. In my opinion this is only a matter of time. . . .

The question whether I would want to hold a seat in the Chamber can be reduced to two others: 1. Do I feel able to assume leadership of a large opposition party? 2. Do I think I can accept the support of the ultramontanists? To the first question I must, for the time being, definitely answer in the negative.

---

8. Kuyper received 767 votes, the liberal candidate 957 votes. Two conservative candidates (one supported by Catholic voters) garnered 599 votes between them. The first round being inconclusive, a run-off election between the two highest candidates was scheduled for Jan. 20.

I cannot see how I am or could ever become equal to the task; the details of the machinery of government are too unfamiliar to me. To the second I may not answer positively either. Thus even if the Catholics help elect me in Gouda . . . I would still feel obliged, on my reading of the present situation, to decline.

I agree fully that my office is too tender to be so involved all the time in politics. Also, my strength in body and soul is too weak for that. Thus declining the seat for Gouda would probably have to be followed by one of two things: either resigning as pastor to devote all my time to being an editor, or abstaining altogether from political engagement. But I shall want to consult with you first, about the course that our party would then have to take.

Kuyper to Groen, January 16, 1874

. . . To my regret I see coming what I was afraid of. Apparently the Catholics in Gouda are going to support my candidacy. They sent a deputation[9] to me. . . . I still hope to escape it. If it turns out differently, may He show me the way, whom to serve is my only desire. May He show it also through you, by your advice and counsel.

Groen to Kuyper, January 17, 1874

. . . I think your election may now be considered quite certain. Less clear to me is what to advise you in that case. In the pros and cons there is much of which you alone can be the judge.

With cordial regards, and the prayer that your decision may be so led as to be a blessing for church and fatherland and for you personally.

Groen to Kuyper, January 19, 1874

. . . I want to leave you entirely free with respect to Art. 194, also for my sake.[10]

9. H. J. Kabel, baker, and H. J. J. Leyen, bookseller, chairman and secretary, respectively, of the Catholic voters' club "Justice for All" in Gouda.

10. Art. 194 of the Constitution made primary education the responsibility of the national government. The liberals held that this provision limited public funding to government schools, an interpretation that was enshrined in the Primary Education Act of 1857. The Anti-School Law League, founded in 1872, agitated for a revision of Art. 194, a campaign that Groen

Many still do not understand that what I wanted has become impossible, in more ways than one. I would look quite foolish if people thought I still did not realize it myself. . . .

Groen to Kuyper, January 21, 1874

Dear friend! I have just received your telegram.[11] I was not surprised. I understand the difficulty of your position. We will have to leave the decision to you alone, while looking Above. We will respect whatever you decide. Cordially, with warm sympathy, yours. . . .

P.S. Of course, given some advance notice, I am available for a consultation at any time.

Kuyper to Groen, January 21, 1874

I have just received the news that I have been elected. May He, whom to serve is my life and my pride, show me His way. I hope to visit you soon, to seek your advice. Thank you for your letter of yesterday. Would you perhaps have any use for my excerpts from [Edmund] Burke? There are even some that speak rather strongly for divine right. If so, I shall take them along.

Groen to Kuyper, January 30, 1874

Dear friend, keep me up to date about yourself. Let me know confidentially if you still have doubts. Otto[12] from Gouda was here yesterday. If you do not accept they will be so discouraged they won't even nominate another candidate. . . .

I was especially struck by the fact that even the warmest of your Amster-

---

had opposed in favor of a more honest interpretation and implementation — and in the long term, legislative revision — of the Act of 1857, thus avoiding the laborious process of amending the Constitution. Acquiescing in the futility of his opposition, Groen now agreed that Kuyper should work for a general revision of the Constitution, including revisiting Art. 194 to end the monopoly of public funds enjoyed by the government schools.

11. Kuyper was elected by a vote of 1,504, against 1,252 for the liberal candidate.

12. H. W. Otto, florist; treasurer of the local anti-revolutionary voters' club, "Fear God, Honor the King."

dam supporters realize that they may not demand of you that you refuse the mandate. I myself am so taken up by the matter since you left that I can hardly attend to my usual business. . . .

Kuyper to Groen, January 30, 1874

. . . My soul is still like a pendulum, swinging now this way, now that. Reasoning I say, "I have to go!" but in my heart there is trembling fear: "What if it be against the Lord's will!"

Meanwhile a strong agitation has developed in the congregation which finds me not unaffected. Will my knowledge not fail? Will my constitution not collapse? Will my soul not be tormented in that unholy atmosphere?

Oddly, especially my opponents are urging me to go. They hope that once in the Chamber I will see things differently. The question of my status is settled.[13]

Groen to Kuyper, February 1, 1874

I eagerly look forward to hearing your decision. Being able to keep your preaching license must be an important matter to you. But I have expressed my opinion to you as strongly as I could, and every objection of conscience can and must, I realize, be resolved by you alone while looking Above.

Kuyper to Groen, February 2, 1874

Yesterday I felt most miserable. Exhausted in body and soul. Today, after a refreshing night's rest, I feel much better. My mind tells me more and more that I must go, but my heart is still not at peace with it. I do not think I can handle it. I am so afraid of abandoning God's way. There is so much in it that appeals to the wrong inclinations of my heart. If I prove a fiasco it would be a fiasco for my whole party. But how to live up to expectations when they are set so high?

One thing would give me courage: if I had a set goal and could see a path plotted towards it. Tomorrow I shall therefore set my thoughts on paper. Then I shall send these to you, to approve, or else to put aside.

---

13. Kuyper would be emerited and retain his preaching license.

Every day now we are threatened with a strike at our printing plant. . . . Yesterday our nurse-maid carrying our youngest child fell down a flight of stairs, and today my boy stabbed me with a pair of scissors right above my wrist up to the bone. Thus the small agonies are added to the greatest anguish of soul and the Lord alone is Light.

Kuyper to Groen, February 4, 1874

I hereby have the honor of sending you my loose thoughts. You will appreciate my purpose. Accepting a seat is to me like accepting a mandate, and therefore I feel the need to know what direction to follow and what to undertake. I cannot take "a leap in the dark."[14] I therefore beg indulgence for my sketch. If it is all wrong, tell me freely. But at least give me the assurance, as I pass through this anxious struggle, that your prudence has gone over the thoughts of a young man. I would have the courage to accept only if I knew you think my line of thought has any future.

May I have your answer as soon as possible? The tension is causing me such agony.

Respectfully, as ever, your humble servant and friend,

Kuyper

Memorandum presented to G. Groen van Prinsterer by A. Kuyper during the latter's deliberation, re: accepting a seat in the Second Chamber

For someone to enter the States General with no political specialty is pointless unless he has a program aiming at an overall change in the political situation, enabling him to know what he wants, to bring the parliamentary battle back to a battle over principles, and to give leadership to public opinion.

The urge to witness for Christ is not adequate for this purpose, for the simple reason that such a witness had already been given more than once and that repeating it too often has the adverse effect.

Such a program must satisfy four conditions: 1) it must continue the line of his party's past; 2) offer a modus vivendi also to the opponent; 3) anticipate the future; 4) follow from the basic principle underlying his endeavor.

Ad 1: We ought to distinguish between the orthodox and the heterodox line in the antecedents of our sympathizers and follow only the former.

---

14. The italicized words are in English in the original.

Ad 2: We ought to distinguish between that which the Antirevolutionaries aspire to among themselves and that which they present as a general political program to the nation as a whole. Only like-minded men can work for a strictly Antirevolutionary program; a national program can be promoted by men of all parties. The former could become the latter only if the whole nation were converted to the anti-revolutionary principles.

Ad 3: To anticipate the future we ought to take our cue from the present situation, in which the conservatives are dying away, the liberals, drawing no recruits from the younger generation, are destined for one part to revert to conservatism, for the other to vanish into the radical wing, with the result that when the generation now being educated at our secondary schools and our universities is ready to take its place in society it will no longer be possible to stop the triumph of revolutionary radicalism unless we at this early stage take up position at the head of the movement and seize the initiative in further developing our constitutional forms in a strictly neutral sense, in order to avert a development in a positively anti-Christian spirit. Failing this, we will inevitably be forced by future developments into the corner of reaction, forfeit our influence on public opinion, and in the end find our shameful place between ultramontanists and conservatives.

Ad 4: Our principle may not be an attempt to impose Christianity by force, openly or obliquely, but rather the belief that by way of the conscience of the nation and of individual persons the Christian religion, provided it regains its free and unhampered place in society, will prevail in state and society and so set them free.

For this reason, no demanding any privileges; no ignoring the new phase political life has entered owing in part to the Revolution; no attempts at subverting our civil liberties, but an effort to make them real and to graft them onto a better root.

Proceeding from these premises, we shall have to acknowledge the fact that our present constitutional order, especially as a result of its interpretation by officials and successive administrations, has not kept pace with the evolution of political life at the grassroots level, that it is a layer of ice underneath which the water has flowed away, and that it lacks even the vitality to catch up to the political evolution the nation is undergoing.[15]

From this it follows that our party (1) should take up position not behind but in front of today's liberalism; and (2) must qualify that liberalism as static

---

15. From this point on, down to the words "fictitious trade," the manuscript has only a single paragraph without any indentations.

and conservative, wherefore we ought to choose as our objective a revision of the Constitution, not in any partial but in a general sense. Our party, too, must be liberal, but in contrast to revolutionary liberalism it must stand for a Christian liberalism, different in this sense that it seeks a liberalism not against or without Christ but a liberalism that returns thanks to Him, a liberalism that is not against or without our historic past but a liberalism that is embraced as the fruit of that past, a liberalism that is not restricted to the confines of our Constitution but in place of that straitjacket offers a garment in which the nation can breathe and grow freely.

To this end, the Constitution is to be purged of whatever tends to have the State, in spite of itself, favor its own form of religion, a religion that must necessarily be anti-Christian in essence and character; purged of whatever separates the State from the life of the nation; purged of whatever restricts the free course of the Christian religion; purged, finally, of whatever obstructs the free development of the organic life of the nation.

To the same end, our system of representation must be changed. The First Chamber, as composed at present, should be abolished and replaced by a chamber of organic representation reflecting the diversified makeup of society. Its complement, the Second Chamber, should mirror the nation in its individual intellectual life, hence in its party divisions. For this purpose the franchise should be lowered to the level where political conviction stops, and by abolishing the electoral districts should allow for the amalgamation of votes over the whole country. . . .

The taking of the oath, now weakened through unholy repetition, is to be limited.

The churches are to be declared free, their financial ties to the State undone. . . .

Education is to be under the direction, regulation, and inspection of the State.

For higher education the State is to endow one state university with fixed assets, in order that it may develop as a corporation solely in accordance with the innermost law of science. No appointment of professors by the State, only curators, by the King, from nominations. To the free universities which one may wish to establish in addition, the same benefits are to be assured in respect of titles and degrees, not as regards endowment. Only in this way can a Protestant university come into existence at Utrecht and a Roman Catholic at 's-Hertogenbosch, as the vital centers of the two large elements of the nation.

Secondary education must pass from the hands of the State to the provinces as concerns its partial regulation. . . .

Primary education must be made compulsory, offset by full or partial subvention by the State to those parents who are unable to pay the normal costs of primary schooling. . . .

Supervision of administration of the colonies must pass from the States General to a Colonial Council, appointed for ⅓ by the King from nominations made by the States General, for ⅓ by the Chambers of Commerce, and for ⅓ by the European population of the colonies.

The state lottery is to be abolished.

Taxes on necessaries must be removed, including taxes on light and air, and replaced by a tax on tobacco, an increased rate on luxury cloth, landed property, and paper assets above a fixed minimum.

The rights of employers and employees must be regulated by law, both bodies to be organized by local government, the individual freedom of employers and employees alike to be guaranteed by severe sanctions.

Corporate law is to be revised to keep the accumulation of capital within bounds and to combat fictitious trade.[16]

By what degrees such a program is to be published depends on the cooperation we receive. . . .

The program has to be comprehensive, to bring about an overall political re-alignment and for the time being hold off any playing for ministerial seats. It has to anticipate the future because only in that way can it get ahead of the revolutionary radicals and because it itself needs time for its realization.

Coming with such a program, at once or in stages, one ought to accept support from whichever side it comes, provided there is agreement with the program in its strict formulation. With all such as accept it one ought to form a caucus and distribute the various tasks. The caucus should resolve not to accept the formation of a ministry unless the realization of this program can immediately be taken in hand.

During elections this program, after publication, should be the sole shibboleth. As soon as a party begins to form around this program, a large political paper should be set up which can, in distinction from *De Standaard* as the popular organ, lead the political discussion.

These ideas are developed in order to arrive at the question whether in the judgment of Mr. Groen an active role in Parliament guided by these goals and moving along these lines might meet with his approval and would in his view be conducive to political results and the well-being of our country.

Or else . . . to know his objections . . . and alternatives.

---

16. In the original, the paragraph begun after note 15 ends here.

The writer is desirous of being so informed, as he will continue to lack the courage to undertake the task so long as he has no fixed goal before him.

Groen to Kuyper, February 5, 1874

I need not let you wait long, since I assume you ask me only for my opinion about the general thrust to work toward a general revision of the Constitution in a Christian-historical spirit. All the particulars . . . cannot be dealt with off-hand. You have coupled your resoluteness with rare circumspection. Qui va piano va sano.[17] You know our people. Provided they are not too rudely shaken they are quite capable of being galvanized in the cause of the highest interests of the nation. Your slogan is, In God we trust, which has proved so sound in the history of our country. In short, it seems to me your Memorandum has brought to light, even more clearly than thus far, the obligatory nature of your forthcoming decision. And, further, may God's blessing, without which we can do nothing but which suffices under all difficulties, rest, dear friend, upon your person and your work!

P.S. I count on a telegram once your decision is made. I add our cordial greetings, in these circumstances, to your dear wife from both of us, with the request to let us know if the fall and the injury had any harmful consequences.

Kuyper to Groen, February 6, 1874

Your quick reply was most welcome to me, and no less your approval of the general tenor of what I would come to regard as my mission. You are right in assuming I did not insist on all the details as a sine qua non. Yet your letter still leaves me unsure. . . . Do you consider what is being proposed to be indeed Christian-historical? I am not asking you to endorse every point so that I could defend them later with the authority of your name. But those details do reveal a spirit, a direction, a course to be taken. Do you consider it to be indicated correctly?

Husen[18] wrote me that an anonymous person has set aside 500 guilders a year for my use in the event that I accept.

17. Easy does it, one step at a time.
18. R. Husen, principal of the parish school in Utrecht, board member of the Association of Christian Schoolteachers.

Fortunately our injuries, after some pain, had no further effect. I commend myself to your prayers and friendship.

Groen to Kuyper, February 7, 1874

I have just received your letter. Do not ask more than I can give. Your premises I regard as excellent. Also the constitutional revision in a general sense; also the idea of a Christian liberalism. But to give my verdict on the rest already now will not do. You should not [in your first term] present a detailed program; you know my principles and my desire to stand by you.

Kuyper to Groen, February 8, 1874

I have not yet come to a decision. Let me add something confidential: I have never taken weighty decisions of this kind without receiving a sign from the Lord. That is what has always made my tone so sure and my step so steady. I would usually receive such a sign only at the peak of my mental strain. You understand that biding of the soul, do you not; that fear to act against His will, to depart from His way and be moving away from Him?

However, if you are not wondering about my decision but about my inclination, then I believe that it will certainly have to come to that and that the Lord will open the way for it.

Upon my entrance in the Chamber, I would not like to broach the subject of a general revision of the Constitution until you have first brought it up. I can live only as a rod on your stem. However, please write of it only in passing. I must have something fresh to divert attention away from my person toward my line of conduct. Would it not be possible, therefore, that your *Nederlandsche Gedachten* contain a hint of a sort that would for the moment be less clear to the public but which I could then pick up to show how I intend to carry on what you yourself have indicated in so many words as the next step in your lifelong campaign?

Groen to Kuyper, February 9, 1874

Just received your letter. I had already composed a directive about a general revision. Now I shall formulate it a bit more enigmatically, so as not to pre-empt what belongs to your entrance.

Kuyper to Groen, February 10, 1874 (telegram)

INVITUS ACCEPI[19]

---

19. That is, have reluctantly accepted.

Kuyper as Emancipator and Christian Democrat

Harry Van Dyke

It has become abundantly clear after more than a decade of renewed study of Abraham Kuyper that two roles in particular define his historical significance. He helped emancipate a large disenfranchised group in his country using means that merit further study. And he grew into an eloquent exponent of that anti-modernity movement in Europe known as Christian Democracy. To adequately understand these roles in their historical setting, we would do well to ask two questions: Exactly in what sense was he a "democrat" as we commonly use that term? And in what sense was he an "emancipator" as that term is often used in social history?

I

Let's begin with his credentials as a democrat. A democrat is person for whom all people have equal status and dignity and enjoy equality before the law. Does this description fit Kuyper?

We may not want to attach too much importance to a third-hand account[1] that relates how Reverend Kuyper in his first charge in Beesd would lace his boots in spring and tramp across muddy fields to visit the ploughboys that belonged to his parish, nor how, when autumn came round, he enjoyed shaking the branches of the apple trees in the yard of the parsonage so that the

---

1. P. H. A. van Krieken to H. Colijn, n.d. (*ante* Oct. 29, 1937); Archief-Colijn, Historisch Documentatiecentrum, Free University, Amsterdam.

poor people of the village could fill up a hamper. Our source is third-hand, yet anecdotes like these fit the man one gets to know when studying his life.

Kuyper's first publication to address the church question — should the church be broad and inclusive, or confessional? — advocated that the men in the pew, not the elders or the local lord, should choose their pastors. Why so? Because, he writes, that would be more "democratic," and a Reformed church is by definition democratic.[2]

During the early years of his newspaper *De Standaard,* as he was taking over the baton from his mentor and predecessor Willem Groen van Prinsterer, he protested that Groen wanted to make a distinction between two factions in the Antirevolutionary Party: Groen's and Kuyper's. Kuyper informs Groen by letter, politely but firmly:

> . . . You are the head of our party and will remain so. You have entrusted me with a flotilla, and I have made ample use of the freedom granted me as a "minister plenipotentiary." But my role was, and is, to minister, called only to assist in winning support for your cause among the lower middle classes, where I am at home and whose language I speak.[3]

By then he had pastored not only the peasants of Beesd but also a ward in Utrecht that included slum dwellings. Currently he was serving a ward in the Amsterdam church dominated by bleak row housing inhabited by dockworkers and longshoremen and their families. Labor activists like Klaas Kater and his friends in the society *Vrienden der Waarheid* had played their part in wooing the pastor from Utrecht to Amsterdam.

The Rev. Dr. Kuyper had already acquired a reputation as a friend and advocate of the working classes. This was the nineteenth century, the age of the awakening of the common man. Kuyper had a keen sense of the direction history was headed, and he ran with it. He resolved early on to "steer in a democratic direction," urging the adoption of social legislation to protect the unfortunate victims of absentee landlords and rugged capitalists. After the First International had held its congress in The Hague in 1872, it invited

2. Abraham Kuyper, *Wat moeten wij doen, het stemrecht aan onszelven houden of den kerkeraad machtigen? Vraag bij de uitvoering van Art. 23 toegelicht* (Culemborg: A. J. Blom, 1867), p. 10.

3. Kuyper to Groen, January 7, 1874, in *Groen van Prinsterer, Schriftelijke Nalatenschap,* Deel 7: *Briefwisseling,* Deel 6 (1869-1876), ed. L. J. Van Essen (The Hague: Instituut voor Nederlandse Geschiedenis, 1992), p. 492. The last clause literally reads: "where I belong, according to the needs of those folk." My rather free translation is warranted by the context in which Kuyper describes the effect in particular of his editorship of *De Standaard.*

Kuyper to participate in a public debate with one of its leading spokesmen. He declined because he realized "how radically we differed in principle."[4] A social democrat he was not.

Of course the test for one's status as a democrat is most pertinent in the area of politics. Very well, if Abraham Lincoln was correct in defining democracy as "government of the people, by the people, for the people," then this Abraham would agree with him for at least two-thirds of the way.

Government *for* the people? Absolutely! From the beginning Kuyper's voice was heard protesting against an oligarchic form of government manned by liberals from the upper middle class and the aristocracy. Their concerns and legislative measures naturally tended to favor the interests of their class and to neglect the material needs of the *kleine luyden,* the people without influence in the land. Worse, they trampled on the latter's spiritual needs, in the belief that religion was irrelevant for public policy and that politics was most reasonable when religion was kept out of it and when laws (e.g., laws for public education) enshrined religious neutrality.

Kuyper excoriated the one-sided system of representation based on a census that privileged the higher taxpayers. If this system continues, he wrote,

> things will come down to this: a liberal coterie, which makes up a minority in the country and among the voters, will nevertheless manage to become the majority in the Chamber as a result of an unjust voting system and an even more culpable division of districts.[5] Using this stolen majority, it makes the work of the States General serve no other purpose than to have this coterie dominate the nation, throttle the voice of the people, and deform this poor people at the expense of its own tax monies. . . .[6]

Government *by* the people? Unquestionably! But only via a broadly based representative system. Kuyper prided himself on being the leader of a grass-roots movement. The liberals, he observed with ill-concealed disdain, recruit their spokesmen from the ranks of academics, industrialists, and especially lawyers, whereas our party has always been active "from the bottom up."[7]

---

4. Abraham Kuyper, *De kleyne luyden. Openingsrede ter Deputatenvergadering van 23 November 1917* (Kampen: J. H. Kok, 1917), p. 493. Reprinted as *Geen vergeefs woord. Verzamelde deputaten-redevoeringen* (Kampen: Kok, 1951).

5. Kuyper was indignant about the periodic gerrymandering that went on.

6. Abraham Kuyper, "*Ons Program,*" 2nd ed. (Amsterdam: J. H. Kruyt, 1880), §94. The last clause alludes to the secularization of the public school.

7. Kuyper, *De kleyne luyden,* pp. 19, 21.

His ideal, based in part on a romantic reading of his country's history, was participatory government.

Small wonder that a perennial theme in Kuyper's public statements was that the right to vote had to be extended to a much broader group of citizens — with one proviso. In 1878 he did not believe that the country was ripe for "government by the people." In his estimation, the Dutch were insufficiently engaged with issues of justice, and a certain level of engagement, he continued,

> is an essential condition for establishing a viable government by the people. . . . And whoever would be foolish enough to dream of a democratic form of government for our country would completely overlook that a democracy is not possible without a strong public spirit and that a "public spirit" of the political kind runs counter to the national character of the Dutch people.[8]

A decade and a half later, however, Kuyper deemed the requisite public spirit to be there. Presumably, the character of his fellow countrymen was not a constant but had undergone an evolution, no doubt as a result of the maturing Antirevolutionary Party, the rallying of Catholics under a banner of their own, and the rise of the labor movement and democratic socialism.

Unfortunately, it was the very franchise question that now led to a schism in the Antirevolutionary Party. The break came in 1895 over a bill before Parliament that would expand the franchise by 75 percent. The proposal did not represent Kuyper's ideal of "organic" suffrage, i.e., head-of-household voting. Nevertheless, he was willing to support the bill since it was a step in the right direction: it would at last give the vote to many of the common people and enable them to share in the country's growing prosperity. What is more, it would give them an increasing role in contributing to the moral tone of politics and the spiritual direction of the country. However, the party's aristocratic wing demurred, claiming that the bill was far broader than the Constitution intended. This did not dissuade Kuyper from supporting the bill. He was inclined to view their objection as hypocritical and self-serving. "A parting of the ways has become inevitable for the party," he wrote in *De Standaard* shortly before the general elections in which the franchise question was the paramount issue. Our battle must be against "conservatism of every stripe." He pointed out that

> of the twenty members that sit for us in the house, only nine are commoners. The other eleven are men of noble birth, . . . chiefly landed gentry, all

8. Kuyper, *"Ons Program,"* §75.

of them millionaires who do not understand the real needs of the common people, the "people behind the voters" whose socio-economic condition cries out to heaven. Our eminent men are welcome to occupy the main floor of the party as long as they do not disturb the house rules. And those rules dictate that anti-revolutionaries are, and always have been, Christian democrats on principle and Christian democrats at heart. They therefore cannot but support proposals to broaden the franchise.[9]

Kuyper was determined to stay the course and "steer in a democratic direction." But just how far was he willing to go? All the way to universal adult male suffrage? Progressive liberals were talking in that vein, betraying their kinship with the French Revolution. However, could the right to vote not also be exercised in a different spirit, from "anti-revolutionary" motives? In any case, when one of Kuyper's associates at the newspaper continued to warn against "the revolutionary notion of universal suffrage," Kuyper reined him in. He took him aside and ordered him to tone down: "We may yet need it," he told him. Kuyper was ever the principled pragmatist, a skillful practitioner of the art of the possible. All the same, he was hard to please at times. When universal suffrage was finally introduced in 1918, he complained that "the atomism of the individual has triumphed over the household."[10]

In any event, Kuyper stood squarely behind "government by the people" — on the understanding that a genuinely "organic" representation of the whole nation would be allowed to participate through a system that honored families and households as the basic building blocks — the "organic" elements — of society.

Now for the third descriptor of democracy: government *of* the people. To that, Kuyper could never subscribe. After all, do the governed confer authority on their government? Hardly. The people are not the source of political authority. To be sure, in a democracy they are involved in choosing their political leaders and setting the overall direction of public policy. But if government is proximately accountable to the people via their representatives, in the final analysis it is accountable to God. Kuyper was an unabashed proponent of the divine right of government, a principle he shared with Christian thinkers like Augustine, Aquinas, Luther, and Calvin, and yes, also with pre-revolutionary rulers like James and Charles Stuart, and Cromwell, and Louis XIV and his

9. Cited in Harry Van Dyke, "Abraham Kuyper and the Continuing Social Question," *Journal for Markets & Morality* 14:2 (Fall 2011): 643.

10. Abraham Kuyper, *Wat nu? Rede ter opening van de Deputatenvergadering, gehouden te Utrecht op 2 Mei 1918* (Kampen: J. H. Kok, 1918), p. 8.

chaplain Bossuet. If Kuyper was a democrat, he was a Christian democrat. The monarch (or a president or council in a republic) is the Sovereign, not a Parliament or a Congress. The people do not govern themselves; they are governed. The political institution that governs them is the State, and the head of a State is the Sovereign. For Kuyper the head of the Dutch State is a king (preferably a member of the House of Orange). Such a Sovereign, in any state whatsoever, does not represent the people and does not rule on behalf of the people. For example, it is the Sovereign who commutes sentences and grants pardons without any involvement of the people. He rules — cheerfully or unwillingly, defiantly or unwittingly — on behalf of Christ the Lord. Such is inherent in the office. "The powers that be are ordained of God." Nothing in the world, no manmade theory, can undo this fact.

Evidently, the third description of democracy — government of the people — was equated in Kuyper's mind with the doctrine of popular sovereignty — and he would have none of it. Adding the modifier "Christian" would not salvage it either. In Groen's writings he had read with approval a quotation from the Swiss theologian Alexandre Vinet who considered the term "Christian democracy" an oxymoron.[11] It was only over time that Kuyper began to pour new meaning into the political term "democracy," allowing it now to be joined to the adjective "Christian."

Yet of critical importance is the fact that Kuyper's perduring opposition to popular sovereignty in no way detracted from the irreplaceable value he attached to popular representation. In the footsteps of his mentor Groen van Prinsterer he was a strong defender of the formidable influence of a body of popularly elected representatives that can check the government. This body can call the Sovereign's ministers to account; that is, they can question the sitting government, put its feet to the fire, refuse to approve its tax bills, vote down its budgets, review its appointments, and so much more. Kuyper wished to be a Christian in politics — but not otherwise than as a Christian democrat.

Equally critical: the political Sovereign is not an absolute ruler. He has to share the stage with other "sovereigns," such as the father in his household, the teacher in the classroom, the scholar in the university, the businessman in his firm, and ever so many other distinctive roles in human society. Each is endowed with a "divine right" and is therefore sovereign in his own sphere.

---

11. Vinet wrote: "In a word combination like that, the substantive devours its adjective." Cited in G. Groen van Prinsterer, *Verscheidenheden over staatsregt en politiek* (Amsterdam: Müller, 1850), p. 245. Groen scholar Johan Zwaan informs me that in his daily *De Nederlander* (which ran from 1850 to 1855) Groen used the quotation on three different occasions: August 21, 1850, and July 13 and 21, 1852.

Sphere sovereignty is endemic to the neo-Calvinist version of Christian democracy. Although Kuyper often lumped disparate "spheres" together, with the State as the overarching supreme sphere, the seed of the doctrine was there when he wrote in his commentary of 1878 on the Program of the Antirevolutionary Party:

> If the liberals are right in proceeding from the false premise that the State represents the plenitude of power, which accounts for their view that a region, a municipality, a church and a family have only as much power as the State hands over to them as a conditional grant — then of course it is entirely appropriate that the State itself controls these subordinate spheres and coerces them to interpret the law in such a way as to always please the Sovereign. . . .
>
> If on the other hand we anti-revolutionaries are right in proceeding from the belief that the family, the church, the municipality and the province are spheres of life that exist by the grace of God and function in their own right — then of course they have all the power and all the rights which have not been reserved for the Sovereign in the interest of state unity and for the sake of supreme authority. . . .[12]

Sphere sovereignty stops statism dead in its tracks. Groen had fought religious neutrality in government schools and political interference with the governance of the national church. Very well, his successor Kuyper would fight political interference with seminary training — the seed idea of a free university — and he expanded the anti-state campaign over the length and breadth of society in order to safeguard the autonomy of home and family, academic freedom for scholars, self-regulation for business and commerce, and so on and so forth.[13] Not surprisingly, at one point he was willing to embrace the label "Christian liberalism." This he did quite early on. In the winter of 1874 he submitted a memorandum (see pp. 178ff. in this volume) to his mentor Groen van Prinsterer in which he summed up what he would see as his mission and program if he were to accept his recent election to Parliament. In the memorandum Kuyper argued that an anti-revolutionary party such as Groen van Prinsterer's

---

12. Kuyper, *"Ons Program,"* §183.

13. His reason for opposing the *Bakkerswet* of 1912 — it was introduced by the Antirevolutionary minister Talma in an effort to protect employees by prescribing that bakeries could start heating their ovens no earlier than 4 o'clock in the morning — was that many such firms were owner-operated and thus had to be respected as sovereign in their own sphere.

should take up position not behind but in front of today's liberalism and must qualify that liberalism as static and conservative. . . . Our party, too, must be liberal, but in contrast to revolutionary liberalism it must stand for a Christian liberalism, different in this sense that it seeks a liberalism not against or without Christ but a liberalism that returns thanks to Him, a liberalism that is not against or without our historic past but a liberalism that is embraced as the fruit of that past. . . .[14]

The reigning liberals, he complained with bitter sarcasm, ought to extend their much-vaunted rights and freedoms to all groups in society. The playing field ought to be level.

Yet, in practical terms, what did Kuyper have in mind with his alternative to classic liberalism? It did not mean that he supported limiting the government to the role of a night watchman or that he relied on some Invisible Hand to keep unrestricted free enterprise from going off the rails. On the contrary. For example, he earmarked "paper assets" and financial speculation for stricter government regulations, suggesting that Dutch corporate law should be revised "in order to keep the accumulation of capital within bounds and to combat fictitious trade."[15]

Behind such proposals lay his concern for that large sector of the working classes that still attended church. These people had to be kept from being lured into the fold of the self-styled "anti-clerical" socialists. They had to be shown that the church — that Christians — cared. "There burned in Kuyper," as James Bratt has emphasized, "a passionate concern for the poor," a concern that was persistent throughout his career, rooted as it was in a particular reading of Scripture; wherever the poor appeared, Kuyper "put God squarely on their side."[16]

Days before the election fought over the franchise bill, Kuyper wrote in his paper: "It is our firm and unshakable conviction that the Savior, if He were still on earth, would again align Himself with the oppressed and against the powerful of our age."[17] From his earliest days in public life, as noted above, he had urged protection of wage-earners, notably through Chambers of Labor that would enable workmen to bargain collectively for wage increases and improved working conditions. His concern for the least in society extended to

14. Kuyper, *Groen van Prinsterer*, p. 736.

15. Kuyper, *Groen van Prinsterer*, p. 737.

16. James D. Bratt, "Passionate about the Poor: The Social Attitudes of Abraham Kuyper," *Journal of Markets and Morality* 5:1 (Spring 2012): 37-38.

17. Kuyper, leading article in *De Standaard*, April 9, 1894; cited in J. C. Rullmann, *Kuyper-Bibliografie*, vol. 3 (The Hague: Bootsma, and Kampen: Kok, 1923-1940), p. 91.

slum dwellers as well. For instance, he advocated strict laws for public hygiene and tough controls on bars and taverns. Factory smokestacks were to be tested for harmful substances and kept at a safe distance from residential areas, and a factory's effluents were not to be allowed to drain onto the soil.[18]

When Protestant Christians assembled in 1891 at the Social Congress he urged "men of wealth" to show love for the poor, and he minced no words when he warned them:

> ... those who are diverted by fear for their money box have no place march- ing in the ranks with us. This is holy ground, and he who would walk on it must first loosen the sandals of his egotism. . . . There is suffering round about you, and those who suffer are your brothers, sharers of your nature, your own flesh and blood. You might have been in their place and they in your more pleasant position.[19]

The gloves came off again four years later, in a series of articles on "Christ and the Needy":

> ... if there are any "practicing Christians" who live off their wealth year in, year out, constantly laying up treasures on earth while hunger and poverty continue to inflict suffering — let them see to it how they may still escape the terrible word of the Lord recorded in Matthew 25: Verily I say unto you, inasmuch as you did it not to one of the least of these, you did it not to Me. These people, so ends the word of Christ, these shall go away into everlasting punishment.[20]

Did outbursts like these make Kuyper a crypto-socialist? He was not afraid of the label "socialism," provided, again, that he would be allowed to define it: not just material needs but all man's needs had to be provided for — what humans need for time and eternity.[21] Kuyper also nursed a somewhat romantic view of a people's collective strength and spirit based on social values like self-help and self-reliance. At no time did he subscribe to wholesale government intervention in the economy. He was no friend of nationalizing industry or of

18. Kuyper, *"Ons Program,"* §197.
19. Abraham Kuyper, *The Problem of Poverty,* ed. and trans. James W. Skillen (Grand Rapids: Baker, 1998), p. 76.
20. Abraham Kuyper, *De Christus en de social nooden en Democratische klippen* (Amster- dam: J. A. Wormser, 1895), p. 44. For the English translation, see "Christ and the Needy," *Journal of Markets & Morality* 14:2 (Fall 2011): 673.
21. Kuyper, *De Christus en de social nooden,* p. 44.

welfare programs that resemble free handouts rather than insurance schemes for which one has to pay premiums. He was no social democrat, no harbinger of the welfare state.

II

Let us now look at the second role he played in his country's history. In what sense was Kuyper also an emancipator? He who emancipates liberates, sets free, lifts restrictions, and removes disadvantages. Kuyper was a champion of the lower classes. Compare their lot at the beginning of his public career in 1867 and toward its close in 1917, and note the progress they had made in the intervening half-century. From a disadvantaged and disenfranchised, disqualified and despised minority, they had become a cultural "pillar" to be reckoned with: a community worshipping in free churches and operating their own university, their own press, trade unions, youth organizations, housing cooperatives and, last but not least, a nationwide private school system. The consensus among historians is that, along with many other figures, Abraham Kuyper contributed in no small measure to their emancipation.

As he celebrated his seventieth birthday, Kuyper reflected on his lifelong exertions at instructing and organizing his followers into a fighting force. With a play on his name and only half in jest, he boasted: "I knew how a cooper makes his barrels, so I arranged the staves in a circle, stoked a fire inside the circle, and as the staves bent inward threw a hoop around them, and presto — I had my organized band to lead to victory!"[22] The loose staves, of course, were the *kleine luyden,* and the hoop was Calvinism.

We have to tread carefully here. Kuyper was certainly not an emancipator in the sense of positivist social-science history. The Marxist historian Jan Romein loved to explain that Kuyper was sociologically predetermined to be the man that would give the lower middle class and the working class their place in the sun.

And indeed, did not his voice champion their cause in and out of Parliament? He was tireless in educating his constituency in forty years of unremitting popular journalism. In one of his earliest speeches in the lower house of Parliament he summarized Western legal history in four great phases: the early church developed its canon law, medieval lords got their feudal law,

---

22. Cited in Jan and Annie Romein, *Erflaters van onze beschaving. Nederlandse gestalten uit zes eeuwen,* 10th ed. (Amsterdam: Querido, 1940), p. 747.

and modern times came with a Commercial Code to protect the rights of the bourgeoisie. Is it not high time, he asked the cabinet minister responsible for social affairs, that we enact a Labor Code for the working classes, to ensure their particular rights and freedoms in an industrializing Holland operating by the rules of free enterprise?[23] Romein agreed: it was time. The time was ripe for such reforms, and the evolution of modern society had given birth to a man like Kuyper to be the agent of such reforms.[24]

Another historian, Carel Gerretson, was not far from that sociological portrayal when he wrote in the opening lines of his 1920 obituary of Kuyper that his one central goal in life had been "to raise a hidden group of people, despised because they were deemed backward, to a coherent intellectual, religious and political consciousness." More to the point is Gerretson's note on the very next page: "The Reformed people in the Netherlands owe it to Kuyper that they became conscious of the wealth of cultural ideas which they possessed in their religion without even being aware of it."[25]

And yet this further note still does not get at the heart of the matter. Raising that "wealth of cultural ideas" to consciousness was for Kuyper but a means to an end. And the end was to bring the country back to its Christian moorings; in Kuyper's own words: "to engrave God's holy order upon the nation's public conscience, till God is once again its Lord."[26]

Did he dream of converting the whole nation? Did he dream, be it ever so remotely, of some kind of theocracy? Of course not. But he believed that the public life of the nation could be brought more in tune with the Christian tradition and with biblical wisdom about justice and morality. This tradition and this wisdom, if patiently explained, should recommend themselves to all lawmakers, he felt, regardless of their personal worldview. A majority of them would come to support such policies, if not from religious conviction, then from self-interest, or from love of the common good.

Kuyper, the man of rock-solid divine principles, was a political realist. His realism convinced him from the start that balancing principle and practice

---

23. Abraham Kuyper, *Eenige Kameradviezen uit de jaren 1874 en 1875* (Amsterdam: J. A. Wormser, 1890), p. 192.

24. See Romein, *Erflaters van onze beschaving*, passim.

25. C. F. Gerretson, "Levensbericht van Dr. A. Kuyper," in *Verzamelde Werken*, vol. 2 (Baarn: Bosch & Keuning, 1974), pp. 107-8.

26. Abraham Kuyper, "Thank-you speech during the celebration of his 25-year editorship of *De Standaard*," in *Gedenkboek. Opgedragen door het feestcomité aan Prof. Dr. A. Kuyper, bij zijn vijf en twintigjarig jubileum als hoofdredacteur van "De Standaard"* (Amsterdam: G. J. C. Herdes, 1897), p. 77.

was not always easy but had to be attempted. One of the points on his agenda, articulated in the 1874 memorandum sent to Groen, was that their party ought not to try and replace a liberal-dominated country with a Calvinist-dominated one. A truly national program had to accommodate all. A viable anti-revolutionary program, he wrote,

> must offer a modus vivendi also to the opponent. . . . We ought to distinguish between that which anti-revolutionaries aspire to among themselves and that which they present as a general political program to the nation as a whole. Only like-minded men can work for a strictly anti-revolutionary program; a national program can be promoted by men of all parties. The former could become the latter only if the whole nation were converted to the anti-revolutionary principles.[27]

Could such a man have been historically and sociologically predetermined? Many factors indeed steered Abraham Kuyper in the direction that his life and career would take. But unless we give up on human freedom and responsibility, we had better replace that fatalist word "predetermined" by the much more nuanced word "conditioned." Like many of his contemporaries (who were never stirred to become emancipators), Kuyper became increasingly aware of the plight of the lower classes. What made him take up their cause? Not some historical mechanism rooted in dialectical materialism, but a unique combination of personal motives. These are what conditioned Kuyper to become what he became. At least three factors, I think, help explain his involvement in the emancipation waves of his day. (1) Compassion for the underprivileged whose daily toil he saw scantily rewarded. (2) Sympathy for the disempowered, whom he experienced as by and large orthodox in their Reformed religion. (3) Zeal for a practical Christianity that entered the public arena to combat poverty, injustice, and immorality in public life, all for the honor of God and for the sake of Christ the King. *Pro Rege* (for the King) is the deepest mainspring of his emancipatory crusade and the keynote of his whole public career.[28]

Kuyper helped emancipate the common man precisely by battling for the historic Christian faith in church and school. Thanks to his campaigns for church reform and private education, the people in the pew no longer had to sit and suffer through worship services while preachers trained at a state university mocked their beliefs from the pulpit, and those people no longer

---

27. Kuyper, *Groen van Prinsterer,* p. 765.

28. L. Praamsma, *Let Christ Be King: Reflections on the Life and Times of Abraham Kuyper* (Jordan Station, Ont.: Paideia, 1985), passim.

had their conscience violated by having to send their children to a secularized government school. Freedom of religion and freedom of conscience: these were the twin goals of the latter-day crusade led by Abraham Kuyper, the Christian democratic emancipator.

Bibliography

Bratt, James D. "Passionate about the Poor: The Social Attitudes of Abraham Kuyper." *Journal of Markets & Morality* 5:1 (Spring 2002): 35-44.

Gerretson, C. F. "Levensbericht van Dr. A. Kuyper." In *Verzamelde Werken*, vol. 2, 107-32. Baarn: Bosch & Keuning, 1974.

Kuyper, Abraham. *Wat moeten wij doen, het stemrecht aan onszelven houden of den kerkeraad machtigen? Vraag bij de uitvoering van Art. 23 toegelicht.* Culemborg: A. J. Blom, 1867.

————. *"Ons Program."* 2nd ed. Amsterdam: J. H. Kruyt, 1880.

————. *Eenige Kameradviezen uit de jaren 1874 en 1875.* Amsterdam: J. A. Wormser, 1890.

————. *De Christus en de social nooden en Democratische klippen.* Amsterdam: J. A. Wormser, 1895.

————. "Thank-You Speech during the Celebration of His Twenty-Five-Year Editorship of *De Standaard*." In *Gedenkboek. Opgedragen door het feestcomité aan Prof. Dr. A. Kuyper, bij zijn vijf en twintigjarig jubileum als hoofdredacteur van "De Standaard,"* 59-77. Amsterdam: G. J. C. Herdes, 1897.

————. *Antirevolutionary Staatkunde, met nadere toelichting op ons program.* Vol. 2: *De toepassing.* Kampen: J. H. Kok, 1917.

————. *De kleyne luyden. Openingsrede ter Deputatenvergadering van 23 November 1917.* Kampen: J. H. Kok, 1917.

————. *Wat nu? Rede ter opening van de Deputatenvergadering, gehouden te Utrecht op 2 Mei 1918.* Kampen: J. H. Kok, 1918.

————. *Groen van Prinsterer. Schriftelijke Nalatenschap,* Deel 7: *Briefwisseling,* Deel 6 (1869-1876). Edited by L. J. Van Essen. The Hague: Instituut voor Nederlandse Geschiedenis, 1992.

————. *The Problem of Poverty.* Translated and edited by James W. Skillen. Grand Rapids: Baker, 1998.

————. "Christ and the Needy." Translated by Joseph M. de Torre. *Journal of Markets & Morality* 14:2 (Fall 2011): 647-683.

Praamsma, L. *Let Christ Be King: Reflections on the Life and Times of Abraham Kuyper.* Jordan Station, Ont.: Paideia, 1985.

Romein, Jan, and Annie Romein. *Erflaters van onze beschaving. Nederlandse gestalten uit zes eeuwen.* 10th edition. Amsterdam: Querido, 1940.